# GREAT GC

# Volume 1

Received through the inner word
by
Jakob Lorber
in 1851 - 1864

This is God's Word and God's Word is free. It may be copied freely on condition that the text will not be altered.

Translator: Jürgen Pless

NOTE: A special word of thanks to all the volunteers who spend years of their free time to translate the books of the New Revelations without compensation. Most of the translators followed the guideline to keep the translation as close as possible to the original old German language in order to preserve content in exchange for English style correctness. Professional proofreading is in progress as funds become available.

# The Great Gospel of John

## Volume 1

### CHAPTER 1

*John 1,1. In the beginning was the Word, and the Word was with God, and the Word was God.*

[1] This verse has already been the subject of a great many misrepresentations and interpretations. Yes, even atheists have made use of this very text to dispute My deity all the more surely since they in general denied the existence of the deity. However, we are not going to once again present such false concepts whereby the confusion would only be increased, but shall bring light into the matter with the shortest possible explanation. This as itself light within the primordial light will automatically fight and conquer all misconceptions.

[2] A main reason why such texts are not understood is unfortunately the very poor and incorrect translation of the Scriptures from the original tongue into the tongues of the present time. But this is for the best. For if the inner meaning of such texts were not hidden as well as it is, that which is holiest therein would long since have been utterly desecrated which would be disastrous for the entire Earth. As things are, however, only the outer shell has been marred while the hallowed life has been preserved.

[3] The time has come to show the true inner meaning of such texts to all who are worthy of participating in this knowledge, about the unworthy will have to pay dearly, for in these things I will not be trifled with and I shall never take part in a trade.

[4] Now the explanation shall follow this necessary prelude, but I will still add that here only the inner meaning pertaining to soul and spirit is to be understood and not the innermost, purest heavenly meaning. This is too holy and can be bestowed only on those in the world without harm who seek it through living their life in accordance with the precepts of the Gospel. But the inner meaning pertaining to the soul and spirit may easily be found, sometimes already by means of the correct translation in the respective vernacular of the time, which shall become evident in the explanation of the first verse.

[5] The expression 'In the beginning' is most incorrect and greatly obscures the inner meaning, for thereby even the eternal existence of the deity could be questioned and disputed, which was also done by some of the older philosophers from whose school the present-day atheists have actually gone forth. But if we now render this text correctly, its cover will be found to be only very thin and it will not be difficult to discover the inner meaning quite clearly and sometimes very accurately through such a thin cover.

[6] The correct translation shall read thus: In the primordial essence, or also in

1

the primal cause (of all life) was light (the great holy creative thought, the existential idea). This light was not only in, but also with God, that is, The light came forth from God as substantially visible and was thus not only in, but also with God and, as it were, flowed around the primordial divine essence. Thereby the basis for the eventual incarnation of God was given, which becomes plainly evident in the following text.

[7] Who or what actually was this light, this great thought, this most holly fundamental idea of all future substantial, utterly free existence? It could not possibly be anything else but God Himself, since God, through God and from God nothing but God Himself could manifest in His eternally, most perfect being, and thus this text may also be read as follows,

[8] In God was the light. The light flowed through and around God, and God Himself was the light.

### John 1,2. The same was in the beginning with God.

[9] Now that the first verse has been made sufficiently clear and can be comprehended by anyone with some measure of enlightenment, the second verse is self-explanatory and only bears witness to the fact that the above described word or light or the great creative thought did not come later into existence out of the primordial being of God, but is as eternal as God, itself God, and therefore does not contain within itself any process of coming into existence. That is why the explanation – by way of giving witness – follows, The same was in the beginning, or in the primal Cause of all existence, and in all later existence, as the First Cause itself with, in and out of God, thus itself God through and through.

### John 1,3. All things were made by Him, and without Him was not anything made that was made.

[10] This verse confirms and substantiates, as it were, what had already in the first verse plainly presented itself as the 'word' or 'light' in the primordial essence of all being or coming into existence, completely present, but not yet fully manifest.

[11] Accordingly, this third verse in its correct rendition should read as follows: All existence came into being from this primal existence which in itself is the eternal First Cause of its existence through and through. The light, word and will of hits existence set its very own light, its eternal idea of creation, out of itself into a tangible, visible existence, and there is nothing in the entire eternal infinity that did not go forth from the same First Cause in the same way assuming a manifest and visible existence.

[12] Whoever has now fully comprehended these three plainly explained verses must find the meaning of verse 4 quite clear.

### John 1,4. In Him was life. And the life was the light of men.

[13] It is obvious that the First Cause of all existence, the light of lights, the original thought of all thoughts and ideas, the archetype as the eternal original form of all forms, firstly, could not be formless and, secondly, could not be dead, since death signifies the very opposite to all existence in whatever form. Thus there was a most perfect life in this word or light or in this great thought within God, fundamentally God Himself. So God was from eternity the most perfect fundamental life in and out of Himself through and through, and this light or life called forth out of itself all created beings, and this light or life was the light and also the life within the creatures, within the human beings that had gone forth from Him. Thus these creatures and human beings were a complete image of the primordial light which gave them their existence, light, and a life very similar to the eternal primordial existence.

[14] The primordial life in God is and must be a perfectly free life, otherwise it would be as good as no life at all. This same life must be one and the same life in the created beings, otherwise it would not be life and, thus, without life also would be without existence. It is obvious that the created beings – men – could only be given a completely free life, which has to be aware of itself as a complete life, but also had to realize that it was not a life that had come forth from itself, but had come forth as fully equal out of God in accordance with His eternally almighty will.

[15] This perception had to be present in all created beings, just as the one that their life and existence must be completely equal to that of God, as otherwise they would not have any life or existence.

[16] When we now consider this circumstance more closely, it becomes evident that two feelings must meet in the created beings, namely, in the first place, the feeling of equality with God or the presence of God's primordial light within them, and then, resulting from this light, also the feeling of having been created at some time through the primordial will of the Creator.

[17] The first feeling makes the created being without fail equal to the Creator and, as if it had come into existence out of itself, completely independent of the eternal First Cause as if comprising it within itself. The second vital consciousness, necessarily arising from the first, must still consider and regard itself as having been called forth from the actual First Cause, an only in the course of time freely manifested being, and thus most dependent on the First Cause.

[18] Now this humbling realization turns the initial feeling of exaltation also into a feeling of humility, which for the feeling of exaltation is a most necessary and unavoidable matter as will be plainly shown hereinafter.

[19] The feeling of exaltation puts up a mighty resistance to such humiliation and wants to crush the other feeling.

[20] Such a conflict then causes anger and finally hate against the First Cause of all that exists and resulting from that against the lowly feeling of humility and dependence, whereupon the feeling of exaltation becomes weak and benighted and the primal light within the created being gives way to night and darkness. This night and this darkness is then hardly able to recognize the primal light within itself and, as blind but still independent, distances itself from the First Cause of its existence and creation unable to recognize the same in its delusion.

3

**John 1,5. And the light shines in the darkness, and the darkness does not comprehend it.**

[21] Therefore, this primordial light may shine in such night as brightly as it may, but since the night, although it has also originated from the light is no longer able to see properly, it does not recognize the light coming into such night in order to transform it once more into the true original light.

[22] Thus also I, as the eternal primordial essence of all existence and as the original Light of all light and life, came into the world of darkness to those who had come forth from Me, but they did not recognize Me in the night of their weakened feeling of exaltation.

[23] For this 5th verse points out how, in accordance with the original standards and circumstances, I have come into the world created by Me and out of Me as fully the Same that I was from eternity and the world fails to recognize Me as its very own fundamental existence.

[24] But I, as the First Cause of all existence, could not fail to foresee in My eternal, primordial light how through the constant conflict the feeling of exaltation, as the primal light within men, kept growing ever weaker and as the vital light also dimmer, finally to end in darkness, and that therefore men, if I came to them in the image they had been given out of Me would not recognize Me. At least very many would fail to recognize Me, especially if I came to them as a *Deus ex machina (a suddenly appearing God)* unexpectedly and without warning in a limited human form, in which case I would have to blame Myself that men could not possibly recognize Me because they would not be prepared for My advent in this way.

[25] I did, indeed, realize this from eternity and, therefore, had this My advent, already beginning with men's first coming into existence, independent of Me, right to the time of My actual arrival, foretold to men through many seers who did not lose My light in the conflict. They faithfully described the circumstances and even the place and time of My advent. At the time of My actual arrival I caused great signs to take place and awakened a man, in whom dwelt a high primordial spirit, that he might announce to all the blind people My advent and full presence on Earth.

## CHAPTER 2
### John the Baptist bears witness to the Lord

**John 1,6. There was a man sent from God, whose name was John.**

[1] This man, who preached repentance by the Jordan and baptized the converted with water, was called John. In this man dwelt the spirit of the prophet Elijah, and this was the same angel spirit who in the very beginning defeated Lucifer and later on the noted mountain wrestled with Lucifer for the body of

4

Moses (*as Michael*).

**John 1,7. *The same came for a witness (from above) to bear witness of the light that all men (benighted men) through him might believe (i.e. through his light might recognize the primordial light that had come to them).***

[2] This one came as an old as well as a new witness from above, that is, from the primordial light as a light that he might bear witness to the primordial light, of the primal essence of God, who now took on the flesh Himself and in the full likeness of the human form, Himself as a man, came to His human being, who are out of Him, in order to once more illuminate them in their night, thereby to return them to His primordial light.

**John 1,8. *He was not that light (out of himself), but was sent to bear witness to that light (that is, he bore witness to men's benighted feeling of exaltation that now the primordial light Himself had descended from His eternal height to men as a lamb in humility to voluntarily take all their weaknesses (sins) upon Himself thereby to give back to men the original light and make them His equals).***

[3] This man was, of course, not the actual primordial light itself, but like all beings only a partial light out of the primordial light. But because of his extreme humility, it was granted to him to stay united with the primordial light.
[4] Since he was, thus, in constant contact with the primordial light and was well aware of the difference between It and his own light – although having gone forth from the primordial light, but not being that light, but only a light derived from it that he might recognize it and bear true witness of It – He bore valid witness to the primordial light thereby awakening in men's hearts sufficient of the true light to enable them to recognize, even though initially only faintly, but gradually more strongly and clearly, that the primordial light, now clothed in the flesh, is still the Same that gave all beings and men their independent existence which they may, if they so desire, keep for all eternity.

**John 1,9. *That was the true light, which enlightens all men who come into this world.***

[5] Not the witness, but his testimony and He of whom he bore witness, were the true primordial light that from the very beginning has illuminated and animated all men coming into this world and continues to animate and illuminate them. Therefore, it says in verse 9 that the true and proper light is and was the one that created all men in their very beginning for a free existence and now came to abundantly enlighten this existence and render it once more similar to Himself.

**John 1,10. *He was in the world, and the world was made by Him, but it did not recognize Him.***

[6] It has already been plainly discussed in verse 5 how this world, that is, benighted men who with their entire being have gone froth from Me or, which is the same, from the primordial light (the word) could fail to recognize Me or the primordial light, notwithstanding all the forerunners and proclaimers of My advent. However, it has to be specially mentioned that in this case under 'world' is not to be understood the Earth, as carrier of souls under judgment which actually constitute matter, but only those people who, although partly derived from this matter, no longer belong, or are supposed to belong, to this primeval soul matter under judgment once they have been made independent beings, for it would really be asking too much if I demanded of the stone, which is still in an extreme state of judgment, to recognize Me. This can justifiably only be expected of a liberated soul in which My Spirit is dwelling.

### John 1,11. He came unto His own, and His own would not receive Him.

[7] Thus, as already mentioned, not the Earth, but only men in their soul and spirit nature are here to be regarded as actually the Lord's own – My own, because they are, as it were, themselves primordial light out of My primordial light and thus at one with My fundamental essence.

[8] But since in this particular existence, which within them expresses itself as the feeling of exaltation, they are weakened and because of which weakness I came to them as into My original property and am still coming, they failed to recognize Me as a result also themselves and their very own fundamental essence which cannot ever be annihilated since it is basically My essence.

### John 1,12. But to all who did receive Him, He gave the right to become children of God, because they believed in His Name.

[9] It is obvious that, with all those who did not receive or recognize Me, the original order was disturbed, and with this disorder there remained a state of suffering, the so-called 'evil' or 'sin', whereas with many others who did receive Me, that is, who did recognize Me in their hearts, this evil had to vanish, since they were once more united with Me, as with the original order and primal might of all existence, finding therein themselves and My primordial light as the light within them and in it everlasting, imperishable life.

[10] But they also found in such life that, thanks to it, they were not only My created beings, which was expressed by their lower life-consciousness, but that – since they carry My Self within them which only through the might of My will was given independence of Me – they are indisputably My very own children, because their light (their faith) is equal to My very own primordial light, wherefore it carries within the full might and power that dwell within Me and this might gives them the full right not just to be called My children, but to be it in all fullness.

[11] For, faith is such a light and My name, toward which the mighty beams of this light are directed, is the power and might and the actual nature of My primal

essence through which everyone accomplishes within himself the proper and fully valid sonship of God. That is why it says in verse 12 that all who will receive Me and believe in My name shall have the power within them to be rightly called 'children of God'.

[12] Who were not born of the blood, nor of the will of the flesh, nor of the will of a man, but of God.

[13] This verse is but a closer definition and explanation of the previous one, and in a smoother diction ten two verses together could also read, But those who received Him and believed in His name, to them He gave the right to be called 'children of God', who were not born of the blood nor of the will of the flesh (desire of the flesh), nor of the will of a man, but of God.

[14] It goes without saying that here not a first birth as flesh from the flesh is meant, but only a second birth from the spirit of love for God and from the truth of living faith in the living name of God who is called "Jesus-Jehovah-Zebaoth". This second birth is also called 'the rebirth of the spirit through the baptism from the Heavens', this being a good definition.

[15] The 'baptism from the Heavens' is the complete transition of the spirit and the soul with all its desires into the living spirit of love for God and the love in God Himself.

[16] Once such a transition has taken place of man's own accord and all his love is now dwelling in God, then through such sacred love the whole person is dwelling within God where he is brought to maturity and strengthened as a new being and thus, after attainment of proper maturity, reborn of God. Only after such a second birth, which is preceded neither by the desire of the flesh nor man's procreative will, has man become a true child of God thanks to God's grace which is a free power of God's love in the human heart.

[17] This grace is actually God's mighty prompting in the spirit of man through which he is drawn by the Father to the Son, that is, to the divine primordial light and thus which is the same, attains to the proper and living mighty wisdom of God.

### CHAPTER 3
### Toward spiritual rebirth. First and second grace

*John 1,14. And the Word became flesh, and dwelt among us, and we saw His glory, a glory as of the only begotten Son of the Father, full of grace and truth.*

[1] Once man in this way attains to the true sonship of God into which he is as if born of God, the Father or the love within God, he attains to the glory of the primordial light in God which actually is the divine primal essence Itself. This essence is the actual Son begotten of the Father just as the light rests latent within the warmth of love, as long as love does not stir it up and radiate it out of

itself. Thus this holy light is actually the glory of the Son from the Father which is attained by everyone who is reborn and becomes equal to this glory, which is forever full of grace (God's light) and truth, as the true reality or the incarnated word.

**John 1,15. John bears witness to Him, and cries, saying, "This was the One of whom I said: After me will come the One who has been before me, for He was there before I was."**

[2] To this again John bears true witness and immediately after the baptism in the river Jordan – in order to give Him a worthy reception – he draws people's attention to the fact that the one whom he had just baptized is He of whom he had spoken to the people all the time during his sermons on repentance, that He who would come after him (John) had been before him. In a deeper sense this means as much as: This is the original fundamental light and First Cause of all light and existence that preceded all existence, and all that exists had come forth from it.

**John 1,16. And of His fullness we have all received grace upon grace.**

[3] This primordial light, however, is also the eternally great glory in God, and God Himself is this glory. This glory was from eternity God Himself within God, and all being have received their existence and their light and independent life from the fullness of this glory.

[4] Thus all life is a grace of God filling the life-bearing form through and through. Because in itself it is the same glory of God, the primal life in every human being is a first grace of God, but this had been harmed by the weakening of the feeling of exaltation by the lowly feeling of coming into existence and the thereby resulting inevitable dependence on the primordial light and First Cause of all existence.

[5] Since this first grace within man was in danger of being completely lost the primordial light itself came into the world and taught people to once more leave this first grace to the primordial light or rather to completely return into this primal existence there to receive a new life for the old light. And this exchange is the receiving of grace upon grace or the giving away of the old, weakened, quite useless life for anew, imperishable life in and from god in all fullness.

[6] The first grace was necessity in which there is neither freedom nor permanence. But the second grace is complete freedom without any compulsion and, therefore, since not urged or coerced by anything also forever indestructible. For where there is no enemy, there is also no destruction. By enemy is to be understood all that in any way impedes a free existence.

# CHAPTER 4
## About the law, judgment, grace and salvation

*John 1,17. For the law was given through Moses, but grace and truth came through Jesus Christ.*

[1] The law had to be given to the first life, namely, in the beginning already to the first man in the course of things through Moses who in this verse is also mentioned as a representative of the law. But since the law is an impediment rather than a furthering of life, no one could ever gain the true freedom of life through the law.

[2] The first ideas of creation were placed in an isolated as if independent existence by a positive 'must' from the immutable will of the primordial might. Therefore, as concerns the separation and forming of the existence limited by space and time, this was accomplished by an immutable 'must'.

[3] Now the entity, man, was there, in his inner being to a certain degree the deity Itself or, which is the same, the primal essence of God, only separated from his First Cause, although conscious of it, but still bound in a limited form and restrained by an immutable 'must'. The thus placed entity did not relish this state, and his feeling of exaltation came into a mighty conflict with his inevitable limitation and separation.

[4] Since in the very first line of beings the conflict kept growing in intensity, the great fundamental law had to be tightened to hold the beings temporarily in a firm judgment which consisted in the manifestation of the material, solid globes and the thereby effected greater division of the primordial beings.

[5] In the second line of beings man appears, clothed in the flesh, standing on the ground of his first judgment. Notwithstanding his now threefold separation from his First Cause, he still soon recognized Him again within himself and became defiant, arrogant and disobedient to a mild law, no longer given with a 'must', but only a 'you shall'.

[6] But because he refused to submit to this mild 'you shall', he was given a more severe and mightily sanctioned law, and the sanction promptly executed when this second 'shall' was disregarded (see the deluge and similar cataclysms).

[7] After this disciplining the Divine Being descended to the Earth in Melchizedek and guided men, but they soon began once more to fight and had to be bound through new laws and returned to order, so that they were left with only a kind of mechanical movement limiting all their inclination.

[8] Thus through the law a wide gulf had been created and no spirit or entity was able to leap across it. This is caused the prospect and the inner awareness of an eternal existence of the inner, thus considerably limited, life to become seriously doubted.

[9] Following this limitation the divine primordial being then appears in its own fullness, namely, in the person of Christ.

[10] Thus the original grace returns once more, takes all the weaknesses of the

9

human life upon Himself, giving men a new grace, a new life full of true light and showing them in this light and through His example the right way and the true purpose of their existence.

**John 1,18. No one has ever seen God, but the Son within the Father's Bosom, He has made Him known.**

[11] Only now those who recognized Him obtained true knowledge of God and were for the first time able to see and recognize God - whom previously no being could ever see in His fullness - beside and outside of them and through Him also themselves and the freest destination of their own life.

[12] And now also the insurmountable gulf that had been created through the law was once more abolished and every man could and can now at any time free himself from the burden of the law, if he exchanges his old nature for the new one out of Christ, wherefore it is also said that one should put off the old man and put on the new one. Or, who loves the old life will lose it, but who flees it shall receive it as a new one. That is the annunciation from the bosom of the Father and the living Gospel of God.

[13] The phrase, however, 'Who is in the bosom of the Father', means as much as, 'the primordial wisdom of God or the actual innermost essence of God is within love just as light dwells in warmth, originally arises and goes forth from the love of mighty warmth and, finally, by its existence again creates warmth and this again always light. In the same way from love, which is equal to the Father and basically the Father Himself, goes forth the light of divine Wisdom, which is equal to the Son or the actual Son Himself, who is not two, but fully one with what is called 'Father', just as light and warmth or warmth and light are one, since warmth keeps producing light and light keeps producing warmth.

## CHAPTER 5
## NEAR BETHABARA
### John the Baptist's testimony of himself and the Lord

**John 1,19. And this is the testimony which John gave to the Jews when they sent priests and Levites from Jerusalem to ask him: "who are you?"**

[1] This verse deals with a purely external fact and therefore has no deeper meaning. Just one thing can be plainly understood from this mission, that at this time the feeling of exaltation of the Jews began to sense already that the primordial light or the primordial life of God was beginning to draw close to men on Earth and would already have to be on Earth. And it presumed that this primordial life of all life might be dwelling within John and he be the promised Messiah.

[2] That is why - due to the above mentioned assumption rather than John's reputation as a preacher - they sent emissaries to ask him who he was, whether

the Christ or Elijah or another prophet.

*John 1,20. And he confessed, and did not deny it, saying: "I am not the Christ, the promised Messiah."*
*John 1,21. But they went on asking: "What then? Are you Elijah?" And he said: "I am not." And they asked: "Are you a prophet?" He replied: "No."*

[3] The reason why they asked John whether he was either Elijah or another new prophet was the fact that their prophetic Scriptures stated that Elijah would be the forerunner of the promised Messiah and prepare all Israel for the great advent of the Messiah. Besides, at that time also other prophets would be appearing who, too, would precede the Messiah as heralds. This was known to the emissaries from Jerusalem who were well versed in the Scriptures and so they asked John all these question, but he confessed that he was none of these.

*John 1,22. Then they said to him: "Then who are you, that we may give an answer to those who sent us? What do you say of yourself?"*

[4] Thus they had to continue asking him, who he actually was.

*John 1,23. John said: "I am the voice of one crying in the wilderness, preparing the way for the Lord, as predicted by the Prophet Isaiah."*

[5] Whereupon John confessed that he was but a crier in the wilderness preparing the way for the Lord, as predicted by Isaiah.
[6] Here the question would be justified, why John had chosen the wilderness for this work where, one must assume, not many people would be dwelling, and that it would be more advisable to make a forerunner in more densely populated areas. What use could the most powerful crying be in the dead wilderness where the sound of the call would lose itself before it had reached any ear? Even if it did reach a human ear, that why that would be far from sufficient in a matter so vitally important for all men.
[7] In answer to this question it must be pointed out that the term 'wilderness' did not so much refer to the small desert of Bethabara beyond the Jordan, but rather to the spiritual desert in the human hearts. The desert of Bethabara, where John actually lived, preached and baptized, had been chosen only to show man symbolically what it looked like in his heart, namely, quite as arid, empty and bare of noble fruits, but full of thorns and thistles, all kinds of weeds, vipers ad other vermin. And in such a human desert John appears like an awakened conscience, which spiritually he also represents, and preaches repentance for the remission of sins, thus preparing for the Lord the way to the hearts of people who have become arid like a desert.
[8] Now there still remains the question why John denied being Elijah or a prophet since, according to My own testimony, he was one as well as the other, for I Myself told My apostles and also other listeners to My teaching quite plainly,

John was the Elijah who was to come before Me, if you will accept this.

[9] The reason for this denial was that John here describes himself only according to his active, new calling and not the previous one given his spirit within Elijah when he was living on Earth. Elijah had to punish and destroy the Moloch, whereas John had to call people to proper repentance, bestow the forgiveness of sins through baptism with water and prepare the way for Me. And in accordance with such activity he presented himself only as that which he now in fact was.

**John 1,24. And the ones who had been sent were of the Pharisees.**

**John 1,25. And these continued to question him, saying: "If you are not the Christ, nor Elijah, nor a prophet, why then are you baptizing?"**

[10] Since he was baptizing, which was allowed only to the priests and the prophets proven to be called for this, the priests and Levites, who had been sent to him by the jealous Pharisees, asked him why then he baptized people if he was neither one nor the other.

**John 1,26. John answered them saying: "I baptize only with water, He (the Christ about whom you are asking) is standing among you, but you do not know Him."**

[11] But John said, 'I baptize only with water, which means, I wash hearts that have become unclean for a worthy reception of the One who, as it were, has been in your midst already for quite some time, but whom you do not recognize because of your blindness.'

[12] Here also all those who seek Me, the Lord, somewhere outside are represented by the emissaries who travel over lands and seas asking all the sages, 'Where is Christ, when and where will He be coming?' The true One who built a dwelling place for Himself in their hearts, and who can be found only there, (Oh, these deluded seekers.) Him they do not seek, at least not at the only place where He must be sought and can be found.

**John 1,27. "He is the One who is to come after me, who was before me, whose shoe's laces I am not worthy to unloose."**

**John 1,28. This took place at Bethabara beyond the Jordan, where John was baptizing.**

[13] What a most humble witness John bears before the priests and Levites, since he quite aware who had come to the Earth in Christ. But what is that to the so worldly wise priesthood. They ignored John' truest testimony, for they did not care for a humble, poor and unpretentious Messiah, but wanted one to whom everyone would succumb in fear and terror.

[14] At his first appearance – naturally nowhere else but in Jerusalem – descending visibly from Heaven shining more brilliantly than the sun, accompanied by myriads of angels and taking residence only in the temple, the

Messiah would have to immediately abolish and destroy all the then existing potentates, also promptly render the Jews completely immortal, provide them with all the money on Earth and fling at least some hundreds of apparently superfluous mountains with thunderous noise into the sea, at the same time also executing the poor, dirty rabble. Then they would have believed in Him and said: 'Lord, you are so terribly strong and mighty. All have to bow deeply before you and throw themselves into the dust, and the high priest is not worthy to undo your shoe's laces.

[15] But Christ came to Earth quite poor, insignificant apparently weak, did not work any sign before the eyes of the prominent for almost 30 years. He worked hard as a carpenter with Joseph and frequented the company of the lower classes. How could, in the eyes of the proud and so very wise Jews, that be the so long awaited Messiah? Away with such a blasphemer, such a magician who accomplishes his feats with the help of the chief devil. Such an uncouth and vulgar carpenter who somewhere with the help of Satan has learned to practice magic, who walks about barefoot, is a friend to the lowest rabble and walks around with them, accepts harlots and eats and drinks in the company of publicly known sinners thereby plainly opposing the law, - how could he possibly be the Christ, the promised Messiah?

[16] This was the opinion of the eminent and wise Jews about Me during My full presence in the flesh on Earth. And exactly the same view is still today held concerning Me by millions, who will on no account even hear of a meek, condescending God who keeps His word.

[17] Firstly, their God has to dwell high above the firmament and because of His infinite sublimity hardly exists. He is not expected to create lesser things than suns if He wants to be a worthy God. Secondly, He may not dare to assume any form, least of all a human form, but has to be some incomprehensible absurdity.

[18] Thirdly, if Christ could possibly be God, He may make Himself known through the inner, living word only to members of the profession, to certain societies, councils, extraordinary pietists, zealots surrounded by a so-called halo and models of virtue, promptly endowing such a blessed one with the power to move mountains. Otherwise there cannot be any divine messages and revelations by Christ.

[19] The Lord Jesus may never make Himself known to a layman or even a sinner, for in such a case the revelation is already under suspicion and is not accepted, just as I Myself was not accepted by the eminent Jews, because in their proud and ambitious eyes My appearing was by far not sufficiently divine and noble. However, that does not matter. What matters is only John's testimony.

[20] The world does not change and continues to be the desert of Bethabara where John bore witness. -But I, too, do not change and keep coming to men to suppress their pride and enliven true humility and love in the same way as when I came to the Jews. Blessed are those who recognize and accept Me as did John according to his testimony about Me before the eyes and ears of the proud priests and Levites greatly annoying them.

[21] The next day John sees Jesus coming towards him, and says, 'Look, that is

the Lamb of God, which carries the sin of the world.'

[22] The next day, with these emissaries still at Bethabara, there to find out what this John was doing and what he was mainly preaching about, John again bears witness to Me, and that on the known occasion of My coming to him from the desert asking him to baptize Me with the water of the river.

[23] Already as I am approaching him, he draws the attention of the leader of these emissaries, who during the night had pondered on what he had heard from John, to Me, saying, 'Look, the one approaching is the Lamb of God who has taken all men's weaknesses upon His shoulders, so that all men who accept Him will receive a new life from Him and have the power within them, because of such a new life, to be called children of God. For Jehovah does not come in the storm or the fire, but He comes only in the gentlest rustle.'

[24] 'This is He of whom I (yesterday) said, after me a man is coming who has been before me, for Hew was there before I was.'

[25] Here John repeats once more what he had said to the emissaries about Me the previous day. On the one hand, he testifies of Me that I come to men, as it were, as a mirror of man's true and indispensable humility proving by such humility that I come to help men in their weakness and not in their presumed strength, which they do not possess at all. On the other hand, John also testifies that the one he calls the Lamb of God is still He who preceded all existence, for the expression, 'He was before me' means that John - for a moment recognizing the high spirit entity within him - intimates to the emissaries that, although the same primordial spirit of the same nature dwelt within him, yet he was brought into a free and completely independent existence solely by the power of the First Cause - the original Source and Creator - dwelling in this Lamb and not by his own power. With such a bringing into independent existence - a true act of the First Cause - also the first cycle had begun, prior to which there had not been anything in the whole of infinity, except the First Cause Jehovah and, in fact, exactly the Same as now visibly before their eyes in this Lamb of God wishing to be baptized by him (John).

## CHAPTER 6
### John baptizes the Lord

*John 1,31. "I myself did not know Him before, but that he might be revealed to Israel I came to baptize with water (the ones waiting for Him)"*

[1] Naturally, the emissaries thereupon asked John, 'Since when have you known this strange man, and how was what you have just said about him made known to you?' - Here John replied quite naturally that he, as a man, had not known him either, but that his spirit had revealed this to him and induced him to prepare men for This One and to cleanse them with the water of the Jordan of their gross contamination through sins.

14

*John 1,32. And John testified further, saying (after the baptism): "(As I baptized Him) I saw the spirit of God (as evidence for me) descending from Heaven just like a dove that gently lowers itself, and this spirit stayed above Him."*

[2] Here John makes known that he, too, is seeing Me for the first time in person before him, and that My Spirit within observed this man during the short performance of the baptism with water, which John had initially refused to perform on me with the significant remark that I should baptize him rather than he Me. But when I insisted that it had to be done in this way, John gave in and baptized Me. But he saw what I Myself had revealed to him though My Spirit within his spirit as I had sent him to Bethabara, how the Spirit of God, that is, My very own eternal, primordial Spirit, descended upon Me from the Heavens full of light like a shining little cloud in the way a dove descends, and stayed above My head. At the same time he heard the familiar words:

[3] 'This is My beloved Son, or this is My light, My own primordial essence in which I, as the eternal, primordial essence of love, am well pleased. Listen to him.'

*John 1,33. "I would not have known Him either, but He who sent me to baptize with water, said to me: Upon whom you will see the spirit descending, and remaining upon Him, He is the one who will baptize with the holy spirit."*

[4] That is why John says: 'I would not have recognized Him either.'

*John 1,34. "And I saw it and am now testifying that this is truly the Son of God."*

[5] Only after this baptism does John tell the emissaries what he had seen and heard and insist that the Baptized, whom he had already as He was approaching announced as the revealed Lamb of God, was truly the Messiah for whom all Israel had been waiting. This is truly the Son of God, that it, God's actual primordial fundamental essence within God.

[6] He, John, had seen with his own eyes God's Spirit descending upon Him and remaining above Him. Not as if this man had only then received that spirit, but this manifestation took place as evidence for him (John) since he had not known Him before.

[7] Here the question arises whether these emissaries from Jerusalem had not perceived these things with their own eyes and ears. The answer to this is always one and the same: These things shall be revealed only to the babes and the simple, but to the worldly wise they will remain hidden and veiled.

[8] Thus the emissaries from Jerusalem also say here nothing but he baptism with water and were quite annoyed when John told them what he had seen and heard. They did not perceive any of this and, therefore, abused John saying that

he lied to them. However, several of John's disciples who were present joined them and testified that John had spoken the truth.

[9] But the emissaries shook their heads and said, 'John is your master and you are his disciples, wherefore you are confirming his statement. We are learned and wise in all things of prophets and recognize from your words and actions that you and your master are fools, that you do not see and know a thing and with your foolishness drive many people crazy, and that to such an extent that this matter has already for some time been regarded as a nuisance by the high priests of the temple. It would be best to put a stop to your activities by force.'

[10] This angered John and he said, 'You snakes, you vipers' brood: Do you think you can thereby escape retribution? Look, the ax with which you would like to destroy us is already laid to your roots – see how you can escape perdition. Unless you repent in sackcloth and ashes and let yourselves be baptized, you will face destruction.

[11] For truly, this was the One about whom I had told you: After me will come the One who has been before me, for He was there before I was. From His fullness all of us have received grace upon grace.'

[12] Following these forceful words, some remain with him and have themselves baptized, but most of them leave greatly enraged.

[13] These verses deal with purely historical facts and do not have much inner meaning which can be easily recognized from the previous explanations. Here it must be pointed out that such verses are all the easier to understand if given with the then well-known circumstances. For at the time, the evangelist recorded the Gospel it was customary to omit as unnecessary sentences dealing with all kinds of generally known circumstances and record only the main sentences, leaving all secondary details 'between the lines,' as you would say today. In order to throw more light on this for that time most noteworthy matter, we will have a closer look from this angle at the three following verses and the style of that time will become quite clear and recognizable.

## CHAPTER 7
### Examples and explanations concerning the style of the evangelists

*John 1,35. The next day again John was standing (at the river Jordan) with two of his disciples.*

[1] The original text, for instance, of verse 35 reads: 'The next day John was standing again with two of his disciples.' Here raises the question: where was he standing and were the two disciples together with him or were they standing in a different spot, only at the same time? One must notice right away that neither the place nor the action of the two disciples has here been stated.

[2] Why has the evangelist failed to mention this?

[3] The reason why has already been indicated for, especially at the time when it

was customary to write like this, it would have been quite certain and obvious that John was standing at the river Jordan under a willow waiting for someone to come to be baptized. And since he had several disciples who listened to his teaching and also recorded it, usually two, but when there was much work more were with him, assisting with the baptisms and probably also baptizing in his name and in the way he did it.

[4] Since at that time all these circumstances were only too familiar to the people around John, they were not recorded. It was then customary to write like that, but also necessary due to the lack of writing material, wherefore only the main point was recorded and by beginning a sentence with 'and' it was indicated whether the apparently separate sentences were related to each other or not. For this reason such conjunctions were seldom put in letters before the main sentences that had reference to each other, but certain known signs were used.

[5] Although this explanation is as such not an evangelical one, it is still necessary since without it the Gospels would today be hard to understand, not only their external, historical meaning, but even less their inner spiritual meaning and least of all the prophetic books of the Old Testament in which instead of completed sentences only corresponding images are given and there naturally cannot be any question of stating whatever circumstances there might have been. Now that we are acquainted with these rules of ancient times, we should have no difficulty in connecting the following verses and texts, reading them more correctly and at least throwing more light upon their natural, historical part. We will make a short analysis of verses 36 and 37 and the principle in question will become quite clear.

*John 1,36. And as he again saw Jesus walking (on the bank of the Jordan, he said: "Look, there is the Lamb of God."*

[6] The original text of verse 36 reads: 'And as he saw Jesus walking, he said: 'Look, there is the Lamb of God.' The 'And' here indicates that this text has some connection with the previous one and historically states that Jesus, after He had received the baptism with water, for a while still remained in the neighborhood of John and was therefore seen by John's two disciples as well as by John himself walking on the bank of the Jordan.

[7] As John catches sight of Him, he immediately concentrates all his thoughts upon the one subject and speaks with great enthusiasm as if to himself: 'See, there is the Lamb of God.' Today he would have expressed himself roughly like this: 'Look over there. On the bank of the river the supreme God-man is still today walking as unassuming and humble as a lamb.' But John omits all these details and says only what we read in the verse.

*37. And the two disciples heard John speak thus (and left John at once), and followed Jesus.*

[8] Verse 37, actually representing the continuation of the two previous ones, for the above mentioned reason, begins again with 'And' and simply states what happened, just referring briefly to the reason why.

[9] The original text reads simply like this: 'And two of his disciples heard him speak and followed Jesus.' In our time its meaning reads as follows: As the two disciples who were with him (John) heard their master speak thus, they left him at once and joined Jesus, and since Jesus was now leaving this place, they followed Him.

[10] All that was mentioned in this expanded text must also have taken place on this occasion since otherwise the action could not have been carried out. However, as already said, in accordance with the then customary style of writing, only the two concepts 'hearing' and the ensuing 'following' are mentioned whereas all connecting sentences were omitted as self-evident. Whoever understands this given procedure will at least be able to better understand the historical part of the original text and thereby find it also easier to comprehend the spiritual meaning.

## CHAPTER 8
### The Lord's first disciples: Andrew and Simon Peter

*John 1,38. But Jesus turned, saw the two following Him and said to them: "What are you looking for?" They said: "Rabbi (which means: Master), where are You staying?"*

[1] This text also is a sequence to the preceding ones and has historical rather than spiritual meaning: for with it begins the familiar, still quite material, taking on the apostles, and that in the same region where John was active at Bethabara, a most miserable country town inhabited by poor fishermen. This is also the reason why the two disciples immediately ask about My lodging – actually, in which hut I live.

[2] Since I had been staying in this area prior to the baptism for about 40 days preparing my human person for the beginning ministry through fasting and other exercises, it is historically also quite clear and certain that I had to have some place where to stay in this desolate and barren region which I considered the most suitable for My purpose.

[3] The two disciples knew that I had already for some time been living in this region. They may have seen me there a number of times without, however, suspecting who I was. Therefore, they promptly asked, not where I originally came from, but where I was staying in Bethabara which consisted mainly of the poorest fisherman's huts constructed from clay and reeds and often even not high enough for a man to stand upright therein.

[4] And so I, too, lived in a similar hut which I had built Myself rather deep in the desert. The hermitages which exist in practically all Christian lands date back to that.

*John 1,39. He said to them: "Come and see." So they went and saw where that was and stayed that same day with Him. It was about the tenth hour.*

[5] Thus this shelter was not far from the place where John was operating. That is why I said to the two disciples: 'Come and see', where upon the two followed Me at once. We soon reached My hut and the disciples were not a little amazed that God's Anointed was living in just about the most unassuming hut which, besides, was situated in the most desolate part of the desert.

[6] This, however, did not take place at the time during which nowadays the Christian communities usually have their 40-day fast, but about two months later, and as for the time of the day that we reached the hut it was about the tenth hour which according to the new style would be about three in the afternoon, for in those times the sunrise determined the first hour of the day. But since this does not always take place at the same time, the hour of the day mentioned then does not coincide exactly, but only roughly, with the time according to afternoon that I reached the shelter with the two disciples. As these two disciples spent this day with Me until sunset, the question will arise in every inquiring reader's mind what the three of us did from three until about eight o'clock in and at My hut. For nothing has been written about that anywhere. Here it is obvious that I instructed these two concerning their future vocation and how and where I would begin with My ministry, also how I would, in this neighborhood, still take on further men as My disciples, who were inclined and willing similar to them. At the same time I commissioned them to find out from their comrades, who were mostly fishermen and confer with them whether any of them would be inclined to join Me. This is what we discussed during that time. But as it became evening I let the two go and they returned – partly very happy, partly pondering – to their families, for they had wives and children and were wondering what to do with them.

*John 1,40. One of the two who had heard what John had said (about Jesus) and then followed Jesus was Andrew, a brother of Simon Peter.*

[7] One of the two, called Andrew, has soon made his decision and wants to follow Me at all costs. Therefore, he immediately goes to find his brother Simon who was somewhere attending to his nets.

*John 1,41. The first thing he did was to find his brother Simon. He said to him: "We have found the Messiah." (Messiah means as much as: the anointed.)*

[8] When after while he has found him, he hurriedly begins to tell Simon that he has, together with another disciple, who had not made a firm decision to follow Me, found the promised Messiah.

*John 1,42. (Simon wishes to see Jesus) and Andrew takes Simon to Jesus. When Jesus saw him, He said: "You are Simon, Son of Jonas, from now on you shall be called Kephas (that is, Peter the Rock).'*

[9] When Simon hears about Me, he expresses the keen desire to meet Me as soon as possible, for he had not been present at the baptism. **Andrew** says: 'Today it cannot appropriately be done, but tomorrow morning you shall be with Him.'

[10] Upon this, **Simon**, who whatever he was doing kept dreaming of the Messiah and believed that the Messiah would help the poor and completely eliminate the hardhearted rich, says: 'Brother, we must not waste a moment. I shall immediately leave everything and follow Him to the end of the world should that be His wish. Therefore do take me right away to Him, for I feel this strong urge and must still today see and speak to Him. The night is not too dark and it is not far to His hut, so let us go to Him immediately. Who knows, we might no longer find Him tomorrow?'

[11] Giving in to this urging, Andrew leads him to Me. As the two are approaching My shelter at an already rather late hour, **Peter** stops about 30 steps away from it in a state of exaltation and says to Andrew: 'I have a peculiar feeling. I am seized with a sublimely sweet awe, I hardly dare to take another step, but I still have this keen urge within me to see Him.'

[12] Here I step out of My hut to meet the two brothers, which means that I saw him. It goes without saying that under 'being seen by Me' is to be understood My readiness to come to meet one who, like Simon, comes to Me above all in his heart. Therefore, he is immediately recognized by Me, that is, accepted and a new name is his first share in My Kingdom. Here Simon is promptly given the name Kephas, or the rock in his faith in Me, for I had seen long ago by what kind of spirit Peter is, and was, animated.

[13] The way I addressed him was for Peter or Simon sufficient proof that I surely was the promised Messiah. From then on he never yielded to any doubt in his heart and did not ever ask Me whether I was the right One, since his heart was the only sure and valid witness for him. Both men now stayed with me until the morning and afterwards did not leave Me any more.

## CHAPTER 9
### Further callings: Philip and Nathanael

*John 1,43. The next day Jesus decided to go again to Galilee, and he finds Philip and says to him: "Follow Me."l*

[1] In the morning I tell the two: 'My time in this desert has come to an end. I shall ho to Galilee from where I have come. Will you come with Me? I leave the decision to you for I know that you have wife and child whom it is not easy for you to leave. But no one who leaves something for My sake will lose what he has left, but will regain it many times over.'

[2] Says **Peter**: 'Lord, for your sake I would give up my live, not to mention my wife and child. They will survive without me, for I am a beggar and cannot provide

them with much bread. Our fishing brings hardly enough to feed one person, let alone a whole family. My brother Andrew can confirm this. Although we were born at Bethsaida, we had to come for food to these desolate banks of the Jordan, which are comparatively rich in fish, where we have now also been baptized by John. Our father Jonas is still strong and so are our wives and sisters. Added to this the blessing from on high, and they will manage.' I commended both of them, and we started on our way.

### John 1,44. Philip came from Bethsaida, from the city of Andrew and Peter.

[3] On the road, which for a while still followed the banks of the Jordan, we meet Philip, who was also born in Bethsaida, and was now in the early morning fishing for his breakfast in the waves of the Jordan. **Peter** drew My attention to him and said: 'O Lord, this man suffers much and is very poor, but still the most honest and righteous man, full of true piety in his heart. Would you consider letting him come with us?'

[4] Upon such a loving suggestion by Peter I say only: 'Philip, follow Me.' Without hesitation he throws his nets down and follows Me, not even asking whither. Only on the road does **Peter** tell him: 'The One we are following is the Messiah.' But **Philip** says: 'My heart already told me that the moment He called me so lovingly.'

[5] Philip, however, was unmarried and staying with the poor fishermen as a teacher, because he had quite a good knowledge of the Scriptures. He was personally acquainted with Joseph of Nazareth and thus knew me also and many a thing that had happened at My birth and during My early years. He was also one of those who were secretly hoping for the Messiah in My person, but since I, from My twelfth year onward did not perform any miracles and lived and worked like any other ordinary person, also the first amazing impression that had been created by the circumstances of My birth had with many people got completely lost. Even those who had been most excited said that My birth had become so memorable thanks to the as such strange coincidence of various circumstances and phenomena with which My birth was surely not connected in any way. Beside the highly gifted nature of My early years had so completely disappeared that in the years of My manhood not a trace of it could be found. But Philip and a few others secretly still held on to a certain hope concerning Me, for they knew about the prophecy of Simeon and Anna at the time of My circumcision in the temple and thought a lot of it.

### John 1,45. Philip finds Nathanael and tells him: "We have found the one spoken of by Moses in the law, and by the prophets: It is Jesus, son of Joseph from Nazareth."

[6] When **Philip**, who followed Me, meets Nathanael, for whom he had been looking on the road, sitting under a fig tree repairing his fishing-tackle, he says to him with fervor: 'Brother, I kept looking for you along the quite long road and now

rejoice with all my heart to have found you, for look, we have found the One spoken of by Moses in the Law and buy the prophets. It is after all Jesus, the son of Joseph, from Nazareth.'

**John 1,46. And Nathanael said to him: "Can anything good come from Nazareth?" Says thereupon Philip: "Come and see for yourself."**

[7] **Nathanael** thereupon says with just a trace of resentment, 'Everybody knows the miserable hole Nazareth. Can anything good come from this hole? And (in a way quite obviously) least of all the Messiah.' But **Philip** says: 'I am aware that in this respect you have always been my opponent, although I have presented my arguments to you a hundred times. But now do come and convince yourself and you will admit that I have been completely right.'

[8] **Nathanael** rises thoughtfully and says: 'Brother that would be a wonder of wonders, for the rabble of Nazareth is surely the worst in the world. With a piece of Roman tin you can make a Nazarene into whatever you wish. In this place it has not been any belief for a long time, neither in Moses nor in the prophets. In short, you can make a Nazarene into whatever you want to, and the word, 'This one or that one is even worse than a Nazarene' has already become an old saying. And you say that the Messiah whom you want me to meet is from there? Oh well, nothing is impossible to God. We will see.'

**John 1,47. When Jesus sees Nathanael coming, he says aloud: "Look, a true Israelite: There is nothing false in him."**

[9] With these words Nathanael follows Philip to Jesus who meanwhile had sat down for a little rest about a hundred paces away. When both men were already close to **Jesus**, He says aloud: 'Look, a true Israelite. There is nothing false in him.'

**John 1,48. Nathanael asks Him: "How do you come to know me?" Jesus replies: "I saw you under the fig tree before Philip spoke to you."**

[10] **Nathanael** is amazed at his so very true statement coming aloud from My mouth and promptly asks: 'How do you come to know me to be able to say this about me? Only God and I myself can know my innermost nature, and I was never a boaster nor did I brag about my virtues. How then can you know what I am like?' But I look at him and say: 'I saw you under the fig tree before Philip spoke to you.'

**John 1,49. "Rabbi," says Nathanael, "you are truly the Son of god: you are king of Israel."**

[11] This My statement about him amazes **Nathanael** and deeply stirred in his hearts he says: 'Master, notwithstanding the fact that you are a Nazarene, You are truly the Son of god. Yes, You are without any doubt the for a long time longed-for

king                           of                           Israel
who will liberate his people from the clutches of the enemies. O Nazareth, O Nazareth, how small you were and how great you are now becoming. The last will be exalted to become the first. O Lord, how quickly You granted me faith. How did this happen that all doubt has left me and I now fully believe that You are the promised Messiah?'

*John 1,50. Jesus answers, saying to Nathanael: "You believe because I told you: I saw you under the fig tree (before Philip spoke to you). (But I tell you), you shall see greater things than that."*

[12] I answer Nathaniel's question first with the words stated in verse 50, thereby pointing out to Nathanael that he now, to be sure, believes that I am the promised Messiah, but was compelled to believe by discovering in Me the omniscience only God can possess. I also add that in future he will be seeing greater things, whereby I wished to say as much as: now you believe thanks to a miracle, in future you will believe freely.

*John 1,51. And Jesus adds: "In truth, in very truth I tell you all, from now on you shall see Heaven wide open and God's angels ascending and descending upon the Son of man:"*

[13] And in truth, in very truth I tell you: from now on you will be seeing all Heavens wide open and God's angels ascending and descending upon the Son of man, which is to say as much as: In future, when through Me you will attain to the rebirth of your spirit, the doors of life will be opened. Then will you, angels yourselves, see those men who through me were made angels in the rebirth, and thereby also 'children of God,' ascending from death to eternal life. On the other hand you will also see many primordial angelic spirits descending from all the Heavens to Me, the Lord of all life, there to follow the example of the Son of man, according to John's example and testimony.

[14] So his is now the right interpretation of the first chapter, but let no one think that this is a comprehensive interpretation. Oh no, not at all, but hits gift is a practical signpost with the help of which everyone of good will can be guided into various depths of divine wisdom, enabling him to see and recognize much of life's true meaning in every single verse. Besides, as already said, this gift is a true guiding principle by which everything can be evaluated and directed.


## CHAPTER 10
## IN NAZARETH
### New disciples: James, John and Thomas

*John 2,1. And on the third day there was a wedding at Cana-in-Galilee and the mother of Jesus was there.*

[1] The 'and' here already appearing at the beginning of the first verse of the second chapter proves that these two chapters are closely connected. Therefore it

23

appears that this wedding in a family who is on very friendly terms with the house of Joseph takes place already on the mentioned third day, namely, counting from the day when I left Bethabara with my so far only four disciples and together with them spent a full day at the house of Joseph – who was no longer alive at that time – with the mother of My body who, helped by My other brothers, made every effort to show us the best possible hospitality.

[2] In her heart Mary did realize that now the time had come for Me to begin My mission as the promised Messiah. However, wherein My work would consist she did not know either. At this stage she, too, believed in the complete expulsion of the Romans and the restoration of the mighty throne of David and its stable and invincible divinely glorious dignity which would never end.

[3] The good Mary and all My earthly relatives still imagined the Messiah as a conqueror of the Romans and other enemies of the promised land. Indeed, the best of them had a similar idea concerning the promised Messiah, just as at the present time many otherwise honest people have quite a false notion about the millennium. But the time had not yet come to give them a different conception.

[4] Thus, since My own house, beginning with Mary, had this notion about the coming Messiah, it can rightly be assumed that other friendly families could not have a better one.

[5] This is also the reason why many families paid much attention to Me and, of course, to those whom I called My disciples. As a result also James and John decided to become My disciples, in order to rule the nations of the Earth together with Me, for they had already forgotten many a thing I had rather clearly predicted to them in My childhood.

### John 2,2. Jesus and his disciples were also invited to the wedding.

[6] In all the better houses in the neighborhood of Nazareth, practically in all of Galilee, I was considered to be a soon-to-emerge liberator from the Roman yoke, although this had been the case only for the few months since I had begun to make certain preparations thanks to which - like many a thing that had sunk into oblivion during the past 18 years - also certain prophecies concerning My person were beginning to come to life again in the houses of friends. Therefore I was invited with My disciples, My mother Mary and many other relatives and friends even to quite a notable wedding in Cana, a little old city in Galilee not very far from Nazareth, where there was much gaiety, so that the four disciples from Bethabara remarked to Me:

[7] 'Lord, things are much more pleasant here than at Bethabara. Poor John, too, might be very glad if for once in his life he could partake of a meal like this here, instead of his desperately poor fare, which consists mainly of slightly scaled locusts and the honey of wild bees.' (There exists in this region, as also in Arabia, a species of pigeon-sized locusts which are prepared and eaten similar to crabs in this country – Austria.)

[8] To this I replied: 'At this stage you cannot understand as yet why John has to live in this way. He has to live thus, otherwise the Scripture would not be fulfilled.

But soon he will have a better life. Jerusalem will not allow him to continue his in the desert much longer. From now on he will grow less, so that another one may grow greater.

[9] But what about the disciple who came to Me first with you, Andrew? Will he follow or will he stay at Bethabara?' Says **Andrew**: 'Look, he will come, but he had to make some arrangements first.' Say I: 'That is good. For where there is a Kephas, there must also be a Thomas.' Says **Andrew**: 'Yes, that is his name. An honest soul, but always full of scruples and doubts. However, once he as grasped something he will never let it go, although he has an extremely generous heart. Because of his generosity he has been given this nickname. He is coming, Lord, shall I call him in, this Twin?' Say I: 'Yes, do that, for whoever comes in My name, shall be invited to the wedding.'

### John 2,3. And as the wine gave out, Mary said to Jesus: "They have no wine left."

[10] According to the custom of that time, every guest arriving had to be welcomed with a cup of wine. **Mary** had already noticed for some time that the supply of wine had given out and she realized that the newly arrived guest could not be received properly according to custom. Therefore she said secretly to Me: 'My dear son that will be embarrassing. The wine has given out. They have none left. You could create some (at least for the newly arrived).'

### John 2,4. Jesus answered: "Your concern, mother, is not mine. My hour has not yet come."

[11] Whereupon I gave a most ambiguous answer in front of all the guest, but, of course, in a very gently way, saying to her because of the custom of those days, especially around Nazareth: 'Woman, that is none of our concern. It is not yet my turn as an invited guest to supply wine. My time has not come yet.' (At that time and in that region every invited male wedding guest had to make a voluntary gift of wine. However, a certain order had to be observed according to which the gifts of the closest relatives had to be consumed first. Once these had been used up also the gifts of the guests who were no bleed relations were used in order of precedence.) But Mary knew that the available wine had given out. So she turned to Me and, as it were, suggested that I skip the customary order, especially since a new guest was arriving for whose welcome not a drop of wine was left. The mother was very particular in observing the good old custom on such occasions. Although I did not appear too cooperative in this matter, My mother knew Me and that I never refused to fulfill any of her wishes.

### John 2,5. His Mother said to the servants: "Do whatever He tells you."

[12] And so, fully relying on Me, she turned to the servants and said: 'Do whatever my Son will tell you.'

[13] This is as far as the historical part of this verse in the second chapter is concerned. But contained in this historical event or, as it were beyond it, a spiritual and therefore prophetic meaning is also present which with the help of an inner reasoning power is very easy to discover.

[14] Who can fail to observe that there exists one of the most striking correspondences between this wedding, which took place on the third day after My return from the desert Bethabara, and My resurrection which occurred also on the third day after My crucifixion?

[15] Thus through this wedding an indication was prophetically given as to what would happen to Me after 3 years, and – in a somewhat wider concept – that after 3 years I would certainly and surely, as an eternal bridegroom, be holding a true wedding with all My followers and those who truly love Me in their rebirth into eternal life.

[16] In its general practical sense, however, this story of the wedding which – this must be understood – took place 3 days after My return from the desert, points to the 3 stages through which everyone has to pass in order to attain to the rebirth of the spirit or the eternal-life-wedding in the great Cana of the heavenly Galilee.

[17] These 3 stages consist of: first the mastering of the flesh, then the cleansing of the soul through the living faith which has, of course, to prove itself as alive through works of love, as it would otherwise be dead, and finally the awakening of the spirit from the grave of judgment, for which in the raising of Lazarus from the dead surely the clearest analogy is given. Whoever will ponder a little on this little explanation will find what follows easy to understand.

[18] After here having unfolded the spiritual meaning of this wedding story, that is, what is in general meant by it, let us now return to the wedding and look at the different correspondences in this story.

## CHAPTER 11
### IN CANA
### The wine miracle: Symbol of the rebirth (1/11)

*John 2,6. There were six stone water jars, placed in accordance with the Jewish rites of purification: each of these jars held from 20 to 30 gallons.*

[1] After Mary had told the servants: 'Do whatever He will tell you.' I told the servants to fill up with water these 6 stone water jars intended for the Jews' purification which, however, was no longer observed much by the Nazarenes and Canaanites. Thus these jars, each of which held from 20 to 30 gallons, were placed here on display rather than for a specific purpose.

*John 2,7. Jesus said: "Fill the jars with water." And they filled them to the brim.*

[2] The servants complied promptly, but rather in the belief that the newly arrived guest might wash and cleanse himself in accordance with the old custom. The guest entered and was placed at the table without having cleansed his hands beforehand. Having noticed this, **the servants** discuss this with each other, wondering: 'Why did we have to fill these heavy jars with water? This guest did not use it and only caused us unnecessary work.' Hereupon I say to them: 'Why did you not query this earlier, but now grumble about this work? Did you not hear what Mary told Me, namely, that there is no more wine for the guests? Although My time has not quite come yet, neither according to the customary order nor spiritually, I have still – in order to reveal the glory of Him whom they call their God, but have never recognized as yet – changed the water in the jars into wine, not through some kind of magic, but solely through the power of God within Me.'

*John 2,8. And Jesus continued saying to the servants: "Draw some off and take it to the steward of the feast." And the servants did so.*

[3] 'Now fill a cup and take it first to the steward of the feast (the cook) to try. Let him give his opinion about it.' The servants, quite bewildered at the transformation of the water, immediately take this wine to the cook to try.

*John 2,9. When the steward had tasted the wine which had been water, not knowing, as did the servants, where it came from, he called the bridegroom.*

[4] **The cook** is quite astonished, sends immediately for the bridegroom and says to him: 'You probably do not know the customary order?'

*John 2,10. And says to him: "Everyone serves the best wine first and only when the guests have drunk freely he serves the poorer sort but you have kept the best wine till now."*

[5] 'Does not everyone serve the best twine to the guests first and only when they have drunk freely and their palate has become somewhat dulled the poorer sort? But you have done just the opposite.'
[6] But **the Bridegroom** replied: 'You talk like a blind man about color. Look, this wine was not pressed anywhere on Earth but, as once the manna, it came to our table from the Heavens. Therefore, it must surely be better than any other wine on Earth.'
[7] Says **the Cook**: 'Do you take me for a fool or are you one yourself? How can a wine come to your table from the Heavens? Jehovah Himself or His servant Moses would have to be sitting at the table.'
[8] Said **the Bridegroom**: 'Come and see for yourself.'
[9] **The Cook** follows the bridegroom into the dining hall and looks at the 6 jars seeing that they are filled with the best wine. Thus having convinced himself of the

miracle he says: 'Lord, forgive me my sins. Only God can do a thing like this, and He must be here among us, for such a thing is impossible to a human being.'

[10] Now this wine was served to the guests and having tasted it they all said: 'Such a wine is not pressed in our lands. This is truly a heavenly wine. Glory to Him whom God has given such might.'

[11] Thereupon they toasted Me and the newly arrived guest Thomas and welcomed us.

[12] Now all the people present at this wedding believed without a doubt that I was surely the promised Messiah.

[13] But **Peter** says to Me secretly: 'Lord, let me go away again. For You are Jehovah Himself as was prophesied by Your servant David in his Psalms, but I am a poor sinner and absolutely unworthy of You.'

[14] Say I to him: 'If you feel unworthy of walking at My side, whom do you consider worthy of it? See, I have not come to the strong assuming such could be found anywhere, but I came to the weak and sick. One who is healthy does not need a doctor. Only the sick and weak one does. So stay with me and be of good cheer, for I have forgiven you your sins long ago, and even when you will be sinning at My side, I will forgive you that, too, for, because you have recognized Me and are already a rock in your faith, you shall be perfected – not in your strength, but in your weakness – solely through grace from on high.

[15] These My words brought tears to his eyes and **Peter** says with great enthusiasm: 'Lord, if all should leave You, I shall not leave You, for Your holy words are truth and life.'

[16] Having said this **Peter** rises, takes the cup and speaks: 'Blessed are you, Israel, and three times blessed are we, for we are witnesses to the fulfilled promise. God has visited His people. That which was hard to believe, is now fulfilled before our senses. Now we must no longer cry from the depth to Heaven, for the Highest has descended to us into the very depths of our misery. Therefore all glory be to Him who is among us and has provided this wine thanks to His might and grace that we may believe in Him and from now on shall honor God in Him.' Thereupon **Peter** drinks the wine and all drink to him, saying: 'This is a righteous man.'

[17] But I say to Peter secretly: 'This was not given you by your flesh, but the Father who is within Me has revealed it to your spirit. But from now on keep silent still, a time will come, however, when you shall shout so that the whole world may hear you.' Then quiet reigned once more among the guests and because of this act they now all believed in Me and regarded Me as the true Messiah who had come to liberate them from all enemies.

***John 2,11. This deed at Cana in Galilee is the first of the signs by which Jesus revealed His glory. And His disciples now firmly believed in Him.***

[18] This was the first remarkable sign which I gave before the eyes of many at the outset of My great work of salvation, and in this sign I showed – through veiled – the great work that was to follow. However, not a single one of the entire

company comprehended this, for, as my fasting in the desert prophetically pointed to the persecution I would be suffering from the temple in Jerusalem and the baptism by John to My death on the cross, thus this wedding pointed to My resurrection and the sign became a model of the rebirth of the spirit to everlasting life.

[19] Just as I transformed the water into wine, also man his natural being ruled by the senses shall be transformed to spirit through My Word, provided he lives according to it.

[20] But everyone should in his heart follow the advice Mary gave the servants when she said: 'Do whatever He tells you', then I shall do to each one what I did at Cana in Galilee, namely a proper sign by which everyone who lives according to My Word will find it easier to recognize the rebirth of the spirit within himself.

### CHAPTER 12
### IN CAPERNAUM
#### Call to the sons of Zebedee: James and John. Beginning of the Lord's ministry

*John 2,12. After this He went down to Capernaum with his mother, his brothers and his disciples, but they did not stay there long.*

[1] Seven days after this wedding, I left Nazareth and went with Mary, My five brothers - two of whom also belonged to My disciples - and with the disciples I had so far taken on down to Capernaum. This city was then quite an important trade center situated on the border of Zebulon and Naphtali and also in the middle of these two provinces on the Sea of Galilee, not far from the spot where John was baptizing on the opposite bank of the Jordan in the region of Bethabara, as long as there was sufficient water in this often quite parched riverbed.

[2] One may ask what I was actually seeking in this city which had already become quite heathenish. One should read the prophet Isaiah 9:1, etc, where it is written: *"The land of Zebulon and the land of Naphtali on the way by the Sea beyond Jordan and heathen Galilee, the people who walked in the darkness have seen a great light: a mighty light has dawned upon them who were walking in the shadow of death."*

[3] And if one has found this text in Isaiah and knows that I had to fulfill the Scripture from A to Z, it will be easy to understand why I went from Nazareth to Capernaum. Besides, in this region two more disciples had to be taken on: James and John, sons of Zebedee. They were also fishermen fishing in the Sea of Galilee not far from the mouth of the Jordan and also not far from the spot where Peter and Andrew worked, both of whom were also entitled to fish in the Sea.

[4] When I had also taken on these disciples and they had recognized Me from My words and the mighty witness of those who were with Me, I began to teach the people properly, calling them to repentance since the kingdom of Heaven was

upon them. I went into their synagogues teaching there. Some believed, but many were annoyed, wanted to lay hands on Me and throw Me into the Sea from a cliff. But I eluded them with all those who were with Me and visited some small settlements on the Sea of Galilee, proclaimed the Kingdom of God, healed many sick, and the poor and simple believed and received Me with goodwill. Some of them joined Me and followed Me everywhere like lambs follow their shepherd.

[5] In Capernaum I stayed only for a short while since there was as good as no belief there and even less love. This city was a place of trade and mercenary spirit, and where these rule, faith and love have been completely abandoned. Thus where this is the case, there is little or nothing for Me to do.

### John 2,13. As it was near the time of the Jewish Passover, Jesus went up to Jerusalem.

[6] As the Jewish Passover feast had come, I went up to Jerusalem with all who were with Me. But one must not imagine the Passover feast of the real Jews at . same time which is now set for the similar feast by various Christian communities, sometimes already for the month of March. This was almost three months later. For at the Passover, Jehovah was offered thanks for the first harvest of the year consisting in barley, corn and wheat. On that occasion the new bread was already eaten which, according to the Law, had to be unleavened bread, and no one in the land was allowed to eat leavened bread during this time.

[7] Therefore, this feast of the unleavened bread could take place only when the newly harvested corn could already be ground into flour and not at a time when the corn had only been sowed. In a good year the corn in Judea ripens 14 to 20 days sooner than here. However, even in Egypt the corn and wheat are hardly ever harvested before the end of May, let alone in Judea where it is considerably cooler than in Egypt.

[8] But the time of the unleavened bread had come and, as already mentioned above, I went with all who were with Me up to the Jewish capital, which was also called "The City of God", for the name Jerusalem means as much as "City of God".

[9] During that time many people always came to Jerusalem, including many Gentiles, who bought and sold various goods, as utensils, woven articles, cattle and fruit of all kinds. This feast had in those days completely lost its sacred aspect and greed prompted even the priesthood to lease for this time the courtyards and entrance halls of the temple to the traders, where Jews or Gentiles, for a considerable sum, so that such a temple rent for the duration of the feast amounted to 1,000 pieces of silver, which in those days was an immense sum and comparatively more than nowadays 100,000 florins.

[10] I went up to Jerusalem at the time of the high priest Caiaphas who knew how to hold on to this naturally most lucrative office for more than a year. For the observance of the Mosaic Law had in those days degenerated into the emptiest possible ceremony, and no priest had actually more regard for it than for the snow that had fallen a hundred years ago. On the other hand the useless, empty

ceremony had reached its peak in serving to bully the poor people excessively.

[11] He even leased some spots in the inner part of the temple to dealers in pigeons and to some small money-changers. These latter carried small coins, for which those how needed smaller coins could for a certain exchange premium change their silver coins, Roman gold coins and the Roman cattle money (pecunia), for the Romans had a special kind of money for the purchase of cattle. Depending on what animal was embossed on such a coin, the same animal had to be available for purchase with that coin provided its owner had it for sale. For such cattle money it was possible to obtain from the bigger or smaller money-changers also another type of money in circulation, but at a higher premium.


## CHAPTER 13
## IN JERUSALEM. The cleansing of the temple by the Lord

*John 2,14. There he found in the temple the dealers in cattle, sheep and pigeons and the money-changers.*

[1] When on My arrival in Jerusalem I found that because of all the animals and their dealers some people hardly dared enter the temple as it sometimes happened that an ox went wild hurting people and damaging sacred articles, and people visiting the temple could often not bear the stench and noise and not seldom lost all their important belongings, this disgraceful situation had now become unbearable to Me. And **Peter and Nathanael** remarked: 'Lord, have You no lightning and thunder left for this? Just look at it. The poor people are crying in front of the temple. They have come from distant places to honor God and because of all the oxen and sheep they cannot even get in. And many, who with great effort and danger managed to enter the temple and get out again, are complaining that inside they have been robbed of everything and almost suffocated by the stench. Ah, this is really too much and too evil. Such a terrible nuisance should be stopped at all costs. This is even much worse than Sodom and Gomorrah.'

[2] These words were heard by a stranger, an old Jew who now steps up to us and says: 'Dear friends, you do not know everything, but I myself was three years ago working as an ordinary servant in the temple where I learned about things that made my flesh creep.'

[3] **I say**: 'Friend, keep it to yourself, for I know about all that has taken place. But be assured, things have gone too far and still today you shall see God's might and wrath in action in the temple. But do move away from the gates of the temple for a while, so that you may not be harmed when God's power will be driving the offenders from the temple. After that they will no longer dare to perpetrate such sacrilege.'

[4] Hereupon this Jew went away praising God, for after hearing Me speak thus he took Me to be a prophet, joined a group of his friends and told them what he

had heard from Me. This group, consisting of several hundred people of all ages, rejoiced and began to praise God aloud for having again awakened a might prophet.

*John 2,15. And He made a whip of cords and drove them all out of the temple together with their sheep and oxen. He upset the tables of the money-changers scattering their coins.*

[5] But I said to Peter: 'go over there to the rope-maker, buy three strong ropes from him and bring them here.' This Peter did immediately and brought Me three strong ropes which I promptly braided together into a strong whip. Holding this whip in My right hand I said to My disciples and all who were with me: 'Follow Me into the temple now and be My witnesses, for God's might and glory shall again manifest through Me before your eyes.'

[6] Then I went ahead into the temple, and as I walked all in My path retreated, and all those who followed Me had a free passage although the ground was full of dung and dirt.

[7] When I arrived in the last hall of the temple, where the main dealers in oxen and sheep had their animals for sale on the left side, whereas the money-changers were occupying the right side through all three halls, I took up My position on the gate-steps and spoke with a voice like thunder: 'It is written: "My house is a prayer house, but you are making it into a den of thieves." Who has given you the right to desecrate God's temple like this?'

[8] But they shouted: 'We have purchased our right at a high price from the high priest and are under his protection and that of Rome!'

[9] **I say**: 'You are indeed under such protection, but God's arm is against you and your protectors. Who will protect you from Him of His arm is stretched out over you and your protectors?'

[10] Say **the dealers and Money-changers**: 'God is dwelling in the temple and the priests are of God. Can they go against His will? He whom they protect is also protected by God.'

[11] **I say** in a very loud voice: 'What are you saying, you foolish perpetrators?! Although the priests are still sitting on the chairs of Moses and Aaron, they no longer serve God, but they serve the mammon, the devil, and their right and your right is a right of the devils and not ever a diving right! Therefore, get to your feet immediately and leave the halls, or else things will go bad with you.'

[12] They began to laugh and said: 'Just look at the impudence of this lowest of Nazarenes. Do throw him out of the temple right away.' Then they rose and wanted to seize Me.

[13] Here I raised My right hand with the cord-whip and began to swing it over their heads with divine power. Everyone hit by the whip was immediately seized by the most violent, almost unbearable pains. This also applied to the cattle. There immediately arose a terrible howling from both men and beasts and there followed a stampede of the cattle, and whatever got in their way was trampled down. Also the dealers and buyers fled with terrible screams of pain. But I upset

the money-changers' stalls, scattering all the money they contained, and the disciples helped Me with this work.

*John 2,16. Then he turned to the dealers in pigeons, "Take them out," he said: "You must not turn My Father's house into a market."*

[14] Then I entered the temple where still many dealers in pigeons with their cages full of all kinds of pigeons were waiting for buyers. Since these dealers were usually poor people and not greedy for profit and the sale of pigeons in the temple was an old custom, although in ancient times only in the first hall of the temple, I only warned these poor, saying: 'Take them out and do not turn My Father's house into a market. The place for this is in the outermost court. Thus the temple was now cleansed.

*John 2,17. His disciple recalled the words of Scripture: "Zeal for thy house will destroy Me."*

[15] This act caused a sensation and the disciples feared secretly that now the priesthood would soon have us seized by the Roman guard as rebels and we would hardly be able to escape the most humiliating calling to account and punishment. For it is written: "The zeal for thy house will destroy me."

[16] But I told them: 'Do not worry. Look into the halls and you will notice how the servants and priest are eagerly busying themselves with picking up all the money-changers' scattered money to fill their own money-bags. Because of those who have suffered losses they will be interrogating us by whose authority we did this, but secretly they do not mind at all, for this act yielded them about 1,000 shekel of gold and silver and a big amount in other money which they will never return to the owners. At present they are also too busy and have no time to a call us to account. Besides, they will not easily accept complaints in this matter, just as the ones who suffered the losses have learned their lessons and are not likely to bring an action against Me. Therefore, set your minds at rest.

[17] The zeal for My house will indeed destroy Me, but not yet for quite some time. At the most some of the Jews here will question Me, who I am and on what authority I did such a thing and will ask Me for a mark of authority. But I know that things will have to happen in this way, and that there will be no danger for us. Just look toward the curtain. Some are already standing there who want to question Me in their own interest, and they shall get the proper answer without delay.'

## CHAPTER 14
### The destruction and rebuilding of the temple

*John 2,18. The Jews challenged Jesus: "What sign can you show us as authority your action?"*

[1] As I was still talking with the fainthearted disciples, some Jews came up to Me and said: 'You have now performed a mighty act. Men and cattle fled from your hand like chaff in a storm, and no one returned to pick up his scattered money. Who are you, and what mark of authority (by the emperor, they meant) can you present to us which gave you the right to do this? Don't you know the inflexible severity of the laws which could destroy you because of this?'

*John 2,19. Jesus replied: "Destroy this temple and on the third day I will raise it again."*

[2] **I say**: 'Unless I knew them, but did not fear them, I would not have done it. But you demand of Me an official authority and I tell you that I do not have that. But do destroy this temple and on the third day it will be raised again, perfected.'

*John 2,20. Then the Jews said: "It has taken 46 years to build this temple, and you want to raise it again alone in three days?"*
*John 2,21. But they did not know that the temple He was speaking of was His body.*

[3] This My decisive statement amazed the Jews and they did not quite know what to say. After a while **one of them** remembered that the building of the temple had taken 46 years and provided many thousands of hands with permanent work. So this historically versed Jew turns to Me and says: 'Young man, did you realize what a foolish thing you have just said? Look, all of 46 years were needed for the building of this temple and many thousands of hands were fully employed, and you want to do that quite alone without the help of others? Oh, oh, oh, what a testimony you have given Yourself, and that even in the temple where one should speak particularly sensibly.

[4] Your earlier action has surprised us very much and we, as elders of Jerusalem, were already beginning to deliberate out of what power you performed this really most commendable act, whether a worldly or prophetic one, and so we also questioned you about it. If you had told us in wise words, which we do understand, that you are a prophet awakened by God and did this through the might of God, we would have believed you. However, contrary to all expectation, you gave us instead of wise words an indescribably outrageous, boastful and foolish answer without even a grain of truth, and we now regard you as a person who may have learned a little bit of magic in some pagan school and now wished to show off here in the City of David, being either in the pay of Rome or secretly hired by the Pharisees, priests and Levites, for these would have reaped the best temple-harvest today thanks to your act of magic. We truly regret to have been so mistaken in our judgment of you.'

[5] On this **I say**: 'I too regret with all My heart that I had to find you so terribly blind and deaf. For the blind do not see anything and the deaf and dumb do not perceive anything. I work a sign before your eyes which prior to Me no one has

worked and speak the fullest truth and you accuse Me of being either a foolish braggart with some knowledge of pagan magic wishing to show off here before you or being a magician in the pay of Rome or in the despicable pay of the temple-priests. Oh, what an insulting accusation. Look, over there is a considerable crowd of men who have followed Me here from Galilee. They have recognized Me, although you maintain that the Galileans are the worst kind of Jews with the least faith, but these still recognized Me and are following Me. How then could you not recognize Me.'

[6] **The Jews** said: 'We did not want to recognize you and therefore questioned you, for we are neither blind nor deaf as you think. But you have us an answer which with one's natural reason one cannot interpret other than we told you openly. We are of good will, why then, should you be a prophet, do you fail to recognize this? We are wealthy and honorable citizens of Jerusalem. If you were a true prophet, it would be good for you to be in our midst, but you do not realize this and are therefore not a prophet, just a magician who desecrates the temple much more than those who were earlier driven out by you.'

[7] **I say**: 'Go and discuss this with those who have come with Me. They will tell you who I am.'

[8] Now the Jews go to the disciples and talk to them and they tell them what they heard of Me on the Jordan, the witness of John and what they have seen and experienced at My side, but admit that they do not understand what I had said to the Jews.

*John 2,22. After His resurrection His disciples recalled what He had said and they believed the scripture and the words that Jesus had spoken.*

[9] For they themselves understood it only following My most extraordinary resurrection after three days and at the same time also the Scripture which had said this of Me.

[10] Hearing all this from the disciples, **the Jews** returned to Me and said: 'According to all that which we have now heard from your most sincere followers you would evidently be the Promised. The witness of John, whom we know, speaks mightily for you and so do your deeds. Your words, however, are exactly the opposite to all the other points. How can the Messiah be a God in his deeds, but a fool in his speech? Do explain this to us and we all shall accept and support you in every possible way.'

[11] **I say**: 'What could you give me that you had not fist received from My Father who is in Heaven? But if you did receive it, how can you now speak as if you had not? What do you want to give Me that is not already Mine, for I and the Father are not two, but one. I tell you: Nothing but he will is yours, everything else is Mine. Give me your will in the proper love of your hearts and believe that I and the Father are fully one, then you will have given Me everything I can ask of you.'

[12] **The Jews** said: 'So show us a sign and we shall believe that you are the Promised One.

[13] **I say**: 'And why do you want signs? Oh you wicked generation. Don't you

know that signs do not awaken anyone, but judge him? But I did not come to judge you, but that you may gain eternal life if you believe in Me in your hearts. There will indeed by many signs, and some of them you will be seeing. However, these will not give you life, but death for a long time.'

## CHAPTER 15
### The Lord sees through the malice and deceitfulness of the Jews

*John 2,23. While He was in Jerusalem for Passover, many believed in Him when they saw the signs He performed.*

[1] I tell you: it is now Passover and I shall be staying in Jerusalem during this time. Follow Me where I shall be and you will be seeing a great number of proper signs. But see to it that these signs do not bring you death.'

[2] The Jews were astonished at these words, but I left them and with My disciples walked out of the temple into the open. The Jews, however, followed Me secretly, for they did not have the courage to follow Me openly since I had spoken of 'My signs causing death'. They did not understand that this meant the death of the spiritual element, but were thinking of the death of the body, and like all the rich on Earth they were great friends of the earthly life.

[3] However **one of them** joined Me outside the temple and said: 'Master, I have recognized You and want to be with You. Where are You staying?'

*John 2,24. But Jesus would not trust Himself to them. He knew them all so well.*

*John 2,25. He needed no evidence from others about a man, for He Himself could tell what was in a man.*

[4] But I saw that he was not sincere and that his wish to find out where I was staying was dishonest. Therefore I said to him, as I did later on to a number of similarly serf-interested priests, the familiar words: 'Foxes have their holes, the birds their roosts, but he Son of Man has nowhere to lay his head, least of all in this city. But go first and cleanse your heart and then come with honest intention, not with treachery and you will see how you can hold your own at My side.'

[5] **This Man** said, however: 'Master, You are wrong concerning me and my friends. If You have nowhere to stay, come to us and we shall put You and disciples up and provide for You as long as You wish.'

[6] But I saw clearly that this man did not have honest intentions and said: 'We cannot trust you, for you are friends of Herod and like him are keen on spectacles, particularly if you can watch them free of charge. But I have not come to this city to entertain the friends of Herod with comedies, but to announce that the Kingdom of God is close and that you therefore, should repent so that you may participate in this Kingdom. See, that is the purpose of My presence here at this time, and for

that your lodging is not needed. For he who lives in a house can leave it only through the door which is fitted with lock and bolt and by which a guest can also be made a prisoner. But whosoever says in the open is also free and can go where he wants.'

[7] **The Jew** said: 'How can you offend us like that. Do you think we no longer know about the sanctity of the right to hospitality? If we invite you as a guest into our house, you are most sacred therein and woe betides him who should lay violent hands upon you. Thus with us the right to hospitality is upheld and respected above all. How then can you be suspicious of this established order in our houses?'

[8] **I say**: 'With this domestic order in your houses I am quite familiar, but that does not mean that I do not know the other one as well. As long as a guest is in your house, he enjoys the right to hospitality, but when he wants to leave the house, myrmidons and soldiers who have been sent for receive the guest outside the door and put him in chains. Tell Me, is that also part of the old custom of hospitality?'

[9] Says **the Jew**, somewhat embarrassed: 'Who can claim this of your houses with a good conscience?'

[10] I replied: 'The One who knows. Has not a man been thus delivered into the hands of the judges a few days ago?'

[11] Says **the Jew** even more embarrassed: 'Master, who told you that? If this did take place, tell me, has not that criminal deserved it?'

[12] **I say**: 'With you many things are considered a crime which is not a crime with God and with Me, because the hardness of your hearts considers many a thing a crime for which Moses did not give a law. Those are your laws which as far as I am concerned do not make a man a criminal. For your ruling is a sin against the laws of Moses. How, then, can he be a criminal who offends against your rulings, if he observes the laws of Moses? Oh, I tell you: all of you are full of malice and disgraceful deceitfulness.'

[13] Remarks **the Jew**: 'How can that be? Moses gave us the right to introduce laws for special occasions, and thus our well-considered laws are as good as laws of Moses. Therefore, is not he who disregards them quite as much a criminal as the one who offends against Moses' laws?'

[14] **I say**: 'With you indeed, but not with Me. Moses demanded that you should love and respect your parents, but you say, and the priests even bid you do this: "who instead sacrifices in the temple, for him it is better as thereby he redeems himself from this law." But if now a man faces up to you and says: "You are deniers of God and miserable deceivers, abolishing because of your greed the law of Moses, substituting another for it by which you torment poor mankind". See, then that man has offended against you, and at the threshold of the door you delivered him to judgment. Tell Me, had this worthy man deserved it or are not you by far worse offenders against Moses?'

[15] Here the Jew became angry and walked away to **his other companions** whom he told all that he had heard from Me. They shook their heads and said: 'Strange. How could this Man know about it?' But I left that spot and went with My

followers to a small inn outside the city where I stayed for several days.

## CHAPTER 16
## AT THE INN OUTSIDE JERUSALEM
### The spiritual meaning of the cleansing of the temple

[1] As told here, this is a rather brief account of the historical, natural course the two events recorded in the second chapter had taken, for some other things had happened here and there which were insignificant and would only prolong this account unnecessarily and besides would not render the matter more important or provide any deeper knowledge. So only a brief explanation of the spiritual meaning of the second event is required, and this second chapter may be considered finished as far as the two main events are concerned which are described to the reader and listener.

[2] The spiritual meaning of the first event at Cana-in-Galilee has already been given, so that only the spiritual meaning of the second event must be dealt with. And this is as follows:

[3] The temple represents man in his natural-worldly sphere. In the temple, as also in man, there is the Holy of Holies. Therefore also the exterior of the temple should be kept hallowed and pure so that the innermost, as the Holy of Holies of the temple as well as of man, many not be desecrated.

[4] The Holy of Holies of the temple is, to be sure, covered by a thick curtain and only the high priest may on certain occasions enter the Holy of Holies by himself. But the curtain and also the rarely allowed visit to the Holy of Holies is a protection against its desecration. For if someone sins with his body he not only defiles his body, but also his soul and through it his spirit which in every human being represents, and really is, the innermost and holiest. This Holy of Holies in man, just as the same in correspondence in the temple, has been placed as the same in correspondence in the temple, has been placed deeply behind a thick curtain, and only pure love for God, which in every man is God's truest high priest, is allowed to penetrate into this Holy of Holies unpunished and lift the curtain. If, however, this sole high priest in man becomes defiled by attaching himself to impure worldly things, making common cause with them, how can the Holy of Holies remain undefiled if it is visited by an unclean high priest?

[5] If, therefore, in the temple as well as in man everything has become unclean, man is no longer able to cleanse it, for if the broom is full of filth and dirt, how can it be used for cleaning a room? Then, I am afraid, I Myself must take this work in hand and cleanse the temple by force, and that through all kinds of painful experiences like various illnesses and apparent accidents, so that the temple might be cleansed.

[6] "Dealers" and "buyers" are the low, unclean passions in man, the cattle offered for sale represents the lowest animal sensuousness and at the same time also the resulting great foolishness and blindness of the soul whose love may be

compared to that of an ox that even lacks the sensual procreative and sexual love and is only motivated by the grossest polyp-like gluttonous love and whose cognition is equal to the well-known intellectual power of the sheep.

[7] And what do the money-changers and their money dealings denote? They denote and represent in man all that emerges from man's already quite brutish self-love, for the animal loves only itself, and a wolf will devour another if he is hungry. These "money-changers", or such brutish self-love, must therefore also be painfully and forcefully removed from man, and everything that animates this love must be upset and scattered.

[8] Why not completely destroyed? Because also this type of love must not be deprived of its freedom, for the noble seed or the grain of wheat will grow best in a field well fertilized with such dung and yield a rich harvest. If all the manure were removed from the field to cleanse it, as it were, from all the dirt, the grain of wheat would prosper only poorly and be sure to yield a very bad harvest.

[9] The dung which is initially carried onto the field in heaps has to be spread so that as to serve the field. If it were left lying in great heaps, it would suffocate everything where it is lying and be of no use to the other parts of the field.

[10] This is at the bottom of the story of the cleansing of the temple in the Gospel. And because of this I only scattered the money of the money-changers and did not destroy it completely, which I could easily have done.

[11] What then do the pigeon-dealers inside the temple denote who too had to withdraw and return to the places originally allocated to them?

[12] They are to be understood as the external virtues consisting in all kinds of ceremony, custom, courtesy, etc, in a purely worldly sense which, however, men's blindness raises to an inner life value and tries to make true life to strike roots therein.

[13] The pigeon is a creature of the air, and since it was used in the orient often as a carrier of mail, especially in matters of love, and because of that already with the ancient Egyptians as a hieroglyph represented tender and nice conversation, it served as a symbol for such conversation in the temple and was at the same time an ordinary and correspondingly symbolic sacrificial creature, which was usually sacrificed in the temple by young married couples when their first child had been born, as a sign that they now had done away with such external messages, niceness and ceremonial airs and passed into true, inner, life-giving love.

[14] However, according to the order of all things the outermost belongs to the outermost. The bark being something quite dead, must never be contained in the marrow of the tree, but everything that belongs to the bark must also be deposited in the bark. The bark is most useful to the tree when in a proper measure in its rightful place. If someone would push the bark into the marrow of the tree having first removed the marrow, the tree would soon have to dry up and die.

[15] And thus as an indication that men should not make external virtues a matter of inner life, whereby noble man would become no more than a conversation-puppet (warehouse), these pigeon-dealers, as in a broad sense all formalities, endeavoring to raise their merchandise to the status of inner life-values, were also expelled from the temple by My and ordered to their proper

place, only in a somewhat gentler way.

[16] So this is the spiritual meaning of the cleansing of the temple. And from the correct and unchangeable correspondence between man and temple, it can also be recognized that no man, but only God alone, as eternal wisdom, who sees and knows everything can ever act and speak like this.

[17] But why does not the Lord remain in the temple after such a sweeping?

[18] Because He alone knows what man's inner being must be like so that He may take up permanent residence in man. Besides, after such a cleansing, man must not be deprived of his freedom lest he become a puppet.

[19] Therefore, the Lord cannot yet entrust Himself to such a forcefully clean swept inner man, for He alone knows what is required for a full restoration of the inner man. That is why the sweeper walks out of the temple and, as if accidentally, flows from the outside into man's within not submitting to man's request to stay with and within him which would only support man's indolence. Man has to awaken to complete spontaneity, thereby only becoming a perfect man, which will be described in detail in the next chapter.


## CHAPTER 17
### Healing miracles and late guests at the inn

*John 3,1. There was one of the Pharisees named Nicodemus, a member of the Jewish Council.*

[1] That after the cleansing of the temple I spent some time at a small inn outside the city together with all those who had followed Me has already been mentioned in the previous chapter. But everybody might come up with the question:

[2] "What were You doing there, Lord, for You surely did not spend that time in idleness?"

[3] To that I say: 'Of course not. For a great number of people from all walks of life came to Me from the city by day and night. The poor came usually by day, the great, distinguished and rich mostly by night, for they did not want to appear weak and treacherous to their own kind.

[4] But since they – motivated partly by their curiosity, partly by a kind of credulous feeling for the possibility that I might after all really be the Messiah – were prompted to get better acquainted with me, their visits which took place during the night usually ended with considerable sulking on their part. For these distinguished, great and rich were greatly annoyed that I did not treat them at least as gently and well as many of the poor who had no end of praise for My kindness and friendliness.

[5] Besides, I worked many a miracle for the poor as a doctor, freed the possessed from their tormentors, made the lame walk, the palsied straight, the leprous clean, the dumb hear and speak, the blind see, and all this mostly through

the Word.

[6] Those who came to Me by night knew of all that and wanted similar signs from me to which I always remarked, 'The day has 12 hours and so has the night. The day is meant for work, but the night for rest. Who works during the day does not knock against objects, but this easily happens to the one who works at night, for he does not see where he sets his foot.'

[7] But some asked Me by what might and power I performed such miracles. The quite short answer was this: 'Out of My very own, and I do not need anybody's help for it.'

[8] Again they asked Me why I did not take quarters in the city, as such great deeds required a large place and not just a small, insignificant village which, although close to the great city, is quite ignored by it.

[9] Thereupon I again said: 'I do not care to stay in a place where at the gates of its self-conceited citizens soldiers are keeping watch, admitting only the distinguished, but mercilessly refusing admittance to the poor and where a person, if his face is not familiar and his attire not sufficiently magnificent, is stopped at least seven times in every street and interrogated as to who he is, where he is from and what he is doing there. Besides, I only like what is small and despised by the world, for it is written: "What is great before the world is an abomination before God.'

[10] And they asked saying: 'Is not the temple wherein Jehovah dwells great and magnificent?' Say I: 'He is supposed to dwell therein, but since you desecrated the temple He left it and does not dwell there anymore, and the Ark of the Covenant is empty and dead.'

[11] Say **the night-visitors**: 'What is this sacrilegious nonsense you are talking about? Don't you know what God has spoken to David and Solomon? Can what God has spoken ever become untrue? Who are you that you dare to speak before us like that?'

[12] Say I: 'Just as I have within and out of Myself the might and power to heal all the sick who come to Me solely through My will and My Word, I have also the might and power and the fullest right to speak to you of the temple as I did. And I tell you once more that now also your temple is an abomination in the eyes of God.'

[13] Here some began to grumble, but others said: 'This is obviously a prophet and these have always spoken unfavorably of the temple. Let us leave him alone.' And so the night-visitors left again.


## CHAPTER 18
### The Lord's discussion with Nicodemus. Purification of the soul through humility

[1] During the last but one night of My stay in the vicinity of Jerusalem, a certain Nicodemus came to me, also by night because he was a person of high rank in

Jerusalem. He was not only a Pharisee – who as far as his office, high rank and reputation were concerned could be roughly compared to what at the present time a cardinal in Rome stands for – but he was also a very rich citizen of Jerusalem and chief of the Jewish Council in this city. He was the lord mayor over the entire city, appointed for this office by Rome.

**John 3,2. He came to Jesus by night and said to him: "Master, we know that You are a teacher (prophet) sent by God. No one could perform these signs of yours unless God were with him."**

[2] This one, as **the head of Jerusalem** in civic matters, came personally to Me by night and said: 'Master, forgive me that I come to you so late at night and disturb you in your rest, but when I heard that you will be leaving here tomorrow already, I did wish to pay my respects to you, because I and several of my colleagues, after observing your deeds, are now convinced that you have come to us as a true prophet sent by God, For no one can perform the signs you do, except Jehovah be with him. Therefore, since you are obviously a prophet and must see in what a bad way we are, although the Kingdom of God has been promised to us by your predecessors, would you be good enough to tell me when this will come and, if it does come, what will be required of one to enter it?'

**John 3,3. Jesus answered, saying: "In truth, in very truth I tell you: Unless a man has been born over again he cannot see the Kingdom of God."**

[3] My answer to this question of Nicodemus was quite as brief as quoted in the verse, namely: 'In truth, in very truth I tell you: unless a man has been born over again, he cannot see the Kingdom of God, least of all enter it', which is to say: 'If you do not awaken your spirit through ways I show you by My teaching and acts, you cannot even recognize the divine life within My Word, let alone penetrate into its life-giving depths.'

[4] That the otherwise upright Nicodemus – as is shown in the following – did not understand My words and promptly proved them to be true, namely, that the divine life of My Word cannot be comprehended from a distance unless one's spirit is wide-awake, is clearly and plainly shown by the next verse according to which Nicodemus asks Me, quite disconcerted by My words:

**John 3,4. Nicodemus says to him: "How can a man be born again when he is old? Can he enter his mother's womb a second time and be born?"**

[5] 'But dear Master, what a peculiar thing have you said? How is it possible for a man to be born again? Can a man who has grown tall, old and stiff enter his mother's womb through the narrow little door and then be born a second time? This, dear Master, is quite impossible. Either you do not know anything about the coming Kingdom of God, at least not the right thing. or you know, but do not wish to tell me, fearing that I might have you seized and thrown into prison. Oh, do not

42

fear that, for I have never yet had anyone deprived of his freedom, except a murderer or bad thief. You are a great benefactor of poor mankind and have healed almost all the sick in Jerusalem in a miraculous way through God's power within you. How could I then lay violent hands upon you?

[6] Do believe me, dear Master, I am, taking the expected Kingdom of God very seriously. Therefore, if you do know any details about it, tell me in a way I can understand. Present heavenly things with heavenly and earthly things with earthly words in well comprehensible pictures, otherwise your information is of less use to me than the ancient Egyptian hieroglyphs which I cannot read, let alone understand. I only know from my calculations that the Kingdom of God must already be here, but so far I do not know where and how one can enter it and be received into it. I would like you to answer this question for me quite clearly, so that I can understand it.'

**John 3,5. Jesus answered: "In truth I tell you: no one can enter the Kingdom of God without being born from water and spirit".**

[7] To this reiterated question I gave Nicodemus exactly the same answer as it appears in the above quoted fifth verse. It differs from the previous one only in that here it is stated out of what one must actually be reborn in order to enter the Kingdom of God, namely, out of water and spirit which means to say as much as:

[8] The soul must be cleansed with the water of humility and self-denial (for water is the most ancient symbol of humility, it allows everything to be done with it, serves in all things and always seeks for itself the lowest places on Earth, fleeing the heights) and only then by the spirit of truth, which an impure soul cannot ever conceive. An impure soul is like the night, whereas truth is a sun full of light, which causes to be day all around it.

[9] Therefore, whoever absorbs truth into his soul cleansed through humility and really recognizes this as such, is set free in spirit through this truth. This freedom of the spirit, or the entering of the spirit into such freedom, is then also the actual entering into the Kingdom of God.

[10] But I did not give Nicodemus such an explanation, because in his sphere of cognition he would have comprehended it even less than the short, veiled principle itself. Therefore, he asked Me again how this was to be understood.

## CHAPTER 19
### Earthly images of spiritual things

**John 3:6. "That which is born of the flesh is flesh and that which is born of the Spirit is spirit."**

[1] But I answered as is written in the above quoted sixth verse, namely: 'You should not be at all surprised that I speak to you in this way, for see, what comes from the flesh is again flesh, thus dead matter or an external envelopment of life,

whereas what comes from the spirit is also spirit or eternal life and truth in itself.'

[2] However, Nicodemus is still unable to grasp this, He shrugs his shoulders and is increasingly astonished, not so much at the matter, but at the fact that he, as a most wise Pharisee versed in all Scripture is unable to comprehend the meaning of My words, for he thought a great deal of his own wisdom and had been promoted to the office of Chief of the Jewish Council because of his great wisdom.

[3] Therefore, he was all the more astonished that in Me he had now unexpectedly found a master, who offered him very strange wisdom-nuts to crack. Since he found this quite beyond him, he asked Me again: 'Well - how is this again to be understood? Can a spirit become pregnant and give birth to one of its kind?'

***John 3,7. Say I to him, "I have already told you that you should not be so astonished when I say: You must all be born over again."***

[4] Say I to him: 'I have already told you that you should not be so astonished when I say: You must all be born over again.

***John 3,8. "And the wind blows where it wills, and you hear the sound of it, but you do not know whence it comes or whither it goes;"***

[5] For see, the wind blows where it will. You hear its sound, but you still do not know where it originally comes from. It is the same with everyone who comes from the spirit and speaks to you. You do see and hear him, but since he speaks to you in his spiritual way, you do not grasp it, nor do you understand from where he received it or what he actually says and means. But because you are an honest man of wisdom, it will be given you in due course that you can grasp and understand such things.'

***John 3,9. Nicodemus replied: "Master, how is this possible?"***

[6] Here **Nicodemus** shakes his head doubtfully and says after a while: 'Then I would like to hear from you how this is possible. For what I know and understand, I do know and understand in my flesh. Once my flesh has been taken from me, I shall hardly be able to grasp and understand anything any longer. How, oh how do I as flesh become a spirit, and how will another spirit then absorb my spirit and this be born again? How, oh how can this be possible at all?'

***John 3,10. Jesus answered and said to him: "You as a master of Israel do not know that?"***

[7] Say I to him: 'What? You are a wise master in Israel and cannot comprehend this? But if you, as a master of Scripture, cannot grasp this, what shall become of the many others who hardly know from the Scripture that there have once been an Abraham, Isaac and Jacob?

*John 3,11 "Truly, truly, I say to you, we speak of what we know, and bear witness to what we have seen; but you do not understand and accept our testimony."*

[8] In very truth, believe Me. We, that is I and My disciples, who have come from the spirit, are here not speaking with you purely spiritually, but quite naturally, and convey to you in natural earthly pictures what we know and have seen in the spirit, and you all cannot grasp and understand it.

*John 3,12 . "If I have told you earthly things and you do not believe, how can you believe if I tell you heavenly things?"*

[9] If you are already unable to grasp such an easy thing in comprehensible words, when I talk to you in the earthly way of spiritual things which thereby become as if earthly things, I would like to know how your belief would react if I talked to you of heavenly things in a purely heavenly way.

[10] I tell you: only the spirit that is spirit in and out of itself knows what constitutes spirit and what its life. The flesh, however, is only an outer bark unaware of the spirit, except the spirit reveals itself to the cover, the bark. Your spirit is still too much dominated and covered by the flesh and, therefore, not aware of itself, but the time will come when your spirit, as I already told you, will become free. Then you will comprehend and accept our testimony.'

[11] Says **Nicodemus**: 'Dear Master, you wisest of the wise. Oh, do tell me clearly when, oh when this so ardently awaited time will come.'

[12] Thereupon I answered, saying: 'My friend, you are not yet mature enough that I may tell you the time, day and hour. Look, until the new wine has not properly fermented it remains turbid, and if you pour it into a crystal cup and hold the cup against the sun, its mighty light will be unable to penetrate through the turbidity of the new wine. It is the same also with man. Not until he has properly fermented and through this process of fermentation eliminated all impurity from his within, can the light of the Heavens permeate his being. But I will now tell you something. If you do understand, you will know the time. So listen.'

## CHAPTER 20
### Nicodemus and the Kingdom of God on Earth; Earthly images of spiritual things; Continuation of the discussion: Nicodemus fails to understand.

*John 3,13-15 "No one has ascended into heaven but he who descended from heaven, the Son of man. And as Moses lifted up the serpent in the wilderness, so must the son of man be lifted up, that whoever believes in him may have eternal life."*

[1] The Lord, 'Behold, no one ascends to Heaven except the one who has come down from Heaven, namely, the Son of Man who resides in Heaven. And as Moses in the wilderness lifted up a serpent, thus also the Son of Man must be lifted up, so that all who believe in Him may not be lost, but have eternal life. Tell Me, do you understand this?'

[2] Says **Nicodemus**: 'Dear Master, how could I understand it? You possess a strange kind of wisdom. As I mentioned before, it might be easier for me to read the ancient Egyptian hieroglyphs than understand your wisdom. I must now honestly admit that if I were not captivated by your mighty deeds, I would have to regard you as a fool or one who likes to play tricks, for no sensible man has ever spoken the way you do. But your deeds show that you have come to us as a teacher from God, and you must possess an abundance of divine might and wisdom without which no one is able to perform such acts.

[3] And where the 'one' is purely divine, also the 'two' must be of God. Your deeds, dear Master, are divine and so must also be your teaching about the Kingdom of God on Earth, whether I understand it or not. If I now, form a somewhat worldly viewpoint, look at the thesis 'No one ascends to Heaven, except the one who has come down from Heaven,' and this should be the Son of Man who always resides in Heaven – then I am at a loss to understand. Dear Master, since Enoch and Elijah hardly any man on Earth would have been so fortunate as to visibly ascend to Heaven. You may become the third. And if you perhaps do become the third, would that be of any use to all other men who, because they had not come down from Heaven, could not ever attain to the Heavens?

[4] Besides, you said that the One who had come down from Heaven is only apparently on Earth, but in truth still in the Heavens. According to this, for the present just Enoch, Elijah and maybe late on also you would be the only ones to participate in the Kingdom of God that is to come, whereas all the other millions upon millions may lay themselves in their damp dark grave for all eternities and thanks to God's grace and mercy once more turn into Earth and finally vanish.'

[5] Dear Master, such a Kingdom of God on Earth is declined with thanks by the poor earthworms who – ridiculous enough from every aspect – are called 'men'. Who does not know that this is how it is and has always been? One swallow does not make a summer, nor do three. What had Enoch done and what Elijah that they were received into Heaven form Earth? Actually nothing else but what their heavenly nature made them do. Thus they had no merit, and according to your explanation just now, they were only received into Heaven from the Earth because, like you, they had come from the Heavens.

[6] Look, this offers poor mankind on this harsh Earth very little hope and practically no comfort. But as I already told you earlier, this does not change the fact that I consider your teaching still divine and supremely wise, although, as I already proved in one of your assertions, looked at with the natural reason it is and must be plain folly, which you will realize as well as I do.

[7] But what you mean with the lifting up of the Son of Man, similar to that of the brazen serpent of Moses in the wilderness and how and why all those are to have

eternal life who believer in the serpent-like lifted-up Son of Man, that already borders on the parabolic, that is, on something that in itself is utter nonsense. Who is this Son of Man? Where is he now? What is he doing? Does he, too, like Enoch and Elijah, come from the Heavens? Is he still going to be born? What are people who have surely never seen him, like I, supposed to believe concerning this Son of Man. How can he come to this Earth if he is still in Heaven? Where is he going to be lifted up and when? Will he thereby become an invincibly mighty king of the Jews?

[8] Look, dear Master, this surely sounds most peculiar from the mouth of a man who proves by his acts that he must be filled with divine power and might. However, as already said, I shall not let all this confound me and am still regarding you as a great prophet sent by God.

[9] You may see from this that I am not one of those who promptly reject a teaching they do not comprehend. Therefore, I still ask you to give me a little more explanation, for as things are I cannot possibly understand you. Look, I am much respected in the land of the Jews, especially in the City of Salem, where I am the head of all the Jews. If I introduce you and your teaching, this will be accepted and introduced whereas if I drop it, it will really be dropped and find no acceptance. Therefore, be good enough and give me a little bit more light.'

[10] I say: 'That was a lengthy discourse, and you have spoken like a man who knows nothing of heavenly things. But it cannot be any different, for you are in the night of the world and not inclined to see the light that has come from the Heavens to illumine the darkness of the world's night. You do possess a slight gleam, but still do not recognize what is practically under your very nose.'


## CHAPTER 21
### About the mission of the Messiah. Judgment and punishment

*John 3,16. "For God so loved the world that he gave his only Son, that whoever believes in him should not perish but have eternal life."*

[1] I say: 'I tell you: God is love and the Son is His wisdom. And God loved the world so much that He gave His only-begotten son, that is, His wisdom, emanating from Him from eternity, into this world that all who believe in Him may not die but have eternal life. Tell Me, is this too incomprehensible to you?'

[2] Says **Nicodemus**: 'I have the feeling as if I should understand it, but then I really do not understand. If only I knew where the Son of Man fits in, then I should be all right. You also spoke of God's only-begotten Son, whom God's love gave into the world. Are the 'Son of Man' and 'God's only-begotten Son' one and the same individual?'

[3] I say: 'Look here. I have a head, a body and hands and feet. The head, the body, hands and feet are flesh, and this flesh is the Son of Man, for what is flesh comes from the flesh. But in this Son of Man who is flesh there dwells God's

wisdom, and that is God's only-begotten Son. Not God's only-begotten Son, but only the Son of Man will, like the brazen Moses-serpent in the wilderness, be lifted up, and many will be taking offense at that. Those who do not take offense but believe and will adhere to His name, to them He will give the power to be called children of God, and their life and kingdom will be everlasting.

**John 3,17. "For God sent the son into the world, not to condemn the world, but that the world might be saved through him."**

[4] You must not expect some judgment of the world as for instance wars, floods or even a fire from the Heavens consuming all the heathens. For see, God did not send His only-begotten Son (divine wisdom) into the world (into this human flesh) to judge (destroy) this world, but to fully save it, that is, that also the flesh might not perish, but may rise to eternal life together with the spirit. (Under flesh in this case not so much the actual flesh of the body is to be understood, but rather the fleshly desires of the soul.) However, in order to attain to this, the material feelings of exaltation in the flesh must be eradicated by belief, namely belief in the Son of Man that He has come into the world, born from eternity out of God, so that all shall have eternal life who believe in His name and adhere to it.

**John 3:18. "He who believes in him is not condemned; he who does not believe is condemned already, because he has not believed in the name of the only Son of God."**

[5] Whosoever, be he Jew or Gentile, will believe in Him, shall not ever be judged and thereby perish, but the one who will take offense at the Son of Man and not believe in Him, then already judged, for the fact that he will not and cannot believe because his feeling of exaltation causes him to take offense at the name and nature of the Son of Man, is already such a man's judgment. Do you understand this now? I have presented it to you with great clarity.'

[6] Says **Nicodemus**: 'Yes, yes, I halfway do understand the meaning of your highly mystical words, but they appear to have been spoken to no purpose, as long as the by you so highly regarded Son of Man in whom there dwells the fullness of God's wisdom is not present and you are either unable or unwilling to give details of the time and place where he will be appearing.

[7] Thus also your judgment, which you connect mainly with unbelief, sounds rather mysterious. If the judgment is neither a flood nor war or pestilence and also not a consuming fire, but only unbelief as such, to tell the plain truth, dear Master, I still cannot grasp the meaning of your words. For whoever does not comprehend just one or maybe two points of a speech fundamentally does not comprehend the entire speech. What actually does your "judgment" mean? What new meaning do you ascribe to this concept?'

[8] I say: 'My friend, soon I too could say to you: I find it hard to understand why you are unable to grasp the perfectly clear sense of My words. You say you do not understand the concept of "judgment" and I have made it so plain to you.

**John 3:19.** *"And this is the judgment, that the light has come into the world, and men loved darkness rather than light, because their deeds were evil."*

[9] See, this is the judgment that not the God-light from the Heavens has come into the world, but men having been released from the darkness and set into the light still by fare prefer the darkness to the God-light now in abundance before their eyes. That men reject the light is proved by their works which are evil all through.

[10] Where can you find an initial complete faith, where the right piety? Where does one love another, except he has some selfish motive? Where are those now who loved their wife for the sake of fertility? They love the young harlots for sensual pleasure, lechery and harlotry, for he who carries on with the other sex in downright idolatry of lust and fornication commits true harlotry, and this the evil of all evils. Where is there a thief who would take a lamp and steal visibly?

**John 3:20.** *"For everyone who does evil hates the light, and does not come to the light, lest his deeds should be exposed."*

[11] See, all those who are ill-disposed and act accordingly are the ones whose works are bad. Whosoever loves and practices such acts is an enemy of the light, hates it and will do all in his power to avoid it, so that his evil works, which he knows are tabooed by the light and judged, should not in the light be recognized in their ugliness and punished.

[12] And see, therein consists the actual judgment, but what you understand as judgment, is not the judgment, but only a punishment following the judgment.

[13] If you enjoy walking in the night, that is already a judgment of your soul, since you prefer the night to the day. But if you then knock against something and hurt yourself badly or even fall into a hole or deep ditch, such a knocking or fall is not the judgment, but only the consequence of the judgment within you who love the night and hate the day.

**John 3:21.** *"But he who does what is true comes to the light, that it may be clearly seen that his deeds have been wrought in God."*

[14] If, however, you are a friend of the light, the day and the truth out of God, you will also act in accordance with divine truth and will surely long for your works to come to the light and be revealed to everyone, for you know that your works, because they were done in the light of truth out of God, are good and righteous and thus deserve appreciation and visible reward.

[15] Therefore, who is a friend of the light will not walk in the night but by day, and he will recognize the light immediately, because he is from the light, and this light is called – faith of the heart.

[16] Thus, whoever believes in the Son of Man that Jew is a light out of God,

has already life within him. But who does not believe, has already the judgment within him, and the judgment is the very unbelief.

[17] I think you will have understood Me now.'

# CHAPTER 22
## There is no truth in man, except only love

[1] Says **Nicodemus**: 'Except for one thing everything is now clear to me, but the One is still missing, and that is the remarkable Son of Man himself without whom all your wise words with the splendid explanations are completely lost. What use is to me the belief or the best and firmest will to believe in the son of Man if he himself is not there? One cannot create for oneself a Son of Man from the air or purely an idea. Tell me, therefore, where I may find this eternal Son of God and be assured that I will fully believe in him.'

[2] **I say**: 'If I had not realized that, you would never have received these explanations from Me. But you came to Me by night and not by day, although you had heard and seen much of what I have done. However, since you came to Me during the natural night as well as the corresponding night of your soul, it is not hard to understand that you do not yet see your way concerning the Son of Man.

[3] I tell you: if someone seeks the Son of Man by night, afraid to do so during the day in front of all the people, thus risking his reputation, he will not find what he is seeking, for you, as a very wise man among the Jews, will surely know that the night, whatever kind of night it may be, is not at all suitable for seeking and finding. Therefore, who seeks the Son of Man must seek him by day and not by night, then he will allow himself to be found.

[4] Only that I tell you: go to John who because of the water is at present baptizing at Enon near Salim. He will tell you whether the only-begotten Son of God is already here or not. There you shall get to know him.'

[5] Says **Nicodemus**: 'Oh, oh, dear Master, that will not be easy, for all my days are too busy. Bear in mind that in the city and nearest surroundings there are dwelling, including aliens, over 800,000 people whom I, as there head, have in my care. In addition to that I have to attend daily to temple business which cannot be put off. If this grace is not bestowed upon me here in Jerusalem, I shall have to forgo it. Look, I need for this undertaking at least three full days, and in my business this would be like three years for another person.

[6] Therefore, you must forgive me if I cannot follow your advice, but whenever you should come to Jerusalem with your disciples, do come to me and I will provide good lodgings for all of you. You and all those who are with you shall always have a sincere friend and well-wisher in me. My house, which is large enough to put up a thousand people, is situated on the David Square inside the Gate of Solomon, also called the Golden Gate. Whenever you come, it will be completely at your disposal. Whatever is in my power shall always be done to serve you. If you ever need something, tell me, and I shall provide it.

[7] For see, a great change has taken place within me. I love, my dear Master, more than anything I have ever valued, and this love tells me in a way: You yourself are the One for whose sake you bade me to Enon to John. Maybe it is not as I feel it within me, but be that as it may, I love you with all my heart since I recognize in you a great Master of true divine wisdom. Your deeds, the likes of which no one before you has ever performed, have filled me with deepest wonder, but your great wisdom had captivated my heart even more for you, you dear Master. I love you. Do tell me whether my heart gives a right testimony about you?'

[8] **I say**: 'Have a little more patience and everything will become clear to you. In a short while I will return to you and be your guest, then you shall come to know everything.

[9] But do follow the prompting of your heart, which will teach you in a moment more than all the five books of Moses and all the prophets. For see, nothing in man is true, except love. Therefore, adhere to it and you will be walking by day. But now about something else.

[10] I will now go into Judaea where I shall preach the Kingdom of God. You are the highest administrator over this land. Not for My own sake, but for the sake of My disciples, do let Me have a security pass as used among the Jews in accordance with the Roman law, so that they do not have any trouble with customs and tolls. Children are, of course, free, but they must be registered as such. It would actually be easy for Me to pass everywhere free and unhampered with legions, but I do not wish to cause annoyance to anyone and, therefore, submit to the law of Rome.'

[11] Says **Nicodemus**: 'You shall have that immediately, dear Master, I shall write it out myself and bring it to you in an hour, for it is not far to my house from here.'

[12] Nicodemus now hurries home and already in half an hour brings the requested security pass. When we were in possession of this pass on a piece of parchment, I blessed the uptight Nicodemus in My heart. He took his leave with tears in his eyes and asked Me once more to make use of his house on My return to Jerusalem which I also promised him. But I advised him to keep the temple clean and he promised this solemnly. Thus we parted in the morning.


## CHAPTER 23
## IN THE JEWISCH LAND SURROUNDING JERUSALEM ON THE WAY TO SAMARIA
### Baptism with water and with the Spirit

**John 3,22. *After this, Jesus went into Judea with his disciples, stayed there with them, and baptized.***

[1] When day had fully dawned, we got on our way and went into the Jewish

land which, actually belonging to Jerusalem, surrounded this city in the same way as today a district lies around its principal city. One could easily walk through the whole land in a few days.

[2] And what did I actually do in this land? The verse says that I was staying there with them and then baptized. Here arise the questions who in fact 'they' were and what it means that I stayed with them. "They" are above all the disciples, whose number had again increased by a few in Jerusalem, but then also all those who believed in and sympathized with My teaching.

[3] And all those who adopted My teaching in full faith were openly baptized by Me with water, but secretly with the spirit of My eternal love and wisdom and thereby obtained the power to be called "God's children". That is what I was doing as I was staying there. The teaching and what I did was partly recorded by the other three evangelists and need not be stated here. This actually consisted mainly in illustrating all the serious defects from which the Jews and Pharisees were suffering and in preaching the love for God and one's neighbor.

[4] First I described all the weakness, admonished the sinners to repent, warned all who adopted My teaching against reverting to the old leaven of the Pharisees and, in corroboration of My most gentle teaching, performed miraculous acts needed for these so very materialistic times. I also healed many sick, freed the possessed from the unclean spirits and took on more and more disciples.

**John 3,23.** *John too was still baptizing at Enon, near to Salim, because water was plentiful in that region, and people were constantly coming for baptism.*
**John 3,24.** *This was before John's imprisonment.*

[5] As I was traveling through the Jewish land, I also came to the area where John was baptizing in the small desert at Enon near Salim because there was plenty of water, whereas in the region of Bethabara the Jordan had very little water and the same was muddy, dirty and full of foul-smelling vermin. This is why John had changed his location, preached his severe penitential sermons at Enon and there baptized the people who adopted his teaching and did true penance.

[6] Among those there were also many who had already adopted My teaching, but had not yet been baptized by John. These asked Me whether it was necessary to be baptized by John beforehand. And I said to them: 'Only one thing is needed and that is to actually comply with My teaching. But whosoever wishes to be cleansed by John beforehand, while he is still doing this work, will only benefit from such a cleansing.' When I had spoken thus, many went to have themselves baptized by John.

**John 3,25.** *Some of John's disciples had fallen into a dispute with Jews (who had come there) about purification (i.e., about My baptism with water compared to John's testimony).*

[7] A dispute arose about the purification by John and My baptism, for John's

disciples could not understand that I, too, baptized with water, since they had heard John's testimony that I would not baptize with water, but with the Holy Spirit. Many Jews, who were already My disciples, maintained that My baptism was a true baptism. For, although I baptized with water like John, My baptism was the only valid one as I did not baptize with natural water alone, but at the same time also with the water of God's Spirit, giving the baptized the obvious power to be called God's children.

**John 3,26.** *And they came to John and said, "Rabbi, the man who was with you on the other side of the Jordan, to whom you bore witness (that he would baptize with the Holy Spirit), here he is, baptizing (with water), and crowds are flocking to him."*

[8] Following these discussions, **John's disciples** went with the Jews to John and said: 'Listen, Rabbi, the same man who was with you on the other side of the Jordan. To whom you bore witness that he would baptize with the Holy Spirit, is now here in the vicinity and baptizes also with water as you do. How are we to understand this? Is this Baptist really the One to whom you bore the great witness?'

[9] **John** however said to his disciples: 'Go and ask him: "Are you the one who is to come or should we wait for another?" Pay good attention to what he will be telling you and then tell me. Only then will I fully answer your query.'

[10] Thereupon several of John's disciples come to Me and ask Me as suggested by John. But I give them the well-known answer, that they should tell John what they have seen, namely, that the blind see, the lame walk, the deaf hear and how the gospel of the Kingdom of God is being preached to the poor. And happy he who does not take offense. The disciples again return to John and immediately tell him what they have seen and heard.


CHAPTER 24
The Baptist's last and greatest witness to the Lord:
"He must increase, but I must decrease."

**John 3,27.** *John's answer was: "A man can have only what God gives him."*

[1] But **John** collects himself and says to his disciples: 'Listen, I am convinced of this: A man cannot take anything, especially in things concerning the spirit, unless it is first given him from the Heavens. The unusual man who had Himself baptized by me on the other side of the Jordan and above whom I saw the Spirit of God descending from the Heavens in the form of a little cloud of light, as gently as a dove alighting upon its nests, and to whom I bore witness, could not as an ordinary man have taken what He possess. He is more than an ordinary man and

does appear to have the power Himself to take from the Heavens and to either keep what He has taken or pass it on to whomsoever He wishes. And I believe that all of us received what we have from His grace. Therefore, we cannot possibly tell Him what to do and how to do it. He gives and we are the ones who take it from Him. He has His winnowing fan in His hand and will sweep the floor of His barn, but burn the chaff with the eternal fire and use the ashes the way He sees fit.

**John 3,28. *"You yourselves can testify that I said that I am not the Messiah, but sent as His forerunner."***

[2] You yourselves are my witnesses that I told the priests and Levites, who came to me from Jerusalem, that I am not the Messiah, but sent as His forerunner. How then could I find fault with what the One is doing who has His own winnowing fan in His hand? In whatever way He should sweep His threshing floor we cannot make rules for Him. For the field (the world) is His, thus also the wheat (the children of God) and the chaff (the children of the world or the devil), and His is the barn (Heaven) and His the fire (Hell), which never goes out.

**John 3,29. *"It is the bridegroom (Lord) to whom the bride belongs. And the bridegroom's friend, who stand by and listens to him, is overjoyed at hearing the bridegroom's voice. This joy is now mine."***

[3] Whoever has the bride (wisdom of the Heavens) is a true bridegroom, but the bridegroom's friend standing by and listening to him is overjoyed, at hearing the bridegroom's voice. And look, this joy is now mine. But when the Lord Himself comes, the herald's mission is ended. For the herald's sole duty is to announce the arrival of the Lord. Once the Lord had arrived, the herald is no longer needed.

**John 3,30. *"As he increases, I must decrease."***

[4] Therefore, I must now decrease, whereas He as the Lord must increase with the men of this Earth. You were always my disciples since I came to you as a messenger. Has any one of you ever heard me boast about it? At all times I reserved the proper honor for Him to whom it is due. When I testified that I was not good enough to unfasten His shoes, I surely did not raise myself above Him, but gave Him all the honor people's blindness wanted to show me. Therefore I repeat: Now my mission is ended. Once the Lord has come Himself, the forerunner is no longer needed, wherefore the messenger (the flesh) must now grow less, whereas He as the Lord (the Spirit) must grow beyond all flesh. There is a vast difference between the herald and Him who out of His own power sends the herald wherever He wishes.

**John 3,31. *"He who comes from above is above all others. He who is from the Earth belongs to the Earth. He who comes from Heaven is above all."***

[5] The one who has the power to give laws is above and the one who must obey is below. No one can rightly be above unless he originates from there. But he who comes truly from above is above all others. He who is from the Earth can never be from above, but belongs to the Earth and cannot speak other than of earthly things. However, He who comes from Heaven is above all, for He is the Lord and can, therefore, do whatever He wishes. He can baptize with water, fire and spirit, for everything is His.

[6] I still do not think that He Himself baptizes with water, but only with fire of the Spirit, whereas His disciples will baptize the people beforehand in the way I do it, that is, all those who did not receive the baptism with water from me. The baptism with water is no use to man unless followed by the baptism with the Spirit of God.

**John 3,32.** *"And bears witness to what he has seen and heard, yet hardly anyone accepts his witness."*

[7] Water gives evidence of nothing but water and cleanses the skin from the earth's dirt. The Spirit of God, however, with which the Lord alone is able to baptize, since God's Spirit is His Spirit, testifies to God and that which only He at all times sees and hears in God.

[8] Unfortunately, so far hardly anyone accepts this holy witness, for what is mud stays mud and rejects the Spirit, unless the mud first passes through the fire there to become itself Spirit. A proper fire consumes everything except the Spirit, which is a mighty fire itself. Therefore, the Lord's spirit baptism will destroy many, and because of that many will fear to accept it.

**John 3,33.** *"But he who accepts keeps it sealed (within him) that God is true (naturally within the One who bore witness to Him through the baptism with the Spirit of God)."*

[9] However, he who will accept this baptism and its holy witness will keep sealed within him from the world the knowledge that the One who baptized him with the Spirit is truly God and alone able to give eternal life. Now you say within yourselves: 'Why keep sealed within oneself the Heavens' witness of God through God?' I have already told you: Mud is and remains mud and spirit is and remains spirit. If, however, mortal man, who is fundamentally mud, receives the spirit into his mud, will he be able to keep the spirit, unless he preserves it carefully within, that is, in his heart?

[10] Or is there a certain measure according to which spirit is distributed so that everyone may know how much spirit he received? If there is not such a measure, it is up to temporal mud-man to establish in his heart such a measure for the received spirit. And once the spirit has in this measure retired to permanent rest and thus filled up the new measure, only then does the mud-man realize within himself how much of the spirit he has received.

[11] What use would it be to you if by the sea you filled water into a perforated

barrel? Could you ever claim and recognize that you have drawn a given amount of water from the, for you, immeasurable sea? If the barrel is well hooped, you will be able to judge how much of the sea-water is contained in it. The water of the sea, however, is the same throughout, whether in a large or small quantity is of no importance. Thus the sea as such is sea throughout, and wherever one may draw water from the sea, be it much or little, he draws in every part sea-water and will only later know the measure.

**John 3,34. *"For He whom God has sent utters the words of God. God gives His spirit (to Him whom He sent) without measure (not as to a man, but in all His abundance)."***

[12] Thus it is with the One who has come from God to bear witness to God and utter the pure word of God. He Himself is the measureless sea (the Spirit of God). When He gives someone of His Spirit, He does not give it in an endless measure, which only in God can exist in endless abundance, but according to the measure present in man. If a man wishes to obtain the Spirit, his own measure must not be defective and remain open, it must be well hooped and well sealed.

[13] He whom you have just seen and asked whether He were Christ has, although externally also a Son of Man, received God's Spirit not according to a man's measure, but according to the endless measure of God already from eternity, for He Himself is the measureless sea of the Spirit of God within Him. His love represents the Father from eternity, and this is not outside the visible Son of Man, but within Him, who is the fire, the flame and the light from eternity in and form the Father.

**John 3,35. *"The Father loves the Son and has entrusted Him with all authority."***

[14] This loving Father dearly loves His eternal Son, and all power and authority lie in the hands of the Son, and everything we have according to the proper measure, we have drawn from His measureless abundance. He Himself is by His own Word now a man in the flesh among us, and His Word is God, spirit and flesh, and we call it the "son". Thus the Son is also within Himself the very life everlastingly.

**John 3,36. *"He who believes in the Son has eternal life. But he who does not believe in the Son shall not see that life: God's wrath rests upon him."***

[15] Thus, he who accepts the Son and believes in Him has eternal life already within him. For, just as God Himself is in every word His own most perfect eternal life, He is that also in every man who absorbs His living Word and holds on to it. On the other hand, he who does not accept the Word of God from the mouth of the Son, thus does not believe in the Son, shall not and cannot receive life nor see and feel it within him, and the wrath of God which is the judgment of all things that

have no life, except the one of the forever immutable law of compulsion, will rest upon him as long as he does not believe in the Son.

[16] I, John, have now told you all this and have borne all of you a fully valid witness. With my own hands I have cleansed you from the dirt of the Earth. Go now and accept His Word, so that you may receive the baptism of His Spirit, for without that all my efforts on your behalf are futile. I would like to go to Him myself, but He does not want that and reveals it to me through my spirit that I should stay here, since I have already received in the spirit what is still lacking in you.'

[17] This is the last and greatest testimony by John concerning Me and does not require any further explanation as it is already self-explanatory.

[18] The reason, however, why it is not given in the Gospel in such detail is and remains always the same. Firstly because in those days it was the way things had to be written, namely, that only the main points were recorded and everything else, which a person with a wide-awake spirit could easily understand anyway, was omitted and, secondly, to prevent the living holy content in the Word from being defiled and desecrated. Therefore, every such verse is a well-covered grain of seed with a latent germ for an everlasting life and its immeasurable abundance of wisdom.

## CHAPTER 25
## ON THE ROAD TO SAMARIA HALT AT JACOB'S WELL NEAR SYCHAR
### Furious persecution by the temple servants

*John 4,1. When the Lord learned that a report had reached the Pharisees that Jesus was winning and baptizing more disciples than John.*
*John 4,2. Although Jesus Himself did not baptize, but only His disciples.*
*John 4,3. Jesus left Judaea and set out once more for Galilee.*

[1] Following these words of John, his disciples soon joined Me, and the number of My disciples kept growing from day to day, often from hour to hour. For everyone who began to believe in Me and upon whom I, according to the measure of his faith and following the baptism with water which was performed by My first disciples, had laid My hands, became filled with spiritual strength and courage and lost all fear of physical death.

[2] Since many heard of this, they spread the news wherever they went, although I had forbidden it. Besides, all My deeds also, often with additions and exaggerations, were made known all over Judaea and with the Jews, who were always craving for miracles, this naturally resulted in the fact that every day more and more of them came to Me and in many cases also stayed with Me.

[3] But, regrettably, this had also the inevitable result that all this came to the ears of the Pharisees and, as already mentioned, with additions and exaggerations, some of which sounded so peculiar that even some Romans began to think that I would have to be either Zeus himself or at least one of his

sons.

[4] The Romans also, sent investigators to Me, but they did not find what they had been sent for. On those occasions I usually did not do any signs, so as to prevent these superstitious people from becoming even more obtuse than they already were.

[5] From these exaggerations there eventually originated quite a number of false gospels which distorted the true one.

[6] The Pharisees, these malicious and exceedingly jealous chiefs of the temple and the Scripture, promptly began to consult together how to put a stop to our activities. They planned either to do away with us in a seemingly harmless way or at least provide for us a lifelong accommodation in an institution – nicely situated underground – as they later on managed to arrange with Herod for John (the Baptist).

[7] That I was quite aware of these noble intentions is, of course, obvious but, in order to avoid scuffles and annoying rows, I had no option but to leave the ultramontane, dark Judaea and go to the more liberal Galilee.

### John 4,4. He had to pass through Samaria.

[8] It was even not advisable to travel the direct road to Galilee, but rather through Samaria which with the help of the Romans had already long since freed itself from the Priesthood of the temple (an easy and desirable task for the Romans whose principle it was anyway to split up the lands to make it easier to govern them).

[9] Because of this, the Samaritans were in the eyes of the priesthood in Jerusalem also the most despicable and blasphemous people on Earth. On the other hand, the priests of Jerusalem had with the Samaritans such a reputation that they usually described the worst possible thing with the name of a temple priest. If, for instance, a Samaritan in a state of unjustified agitation said to someone, 'You Pharisee' the thus abused sued the offender who often had to pay for his indiscretion with a stiff fine and imprisonment for years. Of course, it is obvious that a Pharisee or other priest would have been ill-advised to enter Samaria. This proved most useful to Me and all those who followed Me, for in Samaria we were safe from the evil persecution by the temple servants.

### John 4,5. He came to a Samaritan town called Sychar, near the little village which Jacob gave to his son Joseph.

[10] The road ran through Sychar, a city near the ancient little village which Jacob gave his son Joseph on his birth, together with the inhabitants of the little village consisting mainly of shepherds whom he received with Rachel as her dowry. The city of Sychar was not exactly a leading city of this land, but many very wealthy Samaritans were living there, as well as many a rich Roman, as this city was beautifully situated and the whole region very healthy.

*John 4,6. Now Jacob's well was there. Since Jesus was tired after his journey. He sat down on the stone curb of the well, and it was about the sixth hour.*

[11] According to the present calculation of time, we set out from Judaea already at about 4 o'clock in the morning, walked briskly without a rest and arrived at exactly 12 noon, which was then the 6$^{th}$ hour, at the ancient Jacob's well which was situated some 40 paces in front of the little village in the direction of Sychar. This well had a very good spring, was enclosed by a curb gracefully chiseled in the old style and surrounded by shady trees.

[12] Since it was midsummer, the day was hot and My body had become very tired after the strenuous journey. All those who had followed Me from Judaea and already earlier from Galilee sought in their exhaustion shelter and a most desirable rest, partly in the little village, partly under shady trees.

[13] Even the first disciples, that is, Peter, My John the Evangelist, Andrew, Thomas, Philip and Nathanael, threw themselves down in the rich grass under the trees. I alone, although very tired too, seated Myself on the stone curb of the well knowing beforehand that there soon would be a good opportunity to have a useful discussion at the well with the stubborn but otherwise more open-minded Samaritans. At the same time, I was already very thirsty and waiting for a vessel to draw water, for which a disciple had gone into the village, but had not returned with it yet.

## CHAPTER 26
### The Lord and the woman at Jacob's well

*John 4,7. There came a woman from Samaria (actually from the city of Sychar: She was born in Samaria the capital of this land) to draw water from the well. Jesus said to her: "Woman, give Me a drink."*
*John 4,8. For His disciples had gone away to the city to buy food.*

[1] While I am still waiting in vain for a vessel from the little village, a Samaritan woman from Sychar comes with a vessel just at the right moment on this hot day to draw a delicious, refreshing drink from Jacob's well. Only after she has drawn up on a cord the vessel willed with water, without taking any notice of Me, I address her saying:, 'Woman, I am very thirsty, let Me have a drink from your water jar.'

*John 4,9. Says the Samaritan woman to Jesus: "What, You who are obviously a Jew ask a drink of water of me, a Samaritan woman? For the (proud) Jews do not associate with us (poor) Samaritans."*

[2] **The woman**, seeing that I am Jew, is quite astonished and says after a

while: 'Are you not one of those whom I met as they were entering the city and asking where one could buy food? They were proud Jews. Judging by your clothing, you must be a Jew too, and I am a Samaritan woman. How is it that you ask me for a drink of water? Yes, yes, you proud Jews, when help is needed, even a Samaritan woman is good enough for you, but otherwise you no longer pay any attention to us. If I were able to drown the whole of Judaea with this vessel of water, I would be only too pleased to let you drink the desired water from this jar. But otherwise I would rather watch you die of thirst than offer you even a drop of water from it.

**John 4,10. Jesus answered her: "If you only knew the gift of God and who it is who says to you 'give me a drink' you would have asked Him and He would have given you living water to drink."**

[3] **I say**: 'You speak like that because you are blind in your perception. If you were seeing and recognized the gift of God and who the one is who is speaking to you and has said: 'woman, let Me have a drink', then you would ask Him on your knees for true water, and he would give you a drink of living water. I tell you: whosoever believes what I say to him, from his body will be flowing streams of the same living water as is written in Isaiah 44:3 and Joel 3:1.'

**John 4,11. Says the woman: "Sir, You have nothing with which to draw the water, and the well is deep. Where else could You get a living water?"**

[4] Says **the woman**: 'You seem to be well versed in the Scripture. But as I recognize from your request for a drink of water from my jar that you have certainly no vessel to draw water from this deep well, where no one could reach the water with his hand, I would like to know how you could manage to procure it from somewhere? Or do you wish to intimate to me in a veiled way that you desire to have an affair with me? I am still young and attractive enough being not yet 30 years of age. But such a proposition on the part of a Jew to a most despised Samaritan woman would be much too surprising since you prefer animals to us Samaritan people. There is not a chance that I could be persuaded to do this.'

**John 4,12. "Are you a greater man than Jacob our ancestor, who gave us this precious well, from which he drank himself, also his children and his cattle?"**

[5] Who and what are you that you dare speak to me like this? Are you maybe more than our ancestor Jacob, who gave us this well and drank form it himself, and so did his children and his cattle? What are you pretending to be? Look, I am a poor woman, for if I were rich I would not come myself in this heat to get a refreshing drink. Do you, as a Jew, want to make me even more miserable than I already am? Look at my clothes, which are hardly sufficient to cover my nakedness, and it will be clear to you that I am very poor. How can you demand of

me, a poor, miserable woman, to even ask you, a proud Jew, to be allowed to serve you in lust? Shame on you, if you are thinking of this. But actually you do not look as if you were like that and, therefore, I do not really mean what I just said to you, but since you did start to talk to me, tell me in plain language what you mean by your living water.'

**John 4,13. Jesus said to her: "Everyone who drinks this water will be thirsty again."**

[6] **Say I**: 'I already told you that you are blind in your perception, and so it is understandable that you cannot and will not grasp the meaning of My words. See, I also told you: whosoever believes in My words, from his loins streams of living water will be flowing. See, I have already been in this world for 30 years and have never yet touched a woman, why should I now suddenly desire you? Oh you blind, foolish woman, And even if I wanted this with you, you would surely get thirsty again and need a drink to quench your thirst. If I offered you a living water, it is obvious that with this I wanted to quench your life's thirst forever. For, see, My Word, My teaching is such a water.

**John 4,14. "Whoever drinks the water that I shall give him will never suffer thirst any more. The water that I shall give him will be an inner spring for him welling up into everlasting life."**

[7] For whoever drinks the natural water of this or any other will soon be thirsty again. But the one who drinks (accepts with faith into his heart) the spiritual water (My teaching), which only I can give, will not ever be thirsty again, for the water I give to anyone becomes an inner spring for him welling up into everlasting life.

[8] You take Me to be a proud, arrogant Jew, but see I am meek with all My soul and full of the deepest humility. Thus, who does not become as humble as I am will not participate in the Kingdom of God which has now descended to the Earth.

[9] At the same time the living water offered to you is the sole true cognition of God and eternal life out of God, thus welling from God, the life of all life, into man as eternal life where it becomes an inexhaustible, ever-present life, flowing back into God's life and producing in God one and the same freely active life. See, such water is what is what I am offering you. How could you misunderstand Me so much?'

**John 4,15. Says the woman: "Sir, give me that water and then I shall not be thirsty, nor have to come all this way to draw water (which I find difficult)."**

[10] Says **the woman**: 'Then give me that water, so that I may never be thirsty and need no longer go to all the trouble to come here to draw water from this well. For I live at the other end of city and have to walk quite a distance to come here.'

*John 4,16. Jesus says to her: "Go home, call your husband and come back (with him)."*

[11] I say: 'O woman, you do not understand. There is no point in talking to you since you are quite ignorant of spiritual things. Go back to the city, call your husband and return to Me with him. I will speak to him, he will surely understand Me better than you do. Or is your husband also like you that he would like to quench his natural physical thirst with the spiritual water of humility?'

## CHAPTER 27
### About true worship of God in spirit and in truth

*John 4,17. The woman answered: "I have no husband." Says Jesus to her: "You are right in saying that you have no husband."*

[1] **The woman** replies to that quite snappy: 'I have no husband', whereupon I say to her with a smile: 'That was brief, good and correct. Now you have really spoken the truth.

*John 4,18. "You have had 5 husbands, and the man with whom you are now living is not your husband, you told me the truth there (how things are with you)."*

[2] For see, My dear *(woman)*, you have already had 5 husbands and, since your nature was not in accord with theirs, they soon fell ill and died, for not one could last more than a year with you. You have bad vermin in your body, and your vermin soon kills anyone who sleeps with you. The man you have now is not your husband, but only your lover towards his and your ruin. Yes, yes, you have really told Me the truth.'

*John 4,19. The woman says to Him: "Sir, I can now see that you are a prophet."*

[3] Here **the woman** is startled, but does not want to commit herself and says after a while: 'Sir, I see that you are a prophet. Since you know so much, you may also know what could help me?

*John 4,20. "Our fathers worshiped on this mountain (Gerizim), but You Jews say that the temple where God should be worshiped is in Jerusalem, (which of this is valid before God?)"*

[4] I am aware that in such things God alone can help, but how and where should He be worshiped? Our fathers say that God must be worshiped on mount

Gerizim where already the first patriarchs worshiped Him. But you say that Jerusalem is the right place where God should be worshiped. Since you are obviously a prophet of God, tell me where one should really worship God effectively. For look, I am still young and people say that I am very beautiful. It would be terrible if my vermin were to consume me while I am still alive. Oh what a poor, miserable woman I am.'

**John 4,21. Says Jesus: "Believe Me, woman, the time is coming (and is already here) when you will worship God the Father neither on this mountain, nor in Jerusalem."**

[5] **I say**: 'Woman, I know your poverty, your misery and your sick body, and I know also your heart which is not really the best, but also not too bad. See, that is the reason why I am now speaking to you. Where the heart is still reasonably good, there is every possibility of help. But you are quite wrong in that you are in doubt as to where God should be worshiped worthily and effectively.

[6] Believe Me when I tell you: the time is coming and it is already here when you will worship the Father neither on the mountain nor in Jerusalem.'

[7] Here **the woman** is alarmed and says: 'Woe upon me, woe upon the whole nation! What will then become of us? Then we must have sinned terribly, just like the Jews? But why did Jehovah not send us a prophet this time who would have warned us? Although you have come to us as a true prophet, what is the use now if you say: In future God will be worshiped neither on the mountain nor in Jerusalem? Does not that mean as much as – which I could read from your suddenly very serious face – God will forsake His people completely and take residence with another nation? Where on Earth may this be? Oh do tell me, so that I may go there to worship God the Father as a true penitent, asking Him to help me, a wretched woman, and not to forsake my people completely.'

[8] To that **I** reply: 'Now listen to Me carefully, so that you may understand what I am saying. Why are you full of doubt and fear? Do you think God is as faithless concerning the keeping of His promises as men are toward each other?

**John 4,22. "You do not know what you worship, but we do know what we worship for salvation still comes from the Jews."**

[9] You do climb the mountain there to worship, but do not know what or whom you worship. The same applies to those who worship on Jerusalem. They do run into the temple and they are wailing there horribly but they do not know either what they are doing or what they are worshiping.

[10] Nevertheless, as God has pronounced through the mouth of the prophets, salvation does not come from you, but from the Jews. Just read the third verse in the second chapter of the prophet Isaiah, and you will find it.'

[11] Says **the woman**: 'Yes, I do know that there it is written that the law goes froth from Zion, since it is also kept there in the Ark of the Covenant. But why do you say then: 'neither on the mountain nor in Jerusalem?'

*John 4,23. "But the time approaches, indeed it is already here (before your eyes), when those who are real worshipers will worship the Father in spirit and in truth, for the Father wants to be worshiped by men in this way."*

[12] **I say**: 'You still have not understood Me. See, God the Father from eternity is neither a mountain nor a temple nor the Ark of the Covenant and thus does not dwell on the mountain or in the temple or in the Ark of the Covenant. Therefore I told you: The time is approaching, and indeed is already here before your eyes, when the true worshipers (as you can see them here resting under the trees in great numbers, some of whom you already met in the city on their way to buy food) will worship God the Father in spirit and in truth, for from now on the Father wants to be worshiped by men in this way.'

*John 4,24. "For God is a spirit, and those who worship Him must worship in spirit and in truth."*

[13] 'For see, God is a spirit and those who worship Him just worship in spirit and in truth.

[14] And for that neither a mountain nor any temple is needed, but only a loving, humble and as pure as possible heart. If the heart is what it is meant to be, namely a vessel for the love of God, a vessel full of meekness and humility, then such a heart holds the full truth. And where there is truth, there is light and freedom, for the light of truth liberates every heart. Once the heart is free, the whole person is free too.

[15] Therefore, he who loves God with such a heart is a true worshiper of God the Father, and the Father will always grant his prayer. He will only look at a man's heart and take no notice of the place of worship which is quite unimportant, be it the mountain or Jerusalem, for the Earth belongs to God everywhere. I think you should have understood Me now.'

## CHAPTER 28
### The Lord makes Himself known as the Messiah

[1] Says **the woman**: 'Yes, sir, now you have spoken more clearly. But tell me: Are you no longer thirsty and do you not want to drink from the water-jar of a sinner?' Say I: 'Dear woman, never mind about that for, see, I do prefer you to your jar and your water. When earlier I asked you for a drink, I did not mean from your jar, but from your heart in which there is a much more delicious water than in this well and your jar. With the water of your heart you can also heal your whole body, for that which I find pleasing in you will heal you if you can believe.'

[2] Says **the woman**: 'O sir, how can I manage to bring the water from my heart to my private parts? Forgive me, sir, that I use such frank language with you, but I

am a miserable woman and misery does not know modesty as such, it knows only itself and loosens the tongue according to the extent of the exigency. If I were not as miserable as I am, I would truly offer you my heart. But as things are – O God, you holy Father, help me – I am miserably sick and must not add to my many sins, for to offer such an impure heart to a pure man as you must be would surely be the greatest possible sin.'

[3] **I say**: 'My dear woman, not that you would offer your heart to Me, but I have taken it Myself when I asked you for a drink of water. Therefore, you may offer me your heart, for I accept also a Samaritan's heart. If you love Me, it is good for you, as I loved you already long before you could think of Me.'

[4] Here the beautiful woman blushes and says, somewhat embarrassed: 'Since when do you know me? Have you ever before been in this city or in Samaria? In truth, I have never caught even a glimpse of you anywhere. Oh, pray tell me, when and where did you see me? Do tell me.'

[5] **I say**: 'Neither here nor in Samaria or any other place, yet I already know you since your birth, even much earlier, and I have always loved you like My life. How do you like that? Are you happy about My love? See, when at the age of twelve you fell into a cistern, it was I who pulled you out. But you could not see the hand that lifted you from the cistern. Do you still remember that?'

[6] Here the woman becomes quite confused and does not know what to say, for quite a fire has already kindled in her heart and her love keeps growing visibly.

[7] After her heart has been active for a while, I ask her whether she knows anything about the Messiah who is to come.

***John 4,25. Says the woman: "I know that the Messiah is coming who will be called Christ. When He comes He will (surely) tell us everything (that you have now told me)?"***

[8] Now **the woman**, her cheeks still flushed, says with great emotion: 'Lord, you wisest prophet of God, I do know that the promised Messiah is to come and that His name will be Christ. When he comes, will He not be able to proclaim to us only what you have now told me? But who will tell us when and from where the Messiah will be coming? Maybe you who are so very wise can give me some more detailed information about the coming of the Messiah. You see, we have been waiting already for a long time, but not a word can be heard anywhere about the Messiah. You would do me a great favor if you would tell me when and where the Messiah will definitely come to save His people from its numerous enemies. Oh do tell me if you know it. Maybe the Messiah would also have mercy upon me and help me if I entreat Him?'

***John 4,26. Jesus says to her: "I am He, I who am speaking to you now."***

[9] Say **I** to the woman briefly, but with loving earnest: 'It is I, I who am speaking to you now.'

# CHAPTER 29
## Continuation of the scene: Healing of the woman and her testimony for the found Messiah

*John 4,27. At that moment His disciples returned (from the city with the purchased foods) and were astonished to find Him talking with the woman but none of them said: "What are You asking (her)," or "why are You talking with her?"*

[1] This statement gave the woman a shock, and that all the more because at that moment the disciples returned with food from the city and were astonished to find Me talking to this woman. But none of them dared ask Me or the woman what we had done or discussed together. The other traveling companions, however, including My mother who was present, too, were so fast asleep that they could hardly be roused. The long march had worn all of them out. Finally, also **the one disciple** returned from the little village, who had gone to look for a vessel to draw water, but had not found one. He apologized and said: 'Lord, the little village numbers about 20 houses, but there was not a single person at home and all the doors were safely locked.'

[2] To this I replied: 'Never mind about that. For see, naturally and especially spiritually this is still going to happen to us frequently, that we, driven by the thirst of our love, shall knock at people's doors (hearts) looking for a vessel to draw the living water. But we shall find the hearts locked and empty. Do you understand this allegory?'

[3] Says the disciple quite moved and disconcerted: 'Lord, my dear Master, unfortunately I have indeed understood You. But if that is so, we are not going to be very successful.'

[4] I say: 'And yet, My brother, look at this woman. I tell you, it is worth more to find one who was lost than 99 righteous, who according to their conscience are not in need of penitence, since they believe to be serving God every Sabbath on Mount Gerizim. They even remove from here on the eve of Sabbath all vessels for drawing water, so that on the Sabbath no one may draw water from the well to quench his thirst, whereby in the eyes of the righteous the Sabbath would be desecrated. Oh for the great blind foolishness of such righteous. But here a sinner is standing with a good water jar at our service. Say, who is better? This one or the 99 Sabbath-observers on Mount Gerizim?'

[5] **The woman**, however, says full of remorse: 'Lord, you Son of the Eternal. Here is my jar, use it. I am leaving it here for your service. But let me hurry back to the city, for I am standing here before you in too unworthy attire.' I said: 'Woman, be healed and do what you think is right.'

*John 4,28. The woman left her water jar behind and hurried into the city where she said to the people:*

[6] Weeping with joy the woman leaves her water jar and the well and hurries into the city, but on her way looks back many times, saluting, for she loves Me mightily. Almost out of breath the woman arrives in the city, where she meets a group of men walking up and down a shady lane as they usually do on a Sabbath. **The men**, who knew the woman, asked her jokingly: 'Well, well, why in such a hurry? Where is it burning?' The woman looks at them with loving earnest and says, 'Oh do not joke, you dear men, for our time has become more serious than you may imagine.'

**John 4,29. *"Come and see a man who (sitting outside at Jacob's well and told me everything I ever did. Could not this be Christ (the promised Messiah)?'***

[7] Here **the men** interrupt her and ask full of anxious curiosity: 'Now, now, what is it? Are enemies coming into our land or is a swarm of locusts approaching our district?'

[8] **The woman**, quite exhausted, says: 'Nothing of that kind. The matter is much greater and most extraordinary. Listen to me quietly.

[9] Already an hour ago I went to Jacob's well to fetch some midday water and there I found a Man sitting on the stone curb of the well, who first looked definitely like a Jew to me. When I, hardly paying any attention to him, had drawn my water from the well, this Man spoke to me asking for a drink from my water jar. I refused this thinking that He was Jew.

[10] But He spoke again, wise like an Elijah and told me everything I had ever done. Finally, he turned the conversation to the Messiah, and when I asked him where, how and when the Messiah would be coming, He looked at me with loving earnest and said in a voice penetrating to my very marrow: 'It is I, I who now speaks to you.'

[11] Already earlier, when He had told me how sick I am, I had asked Him whether I could not get well gain. And now in the end He said to me: 'Be healed' and look, my malady flew out of me like the wind, and now I am in compete health.

[12] Do go out there and see for yourselves whether that is not truly Christ, the promised Messiah. I am convinced that He is, for greater signs that this Man is performing also Christ could not perform. So do go out and convince yourselves. But I am hurrying home to put on better clothes, for as I am now I could not face His glory. Even if He is not Christ, He is certainly more than a prophet or a king of the people.'

[13] Say **the men**: 'Yes, if so, this time would really be most serious and of the greatest importance. We should go out there in greater numbers and among us should be a few who are well versed in scripture. It is unfortunate that today all our rabbis are on the mountain. But maybe he can be persuaded to stay in our midst for a few days, then these also could examine him.'

**John 4,30. *They came out of the city and made their way towards Him.***

[14] Thereupon they invite still others to go with them to Jacob's well, and now a crowd of close on a hundred people of both sexes sets out to see the Messiah.

## CHAPTER 30
### The true Sabbath

*John 4,31. Meanwhile the disciples were urging Him: "Rabbi, have something to eat."*

[1] "While the considerable crowd from the city set out towards the well, My disciples urge Me to have something to eat beforehand, for they knew that as soon as people came to Me, I did not take any food. And they loved Me and feared that I might become weakened and ill. Although they knew that I was Christ, they still regarded My body as weak and frail, wherefore they urged Me to eat.

*John 4,32. But He said: "I have food to eat of which you know nothing."*

[2] But I look at them with loving earnest and say: 'My dear friends, I have now a food to eat of which you know nothing.'

*John 4,33. "At this the disciples said to one another (asking each other): "Has someone already brought Him something to eat?"*

[3] **The disciples** looked at each other, asking: 'Has then someone already brought Him food from somewhere? What kind of food would that be? Has He already eaten it? Nothing can be seen anywhere except the still quite full water jar. Maybe He has changed the water into wine?'

*John 4,34. Jesus says to them: ("Oh do not make such foolish guesses.) It is meat and drink for me to the will of Him who sent me until I have finished His work."*

[4] Say I to them: 'Oh do not make such foolish guesses as to what I have or have not eaten. You have already often seen that while I am with you I have never had Myself served separately. I am now not speaking to you of any food for the body, but of a much higher and worthier spiritual food which consist in that I do the will of Him who sent Me and complete His great work. And He who sent Me is the Father, who you claim is your God, although you have not come to know Him as yet. But I do know Him and because of that am doing His Word, and that is My true food which you do not know. I tell you: not only the bread, but every good deed or work is also food, although not for the body, but all the more so for the spirit.'

*John 4,35. "Do you not say: 'Four more months, and then comes the harvest?' But look, I tell you: Lift your eyes and look round on the field: it is already white for harvest."*

[5] Many of you have fields at home, and you yourselves say: "Another 4 months and the time for a full harvest has come. Then we shall have to go home and gather in the harvest." But I tell you: better lift your eyes. Already now all the fields are white, ripe for the harvest. I do not, however, mean the natural fields, but the great field which is the whole world, where men are the ripened wheat that has to be gathered into God's barns.

*John 4,36. "And the reaper is drawing his pay and gathering a crop for eternal life, so that sower and reaper may rejoice together."*

[6] And see, this gathering-in is true work and this work a true food which I as well as you will get to eat in abundance. He who is a true reaper on this field gathers in the true crop for eternal life, so that at the end of the harvest both sower and reaper may rejoice together.

*John 4,37. "For here the saying is true: One sows and another reaps."*

[7] For after the harvest the sower as well as the reaper will both eat of one and the same fruit and one and the same bread of life. Then the old saying will come true completely: One sows and another reaps, but both will equally live from their work and eat one and the same food.

[8] Look at the great crowd that has come to us from the city to see the Promised in Me, and as you can see, more keep coming. See, all those are already fully ripened ears of wheat which should have been reaped long ago. I tell you with much joy: the crop is heavy, but there are still too few laborers. Therefore, beg the owner to send more laborers to harvest his crop.'

*John 4,38. "I sent you to reap a crop which you have not sowed. Others sowed and you have now come in for the harvest of their toil."*

[9] I have taken you on and thereby already sent you out in spirit to reap what you have not sown, for others have sown and you have now come in for the harvest of their toil, for which you should consider yourselves extremely fortunate. He who sows is still remote from the harvest, but he who reaps also harvests and has the new bread of life already before him. So be now zealous reapers, for your effort brings more bliss than that of the sower.'

[10] Most of the disciples did understand this teaching and started right away to preach My Word of the love for God and the love for one's neighbor to the Samaritans. Also, that I was truly the Christ.

[11] But **a few** in their heart's understanding still rather stupid ones came to Me

and asked Me secretly: 'Lord, where could be get sickles? Besides, it is the Sabbath today.'

[12] Whereupon I replied, 'Did I tell you to reap the natural barley fields that lie before us? Oh you foolish men, how long will I have to bear with you? Do you still not understand anything? So listen and grasp this:

[13] My Word about the Kingdom of God, first in your own hearts and from there passing through your mouths to the ears and into the hearts of your fellowmen and brothers, is the spiritual reaping sickle which I give you to gather the people, your brothers, in to the Kingdom of god, the realm of true cognition of God and eternal life in God.

[14] It is indeed Sabbath today, but the Sabbath is foolish and senseless like your heart, and you think of the Sabbath because in your hearts you look still very like the Sabbath. But since I am also a Lord over the Sabbath, I tell you:

[15] If you want to be and stay My true disciples, free your hearts from the Sabbath as soon as possible. For us every day is a day for work, when the Lord of the Sabbath is at work His servants shall not be idle.

[16] Does not the sun have to rise and set on the Sabbath just as on every work day? If the Lord of the sun and of the Sabbath ceased to work on the Sabbath, would you be satisfied, with a pitch-dark Sabbath? See how foolish you still are. So start now to do what I and also your brothers are doing, and you will be celebrating a truly alive Sabbath pleasing to Me.'

[17] Following these words also the weaker disciples went to the Samaritans, who had already in great numbers come to Me from the city, and taught them what they had learned about Me.

## CHAPTER 31
### The true badge of honor: love of the Lord

*John 4,39. Many Samaritans of that city came to believe in Him, (initially) because of the woman's testimony: "He told me everything I ever did."*

[1] And thus it went on until evening, and many of those who had come to me from the city now believed in me, initially, because of the woman's testimony, who in glowing words told the people of the city how I had told her everything she had ever done. Then, however, many believed because of what the disciples had told them about Me. But those Samaritans who were close enough to Me, so that they could hear My own words, had the firmest belief.

[2] For there were some among them who were well versed in the Scripture. They said: 'This one speaks like David who says: "The Lord's decrees are true and righteous every one, more to be desired than gold, pure gold in plenty, sweeter than syrup or honey from the comb. My desire is to do thy will, Lord, and thy law is in my heart. In the great assembly I have proclaimed what is right. I do not hold back my words, as You know, O Lord. I have not kept thy goodness

hidden in my heart. I have proclaimed thy faithfulness and saving power, and not concealed thy unfailing love and truth from the great assembly", but we know, and that is our witness full of truth and power, that He who thus speaks and acts, as before Him David spoke and acted, and that in His name, is truly the promised Messiah. Until this one, after David no one has spoken and acted like David, therefore this one must unfailingly be the Christ, the Anointed of God from eternity. Therefore, we will wholly accept Him.'

***John 4,40. When the Samaritans had (wholly) come to Him they begged Him to stay with them. And He stayed there two full days.***

[3] After **these Samaritans** had among themselves borne witness to Me, they approached Me most respectfully and begged Me to stay with them. For they said: 'Lord, You who are truly Christ as we have now recognized, do stay with us, for in Jerusalem You will find little acceptance, but all the more unbelief and all kinds of persecution. The vast Earth does not bear anything worse than a Pharisee, neither on the land nor on the water. Here, however, You will be treated as befits the One Moses, David and the prophets have promised us.'

[4] But I said to them: 'Dear men from Sychar. I am overjoyed that I have reaped a good harvest on your field, but it would not be right of Me if I stayed where I have healed the sick who are now in good health and disregarded the many sick elsewhere. I will stay with you for two days, and on the third day continue My journey down to Galilee.

***John 4,41. Many more became believers because of what they heard from His own lips.***

[5] Thereupon many more came who earlier had not believed completely and confessed their now unshakably firm belief. But also **the woman** was there, well dressed, and said to those who now believed: 'Dear friends, you will now accept me as honorable, will you not? For it was I who first showed you the way here when you jokingly asked me where it was burning.'

***John 4,42. And they told the woman: "It is no longer because of what you said that we believe, for we have heard Him ourselves and we know that this is in truth Christ, the Savior of the world."***

[6] **The Samaritans** said: 'Since the Lord has accepted you before us, you are also by us accepted as honorable as is the custom in Sychar. But from now on we do not believe because of what you said, for we have now heard Him ourselves and recognized that this is in truth Christ, the Savior of the world. You will not make us more believing than we already are and, from now on, if you do not sin anymore, you shall be treated by us with all due respect.'

[7] Says **the woman**: 'I have not ever sinned as much as you unfortunately think. Prior to becoming a man's wife, I lived orderly as befits a wife. That I was

barren and that each one of my five proper husbands had to die soon after he had slept with me, for that I could not possibly be blamed, at the most those from whom I receive such a flesh that was disastrous to a man. After I lost five husbands, which caused me unbearable grief, I decided never again to marry. But a year later, as you know, a doctor came to Sychar with herbs, oils and ointments and cured many people. Driven by my greatly felt misery, I too went to him to seek help.

[8] He examined me and said: "Woman, I would give a whole world to be able to help you, for I have never yet seen a more beautiful woman. But, though I cannot cure you, I can alleviate your complaint". He moved into my poor dwelling, gave me daily soothing remedies and looked after me, but he has never yet touched my sick body with evil intentions, as you see, to think erroneously.

[9] And thus I am, of course, always a sinner in the eyes of God, as also all of you no doubt, but in your eyes I do not believe to be such a great and gross sinner as you assume. Ask the one, who is sitting here at Jacob's well and who earlier told me everything I had done. He will tell you to what extent I do or do not deserve the reputation of a public sinner.'

[10] Here the Samaritans look at each other in surprise and say to the woman: 'Now, now, never mind, we did not really think so badly. You shall now become an honored citizen of Sychar. Say, are you satisfied?'

[11] Says the woman: 'Oh, do not worry about the honor of a poor woman. I have already taken for myself the greater part of the honor.'

[12] Say the Samaritans: 'How did you do that? We know nothing of a badge of honor the city has conferred on you. Where did you get this from?'

[13] Says the woman pointing at Me with tears of true love and real gratitude: 'Here He is still resting. He alone is now my greatest honor, an honor neither you nor the whole world could confer on me nor take away from me. For He Himself has given it to me, and from Him I Have taken it. I am quite aware that with all my being I am absolutely unworthy to receive an honor from Him, the Lord of Glory. But He gave it to me prior to you, and I have received it before you and told you about Him, since earlier you did not know anything about Him. Look, that is my advantage over all of you, which you have not given me and cannot take away from me since I now have it. That is the right kind of a badge of honor valid for eternity. Your badge of honor is valid only temporally and for Sychar alone, and that I can do without since I have the eternal one. I hope you will now understand how and from where I have taken the greater part of my honor.'

[14] Say the Samaritans: 'Why should you have an advantage because you happened to come out first and meet Christ here? We have now also found Him and praise Him in our hearts just like you, and He promised us the same as you to stay in our city for two days. In view of this, how can you now speak of a prior honor conferred on you?'

[15] Says the woman: 'You dear men of Sychar, if I were to argue with you we would never come to an end, I have just told you absolutely truthfully what the situation is and I will not repeat it. Several of you have studied the Roman law. They are now judges according to this law and say that it is a wise law. Now this

law, which I have also read because I understand the Roman language, states: *Primo occupanti jus* (I was here first and, therefore, you can never deprive me of my good right.)'

[16] Here the Samaritans were silent not knowing what to reply to the woman, for she had hit upon their weak spot and they were unable to retort. Because of the Jews, they were great friends of the Romans and highly regarded the wisdom and order of the Roman law. Therefore, they were silent when the woman referred to the law of the Romans.

[17] It is no wonder that the woman was proficient in the Roman language for the Samaritans without exception spoke Roman and many also Greek, so as to avoid also through the language any association with the Jews.


## CHAPTER 32
### The Lord sees only the heart. As one sows, so will one reap

[1] It was now getting dark and all those who had come with Me from Judaea and, being very tired, had slept through the entire afternoon, were now one after the other waking up and surprised how quickly evening had come. And they asked what should be done now: should they look for lodgings or would I now during the cooler hours of the night continue on My way?

[2] However I said: 'While men are asleep, the Lord is still watching. The Lord provides for everything, and those who are with Him need not care for anything, except that they stay with Him. Therefore, get ready now, so that we may go to this city of the Samaritans. There all of us will find good lodgings. This woman here, who today at noon refused to give Me a drink of water, has a spacious house and I think she will not refuse to put us up for two days.'

[3] Thereupon **the woman**, sobbing with love and joy, falls at My feet and says: 'O Lord, You my Savior, how do I poor sinner come to be granted this grace?'

[4] **I say**: 'You received Me into your heart, which is much more precious than your house, so you are not likely to refuse to receive me also into your house which Jacob, just as this well, built for his son Joseph. But there are many of us, and for two days you will be very busy caring for us. However, you will profit from this considerably.'

[5] Says **the woman**: 'Lord, even if you were ten times as many, you shall all be well provided for, as far as my means allow. My already rather dilapidated house has many clean rooms and is reasonably well furnished as far as I could afford it. And it is occupied only by me, my doctor and some of his servants. But I tell You, O Lord, the house is Yours. You alone are the legitimate owner of my house, for You have the oldest right to it. From now on it is wholly Yours and shall remain so with all it contains.'

[6] **I say**: 'O woman, your faith is great and your heart delightful. Therefore you shall be and stay My disciple. And wherever this Gospel will be preached, you shall be mentioned in eternity.'

[7] **The Samaritans** were surprised and somewhat provoked at this, and several of them came to Me and said: 'Lord, we have houses too and it would have been more proper if You had taken lodging with us. For look, this woman's house has a bad name here and is more of a ruin than a house.'

[8] **I say**: 'You are already three hours with Me, have indeed recognized Me and it has already been getting dark, but none of you has offered Me or My disciples lodgings, although I granted your request and promised to stay in your city for two days.

[9] But I looked at this woman's heart, and she longed mightily for Me to be willing to take lodging with her. Thus, not I asked to be put up in her house, but her heart did. Since it dared not speak up before you, I met this heart half way and asked for that which it wished to give Me with burning love and full of eager yearning and alacrity.

[10] This is the weighty reason why I shall now take lodging in this woman's house for two full days. Blessed he who will not take offense over this matter.

[11] I tell you: as a person sows, so will he reap. Who sows scantily will also reap thus, but who sows generously will also reap generously. None of you has so far offered Me or My disciples anything, but this woman gives me immediately possession of everything she owns. Which of you had done that for Me? Is it then not fair that I honor her before all of you? I tell you: whoever will argue with this woman about this matter, with him things will go badly in his temporal life.'

[12] At this the Samaritans, visibly displeased, star at each other in surprise, but then pull themselves together and still ask My permission for them to visit Me the next day.

[13] But I reply: 'I do not invite you or expect anything of you. However, those of you who will come to Me voluntarily shall not find the door locked, but will have completely free access to me. Thus, whoever wants to come, let him come and who wants to stay home, let him stay home, for I compel and judge no one.'

[14] On this, the Samaritans go to their feet and went into the city. But I still remained for a little while at the well, and the woman gave all the thirsty who were with Me to drink from her water jar.


CHAPTER 33
IN SYCHAR
**The doctor and the Samaritan Mosaists**


[1] Her doctor however, who earlier also had come out with her, hastened ahead to arrange the best accommodation and an abundant meal for Me through his servants. Entering the house however he was taken aback by his people being nearly finished with everything he had intended arranging. Regaining his spirit, he asked who had requested this. They said however: 'A youth of a most glorious form came and spoke gently: 'Do this, as the Lord who is coming to this house has need of all this'. When we heard this amazing thing we dropped everything

and did and still are doing as asked by this rare youth'.

[2] **The doctor** said in his astonishment: 'And where is this rare youth?' But the servants replied: 'We do not know, for he left the house immediately after requesting this and we do not know what has become of him'. The doctor said however: 'Then do your best, for a great blessing has overtaken this house, and you all shall take part of it.'

[3] Then the doctor hastened again out of the city to tell Me that all is ready now.

[4] He nevertheless ran into some arch-Mosaists, holding him up and saying: 'Friend, it is not right to rush like this on a Sabbath. Don't you know all the ways in which Jehovah's day can be defiled?'

[5] **The doctor** replied: 'You Mosaic men of letters. You count hurrying on a Sabbath a sin, although the sun has gone down already, making this post-sabbatical, but what do you call your violating of your wives and maids, fornicating and whoring and committing adultery on a Sabbath with them? Did Moses command this for Jehovah's Day?' Say **the Samaritans**: 'We would stone you for talking like that if it wasn't for Sabbath, but we let you go this time.' Replies **the doctor**: 'Well, well, your language and manner are of course highly appropriate, especially at a time when the Messiah is in fact tarrying outside the gates of Sychar, with me rushing to tell Him that everything for welcoming Him at His house is ready. Have you not heard what took place outside the gates of our city today?'

[6] Say **the Samaritans**: 'We definitely heard that a Jewish caravan camped outside by the well and that a Jew – probably their ring-leader – was making out to be the Christ. As a doctor you do not know how the Jews are bent on having us purported idiots on in this way? This should be a nice Messiah. Do you think we do not know him? Are we not also from Galilee and of your denomination, staunch in Moses' statutes? But since we are of Galilee we know this Nazarene who is a carpenter's son. This one has lost his taste for work now, so he will let himself be used as a brazen tool of the Pharisees, making use of the magic he learned with which to prove that He is the Messiah. And donkeys and oxen of your type are taken in by him and believe his seductive words. They should all be caught and whipped and chucked over the border like mud and excrement.'

[7] Replies **the Doctor**: 'Oh, you blind ones. Back at my house, angels wait on Him, bringing food, drinks and bedding for Him from the Heavens, and you talk in that way. May the Lord punish you for this.'

[8] When the doctor had uttered this, ten of them instantly became mute and none could speak another word, remaining mute for the two days of My stay in Sychar. But the doctor leaves them and hastens over to Me.

[9] Having come over, he says: 'Lord, your house is ready. There are miracles goings on there, but on the way out to you, oh Lord, I came across some villains who tried to give me a nasty witness of You. But their shrieking did not last long. Your angel smacked them over the mouth and all but two were made dumb. These took terrible fright and took off. All this, oh Lord, occurred in just half an hour.' I said: 'Be of good cheer. This had to come, so that those already believing on My name should not be turned away from us. Let us go now however, and you

My dear Samaritan woman do not forget your pitcher.' The woman immediately draws fresh water to take home with her. A half day had thus been taken up at Jacob's well outside Sychar, reaping quite a rich harvest in this city.


## CHAPTER 34
## The heavenly arrangement of the house

[1] But **My disciple John** asked, saying: 'Lord, if it is Your will, I should like to record still this night all that has taken place here.'

[2] I said: 'Not everything, My brother, but only that which I said unto you to write down. Because if you were to record everything that happened and is still to happen here these two days, then you would have to write many a skin-full, but who could read and grasp it all? If however you duly record only the high points, in the correspondences given you, then the wise in My name shall discover anyway all that took place here and why, and you shall save yourself much effort. Therefore My most beloved brother, take it easy with your work, because you still shall remain the foremost recorder of My teachings and acts forever.

[3] John kisses Me on the chest and, since it had gotten quite dark, we go to the city and Joseph's house, flanked by the woman and the doctor.

[4] As we come to the truly big house, the woman finds preparations for My stay at her house which she had never remotely suspected. Because there are a good number of well-laid tables, with a proper number of chairs, there are well-lit lamps of precious metal on every table. The floors are covered throughout with the most beautiful carpets, with the walls hung symmetrically with flowered rugs, and a most exquisite wine beams towards the guests from the most beautiful crystal beakers.

[5] **The woman** is quite beside herself and says, after interminable wondering: 'But Lord, what have You done? Did You perhaps secretly send Your disciples here to put this on? Where have they gotten it all from? I do know what I have got, but nothing golden and silver for sure, yet here everything is bristling with these metals. I have never seen a crystal beaker like this yet. There are hundreds here, of which each is worth at least thirty pieces of silver. Such wine, food and fruit, the lovely bread and the many expensive carpets, each costing at least a good hundred silver pieces for sure. Oh Lord, please tell me a poor woman whether you brought all this with you, or whether perhaps it is on loan from this city somewhere?

[6] **I say**: 'Look here, dear woman. At the well you said this house belongs to Me. I accepted such a present from you, and since this house is now Mine, it would not have been nice of Me to escort you, the giver, into an unseemly chamber. See, it is here like one hand washing the other. One distinction calls for another. You presented it to Me fully as it was, with all your heart, but I now give it back to you as now furnished. I presume that you can feel at home with this exchange? For see, I too have some ideas about correct decorations and taste.'

[7] And I say unto you: 'All this, like everything else I also learned from My

Father. Because the endlessly many mansions in My Father's house even are full of the most exquisite taste and full of the greatest ornaments, which you can well gather already if you look carefully at the flowers of the field, the plainest of which is more greatly adorned than Solomon in all his kingly glory.'

[8] But if the Father already adorns transient flowers thus, how much more will He adorn His house, which is in Heaven? But whatever the Father does, that I do also, because I and the Father fundamentally are completely One. Whoever receives Me receives also the Father. Whatever someone does for Me he therefore does also for the Father, and you can give Me nothing that you would not soon receive back a hundredfold. Now you know what is necessary.

[9] But let us now be seated and partake of the evening meal, because there are many among us who hunger and thirst. Once we have strengthened our limbs we can discuss this point further.

[10] All sit down at the tables, say thanks and fortify themselves with food and drink.

## CHAPTER 35
### The disciples see the Heavens open

[1] After the meal the woman approaches Me again, but hardly dares to speak, as she had spoken during the meal with the doctor's servants about how all this had been brought in. And **the servants** had said: 'Dear lady, God only knows how this went on. We had the least part in it. The doctor had no hand in it at all, as everything was ready when he came. Well before he came we were about his business, when suddenly a youth of great beauty turned up and told us to do this and that, as the Lord had need of it, and we at once went about doing what the rare youth told us. Yet this truly went on in a peculiar way. Whenever we went to do something it was already done, and we can therefore only tell you: here omnipotence evidently reigned, and the white youth must have been an angel of the Lord. The matter cannot be explained in any other way. The Person who earlier entered the dining-room with you must be a great prophet, as the powers of Heaven serve Him.'

[2] Hearing the servants speak thus she was still more daunted and hardly dared to speak. After a lengthy time she said in a weak voice: 'Lord, You are more than just the promised Messiah. It was probably You who punished Pharaoh, leading the Israelites out of Egypt and thundering the Commandments to them from the High Sinai.'

[3] But **I say** to her: 'Woman, the time for making this known to mankind has not arrived yet. Keep this in your heart for the present therefore. But see to it that the great throng who came with Me from Judea are allocated their sleeping quarters, but remain here yourself together with the doctor and My disciples, of whom ten are counted now. But allocate the cleanest bed to the woman who sat at My side, the mother of My body, so she may rest well, for verily, the already ageing mother

has done a big journey today and needs a good rest to fortify her.'

[4] The woman is overjoyed at hearing that this unpretentious woman is My mother, and looks after her superbly. And Mary praises her for her sensitivity, advising her nevertheless to do as I say to her.

[5] After all is retired and the woman and the doctor, together with My disciples find themselves alone with Me in the great dining hall, I say to the disciples: 'You will remember how at the time of My engaging you at Bethabara in Galilee I spoke to you: from now on you shall see the Heavens open and the angels of God descend to Earth. And see, this is now literally fulfilling itself. None of what you see here and ate and drank is of this Earth, but has been gotten here from the Heavens by the angels. But now open your eyes and see just how many angels are standing ready to serve Me.'

[6] With that the eyes of all were opened, and they saw hosts of angels floating down from the Heavens ready to minister unto Me. Because as their eyes were opened, the walls of the house vanished, and all beheld the Heavens opened.

[7] And **Nathanael** said: 'Of a truth Lord, you are faithful and true. What you had spoken has now fulfilled itself miraculously. Verily, You are the Son of the living God indeed. God spoke to Abraham through His angels. Jacob saw the angels ascending and descending the ladder in a dream but he did not see Jehovah, only an angel who had Jehovah's name inscribed in his right hand. And, Jacob disputing His being the Lord, he started limping through a hefty blow in the ribs. Moses spoke with Jehovah but saw nothing but fire and smoke, and since he had to hide in a cave because Jehovah intended passing it, he was not allowed to look and Jehovah passed. And when he then looked he saw only Jehovah's back, but thereafter he had to cover his face with a threefold veil, because he shone more than the sun and no one could look without dying. After that there was only Elijah who perceived Jehovah in a gentle breeze. And now You are here Yourself.'

[8] Here I interrupt Nathanael and say: 'Let it suffice, My brother, the hour has not come yet. It is given to a pure soul like yours, without guile and falsehood, to sense this. But keep it until the hour is ripe. Because, you see, not all who follow Me are like you.'

[9] But this woman who was not like you is so now. That is why she had a hunch of what you were about to say. But the hour is not come. Let Moses' veil only be fully plucked off his shiny face when the curtain in the temple shall have been rent in twain'.

## CHAPTER 36
### Joram and Irhael joined conjugally

[1] After that, **John** asks Me: 'Lord, this surely I ought to write down. This is more than the sign at Cana. This for once is a true sign of whither You have come.

[2] **I say**: 'This too let go, because that which you are recording is a sign for the world, but the latter does not have the cognition for grasping this. To what end

such effort then? Do you think the world shall believe such? See, those present believe because they see it, but the world, which walks in the dark, would never believe that such took place here because night cannot possibly imagine the works of light. Should you try to tell it about the works of light it will laugh at you and deride you in the end. Let it therefore suffice you to record only that which I work publicly, before the whole world. That which I work in secret however write only in your heart, but not on parchment.'

[3] But there shall indeed come a time when all these secret things shall be revealed to the world, but a lot of unripe fruit shall be falling off trees until then. Because verily, the trees have brought forth much, yet hardly a third shall come to ripeness. Yet the two fallen-off thirds shall first have to be trodden, and rot and wither, so that they may be dissolved by rain and be driven into the stem by a mighty wind for second birth.'

[4] Says **John**: 'Lord, this is too deep. Who should grasp it?'

[5] I say: 'There is no need of it, suffice it that you believe and love Me, the deeper comprehension shall be coming after the spirit of Truth shall have been poured out over you. But until this has taken place, quite a few of you, in spite of all these signs shall be offended by My name.

[6] Because you all have a completely wrong notion of the Messiah and Its kingdom and it will take much learning until you will understand it clearly.

[7] Because the Messiah's kingdom shall not be a kingdom of this world, but a kingdom of spirit and Truth in My Father's kingdom, eternally, and there shall be no end to it for evermore. Whoever shall have been received into this kingdom shall have everlasting life, and this life shall be of a bliss which no man has yet seen, heard of or felt in his heart.'

[8] Said **Peter**, who had long been silent: 'Lord, who shall ever actually become capable of this?'

[9] I say: "Dear friend, the day is already late and our bodies need rest in order to be strong for work tomorrow. Let us therefore bring this day to a close and travel by good light tomorrow. Let everyone therefore seek his resting-places and take full rest on it. Because tomorrow we will get a lot to do."

[10] Here all revert to their natural state and see the walls of the hall in front of which very good resting installations, a kind of canapés, are placed. The disciples, some of whom are very tired, say thanks and at once lay down.

[11] Only I and the doctor and the woman remain awake. And with the disciples soon soundly asleep, both fall down on their knees before Me and thank Me fervently for the unspeakable graces I had bestowed upon them and their entire house. They also asked Me whether I would let them join up and follow Me.

[12] But I say to them: 'This is not essential for your bliss. If you do however want to follow Me then it is enough if you follow Me in your hearts. But you should remain in this country as My witnesses, as many skeptics shall arise around here shortly. To these you shall bear good witness of Me.'

[13] And you, My dear Joram, from now on shall be a perfect doctor. On whoever you shall lay your hands in My name shall get better immediately regardless of how sick they may be. At the same time however you should enter

upon a perfect and indissoluble matrimony, since with your present togetherness you would be an offense to the blind who regard only externals and have no idea about the within.

[14] You Joram need not fear Irhael any more, as she is now fully whole of body and soul. And you, Irhael, now have a man from the Heavens and shall be completely happy with him, since he is not a spirit out of the Earth but from above.'

[15] Says **the woman**: 'Oh Jehovah, how good you are. When is it Your will that we should officially join hands before the eyes of the world?'

[16] **I say**: 'I have already joined you, and this union alone is valid in Heaven and on Earth, and I say unto you, not since Adam's time has there been a more perfect union than yours, since I Myself have blessed your union.

[17] But tomorrow morning a lot of priests and other people and officials of this city shall come here, to these make it known, that they may be aware of your being a proper married couple now before God and the whole world. If you beget children however then bring them up in My teaching and then baptize them in My name, the way you shall see many of My disciples baptize tomorrow, and the way John, of whom you will have heard, baptizes in the Jordan. Thus, My dear Joram, I shall empower you tomorrow to afterwards baptize everyone who believes in My name.

[18] But go to your rest now. But for the sake of chastity refrain from touching one another during My stay in this house. But during this time do not trouble yourselves about table and larder, because for the duration of My stay in this house, as also today, table and larder shall be provided for from above. Do not however tell this to anyone before time because men will not comprehend it. But when I am gone you can make it known to the more enlightened ones. Now however do take your rest, although I Myself shall be watching. Because the Lord must not sleep or rest since such sleep and complete rest would be the death and undoing of beings. Because even if the whole world were to sleep the Lord nevertheless keeps awake and maintains all beings.'

[19] After these words the two thank Me and retire to their separate chambers for the necessary rest. But I remain seated in My chair till morning.

## CHAPTER 37
### With Irhael. The nature of dreams

[1] Early in the morning, before the sun stood hardly a span above the horizon, **a great number of priests** who dwelt in Sychar on account of the proximity of the holy mount (Gerizim) came before Irhael's house and started a great bawling, yelling: 'Hosanna over hosanna!' and 'glory to Him who came in the name of God's glory! Wait, sun, and stand still, moon, until the Lord of all glory with His mighty right arm has smitten and destroyed all His enemies, who also are our enemies! Only the Romans spare, Oh Lord, because they are our friends, as they

protect us from the Jews, who no longer are children of God but of Beelzebub, offering to this their father in the temple, which Solomon built for You, oh Lord. You did right, oh Lord to come to Your true children, who believed on Your promises and yearningly awaited You right up to this hour. Of a truth You came from the Jews, but we have heard how you have now been to Jerusalem and smote the Jews in the temple with cords and overturned their chairs. Oh Lord, in this You did well, and all Heavens should praise You with Psalms, harps and trumpets. We always maintained that when You came You would not by-pass the holy place where Daniel Your prophet proclaimed the horror of the destruction of Jerusalem. And from this place oh Lord, You shall proclaim salvation to Thy peoples. Praised be Thy name, hosanna to Thee on high, and blessing to all children of goodwill.'

[2] This partly suitable but partly nonsensical bawling naturally attracted a lot of people and certainly all those who had been at the well with Me the day before and now wanted to see and hear Me again. The clamor and the throng swelled by seconds, and inside the house all rose to see what went on. The disciples got up first and asked Me what the tumult was about and whether it was advisable to stay rather than flee.

[3] I **say**: 'Oh you faint hearts. Listen to them calling hosanna. Wherever hosanna is being sung there it is without danger to tarry.'

[4] With this the disciples were reassured and I said to them again: 'Now go outside and say to them that they be still now and to move out to the mountain, because I shall come out after the sixth hour (i.e. after 12 hours midday), with you all and shall proclaim salvation to you and them from the mountain. They are to also take scribes with them however so that these may record what I shall teach from the mountain.

[5] But you, John, need not write it, as this My teaching shall be written down several-fold anyway. But a certain scribe – a Galilean too – by the name of Matthew, is resident here. This one has already recorded a considerable amount from My childhood, and because he commands great facility he is sure to write down all that he shall hear and see. Him bring up, call him by his name and he shall follow you at once. But ask the chief priests also to come up, as well as some of the chief ones who you will have seen at the well yesterday. But call Me Matthew first, as I want him to follow us.'

[6] The disciples quickly went down to do as I commanded them.

[7] While the disciples were engaged in the street below all the other guests, together with Mary, came to Me in the dining room and greeted Me most amicably, thanked Me and briefly related to Me the wonderful dreams they had this night, asking Me if one is to think much of such dreams.

[8] But I said: 'Whatever the soul sees in a dream corresponds with its nature. If the soul moves within what is true and good as I taught you to believe and do, then he will in dreams also see what is true, and from this he can take a lot of good things for life. But if the soul is doing what is wrong and evil, then he will also see in the dream what is wrong and make evil out of it.

[9] Since you however move within what is true through My teaching and therefore also follow Me, your soul also shall have seen only the true, from which

81

he can do much good.

[10] Whether the soul is nevertheless also capable of grasping what it sees in a dream is another matter. Because just as you do not grasp and comprehend what you see in the outer world in which you live by day, just so the soul does not grasp what she sees in her world.

[11] When however the spirit shall be reborn within you, as I explained to Nicodemus in Jerusalem when he called on Me by night, then you shall grasp and comprehend and completely understand everything.' With this all are satisfied and move back.

## CHAPTER 38
### Not the hearing but the doing brings salvation

[1] The hostess and her new husband come now, greeting Me with much feeling and asking Me and all the other guests whether we are disposed to now partake of the morning meal, as it is fully prepared.

[2] But I said: 'Dear Irhael, wait just a little. The disciples will soon bring over a number of additional guests and these too will partake of the early meal, and at the same time hear from My mouth that you two, you and Joram now have become a duly married couple, and they are also to see that your house now does not count as one of the last, but, both outwardly and inwardly as the very first house in this city, and that I took accommodation in this house for that reason.'

[3] Even as I am still saying this to the married couple, Peter and My John are already opening the door with **Matthew** entering between them, bowing deeply and saying: 'Lord, I am here fully ready to serve You exclusively. I have a scribe's vocation indeed by which to live and keep my small family, but if You oh Lord have need of me I shall let go of my office at once even while You oh Lord shall not let my small family perish.'

[4] I said: 'Let him who follows Me not trouble himself about anything other than to stay with Me in time and eternity. But see this house, these two owners, these shall take in your family in My name and look after them as also yourself, whether you come by day or night.'

[5] **Matthew**, who had already been acquainted with this house and how it had been more of a ruin than a house, could not have been more astonished, and spoke: 'Lord, here a great miracle must have occurred. Because the house had been a ruin and is now a palace, the like of which there might not be too many in Jerusalem. And this truly regal set-up. This must have cost a fortune.'

[6] I said: 'Just stop and think that with God many things are possible which seem impossible to men, then you will easily understand how this former ruin could have been transformed into a palace. But are you well-supplied with writing materials?'

[7] Says **Matthew**: 'I am all right for two days. If I am to have more I shall at once obtain it.'

[8] I said: 'It shall suffice for 10 days, after that we shall acquire more material elsewhere. Just stay with us and partake of the morning meal with us: after 6 o'clock however we shall betake ourselves to the mountain. There I shall proclaim salvation to these peoples. You record everything verbatim and in three chapters, and sub-divide these into small verses in the style of David. Look around for another couple of scribes however who can copy you, so as to leave a written witness for this place.'

[9] Says **Matthew**: 'Lord, your will shall be followed to the letter.'

[10] After this necessary briefing of Matthew the other disciples enter, followed by the priests and other officials of this city, and greet Me with the greatest of deference. And the chief priest steps forward a little and says: 'Lord, you have prepared this house fittingly, that it should be worthy of accommodating You. Solomon built the temple in great splendor, so it may serve Jehovah as an abode among men, yet men have desecrated this abode with their outrageous vices, and Jehovah left the temple and the ark and came to us on the Mount, even as You oh Lord were in Jerusalem first, finding little acceptance and coming to us, your genuine old worshipers. And thus it shall now come to pass as written:

[11] *"And it shall come to pass in the last days, that the mountain of the Lord's house shall be established in the top of the mountains, and shall be exalted above the hills. And all nations shall flow unto it. And many people shall go and say, Come ye, and let us go up to the mountain of the Lord, to the house of the God of Jacob. And he will teach us of His ways, and we will walk in His paths, for out of Zion shall go forth the law, and the word of the Lord from Jerusalem." (Isaiah 2:2-3)*

[12] We are overjoyed indeed like a bride when her bridegroom comes in to her for the first time. Because verily, Lord, Jerusalem the chosen city of the great King has become evil to piss on and to hiss on and is not worthy of You. We do not really deem ourselves worthy either since what does it not take in order to be found worthy before God? Yet it is nonetheless true that the Lord, now having to choose between two evils, He surely will choose us, the lesser one. And this is now miraculously fulfilling itself before our eyes. You are He whom we have awaited for so long. Therefore, hosanna to You, who comes to us in the name of the Lord.'

[13] Say I to the speaker: 'Yes, you have of a truth spoken rightly, but I also say to you: 'When you hear My teaching then absorb it and remain active in it, for only thus shall you truly partake of the blessing which I shall proclaim to you from the Mount's summit today. Because notwithstanding that grace is bestowed upon you freely from on high, this nevertheless does not suffice, because this does not stay if not seized actively, just as, if standing hungrily under a fruit-laden tree, with the wind having blown down some ripe figs: will these sate you if you do not pick them up and eat them?

[14] Therefore not only the hearing but also the doing of My teaching shall bless you with the salvation going forth from Jerusalem. Do you understand this?

[15] Says **the speaker**: 'Yes Lord, for only God can speak like You.'

[16] 'In that case', say I thereto, 'since you have now grasped this, let us partake

of our morning meal. But make a record for yourself after the meal, that last night I betrothed Irhael and the doctor Joram and blessed them, so that from now on no one should take offence at them. But be seated now for the morning meal. Let it be.'

[17] All sat down, and there were many partaking of the morning meal, consisting of the best milk and bread and honey.

## CHAPTER 39
### Sermon on the Mount

[1] In this land [*Austria - the translator*] such breakfast would not of course be thought of too much, but in the Promised Land, which proverbially overflows with milk and honey, this was a most exquisite breakfast, since especially the honey in the Promised Land was and still is much the best, while the milk too is unsurpassed anywhere on Earth.

[2] Superb fruit was served after the meal, and many delighted in it and praised God who endues fruit with such precious flavor and gives bees the ability to suck such supremely sweet honey from the flowers of the field, carrying it to their artfully constructed beehives.

[3] **One in the Samaritan group** who was a sage spoke: 'God's wisdom, omnipotence and goodness can never be praised highly enough. The rain falls on the Earth, a million species and varieties of plants, trees and shrubs absorb the self-same rain and stand in the same soil, yet every kind has a different flavor, smell and form. Each form is beautiful and pleasant to see and nothing grows without use, and not even the most meager moss upon the rocks grows without a purpose.

[4] Then add all the animals of the Earth, the water and the air. What multiplicity and diversity, from the mosquito to the elephant; from the mite to the most enormous leviathan which could carry mountains on its back and play with the cedars of Lebanon. Oh Lord, what might, what power and endless profundity of wisdom there must be in God, who guides and conducts there the sun, moon and countless stars, holds the sea in its depths, built the mountains upon the Earth and brought the Earth itself into being through the almighty Word.

[5] I say: 'Yes, indeed, you are right, so it is. God is supremely good, supremely wise, supremely just and does not need anyone's advice and instruction when He wishes to do something. But I tell you: Also man on this Earth is called to become as perfect as is the Father in Heaven.

[6] This was impossible until now, since death was ruling on this Earth. But from now on it shall be possible to everyone who will in all earnest strive to live according to My teaching.

[7] And I think that if God offers this to man in return for a small effort, namely, for the easy complying with My teaching, man should spare no pains to reach this supreme goal.'

[8] Says **the high priest**: 'Yes Lord, man should indeed venture everything to attain to this ultimate. Whoever wants to enjoy the view from a high mountain must not shy the effort and trouble of climbing. Whoever wants to reap must plough and sow first, and whoever thinks of gain must take the risk, but whoever ventures nothing out of fear that nothing may be gained cannot possibly ever gain. Therefore Lord, once You have shown us the Ways, it shall not be hard for us to attain to what you have just proclaimed to us, namely to be as perfect as the Father in Heaven is perfect.'

[9] I said: 'Verily so, and I will add: My yoke is easy and My burden light. But mankind until now has had to carry heavy burdens, yet achieved nothing with that. It remains to be seen how their faith will shape up to exchanging the heavily pressing old faith that they learned for the unfamiliar new faith. Shall they not finally say: "If we achieve nothing through strenuous ways and work, what shall we achieve with child's play?"

[10] I say unto you: you shall have to cast off the old man like an old coat and then put on a completely new one. This shall of course be uncomfortable at first, but whoever shall not be driven back to the old, habitual by trivia, but bear up to the small discomfort, shall attain to the perfection of which I spoke.

[11] But let you all get ready now, for I shall shortly start on the small trip to the mountain. Let him who will move up with Me get to his legs, and you, Matthew, go and fetch your writing utensils. But do not tarry as you can see that I am about to go.'

[12] Says **Matthew**: 'Lord, You know how ready I am to follow You. But if I go over to my house or rather to where I am employed and paid by the Romans as a tax collector and scribe, and get tied up near the main barrier before the city, I shall probably find a lot of work as usual, and the Roman guards shall not let me go until I have done the work. Therefore I would prefer it if I could obtain sufficient writing material here for today, and then go and collect mine in the evening, which would then last me for a full two days, because I cannot obtain more than three days supplies from the Romans, which I also nearly use up.'

[13] I said: 'Friend, just always do what I tell you, and you shall always be all right. Just go as I told you and you shall not today find any work or anyone waiting at the barrier. But bring also your other scribes with you, so that My Word shall be recorded here many times over.' Says **Matthew**: 'Well, in that case I may indeed be gone.'

[14] At that, Matthew the tax-collector goes and finds everything exactly as I foretold him. He soon returns with three other scribes and we are on our way to Mount Gerizim, together with everyone else in the house. And as we arrive at the mountain after one hour, the high priest asks Me if he should go up and open the old house of God.

[15] But I point to the area and the many people who followed us, and say to him: 'See friend, this is the oldest and most appropriate house of God, but it is much neglected and I want to restore it, as I did with Irhael's house. But for this, the old house is not needed, and this area at the foot of the mountain shall suffice. There are, besides, a few benches and tables here which will be handy for the

scribes. Open your ears, eyes and hearts therefore and be ready, because now shall come to pass before your eyes what the prophet Isaiah prophesied.'

[16] Says **Matthew**: 'Lord, we are ready to hear you.'

[17] Now follows the well known sermon on the mount, which one can read on Matthew chapters 5, 6 and 7.- This sermon, however, lasted for three hours as I spoke slowly because of the writers.


## CHAPTER 40
### The priests criticize the Sermon on the Mount (1/40)

[1] When the sermon had ended many were shocked, and mainly **the priests and some of the people** said: 'Who can attain to salvation? We teachers of the law also preach properly and justly as once Moses proclaimed from the mountain the commandments to the people. But all that is like dew and a gentle evening breeze compared to this strict teaching and mightiest of sermons. There is hardly a tenable argument against such precepts, but they are too severe and hardly anyone will be able to practice them.

[2] Who can love his enemy, who do good to the one who harms him maliciously and who can bless those who hate him and speak only bad about him? And if a person wants to borrow something from me, I must not turn away and refuse to listen to him nor steel my heart against his words, even if I see clearly that the borrower will never be able to return what he has borrowed? Ah, what a silly thing. If the lazy ones and the shirkers hear about it, will they not promptly go to the wealthy and borrow from them as long as they possess something? Once they have in this way – and nothing is easier than that – lent everything to the poor, who can never return what they have borrowed, and in the end have nothing left themselves, the question arises: who will in the future be working and from whom will the poor then receive a loan?

[3] It is only too obvious that with the observance of such precepts, which oppose the nature of all human institutions, the world would in no time become a real desert. Once the world is a desert, where will men receive any education, since all schools just come to an end if no one has the means to establish and support them?

[4] This teaching will not do at all. The bad people and enemies of the good and their good works must be punished and who slaps my face must be slapped back at least twice, so that he will no longer wish to slap my face again. The careless borrower must be put in a work-house to teach him to work and in future earn his living by diligently working with his hands. The very poor may ask for alms and they will not be refused. That is an ancient but very good law under which a human society can well exist. But the precepts this alleged Christ has now given are too impractical for human life and cannot possibly be adopted.

[5] I did not want to mention all the other things, absurd as they sounded, but the suggested self-mutilation in case of vexation through parts of one's own body

and besides the evidently recommended idleness, according to which no one should be concerned about anything, but only keep seeking the Kingdom of God, as all else would be given him from above. Let us try this only for a period of a few months, during which people do not touch anything or work, and we shall soon see whether fried fish will be swimming into their mouth.

[6] And how stupid is the recommended self-mutilation when limbs cause vexation. If we let someone with a sharp axe in his right hand cut off and fling away the left, what will he do when afterwards the right hand vexes him, how will he cut that off, and how tear out the eyes and finally, without hands, cut off his feet that might still annoy him? Ah, leave us alone with such a teaching. This would not be good enough for a crocodile, let alone for man. If you think only a little of the consequences, it will become clear to you that such a teaching can be nothing else but the result of some ancient Jewish fanaticism.

[7] And if all the angels descended from the Heavens and taught men such ways of attaining everlasting life and the use of such means for gaining Heaven, such stupid teachers should be thrashed out of the world so that they may swallow their stupid Heaven. But what inconsistency. "A tooth for a tooth" and "an eye for an eye" he considers unjust and cruel, preaches utmost gentleness and tolerance, even opens the gate for all thieves by saying: "If a man demands your shirt, let him have your coat as well." What a teaching. But on the other hand people are to tear out their eyes and cut off hands and feet. Which one of you has ever heard a greater nonsense?

[8] Here **the Priest** steps up to Me and says: 'Master, your deeds prove that you can do more than any ordinary man, but if you are able to think correctly, which I do not doubt since at the house of Irhael I heard you speak quite wisely, then revoke certain most impracticable precepts of this your sermon. Otherwise we must, notwithstanding all your deeds, which are truly worthy of a Messiah, regard you as a fanatical magician taught in some ancient Egyptian school and expel you from here as a real Messiah-blasphemer.

[9] Just have a closer look at your mighty teaching, and you will see that your teaching is quite useless for gaining everlasting life and cannot be followed by anyone. For, if a person is to win Heaven in such a way, he is sure to forgo Heaven. It would be preferable not to have been born than thus to win a Heaven which one can enter only as a mutilated cripple. Tell me honestly whether you understand this or whether you are really serious about your teaching.'

[10] I said: 'You are a high priest, but you are blinder than a mole under the Earth. What can be expected of the others? I gave you images here and you swallow only their material part which threatens to suffocate you. You do not seem to have the least idea of the spirit I put into these images.

[11] Believe Me, we are quite as wise as you imagine yourselves to be and know very well whether or not a person could and should mutilate himself to gain everlasting life. But we also know that you do not grasp the spirit of this teaching and will not be able to grasp it for quite some time. We shall not, however, revoke our words because of that. Although you have ears, they do not hear the right thing, also you have eyes, but they are spiritually blind and, notwithstanding your

open ears and eyes, you do not hear and see anything.'

## CHAPTER 41
## Lack of understanding of the image of the Sermon on the Mount

[1] Says **the High Priest**: 'Yes, yes, you may be right therein to, and I will not, and at this stage also cannot, contest whether – and what kind of – spiritual is contained in your educational images. One thing, however, you cannot dispute that if I, for instance, wish to pass a teaching to someone that I want him to understand and practice as my disciple, I must surely give the teaching in such a way that my disciple will understand it in its true sense. Once I know that my disciple has fully grasped the inner truth of my teaching, I have every right to demand of my disciple to act according to my teaching.

[2] If I give someone a teaching in images, which as such are impossible to practice, and if my disciple then asked me: "What does that mean? How am I to take my own life in order to win life? How am I to kill myself, so that as a dead man I may receive a new, even an eternal life, out of death?", then I shall say to him, "Look, friend, you must understand this in such and such a way. For, see, between the given image and the truth it contains there is this and that spiritual correspondence, and you have to arrange your life in accordance with this correspondence, not with the external picture.

[3] Look, Master, then the disciple will understand it and, as already mentioned, I have then every right to demand of him to become active in the spirit of the truth of my teaching. But can I, without being a fool, expect him to act according to my harsh image? And if I in all earnest did demand that, I would appear to all thinking people as a man who carried water in a sealed up vessel and when a thirsty man came to him requesting a drink, the water carrier promptly passed him the sealed up jar, saying: "There you have the jar – drink." The thirsty man then tried to drink, but could not find an opening and asked the carrier: "How can I drink from it since the jar is sealed up from all sides?" And the carrier told him: "If you are blind and cannot find the opening, swallow the whole jar and you will thus also swallow the water with it."

[4] Tell me, you otherwise dear and wise Master, what the thirsty man would have to say to such a carrier? I think he could in this case justly call such a water carrier a fool.

[5] This does not mean that I want to call you exactly a fool, but if you say that because of our spiritual blind-and-deafness we cannot grasp the spirit of your teaching, your teaching would still be like the water in a sealed up jar with the thirsty man would in fact have to swallow together with the water, a demand which could only come from a prophet who has escaped from an asylum. Regard this matter as you please. As long as you do not add a sufficient explanation to your teaching, which in some of its points holds much that is good and true, I and many clearer thinking people abide by what I have expressed, You will never live to see

that, because of your teaching, we shall promptly begin to cut off our hands and feet and tear out our eyes. We shall also continue to work as before and gain our bread by the sweat of our brow, and the one who will deceitfully offend against us, shall not be spared a just punishment.

[6] To the thief who steals a shirt from us we shall not give our coat too, but he shall be seized and thrown into prison, where he will be given sufficient time to repent of his wrong action and live a better life. If you are truly a wise man gone forth from God, you must also be convinced of the sacred need to preserve the Mosaic Law, which God Himself proclaimed under lightning and thunder to the Israelites in the desert. If, however, you want to break the law with your teaching, take care that you can face Jehovah.'

[7] I said: 'I am of the opinion that the lawgiver is entitled to either leave the law alone and fulfill it himself according to the spirit and truth or abolish it completely under certain conditions.'

[8] Says **the High Priest**: 'This now sounds peculiar from your mouth. This morning I would have revered such a word from your mouth, for then it really seemed to me that you were indeed the Promised. But after the teaching you give us you have in my eyes become a madman, whom it pleases to present his fixed idea to us as the promised Messiah's wisdom. Therefore, you had now rather explain your harsh teaching, as without sufficient explanation no one could ever grasp it and act according to it.'

[9] I said: 'So tell me then what confounds you so much in My teaching, and I shall solve the problem for you.'

[10] Says **the High Priest**: 'I have already mentioned that several times, but to show you that I am very reasonable and moderate, I tell you now that I accept all the other points of your teaching as good and wise, but I cannot possible accept the tearing out of eyes and the cutting off of hands and feet. Think it over yourself whether it is possible to tear out one's eyes. Also, will not the one who himself cuts of one of his hands or feet soon bleed to death? And once he is dead, what fruits of betterment will he then be able to produce?

[11] Look, that is the impracticable point of your teaching which can never be reasonably complied with and if there ever should be any fools who do comply with such teaching, they will not achieve any betterment thereby. For if someone should survive, who will not praise God because of the misery such a teaching claimed to be from God has caused him.'

[12] I said: 'Very well, your request is fair enough and it tell you: Among all the priests since Samuel you are the wisest, for you have an honest heart and do not basically reject My teaching, but only wish to have it explained. Therefore, I will also give you a light. This light will not come from My mouth, but from the mouth of one of My disciples. Do now turn to one of My disciples, which will prove to you that My teaching is already understood by people without My explanation.'

# CHAPTER 42
## The Sermon on the Mount clearly explained by Nathanael

[1] Here **the High Priest** turns to Nathanael and says to him: 'Following your Master's direction, I now happen to turn to you. Will you, therefore, explain to me at least the most difficult point of the teaching of your master? But please do use only clear and pure words, for with a haze over a haze, a room cannot be illuminated. And now do speak.'

[2] Replies **Nathanael**: 'Are you of such a closed mind that you cannot grasp a clearly given teaching in its true sense? Have not practically all the prophets predicted that Christ would open His mouth to speak to the people only in parables?'

[3] Says **the High Priest**: 'Yes, you are right, that is how it is written.'

[4] Continues **Nathanael**: 'Well, since you as one versed in the Scripture know that why then do you call the Lord a fool because according to the Scripture He opens His mouth in parables? You may, of course, implore the Lord for a light to help you understand them, but not call Him a fool if you do not understand His allegorical speech, since you are still ignorant in such divine matters.

[5] See, all things in nature have their order and can exist only in their specific order. Thus have also the things of the spirit their specific order, beyond which they cannot exist nor be imagined or expressed in words. However, between the natural and the spiritual things, since the former have gone forth from the latter, there is and exists an exact correspondence which, of course, only the Lord knows in all detail.

[6] Thus, when the Lord tells us – who are all still within the fixed order of natural existence – of purely spiritual things, He can do so only by using images. To be able to understand these properly, we must strive to awaken our spirit through observing God's commandments. Once this awakening has taken place, openly then shall we understand all that the Lord has said and revealed in such a corresponding parable, and that is wherein his divine Word will forever differ from our human word.

[7] But now pay good attention. What the eye is to the natural man, is to the spirit the ability to view the divine and heavenly things, which alone suit the nature of the spirit for its most blessed, everlasting existence.

[8] However, since the spirit, according to the most necessary divine order, has to be for a certain time imprisoned in the matter of the flesh of this world, so that it may become firm in its freedom and almost total independence of God without which it would never be able to see God, let alone exist in, beside and with God - (but when the spirit is maturing within matter and becoming firm in freedom and independence of God, it is exposed to the quite unavoidable danger of being swallowed up by matter and perishing together with it, from which death is an awakening to life in God and must be extremely hard and painful) – the Lord said, not to the physical man, of course, but to the spiritual man: "If your eye offends you, tear it out and fling it away, for it is better to enter the Heavens with one eye,

than Hell with both," which is to say as much as: If you find the light of the world too tempting, make an effort and turn away from such a light, which would draw you into the death of matter. Deprive yourself as spirit of the empty gratification that enjoyment of the world can offer and turn with your soul to the purely heavenly things, for it is better for you to enter the realm of eternal life without much worldly knowledge than be swallowed up by the death of matter – too worldly wise on the one hand and too little spiritually wise on the other hand.

[9] If the Lord here spoke of two eyes, hands and feet, He thereby did not mean the two eyes and the two hands and feet of the body, but only the obviously dual ability of the spirit to see, act and progress. He does not warn the flesh, which has no life, but the spirit not to concern itself with the world, when it feels too much attracted to it. In that case it is better to enter eternal life without knowledge of the world than be in the end swallowed up by the necessary judgment of the world because of too much worldly knowledge.

[10] The spirit shall, of course, also see the world and get to know it, but it shall not take pleasure in it. Once it begins to feel that the world attracts it, it should promptly turn away from the world as danger is already threatening. See, this necessary turning away is expressed by the corresponding picture of the tearing out of an eye and He who is able to give us such an appropriate image must surely be well-versed in all man's spiritual and material circumstances. In my opinion, this could be possible only to Him through whose power, love and wisdom all things spiritual and material have been created. I think you will now have understood me and realize how flagrantly you have sinned against the One who carries yours as well as all our lives in His almighty hand.'


## CHAPTER 43
### Further explanation of Nathanael

[1] Here **the High Priest**, as well as many others, is quite startled and says after a while: 'Yes, yes, now I do understand it. But why did not the Lord speak right away as plainly as you have now spoken? Then I would surely not have sinned against Him.'

[2] Says **Nathanael**: 'If a seven year old boy would ask me that, I would not be at all surprised, but I do wonder how you, one of the principal sages of this place, could ask like that.

[3] Would you not also like to ask the Lord why he put into the grain of seed the limitless forming and developing ability of the tree that will be going forth from it? Why the tedious development of a tree from the grain of seed and following that the long wait for the ripe fruit? Just look how foolish you still are.

[4] The Lord's word and teaching is like all His works. He gives us His teaching in seed-pods. These we have first to sow into the soil of our spirit, which soil is called love. Then the seed will sprout and grow into a tree of true knowledge of God and ourselves, and from this tree we shall then in due course be able to

gather fully matured fruit for eternal life.

[5] Love is the principal thing. Without it no fruit of the spirit can thrive. Sow the wheat into the air and see whether it will grow and bear fruit for you, but if you put the grain of wheat into good soil, it will grow and bear multiple fruit. The right love, however, is a proper soil for the spiritual grain of seed which we receive from the Lord's mouth.

[6] This is the reason why the Lord has now for all of you abolished the harsh Mosaic law of punishment, so that you may soon grow richer in good soil in your hearts. For he who punishes according to the law has little or often no love at all and the divine word-seed will, therefore, develop in him only poorly. The one who is being punished is anyway in the judgment in which there is no love, since judgment is the death of love.

[7] Therefore, it is better if you do not immediately see your fellowman's faults, but are forbearing and patient. And if they in their weakness ask something of you, you shall not withhold it from them, so that love may keep growing in yourselves and also in your weak brothers Once this is present in abundance in you as well as your brothers, the divine seed will thrive within you and the weak will then in his strength look upon you with good will and reward you many times over for what you did for him when he was weak.

[8] But if you are stingy and hard where your weak brothers are concerned, you yourselves will never attain to a divine fruit within you and the judgment of the weak will in the end drag also you into destruction.

[9] When the Lord said: "Give the one who asks you for your shirt also the coat," He only meant to point out that you who are rich and have many possessions should give abundantly to the poor when they come to you. Thereby you will also gain much soil in your hearts and thus be blessed with the possession of such true soil, and the poor will truly bless you, for from your hearts they will receive the most effective sermon of God's true Gospel and thereby become strong for your own eternal support. But if you give miserly and calculate when and how much to give, you help neither yourselves nor your poor brothers, and because of it these will never become a support for you.'

## CHAPTER 44
### Symbolic eyes, arms and feet

[1] Says **the High Priest**, who has listened to this speech most attentively: 'Everything is now in order and I think that I understand all this pretty well. There is just one thing I still want to mention: The Master actually speaks only of tearing out the right eye and cutting off the right hand. Only in my searching zeal I added also the feet, but look, you have now also explained to me the cutting off of the feet just as you did the eye and hand about which alone the Lord spoke as far as I know. You said that there existed correspondence only in the Word of the Lord who speaks to man's spirit. How come then that you found also correspondence

in my addition?'

[2] Says **Nathanael**: 'You are wrong. The Lord spoke also of the right foot, but He hinted to the scribes to omit that about the foot because those who have directed their inner vision heavenward and have activated their love-will – which corresponds to the left arm as the hand of the heart – in accordance with God's will after getting rid of the right arm or right hand, by which the purely worldly motivation is to be understood, no longer need to rid themselves of the right foot. Once the eye is in the right light and the hand, or rather the will, is acting correctly, the progress into the regions of eternal life is automatically there or the right foot, denoting worldly progress, already automatically severed and a special effort is no longer needed.

[3] You Samaritans could as well start with the foot, for although your sight is now directed toward the divine and your hands are engaged in the right action, your foot or your eagerness for progress is directed towards the world. You expect of the Messiah something quite different from what you should expect of Him in accordance with the predictions by all the prophets, and that, spiritually seen, is your right foot which you should sever, so that you can set out on the right road to the Kingdom of God. Only because of you the Lord had spoken also of the right foot, but did not have it recorded because the future followers of the Lord's teaching will know very well where and wherein the kingdom of the Messiah is and consists and what has to be done to enter it. Is there anything else you wish to query?'

[4] Says **the High Priest**: 'Now everything is clear to me as far as I am able to grasp it but, notwithstanding the fact that I now do understand it, I must add that your teaching, the way it is given, is a severe and hard to understand teaching and you will find that many will be taking offense at it.

[5] Not that I wish to make a bad prophet for you, yet I tell you that with the arrogant Jews you will not achieve what you have achieved with us, notwithstanding our stupidity in many points. We do believe now, although still as if in a dream. The prominent Jews, however, will not believe you like this. They will ask for signs and will in the end even persecute you because of the signs. We did not ask you for signs, but you nevertheless worked them voluntarily.

[6] We do not believe you because of the signs, which partly could also be worked by men, but purely because of the teaching since it has now been explained to us. Therefore, you should stay with us, for with the proud Jews and Greeks you will have little success.'


## CHAPTER 45
## Not everyone can follow the Lord physically (1/45)

[1] Says **Nathanael**: 'This far I had to instruct you, from here on everything is in the Lord's hand. What He wills, we also shall will and do, for all of us are spiritually still very poor. Therefore, we must remain with Him, so that we may gain the

Kingdom of Heaven. We will bear together with the Lord all suffering and persecution, so that with and in Him we shall have the proper comfort. In His name let us be meek in all our thoughts, opinions, wishes and desires, also in all our actions, so that we may be able to take real possession of the true soil which is the pure love of god in our hearts.

[2] We shall not shun the land where conditions are harsh and unjust either, we shall be hungry and thirsty for true justice, since we have the One with us who can truly satisfy us everlastingly.

[3] And we ourselves will be most merciful towards everyone, be he just or unjust in his dealings with us, so that in the eyes of the Lord we may be considered worthier of God's great mercy.

[4] We will also everywhere, just as here before you, guard our hearts as much as possible against impurity, so that the Lord may not turn away from us when we face Him. For with an impure heart one cannot approach God and in spirit contemplate in all truth His countenance and the abundant wonders of His works.

[5] If we are of a pure heart, we must be peaceful, patient and gentle toward everyone, for an angry heart can never be pure, since anger always grows out of the ground of pride. But if we are of a peaceful heart, we may confidently approach as children the One who brought us the sonship of god and taught us Himself to pray to God as our Father.

[6] It is of no importance, my friend, if, as you believe, we shall be persecuted in other lands and places on account of our most righteous cause, for we have Him and through Him the Heaven of Heavens. And thus we are happy already here, supremely happy, whether people love us or scorn and persecute us for His sake, because He is Lord over all and over everything. We serve Him above all, whom all the Heavens obey and are always prepared to serve, as we could convince ourselves yesterday and on earlier occasions, and this alone is our highest reward and greatest honor. Therefore, do not be concerned about us, for we know and recognize what we have to reckon with.

[7] **The High Priest** was quite surprised at this speech so full of determination and said: 'Truly, if I were not needed here and did not have wife and children and some other responsibilities, I would go with you.'

[8] Says **Nathanael**: 'We have left wives, children and other things and have followed Him, and our wives and children are nevertheless living. I tell you what I think about this: whoever cannot in this world, for the love of Him, leave whatever it may be, is not worthy of His grace. Whether it offends you or not, this is the position. My heart tells me so, and in the heart everything is truth once the spirit within it has awakened to the living thinking in God. He does not need us, but we do need Him.

[9] Have you ever helped Him to raise the immense sun above the vast horizon and spread its celestial light across the wide Earth? Or have you ever seen, let alone forged, the shackles the Lord puts on the winds, how He constrains the lightning and the mighty thunder and the sea in its depths? Who can claim ever to have helped the Lord in anything? And if this is so, who, when he is called by the Lord to follow Him, can still think of his wife, his children and his things and not

follow unconditionally – Him, the Lord of all life, of all the Heavens and all the worlds, for whom we have waited so long to come and who has now come exactly in the way all the prophets and patriarchs had predicted?'

[10] Says **the High Priest**: 'If I only were not the high priest, I would in truth do what all of you have done. But I am the high priest and since you, as I have heard, will stay here only for one more day, these people, who are so weak in faith, need me like the eye for seeing. So you will understand that I have to remain here, not so much because of my wife, my children and things, but rather because of these weak believers, who for quite some time yet will be unable to completely relinquish their set idea of old about the nature of the Messiah and the purpose of His coming. It will cost me a great effort, but what can I do?

[11] I now believe firmly that your Master is the promised Messiah, but what about my flock? You have seen how already during the sermon many left. These are of a vexed unbelief which they will now diligently spread and many who still remained and yesterday fully believed have now their doubts, too, and do not know what to believe.

[12] Imagine what a job I, being an oracle to all of them, shall have. But if I do not convert them, they will remain to the end of the world whatever you can imagine, but not what they are supposed to be. And look, that is the main reason why I have to stay here, and I am convinced that the Lord will not deny me His grace because of it. Even if I am not bodily in His company, I shall remain so spiritually forever and endeavor to serve Him as a most faithful servant and shepherd in full accordance with His here proclaimed teaching, and I think that He will agree to this.'

[13] I said: 'Yes, I would like that and it suits Me very well. You shall be an excellent tool for Me in this community and your reward in Heaven shall once be great. But now evening has come. Let us go home again. So be it.'

[14] Following these words we walked down from the mountain and homewards. There was still quite a crowd around, although earlier, when I ended My sermon, many had left full of unbelief and vexation.


## CHAPTER 46
### Return to Sychar. Healing of a leper

[1] As already mentioned before, we were not actually at the top of the mountain, but lower down on the first rise because of the larger space there which was suitable for the large crowd that had followed Me from the city among which were many old and already rather weak people who in the considerable heat of the day would hardly have reached the peak of the mountain. But we were nevertheless rather high up and the descent was only slow as the twilight made it hard to see the path for some people with weak eyes.

[2] As we thus slowly and carefully descended from the mountain into the plain, **a man**, covered in bad sores, was lying by the roadside. He immediately got to his

feet, came to me and said in a plaintive voice: 'O Lord, if it were only your will, you could make me clean.' And I stretched out My hand over him and said: 'So it is My will that you shall be clean.' In a moment the sick man was cleansed of his leprosy, all the swellings, scabs and scales had vanished suddenly. As it had been a particularly bad case of leprosy, beyond help from any doctor, all the people were quite amazed when they saw how this man became so suddenly clean of his leprosy.

[3] Now the cleansed man meant to praise Me loudly, but I warned him seriously, saying: 'I tell you that for the time being you must not tell anybody about this, except the high priest. Go to him; he is walking behind us with My disciples. When he will have confirmed that you are cleansed, then go home and sacrifice on the altar what Moses has ordered.'

[4] The cleansed man did immediately what I bade him. **The High Priest** was also greatly astonished and said: 'If a doctor had told me: "Look, I am going to cure this man," I would have only laughed and said: "oh you fool, go to the Euphrates and try to bail it out. Each bucketful drawn will be replaced by a hundred thousand. However, it should still be easier for you to drain the Euphrates than to restore health to this man whose flesh has already begun to decompose." And the man, whom we have now recognized as the Messiah, managed to do this with a single word. In truth, this suffices us. He is definitely Christ. We do not need any further proof.

[5] In truth, if today someone should ask me for a shirt, I would not only add the coat, but all my clothes. For this prize I am truly willing to give away everything right to the shirt, and I now realize that His is a purely divine teaching. Yes, He Himself is as Jehovah now bodily with us. What more could we wish for? I will be a herald all night to announce His presence in all the streets and lanes.'

[6] Following these words he runs to Me, that is, close to the well, falls at My feet and says: 'Lord, do stop just for a moment that I may worship You, for You are not only Christ, a Son of God, but God Himself clothed in the flesh, with us.'

[7] I said: 'Friend, let that pass. I have already shown you how to pray. So pray silently, and that is sufficient. Do not do too much today and as a result maybe not enough tomorrow. There should be a right measure observed in everything. If you add the coat to the shirt, that is quite enough to make the poor your very good friend forever, but if you, when he only asks for a shirt, would add all your clothes, this would embarrass him and he will think that you either want to confound him or that you are out of your mind. And look, nothing good would have been achieved thereby.

[8] However, if someone asks you for one shekel and you give him two, or maybe three, you will make the borrower's heart glad and your own very happy. But if you give a thousand shekels to the one who came to you to borrow only one, he will be alarmed and think: "What does that mean? I asked him for one shekel only and he wants to give me all he possesses? Does he take me for insatiable, does he want to embarrass me or has he maybe become deranged?" And see, such a man will not become a gain for your heart not nor will such an attitude on your part be of benefit for his heart. Therefore, just a fair, full measure

in everything. And that is quite sufficient.'

[9] This instruction has fully satisfied **the High Priest** and he speaks to himself: 'Yes, yes, He is right in everything. If one does exactly as He said, it is quite in order; what is below or above it, is either bad or stupid. For if I today gave everything away and tomorrow maybe an even poorer man came to my door, what could I give him then? How sad it would make me, for I would no longer be able to help an even poorer man.

[10] The Lord is so absolutely right in all things and knows how to arrange for the best measure to be applied everywhere. Therefore, all honor, praise and glory be to Him alone and the fullest adoration from all hearts.'


## CHAPTER 47
### The Lord's celestial servants

[1] By this time however we arrive at Irhael's and Joram's, where, in the manner of the previous day everything had been readied for supper, only more opulently by far. All the many Sycharites who had been to the mountain begin to take their leave in the corridor, but a great host of youths clad in white step among them and implore them to stay for supper.

[2] **The high priest**, astonished at the vast number of youths and above all at their great affability, kindliness and benevolence, immediately steps up to Me and asks in great humility: 'But Lord, who are these magnificent youths? None of them can be sixteen years of age, yet with every word and movement they exhibit extraordinary learning. Oh tell me from where they came and to which school they belong. Of what beautiful shape and how well-fed they are. How exceedingly pleasant and agreeable to the heart just the sound of their voice. Therefore Lord, tell, tell me who and from where are these youths.'

[3] I said: 'Have you not heard it said of old: he who is a lord has also his servants and attendants? You call Me Lord, and it is therefore fitting that I too have My servants and attendants. That they are highly educated evinces that their Lord must be a most wise and loving one. The lords of the world are hard and loveless however, and so are their servants; that Lord however who is a Lord in Heaven and has now come to the Earth and the hard world of men has also His servants from where He came, and the servants resemble Him because they not only are His servants but also children of His wisdom and love. Have you truly understood Me?'

[4] Says **the chief priest**: 'Of a truth, Lord, in so far as one can at all understand your most memorable metaphorical language. There would be a lot of questions of course to clarify this thing, but I leave it there and hope that there shall be ample opportunity yet for that today.'

[5] I said: 'Oh indeed. But let us now go to supper, as all is in readiness.'

[6] The crowd with faith all went to supper; only the part without faith went home, because they regarded all this as a trap. The reason was that those were

mostly **emigrated Galileans**, among them many from Nazareth, who knew Me and also My disciples, whom they had seen often at the fish market. These said also to the native Samaritans: 'We know him and his disciples. He is a carpenter by trade and his disciples are fishermen. He went to school with the Essenes who are well-versed in all sorts of crafts, healing and rare magic. Such he has learned there and now practices his well-learned craft in order to gain for the Essenes a great following and much income. Those youths however are well-bred, Caucasian-bought girls in disguise, belonging to the same Essenes; these would be the main attraction. But we shall not be bewitched so easily, because we know there is no fooling around with the God of Abraham, Isaac and Jacob. But for the Essenes, who think that their ancestors created the world, it is easy to fool around with what they regard as non-existent. So, as long as we believe the God of Abraham, Isaac and Jacob we do not need such Essene deceptions, and if ever we should lose our faith, then the Essenes with their smart errand-boys shall be for us no substitute, but in the end shall make us into Sadducees, who believe in no resurrection or eternal life. But may Jehovah save us from that.' With these comments they returned home.

[7] I and a large part comprising mostly Samaritans sit down to the meal and, after a good day's work take it easy and let the angels serve us, because here too I labored in a desert, and it is written: "*And when Satan was forced to depart, angels came and ministered unto Him.*"


### CHAPTER 48
### Glorious promise for true followers

[1] But only few at the table were aware of being served by angels, with food from the Heavens. They believed in all earnest that I had such servants as part of My retinue, having bought these in Asia Minor for money. But they could not comprehend their great cheerfulness, friendliness and erudition, because such slaves normally had a sour expression and attended to their service slavishly and like machines, and there can generally be no talk about their education or philanthropy. In short, the guests were greatly amused, and the high priest who had gradually come to realize that these many servants were supernatural beings grew steadily more discomfited, since he felt embarrassed for the people who, although well-mannered, in his opinion carried on somewhat loosely with these glorious servants.

[2] But what embarrassed him most of all was that these, in spite of all signs from the wide-open Heavens, hurried home unbelieving. He spoke with trepidation: 'My Lord and my God. What should convert such people ever if such signs are fruitless? You Yourself, oh Lord, and the many angels from the open Heavens were not able to convert this breed; what am I poor rascal to do with them? Would they not spit in my face if I dared teaching them about You?'

[3] I said: 'Do you not also have a great number of believers around you? Make

them your helpers and your task shall be easy. Because if a man is to lift a certain weight but lacks sufficient strength, he engages a helper. If just one does not suffice he engages a second and a third and so becomes master of the burden. Once the number of believers is equal, and here indeed bigger than of the unbelieving, there the work is easy.

[4] Quite different it is in places where no believers are found at all. There indeed one makes an attempt, so that no one should once have the excuse: I never heard a word of it.

[5] If a believer is found, one stays with him and reveals to him the kingdom of God's grace. If however not even one accepts the Word, one moves on, but also shakes the dust off one's feet over such a place, because such place is then unworthy of grace other than bestowed also upon the animals of the field and woods. Here then you have your guide lines for your future stance towards all those non-believers.

[6] But I also urge you to remain strong in your faith yourself, or else you shall accomplish very little for My kingdom. Do not let yourself be diverted by all kinds of news you shall hear about Me from Jerusalem in a couple of years. Because there I shall be handed over to the authorities, and these shall kill this My body, but this I shall revive again on the third day and thereupon remain with you till the end of the world. Because that brood in Jerusalem shall believe only when convinced that there is no way of killing Me off.

[7] And then it shall also come that at sundry places on Earth, obstinate men shall be physically killing the bearers of the Gospel. But precisely such death shall then make believers out of the former, when they see that those who live a spiritual life out of My Word cannot be killed. Because those killed shall sporadically return to their pupils and teach them My Ways.

[8] But to the hard of heart, worldly people who have either no faith or, having some nevertheless do not act according to what faith teaches, neither I nor My disciples shall come to fully remove their night of doubts from their hearts. But when the end of their flesh comes over them they shall taste the evil of their faithlessness and the consequences of not keeping My teaching through deeds, even while those who believe on Me through works shall neither feel nor taste death.

[9] Because when I shall open the door of the flesh to these, they shall step out of their flesh like prisoners from their cells when the leniency of their lord has unlocked them.

[10] Therefore do not be disconcerted when you shall hear one or the other thing about Me. Because he who abides in faith and unshaken in faith and love till the end, as I teach and have taught and shall teach on and on, shall attain to blissfulness in the everlasting kingdom of the Heavens, which you now see open above you, with My angels ascending and descending.'

# CHAPTER 49
## Every day is the Lord's day

[1] Says **the high priest**: 'I am sorted out now and hope that this entire district also shall be so in a short time. But allow me just another question, and this consists in: are we to still honor the mountain and your old House, and honor your Sabbaths there, or should we erect a new House here, to meet in Your name? If the latter is Your will then You might want tomorrow to point out the appropriate spot most pleasing to you, and we should then do everything to accommodate Your desire therein too.'

[2] I said: 'Friend, that which is the right thing for you and mankind at large I have already made known to you on the mountain today.

[3] But for the keeping of same it requires neither the old House on the Mount, and still less a new one in the city, but only your believing hearts and a firm and good will.

[4] When I came here yesterday and took a rest at Jacob's well, encountering Irhael, she too when recognizing Me more closely asked Me whether God is to be worshiped on Gerizim or in the temple at Jerusalem. Let her tell you what answer I gave her.'

[5] Here **the high priest** turns to Irhael, and she says: 'The Lord spoke to me thus:

[6] "The hour comes, and now is, when the true worshipers shall worship God neither upon Gerizim nor in the temple at Jerusalem. For God is a Spirit, and those who worship Him must worship Him in spirit and in truth." This the Lord spoke, you are a high priest and shall know what from now on has to be done.

[7] My view is that since the Lord has bestowed such exceeding Grace upon us all and took lodging in this house, which is not mine but is His and shall remain so, this house should remain a memorable one forever, and we want to assemble in it in His name always and honor the Sabbath in His glory.'

[8] Says **the high priest**: 'Yes, yes, you are quite right, if only we were all believers, but some consideration has to be also given to the weak. These would be offended even more.'

[9] I said: 'Irhael is right. Whoever is offended – well, let him be offended and climb his mountain. Once he no longer finds anything there, he will start thinking of something better.

[10] Do not in future build houses of prayer for Me but guest houses and refuges for the poor who cannot pay you.

[11] In the love of your poor brothers and sisters shall you be My true worshipers, and in such houses of prayer I shall be frequently among you, without you necessarily becoming aware of it, but in temples built for worshiping Me with the lips, as it has been till now, I shall from now on dwell no more than man's intellect would in his little toe.

[12] If notwithstanding you have to awaken your hearts towards Me and enter upon the right humility in an exalted temple, then move outside into the temple of

My Creations, and sun, moon and all the stars and the sea, the mountains and the trees and the birds of the air, as also the fish in the water and the countless flowers of the fields shall proclaim My glory to you.'

[13] Say, is not the tree more glorious than all the splendor of the temple at Jerusalem? A tree is a pure work of God, it has its life and brings forth nourishing fruit. But what does the temple bring forth? I say unto you: nothing but arrogance, anger, envy, the most blatant jealousy and domineering, because it is not God's, but the vain work of man.

[14] Verily, verily I say unto you all: he who shall honor, love and worship Me by doing good to his brothers and sisters in My name shall have his everlasting reward in Heaven, but he who from now on honors Me with all kinds of ceremonies in a temple built especially for this shall also have his temporal reward from the temple. When however after the death of his flesh he shall come to Me and say: 'Lord, Lord, have mercy on me, your servant', I shall then say unto him: 'I do not know you, therefore depart from Me and seek your reward with him who you served.' For this reason you too should from now on have nothing more to do with any temple.

[15] But in this present house you may always assemble in My remembrance, whether on a Sabbath or other day, because every day is the Lord's and not just the Sabbath, on which you can in the future do good just as on any other day.'


## CHAPTER 50
### The honoring of the Sabbath

[1] **The Lord**: 'The most appropriate honoring of the Sabbath however is that you should be more actively engaged in doing good than on any other day.

[2] Servile work, by which I mean to work for wages and reward from the world, you should from now on perform neither on a normal week day and even less on a Sabbath, because from now on every day shall be a Sabbath and every Sabbath a full work day. In this, My friend, you now have a complete rule on how you are to serve God in the future. At that let us leave it.'

[3] Says **the high priest**: 'I now clearly recognize the holy truth of this rule, which I am happy to take as a commandment, but with the entrenched Jews it will take much before this rule, gone forth from the purely divine will, shall become comprehensible to them in its fullest truth. I fear that very many shall not accept this rule before the end of the world, because men already are accustomed to the Sabbath from antiquity and will not have it taken from them. Oh, the effort and work this shall take.'

[4] I said: 'It is not strictly necessary that the Sabbath be completely dropped, but only its follies. God the Lord does not require your services and honoring, for He has created the world and man without anyone's help and is only asking men to acknowledge and love Him with all their strength, and this not only on the Sabbath but every day ceaselessly.

[5] What kind of divine service is it that makes you remember God only on a Sabbath yet never during the week? Is not God the same, unchanging God every day? Does He not every day let the sun go up and pour light over the just and unjust, of whom there always are more than the just?

[6] Does not God Himself work the same on every day? If however God Himself takes no holidays, why should men keep, holidays just for idleness? Because they do regard nothing more on a Sabbath than idling. But with this they give God the worst possible service.

[7] For it is God's will that men shall get more and more used to love-activity, so that once in the other life they will be capable of much work and effort and able to seek and find only in such activity true and supreme bliss. Would men ever be able to achieve this within themselves through idleness? I tell you: never.

[8] On working days, although he does work, man only practices selfishness, for then he works for his flesh and calls what he gains his own. Whoever wishes to obtain that from him must buy it through work or with money, or he would not get anything of significance from anyone. Therefore, if on workdays men cultivate only their selfishness and spend the Sabbath, as the only day on which they should practice love-activity, in the most inflexible idleness, the very serious question arises: when should or would people practice the only true divine service, which consists in loving service to the fellowman?

[9] God Himself is not even for a moment idle, but constantly active for mankind and never for Himself. He does not need an Earth for Himself, or a sun, a moon, all the stars or anything contained therein or going forth from same. God does not need all that. But all the created spirits and men do need it, and for their sake the Lord is continually active.

[10] If the Lord, whose work goes on every day and who is continually active for mankind, wishes men as His children to be like Him in everything, how can it ever have been His will that after six selfishly spent days men should on the seventh serve Him satisfactorily by absolute idleness and honor Him, the eternally active One, through indolence?

[11] I tell you, the high priest, this now quite clearly, so that you may in future – well aware who the One is who has told you this – show your flock the Sabbath in a better light than it has been the case from Moses until now. For in the same way as I have now explained the Sabbath to you it had been given also to Moses, but the people only too soon perverted it into a heathen day of idleness, believing to render a good service to God through inaction and the punishing of those who at times dared to perform also on the Sabbath some small task or give some beneficial help to a sick person. Oh what a great blindness, oh what a very gross foolishness.'

[12] Says **the high priest**, quite subdued by the truth: 'Oh what a holy truth comes out of Your mouth. Yes, now all is clear to me. Only now have You oh Lord taken away Moses' threefold veil from my eyes. Now Lord there is no need of further signs, because here just Your holy Word suffices. And I maintain from fullest conviction that in future those who believe on You only on account of the signs but not Your eminently true Word shall not possess a true living faith but be

102

instead mere idle, mechanistic followers of Your teaching and holy will, but with us it shall be otherwise. Not the signs which Your presence has provided but only your holy and most true Word shall bring forth and awaken the true, living faith and fullest love for You in our hearts, and out of Yourself and solely on Your account also towards all men in the right measure. And thus Your will be done for evermore, which You oh Lord have now made so abundantly clear to us forever.'

[13] I said: 'Amen. Yes, dear friend and brother, thus it is right and good. Because only in this way shall you become perfect even as the Father in Heaven is perfect. When however you are perfect like that then you are also true children of God, and can at all times call out to Him: 'Abba, dear Father'. And whatever you shall, as His true children ask Him, that shall He also give you, because the Father is exceedingly good and gives His children all He has. But eat and drink now, because the food here is not of this Earth, but the Father sends it to you from the Heavens and is now Himself among you.'


## CHAPTER 51
## The Gospel of Sychar

[1] Says **the High priest**: 'Lord, are we to commence eating again? Did we not already fortify ourselves with food and drink at the start of supper? I for one am fully fortified and can neither eat nor drink more.'

[2] I said: 'You have answered rightly, for you are filled with food and precious wine from the Heavens. But there are many here who dared to neither eat nor drink, because they held no regard yet for My name or My Word and were frightened as of witchcraft. But now that they heard our talk and comprehended its lucid truth, their foolish fear left them and hunger and thirst took its place. Now they would like to eat and drink but do not dare for all their reverence. Do you think one should let them go like that? Oh, that be far from us. They shall now eat and drink heartily. Because they shall from now on not eat or drink from this kitchen, except once in My kingdom in the Heavens.'

[3] After this correction I again exhorted the crowds to eat and drink, and also said to the youths: 'Don't let them miss out on anything.' And the youths once again brought a good amount of bread and wine and all kinds of precious fruits.

[4] But some worried about whether to eat the unknown fruits. And **the youths** spoke: 'Dear brethren, eat all these fruits without fear, because they are clean and of exquisite flavor. There certainly are on this Earth a number of fruits, grasses and animals in whose formation unclean spirits are at work, because it is written into the Lord's order, because here also the devils have to serve the Lord, even if they won't or cannot do so voluntarily, because just as a slave has to serve his master in chains, just so the devils also must serve, but the blessing is not in such work.

[5] And so there are upon this Earth, where not infrequently men, animals and devils live under one roof, and active after their kind, all kinds of deeds, works and

fruits of a bad and unclean nature and species, of which men should not partake if they desire to avoid all kinds of earthly diseases; and the Lord has through His servant Moses for that reason determined all those things which are clean and good, and has counseled men against using those things upon which unclean spirits are at work, and this is a splendid order. But everything offered here for your enjoyment is most clean because brought here from the Heavens for you supernaturally; therefore you may enjoy everything fearlessly. Because what the Father gives from the Heavens is most clean and advances the life of soul and spirit forever.'

[6] This instruction on the part of the wise youths cheered every heart, and all praised God for the friendly wisdom of these youths. This teaching also was recorded later, maintaining itself in this city and district for many years.

[7] But when afterwards this city and district were ravaged by sundry foes, much perished and this teaching with it, to which Paul once made a mystical allusion in one of his letters where he speaks of all kinds of spirits.

[8] The entire company now was in good spirits, and discussed Me and My teaching and this meal from the Heavens among themselves, and the youths discussed many things with the guests.

[9] **Nathanael** however got up and spoke to the guests: 'Dear friends and brethren, only a few moons (months) ago I was still a fisherman in the district of Bethabara on the river Jordan, not far from its estuary; a most unassuming man came to John and allowed Himself to be baptized, and John, without ever having seen Him physically on Earth, immediately gave Him this testimony: "See, the lamb of God that takes away the sin of the world." And again, John testified and spoke: "He it is of whom I said: He it is who, coming after me is preferred before me, whose shoe's latch I am not worthy to loosen."

[10] Such testimony I heard from the preacher in the desert, and I became reflective, made off and related it to my wife and children at home, and these were greatly astonished that the strict preacher gave another human such testimony.

[11] Because it was hard to speak with the preacher, and when he spoke his words were rough and he spared no one, whether it was a Pharisee, priest or Levite, all had to jump for life or death over the sword of his tongue.

[12] When however He who is now a Lord among us came then John became a lamb among lambs and became as tender as a lark singing its song of spring. In short, my family could hardly believe my tale, since they knew how John was wont to speak only too well.

[13] Two days later however I went about my day's work quite early, sat under a tree to repair my fishing gear, when He whom John had given this delicate testimony came to me in company of a few who already followed Him, called me by my name and asked me to follow Him. And when I wondered at how He knew me thus, since I had not met Him previously, He said: 'Wonder not greatly, for verily I say unto you, hereafter ye shall see Heaven open, and the angels of God ascending and descending upon the Son of Man.'

[14] And see, what the Lord had spoken to me then has now most gloriously fulfilled itself here. All the Heavens stand open and the angels descend and

minister unto Him and all of us. What further proof do we need that He alone is the One who is to come in accordance with the promises proclaimed to all children of Israel, starting with Adam? I therefore regard Him as more than just the Messiah. He is ....'

[15] Here I interrupt Nathanael, saying: 'My dear friend and brother, for the present only, this far and no further. Only after this flesh shall have been uplifted by the Jews, you can say everything that you know about Me, unreservedly, but not before under any circumstances, because men are not ready for this yet.'

[16] Nathanael accepted that, yet could nevertheless not understand what I meant by the uplifting of My flesh, but he was silent and of sad countenance. But I consoled him and reminded him of what I had told him previously in this matter, and he became cheerful and praised Me in his heart.

[17] But the morning of the following day began to dawn. Yet no one felt any trace of tiredness or sleep, because all were fortified as never before even after soundest sleep. All therefore asked Me if they could tarry with Me for the day. And I acceded to such their devout request.


## CHAPTER 52
### The slandering of the daughters of Jonael

[1] **The high priest** rose and besought Me, saying: 'Lord, since You have blessed us with the inestimable grace of staying with us for another day, how about You and Your disciples, together with also those others who believe on You, and with my own presence, visiting the nearby cities, of which we can count only three? Perhaps some people could be found there who would believe on You if they saw and heard You?

[2] I said: 'On their account, no, but yes on your account. It gives you pleasure and I want to gladly give you that pleasure. But you have a wife and children; do you not want to introduce them to Me? Where are they and how many of them?'

[3] Says **the high priest**, somewhat embarrassed: 'Lord, I have a pleasant wife who like myself is getting on a bit in years, and also seven children, but unfortunately only maidens between 12 and 21 years. But You know that it is not a great honor for an Israelite to have no male descendants; and so, Lord, please bear a little with my weakness. I lacked the daring to come up with my exclusively female folk.

[4] If it pleased You, oh Lord, then I would nevertheless ask You on this occasion to pass by my house, where I could then introduce my womankind to You. But until now it would have hardly been appropriate. Because notwithstanding that I am not lacking in anything and can get on reasonably with my family here, the clothing situation leaves something to be desired. They are indeed clothed appropriately for domestic errands, but to be seen in company such as this would, for a high priest's family be much too unseemly. Under the circumstances therefore they would do well to stay at home, where they shall not

be exposed to ridicule by the world and to their inborn vanity. And it is good for them to have as little as possible to do with the world, because the latter is and remains bad at all times.'

[5] I said: 'I want to comply with your request, but then let them all come with us. But a more suitable apparel for them shall in any case be arranged for them, to the extent of their making a favorable impression in our circle. It nevertheless is good and wise of you to keep them away from the world as much as possible, but with our surely non-worldly company they would have fitted in.

[6] See Mary, the mother of My flesh. She simply is fitted out in white linen, overhung with a very ordinary blue apron, yet she is sufficiently dressed up. On her head she wears normally a square sun-hat like all the other women who followed Me from Galilee and Judea, and they nevertheless make out most fittingly in our company. But regardless of that, your wife and daughters shall be found among our company this day.'

[7] Says **one of the Samaritans**: 'That would all be all right. But although I on my part have no proof, I nevertheless tell you what I heard from people in this area and then you can do what you like. This however is what they are saying about the four elder daughters, that whenever the high priest is not home, they are seen in the streets at night and, since they are most beautiful, they are accepting money from lustful laborers and sleep with them. This is going on in secret. I on my part have no proof, but this much I can say: if this teaching is to find general acceptance in these parts, with all those many unbelievers, then for the sake of the foolish masses the four eldest daughters at least should be kept out of our company. Because you brother Jonael know only too well how gossiping and immensely foolish and unbelieving our folk are. If this got around among them then not even Jehovah Himself could do anything about it. But this is only my humble opinion, on account of the evident malice of our people, to forestall any damage to our good cause.'

[8] **The high priest** gets very sad and says: 'Lord, if I had been only slightly remiss in my daughter's upbringing then it would hardly sadden me to listen to this, but I am only too aware that nothing was neglected for the education of their intellects and hearts, and I hazard to swear that each one of my daughters is as pure as a flower on Jehovah's mountain. So why such shameful slander?'

[9] I said: 'My dear brother Jonael, do not let it grieve you. Let it suffice you that your daughters are pure before Me. Because the world now is purely devilish and thus malicious through and through. Have you ever heard of grapes reaped from briars and figs from thistles? I have known a long time since and therefore also made quite a vivid reference to it on the mountain with the parable of the splinter in your neighbor's eye And see, this quite drove many from the Mount, because they discerned that I meant them.'

[10] But I say unto you: now even more certainly your daughters must come with us, and I shall walk in their midst. Because, let that which is of the devil also remain with the devil, if it will not be converted. But now let us start. I have already made everything known to your wife and daughters. They shall be waiting for us.'

# CHAPTER 53
## The punishment of the liar and slanderer

[1] Along the way **Peter** speaks again: 'Now I am getting really dizzy with all the wonders upon wonders. No, anyone still doubting that this Jesus of Nazareth is the true Son of Jehovah must be either struck with the tenfold blindness of Pharaoh, or he is fully dead. The sick are suddenly healed just through the Word, the blind see, the deaf and dumb hear and the lame walk. And those with the most obstinate leprosy get as clean as if they had never sinned.

[2] On top of that the Heavens open and hosts of the most magnificent angels hurriedly sail down, serve and carry on with us as if they had not left the Earth since the appearance of the first man. And their beauty is such that at their mere sight one could perish with delight. And when He speaks with His unheard of wisdom, how these beautiful servants of Jehovah are all sweetest reverential attention and holy devotion, yet as cheerful as swallows on the nicest of summer days. Truly, whoever still can say: 'This Jesus is a magician pure and simple' ought to be slaughtered like an ox. Because such a man cannot be a man but only a talking animal, and should therefore not die like a man but like a domestic animal.'

[3] While Peter is ruminating thus, not noticing what is going on around him, **one unbelieving inhabitant** of this city roughly taps him on the shoulder and says: 'In that case I as an honest man shall dutifully prophesy that you shall die as a barest ox. Because if you haven't reached the stage of realizing what a real magician is capable of then you shouldn't open your big mouth where experienced and knowledgeable people live.'

[4] Says **Peter**: 'Tell me, you coarse, dark spirit. Can those magicians of yours also heal all the sick with one word, and open the high Heavens where no magician's hand or intellect can reach?'

[5] Says **the local**: 'Oh you stupid, blind Galilean. Don't you know that a real magician can make a fish or snake out of a piece of wood? Only recently there was one here from Egypt who threw sticks in the water and they at once turned into fish, but when he threw the sticks on dry land they turned into snakes and vipers. He then breathed into the air and it filled with locusts and other flying insects. Then he took white stones, threw them in the air and they turned into pigeons and flew off. Then he scooped up a handful of dust from the road, flung it in the wind and watch it, the air was instantly filled with mosquitoes to where the sun could hardly get through. But when he blew into these mosquitoes, a wind came, blowing these mosquitoes off like a cloud. Then he took us to the pond behind the creek from where he first drew fish from sticks. He touched the water with his cane and look, it instantly turned into blood, and when he touched it again it again turned into water. In the evening he calls to the stars and they fly into his hands like tame pigeons. Then he commands them and they fly back to the firmament. Yet you say: where is the man whose hands reach up to the Heavens? But that all this took place here I can testify with a hundred witnesses. What do

you say to your Son of God from Nazareth now, of whom I know only too well whose son he is and where he learned all this?'

[6] Says **Peter**: 'If you haven't in fact lied like a crocodile with its baby-cry, after buying yourself your hundred witnesses for a few coppers, then these many recognizing Jesus as the Christ must also know something of this magician of whose wonders you tell me. I will ask Jonael straight away. You'll be sorry if you lied.'

[7] Says **the local**: 'These won't clear you up because they wouldn't attend such shows in the first place for fear that the magicians did all this with the help of the devil, and he could do them much harm. Only us brave few, not believing in a devil went out, because we are slightly more acquainted with the powers of nature, convincing ourselves with supreme amazement at what man can do.'

[8] Says **Peter**: 'You should be a fine customer for sure. But I tell you that you are not going to get away with it and not escape your punishment. Just follow me to the high priest of this city now. We shall finalize this matter in front of him.'

[9] Says **the local**: 'What have I to do with this high priest? I am a Galilean, and more of a Greek than a Jew at that; this high priest however is a stupid fanatic, even while at night-time his four eldest daughters, with their mother's consent carry on shamefully, so the story goes, surrendering to fornication. What use such idiot to me? I rate art and science above everything and I reserve my highest respect for all true scholars and artists, but they mustn't make out to be more than they are.

[10] If your truly clever and scholarly master in all kinds of art and science had stuck to what he is, he would have been one of the most highly regarded among the Jews, Greeks and Romans. But he makes a god out of himself and this is very stupid and belongs to dark antiquity.

[11] You people however are honest and upright souls in your own right. Only your knowledge and experience doesn't seem to go much over fishing. Therefore we shall leave further argument aside. You can believe what you like, but you won't pull the wool over our eyes so easily, because we are versed in all kinds of knowledge and science and not without a smattering of magic, and know therefore what to think of your master.'

[12] Says **Peter**: 'Friend, you are trying to whitewash yourself in vain. This is not at all about whether you regard my Master as this or that and now with seeming cleverness try to make me forget about telling me a rotten lie before. May the high priest be just a fanatic to you as much as he likes, but as a public person in this small city he is bound to know whether a magician had recently been performing here as described by you. Because on this depends what I am to think of my Master.

[13] I tell you that I and many of us have left everything, indeed even wife and children and unquestioningly follow Him, since we saw Him perform deeds which would not be possible to any human ever, in addition hearing Him speak wisely as no man ever spoke before Him and hardly ever shall after Him.

[14] Yet you introduced another master besides mine who, even though not surpassing Him, nevertheless performs deeds equaling His, which should be

respected by every person. Everything now simply depends on whether it can be proven that such magician in fact performed the deeds you mentioned.

[15] If your witness is true then I give you my holy word that although I fully attribute purely divine power to my Master, I nevertheless shall leave Him at once and go home to my family. Because I don't intend following a questionable magician even one more step, as I am still a true Jew, believing more in Moses than hundreds of thousands of the craftiest magicians. If however, as I fully suspect, from a purely evil will, you lied to me in order to just cast suspicion on my Master, then, as I already warned you, beware. You shall find out that I too out of the grace of My divine Master am quite capable of effecting certain things, without however introducing myself to anyone as a worker of miracles.

[16] Therefore just come with me to the high priest, who right now is conferring with your tax-collector Matthew, who is bound to know something about your magician as well, because he too was here in the city constantly and must know something about it. Therefore come of free will or I shall use force.'

[17] Says **the local**: 'Why force, since I don't feel like it? Just have a look, there are hundreds behind me. Just dare lay hands on me and see what happens.'

[18] Says **Peter**: 'I shall not put my hand on you the way you quite indelicately put yours on me before, yet you shall nevertheless be hauled over. Hosts of angels are traveling with us, whom you don't seem to see. It requires only a hint and they will immediately have you where I want and must have you.'

[19] Says **the local**: 'These boys clad in white are not going to be your angels? Ha, ha, ha! Well, if these are our protective legion then we'll just hand out a few hooks and you and your protection-boys are spread outside the city wall.'

[20] This remark gets Peter quite beside himself and he straight away calls upon one of the youths to punish him. But the youth says: 'I am all for it, as long as it is the Lord's will, but the Lord has not given me a hint yet, and so I cannot accede to your request yet. But if He wants it I shall act.'

[21] Peter moves forward towards Me a little straight away and tells Me his problem. But I said, even while arriving in front of Jonael's house: 'Go and bring Me this person'.

[22] **Peter** was greatly relieved and hurried back and said to the youth: 'It is His will.'

[23] Here the youth gazed at the local and the latter began to quake and, driven by the youth, followed Peter over to Me without protest. But I just looked at him, and the local confessed that he had lied and that he had never seen such a magician, but that he had only heard of such and only wanted to see if this disciple was firm in his faith, having otherwise meant no evil at all.

[24] I said: 'You are one who wants to use a second lie to get out of the first, and therefore of the devil. Go and let him give you your reward, since you are such a good servant of his.'

[25] Immediately an evil spirit steps up to the local to agonizingly torment him. But the local puts out a tremendous yell: 'Lord, help me, as I admit loudly that I have sinned.'

[26] But I say: 'So did you hear that Jonael's four eldest daughters were

whores? Confess it loudly or I let you be tormented till the end of the world.'

[27] Says **the local**: 'Oh Lord, I never heard it from anyone, but I once met the four daughters at night as they were carrying water from Jacob's well and tried to seduce them. But the daughters told me off in a way that made me glad to leave them, but I swore them revenge, invented this shamefulness out of my evil heart and spread the rumor all over the place. The daughters are perfect virgins. Oh, Lord, I alone am evil; everyone else is good and pure.'

[28] Here I command the evil spirit to leave the local. The latter has nevertheless to make up to Jonael. He is a merchant however and goes back and brings the daughters ten times what I commanded him, asking Jonael and the daughters for forgiveness.

[29] But I say unto him: 'The gift alone does not rectify such injustice. Go and recant all evil you spread everywhere, only then shall your sins be forgiven. Let it be so now.'

[30] The local promises to do everything immediately, but asks that I absolve him where in the case of strangers having found out, he doesn't know how to locate them.

[31] But I say unto him: 'Do what is possible; everything else I shall do and you shall then be without sin.'

[32] The local is happy with that and goes off to undo all the evil he has committed.

## CHAPTER 54
### The Lord with Jonael. The disciples criticize the Lord (1/54)

[1] After the local's departure, I call back Jonael's wife and daughters who, when they had seen Me with the local, had fled in fear from the corridor back into the house.

[2] They hurry back in response to My call, hastening towards Me with the friendliest, cheerfully reverent faces, thanking Me with tears in their eyes for giving them back their innocence, smeared through the evil man.

[3] But I lay My hands on their heads, bless them and ask them to walk by My side all this day. But they excuse themselves, saying: 'Oh Lord, we are not worthy of such enormous grace. We are only too happy if we can follow You as the last ones among this great company.'

[4] But I say: 'I am aware of your proper humility, calling upon you to walk in My proximity for that very reason, wherever I shall be taking to the road in this district today.'

[5] The daughters thank Me for such incomprehensible favor. But **Jonael** asks the daughters, saying: 'My dear daughters, where did you get these marvelous dresses, which truly become you in a heavenly fashion?'

[6] Only then do the daughters become aware of wearing dresses of the finest brocade and their heads are adorned with the most precious diadems, giving them

the looks of princesses.

[7] As the seven of them become aware of such splendor they are fully beside themselves. Their hearts are aflame with love and wonder, and with sweetest confusion they are unable to work out what had taken place with them. Only after long astonishment do they ask Jonael how this went on, because they were not aware of anyone handing them such regal clothing and diadems.

[8] But **Jonael**, himself quite delighted by the great charm of his daughters, says: 'Thank Him who blessed you. He has bestowed it on you miraculously.'

[9] Here the children swarm all over Me, crying for love and joy and unable to speak. But **the disciples** behind Me are saying: 'If this only were happening indoors. But here in front of several thousand onlookers the thing is creating too much of a stir.'

[10] But, perceiving that they spoke thus I turned around and said to them: 'I have been with you for a long time, yet you never gave My heart the joy which these seven daughters have done. I verily say unto you these are already along the right way and have taken the best part. If you don't take this way you hardly shall find the portals of My kingdom. Because the children who come to Me thus shall also stay, but those coming with only adulation and praise shall have only My reflection but not Me amongst them.

[11] But My true kingdom is only where I am Myself in actual fact. Understand this also. But the Lord is a Lord also over the whole world and does not have to consider what is fitting before a foolish world. Have you understood this?'

[12] **Peter** replies: 'Lord, have patience with our great foolishness. You are aware of our education not deriving from Heaven but from this world. It is all bound to be set right however, because we also love you above everything, otherwise we would not have followed You.'

[13] I said: 'Do therefore indeed remain within love and take no account of this world, but of Me from the Heavens.' With this the disciples are happy, praising Me in their hearts.


## CHAPTER 55
### Esau's castle. The clever merchant

[1] But we continue with our journey, arriving after one hour in a clean, shady grove belonging to a wealthy merchant of Sychar. This grove is provided with lots of ornaments, small gardens, brooklets and ponds with all sorts of fish and birds; and at the end of the extensive grove there stands an immense castle with massive, fortified walls. This castle had been built by Esau, and he lived there when Jacob was abroad. It had of course greatly suffered with the vicissitudes of time, but this merchant spent vast sums on it, completely restoring its habitability, frequently dwelling there with all his, own and on this occasion too. Although he was of a charitable disposition and owned many other properties, he was quite fastidious about this one and uneasy when seeing too many people entering it, for

he took great pains to cultivate it.

[2] When therefore he espied a large crowd moving through the grove and towards the fortifications, he quickly dispatched his many servants and workers to get us out of the grove, and to also find out what we were on about.

[3] But I said to the workers: 'Go to your lord and tell him, his and your Lord is letting him know that He and those with Him shall stop off for lunch.'

[4] The workers and servants immediately return to their lord with the message. He asks them whether they were able to work out who I was. But **the workers and servants** replied: 'We have already told you how he said to us that he was your and our lord, why do you ask again? Seven regally adorned daughters accompany him, and there is a measureless crowd in his train. He could turn out to be a prince of Rome, and it would therefore be advisable to rush to the portals and welcome him with all honors.'

[5] On hearing this, **the merchant** says: 'In that case bring me my most expensive festive clothing at once and let everyone look as festive as possible, for such a prince has to be welcomed gloriously.'

[6] Everything throughout the castle now is a run-to and fro, with all cooks racing to the larder to move masses of edibles into the kitchen, while the gardeners are rushing to the large gardens to collect all kinds of precious fruit.

[7] After some time the castle lord comes out, splendidly attired and surrounded by a hundred of his most distinguished servants, bows down nearly to the ground before Me three times, welcomes Me in the name of all, thanking Me for the inestimable grace, for he still is of the persuasion that I am in all earnest a prince of Rome.

[8] But I gaze at him, asking: 'Friend, what do you consider to be the highest station a human being can occupy on Earth?'

[9] Replies **the wealthy merchant**: 'Lord, forgive your most obedient slave, but I was unable to understand your question, of a most lofty wisdom; therefore please come down from your immeasurably exalted wisdom and put the question in a manner comprehensible to my unlimited mental dullness.' (He nevertheless had understood the question quite well, but it was in those times a silly form of courtesy to not understand even the simplest question, where the questioner was one of exalted rank, so as to highlight the wisdom of the eminent person.)

[10] But I say unto him: 'Friend, you understood Me quite well, but pretend to not have understood Me, merely on account of the old courtesy rule, which however has already gone out of vogue. Put this old silliness aside therefore and answer My question.'

[11] Replies **the merchant**: 'Yes, if I may dare to answer your exalted question straight out, then with your permission I deem myself to have understood your exalted question, and my answer therefore would be that I naturally regard the emperor and his office as the highest a human can occupy on Earth.'

[12] I said: 'But friend, why do you contradict yourself so immensely in your own heart against your own dictum, running thus: "Truth is highest and holiest on this Earth, and an office-bearer who is a steward of the office of Truth and justice discharges the highest and most exalted office on Earth." See, this is your maxim.

How can you declare as highest the office of an emperor who as commander in chief occupies an office of brute force, which definitely does not always base itself on Truth and justice, thus flatly contradicting your inner convictions?'

[13] Here **the rich merchant** is stunned, saying after a while: 'Lord, exalted one. Who gave my adage away to you? I have never expressed it aloud, yet of course I thought it thousands upon thousands of times. Because we are only too well aware that with plain truth the best results are not always achieved and one has to often sacrifice it for political considerations, to escape unscathed among men.

[14] But it seems that in yourself too, exalted princely son, I have detected a great friend of truth and justice, and you may deem it appropriate for me to meet you with cherished truth, because high-ranking lords never want to hear truth and therefore highly regard flattery after which alone they strive, all human rights being nothing to them. Whatever they want they take, preferably by force. Whether the poor complain about injustice, now or in times past, this is all one to the great who bask in high esteem. That's why one has to be political and talk with them nicely, otherwise prison and galley follow, multiplying mankind's torment and pain.'

[15] I said: 'You have spoken well and truly. In this case I am of similar opinion, but now tell Me for whom you actually take Me?'

[16] Says **the merchant**: 'Lord, this is a ticklish question. If I say too much I shall obviously be laughed at, but if I say too little I end up in the can. Therefore it shall be better to let the question go begging than, for answering it, to while away one's time with torture and pain in jail.'

[17] I said: 'But if I give you the assurance that you needn't fear either, then you shall surely be able to answer? Therefore say it straight out as to who you think I am.

[18] Replies **the merchant**: 'Well if I have to say it: a prince of Rome.'

[19] Says **Jonael** behind Me: 'This might be far too little. You'll just have to guess higher. The prince won't do.'

[20] **The merchant** is startled and says: 'In the end, could it be the emperor himself?'

[21] Says **Jonael**: 'Still far too little; therefore guess a little higher.'

[22] Says **the merchant**: 'This I shall leave alone well and truly, because there is nothing higher than an emperor of Rome.'

[23] Says **Jonael**: 'And yet there is. Something much, much higher. Just think and say it straight out. Because I see into your heart, and this allocates the lowest place to the emperor of Rome. Why do you speak differently from what you think and feel in your heart? Therefore speak the truth.'

## CHAPTER 56
### The result of lies and truth (1/56)

[1] After a little while **the merchant** replies: 'Dear exalted guests, here it is

113

better to put a clamp over one's mouth and say as little as possible. Because one must never – and least of all in front of prominent people – make it known what one thinks and feels in one's heart, because these important people have a sensitive skin which will not take the sharp stroke of truth. It is therefore especially dangerous to come out with the truth in front of such exalted people. Because such lords are, as one would say, of a tempting nature, and one must beware of them more than of snakes, vipers and basilisks, since there are precedents, quite curious precedents. Let everyone think what he will, but in his transactions let him be a good patriot, and he shall get along with all men. But only as little speaking as possible, otherwise one may easily make the most unpleasant acquaintance with the henchmen.

[2] I actually have already spoken far too much about truth. Therefore I keep with the emperor now and say again: there is to be found nothing higher on Earth than the emperor. *'Caesarum cum Jove, unam esse personam'*. What an emperor wants God quietly carries out.

[3] Therefore away with the truth from Earth, if any truth exists, it is not good for the human race. How much trouble has not truth caused already, and its teachers have expired their spirit of truth either on the cross or under the sword. But he who has switched over to lying has always managed to save his skin, unless here and there, where his lying was too stupid he had to look to his feet, but other than that not much happened to him, while with few exceptions, all great friends of truth were dispatched from Earth by violent death.

[4] But if such reward follows truth, what donkey or ox wants to still be its friend? Let it be kept under arrest as a detainee under lock and key, in one's breast, and walk freely among men, rather than through setting free the detainee one becomes such oneself in body and soul, because as long as a body has to languish in prison the soul can't go wandering through meadows.

[5] Neither have I heard of truth ever bringing about anything good. A few examples will shed more light on this:

[6] A thief is arrested as a strong suspect and brought before the strict judges. If he is good at lying he shall be released, due to lack of convincing evidence, but if the ox speaks the truth, he shall be punished with all severity. To hell with truth.

[7] Or someone pays a clever businessman – and this happens many times – too much money for certain goods. The deceived fellow, as an owner of many other businesses and wealth, does not notice the deception and is quite happy. Thereupon, a friend of truth who became aware of the deception comes and shows the deceived one how and to what extent his merchant deceived him. Only then does the deceived one become sad, goes to court at great expense to have the deceiver punished. Did this truth bring him any advantage? No, it only awakened anger and revenge in him, leading him to still greater expenditure. But the deceiver, skilled in lying, not only suffered no harm through the truth of the informer, since lying got him through, but it placed the traitorous informer behind bars for slander. The question is: what reward, once again, did truth yield to its friend?

[8] Therefore away with truth from this Earth. It alone is accountable for all of

men's afflictions, as Moses also says in book one: 'For in the day that thou eat from the tree of truth's diversity thou shall surely die.' And thus it is and remains to this hour. With the lie you rise to the throne and with truth you go to jail. A lovely surprise for friends of truth.

[9] Therefore go and seek truth wherever you will, only leave me out of it. Whatever my larders hold and what grows in my gardens is at your disposal, but the holiest of holies in my heart is mine alone, as a gift from Jehovah. But to you and the whole world I give what I have from the world, and that is the grace of the world. But God's grace I keep for myself.'

[10] Says **the high priest**: 'I concede openly that so far as the situation in the world is at present, your summation is correct. But since you also mention Moses you will no doubt be aware of Moses also receiving a commandment for his people where the lie or false witness is forbidden, thus making truth obligatory? If all men kept this commandment, then admit it: would it not be wonderful to live on Earth?

[11] I tell you, and you have to acknowledge it: not through truth but through the lie every affliction reaches mankind and this because man, with rare exceptions encounter one another domineeringly and arrogantly. Everyone wants to be more than his fellow man, and so man reaches out for every means to make him appear superior to fellow man and making the weaker ones believe that he is more excellent than any other man.

[12] This desire then to dominate with time leads men into all kinds of vice, even to murder and killing, if through other ways of lying and deception they can't gain great status and recognition from others.

[13] Since mankind as a whole therefore wants to appear better than they are, nothing remains to them of course other than to constantly lie to one another, rank and file, to the limit, and truth therefore has an exceedingly hard time among them.

[14] If however mankind were to recognize the endless advantage of truth over lies, which ought to be easy if they actively would obey God and His holy will. Then they would flee the lie more than the plague, and God's righteousness would then punish the liar with death. But mankind, one and all are arrogant and domineering, love the lie and promote it.

[15] But, as seen throughout millennia, men do not live on this Earth forever, their bodies dying within a short time, to become the food of worms, but the soul shall then have to submit itself to God's judgment. There I ask how, with its highly praised lie will it fare before God?

[16] But I on my part maintain it is better to be crucified for the truth in the world than to once be brought to shame before God and hear His pronouncement 'Depart from Me everlastingly'.

[17] If you have now properly understood me and so have realized that we are friends of truth, then speak the truth and do not foolishly fear our punishing you for truth, and tell us openly and truly what you think of us and namely of Him who is now conversing with my daughters.'

# CHAPTER 57
## How the merchant expected the Messiah

[1] Says **the merchant**: 'Friend, you now have conversed with me in the fullness of wisdom, telling me what I have only too often felt within me. But I can't understand your insistence on my saying what I think of you and in particular Him. What I had thought him to be from the start you said he wasn't, yet something much more. But how one can be more than a god of the world, I do not understand. Jehovah alone is terrestrially and spiritually more than the worldly emperor-god. Yet surely he is not going to be that?'

[2] Says **Jonael**: 'I tell you, observe our company more closely; maybe something shall stand out after all. What do you make of the many glorious youths you see in our company? Observe them and then speak.'

[3] **The merchant** says: 'Up till now I took them to be noble lads of the emperor's, and sons of Roman Patricians, although, on account of their fine white skins and color, to rather be disguised girls from Caucasian Asia Minor. Because truly, notwithstanding my former dealing in such merchandise, with Egypt and Europe and mostly with Sicily and its big Romans and their penchant for voluptuousness, forms of such inexpressibly glorious kind nevertheless I have not struck before. Will you not tell me from where they are? Your daughters of course also are of glorious shape, but in comparison with these – one could say radiant figures – they trail behind considerably. Since you are bound to know more about them than I, please tell me how and from where they are.'

[4] Replies **Jonael**: 'It is not up to me but only to Him who stands here amidst my daughters to tell you that. Therefore turn to Him. He will clear you up.'

[5] Here at last **the merchant** turns to Me, saying: 'Lord, all these throngs which seem to follow You like sheep their shepherd, will You not please tell me who I have the privilege of speaking with in your person. Because I was asked and settled for the highest earthly status, yet it was indicated to me that I had erred. Now I have nothing further to say. Therefore please regard me worthy of finding out more about your status.'

[6] I said: 'You too are one of those who will not believe without seeing signs. But when seeing them they say: See, this either is a disciple of the Essenes or a magician from Egypt, or even from the land watered by the river Ganges, or he is a servant of Beelzebub.' What can one do then? But if I tell you straight out who I am you won't believe Me.

[7] You voiced your opinion and it was wrong. But when Jonael told you that I was more than your worldly god, you said: only Jehovah is greater than an emperor, and secretly guard against the supposition that I am more than an emperor of Rome, to whom you concede highest rank only for fear of his worldly power, but whom in your heart you despise more than the plague, and his power more than swarms of locusts.

[8] Yet it is already the third day of My stay in Sychar, and only an inconsequent

walk to the city from here. It would greatly surprise Me if you have not received news of Me from your colleagues in the city.'

[9] Replies **the merchant**: 'Ah, so it is you of whom I was told already yesterday and today that He is the Messiah, supporting it with marvelous deeds. You are supposed to have restored beautiful Irhael's old house and fitted it out miraculously and regally. And I was also told of a pungent sermon you delivered from the Mount, with which many were offended because it was completely against the laws of Moses. Well, well, so You are that One?

[10] Now, I am happy You are visiting me and hope to get to know You better. Do You know that I am not averse to this idea and firmly believe that the Messiah will, and must come? The time would according to my estimation be about right, as the pressure from the Romans is barely tolerable. And why could the long-awaited Messiah not be You? Oh, this I would soon and easily accept.

[11] If you are sure of your power, knowing how to properly present yourself thus, then I am at your service with all of my great wealth. These heathen pigs from the West shall soon clear the land of our fathers. Because verily, I have spent all my powers from my youth exclusively on amassing as many fortunes as possible on account of the awaited Messiah, so that a great army of the most martial and boldly cunning warriors can be bought for good wages. I have already established contact with quite a few of the most valiant peoples of the Far East, and it only needs a few messengers and in the space of a few moons a dreadful might shall be massing in these parts. But now no more of this. In my most spacious house we shall be able to resume our mediations.

[12] But lunch should by now be readied for you all; therefore do come, all of you, to eat and drink to your heart's content.'

[13] I said: 'Right then, let it all stand till then. Then we shall discuss and finalize things. Therefore lead us all to your big hall. But those men at the far back leave here; these don't belong to Mine but only to the world.'

## CHAPTER 58
### He who worries about the Earth and the flesh is a fool (1/58)

[1] Says **the merchant**: 'I know them, they are tough Sycharites who are pagan rather than children of Israel. But the most miserable among them are those from the region of the Galilean sea. These are sheer servants of matter and no longer have an incline of anything exalted and divine. Pure circus heroes. A magician from Persia is more to them than Moses and all the prophets, and a voluptuous whore from central Asia preferable to gold and precious stones. I know them only too well, but to keep them quiet I shall banquet them at the summer house, because not to serve them would be the end.

[2] I said: 'Do what you like and can, because it is more blessed to give than to receive. But in future give only to the needy and poor, and if someone wants to borrow money from you but is rich, and it is obvious to you that he can repay you

handsomely, then don't lend. Because once you have loaned to him he shall soon secretly turn into your foe, and you shall find it hard to get back your money and interest.

[3] But should a destitute come to you and you can see that he won't be able to repay, then lend, and the Father in Heaven shall restore it to you a hundredfold in different ways already on Earth, and then turn the money you loaned to the poor into a great treasure in Heaven, awaiting you high above the grave in the beyond after this earth-life.

[4] I say unto you: whatever was done by love on Earth also remains done in Heaven forever, but what mere worldly intellect does shall be swallowed up by the soil of the Earth, leaving nothing for Heaven. But of what use to man all earthly treasure-work if his soul suffers harm?

[5] He who worries about the Earth and the flesh is a fool, for just as man's flesh has its end, so will it be with the Earth. When however the end of the Earth shall once have come for sure, on which ground shall the poor soul have its dwelling then?

[6] But I say unto you that every man whose body is taken from him also loses the Earth forever. And if he has not created a new Earth in his heart through love, then his soul shall have to expose itself to the mercy of the winds and the clouds and mists and be driven about throughout everlasting infinity without finding pause or rest, other than in the false and insubstantial configurations of its own fantasy, which becomes feebler and darker the longer it lasts, eventually turning into thickest night and darkness, from which the soul shall by itself hardly ever find its way out. Therefore you can in future do as I have just shown you, but for now do as you want to and can do.'

[7] Says **the merchant**: 'You are exceedingly wise and might be right in everything, but I don't quite agree with the money lending. Because if one has earned a lot of money and does not want to see it lying around dead, then one would rather lend it out at reasonable interest than bury it so robbers coming by night can't take it, when breaking closet and chest; one can by all means give to the poor out of the abundance, as appropriate, because if I give everything away at once without managing my wealth properly, then I shall soon be left with nothing and not be able to give to the poor'.

[8] Say I: 'Leave the right economizing to God the Lord and help him who the Lord will lead to you, and your wealth shall not diminish. Do you not have many large fields and meadows and gardens full of fruit and grapes, and your extensive stables full of oxen, cows, calves and sheep? Trading with these shall always, with God's blessing fully restore what you have distributed to the poor throughout the year, but that which you place in the banks of the rich shall not be restored from above, and you shall be troubling yourself much about whether the banks are managing your money properly. Do therefore as I have shown you earlier and you shall have a good and trouble-free life, and all the poor shall love you and blessedly serve you where possible, and the Father in Heaven shall constantly bless everything you do; and see, this shall be better than the ever-growing bank-interest worries.'

118

# CHAPTER 59
## God is to be loved more than feared

[1] On the way to the castle **the merchant** says: 'My Lord and friend, I see that through you speaks pure, devout Godly wisdom, and does so with a gentleness I have not heard from human mouth yet, but to abide by your teaching a strong trust in Jehovah is needed, which I am lacking in spite of my strong faith. I know that it is He who created all and now guides, rules and sustains everything, yet I cannot adequately visualize as to how, as the supremely high Spirit, He could or wanted to get involved in personal affairs. Because for me He is too exaltedly holy, so that I hardly dare to enunciate His holiest name, let alone my expecting Him to offer help with my filthy money affairs through His almighty, holy hand.

[2] Yet I too give to the poor who come to me, without keeping a dog to bark at the destitute so he would not approach my threshold. Only this grove, which is my favorite, I don't like seeing trodden by strangers and the poor, who often wantonly damage the grounds and new plantations, yet being hungry and thirsty, find nothing therein for stilling hunger or quenching thirst. For this reason I have set up a fig and plum plantation some 20 furlongs from here, for the use of strangers and the poor, only they must not damage the trees, wherefore I have placed several keepers there.

[3] From this you can see that I think of the poor, yet be it far from me that I should ask the most exalted spirit to manage my moneys either terrestrially or celestially. If He wants to do something, and really has already done so, which I don't doubt, then that is His holiest free will. But I hold Him in such unlimited reverence that I hardly dare thank Him, as it seems to me that such purely material thanks, through which I would signify Him to have served me as a mere handyman, would greatly profane Him. I therefore act as a most righteous human, in accordance with the law, out of the powers loaned to me by God, not binding the oxen and donkey's jaws when they tread down my grain. But the great Spirit I honor only on His day. Because it is written: 'You shall not take the name of the Lord thy God in vain'.

[4] I said: 'Had I not known you to be a righteous and most reverential man, I would not have come to you. But see, it is not completely right of you to fear Him who you should actually love above all; and therefore I came to you to show you how in future you should love God more than fear Him. In this way God shall then lower Himself down to you and shall then be to you in everything a most sure, powerful and trustworthy Handyman.'

# CHAPTER 60
## With God the right will is already accepted as the deed itself (1/60)

[1] After these My comments we have reached the courtyard of the castle with measured step, even as his entire domestic force come out to meet the merchant, absolutely astonished and lost for words, with **their governor** taking the word and saying: 'Lord, lord, this has been some state of affairs. None of our cooking staff can get any food ready: everything goes wrong. We wanted to at least set the tables with fruit, wine and a proper amount of bread, yet all the rooms are so thoroughly locked that we could not open a single door even with all force. What are we going to do?'

[2] **The merchant**, half surprised himself and half enraged, says: 'This is what it is like when I just set foot outside; nothing but tumult upon tumult. What are the cooks up to? Have I not often hosted ten thousand guests, yet all went well; now there are hardly a thousand of them and there is chaos everywhere. But, what am I seeing? Youths looking out from all the windows, my castle is crowded with people and you and your subordinates say that all the doors of my castle are locked? How now? Are you lying or just beautifying your dawdling, or if the rooms are locked, who locked them?'

[3] The governor is stuck for a reply for his lord, and this castle-lord's entire large domestic team is suffering great embarrassment and consternation on account of his visible rage, but all are at wits end.

[4] But I said to this merchant: 'Dear friend, suffer it to be so for now. See, when earlier on your servants and guards came to Me in the grove, sent by you to inquire about who I am and what I am on about with such big crowd, I as Lord desired of you to give us a good lunch. You were quick to comply, even though you didn't know who he was who took it upon himself to ask lunch for so many.

[5] At first your servants and you took Me for a prince of Rome, and therefore you were at even greater pains to accommodate My request, but when after much instruction on our part you were finally brought to recognize that I am the Messiah, you were happy in your heart and thought even more to host Me and the whole company to the best of your ability, so that I would be pleased to stay with you pending the gathering of your martial host from central and east Asia, against the Romans, so as to under My command drive from God's land all foes, who are all heathens and do not believe in the One true God.

[6] After you had made up your mind about that, I too secretly decided on something, and that is that although in your own house, you shall be My guest and not I yours. I therefore commanded My splendid servants, and see, everything is in prime readiness and you shall partake of the truest heavenly fare at My side.

[7] The fruit of your gardens however and whatever your kitchen has produced serve to those abusers and big-mouths from Sychar who are still beating about in your grove with uncontrollable rage at not also being counted among the invited. I mean, you should have no problem with that, because see, when I am conscious of someone's right will, then I already accept same as the completed deed. With you I had discerned such will, and so I released you from the costly works, since I am wealthier than you and therefore do not want to be satisfied by you but want you to be satisfied by Me.'

[8] At this **the merchant** became wide-eyed, saying after a while of deep thought: 'Lord, this for a sinner is too much all at once. I cannot grasp the miracle in its full extent and depth. If you were just a man like me this would be impossible to you, because I saw no carriers in your company. From where then in a natural way should you have obtained food, most miraculously? I had earlier on indeed noted, and still do, certain most beautiful male servants in your company – with perhaps female servants among them – but from where did they come? The chambers of my castle are many, and these mostly exceedingly spacious, 10,000 people being capable of being accommodated therein with ease. But now I am seeing these most beautiful servants looking down from all the windows. Therefore I ask: where did they come from?'

[9] I said: 'Friend, when you are about to travel abroad to buy and sell, you too take servants with you according to need. And see, so do I. I have exceedingly many of them. You could hardly ever contemplate their number. When therefore I take to the road, why should My servants and workers stay home on such occasion?

[10] Says **the merchant**: 'Lord, this is completely in order, but I would just like to know where you and your glorious servants came from – this is what intrigues me'.

[11] I said: 'Let us first partake of lunch, and the time for your further instruction shall still present itself. But for now we have said enough, and it is time for rest and sustenance. Let us therefore proceed to the big hall which occupies an easterly position in this castle and is out of our view, because we are right now in the western end, from where the great wing of this castle cannot be seen.'

[12] Here **the merchant** almost faints from admiration and after a while of exceeding astonishment says: 'Lord, now this thing is getting almost too marvelously thick for me. There had indeed once been an east wing to this Esau castle, yet at least two centuries might have lapsed into irrevocable history since the existence of that wing, but I and my predecessors hardly know anything about it. How then can You speak of the great hall of this castle's easterly wing?'

[13] Say I: 'Say this only if you cannot in fact find an east wing to your castle, but if you find one then remember that with God all things are possible. But be silent about it with My group, because for such acts My precincts are not ready yet.'

[14] Says **the merchant**: 'Truly, now I burn with the desire to see this easterly wing to my castle, of which my distant ancestors hardly heard a thing. Some of the foundations can indeed still be seen here and there, but that is about all I have inherited from this purportedly gloriously former castle-wing.' Only now does the merchant hastily move forward, and we follow.

# CHAPTER 61
## A miracle does not free the spirit

[1] On reaching the first storey he notices the aforementioned wing and runs delighted through the open door, looks at the great hall and collapses in wonder. But some of the white youths immediately step over, helping him up and fortifying him. Recovering a little, he comes towards Me again and asks Me with a voice tremulous with wonder: 'Oh Lord, please tell me once and for all whether I am awake or whether I am sleeping and actually dreaming.'

[2] I said: 'The way you ask you seem indeed to be more asleep than awake, but you nevertheless are awake, and what you are seeing is solid reality. Outside in the grove you told Me yourself how you had heard how I had quickly restored Joseph's old house, currently occupied by Irhael as owner. Now then, if I could re-erect Joseph's house, then surely I should be able to renew Esau's old fort?'

[3] Says **the merchant**: 'Yes, yes, this can now be seen and is true; yet it is nevertheless unbelievable that a man should accomplish such things. Hear me, Lord, if You are not a prophet like Elijah, then You must be either an archangel in human form, or in the end Jehovah Himself. Because such things are possible only to God.'

[4] I said: 'Yes, yes, if you had seen no sign you would not have believed Me. Now you believe Me of course, but in such faith you are not free in spirit. But so that you would nevertheless become freer in spirit I say unto you: not I but these many youths did this; such power they have from God the Father. These you may ask how they went about it.'

[5] Says **the merchant**: 'That's right. I had already asked Jonael outside where these gloriously beautiful young beings came from, but did not get an answer, and was simply referred to You. When I came over to You I strangely enough forgot all about it; I became concerned only with Yourself, and our discourse took quite a different direction. Only now does it come back to mind, and I should like You to give me a proper explanation as to where these fairest youths come from.'

[6] I said: 'In order not to put you off any longer I say unto you that these are angels of God, if you will accept that. But if you don't want to accept this then take them for anything you like, except for the devil and his servants.'

[7] Says **the merchant**: Oh Lord, what, what is happening to me? I asked You only earlier on whether I am indeed awake, or whether I sleep and dream, but now I ask you whether I still live. Because such things surely cannot take place on the actual Earth.'

[8] I said: 'Oh, indeed you live upon the Earth. I have opened your inner vision, so now you may also see the spirits of Heaven. But now ask no more, because it is time for lunch. All is readied, so let us move over to the tables.'

[9] Says **the merchant**: 'Yes, yes, right so. But I shall not be able to eat much for wonder upon wonder. No, just this morning I would not have been able to suspect anything like it. All this came too fast for me and far too unexpected. Hardly three hours have passed since you entered my sizeable grove coming

from Sychar and what has happened in these three hours?! – The most impossible things. – But they are real! But who else than those who were present will believe it, even with a thousand testimonials?! Lord, Lord, You high master, taught and guided by God Himself, I believe it because I see it with my own eyes now. But if you tell it to thousands they not only will doubt, no, they will get upset and accuse the narrator to be a brazen liar. Therefore do tell nobody about it because this matter is too big a miraculous one. Who has ever seen such magnificence like this hall?! The walls are like of precious stones, the ceiling gold, the floor silver, the many tables from jasper, hyacinth and emerald, the frames of gold and silver, the drinking vessels like from pure diamond and the bowls like from noblest and most fiery ruby; the benches around the tables again of the noble metals and the upholstery of deep red silk, and the aroma of the food and drinks like from the heavens! And all that in – let's say – three hours! No, this is incredible many times over.

[10] Lord, You must be either God Himself or at least definitely God's Son.'

[11] I said: 'Indeed, indeed. But now to the meal. After the meal you shall find out more, but now I add no more before the meal. Just see the many that are hungering and thirsting, as it is quite warm today. Therefore let them first be refreshed and fortified, then everything spiritual shall come into its own again.'


## CHAPTER 62
### The Lord opens the way to Heaven for all (1/62)

[1] Now the merchant is saying no more, thanking the Father with Me and then sitting down at a big table in the centre of the hall. I and all My disciples, Jonael and his wife and daughters, Irhael with her husband Joram, with the mother of My body between them, sit down at the same table.

[2] This makes **the merchant** exceedingly happy, so that he says: 'Lord, for deeming me worthy with Your sitting at the table I set down at, I want to in future give the poor a tenth of all that my lands produce, and pay their taxation to the Romans for ten years in advance. After this time however I hope to God Your and our Father that He shall rid us of this plague through You oh Lord, to which end I have outside already offered You my fullest help with all my resources.

[3] Oh Lord, only rid us of this plague, and make that the Jews of Jerusalem would once again associate with us; they have distanced themselves sky high from the old Truth. With them reign only selfishness, domination and glitter. They no longer think of God and there is no trace of love for fellow man. They scorn Gerizim even while converting Jehovah's temple into a den of money-changers and hawkers. And if accused of despoiling God's holiest of holies they curse and revile him who dares to call them by their proper name. Lord, this must change. It cannot stay like that, and if it does, then another Flood can be expected soon. All around the world nothing but heathens upon heathens, yet in Jerusalem and Judea there are Jews, priests, Levites, scribes and Pharisees and money-

changers ten times worse than all heathens. In short, the world is worse now than in the days of Noah. If no help arrives, with the Messiah taking up a flaming sword, then we shall evidently get to build a new ark. Lord, do therefore whatever is in Your power. I shall always support You.'

[4] On this I said: 'Dear Jairuth, see My youths. I say unto you: I have such numbers of them that they should not have room on a thousand times a thousand earths. Yet just one of them suffices to destroy the whole Roman Empire in three moments. But although you are better than the Jews, you yet share their total misconception about the Messiah and His kingdom.

[5] The Messiah shall indeed found a new kingdom on this Earth, but – mark it well. Not a material one under crown and scepter but a kingdom of the spirit, the truth, the right liberty by the truth, under the exclusive dominion of love.

[6] The world however shall be called upon to enter upon this kingdom. If it responds then everlasting life shall be its reward. If it does not respond however then, although remaining as it is it nevertheless ultimately shall inherit everlasting death.

[7] The Messiah, a Son of Man right now, has not come to judge this world but to only appoint to the kingdom of love, light and truth all those now walking in darkness and death.

[8] He did not come into this world to win back for you what your fathers and kings lost to the heathens, but to only bring you back that which Adam lost for all men who ever lived or shall live upon this Earth.

[9] Up to the present, no soul leaving the body has yet been removed from the Earth. Countless numbers, starting with Adam right up to this hour are languishing in the night of the Earth. But only from now on shall they be liberated. After I shall have ascended on high I shall open the way from Earth to Heaven to them all, along this way all shall enter upon everlasting life.

[10] See, this is the task to be fulfilled by the Messiah, and nothing other whatsoever. And you do not have to call your Far-Eastern warriors, since I shall never need them. But spiritual laborers for My kingdom I shall need many, and these I shall drill Myself. Some are seated at this table already, but quite a few more of them shall be prepared in all love and truth.

[11] See, to accomplish this it is My task. Consider it now and tell Me what you think of such a Messiah.'

[12] Says **the merchant Jairuth**: 'Lord, this I must think over thoroughly.

[13] Because no man has yet heard about this sort of Messiah. But I think such Messiah would be of little use to the world. Because for as long as the world is left as it is it shall remain an offensive foe to everything spiritual. But I shall now think it over further.'

# CHAPTER 63
## The good effect of the heavenly love wine

[1] Everyone is eating and drinking, and even **Jairuth** himself, steeped in thought, eats and quite swills it down. All transformed to love through the glowing heavenly love-wine, he says to Me: 'Lord, a great thought just struck me. If possible I would like to obtain vines from whose grapes I could press a wine of this nature. Because with wine like that in my cellars I shall fill the world with love over love. I experienced it on myself. I am of course normally a man with a special liking for what is good, right and nice, but I can't say that I ever experienced any special love for mankind.

[2] Up till now I always acted from a kind of self-imposed righteousness, which I prescribed for myself in accordance with my knowledge of the law. It concerned me little whether a law is good or bad. I never wanted to brood over such. My motto was, law is law, whether God's or Caesar's. If it can result in punishment, one must comply out of self-interest, so as to avoid evil consequences. But if a law is not sanctioned then it isn't a law anyway, but only some good advice which one can follow, without sanctioned obligation.

[3] There can of course be harm in not following good advice, taking on the sad appearance almost of lawful punishment, yet the non-acceptance of good advice is still not sin of a kind by which numbers of other people could be affected rather than mainly the individual who is not accepting the good advice. But if advice is bad then obviously I sin crudely by accepting it.

[4] But with law it is different. Whether same is good or totally bad, I must abide just for it being the law. Regardless of whether I don't obey it because I think it bad, I sin either against God or ruler, and I shall be punished by both. Therefore it clearly transpires that I am law-abiding not out of love but with inner revulsion at legal compulsion. Now that I have drunk this glorious grape-wine from the Heavens however I see nothing but love over love and could embrace and kiss the whole Earth.

[5] On top of that I see a similar effect on all those who drank from this truly heavenly wine. Therefore I should like to establish a big vineyard from these vines and let all mankind drink from this wine, and they should be transformed to love in quick time, the way I see it. If it were therefore possible to provide myself with such vines I would be the happiest man on God's good and beautiful Earth.'

[6] I said: 'Vines which would yield you such wine I can supply you with quite easily. Such supposed effect on mankind however you shall be unable to bring about. Because this wine indeed enlivens man's love, provided it already resides in man, but where there is no love but only evil in man's heart, there the evil in him is animated the same way love was in yours, and he is then only transformed into an accomplished devil, and shall go about doing evil just as enthusiastically as you want to do good.

[7] Therefore one has to be mindful of whom one wants to serve up this wine for enjoyment. But I intend nevertheless to let you have a vineyard of these vines, but

be most mindful about who you want to drink such wine. Of a truth, much good can be done by animated love. Yet it is better for it to be animated by God's Word because this will last whereas with the consumption of this wine it lasts only for a while and then expires like the wine itself. This keep well in mind or you will do much evil instead of good.'

[8] Says **the merchant Jairuth** on this: 'Lord, in that case there would be no point in cultivating such vine. Because one cannot know whether a person harbors good or evil when handing them such wine, and in addition be placed in a great predicament when by wishing to animate someone's love one were only to enliven his wickedness. No, no, in that case I would leave the raising of such vineyard well and truly alone.'

[9] I said: 'It is all the same to Me. I shall do for you whatever you wish. But I say unto you: each variety of wine grown on Earth has more or less a similar property. Just let various people drink from your own produce roughly the quantity that you have already drunk form My heavenly wine, and you will see how some will go over into love completely while others will begin to rage and throw fits, to the extent of you having to tie them up with ropes. But if terrestrial wine already calls forth such reactions, how much more the heavenly wine.'

## CHAPTER 64
### The will of the Lord is the power of the angels

[1] Says **Jairuth**: 'Lord, if so, as I had previously convinced myself on several occasions actually, then I shall give up all vineyard-keeping, and all wine-consumption in my house. Because according to Your assertion, the right degree of love can also be kindled, and that lastingly, through the Word, something I find very true and good, and evil must thereby stay behind as far as possible. If this is so, then I immediately leave all vineyard-keeping alone, and commit myself to after this heavenly wine never drink an earthly one again. What do You say to this my resolution?'

[2] I said: 'I can neither commend nor reproach you for it. Do what seems best to you. Do what best serves your soul in accordance with an informed view. You can in any case obtain everything good from Me if that is your wish, because you are strict and upright in all goodness and because I have promised it to you.'

[3] Says **Jairuth**: 'Lord, in that case stay with me together with your following, or at least leave me two of these youths behind, who could instruct me in all love and wisdom.'

[4] I said: 'For the present I and My retinue cannot accommodate your good wish, as I have much to do yet in this world, but two of these youths, whom you can select, I want to leave you. But guard against yourself or your family falling into some sin, because then they would become your disciplinarians and leave your house in a hurry. Because, keep in mind that these youths are angels of God and can perpetually see His countenance.'

126

[5] Says **Jairuth**: 'Oh Lord, this is again something bitter, because who can vouch for not sinning either through thoughts, words or deeds at least once a year? On top of that a couple of taskmasters before whom nothing can remain hidden, which would hardly be a very nice surprise. That's why I want to refrain also from this request and leave it as is and was.'

[6] I said: 'Very well, let it be as you wish. You are free and shall not be placed under any compulsion, be assured.'

[7] Says **Jairuth**: 'No, these youths, and actually real angels of God simply look too fair and sweet. It seems an impossibility to commit a sin in their presence. Therefore, come what may, I shall in any case keep two.'

[8] I said: 'All right then, two shall be left you, and visibly dwell in your house, for as long as they are feeling right. My friend Jonael shall faithfully acquaint you with My Ways later. For as long as you and your house shall walk these Ways they shall remain and serve you and protect your house against all adversities, but if you depart from My ways then they also shall depart from your house.'

[9] Says **Jairuth**: 'Very well, leave it at that. No more wine shall be consumed in my house, and with its stock I shall pay the Romans the 10 years taxation of the poor in this area, as stated; the grapes growing in my vineyard however I shall dry and eat as a pleasant, sweet fruit, selling the surplus. Is it right thus?'

[10] I said: 'Perfectly. Whatever you do out of love for Me and your fellow men, who are your brethren, shall be truly and rightly done.'

[11] After this I call two of the youths, introduce them to Jairuth and say: 'Will these two do?' Jairuth, delighted celestially by their looks, says: 'Lord, if You consider me worthy, then I am satisfied to all the depths of my heart, but I feel only too unworthy of possessing such grace from the Heavens. But I shall from now on strive assiduously to make myself worthy by stages. And as for myself, Your will, getting constantly holier to me, be done.'

[12] But **the two youths** said: 'The Lord's will is our being and life. Wherever this is being implemented actively, there we are the most active co-workers, having power and strength for this to excess, because our might extends past all visible creation, the Earth being like a grain of sand to us, and the sun like a pea in a giant's hand, whereas all the waters of the Earth would not suffice to wet one hair of our head, and the host of the stars trembles before the breath of our mouth. But we don't possess this power for boasting before men's great feebleness but for serving them in accordance with the Lord's will. Therefore we can and wish to also serve you in accordance with the Lord's will, for as long as you acknowledge and accept same in deed. When however you leave such then you also have left us, since we are nothing but the personalized will of God the Lord. Whoever will leave, him we will leave also. This we tell you in the full presence of the Lord, whose countenance we see at all times and whose gentlest hint we hear calling us and powerfully drawing us to fresh deeds.'

[13] Says **Jairuth** on this: 'Fairest youths, that you possess a great power, incalculable to us mortals, this I understand and grasp quite clearly, but I also am capable of much, some of which perhaps you may not be capable of yourselves, in that I am proud in my weakness, wherein resides neither power nor strength.

But there nevertheless lies a strength in this weakness due to which I can recognize, accept and carry out the Lord's will.

[14] Of course not to the same measure as you, yet the Lord is certain not to encumber me with more than I am capable of bearing up to. And in this sense my weakness seems quite honorable to me, since it is of great import that in the end man's weakness still can carry out the same will of God as your immeasurable strength and might.

[15] And if I have understood the Lord correctly so far then it may yet be that the Lord prefers the action of weak children, and that ultimately the power and deeds of the great and mighty spirits of Heaven may yet have to let itself be led by the weak little children of the Earth, for coming to sit at the little ones' table, because if the Lord Himself comes to the weak then it seems to me at least that He shall make strong the weak.'

[16] Say the youths: 'Yes, so it certainly is and rightly. Recognize God's will therefore and act accordingly and then you already have our power in you, which is nothing other than purely God the Lord's will. We ourselves have neither strength nor power, and all our strength and power is nothing but God's will fulfilled in and through us.'

[17] I said: 'Right now, from every side. We have now fortified ourselves, and thus, all you beloved, we shall get up from the table and re-commence our journey.' All get up, give thanks and follow Me into the open.'

## CHAPTER 65
### Accused and declared innocent (1/65)

[1] Jairuth nevertheless would rather have Me stay with him for the day, but I show him how there still are sundry sick in this district whom I want to visit along the way. Jairuth therefore asks Me whether he could at least accompany Me back to the city, and I grant this. He immediately gets ready but also asks the youths to accompany him.

[2] But the youths say: 'It is better for us to stay here, because the guests in the outhouse have reported you to the Romans as an insurgent, and your house would fare badly without us.'

[3] This news utterly unsettles Jairuth and he asks with great agitation: 'What Satanic person could have said such to the Romans and what could have gotten into them?'

[4] Says one youth: 'See, there are merchants in Sychar who are not as fortunate as yourself; they cannot purchase castles and even less acquire large tracts of land, the way you have done in Arabia on the Red Sea. Such merchants therefore envy you your worldly fortune and are filled with the desire to ruin you. They would also succeed this time if we were not with you, but because we guard you in the name of the Lord, not one of your hairs shall be bent. But make sure that you stay away from home for at least three days.'

[5] This reassures Jairuth and he makes haste to join Me on the journey.

[6] As we move over the castle courtyard, a detachment of Roman mercenaries and thugs encounter us, making a halt and commanding us to stop. But I Myself step forward, displaying the Nicodemus pass. But **the commander** says: 'This is nothing in face of suspected treason.'

[7] I said: 'What do you demand of us? You were moved to this step through the shameless lie of a bunch of grudgers, but I tell you there is not a true word in it. If you could lend your ear so willingly to a lie then lend it the more to the open truth, for which you find more witnesses here than for that shameless lie of a few dangerous jealous people in the city.'

[8] Says **the commander**: 'These are vain excuses and count nothing with me. Only by facing the accusers at court can truth be established; therefore come unhesitatingly to court, or force is applied.'

[9] I said: 'Over there is the castle. Only the master of the castle was reported to you as a rebel. Go there and see if you discover any trace of a revolt. But if you want to force us to follow you to your unjust court then we can counter you with proper force and we shall see who eats the humble pie. Do therefore what you will. My time has not come yet; I have told you that no guilt resides here. But he who is in the right should also defend it by word and deed.'

[10] The commander looks over our large numbers and gives the order to catch and tie us up. The mercenaries and thugs fall upon the youths first, trying to catch them, but the youths dodge them so smartly that not one can be caught. As the soldiers and thugs are exhausting and scattering themselves in trying to catch the youths, since they seem to disappear in all directions, I say to the commander: 'It seems to me that it is getting hard for you to catch us?' The commander heaves after Me with his sword, but that moment one youth rips away his sword, throwing it beyond visibility and so destroying it.

[11] I said to the commander: 'Now then, with what will you heave and stab at Me now?' **The commander** says with raging fury: 'So this is how Rome's authority is respected here?! Good, I shall know how to report this to Rome, and then look at your area shortly and tell if it is still the same one. Not a stone shall be left atop another.'

[12] But I point to how his soldiers and thugs, tied up in ropes are being driven forward by the youths. Seeing this, the commander starts to implore Zeus, Mars and even the furies to save him from such humiliation.

[13] But I say to the youths to release the soldiers and thugs again, and these do so at once. Thereupon I say to the Commander: 'Now, are you still eager to try your strength on us? The Commander says that these youths would have to be gods, as otherwise it could never be possible to defeat his select warriors with bare hands.

[14] I said: 'Yes, yes, for you and your type they should be gods indeed, therefore leave us to continue our journey and continue your investigation in the castle, or worse shall befall you.'

[15] Says **the Commander**: 'I herewith declare you innocent and permit you to continue on your journey. You my troops however move to the caste, check out

everything and let none leave the castle until you have checked everything. I shall await you here.'

[16] Says **one deputy**: 'Why not examine them yourself in the castle?' Says **the Commander**: 'Don't you see my sword is gone? Such investigation is not possible without a sword.' Says **the deputy**: 'We are no better off by one hair's breadth. How can this be valid without our investigation without a sword?' Says **the Commander**: 'What, you without weapons too?! This is nasty. We can't do a thing without weapons. Hm, how shall we get on?'

[17] I said: 'Over there, towards noon, lie your weapons, under the tall Cedar. Go and get them, as we fear you just as little with your weapons as without them.' With this they move towards where their weapons rest.

## CHAPTER 66
### Healing of the palsied near the village

[1] We nevertheless press on eastwards and soon reach a tiny village, some twenty furlong distance from the castle. The entire community joyfully rushes out to meet us, asking softly what they can do for us. But I say: 'Do you not have sick among you? They affirm it, saying: 'Yes, we have one fully suffering the gout.'

[2] I said: 'Bring him here then, so he may be made whole. Says **one of them**: 'Lord, this will be hard. This sufferer is so paralytic that he has not been able to leave his bed for nearly 3 years, and his bed is hard to move, being fastened to the ground. Would you be prepared to go and see him? I said: 'Since the bed is hard to move, why don't you wrap the sick in a mat and bring him over here.' In response several of them hasten to the house where the gout-stricken is lying, wrapping him in a mat and bringing him to Me in the street and saying: 'Lord, here is the poor sufferer.'

[3] But I ask the sick one whether he believes that I can heal him. **The sick** looks Me over and says: 'Dear friend, you look indeed like you could. You sure seem to be a proper healer. Yes, yes, I believe it.'

[4] On this I said: 'Now then, get up and walk. Your faith helped you, but beware of a certain sin from now on, so as not to relapse into gout, which would be more acute the second time than now.'

[5] And **the sick** gets up fat once, taking up the mat and walking. Noticing only then that he is completely healed, he falls on his knees before Me, thanking and finally saying: 'Lord, in you there is more than human power. Praised be God's power in You. Oh, blessed the body that bore You, and over-blessed the breast that fed You.'

[6] But I say unto him: 'And blessed they who hear My Words, keeping them in their hearts and living accordingly. Says **the sick**: 'Lord, where can one hear You speak?

[7] I said: 'You will surely know the high priest Jonael of Sychar, who sacrificed at Gerizim. See, he has My Word; go and learn from him.' Says **the healed**: 'Lord,

when is he at home?' **I** said: 'He is standing here beside Me. Ask him and he will tell you.'

[8] Here **the healed** turns to Jonael, saying: 'Worthy high priest of Jehovah at Gerizim, when could I enter your house?'

[9] Says **Jonael**: 'Your work till now consisted in just lying down, and in the patient bearing of your suffering; therefore you would miss nothing at home. Journey with us today and hear. There shall be quite a few more happenings, and tomorrow you shall find out everything.'

[10] Says **the healed**: 'If considered worthy of traveling in such society, then I follow you with much joy. Because, dear friend, when one had to languish away in a hard bed for 3 years, with often unbearable pain, and now through a divine miracle suddenly be healed from the nasty malady, then one appreciates health. And what joy it is to walk with straight limbs. That's why I should like to do like a David – dance and leap before you, praising the great goodness of the Lord with exceeding jubilation.'

[11] Says **Jonael**: 'Go and do thus, that before our eyes it should fulfill itself as written from the Lord: "Then shall the lame man leap as a deer" (Isaiah 35:6).

[12] With this the healed throws off the mat, moves quickly ahead of the company and starts leaping and jubilating, not letting anyone hinder him in his joy. Because after only two or three furlongs, those Roman mercenaries and thugs together with their leaders, who were scattered unto a side-track by the two angels at the castle, are disturbing his joyfulness, asking him what he is doing. But not letting himself be disconcerted and not seeming to regard the commander's question, he says while still hopping and leaping: 'When men get merry, the livestock get sad, because man's happiness brings death to the cattle. Therefore make merry, make merry.' Thus the healed carries on. This annoys the commander, and he forbids him such noise.

[13] But **the healed** says: 'Why forbid my joy. I was bed-ridden for 3 years with gout. Had you come to me and said "arise and walk", with me getting well with such pronouncement, as I am now, then I would have divinely worshiped you together with everyone of your holy words from your mouth, but since you are not such, and your power sheer nothing compared to my Lord's, I obey my mighty Lord, and therefore once again, make merry, make merry.'

[14] Now the commander forbids him such spectacle in earnest, threatening punishment, but at the same moment **two of the youths** come to the merry one, saying: 'Don't let yourself be hindered in your joy.'

[15] Seeing the familiar youths, **the commander** yells out to his unarmed band: 'Retreat! Look, two more servants of Pluto!'

[16] At this command the band take to their heels in a manner not seen before. But **the healed** now leaps and jubilates all the more, yelling after the retreating: 'Make merry, make merry; when men make merry the cattle get sad!' Then he keeps quiet a little, and returning to Jonael, he says: 'Friend, if you don't mind us talking while we walk, you could acquaint me with some of this Lord's new Word, who gave me my health? Because if I am to make such Word into my law then I have to know it first.'

[17] Says **Jonael**: 'See, we are nearing another village, which according to the new Roman constitution is a small city. Here the Lord is bound to venture into more. You shall be following us into the city anyway, in my house, or that of Irhael. However, you shall find accommodation for as long as it pleases you. There you shall be familiarized with everything. We are not far from the city now. This locality we are coming to already belongs to the city, according to the new Roman order, but since it serves mainly as a Roman stronghold, they severed it from Sychar, encircling it with a rampart and elevating it to a place with a name of its own. The area is not big, and with a thousand paces we shall have it behind us. Then we turn left, with hardly seven furlongs remaining to Sychar's buildings. Therefore have just a little more patience and your wishes shall be met.'

[18] Says **the healed**: 'Oh by Abraham, Isaac and Jacob. If this area is under Roman occupation then we shall fare badly, since only a few moments ago the Roman centurion had to retreat from us most abysmally.'

[19] Says **Jonael**: 'This we shall leave to the Lord, who is with us now. He shall work out everything extra well. But I already see a detachment of warriors heading our way with a white flag. This seems a good sign to me.'

[20] Says **the healed**: 'Oh yes, as long as it is not the usual Roman battle ruse? Because in this the Roman and Greek legions excel.'


## CHAPTER 67
### The new law of love

[1] Says **Jonael**: 'Such bluffing may carry some weight with men, but against the might of God such dodging avails nothing. Only pure and true love achieves anything with God. Everything else is but chaff in a hurricane. Therefore be not troubled, as God is with us. Who should then prevail against us?'

[2] Says **the healed**: 'Indeed, indeed, right you are. But God was undoubtedly also with Adam, yet Satan knew how to grab him with artful cunning. And Michael, after a three-day battle still had to cede Moses' body to him. God is without doubt almighty indeed, but Satan is filled with the worst cunning and this has already inflicted much harm to the people of God. Therefore caution is necessary near a tiger, as long as it lives. Only after it is dead can one breathe freely without precautions.'

[3] **Jonael** says: 'You have to keep in mind that in former times the Lord allowed Satan to act in this or that way, for the first-created spirit (*Lucifer*) had to be allowed a long time for his freedom-test, because he was not only the first, but also the greatest of the created spirits.

[4] However, this time has come to an end and the prince of darkness will now be considerably restrained and no longer be able to move as freely as before.

[5] Therefore, if the right love for God is dwelling within us, we shall find it easier to walk one Earth than was the case formerly under the hard yoke of the law.

[6] From Adam until our time the law of wisdom was reigning and such wisdom

and a strong and unconditional will was required to fulfill such a law within oneself.

[7] But God saw that men would never fulfill the law of wisdom and so came into the world himself in order to give them a new law of love which they will easily be able to fulfill. For in the law of wisdom Jehovah let only His light radiate among men. The light was not He Himself, it only flowed from Him to men just as men have gone forth from Him, but nevertheless are not Jehovah Himself. However Jehovah Himself does come to men through and within love, takes spiritual residence in man in the fullness of truth and thereby makes created man similar to Himself in everything. Then Satan is no longer able to harm, by his cunning, a man thus armed, for Jehovah's spirit within man sees always through Satan's ever so concealed tricks and has at all times plenty of power to disperse Satan's total helplessness.

[8] The Prophet Elijah described the present situation of mankind, when Jehovah comes to men directly in love, as a gentle rustling passing the cave, but Jehovah was not in the great storm and in the fire.

[9] Thus the gently rustling is people's love for God and their brothers wherein Jehovah Himself is dwelling, whereas He does not dwell in the storm of wisdom and the flaming sword of the law.

[10] And since Jehovah Himself now is with us, for us and among us, we don't need to fear Satan's tricks nearly as much as was the case only too sadly in antiquity and in the past; and you can look the bloodthirsty Roman tiger in the eye quite more bravely and untroubled. Did you not notice how an entire legion just now took to their heels most ignominiously before the two youths? Yet such youths are accompanying us in great numbers, and should we fear Romans approaching us with white flags? Not even in a dream, I say, never mind in actuality.'

[11] **The healed** looks surprised, after a while saying: 'What did you say? Jehovah now among us? I thought this man who helped me was only the awaited Messiah? How can Jehovah and the Messiah be One to you?

[12] I have no trouble understanding that Jehovah's power shall show in greater fullness through the Messiah than all the prophets combined, but I would not have dared to even think, let alone voice it that the Messiah and Jehovah would be One. Besides that it is written that one should not imagine Jehovah under any likeness, and now this human, who of a truth possesses all the attributes of a Messiah, should be Je-ho-vah Himself? Well, this is all right with me, as long as it is all right with you as the chief priest.

[13] That the Messiah could be some special God I thought straight after my healing, because according to scripture, we all are gods more or less, depending on how Jehovah's law is kept. But that He should be Jehovah Himself? Well, if that be so then we should act differently. He Himself has healed me – this means coming up with quite different thanks.'

[14] Here he wants to come over to Me at once. But Jonael holds him back, advising him to do so when we get to Sychar, and the healed is happy with that.

# CHAPTER 68
## The Roman commander and living according to the teaching

[1] But now the Roman war-deputation had arrived, and their leader handed Me a written entreaty from the commander-in-chief of this fort, by which he implores Me for the sake of public weal to take no notice of what occurred, and to persuade the company not to divulge what took place, because it would bring him harm while benefiting no one. But, that it would benefit all more than harm them if they made the Roman commander-in-chief into a friend rather than an enemy. Jairuth too ought to keep silence and be assured of being left in peace at home. But would I in any case visit him at his residence, as he has secret and important things to discuss with Me.

[2] My response to the bearer of the writing was: 'Tell your master that he shall receive in accordance with his request. But I shall nevertheless not come to his residence, but that if he wants to speak to Me about secret and important things, to await Me at the entrance to this area, and I shall tell him what that is which he wants to discuss.'

[3] With this the messenger goes off with his company to convey to his master all he heard of Me, and the latter with his deputies immediately heads for the gate to this place to await Me.

[4] Jairuth however asks Me whether such invitation can be trusted, because he knows this chief commander's great cunning, who is a supreme commander. This one is supposed to already have dispatched many to the other world in this way.

[5] I said: 'Dear friend, I also know him, both as he was and now is. The youths have instilled lasting respect in him and he regards them as genii, and Me as a son of their god Jupiter, and he now wants to find out how much substance there is to it. But I know what I shall tell him.'

[6] Jairuth is satisfied with this, even as we arrive at the gate where the commander-in-chief and his officers are waiting for us. He immediately steps forward, greeting Me friendly, and bent on pressing his concerns immediately.

[7] But I was faster and said: 'Friend, My servants are not protecting spirits and I in no way a son of your Zeus. And now you know everything you wanted to know of Me and intended asking Me.'

[8] The chief is stunned by My openly telling him at once what he had only thought, yet intimated to no one.

[9] Being intrigued for a while he again asks Me: 'If you are not such, then tell me who you and your servants actually are. Because you must by all means be more than ordinary men, and it would please me to accord you the proper honors.'

[10] I said: 'Any man asking sincerely and honestly is worthy of an equal answer. You have now asked Me honestly and sincerely and shall receive a like answer, and therefore listen unto Me. For a start I am that and He standing before you, namely a man. There are of a truth many on Earth who look like Me, yet they nevertheless are not men but merely human shells. But the more accomplished a true man, the more power and strength in his cognition and will, prolific in action,

prolific in effects.'

[11] Says **the chief**: 'Can every man achieve a perfection like yours?'

[12] I said: 'Indeed, if he does what I teach for his perfection.'

[13] Requests **the chief**: 'Then let me hear your teaching and I shall try to do thus.'

[14] I said: 'The teaching I could let you have for sure, but it would serve you little, since you would not live by it. Because so long as you remain that for which you are engaged by Rome, My teaching can be of no use to you, unless you were to leave all and follow Me, or it would be impossible for you to live according to My teaching.'

[15] Says **the chief**: 'Yes, this would be very hard. You could nevertheless give me a few basics from your teaching? Because I have already acquired knowledge in many things, being quite conversant with it, then why should I not also receive some grasp of your teaching? Maybe I could still bring it to some application?'

[16] I said: 'My friend, since My teaching consists in following Me, without which the kingdom of My perfection cannot be entered upon, how should you be able to bring it to application?'

[17] Says **the chief**: 'This sounds strange indeed, yet there could be something in it. Let me think about it a little.'

[18] **The chief** ponders for a while and says: 'Do you mean by that a physical, or basically a moral following?'

[19] I said: 'The much preferred following, where possible, is of course the bodily one, coupled to the moral one, but where due to a necessary vocation a personal following is not possible, there a conscientious moral one suffices. But I Myself and love towards Me and all men must be the foundation of conscience, otherwise mere moral emulation would be spiritually dead. Do you understand that?'

[20] Says **the chief**: 'This is vague. But if it is so, then what am I to make of all my nice gods? My ancestors believed on them. Is it right for me to remain true to the faith of such ancestors, or should I start to believe in the God of the Jews?'


## CHAPTER 69
### The insignificance of the gods. The mystery of love

[1] I said: 'Dear friend, your ancestors mean nothing, and still less the gods they honored, because your ancestors have already been dead for a long time, and their gods never had an existence outside of human fantasy. There had never been a reality behind their names and images. Therefore there verily is nothing in leaving a most void belief in your gods, because they can feed your soul no more than can painted foods your body. There is therefore nothing to all this, as stated, but everything in pure truth and the life in and through this one truth.

[2] Because if you live within the lie then life itself is nothing but a lie, and can attain to no reality in all eternity, but if your life goes forth from truth and is itself

truth, then whatever your life brings forth is also fact and reality. No man can however see and recognize truth through the lie, because to the lie everything is a lie. Only for him who is born anew from the spirit of truth, becoming truth within himself, and that fully, for such even the lie becomes truth.

[3] Because he who recognizes the lie as a lie is himself truth in everything, because he immediately recognizes the lie for what it is, and this also is truth. Do you grasp this?'

[4] Says **the chief**: 'Friend, You speak aright, and there is deep wisdom in you. But the great, glorious truth, where is it, and what is it? Are things true the way we see them or does the eye of a black man see it differently from us perhaps? A fruit can taste sweet and pleasant to one, while to another it is bitter and repulsive. Thus sundry human tribes speak different languages; which one among them is true and good? Much can be true for any specific individual, but there can in my view be no general, all-encompassing truth, and if there be one, then show where and what it is and consists in.'

[5] I said: 'Verily, My friend therein lays the old Gordian knot you well know about, which so far has not been unraveled by anyone other than the Macedonian hero you heard about.

[6] Whatever you can see and feel by means of the flesh has affinity with the flesh and its tools, and is similarly changeable and transitory; so whatever is changeable and transitory, how could same offer you substance for ever-constant and immortal truth?

[7] There is only one thing in man, and this great and holy One is love, which is a proper fire out of God, dwelling in the heart; within this is love, and nowhere else is truth, because love is itself the arch-foundation of all truth in God, and out of God within every man.

[8] If you want to see and recognize things and yourself in their full truth, then you have to see and recognize them from this solely true arch-foundation of your being; everything else is delusion, and man's head and what is in it belongs to the sphere of your familiar Gordian knot, which no one can unravel with mere deliberation.

[9] Only with the cutting power of the spirit of love in man's own heart can he hew through this knot, and then begin to think, see and recognize in the heart, and only then along such path to get at the truth of his own and every other being and life.'

[10] Your head can create countless gods for you, but what are they? Verily I say unto you, nothing but vain, lifeless patterns produced by the brain with its loose mechanisms. Only in the heart shall you find a God, and this One is true, because the love in which you found the only true God is itself Truth.

[11] This Truth therefore can be sought and found only in Truth, but the head has done its share if it has delivered you the key to Truth. Yet everything that urges and draws you towards love can be a key to truth; therefore follow such attraction and urge and enter upon the love of your heart, and you shall find the truth which shall free you from all deception.

# CHAPTER 70
## If love is lacking, there is no truth

[1] An example should clarify this for you.

[2] See a case where you have subordinates who, having sinned against your laws are to be punished. You are indeed holding the prescribed investigations, and are about to elicit their confessions with all kinds of smart questions, but they flatly deny everything as smartly from their minds, as your questions. In this way, one lie gives vent to another, and not getting anywhere with them, you in the end resort to sentencing them without their confessions, and just on the testimony of often hostile witnesses, in whom there is no truth either, with you having to always assume that not even one out of ten defendants received a fair trial, with the innocent and the guilty sharing the same fate.

[3] Alternatively, rather than appearing as their judge, you encounter your poor brethren with love, and awaken a love-response from their hearts, and these sinners shall meet you with contrition and many tears, and faithfully and truly confess how, when and what sin they committed against you. But then let the punishment also be dropped. Because any punishment is itself not truth but the contrary, because not flowing from love but the wrath of the law and its giver. But the wrath is itself a judgment, within which there is no love. But where there is no love, truth also is lacking.

[4] Therefore abide in pure love and act within its truth and power, and you shall be finding truth everywhere, and quite evidently perceive that there is universal truth indeed which penetrates not only this Earth but all of infinity.

[5] If you were to act towards mankind in that way then you would quite legitimately follow Me, and through such imitation win eternal life. But if you remain as you are now, then nothing but night and a void, lying existence shall accrue to you beyond the grave, which is the death of the spirit of love and truth.

[6] Because verily, this earth-life lasts for only a short time; then comes endless eternity. As you fall so also shall you remain prostrated, where genuine truth has not come alive within you.

[7] Now you know all you need to know for the present. If however you want more, then see the High Priest Jonael at Sychar on occasion; he shall impart to you all that he has learned, seen and discovered about Me. Act accordingly and you shall gain bliss.'

[8] Says **the commander-in-chief**, fully taken in by My speech: 'Friend, from your talk I adjudge you a wisest of the Earth's wisest, and I shall therefore do everything you have advised me. Only I should like to now find out from yourself as to who you actually are. Because see, notwithstanding the fact of my most shameful defeat by the youths accompanying you, which I cannot put down to anything other than these youths being either gods or genii from the Heavens and therefore able to supernaturally beat me into retreat, I yet recognize that you must obviously be more than an ordinary human only by your exceedingly great wisdom. You probably have already revealed or indicated it to many of your

disciples as to who you are, but you can see by now that I am fully earnest about my intent to become a disciple of yours at least in spirit. Therefore also tell me what I am to regard you as. Who and what, and where did you come from, basically?'

[9] I said: 'Firstly, I basically have already told you, and that in a way you could easily grasp if you thought about it, and secondly I have referred you to Jonael about it. When you get to him you shall find out all you are still lacking. But now detain us no more, because the day nears its end and I have yet to accomplish much today.'

[10] Says **the chief**: 'Then do let me accompany you to the city.'

[11] I said: 'The road is clear, and if your intentions are good then do so. But if there is still some infernal trace in you then stay home, because such escort would then bring you no blessing. You have already sampled My might.'

[12] Says **the chief**: 'This be far from me, notwithstanding that in these critical times, with the mythical point approaching where the Jews await from their God a mighty savior from the Roman rulers, one's ears being full of Jewish whispers of such savior already being on Earth. Therefore I could quite easily think you to be that savior, yes, I have indeed already secretly thought so. But be it as it may, I regard you as the wisest among the wise and therefore love you as mankind's true friend; therefore such thoughts shall in no way hinder me from following you for the sake of truth, in person to Sychar and spiritually throughout my whole life, notwithstanding my being aware that as a Roman I shall not thereby erect myself a triumphal arch. Now I have completely revealed myself to you, and ask you once more whether I can accompany you. If you say yes I shall do so, and if no, I stay.'

[13] I said: 'Well then, escort Me, together with those standing by your side, so that you have valid witnesses on hand.'


## CHAPTER 71
### The Lord witnesses of the Father

[1] Following this counsel I ask the commander whether there are no sick in this place. Says **the chief**: 'Friend, if you are also conversant with the art of healing, then heal my wife. Because she has suffered some secret malady for a year already, which no doctor could identify. Perhaps the depth of your wisdom could identify this sickness and help my wife out of it?

[2] I said: 'I say unto you that your wife is well. Send for her.'

[3] The commander immediately dispatches one of his servants, whom the cheerful wife already meets at the doorstep, betaking herself with him to **the chief**. The latter is astonished beyond all measure and says to Me: 'Friend, you are a God.'

[4] I said: 'You people then are all the same. When you see no signs, you don't believe. Yet you are blessed that you believe, although on account of the signs.

He who nevertheless does not believe in spite of the signs which I work has sunk into death.

[5] But in future only those men shall attain bliss who believe just on account of the truth of My Word, without signs, living in accordance with it. These shall then discover the only living sign within themselves, called life eternal, and this no one shall be able to take from them.

[6] You are now joyful that I have made your wife whole, just through the will of My heart, and ask yourself unceasingly: how is this possible? But I say unto you: if a man were to live in accordance with inner pure love and then came upon such truth, having no more doubt in his truth, he then could say unto one of those surrounding mountains: arise and cast thyself into the sea. And the mountain would rise and cast itself into the sea.

[7] But since no such truth resides in you or many others, you not only cannot work such deeds but on top of that have to wonder many times head over heels that I, who am imbued with such truth in all fullness, perform deeds before you which can be accomplished only through the might of the innermost living truth.

[8] Only within such truth does faith, which in man is the right hand of the spirit, become living in power-action, and the arm of the spirit reaches far and performs great things.

[9] If through such truth you shall have sufficiently strengthened your spiritual arms, then you shall be doing what I have now done before you, and besides that you shall see that this is much easier than to lift a stone off the ground with the hand of your body, and cast it several paces before you.

[10] Therefore live in accordance with such My teaching. Be doers and not just idle hearers and admirers of My Words, teachings and deeds, and you shall receive within yourselves that which now you so highly admire in Me.

[11] However, all that I show you here I do not do by My own power but by the power of Him who taught Me before the existence of the world. And He is the One whom you call your Father, although you do not know Him and have never known Him. He however of whom you say that He is your Father, the same it is of whom all things are, such as angels, sun, moon and stars and this Earth with everything in and on it.

[12] However, as this Father taught Me before the whole world, even so I teach you, so that the Father, who now lives in the world, would dwell and witness in you as in Me of the arch-primordial pure truth, out of the eternal arch-foundation, which is called the love in God, which is actually the very Being of God Himself.

[13] Therefore do not be overly carried away by the signs that I work before your eyes, that you may not beget a dead faith under judgment profiting nothing, but live and act in accordance with what I teach you, and you shall then come by that which now you admire in Me and wonder at beyond measure, because you all are called to be perfect. Now you know all. Do so, and you shall come to discern from within whether I told you the truth or not. Prove My teaching through the deed therefore, with all diligence and remote from half-heartedness, and only then shall you find out whether this teaching is of man or of God.'

[14] After this important instruction **the commander** says: 'Now it begins to

dawn in me. Notwithstanding the incalculable depths of wisdom in all this, which for us ordinary people is at first hard to grasp, there yet is in the end not that much to it. For if insight can be gained only through the deed, then I leave all further brooding over it, after first getting initiated into the entire teaching by Jonael, then moving earnestly into full action. And this resolution stands.'

[15] I said: 'Good so, My friend; if you attain to the light in this way however, then let this light shine also for your brethren, then you shall prepare a reward in Heaven with this. Now I have to attend to sundries. And so let us move on.'

## CHAPTER 72
### The end of the world and the judgment

[1] A start is made, with the commander-in-chief, together with his healed wife and two of his senior deputies escorting Me. The chief and his wife take Jonael in their midst, discussing and asking him diversely about the Jewish religion and where it refers to Myself, with the one healed from gout in the first village taking part most keenly. I Myself walk among Jonael's seven daughters and his wife. These too are questioning Me much, about what shall soon come over the world, Jerusalem and Rome. And I give them proper answers, showing them how shortly the secret prince of this world shall be judged and soon thereafter all his adherents. At the same time I also show them the end of the world and a universal judgment like that of Noah's time, and they question Me with much astonishment about when and how this will take place.

[2] But I say to them: 'My beloved daughters. It shall be as in the days of Noah. Love shall diminish and go completely cold, faith in a pure life and God recognizing teaching revealed to men from the Heavens shall be converted into darkest, dead superstition full of lies and deception, and rulers once again shall use men like animals and slaughter them cold-bloodedly and most callously if not submitting to the dazzling powers without protest. The mighty shall be tormenting the poor with all kinds of repression, and persecute and suppress any freer spirit by any means, and so a tribulation will come over mankind such as never was. But then the days shall be shortened on account of the elect, otherwise even the elect, who will be found among the poor, could perish.

[3] But until then another thousand and not quite a second thousand years will elapse. Then I will send the same angels which you see here now unto mankind with rallying trumpets. These shall so to speak awaken the spiritually slain mankind of the Earth from the graves of their night, and like a pillar of fire rolling over the world, these many awoken millions will fall upon the world powers, and none shall be able to resist them.

[4] From then on the Earth shall become a paradise again, and I shall lead My children along the right path for evermore.

[5] But during the course of a thousand years following that, the prince of darkness shall be freed for a very short period of seven years and a few months

and days for his own sake, either for his total fall, or possible return.

[6] In the first instance, the Earth in its innermost part shall be converted to an eternal prison, but the outer Earth shall remain a paradise. In the second instance however the Earth would be converted into Heaven, with the death of body and soul disappearing forever. Whether so, and how? That, for the present, not even the foremost angel of the Heavens must know. This only the Father knows. But tell no man at this stage what I have revealed to you, until you will – after a couple of Earth years – hear that I have been raised.'

[7] But the daughters ask wherein such raising shall consist in.

[8] And I say to them: 'When you shall have heard, then your hearts will be sad. But be comforted, for then I shall 3 days thereafter be in your midst, to bring you testimony Myself of the New Testament and the keys to My eternal kingdom. But see to it that I then find you pure as you are now, or you shall not be able to become My brides forever.' They and their mother promise to most diligently keep what I commanded and advised them.


## CHAPTER 73
### John, the healed and Jonael

[1] With this we reach the city, and namely at Irhael's house, now also Joram's. Jairuth and the commander with his wife and the two deputies can't get over its new beauty, and the healed palsied also is astonished beyond all measure, in the end saying loudly: 'This is possible only to God. As a boy I had often mischievously caught lizards within the dilapidated walls of this castle or dwelling, which Jacob had built for his son Joseph, and now it stands here perfected as Jacob himself was certain to not have built better. Any, no human power accomplishes this overnight. Now I know where I stand and know what I shall do. My name is John. Just remember this name.'

[2] This John is he whom My disciples, after My sending them out in the second year to teach the people, once threatened for healing and casting out devils in My name without My explicit authority.

[3] Says **Jonael**: 'Friend, your will, mind and words are good, but you still lack one thing, a proper recognition of God's will. Therefore call on me in the next few days, or even remain here, and I shall acquaint you with God's will more closely. Only then will you be able to put into action in its proper order all you now have a good mind of doing.'

[4] Says **the healed**: 'May God the Lord inspire you for it. I shall do as you shall advise me, because I can see you are a real friend of this great prophet and are bound to have a proper light from Him. This prophet however is above all and I think it is precisely He of whom David prophesied thus:

[5] *"The Earth is the Lord's and the fullness thereof, the world, and they who dwell therein. For He hath founded it upon the seas, and established it upon the floods. Who shall ascend into the hill of the Lord or who shall stand in His holy*

place? He who hath clean hands, and a pure heart, who hath not lifted up His soul unto vanity, nor sworn deceitfully He shall receive the blessing from the Lord, and righteousness from the God of His salvation. This is the generation of them who seek Him, who seek thy face, O Jacob.

[6] Lift up your heads, O ye gates; and be ye lifted up, ye everlasting doors; and the king of glory shall come in. Who is this king of glory? The Lord strong and mighty, the Lord mighty in battle. Lift up your head O ye gates. Even lift them up, ye everlasting doors, and the king of glory shall come in. Who is this king of glory? The Lord of hosts, He is the king of glory." (Psalm 24).

[7] And I, John, who have been healed by Him, here openly testify that it is He in Person of whom David sang and prophesied thus. Therefore all glory to Him forever.'

[8] Says **Jonael**: 'Friend, you now stand upon solid ground. But between ourselves for the present, the time is not yet for speaking thus. But when, as He said Himself, He shall depart from here, perhaps to Galilee, only then shall we start teaching the people, and when He shall then shortly return to us, He shall find our gates of proper width and the doors of the world of sufficient height for His entry, meaning our hearts as wide and our love for Him raised above the stars, because the gate is our heart, which is to be opened wide, and our pure love for Him the door which shall be raised above everything.'

[9] Here I step over to them both, laying My hands on their shoulders and saying: 'It is right so, My beloved friends. Wherever you shall meet in My name thus, there, even if not visibly, I shall be among you, all powerfully fortifying you. But I can hear a racket in the city streets. Let us be quiet. We shall see what spirit fills and leads these people.'

[10] **Jairuth** steps up to Me right away, saying: 'Lord, this is an evil racket and bodes no good. If you like I shall order two legions here at once, and peace shall at once be restored.'

[11] I said: 'Let be. If need be I verily have proper guards on hand, but you could conceal yourself somewhat in the house, that no one would see and recognize you. Because no good spirit resides in this city among men, and they could later do much damage to your properties.'

[12] Says **Jairuth**: 'But I still have the two youths - these shall protect my properties.'

[13] I said: 'Notwithstanding, let it be for the moment, for if I were in need of human help I could ask it of the chief who also is here.' Jairuth is satisfied and betakes himself to Irhael's house.

## CHAPTER 74
### Do not return evil with evil

[1] Soon thereafter a fairly large crowd armed with sticks comes to menace us, with the ten who were made dumb by the doctor on the first day in their midst, and

142

the crowd menacingly demands that the former's tongues be loosed.

[2] **Joram** the doctor however steps forward at once, saying vigorously with manful tone: 'O you children of wickedness! Is this the new way of coming to God to beg for mercy?'

[3] **The crowd** steps back somewhat, yelling: 'Who is God here and where is He?! You are not holding out to be God yourself, or else those magician from Galilee, you wide-shouldered blasphemer?!'

[4] **Joram** replies even more vehemently: 'Who is your magician from Galilee, you miserable wretches? Screams **the crowd**: 'That Nazarene carpenter named Jesus it is, whom we know only too well, and his mother who is here too, together with his brothers and sisters! We know his father too, who is supposed to have died a year ago, from grief we hear, because his wife and children didn't want to obey him and are supposed to have deceived him in every direction!'

[5] At such disparagement **Joram** is filled with rage. He hastily steps up to Me, with Jacob and John joining him, saying: 'Lord, Lord, Lord, will You not let fire fall from Heaven to consume these fellows? The impudent lies these fellows dare yelling screams to Heaven.'

[6] I said: 'There now, children of thunder. Let them lie; is there a fire that burns more fiercely than that of the lie? Do them good on top of that and they shall run off with glowing coals over their heads. Remember that. Never return evil for evil and bad with bad.' The three relent, and Joram asks what he should do for these miscreants.

[7] I said: 'Do what they ask, in My name, and tell them to depart.' And Joram speaks to the crowd: 'In the name of the Lord, let all speak who now are dumb among you, and then go their way home, giving God the glory.'

[8] Upon these words of Joram's the tongues are loosed of all who were dumb, yet none bar one, who at least exhorted them, praised God. But when the others said: 'You fool, did Jehovah make us dumb? An initiate into magic inflicted this harm, and are we to praise the heathen god of magic? If we did this, what shall we expect from the almighty, true God of Abraham, Isaac and Jacob?' Thereupon the somewhat better one also left with the other nine, not daring to give Me the due honor.

[9] Joram and all My followers were angry about that, and **Simon Peter** also stepped up to Me full of anger and said: 'Lord, it is good that it please You, but if I had but a spark of Your spiritual power and might, I would know what I had done with these stupid and evil blasphemers of Your name, over-holy to me.'

[10] I said: 'Simon, have you already forgotten what I taught on the mountain? What good can you achieve by returning evil for evil? If you were to cook a meal which in itself is tasteless, will you gain anything by adding gall and aloe, instead of seasoning it with salt, milk and honey? If you add something still better to an already good meal, then certainly no one will call you stupid, but if you make an already bad meal worse with still more inferior ingredients, where is the man who will not say to you: 'Look at what the fool is doing?

[11] See, that much more is it with men. If you return them evil for evil, then ask yourself whether their wickedness is improved. If however you return good for evil

then you shall soften the evil in your brother and perhaps in the end make a good brother of him.

[12] If a master has a servant to whom he entrusts much, while the latter, knowing the master's goodness, commits a sin against him and therefore merits punishment, and being called to account for his faithlessness, meets his master with rage and vituperates against him, will this soften the master towards his servant? I tell you no; there the master shall only get angry over the faithless servant, have him bound and thrown in jail.

[13] If however the servant sees that the master is about to treat him harshly, and he falls down before him to confess his transgression remorsefully and gently, and lovingly asks his forgiveness, will not the master treat him as formerly? No, I say. Through the servant's gentle contrition the master shall not only become gentle and pliable but shall do good to his servant besides.

[14] Therefore do not repay evil for evil, if you want all to become good. If however you are going to judge and punish those who have sinned against you, then you shall in the end all turn evil and there shall be no more proper love and goodness in any of you.

[15] The mighty shall take it upon himself to punish those sinning against his laws; the sinners however shall in turn enkindle with revenge and attempt to ruin the mighty. Then I ask: what good shall come of all that?

[16] Therefore judge and condemn no one, that you may not be judged and condemned. Have you all now understood this My most important teaching, without which My kingdom can never have a place in you?'

## CHAPTER 75
### Dealing with criminals

[1] Says **Simon Peter**: 'Yes, Lord, we have indeed understood it profoundly; yet this thing has its drawback in that, in my opinion and in line with Your teaching, if all punishment is to be abolished, then the transgressors would soon multiply like the grass on Earth and sand in the sea. Wherever a law is given it has to be sanctioned with a corresponding punishment, or it should be as good as no law at all. Or can a law prevail without sanction?'

[2] I said: 'My dear *Peter*, here you judge like one blind judges the color of light. Go and look at the zoos of the dignitaries; there you shall see all kinds of animals: tigers, lions, panthers, hyenas, wolves and bears. If such beasts were not kept in powerful cages, what life should be safe in the vicinity? But what folly to cage also the gentle lambs and pigeons?

[3] Hell of course requires most severe laws, coupled with the most painful sanctions, but My kingdom, which is Heaven, requires neither law, let alone any sanction.'

[4] I have not come to educate you for Hell through the sanctioned severity of the law, but for Heaven through love, meekness and truth. If I now liberate you

from the law by My new teaching from the Heavens, showing you the new path through the heart to the true, everlasting freest life, who do you want to live always judge and condemned under the law without considering that it is better to die a thousand times bodily in the freedom of love than to walk in the death of the law just for one day?

[5] It goes without saying that thieves, robbers and murderers must be caught and imprisoned, for they are like the wild, ferocious beasts that as images of Hell live in holes of the Earth, day and night on the lurk for prey. To properly hunt for these is even a duty for the angels in Heaven, but no one shall destroy them. They must be kept imprisoned to be calmed and tamed, and only in cases of violent resistance shall they be wounded and, if quite unyielding, their body may also be slain, for then a dead Hell is better than a live one.

[6] But whoever will go on to judge and put to death an imprisoned thief, robber and murderer will once have to face My wrath, for the more severely men judge and punish their offenders, the more cruel, careful, furtive and hard the still free criminals will become, and when they break into a house at night they will not only take whatever they find, but will also murder and destroy all who could betray them.

[7] If, however, you abolish the severe judgment and wisely suggest to all people to give the one who should ask someone for a shirt also the coat, then thieves would still come to you asking for this and that, but they will not rob or murder.

[8] Once men will out of true love for their brothers and sisters, resulting from their love for Me, cease to amass the transient goods of this Earth and instead imitate Me, then there will soon no longer be any thieves, let alone robbers and murderers.

[9] Whoever thinks that through severe laws and increasingly harsher judgment all offenders will eventually be eliminated is grossly mistaken. Hell has never yet lacked those. What use is it to you to kill a devil if instead of the one killed Hell sends ten, each of whom is worse than ten of the previous kind would have been? If the evil one when he comes finds that he is opposed again by evil, he becomes enraged and turns into a complete Satan, but if he finds nothing but love, meekness and patience, he desists from his evil act and continues on his way.

[10] When a lion sees a tiger or another enemy approaching him, he soon gets enraged, leaps at him with all force and destroys his enemy, but he will allow a weak little dog to play with him and becomes quite gentle. And if a fly comes and settles on his strong paws, he will hardly look at it and let it fly away unhindered, for to catch gnats and flies is beneath a lion. That will also be every powerful enemy's attitude towards you unless you oppose him with force.

[11] Therefore, you should rather bless your enemies than catch, judge and imprison them, and you will gather live coals over their heads and thus prevent them from harming you.

[12] With love, meekness and patience you will succeed everywhere, but if you judge and condemn people, who notwithstanding their blindness are still your brothers, you will, instead of the blessing of the gospel, sow only curse and

discord among men on this Earth.

[13] Therefore you have to be fully My disciples in word, teaching and deed, if you want to be and become My servants in the spreading of My kingdom on Earth. If you don't want this however, or if it seems too much effort or not right to you, then it is better for you to return home; I nevertheless am able to raise disciples from stones for Myself.'


## CHAPTER 76
### Man knows what is good but does what is evil (1/76)

[1] Says **Simon Peter**: 'Lord, who would want to leave You, or not serve You? You alone have Words of life such as never came from human mouth before. We will do anything You ask us, only don't ask us to leave You. But have patience with our great weakness, and strengthen us with grace from the Father in Heaven, which also strengthened You Yourself, to where you stand there fully at one with Your Father in Heaven, teaching and acting.

[2] We intend doing as You taught us on the Mount, always asking the Father in Your name and saying: 'Father in Heaven. Thy kingdom come, and Thy alone holy will be done. And as we forgive those who trespassed against us, so also forgive us our weaknesses and sins.'

[3] I said: 'Simon, verily, this language is more pleasing to Me than your previous one of defending the law and its sanction. Of what benefit to a nation or kingdom a peace and order through strictest enforcement? It will do for a little while indeed, but when it gets too much for the oppressed devils, they shall burst forth and trample both law and lawgiver with dreadful scorn. Because whoever has to be kept and led by force still is a devil, only he who lets himself be led with love, gentleness and patience is like unto an angel of God, and worthy of being a child of the most High.

[4] With love you achieve everything whereas through force the evil is woken from his sleep. What good can then come over Earth from the awakening of the devils?

[5] It is therefore endlessly better that love and gentleness should grow and remain wakeful among mankind at all times and with that compel the devils to sleep, so that you would not harm the Earth, rather than to awaken the devils through the roaring din of power, that they then ruin the Earth with everything on it. Tell Me how you can, or want to object to that.'

[6] Says **Simon Peter**: 'Lord, here there can be no objection, because this is all clear and understandable. But how many people living on Earth know anything about this holy truth? Lord, see, here there are legions of angels from the Heavens, send these out to all the people of the Earth, to proclaim such truth. If this could happen then I think it would soon get brighter and better on the sinful ground of the Earth.'

[7] I said: 'Here you think the way you understand it, but I must be of a different

opinion here. See, there always are a thousand times more angels among mankind than you see here, acting upon the inner feelings and senses of men, so that man is not consciously coerced thereby and can without harm to his free will accept such thought, desires and drives as his own, and follow them. But what happens?

[8] Men's secret thoughts indeed are good, they have good desires and make praiseworthy resolutions, but when it comes to action, they look to the world and its goods and the deceptive needs of their flesh, and do and act with commensurate badness and selfishness.

[9] Let Me bring thousands of sheer miscreants before you and ask them whether they don't know that they are doing evil, and they shall all tell you that they know that. But if you ask them why they do evil then many shall tell you: "Because it gives us pleasure". And others shall say: "We would do good indeed, but since others do evil we do it too." And still others shall say: "We recognize the good indeed but are not able to carry it out, for our nature resists it, and we have to hate him who offends us."

[10] See, such answers and more you shall meet with, and from that you are certain to see only too quickly that even the most notorious miscreants are not without the knowledge of the good and true, yet still do the evil.

[11] Yet if men do evil from their innermost convictions, what can you expect from a recognition reaching them from without? Of a truth, there shall from now on be given to men cognition of the good and true from the Heavens, and for that they shall kill Me and you and others who will teach them to do good and abandon and avoid evil.'

[12] Says **Simon**: 'Lord, if so then the whole world may as well become of the devil. What is there to a human world which does not want to recognize and accept good?'

[13] I said: 'Whoever speaks in the heat of the moment like yourself is still far from My kingdom. But after I shall have ascended, you shall speak differently. But now evening has come, and so let us step inside and fortify our tired limbs.'


### CHAPTER 77
### The Lord knows the right measure

[1] Upon these words, many who earlier had moved to this spot during the talk with Simon Peter now thronged towards Me, clamoring for signs, saying: 'If you could work signs before the blind, who have no knowledge or understanding and therefore cannot evaluate them, then do them also before us. If they are genuine then we also shall believe on You, but if they are false and bad, then we shall know what it leaves us to do because we are initiated into all things.'

[2] I said: 'Good, if you are initiated into all things, why do you need signs? If you are so wise as to pretend to God's wisdom in all things, then you shall recognize it anyway whether I teach the truth or not. What for the signs then? But

there have already, these last three and a half days, been signs of a most extraordinary nature aplenty, for whose authenticity hundreds of witnesses stand here. If these don't suffice you then no new ones shall suffice your malicious hearts either. Therefore be gone from here of your own accord, if you don't wish to be removed by force.'

[3] Cry **those being dismissed**: 'Who will, who can and is allowed to remove us by force?! Are not we the lords of this place, living and trading and working and ruling here as citizens of Rome. We can indeed remove and drive you out at once, but not be removed by you simple-minded Galilean, as would please you. And we command you in full authority to leave this city by midnight, as we are fed up with your hanging around.'

[4] I said: 'O you blind fools. How much longer do you wish to live by your full authority? It would cost Me only one thought and you and the fullness of your authority are dust. Therefore return to your houses, or the place you stand on shall swallow you.'

[5] At that moment the Earth cleaves open at their feet, with smoke and flames billowing forth. Seeing this, the blasphemers wail: 'Woe unto us. We are lost, having sinned against Elijah.' With such howling they take off and the gap closes. But we quietly move into Joram's house.

[6] As we all enter the chambers of Irhael and Joram's house, everything there is ready for the evening meal. I bless it and all are seated at the tables, close to a thousand in all. All eat and drink, praising the superb flavors of food and wine, being happy and of good cheer. Only the commander, who had escorted us from the previous place with his wife and some deputies, was gloomy and ate and drank little. Jonael came and sat next to him to ask the cause of his somberness.

[7] **The commander** sighed deeply, saying: 'Noble and wise friend, how can one be cheerful if one finds nearly all of mankind a thousand times too bad for even the lowest Hell, if there be one? Where two hungry wolves find a bone and start a furious fight, one understands. Firstly they are wolves, animals without reason, natural machines, driven by powerful natural needs to satiate themselves; and secondly they are devoid of accountability, like a swollen stream unable to prevent destruction of everything nearby on account of its vast water-mass. But here are people who by their own witness command all levels of education and wisdom, yet are more evil than all wolves, tigers, hyenas, lions and bears. They demand all consideration towards themselves but don't want to give the least of it to fellow man. Say friend, are these also humans? Do they deserve any mercy? 'No' I said 'a thousand times no. Just wait, you coarse people. I shall kindle you a light that you won't know ever again whether you are coming or going.'

[8] Says **Jonael**: 'But what will you do? If you bump them off, you shall make enemies elsewhere. These shall inform on you in Rome, where you may get into ill-repute and possibly suffer expulsion to Scythia. Therefore leave revenge exclusively to the Lord, and be assured that He shall find the exact measure for this people.

[9] Read the story of my people, and it will show you to a hair's breadth how the Lord at all times punished their sins most severely and often relentlessly, and I tell

you, the Lord of Heaven and Earth is unchangeably the same as He was from eternity. He is long-suffering, full of greatest patience and never leaves the nation without teachers and signs from above, but the people beware once His patience runs thin. Once He swings the rod He does not relent until all the nation's limbs are broken and the bones tenderized like thin mush.

[10] Whatever you would accomplish here with only much dangerous effort, He can do with His most feeble thought. But so long as the Lord Himself is minded of tolerating such people, we shall not lay hands on them.

[11] You surely have seen how easy it was for the Lord to split the Earth in front of the villains, and make smoke and fire to go forth from the gaping cleft? To Him it would have verily been just as easy to convert these blasphemers to dust and ashes. But it pleased Him to just frighten them and beat them to retreat.

[12] If it suffices the Lord, let it suffice us, for He alone knows how to at all times find the right measure. But if the Lord is visibly well-disposed while among us, even showing some joy in us few, why should we be sullen and sad? Be happy and of good cheer, and glad of God's grace, leaving everything else to Him.'


## CHAPTER 78
### Gentleness and patience more effective than anger

[1] Says **the commander**: 'Dear wise friend, you have spoken well and good, but what should I as a stranger say to this? I now believe and am convinced from my deepest recesses that this Jesus of Nazareth is no other than the truest deity in human form. And not so much the great signs that He worked tell me that, but rather His unlimited wisdom, because whoever wishes to create a world has to be as wise as He in every Word.

[2] But these scoundrels most heinously call themselves children of God, to whom God has in all ages spoken either directly or indirectly, and now that He comes to them Himself physically, they scorn Him like common street urchins, and even want to remove Him from the city. Friend, I am a Roman, a crooked pantheist by religion, therefore a blind pagan, yet I will give my life for this new faith.

[3] If it were heathens, in these parts, I would forbear towards them, but since they call themselves children of God, who is supposed to be their eternal Father, and they scorn Him thus, I cannot show them forbearance as a stranger.

[4] God the Lord they had a mind to expel. Now it is they who shall be expelled. The vermin and weeds must go, so that on this field, which the Lord Himself worked, a pure and wholesome fruit should prosper. Because if the weeds remain here they shall destroy everything the Lord has so gloriously sown here. Be absolutely honest - am I right or not? What ought to be more to me, the Lord or this street rubble?'

[5] Says **Jonael**: 'That you are strictly right in your view, no one shall dispute indeed, but whether this is essential right now is another question. It is quite

possible that these blasphemers, frightened beyond measure, may turn inward, feel contrition and then fully reform; and then it would not after all be in order to expel them. Because sin only remains punishable in man so long as he abides in sin, but once man fully abandons sin and moves within the order established by God, then sin and its punishment has nothing further to do with man.

[6] But to punish a reformed man because formerly he had on one or more occasions sinned out of blind foolishness or weakness, should be the crown of folly, unworthy of a true human and all divine order, and such action would be exactly that of a foolish doctor who, after his patients' recovery, says to them: 'You are indeed fully recovered now, but you also realize that your flesh and in particular this or that limb has committed a sin on you, and has to now be flogged in proportion to the degree it tormented you.' When those who were healed then start to punish their body, which had just been healed, with all kinds of torments or if they are violently tortured, what shall become of their healing? Well, they shall get ten times more sick than they were before. Then the question is: of what use was such wrongly timed paining of the flesh? Is not the healing process an already sufficient punishment of the flesh? Why such after-torment which makes the healthy flesh sick again? But if such treatment is already exceedingly foolish physically, how much more on the spiritual man, mercilessly carried out?

[7] It is our responsibility indeed to in a brotherly fashion remind those men of the dangers of sinning who had sinned and then reformed, but to also at the same time strengthen and support them in their reformed state with every means at our disposal, so that they would not suffer re-bonding to sin, but to call them to account and punish them in their reformed state would be nothing short of dragging the reformed sinners back into tenfold sinfulness.

[8] And here it can be asked whether such dealing would not be a hundred times more punishable by God than the former sin committed by the offender. Believe me, the punishment which every sin carries with it already is a medicine against the soul-ailment called 'sin', but once this ailment is alleviated through the inlaid medicine, why more medicine without more ailment?' Says **the chief**: 'As a preventative against further outbreaks of the illness.'

[9] Says **Jonael**: 'Yes, preventatives are essential indeed, but they must be of a fortifying and strengthening nature, as stated, and not of a weakening or even killing nature. Anger shall not be assuaged by anger, but only through love, gentleness and patience.

[10] If someone is on fire then water and not boiling pitch or molten ore is to be poured over him. If someone breaks a leg then let him be carried and have his leg set and bound so that his break can mend, but not bludgeon him with truncheons for having walked so clumsily as to break his leg.

[11] I was recently told by a missionary, proclaiming the God of Abraham, Isaac and Jacob to the Scythians, that these wild nomads punish a man for dying. They undress and bind him to a post, flogging him all day naked; and this they do on a corpse even if a victim of a killing, because it is his own fault for allowing himself to be overpowered and killed. The killer on the other hand is praised for triumphing over the other and preserving his own life.

[12] As stupid as this may sound it resembles ourselves if in one way or another we want to make still more dead someone, who through sin – a real sickness of the soul – is already spiritually dead.

[13] A sick verily has need of doctor and medicine, but to punish him for having had the misfortune of getting sick, this, my dear friend, belongs to deepest Scythia. I trust you will now have understood that it is better to follow the Lord of life than to forestall Him with pride and clumsy hands, and to therewith wantonly and either devil-fashion or through sheer stupidity destroy His great, divine plantation.'


## CHAPTER 79
### The treatment of the soul-sick (1/79)

[1] Says **the chief commander**, completely taken in by Jonael's convincingly true discourse: 'Yes, now I am fully in the clear, and I shall desist from my design, and shall do it only if prompted by you; and you shall therefore be a God-sent alderman to this community, with priority in all things. I shall from now on do nothing without your counsel.'

[2] Says **Jonael**: 'Good so, and worthy of the Lord's pleasure. Where someone is sick in body, help shall be provided; if however there be anyone sick in soul, psychic help shall be provided in line with the sickness.

[3] The soul-maladies of children can best be cured through a good discipline where the rod should not be missing. The soul-maladies of adults, however, are cured through wise and loving counsel, through thorough teaching and instruction and pure love-motivated admonitions and drawing of the attention to the inevitable bad consequences that must arise in the near future if the soul's weaknesses are retained. If with very stubborn, or with blind and deaf souls, this has no effect, only then would it be time to subject such being to a more severe and strict treatment, at the bottom of which, however, love for the fellowman must be present in abundance, for the blessing of a more sever treatment can result only from that.

[4] If, however, the leaders act only from anger and a hellish vengefulness, then their effort is futile. Instead of healing the ones with sick souls to become true men, they are turned into devils, whose vengefulness in future no power will be able to appease.

[5] For a time Satan can be restrained by might and force from above, but if the Lord, for the sake of arrogant men who think that by their power and wisdom consisting in relentless tyrannical severity they are capable of preserving the order that suits them, withdraws His might and frees Satan from his fetters, then there will be overnight an end to the power of those who imagine themselves so powerful. For the people who by such wrong treatment have been turned into real devils will like a swollen stream fall upon them and destroy them as if they never existed.

[6] The worst effect has capital punishment. For what is the use to kill a person's

body if one cannot keep this soul and spirit captive, wherein dwells the real force for acting and accomplishing?

[7] Whoever believes that he has rid himself of his enemy when he has slain his body is smitten with tenfold blindness. For thereby he made for himself from a weak enemy whom he could see, a thousand invisible ones, who persecute him day and night and harm him in body, soul and spirit.

[8] Look at a war where not seldom many thousands are bodily slain. The victor believes in his blindness that he has rid himself of his enemies whose bodies he has destroyed. But what a mighty error that is. The souls and spirits of the slain, thanks to their direct influence on the Earth's weather, devastate during several years the various crops thereby inevitably calling forth high cost of foods which causes famine and all kinds of fatal epidemics and pestilence. These then within a short time snatch away more people than soldiers of the enemy had been slain. Now weakened in the power his land should give him, he must, in order to exist, hire for a high price mercenaries from foreign lands. Thereby he and his land run into debt, and when after some years he has completely impoverished his land and people and can no longer pay his debts and soldiers, he will soon be persecuted and cursed from all sides. His people, whom he conquered, will, driven by excessive misery, rise against him and the external enemies will not let this opportunity pass and wage war on him. And he, the celebrated victor, will in such a fight never be crowned victor, but despair will seize him with the claws of a tiger and mangle him spiritually to the innermost fiber of his life.

[9] And look, all this is the doings of bodily slain enemies.

[10] Therefore, it is an ancient rule and custom that when a person is physically dying, all those close to him make their peace with him and have him bless them, for if he dies as somebody's enemy, the one who survives him as his enemy is to be pitied. Firstly, the liberated soul will torment the survivor's mind uninterruptedly through unbearable pangs of conscience and then it will arrange all the survivor's earthly circumstances in such a way that he will hardly be able to get on in the world.

[11] The Lord allows all this so that the offended souls may receive the satisfaction they demand and, besides, it is incalculably better for the survivor to be already in this material world tormented for his actions of pride than if he after the death of his body promptly fell into a hundred thousand hands of hostile spirits who would certainly not treat him kindly, as one completely inexperienced in that world.

[12] That is why it is so extremely important to practice in this world love and true friendship, to do good to any enemy rather than harm him and to bless the one who curses me, for I cannot know when the Lord will call him away from this world. If he was in this world my enemy only in small, insignificant things, afterwards as a spirit he will become that in great things.

[13] Since his childhood David was a man according to Jehovah's own heart, but against the Lord's will he had made an enemy of one man, namely Urias, and what a terrible revenge, with the Lord's permission, Urias' spirit had then taken David. And that is and remains always the certain consequence of a hostile act

against a person opposing God's will.

[14] It is, of course, quite a different thing if the Lord Himself bids you do it, as He bade David beat with martial force and physically destroy the Philistines who had already become satanic enemies of God and men. These are in the beyond immediately subjected to a hard judgment and cannot ever rise against God's arm, for they are humiliated by the Lord's might.

[15] However, it is quite different with those enemies you made for yourself against God's will, possibly through your pride or the most imperfect, man-devised justice about which goes the saying that the greatest right is at the same time the greatest wrong. These will, once they have shed their bodies, become your most irreconcilable enemies.

[16] I would give you a thousand lives, if I had them, if you could show me in the world one happy person who had an enemy precede him into the other world. I have not met such a one. But I do know cases where the revenge of a spirit who had become hostile to a family extended to the tenth generation; also where people in a land or region had been treated very badly, they had then as spirits devastated such a land or region for many years, sometimes even permanently, so that men could no longer live there. Friend, although this my well-meant precept may sound quite unbelievable to you, it is still irrefutably right. If it were not so, how could I ever dare give it to you before the Lord and His angels? But if you should entertain any doubt, do turn to the Lord, the eternal Creator of all things, and He will bear you a fully valid witness to the absolute truth of what I have told you.'

## CHAPTER 80
### Avoid self-esteem

[1] At this, **the Commander**, as also many of the other guests present, is quite astonished and says: 'If this is so, life on Earth is a dangerous thing. Who could hold his own?'

[2] I said: 'Everyone who lives according to My teaching, but whoever lives according to his self-esteem, which is usually saturated with self-love and pride, and cannot from all his heart forgive and bless ten times more the one who offended him in some way, will sooner or later have to taste the inevitable consequences of hostility against which he can by no means expect any protection from Me, unless he has paid his debt to his enemy to the last penny. Therefore, do live in peace and unity with everyone. It is better for you to suffer an injustice than to do even an apparent justice to someone. Thus you will not educate avengers for yourselves, and the spirits, who otherwise would have become your enemies, will then be your guardian angels and ward off many a calamity threatening you.

[3] But why is all this so, and must be? Here I say: because it has to be so in accordance with My will and unchangeable order.'

[4] Says **the commander**: 'Yes, Lord. I now recognize only too clearly your endless and unrestricted love and wisdom, and say: if possibly all men shall once be permeated with Your teaching, then the Earth shall be converted into a complete heavenly kingdom. But – and this an immense 'but' – when will this occur?

[5] When I think of the vast Earth to which no explorer has yet found beginning or end, and the numberless humans inhabiting its unmeasured surface, then I become dizzy to my deepest fibers. The leading attribute of all the many inhabitants of the great Earth seems to be crudest malice.

[6] The vast majority are saturated through and through with animalistic selfishness, and the haughtiness of furies.

[7] Wherever on the wide Earth some small peace-loving people settled, achieving some sort of living-standard through communal action, it was soon sniffed out by the fine snouts of wolf and tiger men and pounced upon; these poor were vanquished and made a thousand times unhappier than in their former, natural state.

[8] But where such peaceful and literate little nations nevertheless through courage, intelligence and energy of spirit asserted themselves as conquerors of their enemies, whom they had to of course largely annihilate by weapon, with the spirits of the conquered dead however becoming their still greater and more harmful foes, then I quite frankly ask, how when and under what circumstances shall Your most salutary teaching ever fully take root on Earth, to determine all mankind in their doings and dealings?

[9] If only a few select societies, most happily, are going to bask in the mild beams of your unsurpassed teaching, then they shall day by day be surrounded by more enemies; if they willingly surrender, they shall be nothing but slaves of their conquerors, having to tolerate every inhuman oppression as well as the proscription in the end of their compliance and practice of Your teaching.

[10] But if by some turn of power they should become the masters of their enemies, then the spirits and souls of those killed in battle shall really become their most invincible foes, and then the heavenly kingdom on Earth shall in my opinion be done for.

[11] Therefore I should leave the question of whether even for the best of the cause, one can simply return good for evil to every enemy, wide open. I should not cast the least doubt on being able to therewith potentially make a seeing friend out of a blind enemy, but whether this rule can also be applied blessedly to great masses of enemies to the benefit of the cause, that, Lord, forgive my weak understanding, I would for stated reasons question somewhat.

[12] This conjures up the hapless Scylla and Charybdis where, upon happily avoiding the first, one is swallowed up the more readily by the second. Lord, only a small light upon that, and I shall embrace all my enemies in a brotherly fashion and liberate all the captives from the prisons, including all thieves, robbers and murderers, regardless of how nasty.'

# CHAPTER 81
## The Lord is the bridge to the spiritual world

[1] I said: 'Friend, if you interpret and understand My teaching in that way, then you are still very short-sighted. Jonael also already told you that in the case of combat initiated by God, or for unavoidable self-defense, the souls of people killed in those circumstances are immediately placed under severe judgment, preventing them from causing any effects upon either their rightful conquerors, or upon the Earth itself. But if this is incontrovertibly the truth, from which you can clearly see where this matter stands, how can you counter My teaching with such misgivings?

[2] Who told you that real criminals, who often are worse than wild jungle beasts, should not be apprehended and secured? This is already gainsaid by true love of neighbor, because if you are certain to kill a hyena with a sharp weapon if it attacks a human, so also you would leap to the aid of a just person if attacked by a robber-murderer in the open street, or in a house.

[3] Since however such human hyenas, if proliferating, can endanger not only individual wanderers but entire districts, it is even the unavoidable duty for the powers that be to initiate hunts after such dangerous people, and securely imprison them.

[4] Capital punishment shall be inflicted only upon those with whom during a period of ten years every means to achieve any true betterment has failed. If the criminal promises betterment on the scaffold for execution, he shall be allowed another year. But if also then there is no improvement, the execution is to take place, for in that case the betterment on Earth of such a man cannot be expected and it is preferable to remove him from this Earth.

[5] If, however, the lawful authority in power wishes, in agreement with the community, to change such a criminal's well-deserved death-penalty to life-imprisonment and continue their efforts at betterment, they have the right to do so and I will not call them to account for it.

[6] These types of enemies of those men living in accordance with My teaching have no retroactive power after their physical death. This is a recourse open only to spirits who, while striving for higher aims on Earth, nevertheless were killed in a most cruel fashion by tyrannizing, exceedingly arrogant and self-seeking and domineering and therefore illegitimate rulers.

[7] Where such executions, bereft of all finer feelings, make enemies through such judicially most unjust proceedings, then such enemies shall as spirits take revenge on these executioners, because I grant retroaction to such spirits, but never to basically evil spirits. I trust that your doubts are now cleared up?'

[8] Says **the chief**: 'Yes, the Scylla together with Charybdis have now been removed, and I am now in the clear on this.

[9] But how Your truly holy teaching is to move along a path free of obstacles, through the night in which mankind now lies buried, is to me as unclear as ever. According to Your own statements, a supernatural passage on the one hand

would not be much help to men, because it would only create machines out of a mankind that should and is due for liberation. Along a natural path however it shall cost much blood and require an exceedingly long time. Indeed, I would assert that, although not imbued with the gift of prophesying, the way I know the human race quite extensively in Asia, Africa and Europe, that in two thousand years from now, not even half by far of Earth-dwellers shall bask in the light of Your teaching. Am I right or not?'

[10] I said: 'There, fundamentally, you are by no means wrong. But there is not as much to this as you think, because it is not so much the most widespread acceptance of My teaching on this Earth but rather the erection, at long last, through My present advent and My Word and teaching, of a bridge between this material and that spiritual world, whose everlasting realm lies beyond the grave.

[11] Whoever in this world shall accept My teaching in all earnest shall cross this bridge in the flesh already, but whoever shall receive this teaching either lukewarmly, incompletely or not at all, shall arrive in that other world in great darkness and have much trouble finding this bridge.

[12] But those men who may never be in a position to find out anything about My teaching shall in the beyond be given leaders who will lead them to this bridge. If these spirits, still ignorant of My teaching, shall follow these leaders, they shall also cross this bridge into true eternal life, but if stubbornly clinging to their doctrine they shall be judged as mere creatures and not attain to the childhood of God. See, that's how things stand. Think it over and tell Me how you like it, only soon, because verily, My time in this place is nearing its end.'

[13] Says **the chief commander** after a while: 'Lord, now everything is clear and lucid for me, and for any potential further problems, You have awoken a man for us here who can instruct us all about everything. Therefore let Your name be glorified and praised above all measure by myself and us all, always. Please accept only one more humble request, that when You now depart from us, You would return to us soon, as it shall be my main concern here that, should You return here, You will find hearts more worthy of You than is now the case.'


## CHAPTER 82
### Farewell to Irhael and Joram

**43.** *"Now after two days He departed from there, and went into Galilee".*

[1] I said: 'I shall come again for sure, but secretly. Not all of the district shall then be finding out about My presence, because more people shall continue to settle down here due to the great oppressive taxation in Judea and Galilee, this land being the least burdened, with My Jairuth paying nearly all the taxes for the poor.

**44.** *"For Jesus Himself testified that a prophet hath no honor in his own* *country".*

[2] But where there are too many fellow countrymen, there a prophet is not very valuable, unless he is an old man. Only that which is said by an old man the fools take as God's Word, while the wisdom of a young man is the play of fantasy, occasionally mixed with some good sense. But regarding the miraculous signs, these are one and all consigned to the sphere of magic which in these times unfortunately is all too common. People now are too blind to distinguish the false from the true, and therefore dismiss one and all.

[3] It is therefore better for a prophet to travel abroad, because he is bound to still accomplish more where he is unknown. Therefore I and My disciples shall leave you now, yet also visit you again shortly as promised.

[4] But a man, who had been engaged here as a tax-collector, by the name of Matthew, I shall be taking with Me, on account of his fast and good writing, so that he would record My teachings and deeds, to him issue a passport for worldly reasons.'

[5] The chief does so at once, thanking Me fervently for everything. All the remaining guests, inspired by his example, also do so. But quite a few, exhausted from the day's journey, had fallen asleep at the tables. Those awake were about to waken them, but I say: 'Let them rest till day break. But it is more expedient for Me to depart quietly, at midnight, so as not to arouse too much of a sensation. Remain here yourselves till day-time too, not escorting Me or anyone traveling with Me, except in your heart.

[6] You My Jonael however, see to it that My teaching takes root here and then bears much fruit, just as a new tree of life bears much and good fruit. But I give you, through My name, also an extrasensory power from the Heavens, but do not allow your zeal to draw you into ill-advised use thereof, because then you would do more harm than good. I shall leave you an angel in your house for a while, from whom you shall learn the wise use of heavenly power. But tell no stranger that an angel from the Heavens dwells at Jonael's.'

[7] At this point Irhael and Joram also come to Me weeping, unable to speak for love and gratitude. But I bless them and say, 'Be comforted. Shortly I shall be coming to you again.'

[8] Both of them embrace My feet, covering them with tears, with **Joram** exclaiming: 'O you holy time, hasten to bring the Lord of glory to us in His house for evermore. O Lord, remember those of us who love You from the fullness of our hearts, and come soon to stay with us for good.'

[9] I said: 'Yes, I shall come again, but, as said, only in secret, because from now on no one must through My presence be coerced into believing in My having been sent from above, and therefore in My Word.

# CHAPTER 83
## The power of the Word. Departure from Sychar.

[1] The teaching itself must justify the truth. Whoever will from now on fail to live according to the Word will die in the judgment of the same Word that was spoken to him and which he had not believed and trusted.

[2] For just as I, out of Myself, have received the power from the Father whether or not to give eternal life to everyone who has the will, the same can be done also by My Word. For My Word is invariably the almighty and everlasting expression of My will.

[3] He who fully absorbs My Word and unfailingly acts and lives according to it, thereby absorbs Me with all My love, wisdom, might and power and has thus become a true child of God from whom the Father in Heaven will not withhold anything He has.

[4] The Holy Father cannot do any more than reveal Himself in person in Me, His Son, making of you, created beings under judgment, absolutely free gods and calling you His friends and brothers.

[5] Do consider at all times who He is who is now revealing this to you and what you are receiving with this revelation, then the material world will no longer tempt you and you will easily overcome it. This is all the more necessary since you cannot become children of the Father in Heaven unless you have completely conquered the world within yourselves.

[6] I do not intend thereby to make of you low-spirited condemners of the world, but only wise users of it.

[7] Would you not call him a fool who became so attached to some well serviceable tool he needs for his trade, that he does not want to use it for the purpose for which it is intended, but only keeps gaping at it with intense pleasure, keeping it in a cabinet to prevent it from rusting and thereby becoming less beautiful which would lessen his empty pleasure in it?

[8] The world is also a tool for you with which, if appropriately used, you could produce much that is good and magnificent. But being My disciples now you must use this tool in the way I, as your sole and truest Master, have taught you during three and a half days.

[9] Used and applied thus, this tool will prepare and secure for you eternal life, but if you use it in a different way, this tool will become like a very sharp knife in the hands of small children who could only too easily deal themselves a deadly wound with it which hardly any doctor will be able to heal.

[10] Receive also My full blessing with these words and do pass them on to all those who have not been able to hear them, so that in the end no one will be able to plead ignorance of My teaching.

[11] And now, those few disciples of Mine, and also those of you who followed Me here from Galilee and Jerusalem, make ready for the journey and namely Galilee, where you can once again attend to the tilling of your fields.'

[12] With this exhortation I arise, giving also the remaining angels a sign which

only they can understand, whereupon all but the one assigned to Jonael disappear. The visible portals of Heaven also close, but Irhael and Joram's house remains with all its heavenly outfit, as does Jairuth's castle. All the awoken ones see us out to the gate. The chief commander however would not miss out on escorting Me to the town's precincts, then turning back to Sychar.

## CHAPTER 84
### An eclipse

[1] We continue our journey however, reaching the borders of the Samaritan's land by sunrise, entering the land of Galilee and finding a necessary rest on a hill without trees, on a beautiful grassy field.

[2] The glorious view could not be praised highly enough by all, and the scribe **Matthew** says: 'Lord, if all men were suffused with your teaching in all things then such country should be sufficiently beautiful to be a Heaven to men. But when I think of how mankind at large is more evil than the most bloodthirsty predators, then I would almost reproach God the Lord for creating this Earth so gloriously for such evil rabble.'

[3] I said: 'In that case your reproach is directed at Me, because the Father and I are One. Because the eternal Son's wisdom, which actually is the Father's, brought forth the great plan of Creation, while the Father's love added the 'let there be', and thus the Earth, sun, moon, and the stars came into being.

[4] The people dwelling upon this Earth however also were created by Me, and shall and now will be recreated.

[5] If however things stand thus, how will you reproach Me? And besides, this Earth is not quite as beautiful as it seems to you. All these areas you view from here appear so pleasant only from a certain distance. Go over and you shall find little or nothing beautiful or charming to these areas, other than perhaps an occasional tree or garden, containing maybe a rich man's palace. Will you also call these things beautiful?

[6] Look towards the sun – there are quite different districts there. There a desert is more glorious than a paradise here. Because if it is exclusively the sun's light that makes the Earth-region appear beautiful and friendly, since without sunlight the Earth would be a valley of wretchedness and fear, how much more glorious must be the regions of the great sun itself, from which this Earth borrows its pale shimmer.'

[7] Says **Matthew**: 'Lord, what are you saying? The sun also a whole big world, with unspeakably more beautiful deserts than here a paradise? See the great Earth compared to the tiny sparking disc of the sun. How many times over surely would it fit into the spot we can see, which surely is one of the smallest on the Earth, and therefore how many times over unto the entire Earth?'

[8] I said: 'Listen, the thing is, not comprehending even the earthly things I tell you about, how shall you understand Me if I begin to speak of heavenly things?

See and comprehend.

[9] Look, in the south there, a cedar at the furthest edge of the mountain-chain. Compare its seeming height with a blade of grass here a span in height, and you will see that if held to your face it shall rise many times the height of that distant cedar, which latter is actually the higher by a hundred times a hundredfold. And this is affected by the distance. If you are fast of leg you would reach that cedar in ten hours. How great an effect upon the eye therefore just 10 hours of distance?

[10] But now think of the distance between sun and Earth. See, if a bird had left the Earth in its fastest flight at the creation of Adam, it would still have years to reach the sun. If you can grasp this then you will realize why the sun, thousand times thousand fold bigger than the Earth, can appear so small from here.'

[11] **Matthew**, quite beside himself about such distance and size, says: 'O Lord, if so then how are you able to guide and maintain such a world from the Earth?'

[12] I said: 'Yes, what may appear to you ever so impossible is, between you and I, exceedingly easy for Me. This you cannot of course grasp yet, but there shall come a time when you will comprehend all this.

[13] But so that you may see that through the might of the Father in Me I can instantly reach up to the sun, watch. I shall now cover up the sun for two moments, so that no eye upon the Earth shall see it, from which it shall be clear to you that I can reach the sun even from this Earth.'

[14] Says **Matthew**: 'O Lord, do not do so, or men shall perish for grief.' I said: 'Be not troubled. Men will think it an ordinary eclipse, which at times occurs in the ordinary course of things, and in a few moments they have their sun back. Watch now. **Matthew** says with some trepidation: 'Lord, should not all those present here be made aware of it?' I said: 'Let them sleep and rest; it is enough that you should experience it, because a scribe has to know more than those not yet called for such. And see, I now say, Sun, hide your face from the entire Earth for 7 moments. At that moment it gets pitch-dark. Only some of the brighter stars feebly appear.

[15] **Matthew** trembles for fear and says: 'Lord, you almighty. Who may abide beside you if your divine arm can reach such endless distance in a moment? Matthew hardly finishing those few words, the sun already is shining in its full brilliance again, and My Matthew breathes more freely again, but cannot utter a word for amazement. Only after a good while he gathers up courage to say: 'No, Lord, this I cannot take in. Your might must be limitless. But in future please spare us such terrible proof of Your might, O Lord, because the whole Earth could shortly die and perish therewith.'

[16] I said: 'Be not troubled. Has anyone died so far? But a little fear does no harm to sensual man. But now awaken those asleep, because we shall shortly move on. But tell no man anything about this sight and sign.' Thereupon Matthew awakens those asleep and we get ready to continue our journey, which from here on is of a fairly deep descent and therefore faster than the former ascent.

**45.** *"Then, when He was come into Galilee, the Galileans received Him, having seen all the things He did at Jerusalem at the feast, for they also went unto the feast."*

[1] Having arrived in the valley we soon reached a Galilean village, where many of those Galileans dwelt who had attended the feast at Jerusalem, when I had cleansed the temple. Neither had it been a long time since that occasion in Jerusalem, and therefore everything still was fresh in their minds.

[2] Seeing Me pass through the streets of their village, they soon came out of their dwellings into the street, greeting Me very amicably and not being able to praise Me too highly for what was to them a daring deed in the Temple. And their joy at seeing Me was heightened in that they had nearly all thought that the Pharisees at Jerusalem may have secretly dispatched Me from this world. For these Galileans hardly knew more of Me than that I was the son of the pious Joseph and that God was with Me the way He was with Joseph. I and My company had to stay with them all of the day and finally the entire night. They hosted us to the limits of their ability and there were many questions and much consultation, and the subject of the Messiah also came up, and many saw and recognized Same in Me.

[3] Because they said: 'He who can demonstrate such courage in front of thousands in the Temple must be conscious of a great power, which is given Him from above. Because if an ordinary human being tried this he would fare badly. Neither would he have accomplished anything against the rusty old practices prevailing in the Temple. But it was different with You. They ran out of the Temple as if hit by a mighty storm, and no market has been held in the Temple since then.' And I said: 'And none shall be held there from now on, because its end is near.'

[4] Here **the Galileans** were astounded and answered: 'If so then it shall fare badly with us. What then is to become of the everlasting dominion of David's descendants as promised by the prophets and which the Messiah is to re-establish?'

[5] I said: 'He shall indeed found a new, everlasting kingdom for the true children and descendants of David, and therewith for all men of the Earth, but not on this Earth but above it – in Heaven. Whoever interprets the prophets otherwise shall walk in darkness'.

[6] With these Words several leave, since they believe in an earthly Messiah, but many ask for a more detailed explanation.

[7] But I say: 'You too have to see signs, otherwise you believe nothing. Therefore follow Me to Cana and then thereabouts, and you shall receive doctrine and signs.'

[8] But there were many among My company from Cana who had most devoutly accompanied Me throughout this entire educational tour since that feast. These

wanted to start telling about all the doctrines they had heard and seen from Me.

[9] But I say: 'For these it is not time yet. But let them follow us, there we shall mention some of it, and they themselves shall see and find out more. And so let us continue our journey. But let there be no talking along the way, as there are encampments of Pharisees.'

[10] The Galileans confirmed this, saying how there are now pharisaic spies lurking everywhere, stopping travelers along the road to question them in all sorts of ways and now and then also about the whereabouts of a certain Jesus of Nazareth, and whether He teaches among them. And I said: 'For this very reason we shall move to Cana in silence; they shall very wisely not put questions to our numerous company.'

## CHAPTER 86
### The Lord back in Cana of Galilee. Satan's trick.

**46. 'So Jesus came again into Cana, of Galilee, where He made the water wine.'**

[1] After these Words the journey continues and we reach the little city of Cana without trouble. Arriving there, we at once move over to the house where I had worked the first public miracle. An hour hardly passes when nearly the entire place knows that I and all who journeyed with Me arrived happily and in good shape; and all rush over to see, greet and welcome the arrivals. And seeing me they cannot find sufficient words of praise and glorying at the decisive way I cleansed the Temple at Jerusalem. Because many had come to the feast from Cana and had seen what I had affected in Jerusalem, and had also heard how I had healed many sick there, praising Me tremendously.

[2] I asked them if there were no sick here. But they said that strangely enough there was not one sick at this place.

[3] Then I said that they were indeed healthy as far as their body was concerned, but not in their soul: 'For whoever practices harlotry and fornication is very sick in his soul. Through this sin a person's heart hardens from day to day, becomes ever more unfeeling and merciless towards its fellowmen and in the end loves nothing but itself and the object of its lust, not for the sake of the object though, but only for the sake of satisfying its lust. Such a heart then flees God's Word which admonishes it against its evil desire and in the end even becomes hostile to those who carry the Word of God in their heart and live accordingly. Many of you suffer from this sickness and that is why I returned to you to heal you from this very bad and fatal disease. Those of you who know that they suffer from this deadly disease should entrust themselves to Me and I shall heal them.'

[4] At this My announcement many promptly leave the house, for the offenders fear that I may divulge their secret and so they take to their heels. Among them were some adulterers, some guilty of incest and many of both sexes who defile

themselves, and they were relieved to be out of My sight.

[5] Not that there were not many who would have liked to be healed of this vice, but it was the disgrace. Because they counted as honorable, well-regarded people, and it would have been embarrassing to have their neighbors find out about their infirmity of flesh. Yet they did not consider that they gave themselves away by taking to their heels in response to My offer.

[6] **Many who remained** behind said: 'No, I could never have thought that about this or that one.' **Others** however could not resist laughing, saying: 'Quite smart of You. These would have given no answer even if asked for ten years straight, yet You only offered most kindly to heal them of this affair, and look how they all shot through. They probably thought that He who could convert water into wine could also call them by their name, You there sinned this way and so many times, and you there this way and this often. And this they could not bear of course and thus made off. But they did not consider that this way they gave themselves away most of all. We don't wish to judge them, since we know our own weaknesses, and know it is better to first sweep before your own house, but it is funny how they thought that by running off they would not be recognized the way you described the sins. No, these are sillier than Persian rhinos'.

[7] I said: 'Let them go, the blind fools. Before men they feel ashamed, but before God who at all times sees and tries the hearts and kidneys of men they are not ashamed. I tell all of you: This worldly sense of shame is idle. How long will it last in this world anyway? Soon the body will be taken from them whose flesh gave them so many sweet hours. Then they will arrive naked in the other world where everything they did ever so secretly in this world will be revealed in all detail. Only there a true and lasting shame will be theirs of which they will not be able to rid themselves as easily as here.

[8] In truth, I tell all of you: Those who are lascivious, unchaste and fornicators shall not enter the Kingdom of God unless they have drastically changed their most wicked way of life. For see, all other sins man commits outside his body and can, therefore, rid himself of them more easily, for what takes place externally does not cause as much damage to a person as that which takes place within him. Fornication takes place within man, damages his soul and spirit and is thus the most dangerous of all evils. Therefore, shun it above all and flee it like the plague, for the appetite for sensual pleasure is Satan's trick. Woe betide him who has allowed Satan thus to take hold of him. He will find it extremely difficult to free himself from Satan's claws. Unspeakable suffering and pains will be his share. Do heed all this, or else the time and the days will come which you will not like at all. But now let us retire.'

[9] Several who had travelled with Me moved over to their dwellings. My disciples however and mother Mary and My brethren, i.e. Joseph's five sons, remained with Me.

# CHAPTER 87
## The Jewish skeptics

[1] After all the others had left, **the young host**, at whose wedding I had converted the water into wine, came to Me saying: 'Lord, those who had followed us from Judea and Jerusalem and fortified themselves with food and drink in the larger guest-room, would like a word with You, because from what I can make out, several are ready to depart to their homeland and look after their businesses. If you will allow me I shall go and tell them.'

[2] I said: 'I do not think that is necessary. Whoever is and remains with Me is in his true homeland, and whoever does not earn himself this one and only true and lasting homeland shall wander about like a fugitive beast searching the desert for fare and shelter, finding neither, finally to languish from hunger, thirst and cold, becoming a prey to predators from such barren desert.

[3] Has anyone around Me gone without? Were not all sated daily from the Heavens physically and spiritually? Did anyone suffer hunger or thirst traveling with Me? I say unto you: he, who wants to leave, let him leave, but whoever wants to remain, let him. He who leaves Me shall also be left by Me, and whoever does not seek Me, him I shall in no way seek over zealously. Go and tell them this.'

[4] Says **the host**: 'Lord, I am troubled, You shall no doubt also be displeased with these citizens of Cana who have gone home to rest?'

[5] I said: 'You did not understand Me. See, these folk have already fully received Me into their hearts, and My teaching has become sacred to them, but to those Jews the teaching that I gave at Sychar is not fully agreeable, and they yearn even more for their leaven than their households, and therefore to leave for home. But they want to give Me the honor, so as not to be regarded as churls here. Therefore go out and openly tell them everything I said to you.'

[6] Directed thus, the host goes and acquaints them verbatim with what I said to him. All are startled and feel personally pilloried by turns. Some are offended, but others take it to heart, turning it over in their minds and saying: 'He has got us, and it unfortunately is so. Hopefully He will forgive us, let us stay.'

[7] But **the offended ones** say: 'Yet we are going. Although we lacked nothing with Him we are fed up with this Scythian indigence, and besides one has to always watch one's words very carefully, for the verdict is not long-a-coming, and then one can see how to get back into favor, for leniency there is none with him. Whatever He has pronounced accommodates no compromise. Therefore we shall stay with Him no more.'

[8] But **the remorseful** say: 'This might be true, and the priests are certainly accommodating in Jerusalem, particularly where the offerings are liberal. But He will not compromise by a hair's breadth even if offered the entire Earth. Therefore it is somewhat hard to get on with Him, yet He is bound to be one of the greatest prophets at the very least, full of power and life, and even mute nature responds to His nod. What is left us other than to remain for as long as he Himself does not remove us? Because the signs He worked before our eyes no man has done

before him, and we therefore are staying with Him, come what may.'

[9] **The offended ones** however say: 'Do what you will, but we go. If we owe the host anything, let him give us the bill.'

[10] But **the host** says: 'I keep no accommodation for strangers, but only for native children of Jacob, and these are free just as elsewhere in Canaan, where the brooks are flowing with milk and honey.'

[11] Hearing this they arise, take to the road and are gone. But after several hours journey from Cana, they are too exhausted to lift their feet, sinking down on the road, some hundred in number, to take their night's rest.

[12] But a strong detachment of Roman mercenaries coming the other way from Jerusalem bumps into this caravan. Not being capable of being shaken awake however, the exhausted are guarded till morning. Awakening in the morning however they find themselves bound by the hands, and being without travel passes they are arrested one and all and brought before the court at Jerusalem, being examined there for seven days and then released, after paying the necessary fines, having been identified as Jews.

[13] A segment of these soldiers also arrives at Cana the same morning. After searching our house, and after our clearing ourselves with our travel passes from Jerusalem, they raise no further obstacles and depart for Capernaum, their chief commander having recognized Me and discussed several matters with Me and acquainting Me of his projected extended stay at Capernaum, his family already having moved there two days earlier, where he is meeting them. Therewith he invites Me to drop in on him at Capernaum, which I agree to in a few days time.

[14] He also asks Me about the large caravan he came across sleeping on the road.

[15] I tell him what kind of caravan it is, and he replies with a smile: 'Did I not guess that I bumped into such breed, who basically are pharisaical spies, and it would greatly surprise me if You did not identify them so at first glance.'

[16] Whereto I replied: 'You are not altogether wrong in suspecting them to be so. But they were not yet so when following Me from Jerusalem and Judea, but now some of them shall be so, to their own great detriment. Because the Temple-breed covets betrayal indeed, but actually fears the informer more than the betrayed enemy, and therefore does not let informers go. Nearly all get to drink of the accursed water and hardly one in ten survives this, but the burst ones then are usually branded false accusers and buried at Jehoshaphat in the accursed soil. And this shall also be the fate of some of those turning informers on Me, because My time is not yet come.'

## CHAPTER 88
### The chief commander Cornelius. The Lord's cleansing of the temple.

[1] Says the chief commander, by the name of **Cornelius**, who was also a brother of the emperor Augustus: 'Well, serves them right. Because I cannot tell

you how I abhor this Temple brood. I tell You, dearest and most exalted friend, the most evil of all evils on the entire Earth is a Jewish temple cleric. Our quasi-Egyptian priests are bad, but occasionally they still display hallmarks of humanity; not much is heard there about atrocities, while their business with very few exceptions is to exhort mankind to humanness and to martial chivalry.

[2] But these fellows are hypocrites through and through. Outwardly they act as strictly and piously as if carrying bagfuls of living gods. Inwardly however they are too evil even for our lowermost mythical Hell. Verily, if our three main mythical furies, before whose heinousness everything is supposed to turn to stone in terror, were to catch sight of such Jerusalemite Temple-churl, then they would themselves have to turn to diamond from trepidation. I tell You, for the ultimate unfurling of this most supremely malevolent, depraved Temple and priest knot, same must soon be put to the sharpest sword of the Macedonian king, or the entire Earth should shortly be entangled in it. O friend, I could tell you things about these churls that through this alone the entire Earth would turn feverish. But let this suffice You for now, after you come over we shall have much to discuss.'

[3] I said: 'O let be. I know this brood from the lowest root fibers. But I have already selected a 'Macedonian king' from your Roman race; to him shall be granted the hewing in twain with red-hot sword of this most solid knot. I nevertheless shall prior to this be doing everything possible towards the reformation of some of them.'

[4] Says **the chief**: 'Do not do it. Because they shall know how to kill You, for as long as there is human mortality-potential in You, even if You are a true Son of God. For I tell You, not even a God is safe with them. Believe Me, dearest young friend.

[5] I said: 'Let's leave that. What the Father wants shall be. It would take only one breath from My mouth and they should be no more. But this is not the Father's will, and so we shall let them be for a while.'

[6] Says **the chief**: 'If these churls should carry on for another ten years, not many people should survive in Judea. If it was not for one moderate at their top then soon after Your most courageous cleansing of the Temple of its vermin, there would already have been immense trouble. But a truly upright man by the name of Nicodemus knew how to make these churls, who are now nearly as numerous as the grass of the Earth, keep their distance. It was really funny how with great cunning he was able to make it clear that this Temple-cleansing was permitted by God only so that His servants should acquire much gold, as it was precisely those merchants, money-changers and sellers of pigeons who never, apart from their small stall's fees, ever laid offerings into the Temple offertories, even while being considered the wealthiest in all of Jerusalem.' With this most of them agreed and some said: 'Well, let's hope this one comes also to the next feast with his magic power – he comes in handy.' But some, who secretly, through confidential agents, had also participated in the money-changing, were of course not so happy. 'But notwithstanding this I guarantee You that, upon a repeated cleansing at the next feast, not a hair shall be bent upon Your head, since you had helped them to a considerable sum at the last one. But should You again go to Jerusalem for a

similar affair then sneak in most secretly, or You should find the Temple cleansed by itself, as these hawkers, money-changers and livestock traders have sent out spies after You everywhere, who are to watch all Your paths, similarly to those notorious Temple-servants. Most of those I had arrested belonged to these chaps, and there would hardly have been two honest ones among them.'

[7] I said: 'Well, this favor I could of course do them again, but be assured that no such money-changers or vendors shall set up business in the Temple after that. Upon My final move into Jerusalem I shall get to cleanse the Temple again the way I did recently.'

[8] Following this assurance a troop-commander came to report the troop's readiness for march-off to the chief. The chief takes leave of Me, reminding Me to be sure to drop in on him at Capernaum. Thereafter the host serves up a good morning meal, at which all take part.

## CHAPTER 89
### Two days of rest in Cana

[1] After the morning meal I say to all those present: 'If there is anyone who has domestic affairs to attend to, he is welcome to take a couple of days leave for the purpose, but you need to attend again on the third day because I intend to spend a couple of days here in Cana and also take a little rest. But those too far from home can stay here, as also those not wishing to leave Me. But I propose during these two days to neither teach nor work things but, as said, just to rest and to pray to the Father for you all.'

[2] Mary and My 5 brethren however also come over to Me and ask whether it would be all right for them to go to Nazareth for a couple of days, to put domestic affairs in order.

[3] And I say: 'Yes, go and do so, because My disciples need to also have their worldly affairs in order. But organize your domestic affairs for a couple of years, and let out to someone poor, but mark well, without rent. Because as My brothers and disciples you should in future never seek rent or wages from anyone, but only accept what is handed to you voluntarily.' The brethren together with Mary promise to do so, and leave for Nazareth.

[4] But of My disciples it was only Thomas who went home, with the resolve to seek out disciples for Me, which he also did. There was however among them a certain Jew, not an actual Galilean, by the name of Iscariot, who subsequently betrayed Me. Up to a certain time he was the most industrious of My disciples, he played the purser, paying everything everywhere, and acting as it were as forerunner and stage-manager wherever I went. Yet he also knew how to secretly make money out of My deeds and teaching, and this money-greed in the end made him what he eventually became My betrayer. But Peter and the other disciples who had followed Me from Bethabara remained.

[5] To My asking him whether he was not inclined to go home for a couple of

days, **Peter** replied: 'Lord, only death can part me from You, or a commandment from Your mouth. I arranged with Thomas for my son Mark to come here, he could be of use, because with writing he is almost as good as Matthew. But that's about all that I have to attend to domestically, everything else You my Lord and my God are taking care of anyway.' I said: 'Not so loud, My Simon Peter, because here we are not at Sychar. There are also some here who are not at your stage yet – these could be offended. Therefore it is enough if in future you call Me 'Lord', the rest for the time being keep in your heart, which I know quite well.'

[6] Peter is satisfied with that, asking Me whether we are to undertake nothing at all during the two days in Cana. But I say: 'This be far from us. But we shall not strain ourselves as we did at Sychar. In a worldly sense we are here in our homeland, and you know how much a prophet is worth in his homeland. Therefore we shall be doing and teaching very little here in our actual sphere. Because where faith is lacking there is little work for us. Therefore we shall, as they would say, take it easy for a couple of days, and prepare a little for the time ahead.'

[7] After these words Matthew comes asking Me whether to perhaps now record some of the things he has seen and heard at Sychar.

[8] But I say: 'If you are intent on doing something, then you could twice copy the Sermon on the Mount, and a copy can then be left with the host here in Cana, and one at Capernaum, because there too we shall not get to do much.'

[9] But now the host comes to ask what I should like for lunch. And I say to him: 'Friend, why such an idle question? Not having asked Me before the morning meal, I still quite enjoyed it. Therefore I shall also find lunch excellent. Verily I say unto you, every meal seasoned with the noble and loving heart of the giver is the tastiest – better than the most sumptuous and resplendent things upon the tables of selfish gluttons, filling the halls with their Ambrosian scent. With this advice the young host was fully satisfied, and with the most joyful heart then did everything to serve us with lunch as well as possible.

[10] Thus, the two days passed with many a good discussion and visits by citizens of this small city.

[11] Some sick people were also healed merely by the laying on of hands, and to an honest doctor there, who understood nothing about the healing power of the laying on of hands, I pointed out quite a number of healing herbs with which he then achieved the best cures and by which he received a good reputation.

[12] On the third day however all but mother Mary and the four eldest brethren returned from home, bringing new disciples on all sides. Thomas in particular in this respect had made a big catch of fish, and brought a great many fried fish with him, for he knew how I liked eating such fish.

[13] The young Mark thus also brought his father Simon many greetings from home, and many fried fish as well, and Iscariot brought much money and much life into the company, since he was very lively and active, organizing everything and being exceptionally pleased with Me, and had much to relate about diverse happenings occurring all over the great Roman empire.

[14] After we were all gathered up thus I was bent on re-commencing the journey. But the host asked Me to remain till evening, since it was very hot. And I

remained till evening. But when the sun came close to setting I reminded the company to be ready for travel, as I was intent on re-commencing the journey at sunset.

## CHAPTER 90
### Healing of the son of a royal nobleman

**47. There was a royal nobleman whose son was lying ill at Capernaum. When he (the sick son's father) heard that Jesus had come from Judaea into Galilee, he came to Him (to Cana) and begged Him to go down (to Capernaum) and help his son who was dangerously ill.**

[1] As we were on the point of setting forth on our way a man of royal descent and a close relative of the commander, who a few days ago had gone to Capernaum, came hurrying towards Me almost out of breath for he had learned from the commander that I had again returned to Galilee from Judaea. This royal nobleman had an only son who suddenly had been attacked by a bad fever and the doctor in Capernaum had realized as soon as he saw the patient that he was quite beyond help. The father was in despair and did not know what to do in his grief. Then **Cornelius**, the commander, came to him and said: 'Brother, there is a way. It is less than an hour's brisk walk from here to Cana, where the famous healer Jesus of Nazareth is staying. I myself met Him there and spoke to Him on my journey here. He will surely still be there for He promised me to come from there directly to Capernaum and visit me. What He promises He also keeps without fail, and since He has not yet come to me He is definitely still in Cana. Therefore, hurry to Him personally and beg Him to come to your son and help him. And I can assure you that He will come immediately and help your son.'
[2] Having heard this from his brother Cornelius, the royal nobleman hurries to Cana and, as already mentioned, arrives there quite out of breath as I was just setting forth on My way. On reaching Me, he falls at My feet begging Me to hurry with him to Capernaum as his only son who is everything to him was dying and no doctor in Capernaum was able to help him. If I did not come quickly to Capernaum, his son would die before I got there if he had not died already.

**48. And Jesus said to him: "Unless you see signs and miracles, you will not believe."**

[3] I said: 'See, My friend, it is not easy with you people, for unless you see signs and miracles already in advance, you do not believe. I help only those who believe even if they have not seen any signs and miracles beforehand. For where I am approached with unconditional faith, I also heal surely and certainly.'

**49. The nobleman said to Him: "Sir, come down before my son dies."**

169

[4] Here **the royal man** exclaims: 'O Sir, do not discuss this at such length with me poor man; you can see that I do believe or I would not have come to you. I beg you, O Sir, just to enter my house and my son will live. But if you delay, he will die before you arrive. Look, I have many servants, and if I say to one or the other: do this or do that, he will do it. If I did not believe in you, O Lord, completely, I would have sent one or the other of my servants to you. But since I am filled with the firmest faith, I came myself. For my heart told me: "If only I find and see you, my son will become well. Lord, I also confess that I am not worthy to have you under my roof, but if you would only say one word, my son will become well and live.'

**50. Jesus says to him: "Go home, you son will live." The man believed what Jesus said and went home.**

[5] I said: 'Friend, such a faith I have not found anywhere in Israel. Go home confidently; you will receive according to your faith. You son will live.' And the nobleman went home in tears of gratitude and joy, for he believed My word without any doubt, but I still spent the night and the following day in Cana to the great joy of the host.

**51. When he was on the way down (towards Capernaum) his servant met him with the news: "Your child lives."**

[6] As the nobleman – who was much respected in Capernaum, on the one hand because he, like the commander Cornelius, was related to the ruling house in Rome and, besides, was a high-ranking officer appointed by Rome – approached the city his numerous servants were coming towards him announcing loudly: 'Master, your son lives and is perfectly well.'

**52. He asked them what time it was when he (the son) began to recover. They said: "Yesterday at the seventh hour the fever left him."**

[7] Then the man almost fainted with joy and asked at what time he had recovered. And the servants told him unanimously, 'Yesterday at the seventh hour the bad fever left him.'

**53. The Father noted that this was the exact time when Jesus had said to him: "Your son will live." And he and all his household became believers.**

[8] Hearing this from his servants he began to work out the time and found that it must have been the exact time when I had said to him "Your son will live." So he walked home at ease, and when he arrived the commander **Cornelius** already led the completely healthy and happy son towards him, saying: 'Well, brother, did I send you to the proper healer or not?'

[9] And **the royal man** said: 'Yes, brother, through your advice you have

restored my life tenfold. But this healer Jesus of Nazareth is obviously more than an ordinary healer who ever so skillfully knows how to cure diseases by means of medicinal herbs. Just imagine. Without ever having seen my son, He simply said "Your son will live", and the boy recovered at once. Listen, this is of great significance. I tell you: this is not possible to any man, but only to a god. And from now on I believe, and so does no doubt my whole household, that this Jesus is beyond any doubt a true God and for the salvation of all men walks among them in a human form and heals and teaches them. When he comes here he must be shown divine veneration.'

[10] Says **Cornelius**: 'I know Him already as that and am fully convinced, but He does not allow people to approach Him like that.'

[11] Says the father of **the healed boy**: 'Brother, where one has such evidence in hand, I think, one cannot do too much.'

[12] Says **Cornelius**: 'I fully agree with you, but as I have already told you it is a fact that He is a declared enemy of public and external marks of respect. As far as I know from His earliest childhood, only the silent, innermost mark of respect expressing itself in the love of the heart is acceptable to Him. All that is only external He even regards as irksome and if He came here, as he promised me, you might by a public worship drive Him away from this place forever. Therefore, do whatever you wish within your heart, but avoid all public ceremonies, for I know Him already since His birth in Bethlehem and have heard and seen much of Him since that time.'

[13] Says **the royal man**: 'All right, I followed your advice yesterday by day and will, therefore, listen to you and follow it also now at night.'

[14] (In order to avoid giving cause to hair-splitting, there should here be added a brief explanation regarding the word "yesterday". A day – in particular in Galilee – lasted only until the respective sunset and after the sun had set actually the next day already began a few minutes after sunset the previous day was already described as "yesterday". With the sunset began the first night watch for the coming day. A night watch, however, was a period of three hours and an hour of day was in summer equivalent to almost two of today's hours and in winter to not quite one, for the daylight time had to have always 12 hours whether the day was short or long. If here it says that the nobleman walked from Capernaum to Cana in one hour, it would nowadays amount to almost two hours. This brief explanation is all the more necessary as some things in this gospel could hardly be correctly understood, since the respective time references were only according to those times and not according to the present chronology.)

## CHAPTER 91
## 2,000 years of Gospel

**54. *This was now the second sign which Jesus performed after coming from Judaea into Galilee.***

[1] The following day in Cana I told John, who had recorded the first sign at the wedding, to record also this second sign performed in the same place. And this John also did with few words in eight verses as it is written.

[2] Also Matthew asked Me whether he too was to record this event, but I say to him: 'Leave it. When tomorrow we come to Capernaum where I shall again teach and perform signs, those you shall then record. But add to My Sermon on the Mount also the healing of the leper at Sychar, whom I healed as I was descending from the mountain.'

[3] Says **Matthew**: 'Lord, as far as I know two lepers were healed by You at Sychar. Which one should I record?'

[4] I said: 'Actually more than two were healed, but it is sufficient to mention the one I healed at the foot of the mountain and whom I bade show himself to the priest Jonael, whose name you need not give, and offer the sacrifice Moses has laid down for a witness. For who does not believe Me because of the one sign will not believe if I worked a hundred signs. Therefore, record from the many signs only the one I now told you about.'

[5] Says **Matthew**: 'Oh yes, Lord, now I know which sign You mean. I did make a note of it, but did not write it down in detail. This I will now do and start a new chapter with it. For I divided the Sermon on the Mount into three chapters and this will now be the fourth.'

[6] I said: 'For the time being this arrangement of yours is good, but after I shall have been lifted up from this Earth into My eternal Kingdom, you will have to write another 4 chapters preceding these. Therefore, you can already now give the 3 chapters on the Sermon on the Mount the numbers 5 till 7 instead of 1 to 3, and the new one will then become number 8.'

[7] So Matthew immediately arranged his notes in this way, and thus nowadays the Sermon on the Mount, although the first thing recorded by Matthew, is not contained in the first chapter, but only in the fifth, sixth and seventh chapters.

[8] To be acquainted with this fact is also needed for the better understanding of the Gospels of John and Matthew, for both of them were written under My personal supervision. The object here is mainly to bring the two outwardly apparently so different records into proper harmony, because it has almost always been the case that even good interpreters of the Scripture have regarded the miracles which appear similar in Matthew and John as the same, but have nevertheless been wondering "How come that Matthew says this and John that although the fact seems to be one and the same?"

[9] Many errors resulted from this and not seldom a complete turning away from My teaching as it is written in the Gospels.

[10] Here once could say indeed: "But why, O Lord, did You allow this to happen through so many centuries without enlightening anyone?" There I say:

[11] Not a century passed in which I did not, wherever My teaching is more or less accepted, choose and awaken men to give people the facts and necessary interpretation of the Gospels. The chosen have always done that and also historically supplemented in the records what had got lost, partly through human

negligence, partly through the obstinacy and not seldom evil intent of the various sectarian churchwardens and priests of the Gospel where My teaching was concerned, and only very few accepted that.

[12] The churches, which in the course of time had systematically developed naturally, rejected it declaring it to be "heresy" and "devilry" because it did not suit their greedy and tyrannical purpose.

[13] Scientists and artists on the other hand described such phenomena as "fantasy" and "dreamy nonsense" of a poor wretch who wants to be something too, but without having acquired the necessary qualities through effort, diligence, and profound study.

[14] In the place, however, where the chosen and awakened prophet lived and was known he was accepted least of all and, therefore, did not have much success. For according to people's notions, as they generally are, a prophet should actually not live on Earth at all, should not have a human shape, eat and drink and wear clothes, but should at least drive around in the air in a fiery chariot like Elijah and from there announce to each person only what he in his self-love likes to hear and what flatters him. That would then be a proper prophet at whom all eyes and ears would be directed, particularly if during his air travels he would miraculously throw great quantities of gold and silver coins to the rich, but small copper coins to the proletarians, at the same time praising the great, rich and mighty, but frequently severely disciplining the poor devils (proletarians), especially if they dared to grumble at the rich, great and mighty. Such a prophet would, of course, not be very popular with the poor, and they would not praise him.

[15] However, if the prophet is a man like any other man, if he eats and drinks, has even a home and besides maybe follows some worldly trade, oh, that is already the end where his prophesying is concerned. He is pronounced either a simpleton or a hypocrite and has not much chance of achieving anything in his homeland.

[16] Thus I have during the almost 2,000 years always made up what was missing. But who accepted it? I tell you: always only very few and these seldom actively enough. Notice of it was taken, but that someone should have changed his way of life accordingly and then in his spirit convinced himself that the otherwise natural man was really chosen by Me to bring a new light from the Heavens to men in the world that had gradually become so dark, that was never done for all kinds of idle reasons.

[17] One has bought himself a team of new oxen which he has now to break in for plowing, so he has, of course, no time. Another must cultivate a new field and cannot come because of that. A third has taken a wife and, therefore, has no longer any time or opportunity. A fourth must build a large house and has so many worries now, he cannot possibly have time. And thus everyone has some excuse and a new light from the Heavens then again burns in vain during a whole century in some hidden corner of the Earth. And if in the next century I again send a new light for illuminating the ancient records, it will have the same fate.

[18] If this is certainly so, judging by the experience at all times, the question

arises whether I can be blamed if the ancient records show to this day the same deficiencies that were already a thousand years ago discovered by idle rationalistic researchers and over-subtle brooders as a result of which always many doubters and, finally, rejecters of My teaching and its – and My – fullest divinity have gone forth like mushrooms from the ground.

[19] The reason why I am now giving a full light in this matter is so that in the end no one may be able to excuse himself as if since My bodily presence on Earth I had bothered neither about the purity and completeness of My teaching nor the people who accepted it.

[20] When I shall come again to Earth soon, I shall undertake a thorough sifting and not accept anyone who will come to Me with whatever excuses, for everyone who seeks in all earnest can and must find what he seeks. However, the sick sheep and asses feeding at the crib shall be administered medicine after which they are sure to become greedy for the feed from the Heavens, but then they will as convalescents be fed homeopathically for a long time. But now once more to the Gospel.'

## CHAPTER 92
### God's omniscience and His guidance

[1] When Matthew had finished his several verses the day after I had healed the nobleman's son from Capernaum, he showed Me his work, which I commended, as it was concise and to the point. But after packing his writing utensils he comes to Me asking how much writing material he shall need at Capernaum. If he is to keep more tablets unpacked then it should be easier to remove them from the main pack now rather than at Capernaum.

[2] I said: 'The 4 shall suffice, but I nevertheless have to make you aware of a small error in the ordering of your things. Basically there is not much to it, but since with Me everything has to have its proper order, it is unwise of you to first tie up your pack and ask Me only afterwards how many tablets you shall need. Had I now said "You shall need 5 at Capernaum", then you would now have had to untie the entire pack for just one tablet, which would have caused you unnecessary effort. But, prompted by My secret inspiration, you had to keep the exact number out and thereby save yourself the effort of re-opening the pack. But as I remarked already, there is not much to it, but often the advantage of the right order in all things, even if seeming ever so trivial, can be of great benefit.

[3] See, if someone washes in the morning, at midday and evening, starting with his face and only then the hands, then he won't get his face clean so soon, because going over same with dirty hands, but washing the hands first he shall be finished with his face more quickly, by rubbing it with clean hands.

[4] A man with a stony field cleared same with much effort, but he kept the following good order. First he gathered the largest stones, stacking them out of the field in a rectangular pile. This he did with the smaller stones also and so on down

to 10 different piles holding stones of similar size.

[5] **Neighbors** who saw him do it and who had cleared their fields by just tossing all their stones into one ordinary heap remarked: 'Look at the fool fussing with his stones.'

[6] But **a builder** passed by the road adjacent to his field. Seeing the 10 regular heaps he went to the man whom his neighbors called a fool and bought the stones off him for 40 silver denars, because in this order he was able to use them straight away. When the neighbors saw it they came up and said: 'Sir, why didn't you come to us? See, we have similar stones and would have given them to you for just a few dinars, whereas here you paid 40 silver dinars for the same stones.' But **the builder** said: 'Your stones I would have to first sort out, which would take much work, time and effort, but these here are already sorted, just as I need them now, and so I rather overpay for these than accept yours free.' Thereupon the neighbors of course started sorting their stones, but it was too late. Because the builder had enough with those he bought from the first, and these neighbors went to much effort for nothing.

[7] Therefore always keep the best order in all things. When someone then comes with an offer he is sure to always go for the best order. A later effort is often and many a time in vain. Do you follow this picture?'

[8] Says **Matthew**: 'O Lord, how should I not understand it? Is it not as bright and clear as the midday sun?

[9] But only one thing I would still like to find out from You, how was it possible for You to know that I shall require just four tablets at Capernaum? Because divine omniscience still is the greatest puzzle to me. Sometimes You know everything and arrange Your ways without asking anyone, yet at other times You ask and act like one of us, as if You did not know what happened or will happen. How come? Lord, please give me a little light on this.'

[10] I said: 'Friend, I would very much like to reveal this thing to you, but you could not grasp it; therefore let us leave it. But a time shall soon come when you shall easily grasp and comprehend such secrets.

[11] But this much I can say to you for now, that although God can know anything He likes in spite of man's freedom of will, yet when He chooses not to know, so that man would act freely, then He will also not know. Do you understand that?'

[12] Says **Matthew**: 'Lord, if so then man's life on Earth is most dangerous indeed. Which moderately knowledgeable person does not know the many enemies which confront poor mankind everywhere with all sorts of adversities, causing man's demise therewith? If without knowing so You permit this to go on just like that, then the health of the soul should fare badly.'

[13] I said: 'Not quite as badly as you think. Because firstly everyone shall be living in accordance with his beliefs and loves; and secondly man is free to at any moment call upon God for protection, and God shall turn His countenance towards him who pleads and help him in every adversity.

[14] Besides, everyone has been assigned a guardian angel anyway who has to guide him from his birth to his grave. Such a guardian angel always influences a

person's conscience and only begins to keep further and further away from his ward when the latter, guided by his self-love, has voluntarily relinquished all faith and all love for his neighbor.

[15] Thus man on this Earth is by far not as forsaken as you think, for everything depends on his free will and actions whether he wishes to be supervised and guided by God or not. If he wishes it, God will wish it too, but if he does not wish it, he is absolutely free as far as God is concerned and God does not take any further notice of him, except that he receives what according to universal order every natural man is destined to have as the natural life and what is needed to support it. But that is as far as God will and can go with such a person because of his inviolable freedom. Only when a man with his heart's free will seeks and implores Him, God will always come to meet such a man on the shortest possible way, provided he seeks and prays in downright earnest.

[16] But if a person only seeks and prays tentatively in order to convince himself whether where God and His promises are concerned there is anything to it, he will not be considered by God or his prayer granted. For God is in himself the purest love and looks only upon those who come to Him in their heart's pure love and seek Him for His own sake, wish to learn to know Him with gratitude as their Creator and have the fervent wish to be guarded and guided by Him personally.

[17] Oh, as concerns those who come to God in this way, He knows every moment only too well how things are with them, and He teaches and guides them personally in everything. However, of those who will have nothing to do with God He certainly does not take any notice.

[18] And when once in the beyond they will be standing before God, calling fervently and saying: "Lord, Lord", God will answer them: "Out of My sight, you strangers, for I have never known you". And such souls will then have to suffer and struggle considerably until they will be able to approach God as recognized by Him. Do you now understand this?'

[19] Says **Matthew**: 'Yes Lord, this I understand now quite well, plainly and clearly. But should I not at once record this great teaching, which ought to and must greatly encourage men to constantly search for and pray to God, that He would guide and lead them along the right paths?'

[20] I said: 'No, My dear friend and brother, because man would never grasp such teaching in its right and living fullness. Therefore you need not record it, except perhaps at a later stage, for yourself or a few brethren.

[21] But now, if you all are ready to continue our journey to Capernaum, then let's be on our way. Whoever will, let him follow us, but whoever prefers to stay, let him stay. I must go there, as there is much misery there, as well as in the small cities around the lake, which is a Galilean sea.'

# CHAPTER 93
## The Lord forces no one

[1] We are ready to go, but the young host once again comes to ask Me to stay with him for the evening.

[2] But I say: 'I shall come again soon, because before going to the next feast at Jerusalem, I have to visit Nazareth, and shall stop off on the way there and back.'

[3] Replies **the host**: 'Lord, this shall be my greatest pleasure. But as You intend not staying any longer today, be so good and allow me to accompany You again.'

[4] I said: 'This is up to you, because no one shall on My part be coerced into anything. Whoever receives Me, let him do so, and whoever wants to follow Me and My teaching, let him do likewise, because I and My kingdom are voluntary and therefore need to be gained in all freedom.

[5] Only the freest self-determination counts with Me. Whatever is over or under that is without worth before Me and My Father, who is in Me, as I am within Him.

[6] Every compulsion other than from the very own heart is foreign and cannot possibly be of any value for a person's very own life according to My eternal and, thus, freest order.

[7] Of what use would it actually be to you if you claimed some work of art, which was created by another hand, to be your work? If then someone came and asked you to reproduce this work for a high reward, you would be ruined and have to put up with being called before the whole world by the one who ordered the work, a liar, cheat and boaster with another person's success.

[8] Thus also the full cultivation of his own life has been put into every person's very own hands.

[9] That which before God's eyes will once at every individual person's great life-trial be recognized as foreign to him, will be of no value to him and will be taken away. Then it will be said: "Who has, will keep what he has and will be given even much more, but who does not have his own, will forfeit what he has, since it is not his own, but only something foreign."

[10] I tell you that it is now not even necessary that you go with Me, but if following an inner prompting you want to do so out of love for Me, you will thereby not only lose nothing, but gain tenfold in everything. For whoever does something out of true love for Me will here be rewarded tenfold, but one in My Kingdom a hundredfold, also a thousand fold and endlessly.'

[11] Says **the innkeeper**: 'Lord, if this is so I shall definitely go with You, for my own heart prompts me to do so and, therefore, I will strictly follow my heart.'

[12] I said: 'Very well, do that and you will be living according to your heart which is the sole proper life, for every other kind of life that does not stem from the heart is not life, but a death of every man's own life. I as the sole Lord over all life am telling you this.'

[13] The innkeeper is very happy with this, takes immediately his knapsack and some money and is getting ready for the journey.

[14] But I say to him: 'Free yourself from everything and you will travel much

lighter, for thieves fall only upon those whom they know to be carrying something with them. If you do not have anything, they can also not take anything away.'

[15] Thereupon the innkeeper hands his knapsack and money to his wife and follows Me without money and knapsack.


## CHAPTER 94
### The curse and the dangers of money

[1] But **Judas Iscariot**, standing next to him says: 'But I maintain that a small amount of money on a journey surely can harm no one?'

[2] But I say:, 'He who knows Me the way this host does, having been with Me also at Sychar, knows that one can do quite well at My side also without money. See, I have neither pockets in My coat, and even less any trace of money, yet I led many hundreds through Judea and Samaria to here. Ask them how much this journey cost everyone.

[3] On top of that I tell you that shortly I shall be feeding many thousands while not having more money than now.

[4] I tell you, a proper trust in God is worth more than all the treasures of the world, with which you can help your flesh indeed for a short time, but not your soul. But if you have ruined and therefore lost your soul, what can you give later to ransom your soul?'

[5] Says **Judas**: 'Yes, yes, You are right indeed, but man has to have money for some things.'

[6] I reply: 'How much money did Moses have when he led the Israelites out?' **Judas** says: 'He was in possession of gold, silver and precious stones aplenty.'

[7] Say I: 'That he had indeed. But this also held him back from entering the promised land. Can you actually grasp this?'

[8] Says **Judas**: 'Here I should think that with Moses, the prophet of all Jehovah's prophets, not the gold and silver which he had to bring from Egypt on Jehovah's prompting was responsible, but that in a weak moment he failed to build upon Jehovah's faithfulness sufficiently.'

[9] Say I: 'And what was the reason for his weakening one day? He who caused Moses to weaken due to his thought about the gold and silver now stands before you telling you this. It is however written allegorically, but in reality it is and was as I now explained it to you.'

[10] Says **Judas**: 'All right, I believe You that it was then so. But now, half way around the world, through the king of Rome money has been introduced as a lawful means of exchange for facilitating interchange among people, and we are obliged to make use of same, and thus I think that if it is not a sin to drop money in God's offertory, it neither is a sin to give such money to some poor person, that he may provide for himself for a few days, and therefore even for the benefit of the poor it is already proper to carry money, once lawfully introduced by the state, and

so the host Koban could have hung unto his few silver dinars.'

[11] Say I: 'You do indeed carry with you a well-stocked purse, yet you refused to give any alms to the three poor who begged you for alms yesterday, and therefore I don't think you make that commendable use of money for which you are praising its virtues to Me.

[12] But regarding the money in God's offertory, I tell you plainly, this is a ravaging abomination, not so much on account of some spiritually deprived who think to have secured Heaven therewith, but for those who take the money out of the chest and squander it on harlots by night. So long as there was no money, there were no public whores, as it is now. But since there is money now and many small coins there are now at Jerusalem as in all other cities prostitutes in great numbers, with the men sinning with them day and night. And when those who possess much money lose taste for the local ones, they let them be brought from the uplands, buying them in Greece, to then carry on in Judea the most ignominious harlotry with them. And look, all this and a thousand fold more is the blessing of your highly praised money.

[13] But this is only the start of the curse hanging over money.

[14] But there will come times worse than when Noah built his ark, and they will have to attribute their misery to gold and silver, and nothing short of a fire from the Heavens which shall consume all that excrement from Hell shall save mankind from that tribulation of all tribulations.'

[15] Says **Judas**: 'Yes, yes, You are a prophet without equal and are capable of knowing that, but if money is used correctly then surely it can do no harm?'

[16] Say I: 'I say unto you, indeed, if applied correctly, just as one can use everything else on Earth the right or wrong way. But the big difference consists in, when you go to a city, you have to carry all sorts of things on your back, either tools or food, and you shall obtain other things or food and drink therewith, in accordance with your requirements. This of course is a bit inconvenient, yet at the same time hard or being seduced into sin. Because if you arrive with junk and bundle, or pulling a cart, and come to a whore to sin, in exchange for a few pots and pans, she will deride and laugh at you, and you shall be saved from sin. Coming to her with gold and silver however, she shall neither deride nor laugh at you, but guide you to her brothel and seduce you to sin, with all sorts of attractions, in order the more to relieve you of your gold and silver. Therefore money is a most convenient object, yet also seductive and convenient for sinning.

[17] And for this reason Satan introduced it into the world, so it is easier to sin in the world. Are you not aware of how opportunity breeds thieves?'

[18] Says **Judas**: 'Sure, sure, this is true. But if all this is just to discourage thieves from finding anything around men for arousing their fancy, then immense changes would have to be introduced among mankind. Firstly, all men should have to be equally poor in worldly goods, secondly resemble each other like male and female sparrows, and thirdly not be wiser than anyone else. So long as this is not the case however all talking, teaching and working of signs is in vain. Many shall of course reform, but ten times that many shall remain the same in spite of all teaching and signs, if not worse, and quite easily ten times so, because surely,

every man has self-love and likes to be reasonably well-provided. Therefore, quite naturally, every man first thinks of himself and only then of others. And this surely cannot be held against him. House and land not everyone can have, otherwise God would have to bring house and land into the world with every new-born, to grow up with him. Since this is not the case however, with all the previously born already taking possession of every spot of land, making it impossible for newly-born to possess even a foot-wide piece of land, then nothing remains for them to do in the end but to either make themselves indispensable to the lazy owners through all sorts of education and service, or turn to thievery in order not to be reduced to beggary. If then the more advantaged part of those without land and home receive nothing but money, and then save as much as possible for the old days, then I find nothing wrong therewith, and discover a new creation therein of land and soil, for all those born unto this Earth through procreation and birth without the least landed hope. And I must openly maintain that God, being either unable or unwilling to create land for every new-born, has given the rulers the idea of coinage, whereby children of the landless can acquire a necessary living, often better than that consisting in land ownership. And surely it cannot be God's will that children of the landless should perish? For surely it is not their fault to be born into the world with the same needs as those landed gentry.

[19] Even if You may be the greatest prophet that ever walked this Earth and I concede everything You have taught and are still to teach, this Your appraisal of me regarding the harmfulness of money I cannot concede. Because however harmful money can be in Your view, so can everything else be harmful. If I possessed all the sheep, oxen, cows, calves, donkeys, poultry and pigeons, and all the fruit and bread, stolen in our country just since David, then I would be the wealthiest man in all Israel. And fornication was carried on as badly and worse than today when there was no money, such as in Sodom and Gomorrah and Babylon.

[20] I do not want to say that You are altogether wrong in what you said about money, but where, on this poor Earth, is there an object with which thousandfold wickedness has not already been committed? But if God does not altogether condemn such misuse, why should He suddenly be so angry and cursing about money?'

[21] Say I: 'Whatever someone loves, that he also has the intellect to commend. You love money excessively and therefore well know how to praise it. Therefore I shall say no more about it to you, because what one loves, one also knows how to praise. But you nevertheless shall in the not too distant future learn about the curse of money. But now no more about it. The road to Capernaum is long and we must get there before dark and look for an inn.'

180

## CHAPTER 95
### The nature of Judas

[1] There Thomas stepped over to Judas Iscariot, reproaching him for daring to come to Me with his foolish money-ideas, since I am Jehovah Himself in Spirit and work deeds possible only to God.

[2] Says **Judas** to him: 'You still are as stupid as you have always been. Because you believe either every old wives' tale, or, when you feel like it, nothing at all. Not seldom when taking fish to the market you sell the small like the big, the buyers laughing in your face. But you still are as you always were, neither thinking nor speculating, living foolishly into the day by habit.

[3] I have been here only a few hours in the company of this great prophet and it is my sacred duty to probe Him as much as possible in His attitude and the thrust of His mandate. You have been around Him already for about a half year and would have to therefore know Him better then I. Ought I however, just because you know Him already, make no effort to get to know Him at least as well as you know Him by now?'

[4] Says **Thomas**: 'Surely you are not thinking of going back home again tomorrow, since you are trying to find out everything today? Just as well the Lord has started at last to move again, otherwise you would not have been in the clear about your foolish money even by tomorrow. The Lord is right. Cursed money will be the death of you, since you see such glory in it. The Lord surely has made it clear to you what there is to money and how much it can be to the detriment of man's spiritual life, but you have long been wiser than God Himself and therefore put on your crown of wisdom right in front of God. But be careful not to suffocate in wisdom once.

[5] But what have you to say about my fish sales. Was I not always the first to sell all my fish, whereas you with all your clever talk had to still carry half of yours home. I sold the ten big as well as the ten little ones for two pence each and could have always sold five times that many, had I brought that many to market. And here my reckoning was evidently better than yours, thinking yourself wiser than God, yet a miser seeking your salvation in money. I pay no penny for such wisdom.'

[6] **Judas** says, somewhat bewildered: 'All speak the way they understand it. Says **Thomas**: 'That's right. You understand this with your foolishness and therefore speak accordingly. But, take a look over where that destitute is squatting. Give him your purse and for once in your life you shall have acted wisely.'

[7] Says **Judas**: 'That I shall leave well alone, no one having ever actually given me anything in the real sense of the word; and therefore I shall give no one a thing.'

[8] Says **Thomas**: 'This is a most commendable code, fit to be cursed on the dot. You'll get really far with our Savior and Master with these principles, I can vouch for you. He in Himself is the highest generosity and you a miser without

equal. A good match.'

[9] Says **Judas**: 'Once I shall have worked Him over and He sees how one has to live in the world, He shall come down from His generosity somewhat. Besides it is not all that hard to live generously at the expense of those who have something and prepare good meals for one's disciples. Listen, if I come across fools like this young host, then I too shall be as generous at his expense as anyone shall ever be. But let this Jesus, who was penniless from birth, sustain and maintain His many disciples from His own means, then we shall see how generous He is going to be and whether He won't soon be getting rid of all these followers.'

[10] Says **Thomas**: 'I say to you nothing other than that you are of the devil, because only the devil can talk the way you just did. It may sound as though it had some sense in it, but it isn't so and quite otherwise and your talk is the most shameless in the world. It grieves me to have shown you the way over here. At Sychar there were so many hundreds, yet all were fed from the Heavens. And in a few moments He rebuilt Irhael's house to the most luxurious in the city. And you immense, shameless, very dumb fool, want to as it were demonstrate to me, who have with my physical eyes seen the Heavens open, with countless myriads of angels of God ascending and descending, that Jesus is a poor devil who is enjoying Himself at the expense of others? Oh you poor beggar, you. He to whom belong Heaven and Earth, because He has founded them with His all might, should have need of your or my treasures, to enable Him to live on this world, on which He makes the fruit to grow and ripen? Oh you blind fool. Go to Sychar to convince yourself and we shall see whether you will still blubber that way.'

[11] Here **Judas** with a cunning smile says sarcastically: 'You actually saw this with your eyes? Or did you by chance borrow some oxen and donkey eyes, giving you such extraordinary sights and overviews? I am glad, by the way, that the Nazarene-wise also got to know beautiful Irhael, who, I heard just recently, is supposed to be living with her sixth man already, because the other five died, of her body as it were. There, with that fair one, Heaven standing nicely open for you. Sure, sure, Irhael has transferred quite a few to Heaven. Why should she make an exception with you? But I shall nevertheless not be going to Sychar for her, because I keep Moses' statutes and shall have nothing to do with such sinful stuff.'

## CHAPTER 96
## IN CAPERNAUM
### The Lord's hints about Judas

[1] Thomas gets quite beside himself with rage at these Judas' caustic remarks and is about to heave into Judas with all energy. But, nearly half-way towards Capernaum, I step up to Thomas and say: 'Brother, so long as you still see Me calm and collected, remain the way you can see Me, if only you will keep looking My way. Certainly if you once see Me start hitting out, then you can by all means

jump in and hit with all you've got. But now there is no need of it by a long shot. Come what may, right stays right and Judas stays Judas. He is by no means condemned to this the way night is, being the Earth's natural shadow, but if he wants to remain Judas, let him, but we remain what we are. Yet time will tell how far he shall get with his Judas spirit.'

[2] Says **Thomas**: 'But this much You could do, Lord, that You get him away from Yourself, otherwise he shall be a lot of trouble to us, because he has a swinish and evil mouth.'

[3] I said: 'I did not tell him to come and therefore will not tell him to go, but if he wants to go whither he came, we shall not be weeping for him. But keep away from him, because you two shall not be getting along. But forgive him as I forgive him and your heart shall be free.'

[4] Says **Thomas**: 'When it comes to forgiveness on my part there is no problem, for I never bore him a grudge, even though I have always known him as one human not easy to get along with, not even the prophet John, with whom he frequently quarreled. But I would honestly be much happier if he didn't belong to our company.

[5] When I was home recently I related quite a few of Your deeds to my acquaintances, who could not have been more amazed. This came to Judas' ears and who could have made up their minds more quickly to become Your disciple than Judas? For John's teaching did not satisfy him, because the former preached nothing but the most profound repentance, proclaiming God's strictest judgment to all who did not truly repent – the cause of the repeated quarrelling between him and John.

[6] John was all repentance and Judas the extremist opposite. He kept telling John to his face that so-called repentance in sackcloth and ashes was the greatest silliness in human life and man should reform in deed and not sackcloth and ashes.

[7] John did not really make true repentance dependent on sackcloth and ashes, presenting it only so metaphorically in his sermons, so to say, but the seemingly more understanding Judas would have none of this, saying that teachings of such grave import to humanity should be in clear, understandable words.

[8] According to him, the prophets all were donkeys talking in images which could be interpreted in any old way; none other than they had ruined the priests, kings and entire nations therewith. In short, all were donkeys high or low if not thinking and acting as did he; that's why I think he won't fit in with us'.

[9] I said: 'My dear Thomas, what you told Me I have known for a long time; yet I say to you, if he wants to go, let him and if he wants to stay, let him. I know much more about him yet and even what he shall shortly do to Me; nevertheless, if he wants to, let him stay. Because his soul is a devil desiring to learn wisdom from God, but this bent shall yield this soul a wretched gain. But now no more about it. Only too soon we shall have occasion to get unto him. With this we have also arrived at Capernaum's walls and I see a Roman centurion rush towards us through the gates, accompanied by the chief commander Cornelius and the

nobleman; here there is another sick to heal.'


## CHAPTER 97
## The sick servant of the centurion

[1] Matthew Chapter 8. It is here that Matthew begins to record a condensed version, writing to where I go to another feast at Capernaum.

[2] We quietly proceed the remaining hundred paces or so and entering the city precincts, **the centurion** steps up to Me, beseeching Me: 'Lord, my servant lies at home sick with palsy, grievously tormented, unable to do a thing.'

[3] Say I to the centurion: 'I will come and heal him.'

[4] But **the centurion** replies: 'Lord, I am not worthy of Your coming under my roof, but say only a word and my servant shall be well. For see, I am a mere human, subject like many to higher authority, notwithstanding that I have many soldiers under me who obey me. If I say to the one, do thus, he does it, or if I tell him to go, he goes. And I tell another to come and he comes. And if I tell my servant to do this or that, he does it immediately.

[5] But to Yourself all spirits are subject and You are a Lord in all fullness over all in Heaven, on and in the Earth. You have therefore only to intimate it to Your powers, invisible to us humans and they carry out Your will instantly.'

[6] The reason for this centurion's so trustful request on behalf of his servant is his having convinced himself, both through the quick healing of the noble official's son, as well as the chief commanders many a tale of how I could just through the word heal from afar; and this led him to approach Me in the manner of the noble official, when hearing of My nearing his city.

[7] Hearing such trustful talk from the centurion, I marveled aloud. Not for Myself of course but the disciples, saying not so much to the centurion as to those who were with Me: 'Verily, I have not found so great a faith in Israel yet. But I say unto you that many shall come from the East and West and shall sit down with Abraham, Isaac and Jacob in the kingdom of Heaven (i.e. those possessing the glory of the father). But the sons of the kingdom shall be cast out into outer darkness; there shall be weeping and gnashing of teeth.'

[8] Many were startled by this prelude, saying: 'Lord, are You going to actually cast out the children and put the heathen in their place?'

[9] And I said: 'Neither the children, nor the heathen. He who believes and has the love in him, whether Jew, Greek or Roman, shall be accepted.'

[10] Thereafter I turn to the centurion and say: 'Go your way, be it done to you in accordance with your faith.'

[11] The centurion thanks Me from the fullness of his heart, betaking himself to his house, finding fulfillment there of everything he had asked in faith, the which was undoubting before, as well as afterwards, because his servant was made whole in the same hour I said to the centurion, be it done to you in accordance with your faith.

[12] This sign in Capernaum itself, together with the former with the noble official, who was a councilor of Capernaum, aroused great sensation in this city, mostly among the Romans and Greeks who were domiciled there, but among the Jews and the priests and scribes placed there by Jerusalem so to speak, permanently, it only provoked annoyance, wrath and rage.

## CHAPTER 98
### The people challenge the priests

[1] Because the ordinary people who had seen the signs, too fearful of the priests and scribes to convert to My teaching and follow Me, devised a clever trick, they soon brought several sick to the priests, saying: 'Hear us, you exalted priests and scribes, who according to your own testimony are initiated into all God's mysteries. The man Jesus of Nazareth is working wonders such as no man has done before him and his speech and teaching are like a torrent of fire which almightily consumes or carries away everything that would oppose it. Without medicine and only through the word, akin to a god, he heals every sickness and is supposed to even bring alive the dead through just the naked word.

[2] After convincing ourselves of the truth of all this, a good thought struck us and being mindful of you we spoke among ourselves. Why are we wondering so mightily at this? Do we not have priests and scribes initiated into all God's mysteries, who are sure to be capable of just like this Jesus heal the sick through the mere word, if only they want to. We were already on our way to take our sick to the Nazarene, but we thought of our circumcision and the covenant and of not straying from same as long as it can in all truth give us all we have need of, physically and spiritually. But since this Jesus is working such immense signs we are imperiled unless we can confront him with equal signs-power.

[3] Therefore we brought several sick with us and would ask you, for your own as well as our good that you would, through your spiritual power, which according to your testimony you are given directly from God, to just through your word heal these sick, who are not actually counted among the most serious cases.

[4] We shall criss-cross the whole city with these, healed by yourselves, and glorify God before each house and proclaim your fame with strong voice. Then the Nazarene shall not find much of a reception here and in the end be forced to so to speak make off shamed and ridiculed.'

[5] **The priests and scribes**, only too conscious of their total impotence, to hide same speak with gravity: 'You fools. How are you asking of us what befits only God? When did a priest or scribe ever work miracles? This only God and the high priest in the Jerusalem Temple can do, when the latter enters the Holy of Holies. Therefore take your sick to Jerusalem. If you will make the right offerings, they are bound to find healing, God willing of course. Should God not will it however, then you will just have to put up with taking your sick home again, sick.

[6] We indeed have been initiated into the most diverse mysteries of God, but

not into His might, which is holy and which He bestows upon no mortal.

[7] But whoever like this Jesus still performs deeds, as we have heard, either through magic or with the help of Beelzebub, is a monster of Hell, which is the most cursed dwelling-place of God's adversary. And whoever is converted by his teaching and signs, is also then in relation to God and His servants that which such servant of the devil is himself. This is the fullest truth. Woe betide you if you go over to Jesus, accepting his teaching and help.'

[8] Say **those who brought the sick** to the priests and scribes: 'You are liars all when you talk like that. How can he be of the devil and a servant of Beelzebub who only does exceeding good to mankind, preaching only love and gentleness and patience to his disciples, fully practicing what he preaches?

[9] You yourselves are indeed of the devil when you give him testimony like that; he however is of God, in that he does the will of God as he teaches.

[10] You have called us fools for sure, for having for your own good asked of you something which after all you had a thousand times claimed to be capable of doing through prayer and the word of God, but now, when as never before it comes to demonstrating your old doctrine, you call us fools for taking you at you word. Oh you wicked servants of Beelzebub. We shall kindle you a light, from whose glitter you shall all die.'


## CHAPTER 99
## IN BETHABARA
### The temple servants' anger. Peter's daughter-in-law.

[1] On hearing such speech from their co-religionists, the priests and scribes quickly withdraw. Because the number of those who had come to them was about a hundred, and deadly earnest was flashing from their eyes, for these had long since seen who was behind the Jewish priests and scribes, hating them more than pestilence.

[2] But since the priests, Pharisees and scribes were only too well aware of how the Jews were just subtly challenging them, to have a stronger case against them for the purpose of then following Me more determinedly (because in those days it was even harder to leave the Jewish church for another than it is today to leave the Roman Catholic for the Reformed), the former now watched Me closely, secretly plotting My ruin.

[3] But the centurion with whom I had now been staying in Capernaum for two days had confided in Me what went on and how the Jewish clergy was outraged with Me and even secretly strove after My life.

[4] I said: 'They shall indeed be achieving their evil aims with Me, but time is not yet. But to avoid giving them too much opportunity for their vengeance, I shall move to another city for a short while, but come here again at a later stage, when these infidels shall have somewhat cooled down in their rage.'

[5] Although he would have endlessly preferred to have Me stay, the centurion

commended My plans, since his fear of these priests, scribes and Pharisees was not inconsiderable, in that he was well aware of the artful, secret denunciations in Rome, which this brood of vipers was capable of.

[6] I then, with My entire company of followers, the following morning left the exceedingly hospitable centurion's house, moving to Simon Peter's house in the vicinity of Bethabara, where John had formerly been at work. On entering Peter's simple but quite spacious house, Peter's daughter-in-law, a good and normally hard-working and chaste maiden of some 20 years, lay bed-ridden with heavy fever and in exceeding fear and pain. Peter stepped over to Me, asking Me to help her.

[7] And I immediately went to her bed, taking her by the hand and saying: 'Arise, little daughter and prepare us a meal, rather than suffer here in bed.'

[8] Instantly the fever left her and the girl got up, serving us with much diligence and attentiveness.


## CHAPTER 100
### The miraculous catch

[1] Here Matthew comes to Me and asks Me whether he should record also this sign and many an instruction and speeches I had given during the few days at the house of the chief of a synagogue.

[2] I said: 'The sign with the centurion outside Capernaum and what I said there, and this present sign at the house of Peter, too, but omit the words spoken which do not belong to the open teaching. However, the discussions at the house of the synagogue chief and the fact that I stayed with him for two days, do not mention at all.

[3] We shall soon be once more at the house of this man at the time when his favorite daughter will die whom I will then awaken and restore to him. Then you may write about him and the sign in such a way that you give no details regarding him or the place, otherwise we would prejudice him in a worldly sense as the priesthood is already watching him, and this we will and shall not do.

[4] Until the next feast in Jerusalem I shall work many more signs and teach a good deal in this region of the sea, which I like best, and you will have to record all the precepts in full.'

[5] **Matthew** now prepares for writing, but John is quite sad and says: 'But Lord, You my supreme love. Shall I not get any more to write?'

[6] I said: 'Do not be sad, My beloved brother. You will still get many things to write down. But I have destined you for the most important and most profound things.'

[7] Says **John**: 'But the sign You worked at Cana on the son of the royal officer does not seem to be greater and more important than what You did for the centurion outside Capernaum?'

[8] I said: 'If you think this, you are quite wrong, for the son of the royal officer

represents the entire, extremely depraved world and how it is now given help from a distance through My teaching and My spiritual influence. The servant of the centurion, however, represents for the present just the palsied servant whom I healed and only then also some community or society in My name which because of all kinds of political considerations completely lacks activity according to My teaching in one or the other point and thereby gradually becomes inactive also in the other points. That is then also a palsy of the souls which can be helped only by a firm belief in My word.

[9] See, My dear brother John, this constitutes a considerable difference between the two signs. The first one represents the entire world's condition of spiritual sickness, and I tell you, in an even more profound sense also of all infinity. The second sign, however, represents only that which I have just explained to you. Thus you now know what you have to describe and what Matthew.'

[10] But now the girl with Peter's other servants have prepared lunch and we therefore shall tuck into same and then in the afternoon help Peter to catch some good fish. But towards evening we shall have plenty to do.'

[11] We now partook of an ample meal, sufficiently plenteous for the large company and then betook ourselves to sea, named also the sea of Galilee, catching in a few hours an enormous lot of the most choice fish, to the extent that these could hardly be accommodated in the fish tanks.

[12] This scared **Peter**, making him exclaim in a kind of pious daze: 'I beg You to depart from me O Lord, for I perceive myself too much a sinful man. You had already once scared me when, still unknown to me, You turned up from nowhere to find me fishing with my helpers. Already then I had recognized Your deity, but now I am getting even more scared, seeing only too clearly What and who basically You are. Then, as now, there was fishing all night without gain, so to speak, but upon Your Word and presence the nets were overstraining with the vast catch. This now truly scares me, for You are ...'

[13] I said: 'Be still and do not give Me away, because you know that 'one' among us. This one is and remains a betrayer.'

[14] Now Peter is quiet, getting on with stocking the fish. And it being evening, we betake ourselves home, where through Peter's healed daughter-in-law, an abundant dinner awaits us. All now are happy and in good spirits, and Peter starts up a song of praise, with the others responding in accord.

## CHAPTER 101
### The unusual wine-miracle for Judas

[1] When **Peter** had finished the song, he spoke in a most somber tone: 'My friends and brethren, what a contrast between us and David once, when he gave the nation this glorious song of praise. As he sang, he lifted up his eyes to the stars. Because then, according to men's concepts, Jehovah dwelt in the

unapproachable light above all stars. But what would David now do here, since He to whom he lifted up his eyes above all stars...' I said: 'Halt Peter, friend, let it suffice and consider all those we have among us.'

[2] Peter remembers at once and invites the guests to partake of the evening meal, consisting mostly in bread and well-cooked fish.

[3] But Judas inquires of Peter whether wine could be bought for money in this vicinity. And **Peter** replies: 'A couple of furlongs distance, at the inn, wine is sold.' Hearing this, Judas further asks whether he has no one to send down for a barrel full.

[4] Says **Peter**: 'You know as well as I do that I have no one to send. But if you want wine then go to the publican yourself and strike a deal and you shall come off the better.' Says **Judas**: 'I shall rather do without than go myself.' Says **Peter**: 'Do as you like. I can't spare you servants, as my fishers are still busy at sea and my wife and children and in-laws have their hands full, as you can see. You are not going to ask me to cart a whole barrel here at night by myself?' Says **Judas** somewhat annoyed: 'Now, now, I only meant well, seeing you have no wine, because I myself would have paid for it, no matter what price.'

[5] Says **Peter**: 'There is One among us who converted water into wine at Cana at the wedding of Simon, who also is here. The One could also do so now, if necessary. Since however it surely is not necessary, we can also make do with the very choice water from my well.'

[6] Says **Judas**: 'Right enough, right enough, I am happy therewith too, since I myself greatly commend good water. Yet precisely on an occasion like this wine would not go amiss. But since this One, whom I too deem myself to know, is capable of making water into wine, He surely could also do you the favor?'

[7] I said: 'So go down to the well and drink. Because to you the well shall supply wine, but to us all, just water.'

[8] Judas at once went down to the well and drew. But as he drank from the water drawn, it was wine of the best kind and he got so drunk as to be prostrated by the well, in danger of falling into the well, which was deep, had not some of Peter's servants spotted him, bringing him into the house and into a bed. But it was good thus, because that evening I healed many of all kinds of sicknesses and plagues and exorcised many of their evil spirits, and in the face of such signs Judas would have been a nuisance.


## CHAPTER 102
### The healing of all sick people in Capernaum

[1] When all who were with Me had finished supper, while Judas slept on a straw mattress in the outhouse, those same Jews who the previous day had put the priest, scribes and Pharisees to the test, brought a great many possessed and a great many others suffering all kinds of ills, imploring Me to heal them all.

[2] And I asked them in a lovingly earnest manner whether they believed that

189

the Nazarene carpenter's son was able to do so. Because these people knew Me so to speak from birth.

[3] But they answered and said: 'What have we to do with the carpenter's son? If the carpenter's son was chosen of God to become a prophet to the people of Israel, then he is a prophet even if a thousand fold carpenter's son, because each man is what he is out of God and never what his parents were. And so we believe without doubt that you are firstly a God-tutored prophet and that you therefore secondly can help everyone, as you helped the son of the city councilor and the centurion's servant.'

[4] And I answered them: 'Now then, since your faith in Me and your assessment of Me are such, be it done to you according to your faith.'

[5] Upon this word, all the spirits left the possessed and those suffering all kinds of sickness and plagues became well instantly.

[6] It hardly needs to be described how astonished and grateful they were.

[7] After that, many fitting but also bitingly sharp remarks were made about the Jewish priesthood, but I rebuked the accusers and showed them it is unwise to awaken a brood of sleeping vipers. For as long as they are hibernating they are without harm and danger to anyone, but on awakening they are more dangerous than at other moments when they are not asleep.

[8] Those temple servants, full of cunning and malice, had indeed been sleeping like a brood of vipers in winter, but through your bold request, you have forcibly roused them from sleep. Guard against their harming you therefore, because this adulterous kind derives lascivious pleasure from doing harm.'

[9] All recognize the truth of this lecture and regret the mischief they brought about by their rashness. But I comfort them and tell them not to divulge the sign worked here at Capernaum, except to some trusted friends of truth, who also know how to keep silence. And they assured Me of it.

[10] But there was one amongst them who, although not counted among the priesthood, nevertheless was very well versed in the scriptures.

[11] This one stepped in front of the crowd, speaking in an earnest manner: 'Listen, beloved friends and brothers! In this deed I have discovered something which bespeaks more than just saying "see, this man is a true prophet." I believe that this act took place in fulfillment of the prophecies of Isaiah, when he spoke, *"Surely He has borne our grief and carried our sorrows."* Don't you notice anything?'

[12] The people looked at the speaker in astonishment, not understanding him. He repeats his question and with the people still not grasping his quotation from Isaiah, he says: 'It is not easy to preach about the colors of the rainbow to the blind.'

[13] I said: 'Calm down, it is better for these people not to grasp it for the present. Because if these people were to grasp this immediately, they would run over to the priests and start a mighty argument and this should be good neither for yourselves nor from the viewpoint of My teaching. But when the right time comes they shall grasp even with the hands what the prophet was saying.'

[14] The speaker settled down with that, while the crowd whose possessed and

sick I had healed this evening, left with their healed.

[15] But when the crowd arrived at home in Capernaum they caused a furor among their acquaintances, and when the next morning hardly began to dawn, Peter's house already was surrounded by an immeasurable crowd, wanting to see Me who had performed such incomprehensibly immense wonder. And Peter asked Me what should be done, since the crowd continued growing.

[16] I said: 'Get the large boat ready and we shall go to the other side of the sea, otherwise there will be trouble here. Although the people are here with the best intention, also the priests are sneaking up behind them, and at this stage we do not want to have anything to do with them.'

[17] Peter immediately made the largest ship ready, which we soon boarded and began to sail fast across the sea, helped by a fair wind.

[18] However, before I had boarded the ship with the disciples **a teacher of the law from Capernaum** came up to Me and said: 'Rabbi, allow me to follow you where you are going.' But since I saw that his secret motive in wishing to follow Me was by no means an honorable one, and that he was not much interested in My teaching and all My deeds, but only wanted to be provided for and if profitable commit secret acts of treachery, I shook My head and said to him: 'The foxes have their holes, the birds under the sky have their nests, but the Son of Man has in this world not even a stone belonging to Him upon which He may lay His head.'

[19] And the man understood Me, turned away and went home. For thereby I gave him to understand that he, too, was a cunning fox and had his hole (a paid position) and that birds of his kind living under the sky, i.e. a feeding and resting place, where they consumed their prey, but that with the Son of Man nothing is to be found of all the worldly deceit, not even a so-called political emergency-trick (stone), upon which one could occasionally rest the head of one's mind. The teacher of the law, as already mentioned, did understand Me correctly and quickly returned to Capernaum without any further argument.


## CHAPTER 103
### Jesus and the storm

[1] Before we boarded the ship, one of My disciples came to Me asking for My permission to bury, before we left, his father who had died so suddenly the previous night. I however said to him: 'You better follow Me and let the dead bury their dead.' And the disciple immediately refrained from his request and followed me into the ship, for he understood that it is better to be concerned with life than with death – a futile concern – indeed, best suited for the dead, for all those who make much of funeral pomp are more or less dead. They pay their respect to death and the honor of death is most important to them.

[2] Man's true death is selfishness and its spirit is pride which above all craves for glory. Thus, the pompous funeral of a deceased is nothing else but the last display of pride of a person who has been spiritually dead for a long time.

[3] When the disciple had grasped the full depth of the truth I spoke to him, he followed Me into the ship without misgivings, as already remarked and we quickly sailed off with a good wind, escaping the growing onrush of the crowd.

[4] Some indeed boarded the small craft, following us for a short distance. But as the wind grew mightier, they quickly turned back and reaching shore safely, before the start of the storm.

[5] But we already had reached the high sea when the former favorable wind turned into a mighty storm. Having been somewhat tired already at boarding-time, in that I had been awake all night, I therefore said to Peter in the boat: 'Prepare Me a resting-place, as I intend to take a little rest during the voyage, having as you know found no rest during the night.'

[6] Peter at once brought Me several mattresses, making Me a good place of rest and adding a pillow under My head, whereupon I soon fell asleep good and proper, physically, although knowing the wind would soon turn into a mighty storm, menacing the ship with waves soaring.

[7] When we were some two hours off shore, the rage of the storm was peaking and the swell began to surge over the deck. [Mt.8,24] Even My most tried disciples became faint, as they saw the ship take water with the swelling surf, especially over the middle section – the lowest part in accord with prevalent ship-building style. As the storm showed no sign of abating, but instead only whipping the sea higher, the disciples stepped over to Me, on the most elevated spot where **Peter** had made My resting place, out of the waves' reach and started shaking Me awake, yelling with trepidation: 'Lord, help us, or we all perish!'

[8] Whereupon I rose from My resting place, saying to them: 'O ye of little faith. Why are ye fearful when I am with you? What is more, the storm, or He who is Lord also over all storms?'

[9] Nevertheless, since the disciples as well as several others on board became practically speechless from fear and even a Peter could only stammer, I immediately rebuked the storm and the sea, and all was suddenly becalmed. The storm was as if cut off, while the sea became mirror-smooth, save for a small ripple where the oarsmen stirred it. [Mt.8,26] The fairly large number of people however who had not been more closely associated with Me, having only arrived that morning, making this journey for business rather than on My account, began to marvel beyond all measure, saying to the disciples and asking: 'What manner of man is this in Jehovah's name, that even the winds and the sea obey him?' [Mt.8,27]

[10] But I gave a sign to the disciples not to give Me away and **Peter** said: 'Ask not, but all of ye be about bailing out the exceeding waters from the boat, lest we perish from a follow-up storm, which often follows a quick becalming like the present!' Whereupon the strangers asked no more but grabbed hold of the buckets and nimbly ladled the water out, being fully occupied therewith until we reached the extensive opposite shore.

# CHAPTER 104
## The healing of the possessed

[1] The tiny country or rather district we came to was inhabited by a small race known as the Gergenese or Gadarenes, which occupied the entire opposite length of the sea of Galilee.

[2] When we had all stepped ashore there and were about to head for the small city of Gadara, situated on a rise some 6,000 paces from our landing place, there came running, from a hill topped by this city's cemetery, opposite the town and along the seas, two naked men of a terribly contorted appearance, who were possessed by an entire legion of spirits, of such fierceness that hardly anyone could get through along this road because of them. Their dwelling place was the graves of the above cemetery. None could catch or shackle them with chains. Because even where a crowd of the strongest people managed to subdue them, putting them in heavy chains and shackles, the chains were broken instantly and the shackles rubbed to powder. They were on the hill and in the graves day and night, screaming dreadfully, and mightily beating themselves with the stones.

[3] When these two became aware of Myself among the disciples however, they ran straight towards Me, falling down before Me and yelling: 'What have we to do with thee, thou son of the most high?! Art thou come to torment us before the time?! We beseech thee by the most high not to torment us.'

[4] But I rebuked them, saying: 'What is your name, evil spirit, who torments these two as if they were one man?'

[5] And **the evil one** cried: 'My name is legion, for there are many of us!'

[6] But I commanded the evil one to depart from these two. Instantly a vast number of evil spirits departed visibly from the two, in the shape of large, black flies, but pleading with Me that I would not drive them out of this district.

[7] There was along the hills straddling the sea however a great herd of swine belonging to the Gadarenes, because this little race, consisting mostly of Greeks, ate the flesh of these animals, trading therewith mainly with Greece.

[8] When the evil spirits spotted these pigs, they once again implored Me for their entering into this herd.

[9] And when I acceded to their request, for reasons secret and concealed from the world, the devils instantly entered the pigs, some two thousand in all.

[10] As soon as the devils had entered the swine, these animals ran up a hill which ended with a great cliff jutting into the sea, with a sheer drop of about three hundred yards, with all the two thousand swine properly storming into the sea, where it was very deep.

[11] When however the shepherds who watched over the swine saw what had taken place with the possessed, they fled appalled, rushing into the city, telling especially their employers what took place down at sea.

[12] The inhabitants of this little city took fright and one who like many in this city still was **a pagan**, placing much store by Jupiter and all the other pagan gods, spoke, saying: 'Did I not tell you this morning: once the two tormented by the

furies calm down, with the sea going strong beyond measure in spite of a bright sky, a god comes down and judgment follows, because the gods never come down to Earth from the stars without the rod and the sword. And we have it right here before us. The furies who tormented the two sinners first stir up the sea, as they were certain that a god would come down from above and drive them out of the two sinners. That they then threw themselves upon our swine in the form of black horseflies, storming these animals into the sea, is now clear to me as the sun in broad daylight! We have now no choice but to betake ourselves in all humility and remorse down to the god, probably Neptune or Mercury and beg him to soon leave this area again, for as long as a god tarries in a district of the Earth visibly, there can be no thought but of misfortune upon misfortune. Because, as said, a god never comes down to Earth from the stars without the rod, sword and judgment.

[13] But not even with the most secret thoughts let any of us reproach him for the damage inflicted upon us, because that would be the end of us. For a long time now we have not brought the old gods a proper sacrifice, from which the foolish Jews held us back more than anyone else, by wanting to know everything better than us, and therefore an offended god took his own sacrifice. Thus it is. Therefore we must not allow even a thought of dissatisfaction to surface in us. But down we must go to greet him and then implore him to leave this district again at once.'

[14] But quite **a few Jews** listened to this lecture as well and said: 'You indeed consider us stupid, yet this thing we know more about then you. See, this your purported god is none other than either a Persian magician, or it is the renowned Jesus of Nazareth, of whom we already heard great things. But we otherwise agree with you that we should implore him to leave this area. Because such people never are a blessing for a country – this we know from the days of our prophets. Where God awakens certain people in some nation as prophets, the misfortune for such country is sealed.'

[15] Thereupon the whole city got together and moved down to Me, leaving behind only a few sick. When the arrivals caught sight of Me and saw that I had a completely natural human appearance, they took courage to approach Me and although still fearful, stepped up to Me begging Me to leave their borders soon.

[16] Some however studied the two whom they formerly had well known as possessed. Both were clad now and conversed with them intelligently, relating to them how I had freed them from their plague and how they immediately were clad by those who had come with Me. But none of this could diminish the fear, especially that of the pagans and they asked for nothing but My departure and no return.

[17] And I acceded to their request and then said to Peter: 'Friend, get the ship ready again at once, that we may leave this area as soon as possible.'

[18] And Peter and his servants got the ship ready at once. But as I boarded the ship, the two healed hurried after Me, asking Me whether they could follow Me, because they would obtain no work or living in this city, and their relatives at home were bound not have to them, due to their great fear of them. But I turned them

away in a friendly-earnest manner, saying: 'Return to yours cheerfully, as they shall receive you with joy. But go and proclaim it to yours and to the entire region too, what great thing the Lord has done for you and what mercy He has shown you. And in this way you shall do greater good than by following Me now. Because in this area, where you are known by one and all, you are to bear proper witness and thus become useful to men. And people shall, as before when they still feared you, not let you starve.'

[19] With that, the two healed departed as one man and eagerly did as I commanded them.

[20] The two of them in a short time glorified My name not only in their native land, but in the 10 cities straddling the upper sea-coast too, everywhere proclaiming with much zeal what great thing I had done for them and the great mercy I had shown them. And many therewith believed on My name, generating much longing for Me in Jew and Greek alike.


## CHAPTER 105
### Disbelief prevents miracles

[1] But we now head straight for Nazareth, because I was determined to visit Nazareth once again and to rest a little at home and on this occasion to kindle the light of truth for the very unstable Nazarenes.

[2] The return voyage however took somewhat longer than the outward journey and many became hungry. But I fortified them and they felt a marvelous satiety, so that **some** said: 'Verily, each breath gives bread and each second one tastes like wine.' And so we reached shore the following morning. It was another 20 field ways (about 3 kilometers by today's measures) to Nazareth from the shore and we thus continued our journey unhindered and reached it in a short time, while Peter's servants looked after the ship of course and then sailed home.

[3] It was however a major port of call where we had landed, where many people had converged, some having to travel over the sea, trading in every direction, while many others from many districts, including Jerusalem, came to the Nazareth market, because just then a big market was held in this city.

[4] But when it became known in port that I had arrived in Peter's boat, those who had intended to travel over the sea for business remained and a huge crowd therefore moved to Nazareth with Me.

[5] I and My disciples betook ourselves to My, i.e. now mother Mary's house, who was at home with the three eldest sons and four maidens who had already in Joseph's time, when I was still a child, been taken on and reared as children.

[6] Mary and the entire household now put their hands to preparing an abundant morning meal, of which we already had much need, especially the disciples, who had already gone a day and nearly a night without food. The meal was soon ready and we sat down and ate and drank. After the meal we said thanks and rose to go to the city to watch the tumult a little. But we could hardly get out of the house

because of the great crowd that had quartered itself there, mainly from curiosity but also partly for contemptuous spying, with only an inferior part out of real need.

[7] As we stepped before the house therefore, several Jerusalemite Pharisees and scribes asked if I am not going to work wonders and signs here. But I said to them earnestly and decisively: 'None, because of your unbelief.' Upon this decisive 'no' they began to scatter and some murmured and whispered into each other's ears: 'He is scared of the Jerusalemite lords and does not dare'. Others said: 'He probably hasn't got his magician's paraphernalia with him'. And still other's said: 'Here he does nothing on account of his compatriots, as he is bound to know that he is not especially esteemed by them.' With these and other comments they scattered and in just a few moments there were no people before the house of Mary, mother of My body and we immediately had room to make our way to the city.

[8] There we dropped in on a Synagogue, where every Jew who had something to say was able to contribute before three scribes seated on high, or voice any complaint either personally or on behalf of a community against any priests or scribes appointed there by Jerusalem.

[9] On entering the Synagogue, **Simon of Cana** said to Me in secret 'Lord, here we could bring up something too? We should not be short of complaints.'

[10] I said: 'My friend, it is good to speak truthfully at the right time, but even better to keep silence at the right time. You shall not make gold from iron or silver from mud, no matter how hard you try. This kind, conducting judgment and hearings, is inwardly quite different from their outward demeanor. Outwardly it is a lamb and inwardly a rapacious wolf.

[11] Do you think that these here conduct inquiries in order to redress complaints? O, here you would be greatly mistaken.

[12] This kind holds public sittings with friendly faces only to sound out the people's attitude towards the priesthood. Believe Me: today you obtain a friendly hearing and tomorrow you are put in prison for a year of flogging with serpents, because these priests are as the ravens and crows, not in the habit of poking the eyes out of their own with their sharp beaks.

[13] Therefore we shall just make listeners and take note in what way if any they make mention of us. They shall not notice us and even if they did they would not recognize us too easily and so our listening shall be easy and we shall go by what we hear'. Simon of Cana was happy with that and we took our seats in a somewhat dark corner of the Synagogue and listened to what went on.

[14] Individuals as well as communal spokesmen were bringing a great many of the most glaring complaints against the Pharisees and were receiving a friendly hearing.

[15] When however the people's complaints were over, with the three scribes and Pharisees who had come down from Jerusalem reassuring them that all measures shall be taken to investigate and punish any priests found guilty. One scribe kindly asked the people what if anything knew of Me, i.e. the notorious agitator Jesus. Because it had come to their ears right up to Jerusalem that he was roaming around Galilee, doing great signs as never done by man before him,

whether it be true and what they and others thought of it.

## CHAPTER 106
### Life, deeds and teaching of Jesus of Nazareth

[1] Here **a reputable man** from the Capernaum area steps up and speaks: 'Highly esteemed servants in Jehovah's Temple at Jerusalem, the Jesus about whom you have queried us was so to speak born in this city, having always behaved in a most proper and thoroughly God-fearing manner. One saw him pray often and at great length. No one has ever seen Him laugh, but rather weep in secluded places that He frequented often.

[2] From earliest times in His life already, the most peculiar things were happening. And now, having taken to traveling as a proper doctor without equal upon Earth, He is accomplishing through the mere Word healings which Jehovah alone can accomplish.

[3] In comparison, all deeds from Moses onwards till our time can be regarded as next to nothing. Cripples, totally withered for many years, He makes whole instantly. Every fever, ever so intense, has to bend to His Word, and the dumb, deaf and blind from birth speak, hear and see like unto any of us. The most advanced leprosy He chases away instantly, from the possessed He casts out legions of devils by the mere Word and He calls out to the dead and they rise, eat and drink and move about as though there had never been anything wrong with them. Similarly He commands the elements and they obey Him as if His most faithful and ready servants.

[4] His teaching in general can be summed up thus, love God above all and your neighbor as yourself, indeed.

[5] Since He does however perform such deeds, proclaiming the purest teaching to His disciples, we are taking Him for an extraordinary prophet whom Jehovah, as He once did with Elijah, has sent us from the Heavens, in our greatest extremity! This is all that I and many others know of this glorious Jesus and we can't thank God enough for having once again thought of His poor and exceedingly troubled people.

[6] Many hold Him to be the great promised Anointed of God. I myself however am neither for nor against this, but would ask whether Christ, who is to come, shall perform greater works once?'

[7] Says **the priest**: 'You speak the way a blind judges colors. Where is it written that a prophet shall be called out of Galilee? We tell you that this your Jesus is nothing but an evil magician who should be consumed by fire. His teaching however is a mask behind which he hides his blasphemous nature. He performs his wonders not through God but the devils' chief – yet you blind ones take him for the Promised one even. Truly, you are for this worthy of a fiery death with him.'

[8] But **the man** takes up an imposing stance and says: 'Indeed, as far as you are concerned, if we were not Galileans and I myself fully a Roman and if you

yourselves were still masters instead of the Romans, we would have been burnt long ago. But fortunately your glory with us Galileans had long since come to an end. We are fully Roman subjects and therefore have nothing more to do with you, other than perhaps show you the way out of Galilee once and for all, should you dare to lay hands on even the least of us Romans.

[9] But in relation to our great prophet Jesus I tell you yet more, beware of a temptation to lay your evil hands on him in this country!

[10] Because to us verily He is a God. He has done things in front of us which can be possible only to God.

[11] A God who does good to poor mankind must be a right and true God. A god like yours however who can be appeased only with gold, silver and all sorts of other fat sacrifices, doing next to nothing in response to long and exorbitantly-priced prayers, is like yourselves, who call yourselves his servants, evil through and through and deserves like yourselves to be tossed out of the country.

[12] You say Jesus is a ravenous wolf in sheep's clothing. What then are you? Truly, you yourselves are in fullest measure just what you say of Jesus, a man of lamb-like devoutness.

[13] With friendly mien you hear our complaints, but deep down you plot for us complainants the dastardly revenge and if it were possible, wipe us out with Sodom's fire from the Heavens. But not to worry, you evil brood of vipers and scorpions, here we Romans are the masters and shall know how to show you the way from here to Jerusalem, if you don't get yourselves going immediately on your own accord.'

[14] This talk had of course cast the three scribes into the most glowing fury, but they did not dare to come up with anything else in front of so numerous a crowd and therefore now tried to make off through a small back door and more exactly for the road to Capernaum, where most of the Jerusalemite Pharisees and scribes were want to stay, abandoning themselves unhindered to every imaginable vice and fornication and every possible racket.

[15] When the three had so to speak cleared the Synagogue, **one other** came forward, thanking the speaker on behalf of all spokesmen and individual complainants present, adding however and saying: 'If we don't do as the Samaritans did, we shall not be left in peace by these beasts. Their names shall have to be more odious to us than Gog and Magog and Jerusalem a place to piss on, otherwise we shall not be rid of this plague, worse than pestilence.'

[16] **All** chimed in with him and said: 'If only our miracle-working Jesus could now be located, then He should have to come along at once and we could make Him our only true teacher and High priest.'

[17] Says **the speaker**: 'I am all for it, yet we should first have to ask the Roman governor whether it is all right with him. Because the Romans don't have it all that easy with our priesthood, because the Temple is supposed to be constantly in touch with the Roman Emperors secretly.'

[18] All agreed to this suggestion, gradually leaving the hall where the Synagogue (meeting) was held.

# CHAPTER 107
## The comedy of the world is a tragedy to God's children

[1] But I say to Simon of Cana: 'Have you now seen the advantages of being able to keep silent at the right time? Where others speak and act on our behalf it is better for us well to keep silent. Do you understand that?'

[2] Says **Simon of Cana**: 'Yes Lord, I understand and clearly see the advantages of keeping quiet rather than speaking, although sometimes one feels as if pulled by the hair to on such occasion let one's tongue go into spasms. Yet here it has been clearly demonstrated that to keep quiet at the right time is better than the most pertinent speech But we nevertheless found it easy to keep our silence, since we had a most courageous eloquent and knowledgeable representative in the one who introduced himself to the priests as a Roman.

[3] I was close to laughter at the retreat of the three Templers, which would have cost them almost all of the little regard they still had in this country. Their faces grew steadily longer and their feet became markedly restless with the steadily thickening speech of the Roman, afterwards finding most appropriate arrangements for their escape. When I noticed the peculiar disquiet of the three Templar's feet, my spirit said to me: "now they shall shortly become invisible" – and they in fact became invisible.

[4] It surely won't be a sin, o Lord, for the heart to feel unavoidably good at an occasional thwarting, like now, of the intentions of such arch-evil and utterly incorrigible thugs. I would on my part have chosen the Roman's every word myself.'

[5] I said: 'Every honorable breast can feel a righteous joy and a fortifying cheer at the exposure and destruction of ever so secret evil, but mark well, only at the fortunate thwarting of wickedness, falseness and evil, but never at the person who, usually in his blindness, has been a servant of such sin.

[6] You surely saw the two Gadarenes and how evil they were, but how, after I drove the legion of devils out of them, they became good and gentle, praising God for giving man such power. Would it have been right to only feel elation there at the two loathsome ones, having been a terror to the entire region, at the mere stopping of their game and at the simultaneous plunging into the sea of the pig-profiteers' stock-in-trade? O, such elation should have been most unworthy of all true humans. Yet if the joy were felt at two exceedingly tormented individuals having the plague taken from them and the tormenting spirits, through the destruction of their own spirit of usury – carefully nurtured in the Gadarenes, having to serve Heaven's good cause, then the joy and cheer would be of a celestial nature and therefore fully good.

[7] I say unto you as a matter of profoundest living truth: he, who laughs over a foolish person, shows his own fullest leanings thereto, because here the one acts foolishly owing to his foolishness, while the other laughs out of foolishness. And thus one foolishness finds pleasure at another, to the extent of not being pleased

if the first rids himself of his foolishness and starts acting sensibly.

[8] But quite another thing it is if in a brotherly fashion you reprimand the one asking foolishly and then laugh joyously and lightheartedly when the foolish one begins to act wisely. Then your joy and lightheartedness are of a celestial order and therewith good, right and just.

[9] But what kind of joy and cheer, by any wisdom, could it give to anyone at all if a blind one, walking along the way, having spoken to a seeing one going the same way, as follows: "Friend, I have lost my way and don't know in which direction I'm going. My home is supposed to be straight ahead. According to the paces I have counted I should be close to it. But if by mistake, as one fully blind, I turned the wrong way, then I would be further from my house than at the point when I set out for home. Please be good enough and set me on the right track."

[10] If the seeing one were then to laugh, even while finding himself in the vicinity of the house, having only ten paces to go, he says to the blind: "O, here you've gone way out. Give me your hand and I'll lead you to your home, although it is out of my way." The blind man happily thanks the seeing one in advance. The latter, constantly laughing to himself, leads the blind one around his house twenty times, saying to him full of inner glee: "Now, my friend, we are here. Here is your house." The blind thanks him no end, yet the seeing one is full of derision because his dodge came off.

[11] I ask, who is in this case blinder, the blind or his seeing leader? Verily I say to you: the heartless leader, because he is blind in his heart and this is a thousand times worse than blind in the head.

[12] In like manner people also laugh at witty talk, especially at crude and filthy public allusions to the weaknesses and sins of their brethren.

[13] Verily I say unto you: whoever can laugh over such-like or even watch some funny crank really take down some weakling, by flogging him a faintly-silvered bean as a pearl, in such a one's heart the devil has sown a fill of all kinds of evil seeds from which no fruit of life shall go forth.

[14] Therefore it is better to turn away from all this and rather mourn where the world is abandoning itself to impudent laughter, because the world's comedy constantly is tragedy to the true children of God and God's angels only too often weep at the worldly men's laughter out of their wicked nonsense.

[15] Therefore let us forget the three Temple servants, who indeed are full of wickedness owing to Satan's workings and their own worldly and self-love, which are their attributes, yet who nevertheless are yet humans and merely wayward children of the same Father who is your Father. Their wickedness alone is to be condemned, but as men and brethren they are to be bewailed.'


## CHAPTER 108
### Mary, the mother of the Lord

[1] We now are on our way and many who meet us, although greeting us, are

not asking where we have been or where we are going.

[2] But Judas also runs into us along the way. This one asks us where we have been and where we are going, because he had not been to the Synagogue, since he was marketeering with his fish and earthenware, having made much money, which gave him great joy. But he nevertheless came along to My house, spoiling his palate there since it cost him nothing. But after the meal he at once returned to his stand, getting down to making money, for the market lasted three days and many merchants made good business, charging steep sums for their wares.

[3] The next day the mother Mary asked Me whether I planned any public activity here and how long I would this time be staying at the house and whether any more visitors were expected, so that she could look for some more provisions as there was at present nothing much left.

[4] I said: 'Woman, do not concern yourself about Me or My companions nor about sufficient provisions. For see, He who nourishes the entire large Earth and with His love appeases the sun, the moon and all the stars is quite familiar with this little house and knows exactly what this house needs. Therefore, do not trouble your head about it and do not worry, for that about which you are worrying has already been taken care of from above.

[5] The Father in Heaven does not let His children go hungry, except when it is necessary for their salvation.

[6] You did see it in Sychar where it became sufficiently evident how the Father in Heaven provided for His little children. Do you think that after these few days He has become any harder? Go to your larder and you will see that you have been unnecessarily concerned.'

[7] Now Mary hurries to the larder and finds it filled up with bread, flour, fruit, smoked and fresh fish, with milk, cheese, butter and honey. When the mother sees such abundant provisions in her larder, she anxiously hurries back to Me, kneels before Me and thanks Me for so richly providing her larder. But I quickly bend down, raise the mother to her feet and say to her: 'What are you doing to Me? This is due to the Father alone. Rise, for we have known each other already for 30 years, and I am still always the same and unchanged.'

[8] But Mary weeps with joy, greets all My disciples and then quickly leaves the room to prepare a good midday meal.

[9] **The disciples**, however, step up to Me and say: 'Look, what a dear woman and what a loving mother. She is now already 45 years of age and looks as if she were hardly 20. What great loving concern, and how her truly holy purest bosom swells with mother-love. In truth, a woman of women of all the Earth.'

[10] I said: 'Yes, indeed, she is the first, and there will never be another like her. But it will also happen that more temples will be built to her than to Me and she will be worshiped ten times more than I and people will believe to be able to attain salvation only through her.

[11] Therefore, I now do not want her to be praised too much. She knows that she is the mother of My body and is also aware of who is behind this body which she has brought forth.

[22] Therefore be very good and nice to her, but beware of according her any

201

divine adoration.

[13] For, notwithstanding all her very best qualities, she is still a woman, and the gap from the best woman to vanity is only very narrow.

[14] And any kind of vanity is a seed of pride from which has come, is still coming and will always be coming all evil into the world. Therefore, keep in mind what I have now told you also where the mother is concerned.'


## CHAPTER 109
### You are a winnowing fan in the Father's hand

[1] Peter is shaking his head and shrugging his shoulders. **Simon of Cana** wants to know why, saying: 'Then what do you think? If the Lord has foretold it, then it shall also surely come to pass, while we for our part now know how to take it, believing accordingly. Then why are you shaking your head in disbelief and shrug your shoulders?'

[2] Says **Peter**: 'Dear brother, my shaking of my head and shrugging my shoulders mean something totally different from what you thought.'

[3] Says **Simon**: 'What then, dear brother?'

[4] Says **Peter**: 'Of a truth, the Lord's Word is holy. How happy mankind, if they already were in possession of this teaching, acting accordingly. If so however, then how shall in the end this doctrine become the holy property of all men on Earth? Yet if the Lord allows all sorts of things to go on, then how will this teaching look after a short time? Truly, this most precious soul-food shall eventually become the fodder of dogs and pigs. And that is why I was shaking and shrugging, beloved brother.'

[5] I said: 'Peter, let it be. You shall do whatever has been assigned to you. You don't need to concern yourself with the result. Whatever shall come and one way or another has to come, on account of the profundity of wisdom and love, only the Father knows and he to whom the Father wants to reveal the how, when and why of His permitting it so.

[6] If you should come to a craftsman's workshop, seeing all sorts of tools, shall you know how the craftsman applies them in bringing forth his manifold works? You shall indeed shake your head and shrug your shoulders, but you shall not that way work out how the craftsman uses his manifold tools and how a particular work shall come about therewith. If however the craftsman has a mind of explaining it to you, then you too shall know in accordance with his explanation.

[7] But I say unto you: God is above all craftsmen and the greatest craft is to, out of oneself create the first independent life within countless distinct beings. For this truly, a myriad of spiritual tools are needed, and to this end, you and Mary and all men are divine works and tools, whose application only the Father in Heaven most wisely knows.

[8] Therefore do not trouble yourself about anything other than that to which you have been called. Then, as a tool in the Father's hand you shall be performing the

right service.

[9] Or, is the winnowing fan above him who utilizes it as a cleansing tool? If fit, it shall be used for cleansing wheat, barley and corn. If unfit, then it shall be either made fit or thrown in the fire. If the Father has made you into a winnowing fan, then remain what you are and don't try to be also a pot. Do you understand this?'

[10] Says **Peter**: 'Lord, this is a bit obscure. It indeed seems as if I understood it. Yet when I try to fathom it, I can't grasp this peculiar parable. How can one be simultaneously a work and a tool?'

[11] I said: 'Is not every tool, before employed by the craftsman, an accomplished work in itself, for the purpose of bringing forth another work or an expeditious performance of some work?

[12] I said however that in the heavenly Father's hand you are a winnowing fan, because you and the other disciples are being instructed by Me on how to raise men to the true recognition of God.

[13] The men of the world are like wheat, barley and corn. This living grain however does not grow without chaff and the offensive dust. In order however for this grain, i.e. these worldly men to be cleansed of their worldly chaff and filth and then, as a fully cleansed grain be gathered up into the Father's eternal barns, you are being transformed into proper and living winnowing fans through whom the Father in Heaven shall cleanse His grain. Do you all understand this now?'

[14] Says **Peter**: 'Yes, Lord, now the thing is completely clear to us, but we would also like to know, as You always speak of the Father in Heaven as if of a second person, although, since Sychar, we have always secretly taken You to be the Father Yourself, who in that case You Yourself actually are. Could You be also perhaps Yourself someone else's winnowing fan?'

[15] I said: 'I am firstly He who I am, but then I am also He who I don't appear to be. I sow and reap as the Father sows and reaps and whoever serves Me as a winnowing fan serves also the Father as such, because the Son is where the Father is, and where the Son is, there is the Father. Notwithstanding, the Father is above the Son and the Son proceeds from the Father. No one knows the Father nevertheless save the Son and he to whom the Son wants to reveal Him. Do you all understand this?'

[16] Says **Peter**: 'Lord, this no angel understands, let alone us. But You could once, if you wanted to, show us the Father.'

[17] I said: 'For this you are not ripe yet, but not too long therefore you shall be ripe and then you shall also see the Father.'

[18] With these words, Mary and her helpers come in and announce the morning meal ready. The tables are set at once and the meal brought in.

## CHAPTER 110
### The Lord and the three Pharisees

[1] We sit down to start enjoying the meal cheerfully, when Judas enters,

reproaching us good and proper for not letting him know, since we know how busy he is and not able to constantly find out when we have meals, even while counting himself as one of us. **Thomas** gets furious at such talk, saying: 'Lord, here my moderation is at an end. It's time for him to taste my fists again.'

[2] I said: 'Let that go. Have you not heard that where 12 angels dwell under one roof, the twelfth is a disguised devil? Let him be, because him you cannot change.' Thomas is seated and Judas goes off without a meal.

[3] As we thereupon continue with the well prepared meal, Judas returns, soft-pedaling us and asking for a meal, because nothing was obtainable in the city, as the many visitors had consumed everything.

[4] I said: 'Give him to eat then.' And brother Jacob gave him bread and salt and a whole well-cooked fish. And Judas consumed the whole fish, weighing about seven pounds, and thereafter much water, whereupon he began to feel somewhat unwell. Then he started complaining, maintaining that the fish had been off, which always gave him trouble.

[5] **Thomas** however got angry again, saying to Judas: 'You sure still are the same old hulking and crude man you always were. Go to the larder and see whether our fish are off. If you voraciously consume a seven pound fish like a wolf, swilling it down with a jug full of water sufficient for twenty people and on top of that eat a loaf of bread none too small, then you have to feel congested in your stomach. If then you are aching so much, we have the best Doctor in our midst. Ask Him and He surely shall help you.'

[6] Says **Judas Iscariot**: 'You all are dead set against me and call me a devil, how would you believe me as a devil that I'm suffering and how help?'

[7] Says **Thomas**: 'Were you not with us at the Gergenseans (Gadarenes), seeing how the Lord heard even the devil's request, consenting to it? If you earnestly take yourself for a devil, then ask like a devil and some herd of swine shall be found for you to possess, after the Lord has heard your request.'

[8] Says **Judas Iscariot**: 'O, you certainly mean me quite well. I never thought you such a great friend. See, I nonetheless shall ask Jesus, the son of this house, for proper help and shall see whether like you he shall send me into a herd of swine.' Here Judas turns to Me, voicing his plight. But I say: 'Go to your pots. There it shall be better with you.'

[9] **Judas** goes, remarking to Thomas on the way out: 'Not a herd of swine after all.' Replies **Thomas**: 'But not all that much better. Because your pots are as much a tool of usury to you as the pigs for the Gergenese.' Judas says no more and quickly departs.

[10] But soon thereafter three Pharisees from Capernaum arrived, asking if I were home. Upon being told that I was home indeed, they at once enter the dining room, asking around for Me, since they didn't know Me personally.

[11] But I say with full force: 'I am He! What is it that I should do for you?!'

[12] But they are too terrified by My address to dare asking anything at all, because My powerful Word had the effect of lightning within their heart. And I asked them yet again what they were after.

[13] **One of them** steps up, speaking timorously: 'Good master!'

[14] But I say: 'How are you calling Me good? Do you not know that none besides God is good?' Says **the Pharisee**: 'I beg you not to be so hard on me, for I have need of your well-tested help.' I said: 'Don't start holding Me up, because I have to go down to the sea this afternoon to catch fish. You shall find Me down there.'

[15] With this information the three left. The one who spoke to Me however was a principal of the school and Synagogue at Capernaum, by the name of Jairus.


## CHAPTER 111
### The healing of the Greek woman

[1] When Peter heard that I intended going to sea, he asked Me whether to go ahead and prepare the big boat. But I said to him: 'No need to trouble yourself. It shall be ready for us when we get there.'

[2] But Mary also asked whether to prepare any lunch or dinner. And I say to her: 'Neither for lunch nor dinner, because we shall not return until late at night.'

[3] After that I tell the disciples to get ready, if they wish to come along. And all get up quickly to go with Me to sea, which, as is known, was not a great distance from Nazareth.

[4] A great crowd was assembled there when we got to the sea. There were several ships there, not excluding Peter's. We boarded Peter's at once and pushed off to sea.

[5] When however the people saw Me head for the sea, they boarded many boats to paddle after Me.

[6] But one of the boats also carried one of those three Pharisees who was a school principal and who had an attractive country property near Capernaum and who on that day had been at My house at Nazareth. When his boat had caught up with Mine, he fell on his knees in his boat, imploring Me and saying: 'Lord, My daughter is in her last stages. If only You had a mind of coming there to lay Your hands on her, so she would get well again.' We were not far from shore yet and I asked Peter to steer back.

[7] Having stepped ashore again, the crowd there was so enormous that we could move only with difficulty, battling for three hours to reach Jairus' house, what the average pedestrian would have done in an hour.

[8] As we were gradually pushing rather than making our way forward, led by Jairus, a woman who had been suffering from an issue for twelve years, having given over nearly all her fortune to doctors to get well, pushed her way towards Me from behind, touching My garment in the belief of getting well therewith, since the woman had heard much about Me.

[9] She did not venture to approach Me openly however, for being a Greek woman rather than a Jewess, since there was at that time tension between Jews and Greeks, by way of trade and due to competing for favor with Rome, where each nation wanted to enjoy precedence.

[10] The Greeks, as a refined hero-nation, had a far greater standing with the Romans and enjoyed much greater advantages with Rome than the Jews, who had a very low reputation in Rome. In a sense the Greeks also were so to speak secret agents over the Jews and therefore tolerated even less by the Jews.

[11] Therefore the fear, particularly that of the Greek women, of the Jews, especially because of the tale spread among the Greeks by shifty Jews, that the Jews, initiates into all kinds of magic, only needed to fix Greek women with their stare to make them barren. And this was also the reason here for this woman pushing towards Me from behind.

[12] But no sooner had she touched Me when she realized herself completely well. The fountain of her blood was at once stopped and a great reassurance in relation to her malady overcame her and her whole being told her that she was completely mended.

[13] But I soon turned around, asking the disciples nearest to Me, 'Who touched Me?'

[14] The disciples however were irritated by this question, saying: 'How could You ask who touched you, seeing how the crowd is pushing?''

[15] But I said to the disciples: 'Not quite so, for he who touched Me had faith and a certain reason for touching Me, because I became well aware of power leaving Me.'

[16] Here the woman, whom I held steadfastly in sight while asking, since I knew only too well within Myself that this very woman touched My garment and why, took fright. She fell down before Me, admitting all and asking forgiveness, because her fear was so great that she shook uncontrollably, bearing in mind the above mentioned tale.

[17] But I kindly looked at her and said: 'Arise, daughter, your faith has helped you. Go to your country in peace and be well and free of your plight.'

[18] And the woman arose happily and cheerfully and departed to her country, a half day's journey away, because she was the daughter of a tenant-farmer beyond Zebulon and single. She had once transgressed in her thirteenth year with a sensuous man, who gave her two pounds of gold, for this however she had to suffer 12 years and use up the whole 2 pounds of gold, which in those days represented a sum more than 30,000 florins of today's paper money, because for one silver penny one could obtain more in those days than for 10 coined florins of the realm today. Such present therefore made her rich, yet she had to spend all her wealth to get well.

## CHAPTER 112
### The daughter of Jairus

[1] But while I was yet telling the disciples about this woman, the principal's domestics came running almost breathless, to bring him the sad news of his daughter's death.

[2] **The principal** became grief stricken, saying to Me: 'Dear Master, since it is grievously too late for me now for helping my daughter, who was my everything, do not further trouble yourself.'

[3] After these words he started sobbing loudly. He had much loved his daughter, who was very shapely and well-bred, with the build of a 20 year old and was also this principal's only child.

[4] After hearing his domestics and then the exceedingly grieving principal himself, with whom My heart commiserated, I said to him: 'Fear not, friend, but believe. Your daughter has not died but only fallen asleep and I shall awaken her.'

[5] On hearing Me thus, the principal began to breathe more easily.

[6] When we were still some thousand paces from the principal's house, I said to the crowd, as well as to those disciples still of a more feeble faith, to all wait here. And only Peter, Jacob and his brother and John were allowed to come, for on their faith one could already build houses.

[7] Arriving at the house with the school-principal, there was a great turmoil there and much weeping and wailing in accordance with Jewish tradition, with mourning hymns sung.

[8] Entering the room where the deceased lay on an adorned bed, I said to the many mourners: 'What are you carrying on and wailing for? The little daughter has not died but only sleeps.'

[9] But they laughed Me off and said: 'Yeah, that's what the sleeping look like. When there has been no breath or pulse for three and a half hours and the body cold and colorless and the eye lifeless, then according to your knowledge one sleeps? Yes, yes, that also is sleeping of course, only no one awakens from it except on judgment day.'

[10] But I say to the principal: 'Get them all out, because their unbelief is no good to Me.' The principal did so. Yet the troublemakers would not obey him and he asked My help. So I drove them out by force and they ran out and scattered.

[11] I then went back with the principal and his grieving wife and the 4 disciples to the chamber where the deceased little daughter lay, stepped straight to her bed, took her left hand and said to her, 'Talitha kumi', which is to say 'I say to you little maiden, arise.'

[12] Immediately the little maiden rose, leapt cheerfully and merrily from her adorned bed and went around the room in her former liveliness, caressing her tearful mother and father. At the same time the merry little maiden felt empty in the stomach and therefore hungry and that she therefore wanted to eat a little.

[13] The parents, elated beyond all measure, turned to Me with many a tear of joy and thankfulness, asking whether and what to give her to eat. But I said: 'Indeed give her to eat, whatever she likes and whatever is close to hand.'

[14] There were some figs and dates upon a dish and the little daughter asked if she could eat these fruits. And I said: 'Eat whatever you like, for you are now completely well and shall not get sick again.'

[15] So the little maiden leapt over to the bowl, nearly emptying it. But the parents were concerned it may harm her.

[16] But I comforted them, saying to them: 'Do not be troubled. When I say unto

you that it can never harm her then it shall never do so.' And the parents firmly believed.

[17] After the girl was filled and had said thanks, she went over to the parents and asked them softly who I was, actually. Because while on the bed, she had seen the Heavens open and a vast number of radiant angels. 'And amidst the angels there stood a very friendly man looking in my direction, then approaching me, seizing me by the hand and saying 'Talitha kumi', after which call I woke up immediately. And see, this man here looks exactly like one I saw among so many angels. O, this must be a most wonderful man indeed.'

[18] The principal understood the daughter's question only too well but, having received a hint from Me, he said to the daughter only that she had a beautiful and true dream, which he shall shortly explain to her. And the little girl was happy with that.

[19] But I asked the principal to come with Me into the open, together with the daughter and mother, so that those tarrying outside should be put to shame on account of their unbelief. And we went outside. And when **these unbelieving** saw the daughter and how well same looked and cheerfully proceeded to question them on why they stood there so puzzled and frightened, these were horrified even more and said: 'This is a miracle above all miracles, because the girl truly was dead and now lived.' And they were determined to spread this all over the place at once.

[20] But I rebuked them all and commanded them to keep it to themselves, for the sake of their physical and spiritual lives. And they kept their silence and departed.

## CHAPTER 113
### Details regarding the different nature of the biblical Gospels of Matthew and John (2/13)

[1] The scribe Matthew, who followed Me at a certain distance in order to see what was going on, so that he could then record it, stepped up to Me and asked whether he was to record these events.

[2] But I said: 'Leave that be, so that there may not be a mix-up later on. For the day after tomorrow we shall again be going towards the sea, where exactly the same will be happening and that you shall then describe in detail. Anyway, beginning with tomorrow you may record all that is extraordinary whatever that may be.'

[3] Matthew is quite satisfied with this, but also John, who was particularly impressed by this deed, asks Me whether he may not make at least a short note of this deed also.

[4] And I say to him: 'That you may do. However, it must not follow immediately upon that which you have so far written, but only at a later stage, for in 6 months we shall have to sort out still another affair exactly like this one, and that you may

then record for this or this for that one.

[5] It is not really important whether one or the other sign, which is very similar to a previous one, is written down or not, for that could easily cause confusion for the later followers of My teaching, and such confusions could then give rise to all kinds of speculations and doubts. This would then do damage rather than promote the main issue, which is solely My teaching.

[6] As long as I and you, who can witness to the whole truth of the different signs, are living on this Earth, any doubts can easily be prevented. But in later times, when, because of the freedom of man's will, only what was written shall bear witness to Me, the Scripture must be pure and well ordered, otherwise it would harm rather than be of any use.'

[7] Says **John**: 'Lord, You my love. What You have just said is no doubt absolutely true, but would it not because of that be of great benefit if I, exactly like brother Matthew, recorded everything You do and teach?

[8] For if in later time men would compare my records with those of Matthew and not find in mine what is recorded in Matthew's, would they not begin to speculate and doubt the authenticity of the whole Gospel and say "Has there not been one Jesus who taught the same and no doubt did the same? Why did Matthew write this and John that, - things that differ, and yet both are said to have been with Him constantly?"

[9] I said: 'You are quite right, dearest brother, but look, the reason why I allow this to happen is at present still incomprehensible to you. It will become clear later on.

[10] What Matthew writes is especially for the benefit of this Earth, whereas what you write is aimed at all of eternal infinity. For in everything you write there is veiled the purely divine, working from eternity to eternity through all the already existent creations and also through those that will in future eternities replace the now existing ones. And if you wrote into many thousands of books what I am still going to tell all of you, the world would never be able to understand such books which would then also be useless to the world.

[11] Whoever will live in accordance with the received teaching and believe in the Son will be reborn in the spirit anyway, and the spirit will guide him into all the depths of eternal truth.

[12] Now you know the reason why I do not let you write everything. So do not ask Me any further about it in future. For this must never be made all too clear to the world to prevent it from falling into an even greater judgment than is the ancient, necessary one wherein it is already finding itself.

[13] I will arrange My teaching in such a way that by merely reading or hearing the Gospel no one shall get to the bottom of the living truth, but only by acting in accordance with My teaching. Only the action will become a guiding light for everyone.'

# CHAPTER 114
## A lesson for Judas

[1] After this instruction, **Jairus** once again stepped over to Me, saying: 'Dear Master, by giving me back my daughter, You have given me more than if You had given me my own life a hundredfold, if it were possible. How can I thank You for this and how reward You? What can I do for You?'

[2] I said: 'Nothing more than that in future you should not be offended in Me when hearing this or that about Me, therefore! Because the whole world cannot give you and do for you what I have given and done for you! You shall once understand how and why I was able to do that for you. Remember Me in your heart.'

[3] Jairus wept for joy and his wife and daughter sobbed as I resumed My journey back to Nazareth with My disciples. They accompanied Me to where the other disciples and a great crowd were tarrying for Me.

[4] Arriving, there was many a questioner who had nothing better to do than regale us thick and fast with questions about the state of the school-principal's deceased daughter.

[5] But **Peter** spoke, saying: 'You blind ones. Here, see, this is the maiden who was dead and now lives. What more do you want?' Thereupon many turned to the principal, asking him if this were true.

[6] And **the principal** spoke strongly: 'Yes, you blind and unbelieving fools. An hour ago I was weeping the loss of this my beloved and only daughter. And now you see me happy beyond measure, as I once again have my daughter. Is this obvious proof not enough for you?'

[7] Upon these words all were exceedingly amazed. And when I started to move on with My disciples, the whole huge crowd of some three thousand accompanied Me to Nazareth.

[8] It was however quite late at night by the time we arrived home. Yet Mary and the brethren and sisters were still up. A well cooked dinner was awaiting us, coming in handy for quite a few of us – not having had anything since the morning, our considerable hunger was excusable.

[9] Judas however also was in the house, sleeping on a bed of straw. Being woken with our talk, he got up, asking us no more than how the catch had been.

[10] **Peter** said to him: 'Go outside and look.' Judas went outside, seeing nothing other than the huge crowd settling down around My house. Soon he returns to the room, asking Peter where the fish were, because he had been around the house, seeing no fish.

[11] To this **Peter** says: 'Have you never heard that the blind see nothing, the deaf hear nothing and the foolish understand nothing besides the needs of the stomach? See, you blind usurer, those people camping out there by the thousands are the choice fish I mean.'

[12] Says **Judas**: 'Is that so. Well, this of course is no mean catch for a particular purpose, but for ordinary life I prefer a one hundred pound whaler to all

those people out there. Because for such fish I can get 4 denari everywhere, but for those out there no one would give me a stater.'

[13] Says **Peter**: 'You will become fully Satan's yet, with your profiteering. Are you actually above the human race, to which the likes of us still belong? We all live without profiteering and you are living with us, eating from the same platter, which costs you no more than the actual effort of eating. If however you subsist here without your foolish money, of what use is money for you then?'

[14] Says **Judas**: 'Do I not have wife and children? Who would maintain them if I were to earn nothing? Do you expect these to survive on air?'

[15] Replies **Peter**: 'Look here, I can put up with just about anything, but not an outrageous lie. You might indeed in Jerusalem, where they know of you no more than being a Galilean, pose as a caring family man, but it will do in no way with me here, because I and all those who were and still are our neighbors know you and your domestic affairs only too well for believing a single word of yours. Your wife and children have always had to live in want, earning their meager daily bread through hard labor. They enjoyed mighty little of your catch of fish. Their clothing they got off me and how long is it since from our mercy we almost completely restored your family's totally dilapidated house, while you were roaming the markets? How much did you give us for it? And this you call caring for your wife and children? You should be ashamed of yourself for ten years for daring to so impudently lie to us, who know you so intimately.'

[16] Here Judas' face looks stunned and he says not another word, as Peter had cut him to the quick. He went outside to think about it, returning after a while to ask us all to forgive him. He promised to completely change from now on, wanting quite seriously to be My disciple. Only, would we not cast him out. Here **Nathanael**, who spoke little and rarely, said: 'The spirit of Cain dwells in you, do you get me? And this spirit shall not change on this Earth, because Cain's spirit is the world and no improvement can be expected from same.'

[17] Says **Judas**: 'Yes, yes, yes, you with your old spirit of Cain. Where is Cain and where are we? The generation of Cain perished. Noah alone remained, and in his descendants there is no longer even a drop of Cain's blood, but only the pure blood of the children of God flows in our veins. And where the blood is pure, there the spirit is pure too, for man's spirit always originates in his blood, and thus the spirit is always quite as pure as the blood.'

[18] Says **Nathanael**: 'That is your old, already familiar nonsense and does not count with me. Go to the Sadducees. There you can cause a sensation with your nonsense. With us, however, the blood is putrid matter and the spirit is and remains forever spirit. What use is to you the blood of a child of God if a most impure spirit dwells within it as is the case with you? Do you understand me?'

[19] Says **Judas**: 'Indeed, indeed, you could be right and I shall endeavor to follow your teaching. Yet if your teaching is built on altruism, coming over with patience and gentleness, then I don't think it necessary that you should all constantly try to get rid of me with all kinds of quarreling. Because, what is any teaching without disciples? Thin air, going unnoticed. Therefore every teaching needs its disciples just as much as all disciples need a good teaching. And

therefore I maintain that every disciple is worth whatever any teaching in itself is worth. And so I don't think it would be too remiss on the part of you all to show me, your fellow disciple, a bit more patience.

[20] As quite wise people in your own right, you hopefully shall understand my still being grounded in my old precepts, for this very reason I want to grasp your teaching, in order to therewith shed my old teaching of not much faith. If then I sometimes bring up something here and there against your new teaching, since I am not yet an initiate, I trust you are going to find this natural?

[21] Once I shall, like yourselves, become initiated into the principles of your teaching, finding them like yourselves incontrovertibly good and true, I shall become a proponent tenfold of you all in aggregate, since I possess courage and can confront all, fearing no humans. And if I were fearing, I would have stopped coming over to you a long time since, because you have been, together with your Master, showing me only too clearly that I should spare you my company. But I once and for all do not fear and so I keep coming. You are of course always thoroughly annoyed about it, but this does not bother me and I remain a disciple of this new teaching just like yourselves. What can you put against that?'

[22] Replies **Nathanael**: 'Much and nothing, whichever way you want it. Your virtue of fearlessness is not worthy of much praise, since Satan also must be fearless, otherwise he would not remain disobedient to God the Lord eternity after eternity. We can observe something like that also in the animals of this Earth, of which some obviously are more daring than others. See a lion, a tiger, a panther, wolf, hyena or bear and compare these to a lamb, a goat, a deer or rabbit and other such timid animals. Tell me to which of these animal groups you would count yourself?'

[23] Says **Judas**: 'That surely should be obvious that, like everyone else, I should incline towards the gentler animals and not towards the rapacious, wild beasts, because the lion's courage is everyone's death.'

[24] Says **Nathanael**: 'And yet you praise courage, thinking to become a competent disciple therewith? Courage, in the actual sense of the word is, I tell you, a great vice, because it is the fruit of arrogance, which is contempt for everything not part of one's own self. Therefore in our teaching, fearless human courage shall never be regarded as a virtue, as it is the exact opposite of what our teaching demands of man.

[25] Who is it that wages warfare? See, all those so-called heroes, not fearing even death. Let the world be filled with heroes, and eternal war shall be passing over the Earth's fields constantly, because every hero not only wants to be a co-hero of the other heroes, but a hero of his own, and shall not rest until all other heroes either submit to him or he has dispatched them from the world one by one.

[26] Compare this with a mankind innocent as lambs and you have a paradise on Earth.

[27] When a hero faces the timorous, he will not pursue him, because the timorous does not contest his fame. But where one hero confronts another, they soon shall challenge each other to a fight and neither shall rest until one or the other has subdued the adversary. And see, this in a nutshell is the blessing of

courage.

[28] If therefore you want to be our fellow-disciple, then put aside your most superficial courage and rather be full of love, patience and gentleness, and you shall be as befits a disciple of the Lord.'

[29] Says **Judas**: 'Very well, you are not altogether wrong. I shall consider the matter further and let you all know tomorrow what I intend doing, whether to stay with you or leave.'

[30] With these words Judas goes outside, seeks out several acquaintances among the big crowd, discussing nearly all night what he heard of Nathanael, but they all are on Nathanael's side, saying: 'Nathanael is a true sage.' And they know there is no guile in his soul. We in the house however took our rest.


## CHAPTER 115
### The people's intention to proclaim Jesus king

[1] The following morning however there was much excitement in front of the house, because by daybreak already a great many people were streaming in from all sides and there was also no shortage of bread and milk vendors. And thus a very great commotion got under way, daunting all those within the house.

[2] But I said: 'Let us partake of our morning meal and then move to a house of My acquaintance, a few furlongs beyond Capernaum, so that this thing would not arouse too great a sensation in Nazareth.'

[3] Even while still announcing this to the disciples, **Judas** enters, saying: 'Brethren, I am staying with you for good. My business is finished. I finished it already today instead of tomorrow, on your account, but, to change the subject, the crowd around here, swollen to several thousand, wants to do nothing less than proclaim the good Master Jesus king. And this I would call quite risky, given the strong Roman presence, because it may be rather hard to trust the otherwise humane Romans under these conditions, nor the High Priests, Pharisees and scribes of our people.'

[4] I said: 'Now then, bring in the morning meal quickly. It also is Sabbath and more folk could arrive, therefore we shall get away from here quickly.'

[5] There was a well-fenced garden to both sides of our house, which could be reached only through a small back door to the house. We therefore used this door and got away from the thousands of curious eyes, so to say, of whom more than three quarters were driven there by idle curiosity, to gape at miraculous happenings there.

[6] After the one hundred-odd of us got away from the great crowd unseen, even while they were still waiting for Me and My disciples to come out in order to work some miracle or make a speech, with their then being able, as planned by many, to proclaim Me king of the Jews, one maid of My house stepped out to the crowd, asking a man who especially appealed to her, what the great crowd was after. And **the man** spoke: 'We are here to make Jesus, the mightiest of the mighty and

wisest of the wise, our King. Because we were witnesses of how the sea and the winds obeyed Him and how the worst devils and men and spirits must flee before Him. He irrefutably is the Promised Anointed of God, to redeem the people of God from the hard yoke and tyranny of Rome. It therefore is time to elevate Him to king of the people of God, recognized and worshiped universally by all Jews. See, that's why we are here. What is He doing inside the house that long, not even coming out to see us?'

[7] Says **the maid**: 'Here you are waiting in vain, because he already left early for the district of Capernaum, maybe for someone sick and together with all His disciples. Thus, as said, you are waiting in vain.'

[8] The man asks her whether she knew the house I went to. But the maid is sorry that neither she nor anyone else in the house knew. Because I had confided it to no one as to which house I had gone.

[9] In order to convince himself of the maid's statement, the man goes to check out the house, and not finding anyone there other than the few people helping Mary clean the cooking and table crockery, he goes back outside to inform all that I had headed in the general direction of Capernaum to heal a sick.

[10] When **the crowd** found that out, they took off, yelling: 'Let's be off to Capernaum! There we shall find out the house He went to!'

[11] All but a few Nazarenes head for the road to Capernaum and My house is free of the huge public encampment.

[12] But the people of Capernaum in turn are startled on seeing this outsize crowd moving on the city. The Roman chief at once dispatches orderlies to find out the reason for such numbers moving into Capernaum, particularly on a Sabbath, whose keeping it is the chief's lot to uphold.

[13] Say **the asked ones**: 'We are seeking Jesus of Nazareth, having heard of His presence here.'

[14] And the chief notifies them that Jesus is to be found not in Capernaum, but in the vicinity of Bethabara, where He had moved 2 hours earlier.

[15] Hearing this, the multitude quickly moves toward Bethabara. But on the way between these two localities along the Galilean Sea, the ringleaders spot another multitude surrounding a house, and inquiring there are told that I was within.

[16] The house is thereupon beleaguered on all sides and the people are figuring out how to make Me king. But here the commander does Me a favor, by dispatching a whole legion from Capernaum, who is to oversee the multitude. And the host holds back from their undertaking.

[17] This commotion however was, because of Myself, attracting to this house several Jerusalemite Pharisees and scribes, detained at Capernaum at the time, as well as some from Nazareth and the surroundings, as they had heard from Jairus how I had awoken his daughter from sheer death. For these the crowd was making way to enter the house.

[18] No sooner do they locate Me in the house when they start regaling Me with a host of questions. But I refer them to My disciples, saying: 'These here are My witnesses. They know about it all, ask them.'

[19] And the Pharisees and scribes then storm the disciples and these give

them well-measured answers.

## CHAPTER 116
### Healing of the man with gout

[1] While the Pharisees and scribes are trading all kinds of words with the disciples, a man with gout is brought upon a bed by some 8 persons, for the purpose of My helping him. But the house was so densely beleaguered that it was not possible for the 8 men to bring him into the house and over to Me. But they also feared that owing to the crush, I would shortly leave through the small door facing the sea and then make off over the sea. **One of them** therefore went to the owner, whom he knew, saying: 'Friend see, we 8 brothers have just brought our mother's brother together with his bed. He was not able to leave his bed for 8 years because he had gout after gout, and for probable healing by the famous Savior Jesus, who is in your house just now. Due to the immense crowd however it is impossible to bring him into the house and before Jesus. Give me a clue, friend, what I should do.'

[2] Says **the landlord**: 'This is of course a problem, because the room where Jesus finds Himself is thronged with people. Over one hundred of His disciples as well as a great many priests, Pharisees and scribes from all places and districts are in there having discussions. Yet I shall nevertheless on this extraordinary occasion, as between old friends try to do something for you.

[3] Watch, my house, like most fisher-huts, is covered with thatches. Let's put up a couple of ladders to the roof and uncover it sufficiently for you to get the sick through it. Once you have him in the attic, you can put four heavy ropes, of which I have plenty up there, around the bed legs, while I open the trap door situated in the middle and we shall let the sick down with the roped bed and he can then himself ask Jesus to make him whole. The ones right beneath the opening shall be making room, unless they want the bed to land on their heads.'

[4] This impresses the one from the outset and to the derision of the big crowd, it is put into action and the whole thing goes off well, without disturbance. Only one person, a properly foolish ultra-orthodox temple servant, who measures the law with the precision of the compass, remarked to those who uncovered the roof conscientiously that they ought to be mindful of it being high Sabbath.

[5] But **the 8** said: 'Ay, what should you old temple ox have to say here? Shut your toothless trap and go crawling up to Jerusalem to the Solomonian ox, donkey, calf and sheep barn and there bawl your Jeremiah lamentations to these customary occupants of the house of God. We have for a long time now been wide awake to your beastly divine service and know that God is pleased with good works rather than the braying of your oxen and donkeys.'

[6] This sharp comment from one of the 8 silenced the temple servant quite expeditiously, with the echo of the whole crowd leading to great spontaneous cheering, since for a long time already to the Galileans, the temple machinations

215

meant nothing.

[7] The young man had in just a few words told the full truth in a rather funny way and more for this than anything else received the accolade. Because on great feasts, big hordes of cattle were herded into the temple, together with donkeys and sheep, for the very purpose of the loudest braying and bleating of these animals, usually also letting these animals starve for a couple of days, so as to have them make the peak noise during the offering, making the people shake and tremble.

[8] Verily, the high Mass in the Temple, especially on the great feast days, was something so foolishly hideous and swinish, as is not to be met with on the entire Earth, not even among the fiercest peoples. And therefore the young man answered the strict temple servant quite correctly, with which even I was pleased, as I knew quite well within Me how it came about.

[9] Soon thereafter, the trapdoor of the room, or rather the attic, was opened. **A self-important Pharisee** inquires loudly: 'What's going on up there, what's happening?!'

[10] Says the former **clever speech-maker**: 'Have a little patience and you soon shall see. See, today is Sabbath. Upon this day, according to your customary teaching in the Synagogues and schools, grace comes from above. This time however, mankind's grace is below and so, there being one who having not yet received grace, comes from above down to you to seek his grace down there. Therefore nothing contrary to the Sabbath is taking place here, for surely it shall not make any difference whether on a Sabbath grace comes from above, or whether someone seeks grace down below, if it has already come down to blind men who are not capable of seeing it, although already bumping into it with their noses.'

[11] This address once again draws great cheers from among the disciples, but anger from the Pharisees, priests and scribes. **The disciples** nevertheless call out loudly: 'Then down with the graceless one from above, who seeks grace only down here.' And the sick is lowered down at once.

[12] As he now lay on the bed in front of Me, he begged Me to help him, sobbing. I however, seeing that he and those who brought him had the right and true faith, said to the sick, 'Fear not, My son, your sins are forgiven you.' But this I said initially only for the scribes' self-examination, who had become favorably disposed towards Me, because the resurrection of the daughter of Jairus, who was their superior, had made this sort into My friends.

[13] When however I had said to the sick: 'Your sins are forgiven' [Mt.9,3], anger was immediately kindled with some strict scribes and they said to themselves in their hearts: 'what's this, what do we hear? How can he be a proper Savior (doctor)? He blasphemes.' [Mt.9,3] Because they regarded Me merely as an exceptional doctor, but that divine power could indwell Me was to them *crimen sacri leasi* (blasphemy), since God's power resided only in the priests, Levites, Pharisees and scribes and furthermore only in the Temple at Jerusalem.

[14] Having of course discerned their innermost thoughts only too quickly, I spoke to them at once, saying: 'Why think ye so evil in your hearts? For, which is

216

easier, to say "your sins are forgiven you", (which of a truth you yourselves always say, especially to those who come to you with rich offerings, yet none being actually helped), or to say with effect: "arise and walk".

[15] Says **one scribe**: 'With this one you won't be getting beyond the forgiving of sins, surely, because whoever has been ravaged by gout like him, only death can help.'

[16] I said: 'Is this your opinion? Yet I say unto you, so that you may see and know that the Son of Man also has power on Earth to forgive sins, I now say, full of effect, to this sick one, who is to you who arrogate to yourselves the exclusive power from God to forgive sins, yet saying he can be healed only through death: Arise, take up your bed and go home without fear, completely sound.'

[17] With these words, the sick stretched out his fully sound limbs, which had previously been most miserably contorted and partly withered away. And instantly also he gained all flesh, thanking Me while sobbing with over great joy, standing up sufficiently firm and powerful to loosen the ropes from the bed at once, then carrying the bed under his left arm, making his way through the immense throng with the fairly heavy and large bed with great ease, carrying it home all the way to Capernaum.

[18] The multitude however who were present and saw this deed, began to praise God loudly for giving a man such power, as was only within God Himself and with which all things were possible to him.

[19] This deed again fortified **the Pharisees and scribes** in attendance, to the extent of dropping their evil thoughts and saying: 'This truly is unprecedented. How this is possible for you, verily only God can know and otherwise no man upon Earth.'

## CHAPTER 117
### Speech of the young Roman

And **the young man** who had previously spoken so well, said through the attic: 'I wonder whether the High priest in Jerusalem can bring this about, even with a thousand oxen, ten thousand donkeys and a hundred thousand sheep?'

[2] This comment provoked great derision even among the Pharisees. Yet **one scribe** nevertheless became vocal, saying to the worked up speaker in the opening above: 'Good friend, I wouldn't take this too far, because the High Priest's arms encompass the entire Earth and he who gets under the High Priest's arms shall be crushed. Besides, the High Priest does not need to resurrect the dead or heal people with gout, because all this concerns man's flesh and not his spirit and is the concern of doctors and not priests. Do you understand that?'

[3] Says **the speaker**: 'Friend, this certainly would be the concern also of priests, if only they were capable of bringing it about. But because they are for all the treasures of the world incapable of doing so, they have to in the end admit with proud mien and say: "This is no concern of priests, who are called upon to

only care for man's spirit." But I say, if it is possible for a doctor to give back the spirit and soul of a young maiden who died after a high fever right before our eyes and therefore from a malady from which no man ever even half died, then this surely is also going to be a very powerful spiritual care too?

[4] When God created Adam merely from the dust of the Earth, then this creation was a merely material one and there was nothing spiritual, besides God Himself.

[5] When later however God breathed into the dead form a living soul and into same a thinking spirit, then this was not a material but a highly spiritual work of God, upon the first man of the Earth. And if here right before our eyes this wonder-doctor Jesus of Nazareth carries out the same upon the little daughter of the principal, then this surely would be a most spiritual work and care?'

[6] Says **the scribe**: 'This is something you don't understand, therefore you should be quiet.'

[7] Says **the young man**: 'If I were still a Jew, I should indeed be quiet. But since I am a Jew no longer, but an honest Greek and follower of Socrates' glorious teaching, I see no reason for being silenced by Jewish priests, whose current and exceedingly stupid teaching I unfortunately know only too well.'

[8] Says **the scribe**: 'And what should you heathen find stupid about the old, purely divine teaching of the Jews? Are Moses and the prophets perhaps insufficiently exalted for you and do you find their teaching stupid?'

[9] Says **the young man**: 'No, Moses and all the prophets who spoke that of you which I now say, I regard as exceedingly and purely godly-wise men. But your statutes, of which neither Moses nor any of the prophets ever dreamt of, I regard stupid to full excess.

[10] How do you serve God? Dung, excrement and filth you burn upon the altar consecrated to God, while the fat oxen, calves and rams you consume yourselves, offering them to your omnivorous paunches. The purely divine part of your teaching you have discarded and whoever among you dares to teach the pure, to such you do what you have always done to your prophets.

[11] How long is it since the days you murdered Zacharias in the Temple?

[12] At Bethabara, his son preached the truth, exhorting you treacherous blasphemers in the Holy of Holies to repent and to return to Moses and his most pure teaching. What did you do with him? Where did he get to? He disappeared. As far as I know he was taken away by thugs at night.

[13] Now at Nazareth, Jesus has been awoken by God as a prophet, accomplishing deeds which are possible only to the almighty gods, yet you watch Him with Argus eyes. Let Him beware if He should dare to, like myself, hold forth with even one word against your own most obscene teaching, not initiated by Moses. You would at once accuse Him of the ultimate crime of blasphemy and out of gratitude for resurrecting your dead and making straight your cripples, stone and even bind Him to the cross.

[14] Because what you are on about is ruling and to at the same time luxuriate in the fattening of your paunches. Whoever would restrict you therein or turn you back to Moses is your enemy and you have the means to get him out of the way.

[15] You all I despise like a decayed, stinking ass, because you are and will remain actually, the greatest enemies of God and all his people. I am a heathen, yet I recognize the purely divine power in the man Jesus, the fullness of which the world has not experienced to this day.

[16] Not his flesh affects these unheard of deeds, but the almighty, pure spirit of God, which must be indwelling in Him in all its fullness.

[17] See, this do I recognize as a heathen, declared blind by you. What however do you recognize in Jesus, who through the mere word, without any medicine, resurrects your dead and makes our cripples leap like young stags?

[18] And I ask you blind ones: who must be He whom it takes only a word of will, and storms and winds are silenced, the dead arise and the lame start leaping as if transformed to stag-nature?'

[19] Through this really true and bold speech he had brought the Pharisees and scribes one and all to such rage that they would have torn him to pieces if they could have laid hands on him. But this was not possible and no proposition, because the people were jubilant about this young man, who had at last the guts to thoroughly rub the full truth into the noses of the swollen-headed Pharisees and scribes.

## CHAPTER 118
### Revelations about the temple

[1] But **one Pharisee** turned to Me and said: 'How can you, as a true Jew, keep silent when a miserable heathen like that, to whom you have done such good, has the audacity to so blasphemously slander the holy teaching of our fathers?'

[2] I said: 'But he slandered neither Moses nor the prophets, but only yourselves and your new statutes, letting Me off. With what should I reprimand him? He described only yourselves and therefore only abused you. It is your own business to get even with him. If he has nothing against Me, what should I have against him? See to it yourselves as to how to settle with him. I am on good terms with him at this stage.'

[3] Say the **Pharisees and scribes**: 'Too right has he not abused you of course, but us, but we thought you had now become our friend and knowing what power dwells in Your word and will, you could for comradeship have told this heathen off, at least on account of the people. But you let him talk and put us to shame in front of the people and you see, that was not too praiseworthy of you. We don't want to hate You for it, but cannot be favorably disposed towards you either.'

[4] I said: 'Choose the way you want to be and I too shall be the way it seems discreet to Me. By the way, it is rather odd of you to deny Me your friendship now, since you have never shown Me any yet. I however, who should have the full right to deny you My friendship, since only a short while therefore the thoughts about Me in your hearts were not exactly commendable, still am not doing so.

[5] What can I actually lose with your friendship? I say unto you: verily, nothing.

But when you enjoy My friendship no more, who shall call your dead children to life in My stead?

[6] If however you carefully consider the young man's speech, then by any true intellectual standards you must admit it within yourselves that the man has spoken the truth most fundamentally. You know the scriptures and know Moses and the prophets. Do you ask yourselves whether any trace of Moses or any other prophet is to be found in the Temple?

[7] Was I not in Jerusalem Myself this year and to My great annoyance saw how the prayer-house of God had been turned into a murderer's den?

[8] The forecourts are full of slaughter-cattle for sale, as well as other unclean creatures, so that people cannot get into the actual Temple without gravely endangering their lives. Slaughtering proceeds in the forecourts on one side as in a slaughter-house, with meat being sold. On the other side, brokering booths and money-changers are situated, there being a racket and yelling where hardly a person can hear their own word.

[9] When one then gets to the actual main Temple, one cannot move at all for all the pigeon and other bird merchants, yelling out their sale offers. And inside the Holy of Holies, to which once only the High Priest had access once a year by God's command, anyone, including even a heathen, for payment called offering, can be guided around, behind Jew's backs of course, under seal of secrecy. Yet the Holy of Holies is as well-known in Rome as to the High Priest in Jerusalem. And thus, for money, all Temple-secrets are revealed to strangers. If a poor Jew however should dare to step behind the curtain, he is at once stoned behind the Temple wall, at the accursed spot, as a blasphemer and profaner. And not a week passes when not at least one person is stoned and two have to drink the accursed water.

[10] What kind of system is it however where strangers are initiated, but one's own children killed?

[11] Tell yourselves that Moses and the prophets commanded this and that Solomon in all his wisdom, when he had completed the Temple, consecrated it for the purpose it now serves. In short, the prayer-house of God has become the barest den of murderers, and Jehovah's Spirit no longer dwells in the shape of the pillar of fire above the Ark of the Covenant.'

[12] Here the Pharisees and scribes grow suspicious, saying to Me: 'You always stayed in and around Nazareth. How can you know all this? Who betrayed the Temple to you?'

[13] I said: 'O for the great silliness of your question. If I know your most secret thoughts, how should I not know what is and happens in the Temple? Yet not I alone, but every person knows it.

[14] You yourselves however are the actual betrayers of it all and your great money-greed tempted you to it. For money you initiated strangers into Temple secrets and those then loudly proclaimed it to the Jews in the streets. Are you asking Me who betrayed the Temple to Me?

[15] If however, like many thousands of people, you know how matters stand in the Temple, knowing at the same time what Moses and all the prophets taught,

who all were filled with the purest and truest Spirit of God – such Spirit alone speaking through their mouths – what kind of faith in God is yours then, that you should so easily sell God's Word down the river and with the most brazen and haughty conceit substitute and proclaim as if from God, your own statutes to the poor blind people, together with threats of death, to keep and worship your statues?'

## CHAPTER 119
### The example of the road to Rome

[1] Says **one scribe**: 'Friend, you take much upon yourself saying such things to us, on the betrayal of which the Temple has set the death penalty. You are lucky to have rendered our principal such favor, otherwise you might not fare too well, for we are bound to the Temple by a mighty oath.'

[2] I said: 'Which you can break any time you like, because it is not God to whom you swore the oath, but to the Temple, which is made by human hands and within which God no longer resides.

[3] But where God does not reside, there the old prince of the lie and all evil resides and to this prince and current lord of the Temple you can break your oath without fear.

[4] Were you to break your vain oath with the Temple, God the Lord would take pleasure in you and He would give you what He has given Me from the foundation of the world: that which you are now marveling at but cannot grasp, how I accomplish works which according to your own testimony, are possible only to God. But if you fear the Temple more than God, whom you don't know, then you shall remain bonded to the Temple and be an abomination before God.

[5] If however you do not believe My simple Words, then believe on account of My works, which I perform before you for your good and of which you yourselves say they are possible only to God.'

[6] Say **the Scribes**: 'How can you know God better than us, since you have not learned the scriptures?'

[7] I said: 'The dead letter you know indeed, but God is not to be found in that. Therefore you are unable to recognize God from the Scriptures, because the Scriptures only show the way to God and this only if you follow this way undeviatingly.

[8] Of what benefit is it for you to know the road to Rome, if you don't set out upon it in order to get to Rome and there to see the great city of the king? Who is he that can claim to know Rome because he knows the way, upon which however he has never set out by even a single span? Of what use is in this respect the knowledge of the Scriptures, which are a way to God, if you have never taken a step along same?

[9] I however am familiar with all of Scripture, like yourselves and have always acted in accordance with God's commandments contained therein and therefore

within the fullest knowledge of God and can therefore say unto you from the first wellspring, that neither among you, nor the likes of you had there ever been even one who has recognized God and never shall do so along your evil ways, for you are atheists, one and all.

[10] You yourselves did not want to recognize God, yet you will block off with death and ruin the way for those who would still walk the right way. For this you shall therefore in the other life once be overcome that much more by damnation. Because all those you have and still are perpetually persecuting, shall once be your eternal judges.'

[11] As I proclaim this to the Pharisees and scribes, there arises among the people a mighty storm of applause and they are about to lay hands on the Pharisees and scribes. But I prevent it and make My way to the sea through the small seaward gate, together with the disciples and all the Pharisees and scribes. And with several boats lying in readiness there, these are immediately boarded and with moderate wind we sail away from the coast, the great crowd having been unable to catch up with us.

## CHAPTER 120
### Matthew the tax-collector

[1] Once we were out of view to the people, I called for a landing, as it was high noon and there was nothing to eat in the boat. After a good two hours from the previous house, we disembarked and had to go back some way to a village where we intended spending our lunch-time.

[2] Just before the village there was a principal toll-gate. And see, at the desk sat that same young man (he was only 35 years old, which was regarded as young by the Jews) who at the previous house was one of the eight brothers who had brought the palsied and who had spoken so wisely.

[3] When **the scribes and Pharisees** caught sight of him, they said: 'This does not look too good. This one turns out to be a Roman tax-collector. He is going to hit us hard with the tax. What are we going to do?'

[4] I said: 'Don't be troubled, for here it will not be necessary. I shall arrange it best.'

[5] With these words I step up to the tax-collector, saying to him: 'Matthew (that was his name), hand this table over to someone else and (you) follow Me. And at once he got up, delegated the table and followed Me without comment. And when the disciples and Pharisees and scribes at the gate asked what the charges were.

[6] **Matthew** said: 'This time the Lord has fixed up your tax, for He has healed my uncle. How should I now accept tax from Him, the godly Master?'

[7] Therewith the barrier was opened and all passed through free of charge.

[8] When we reached the village however, Matthew led us into his house, where all those tax-collectors employed at the principal toll-gate, together with a great many officials and other "sinners", according to the assessment and judgment of

the Jews, Pharisees and Scribes, were having their lunch. For Matthew's house was big and also a guest-house, where only those Jews who paid could eat and drink, whereas the tax-collectors, officials and "sinners" were not charged, as they were one and all employees of the house leased by the Romans for tax-purposes.

[9] I was however immediately invited to lunch by all the tax-collectors, while bread and wine in adequate quantities were served to My disciples and also to the Pharisees and scribes outside. And the disciples were happy with that. Not so the Pharisees and scribes with them, for these were peeved at not also being invited to the table.

[10] But while I was already seated at the table with a great many tax-collectors and sinners, another large number of them were arriving from other areas, because Matthew's house was known far and wide as a well-to-do and hospitable one and there were large gatherings there, particularly on Sabbaths. They all greeted Me most friendly, all saying that a greater honor could not have come upon the house than to have Me as their guest, even as they were extending the table and all accommodating themselves at My table.

[11] But **the Pharisees and scribes** crowded the big open doorway, to watch what I should do and say. Seeing that I got on most friendly with the tax-collectors and sinners however, they were secretly enraged, asking My disciples who were outside with them: 'Why does your Master dine with tax-collectors and all those obvious sinners? Is he perhaps one of them?'

[12] As I perceived such question, I turned to them from the table and said, briefly and with abandon: 'They that are strong and well need no doctor, but only the sick. But go and learn what it means:

[13] 'For I desired mercy and not sacrifice'.

[14] For I have come to call the sinners to repentance and not the righteous, who need no repentance'. (Mt.9,13)

[15] These words the Pharisees and scribes interpreted in their favor and said nothing more, as they felt flattered.

[16] I then engaged the company's attention with all kinds of parables, shedding light on how human life and its weaknesses can end in degeneration. I thus also gave them firm outlines for the rearing of children, showing them how deficiency in rearing children has, with time, resulted in every kind of evil, spiritually and physically.

[17] In this way I also taught the company the reason for God's creation of man and how as a free being he should try to meet God's purpose, in order to therewith become a perfect, indestructible spiritual being.

opposite always of what it preaches. Instead of friendship, love and peace, it often creates irreconcilable enmity, hate and the most furious wars. And these have always been the fruits of all religious revivals upon Earth. But if the fruits after such happenings, as experience always teaches, are the same ones, then it becomes the imperative responsibility of us enlightened ones and leaders of the peoples to in time cut the path of such revivalists, along which thousands are threatened with downfall and ruin. Is it not better that such domineering magicians should be dispatched from the world, rather than thousands having to be led astray by such eccentrics and be bumped off and destroyed?'

## CHAPTER 121
### Conversation about Joseph, Mary and Jesus

[1] It shall be realized that such instruction of the company, although not understood by all, nevertheless went down well and with gratitude. Even **the Scribes and Pharisees** were astonished at My wisdom, asking among themselves how such wisdom came My way. Because they had known Me and Joseph, Mary and Joseph's children, saying to the disciples: 'It truly is incomprehensible. His father was indeed a highly competent craftsman in his own sphere and exceedingly faithful, fair and honest and a strict Jew as well, who concerned himself with Moses and the prophets to the best of his knowledge of same. Yet there never was any special wisdom about him, and his4 other, actual sons who had been engaged by us several times, are as far removed from any trace of wisdom as the sun, moon and stars from the Earth.

[2] The good mother Mary herself, a woman still pretty, hard-working and virtuous, on whom none can cast aspersions, was indeed, as we were informed, brought up in the Temple, but we know all about such training, knowing only too well how much wisdom is expected of it, particularly for girls. And he cannot have absorbed much wisdom from his mother. And he has to our knowledge never attended any school either!'

[3] 'On the contrary', says **one Scribe**, a good acquaintance of Joseph's, 'Joseph has more than once told me about the problem with his boy, complaining and saying "I don't know what to do with this boy. His purportedly very peculiar birth, seemingly closely intertwined with those appearances, from which one should have expected the divine being itself to manifest itself through such a child on Earth, to which several most extraordinary appearances in his earliest childhood clearly attest, as well as his sayings of the most exalted wisdom, had truly filled me with the greatest expectation, the more so on account of my most direct lineage from David. Yet in this very time when the child should be learning something, nothing can be accomplished with him and there can be no mention of any learning. Even if I place him with a teacher, same can't get anywhere with him. The boy knows and understands everything much better and if a teacher is about to get strict with him, that's the end of it.

[4] What has remained with him from his earliest youth is a most incomprehensibly unbending willpower, with which, where he deems it necessary, he can work most obvious miracles. But precisely on account of this very trait, nothing is to be done with him. He otherwise is pious, obedient, well-behaved, gentle and as unassuming as his mother. Only he must not be confronted with learning.

[5] See, this is how the old Joseph complained to me not once but several times and therefore it is even more certain that he has never, besides his carpentry, in

his life learned anything, neither reading and still less writing. Therefore, an excusable question: where does this wisdom come from?'

[6] Says the Gospel writer **John**: 'Friends, I know it only too well and feel easy about it, but the time for telling you this is still far off. But the time shall come for you to hear it from His own mouth. Until then however, let His works and wisdom suffice you.' The Pharisees and Scribes tried indeed to get more out of John, but he would not be moved. But now several taxation employees and officials went back to work, creating room at the big table.

## CHAPTER 122
## The doubt of John the Baptist

[1] And the young landlord Matthew, the tax-collector (who is not to be confused with the Matthew who was only a scribe, wherefore in the Scriptures, 'tax-collector' is added when referring to him) went and called My disciples, the Pharisees and the Scribes in and they came and were seated and quite heartily tucked into the food and drink, with the exception of Judas, who held back this time for fear of a large bill. And, as known, he was no good friend of payment.

[2] When we were all together cheerfully, with the Pharisees and Scribes also gradually finding some rapport with the tax-collectors and so-called sinners, a young **kitchen maid** comes in to the landlord, saying: 'What is to be done? The fishermen have just arrived with fish and are asking to eat and drink, but having had all these guests by coincidence today, consuming nearly all our stores, we in the kitchen don't know what to do'. Says **Matthew, the tax-collector**: 'How many are they?' Says **the maid**: 'There are about 20 of them.' Says **Matthew, the tax-collector**: 'Then let them come in here. There is still plenty of provision here.'

[3] The maid goes and tells the fishermen and these betake themselves to the large dining room, taking up a small table from which the lunch guests had already departed.

[4] But when the fishermen caught sight of Peter and several others of their former mates, they exchanged greetings and **the fishermen**, somewhat moody because of the relative lean look of their table, say to Peter: 'For us this will do, no doubt, as we still are true disciples of John and our law is fasting. But you new disciples of Jesus can eat to your heart's content, as we see, since with you, fasting is no longer a problem.'

[5] Says **Peter**: 'John fasted on account of what we have and we used to fast with him in accordance with his doctrine and strict sermons. John proclaimed Him with whom we are now, testifying of Him. When this One came however and even accepted John's baptism with water, John did not fully trust his senses, nor did you. Because even while John, prompted by the Spirit, testified of Jesus as He was approaching, saying: "See, this is He of whom I said, after me cometh a man who is preferred before me, whose shoe's latchet I am not worthy to undo", he yet secretly doubted, like yourselves and still does to this hour. Wherefore he still

fasts and you fast also. But with us believers, fasting is at an end. It is your own fault that you still fast. It suits you thus, for just as the blind cannot fortify his vision with the light and its colors, just so the blind in heart shall fortify neither his heart nor his stomach. Do you understand that?

[6] Had John believed, he would have followed the Lamb, which according to his testimony, takes away the sins of the world. But because his soul itself doubted Him of whom his spirit thus testified through her, he stayed behind in the desert until Herod arrested him, as we heard.

[7] Why did he not follow Him, since he said to us through his spirit: "Hear Him"? Why did he not want to hear Him? Why did he not follow Him, since it was on account of His coming that he lived his whole life so strictly? We are not aware of Him who we followed ever forbidding him to follow Him. Therefore give me one solid reason why John did not follow Jesus.'

[8] Here John's disciples were perplexed, not knowing what to reply. Only one of them says that the news that John was arrested by Herod is wrong. Herod had only summoned him to his residence at Jerusalem in order to find out from him about the coming of God's Anointed. Herod regards John too highly to put him in prison.

[9] **Peter** however said somewhat humorously: 'If it has not yet happened in actuality, it is bound to do so soon. Because Herod is a cunning fox and is to be trusted no more than a snake.'

### CHAPTER 123
### The testimony of John the Baptist

[1] After this conversation, John's disciples carry on eating and we do too. Only some of the Pharisees properly fasted and were not prepared to eat until sunset, for unleavened bread they could obtain none among the Greeks here, whereupon they fasted, even while the majority of their colleagues and the Scribes were heartily tucking into the food.

[2] When the wine after a while had made John's disciples more talkative, **one of them** rose, wanting to know from Myself why they, as John's disciples, had to fast so much and so strictly, yet I and My disciples not, asking Me: 'Lord and Master, why do we fast so much and the Pharisees also, whereas Your disciples are not fasting?'

[3] And **I** say to him: 'Friend, you were with John when the news was brought to him that I was baptizing and that many were following Me. Say it aloud in front of everyone, what was John's reply?' Says **the disciple of John**: 'Here John said and replied: "A man can take nothing unless it were given him from Heaven. You are my witnesses to my having said that I am not Christ, but only sent before Him. He who has the bride is the bridegroom. The bridegroom's friend however is with him and listens to him and rejoices with the bridegroom's voice. This my joy now fulfils itself. He must wax but I wane. He who is from above is over all, but he who

is of this Earth is only so and speaks only of this Earth. Only He who comes from Heaven is above all."

[4] Here John paused, relating all that he had beheld and how he had witnessed of Him, but regretted, with a deep sigh, that his testimony, being totally true, was not accepted by anyone. But he who nevertheless accepts it let him tightly seal the immense actuality of God, for fear of the world.

[5] Although he knows it that He who was sent of God Himself speaks only the pure Word of God, he nevertheless does not dare to confess it before the world, fearing the enemy of God more than God Himself, on account of his miserable body, which also is of the world, thus paying tribute to the world. Of what good is it however to know God's true measure, yet stick to the measure of the world? God however never gives man the spirit by the world's measure. Let those be condemned therefore who have recognized God's Spirit, yet stick to the measure of the world, having no life eternal within them.

[6] Only, continued John, he who believes on the Son has life eternal within him, because the son Himself is the life of the Father. He who does not believe on the Son therefore has not eternal life and the old wrath of God remains upon him.

[7] See, this is what John said at the time. Yet right up to this hour none of us has been able to fully grasp its meaning. That much we gathered indeed, that he meant You, but how all this relates, how should we have been able to grasp and fully understand it?'

[8] I said: 'Now then, since you heard this about Me from John, you must know that I am the bridegroom who John meant. But if I am the self-same Bridegroom, then surely these will be My wedding-guests?'

[9] Says **John's disciple**: 'Where then is the beautiful heavenly bride? How are you a bridegroom without a bride?'

[10] I said: 'These My wedding-guests are also My bride at the same time. Because those who hear My Word, preserving it in their heart and acting accordingly truly are My bride, as they are also My wedding-guests. How could and should the wedding-guests suffer among themselves even while the Bridegroom is with them? But comes the time when the Bridegroom is taken from them, then they shall also be fasting.'

[11] John's disciples greatly marvel at this and are somewhat annoyed, thinking they detected a sneer, since I said these Words with a slight smile. And so that same **disciple of John** then tried to also make a somewhat snide remark, saying: 'This seems strange. It was God's Spirit that spoke through John and it should speak that much more through you, since John's testimony applied to you. Yet it is odd that the self-same Spirit of God, speaking through Moses and the prophets right through to John, always proclaimed a life of strict repentance to poor mankind on Earth, demanding the strictest compliance. You however seem to be and teach the actual opposite of all this. Whoever according to Moses so much as entered the house of a sinner was unclean and had to cleanse himself. He who touched a maiden on a Sabbath, or any woman having her period on some other day, had to have himself cleansed, and much more of the like and of even greater strictness. You and all your disciples however seem not to regard the Sabbath or

personal cleanliness at all. How then is your teaching of God, the way it was through the mouth of the prophets?'


## CHAPTER 124
### Parable of the new and old garment and the new wine in old skins

[1] I said: 'My teaching is like a new garment. Yours however is the old, torn and damaged, wherefore, it was for you also quite in order to go catch fish today, on a Sabbath, in spite of Moses and John. My teaching therefore is a new one and one cannot take parts of it to patch up your old, torn garment therewith. And even if done, it would only result in bigger tears than they were already, because the new patch shall come off the old, brittle garment, resulting in greater damage.

[2] My teaching furthermore can be likened unto a new wine that can't be poured into old skins, or they would be rent, spilling the wine, but to preserve both wine and skin, one pours it into new skins. Do you understand this?'

[3] Say **John's disciples**: 'One can let that pass indeed, although it is not immediately apparent, what you would say therewith. Therefore you could perhaps express this in plainer terms?'

[4] I said: 'Could I, or should I be plainer still? Sure, sure, I could, if I would. But here I intend to be no plainer and therefore I tell you no more than that you are old, brittle garments and skins, unfit for My Teaching. For would this not deprive you of your sweet earth-life, which of a truth is your greatest possession and for the improvement of which you leave no stone unturned, going for large fish-hauls even on a Sabbath, to simply provide your earth-life with an existence of ease and a spot of splendor besides. But the poor you don't see, nor the sick and hurting, nor the hungry and thirsty.

[5] What worry, to the one filled, the poor, hungering and burning of stomach? Likewise, you who are well-clad do not feel the cold in winter, for do you not have means to make winter cozier than the hot summer? And if one half-naked and shivering meets you, telling you of his plight and asking for some warm garment, you get annoyed, serving him with hypocritical words: "Depart, you sluggard. Had you worked in summer, you would not be wanting in winter. Besides, it's not all that cold and as a beggar one should not be all that soft and delicate."

[6] **The beggar** however says: 'Sir, I worked all summer and fall, but my hard work's wages were not even a thousandth's part of what my master gained from my work. Therefore our master can walk about well-dressed even in winter but us his poorly-paid workers who already easily used up our meager wages in summer, now have to suffer in winter, not because not working in summer, but simply because we can't make ends meet. Our master's profit is our want.'

[7] See, this is what the beggar is saying, notwithstanding the fact that there are among the beggars those sinners who deserve their poverty.'

[8] Say **John's disciples**: 'Ah, you are exaggerating. It is not so. A faithful and proper worker has never had cause for complaint about his employer. Those who

want work will get it winter and summer, wages, food and clothing. But we all think it right that the lazy should be shown the door.'

[9] I said: 'You indeed, that I know only too well. But not I, that I tell you. The "why" you shall hear at once. Tell Me, who was it that created the sea with all the good fish?'

[10] Say **John's disciples**: 'Now, what a question. Who but God alone could do so?' I said: 'Good then, tell Me, have you perhaps received advice from God according to which you alone have sole right to catch the good and expensive fish of the sea, selling them at a high price, then putting the entire profit in your bags, hardly passing the thousandth part to your good workers, who alone did the heavy work under life-endangering conditions.'

[11] Say **John's disciples**: 'This again is a silly question. Where on Earth is the man who can produce a property deed from God? For this, God has appointed a head of state and same issues property-rights in God's stead, whoever is recognized by the state as a property owner is so also before God. Besides that, every legal property owner has to annually for his dearly paid-for right to pay all kinds of tithes and rates to the state and is therefore doubly entitled to make the necessary profit from his property.'

[12] I said: 'Yes, indeed is it so on Earth, but not through God, but through mankind's selfishness and domineering. It is they who have instituted such laws and order, but in the beginning of the world, this was not so, for a long time the Earth was then the common weal of mankind.

[13] But when from among mankind the children of Cain made a part of the Earth subject to inheritance, making it into law and into a selfish, domineering order, it then did not take another thousand years.

[14] God allowed the Flood to take place, drowning them all but for a few who were saved. And thus it shall be again.

[15] God indeed is long-suffering and exceedingly patient, but shall soon get tired of your doings. And then watch who shall become owner of the Earth after you.

[16] But that you should speak like that is only too clear proof that your faith and your teaching of righteousness is an old, torn garment, tolerating no new patches, and like an old skin, into which no new wine can be poured, because you are one and bad and selfish people. Do you understand Me now?'


## CHAPTER 125
### The trust of Matthew the tax-collector

[1] Say **John's disciples**: 'Are we then doing wrong by living in accordance with John's teaching? John surely was a severe preacher, yet he never gave us such teaching.

[2] See, the Essene Order, with which we are familiar, also is strict and the first law among them is truthfulness, but of what use to them their truthfulness and

their other strict rules? Who takes any notice of them? They are regarded by neither the Greeks nor us Jews and are supposed to have just a few adherents among the Romans. May the teaching by which they live be ever so good and pure, being excellent for those few who have separated themselves from the world, yet it is totally unfit for mankind at large.

[3] Of what benefit to us ever so many nice and forceful words about the brotherhood of man?

[4] See, this house is a big house, a hospitable house and second to none in the brotherhood spirit, but can you seriously expect of same to be at all times ready to receive and care for all men, who surely are our brethren as well? Even with the best of spirit and will, it surely lacks the necessary means, such as space, food and the like.

[5] Furthermore, suppose some poor people struggled to build themselves a hut and gather a most meager provision for winter, barely sufficient for their own needs and 10 people suddenly come to this couple, who hardly have enough room to themselves, asking for admission, lodging and provision. Say, can any teaching demand of these two, or even advise them that it is good and a blessedness to meet the demands of the 10 newcomers, therewith to be ruined good and proper?'

[6] I said: 'Every bird sings and chirps in accordance with its beak and you talk in accordance with your worldly sense and cannot do otherwise, as you don't know how to. Because even if I were to tell you something higher and fully true from the Heavens, you would still not understand Me, because your hard heart lacks the intellect.

[7] Fools. Who is it that lets the fruit grow and ripen upon the Earth? Who maintains them constantly and gives them their consistency. Do you think that God cannot or will not reward him who sacrifices unselfishly for his brethren's sake? Or do you think that God is unjust, demanding of man the impossible?

[8] Yet I say that a truly honest goodwill and a keen desire to do a poor brother some good is easily possible for all.

[9] If everyone were thus imbued through and through, then there also would be no more such meager huts upon Earth, inhabitable by just two people.

[10] See, this My friend Matthew's house has fed many people today and gave away its entire store from true goodness of heart, and if you don't believe it, then go and see the larder and the granary and you shall find no provisions. Here however stands the landlord. Ask him whether I speak untruthfully.'

[11] **Matthew** fully supports My statement, saying: 'Lord, it unfortunately is so today and I don't know how I shall sustain the guests tomorrow. But I have often fared that way and I trusted in God, and see, it was fully replenished, so that I could quite well provide the guests.'

[12] 'See,' say I thereto, 'thus acts a righteous person in this world and does not complain that God abandoned him. And so it has always been and eternally shall be!

[13] If a person trusts in God, he is trusted also by God who does not forsake him and does not let him be confounded. But those who like you do believe in

God's existence, but do not fully trust Him because their own heart tells them that they are unworthy of His help, are not helped by God either, for they have no trust in God. They trust only their own powers and means, which they regard as holy and inviolable as it were, and say: "Man, if you wish to be helped, help yourself, for charity begins at home and thus you have to look after yourself first." And by the time he has provided for himself, the one who needs help has perished.

[14] But I say: If you provide for yourselves first, you are abandoned by God and are without His blessing and His otherwise so certain help. For God did not create men for selfish reasons, but out of pure love and, therefore, men must in everything fully correspond to the love that gave them their existence.

[15] If, however, you live and act without love and trust in God, you voluntarily reverse the heavenly element within you into a hellish one, turn away from God and become servants of Hell, which in the end will not fail to give you the reward you have deserved, which is death in the wrath of God.

[16] You also state that the Essenes, who live in accordance with Pythagoras' school, are not with all their philanthropy, given any regard, other than by a few Romans.

[17] I don't have any regard for them either, because they don't acknowledge the immortality of the soul, yet the meanest among them is better than the best among you.

[18] I now say unto you openly: among all who were born of woman since the beginning of the world, no greater emerged than John, but from now on, the least of My disciples in the true Kingdom of God shall be greater by far than John whom you call your master, yet whom you have never understood. Because he showed you the way to Me and made straight the way before and to Me, but the world in you has blinded your heart, wherefore you are not capable of recognizing Me when you already find yourselves with Me.

[19] Therefore go and care for your world, for your women and children, so that they would not go naked and not ever be plagued by hunger or thirst. But it shall soon emerge how well you provided them therewith. This I can tell you, by fullest right and deepest truth:

[20] Whoever possesses property and has a trade which can give him a good profit, but saves the profit for himself and his children and looks with unkind eyes and heart down at the poor brothers and avoids the poor children who, because they lack all earthly goods, suffer hunger, thirst and cold and sends them away if they come to him asking for alms, and who says to a brother: "Come to me in a few days or weeks and then I will do this or that for you" and when the hopeful, on help relying brother comes and reminds the one who promised of his promise, the latter excuses himself that also now he could not possibly help, while actually having the means to do it, in truth, I tell you: that one is an enemy of God, for how will he love God whom he does not see if he does not love his brother whom he sees before him and is aware of his misery?

[21] In truth, in very truth I tell you: whoever forsakes his brother in need simultaneously forsakes God and Heaven also. And God will forsake him in the twinkling of an eye.

[22] However, who does not forsake his poor brothers, not even if God sent him trials, shall be unexpectedly blessed temporally and eternally more richly than here our host's larder and granary have been blessed.'

[23] Say **John's disciples**: 'This we should believe for sure. They are totally empty.'

## CHAPTER 126
## God does not change

[1] Here **the kitchen-maid** comes breathlessly, saying to Matthew: 'Lord, lord, come and see! Lots of young men just came and brought all kinds of foodstuffs in such amounts that we would hardly consume them in a year! And everything appears so fresh and good! The granaries also are filled from top to bottom and the skins in the cellars filled with the best wine. Lord, lord, where did this come from today, on a Sabbath for the Jews?'

[2] Matthew and everyone in the room are quite beside themselves and John's disciples, of whom two had previously convinced themselves that the larders were empty, at once asked Matthew whether he had ordered such foodstuffs.

[3] Says **Matthew**: 'Not me, since I would have to be the first to know about it. And not my wife either, because she was the one who notified me through this maid that our small stock had been as good as consumed. Because apart from a garden and a few rented fields, I have no ground for the planting of much fruit and would also have very little time for it, being firstly busy with the toll and having to secondly host my guests in this guest-house. Therefore I stocked my guest-house week by week with rations, having them usually purchased and delivered for my own money from Capernaum, while having the fish supplied by you. The wine and grain however I usually bought off my own co-religionists, the Greeks. This in short is the way I usually kept my house stocked with necessities, but I and my house know not a thing about this order.

[4] Some great unknown friend therefore would have to have done this for me, otherwise it obviously is a great miracle. Where and who this great friend should be however I know no more than yourselves. But I shall summon all my people in here and question them in your presence as to whether they recognized any of the delivery men.'

[5] His wife and **all the maids and servants** are called in and asked, but they all deny with one voice ever having remotely recognized anyone: 'The men looked like delicate youths, as none of them was bearded, but all had beautifully curled long hair and their garb was more Roman than that of the Jews. There were many of them, in the larder as well as in the loft and cellar. They laid down the deliveries quickly and said: 'This is a gift for the tax-collector Matthew, who was called by the great Master this day.' They then departed in haste and we did not see which way they turned.'

[6] Says **one Pharisee**: 'This thing sounds exceptionally rare and yet is true. In

that case we should be most inclined to get to the bottom of it.'

[7] Turning to Matthew, **the same Pharisee** says: 'You host, let them bring us samples of wines and we shall tell you where they come from, for we can tell you by the flavor and color where it was grown.'

[8] They send to the cellars and bring all the drinking vessels filled. And as **the Pharisees and scribes** sample the wines, they say full of astonishment: 'No! Such wine as this we never tasted before. It is indescribably good and delightful. Have we not drunk of all the wines grown upon the known Earth, among these very good and flavorsome ones indeed, but they would have to be hardly lukewarm water by comparison to these. Therefore it is and remains a riddle.

[9] But since you now have a great stock of these unsurpassable superb wines, how would you like to let us have some skins for money and a bit of persuading? It would be worth sending a consignment to the High Priest at Jerusalem.'

[10] Says **Matthew**: 'Free it came my way and thus will I give it, but not one drop to the High Priest in Jerusalem. Unless he were to come here by chance as a guest, then he shall be served like everyone else, but understood, only as a human equal to all others, but never as a Jewish High Priest, who is an abomination of the desolation to me and a murderer of the spirits of those men who are of his faith.'

[11] Says **one scribe**: 'Friend, here you quite misjudged the High Priest of Jerusalem, having no knowledge of his nature and office.'

[12] Says **Matthew**: 'Let's leave this subject, for it gets me into a just heat under the collar. You are his eyes and therefore see least of all what is nearest to you, namely your own nose, brow and whole face. We who are situated opposite you see it only too well and truly. But no more about it, or I could get upset and be obliged to offend you, my respected guests.'

[13] Says **a more sedate Pharisee**: 'Now, let us indeed give the matter a rest and instead consult with the Master Jesus. He shall be the one most likely to clear this matter up for us, because he loftily exceeds us all in knowledge and wisdom.' Turning to Me: 'What do you actually say to this story? Because you seem to have some hint about it, as your foregoing conversation with John's disciples almost pointed to it. Because this was occurring almost in the same moment you were telling John's disciples how God provides for those who truly love Him and animatedly trust Him, and after you properly flogged the ugliness and repulsiveness of selfishness. And therefore it seems to me that from somewhere you received knowledge about it, or even secretly were the instigator of it.'

[14] Say I: 'Good. If you suppose that about Me, then apply it also to what I said to John's disciples and admit it in your hearts that I spoke the fullest truth.'

[15] He who among you shall act accordingly from the bottom of his heart shall experience with God what our friend and brother Matthew has just experienced.

[16] For of a truth, believe Me: God in His heart steadily remains the Self-Same. As He was when no sun, moon or stars were shining yet for a long time upon the firmament, just so is He still this moment and shall be into all eternity.

[17] He who seeks Him along the right path also shall find Him and be blessed into all eternity of eternities.'

[18] These words stir their hearts and **John's disciples** began to ponder deeply, saying: 'He must be a far greater prophet than our John was. For we were around him a full 10 years, yet never felt like this. The Pharisee is right in saying this Nazarene knows about it. - I would maintain that all this originates from Him, along paths unknown to us and the whole thing is blatant proof of our blindness, including our great master John.'

## CHAPTER 127
### In Capernaum and Nazareth (ch. 127-131)
### The death of Cornelius' daughter in Capernaum

[1] But now Judas, whom the wine had heated somewhat unduly, also wants to have his say with his table-neighbors, the disciples of John. But **Thomas**, his perennial opponent, beats him to it, saying: 'Friend, when the Master speaks, the disciples must be quiet and listen, but not speak, because words out of our mouth here would be the greatest folly. But should you feel the urge to speak, then step outside and yell to your heart's content, returning when your mouth gets tired.'

[2] Says **Judas**: 'What do you want of me? I did you no harm. Shall I not get to speaking at all?'

[3] Says **Thomas**: 'We are familiar with your wisdom through and through over the years, and are not at all inclined to, right next to our great Master, listen to it for the thousandth time, and we are all imbued with as much homespun wisdom as yourself. Therefore you can give no greater teaching than we already have and you will hopefully see that it is not necessary for you to talk here. We disciples are to only speak when asked, we can of course ask as well, but then watch it that our question is well founded in need. But if we ask only out of idle curiosity, to give our tongue free reign, then we are worthy of flogging, because mad fools should be always punished with the whip.'

[4] Says **Judas**: 'All right, all right. I'm quiet already, knowing that in your presence I cannot and must not speak, since you are the prophet Elijah's wisdom. What a pity you did not live before Solomon. What heights of wisdom Solomon could have reached in your school. But now no more, I'm quiet.'

[5] Thomas would have liked to add more, but I winked to him that it sufficed and he kept quiet.

[6] But one of John's disciples still could not get the hang of his colleagues being compared to old, torn garments patched up with new patches, and old wineskins not capable of taking new wine. Therefore he turned to Me with a rather clumsy question, saying: 'I can see now that you too might be a prophet, but I see that the wine from the old skins suits you better than the new one in the new skins and it seems to Me that your coat is none too new either. Should it need a few patches, then I can help you out, as I have a great many of them. If I can be of assistance there, let me know.'

[7] His companions felt like throwing him out for such an awkward question. But

I took his part, explaining the comparison to him more comprehensibly and it put him at ease.

[8] But to the others I said: 'If you see one blind stumbling over a ditch, who through his fall has flattened the high grass around the water-ditch, will you hold him to account, fining him for the damage? See, this your brother like yourselves can see with the eyes of the flesh, but is still quite blind in his soul-eyes and it should be over-rough to punish a brother because he stumbled somewhat in front of us.'

[9] For these words all sang Me a proper three cheers and 'hail thee', saying: 'That's proper talk, and anyone who acts in accordance with how He says commendably and wisely is worthy of being called a man among all men. Hail thee and three cheers to you, man of all men.'

[10] With the sound of these words and a few of My further comments on old garments, the new wine and wine skins having only just died down, one of the chiefs of Capernaum (in fact the Roman Commander Cornelius) comes in hastily, properly storming Me, falling on his knees and saying breathlessly: 'Lord! Friend! You godly Master and Savior! My most beloved daughter, who bears my name, my glorious, good and most beautiful daughter, has died. Here the chief weeps and for a while is unable to speak. Recovering after a while, he continues:

[11] Lord, to whom nothing is impossible, come with me to my house and lay Your miraculous hands upon her and she shall surely live again, just like the school superintendent Jairus' little girl also was fully dead and lived again. I beg you, my most exalted Friend, come and do me this favor.'

[12] I said: 'Never fear, I am coming to do according to your request. Although the daughter is indeed fully dead and cold, yet I shall nevertheless awaken her, so that she may then proclaim God's glory to the poor. And so let us go.'

[13] But My disciples asked whether to wait for Me here, or whether to also come along. But I said: 'All those of you who are My disciples and you also, Matthew, who have been a tax collector, follow Me. I have taken care of your earthly house and shall do so in future, but for this you are to become My disciple, like these.'

[14] Matthew casts off his host's vestment at once, putting on his good coat, and follows Me without first making the usual host's arrangements with his own for his absence.

[15] Nota bene: This is what everyone must do who wants to follow Me. He has to become dead to all worldly living and not think about his worldly state, or he is not fit for My Kingdom. Because he who lays hands on his plough but looks over his shoulder is not fit for the Kingdom of God.'

## CHAPTER 128
### Resurrection of Cornelius' daughter

[1] And now to continue with the Gospel.

[2] Half way towards Capernaum from Matthew's house, quite late in the afternoon and once again, as with the Greek woman previously, another woman, with 12 years bleeding which no one was able to heal, came rushing up from behind Me. This woman, having found out from the previous Greek woman, touched only the hem of My top coat and was instantly healed. Because she said to herself: "If I can only touch the hem of His raiment, I shall be made whole". And so it happened instantly, in accordance with her faith. And she perceived at once that through her touching of My raiment, believing, the fountain of her 12 years plight was stopped.

[3] But I turned around and said to the woman: 'Fear not, My daughter, your faith has helped you. Go your way in peace.' And the woman went home amidst many tears of thanks and joy and remained well for good.

[4] This woman, although not Greek but a Jewess, nevertheless lived not far from a Greek settlement, paying many visits there and finding out much from them and therewith also about the healing of the previous, Greek woman, about which later Mark and also the painter and poet Luke made mention, wherewith, due to the similarity of the occasion, grit had been thrown in for the mills of the doubters, causing even the most informed theosophists to regard this as one and the same event.

[5] And Matthew the scribe immediately asked whether to record this event as well as further ones this day.

[6] And I said to him: 'You are to record everything that happened today, with the exception of My provision for your namesake's house and the many conversations held there. In short, we shall again be turning in at home today and shall have ample time tomorrow to determine in detail what to record about this day.

[7] Matthew the scribe was happy with that, and we soon also reached the chief's house and moved at once to the chamber where the deceased daughter lay upon a bed adorned in the Roman style.

[8] There were however many pipers and other noise makers, because it was tradition to make a lot of noise around the deceased, to either awaken them, or if not possible, to in accordance with the opinion of the blind, common and mostly heathen folk to, at this of all stages, go to the greatest length to scare away the messengers of the prince of Hell, Pluto.

[9] Entering the big chamber with the disciples however and seeing and hearing the ridiculous noise making, I commanded them to above all immediately cease their noise-making and to completely clear the chamber, as well as get out of the house, because the daughter did not die, but only slept.

[10] Here the engaged noise-makers (for money of course, because none could obtain noise without money) started laughing Me off, and one of them confided to Me: 'Here you are not likely to succeed as with Jairus. Just look at her more closely and you as a doctor shall at once have to acknowledge that fullest death sits on her nose, as would have been taught by the famous Greek doctor Hippocrates – and you declare that she sleeps?'

[11] But the chief sensed that the noise-makers did not intend to move. He therefore commanded them to clear out, threatening them with punishment,

ordering his centurion guards to drive the people out. And the chamber soon was free of the noise-makers.

[12] Only after the chamber as well as the entire house were rid of these tiresome guests did I fully proceed into the chamber with My disciples and the chief's relatives, stepping up to the death bed and taking hold of the daughter's hand without saying anything, the daughter at once getting up in full strength and health, as if there had never been anything wrong with her.

[13] But when the daughter saw that she had lain upon the familiar bed on which only the dead were laid, she asked how she came to lie upon the death-bed.

[14] **The chief** however went over to her overjoyed, saying: 'My overly beloved Cornelia. You became very sick and also died from your sickness, and you were dead and would have remained irretrievably dead, had not this truly almighty Savior of all saviors awakened you with his godly power, just as he also awakened the little girl of the school superintendent Jairus, with whom you were well acquainted. Therefore be joyful again with beautiful life and be forever grateful to this Friend of all friends, who alone gave you back the greatest possession, dear life itself.'

## CHAPTER 129
### The experiences in the hereafter

[1] Says **the daughter**: 'Yes, yes, now I remember clearly that I was very sick, but a very sweet slumber came over my eyes. I fell asleep and had a most wonderful dream. Wherever I turned, there was light and nothing but light and a most beautiful world shaped itself out of the light. Indescribably beautiful gardens, streamed by the light, became visible and one splendor after another came into view. But no living being seemed to inhabit this splendor and as I beheld these splendors with astonishment, without a living being showing up, my heart started sinking. Amidst these splendors I began to cry and yell out, but not even the faintest echo wanted to answer me from any direction, and I became sadder and sadder amid the mounting splendor.

[2] And as I sank down in sadness, starting to loudly call out for you, my father, see, this friend here suddenly came from the gardens, grasped my hand and spoke: "Get up, my daughter", suddenly all the splendors which had made me sad vanished and I awoke, even while this friend still held me by the hand. I could not immediately remember all that I had seen, but when consciousness was given back to me, as if from the Heavens, I recalled everything that I had seen and experienced in the dream, just as I related it to you.

[3] What amazes me however is that although I have to conclude from this bed that I was actually dead to the world, I nevertheless continued to live in my dream. And still more amazing is it that this glorious friend who came to me in my dream now is present exactly as I saw him in the dream.

[4] But now I ask you, my dear father, whether perhaps this my life that he gave me anew belongs to him? My heart is deeply moved and it seems to me that I could not ever give my love to any man other than him. May I love him above all, more than you, my father and more than everything in the world?'

[5] This question embarrasses Cornelius and he can't find an answer. But I say to him: 'Leave the daughter to feel the way she does now, because only this shall give her the fullness of life'.

[6] Says **Cornelius**: 'If so, then indeed love this Friend above everything. He who could give you life from His strength and power when you were dead, shall never be capable of harming you, because if you were to die again, He would be certain to give you life again. May you therefore love him above everything, as I also love Him with all my strength.'

[7] I said: 'He who loves Me loves also Him who is in Me and this One is life eternal. If he were to die with love for Me even a thousand times, yet he shall live eternally.' **Many** who hear this say within themselves: 'How, what is this? Can a man also say that? But, can a human being do what he did?'

[8] Says **one Roman** who was staying with Cornelius as a guest: 'Friends, a wise man once said that there isn't a great man whom the gods have not filled with their breath. But if ever a man had been most strongly breathed upon by the gods, it is this Jesus, who, at least terrestrially, appears to have been of very low birth, but the gods do not love the pomp of the world. Whenever they walk the Earth they always hide within a most inconsequent exterior and let mortals in on who and what they are only through their deeds. And this will probably be the case with this most plain man. You all can opine and think, but I take him for a god of the first order, because no mortal reawakens the dead.

[9] Wherever a son of Asclepius nevertheless had reawakened one seemingly dead, with all types of balm, oils and ointments, such a purported re-awakened one never was vigorous and sound like Cornelia, who appears to be more vigorous now than ever before. That is my opinion and conviction and you may all think what you like.'

[10] I said: 'He who is right also believes that it is right so. I tell you this and ask all those who have heard and seen this to be so good as to remain silent about it for now and not tell anyone, for you know how wicked the world is.' They all promise to strictly keep it to themselves.

[11] They indeed kept quiet during the 2 days of My stay with My disciples at the chief's. But as soon as I departed, this thing became known all over Galilee. I verily could have prevented this, had I bound man's free will, which would have been the easiest thing for Me to do, but since I have to respect man's free will, without which man would turn into an animal, I had to of course put up with it, in spite of it not being within the proper order and of no use to the cause.

## CHAPTER 130
## The 2 blind beggars

[1] There were however at Capernaum 2 blind-born, who had never seen daylight or the glitter of the stars. These two also had heard of Me and My deed. As I was on My way back from Capernaum to Nazareth, accompanied by the chief and his wife and all his children and many of his friends, we unhurriedly passed a spot where several roads crossed. Here the two blind usually sat, begging. When these two found out from passers-by that a large crowd was approaching, including the foremost lords of Galilee and amidst them the Savior Jesus of Nazareth, about whom as well as His father the legend had it that they were direct descendants of David, the said two quickly got up from the ground, running after Me as fast as they could, crying and saying: 'Jesus, you son of David, have mercy on us!' They gave Me that title thinking to flatter Me, that I should be even more mercifully disposed towards them.

[2] On account of this however I let them follow Me all the way to Nazareth, to show them that I laid no store by such worldly titles and vain flattery.

[3] Two hours later, on hearing that I was arriving home, the two asked those they perceived closest to them to take them to Me. And My disciples immediately brought them to Me inside the house.

[4] When the two felt themselves in My vicinity, they came over and wanted to ask Me to make them seeing. Knowing full well what they wanted, I beat them to it, saying: 'Do you of a truth believe that I can do so?' They spoke with brevity: 'Yes, Lord.' I touched their eyes with My fingers, saying, 'Let it be with you in accordance with your faith.'

[5] And their eyes were opened, so that they could see like all those with sound eyes. As they now felt the blessedness of sight, viewing the creation with wonder, they also in their hearts remembered their endless thanks to Me, intending to give Me all they acquired through begging, for they would in future not be begging, but earn their living with the strength of their sound hands.

[6] But I said to them: 'It verily is right and good that you want to serve your brethren and earn your living through the strength of your hands. Because he who has sight and can work should not go around with idle hands and be a burden to his brethren, but serve them and be of help to them one way or another, so that love among men would grow.

[7] This your resolution therefore is fully right and good, but while it is commendable that you want to present Me with your savings, out of gratitude, neither I nor My proper disciples have a need of it and so you may as well keep them.

[8] But what I ask of you for opening your eyes to light, is that you firstly keep God's Commandments, loving God above all and your neighbor as yourselves, serving them in everything as best you can and gladly help them. And secondly and on My own account, I command you to tell no one, ensuring that this spreads no further.'

[9] But they said: 'Lord, this shall be rather difficult, because everyone in the surroundings knows that we were blind. If therefore we are asked how we, who had been blind, became seeing, what kind of answer shall we give them?' I said: 'One that is grounded in silence.' They indeed promised to heed it, yet did not keep their promise and soon went to all adjacent areas and spread My renown.

## CHAPTER 131
### Healing of the possessed deaf and dumb

[1] But these two had hardly left the house when new arrivals brought a man who was both dumb and possessed. Several Pharisees and scribes whom we had left behind at Matthew's house had also followed them, to see what I should do inside the house and to where I would turn. In front of the house they encountered the two blind, who immediately told them that one dumb and possessed is about to be healed, but they told them nothing about themselves, for they still feared in their hearts.

[2] In response to this **the Pharisees** hurried, lest they should be late. On entering the room, they recognized the possessed, who also was dumb and they said: 'O, this one we have known for a long time. With him no power has any effect. When his devil gets wild, he uproots trees and no wall or chain is too strong for him. He does not burn in the fire and let the fish beware if he enters the water. The best thing about him is that he is dumb and deaf, if he could also hear and talk, then no creature on Earth would be safe with him. O, this man is terrible. Everything flees before him, even the most rapacious animals. And this one he intends healing? This one only the devils' chief can heal.'

[3] I said: 'And yet shall I heal him, that you should at last recognize that all beings must obey God's might'.

[4] Therewith I stretched out a hand over the possessed and spoke, 'Come out of this person, you unclean, evil spirit!' Here **the spirit** cried: 'Where should I go?' I said: 'Where the sea is deepest, there a monster awaits you!' The evil spirit cried out again and at once left the man.

[5] Thereupon the man at once assumed a friendly appearance, began to talk full of gratitude, answering everyone with propriety and the gentlest of words: all became convinced that he had also lost his deaf and dumbness.

[6] The disciples however and all folk present began to greatly marvel, saying: 'Truly, this surpasses everything. This has never been heard of in Israel. There has been banishment of wind and storm, even if on a much smaller scale, and there have been revival of the seemingly dead, while rocks had to yield water and Manna came from Heaven in response to Moses' prayer, of course nothing to that high degree of perfection.

[7] When Solomon was building the Temple and no workers wanted to lend their hands for a month, he prayed to God for workers and a great many youths came and offered Solomon their service and Solomon took them on, working with them

for a month, as tradition would have it.

[8] In short, since Abraham, quite a few wonders have taken place, but, as God truly lives and reigns, nothing equals this wondrous deed.'

[9] This wonderment thoroughly angered **the Pharisees**, and not being able to contain themselves, they spoke to the people: 'How can you be such blind fools! Did we not upon entering the room immediately indicate to you who could be the master of such possessed? We told you that only the devils' chief could do this! He also healed the possessed of course, but how? He cast out this devil through the devils' prince!

[10] This testimony to Me in front of the people by the furious Pharisees was the last straw to the commander **Cornelius**, also in attendance. Utterly outraged at these remarks, he thundered a sentence over the Pharisees and scribes: 'Even this very day the cross shall be your lot! I shall make you tell the difference between God and the devil!'

[11] Hearing such thunder, the Pharisees began to dreadfully howl and despair. But **the people** were jubilant, saying: 'Ah! Have you at last found the right one to drive out your old devil? Serves you right all the way. For you are yourselves fully the equals of the devils' prince, you continue to fight the way he once fought the archangel Michael for Moses' body, i.e. about the dead matter of his teaching and persecute all with the curse, fire and sword, everything that even remotely scents of spirituality. Therefore it is you who always act with the devil's help, lending a hand to the lying spirit. Therefore the devils' sentence is a fully just one for you Satan henchmen, and no compassion stirs our hearts.'

[12] Here **Matthew** the tax collector steps over to the Pharisees, saying: 'It is about 4 days since on the last Sabbath the Master Jesus freed the old brother of my mother from palsy, how much was said to you then by way of fundamental truths. Children understood it almost with their hands and pointed their fingers at you. The Master Himself spoke to you with such wisdom that you were filled with astonishment and were forced to ask how He came by such wisdom. Yet neither His Spirit nor instruction filled answers, nor His unheard of deeds were able to open your eyes.

[13] If such deeds and teachings are not capable of opening your eyes, even while your wicked hearts only get steadily more furious and vengeful, say, what do you still lack for accomplished devilry? I tell you indeed, as I already told you, that you are worse than all devils put together and it is therefore right before God and all better mankind that you be extirpated like ravenous beasts.

[14] Even if I am an exceedingly sensitive person, unable to hurt a fly or tread upon a worm, yet I could quite easily myself strike off your heads without feeling uneasy about it. Therefore I praise the chief Cornelius for condemning you to the gallows' (synonymous with cross).'

[15] When the Pharisees in their great fear saw that no one felt mercy for them or were about to intercede with the Commander, who held the inexorable *Jus Gladii* over all Galilee, they fell on their knees before the commander, averring that they had not meant Jesus harm, the way it was taken, but had only wanted to highlight how the obviously divine power within the Master of all masters Jesus,

241

could and has to also manifest by making the prince of the devils subservient to it, for it should be bad for mankind if God had no power over the devils. If undisputedly however God's supreme power is acting through Jesus, then it has to be able to reign over all devils as over all angels and be capable of enforcing their strictest obedience. 'Therefore we only wanted through our pronouncement to emphasize that his godly power extends over everything in Heaven, on and under the Earth. Since however we had meant only that and not possibly anything else by our exclamation, for which you have condemned us to death, how is it possible that you as an exalted lord of Rome, could have pronounced such sentence over us? We therefore beg you in the divine name of Jesus that you would most mercifully retract the pronounced sentence.'

[16] Says **the commander**: 'If Jesus, the Master, is willing to put a word in for you, then I shall retract my word, but if He keeps His silence, then you die without further ado even this day. For I put no trust in your words, because your hearts don't tally with your mouths.'

[17] After these words from the chief, **they all** rush at Me, clamoring: 'O Jesus, you good Master, we beg you to rescue and save us. Have us flogged if you don't trust our words not to place any further obstacles in your path. For we all are convinced now that you are a purest servant of God to us, His unfortunately profusely degenerated children. O, Jesus, do not overhear our plea.'

[18] I said: 'So go home in peace! But beware of more exploits, or I would no longer say to you then: go home in peace.'

[19] They all promised, and **the commander** said: 'As He gave you the peace, so give I, taking back the sentence for now, but beware if I find out even the least about you.'

[20] The Pharisees thank Me and the chief exceedingly and fervently, departing hastily and keeping utter silence, for they all dreaded Cornelius terribly. But in their hearts they hatched that much harder how to ruin Me and revenge themselves on the chief. Yet they had to, due to lack of opportunity, grin and bear it, their survival depending on it. This nevertheless was good for My cause, for I now could for a lengthy period, until late autumn, preach the Gospel of the Kingdom of God without hindrance in all the cities and market places of Galilee, healing all kinds of diseases and sicknesses among the people.


## CHAPTER 132
### The greed and hardness of the tributary king Herod

[1] There was much misery to be found among the people languishing under all kinds of oppression, especially in the markets and villages. Physically and psychically they were scattered and dying like sheep among the wolves without any shepherd. Since I deeply regretted the poor people's desperate plight, I spoke as I did in Sychar at the well: 'The crop is heavy, but laborers are scarce. Therefore, beg the Lord to send laborers to harvest His crop. For these poor

people are ripe for the Kingdom of God and the field where they are is large. They languish and thirst for light, truth and salvation. But laborers, laborers. Where are they?'

[2] Say **the disciples**: 'Lord, if You should consider us capable, could we not spread out and each of us take a city or a market?' I say: 'We are now on the way to an extremely poor village. Once we have reached it I shall select the most capable and strongest among you and send you out into the different regions and places, and then you will be doing all that which I am doing and have done in your presence. But now let us hurry towards the village.'

[3] In less than half an hour we had reached the little village where we found truly indescribable misery. Parents and children were walking about literally naked, covering their nakedness with foliage. When the people saw us approaching everybody, big and small, young and old, came hurrying towards us begging for alms, for they suffered great want. Children were crying, holding their hands over their tummies, for they were very hungry having had nothing to eat already for 2 whole days. The parents were in despair, partly from their own pangs of hunger, but even more so because their little children were asking for bread and milk.

[4] **Peter**, who was very deeply moved by this sight, asked a staunch-looking old man: 'Friend, who has made you so extremely miserable? How did you get into this plight? Did some enemy come and rob you of everything, even disgracefully ruining your houses as I notice? For I see only walls and no roofs and lofts above them and your granaries, which I knew, are completely destroyed. How did this happen?'

[5] Says **the man** in a tearful voice: 'O you dear and no doubt good people. This was done by the harshness and greed of the tributary king Herod. His father was Satan's left, and he is his right arm. We could not raise the taxes which he had demanded of us 10 days earlier. His bailiffs gave us a deadline of 6 days. But what were 6 days? During this time the bailiffs consumed almost all our better provisions and on the seventh day – since we could not possibly raise and pay the exorbitant tax – they took everything we had and we only barely escaped with this miserable life. O friends, this is hard, immensely hard. If God does not help, we shall still today die of starvation together with our children. Do help us in whatever way you can. If only the wicked servants of Herod had not taken all our clothes we could have gone begging, but where could we go in this state? For our children it is too far in all directions and as you can see we are as naked as in the womb. O God, O God, why did we have to be made so terribly miserable? Which one of all our sins before You, O Jehovah, has brought such punishment upon us?'

[6] Here I step up to the old man and say: 'Friend, the cause for this is not your sin, which before God is the most insignificant in all Israel, but God's love.

[7] You were the purest in all of Israel, but some worldly desires were still clinging to your soul. God, however, who loves you, wanted to free you all at once from the world to make you fully capable of absorbing your heavenly Father's grace. This has now happened and you are now safe from Herod for all times, for from those who have been completely robbed by his greed he never again

collects taxes because those subjects who have been made beggars are struck off the tax register.

[8] And so you see, you have been freed from the world at a single stroke. That is God's greatest blessing for you and you can now begin to care for your soul in all earnest.

[9] However, I tell you: Do not in future build wealthy looking houses, but erect for yourselves scanty huts, and no one will demand taxes of you, except the exclusively privileged king of Rome. And he demands only 2 to 3 percent. If you have something, you can give it. If you have nothing, you are free. But we shall speak about that later.

[10] Now go to your roofless houses. There you will find food and clothes. Refresh yourselves, put on clothes and then come back here and I shall discuss further things with you.'


## CHAPTER 133
### A food and clothes miracle

[1] Hearing this all the poor people hurry with gratitude and faith into their half-destroyed houses and are amazed when they find the tables laden with plenty of good food and also all kinds of clothes for old and young, big and small and for both sexes separately. They ask each other how this has come about, but no one knows the answer.

[2] When they find even their larder fully stocked, **woman and children** say to the men: 'That has been done by God. He who in the desert had for 40 years manna rain and thus fed His children in an area of rock and sand where no grass grew. He would not have let us die since we have always prayed to Him. O, this is certain: God does not ever forsake the ones who implore Him.

[3] David, the great king, prayed to God when he became wretched, and God helped him out of his great misery. God has never been known not to give a favorable hearing to those who sought His help. It would have been an unprecedented case if God had not granted our prayers in this our greatest distress, for God is always full of love for those who call to Him: "Abba, dear Father." Therefore, let us from now on love Him above all. He alone is our deliverer. Our most holy Father sent us all this from the Heavens through His holy angels.'

[4] Says **the old man** who happened to belong to this particular family where the whole village used to gather to listen to his wisdom, for he was well versed in the Scripture: 'My children, friends and brothers. It is written: "From the mouth of the little ones and babes I shall have myself praised." And look, here we have it before our eyes and ears. The dear Father has looked at us in His great mercy and had done this for us. To Him be therefore all our love and praise from the mouth of our babes, for the praise from our mouths is not sufficiently pure to be pleasing to the Almighty. That is why He has prepared for Himself the mouth of our

babes. But now let us go outside to the young who sent us to our houses and no doubt knew what God had done for us. He must be a great prophet. Maybe even Elijah who is to come once more prior to the hoped-for and already long since promised Messiah.'

[5] Says **a little child** that has only recently started to talk: 'Father, could not this Man himself be the great Promised One?'

[6] Says **the old man**: 'O child, who loosened your tongue so clearly? For you did not speak like a child just now, but like a sage at the temple in Jerusalem.'

[7] Says **the little child**: 'I do not know about that, only that prior to this talking was so difficult for me and now so very easy, that I do know. But why should this surprise you, since we are surrounded by God's wonders?'

[8] Says **the old man**, pressing the little child to his heart: 'Yes, yes, you are right. Everything here is a wonder, and you are surely not wrong if you even take the young Man to be the Messiah. For us He is certainly that. But let us now go outside to Him and dutifully render our gratitude also to Him in the name of Jehovah, for He was obviously sent to us by God. So let us hurry outside to Him.'

[9] Now they all hurry outside to Me and the little children are the first to throw themselves at My feet bedewing them with their innocent, purest tears of gratitude and joy.

[10] But I gaze up at the firmament and say in a loud voice: 'You Heavens! Do look down and learn from these little children how your God and Father wants to be praised! O creation, how endlessly vast and ancient you are and how countless the number of your wise citizens, and yet you could not find the way to the heart of your Creator, your Father, like these little children! Therefore, I tell you: who does not come to Me like these little ones, will not find the Father!'

[11] Thereupon I sat down and blessed and caressed the little children. And **the little child** said to the old man who called out in some confusion: 'How is that? Why? How are we to understand this? Father, there is more than Elijah here, more than your Messiah. Here is the Father Himself, the good Father who brought us bread, milk and clothing.'

[12] The old man begins to weep, but **the little child** leans his head against My bosom which he begins to kiss and caress, and after a while he says: 'Yes, yes, I hear it, here in his bosom the true, good Father's heart is beating. O, if I could only kiss it too.' Says **the old man**: 'But little one, do not be naughty.'

[13] I said: unless all of you become that naughty, you will never come as close to the Father's heart as this dear little child.'


## CHAPTER 134
### Calling of the 12 apostles

[1] Matthew, the Evangelist, **and John** come to Me and say: 'Lord, this deed should really be recorded since it is so extraordinary and purely divine.'

[2] I said: 'Did I not accomplish the same at Sychar, did I not just a few days ago

provide also My house in the same way the house of My disciple Matthew? You wanted to record all that and I did not allow it, for which I have My very good reason. Why should this deed which is equivalent to the previous ones now be recorded? Leave that be. I alone know best what the world needs and shall tell you what you may again record of a new deed and when. And your turn, My brother John, will not come for quite some time.

[3] But now, My dear disciples, I shall choose from your midst some whom I shall already now send out into the cities of Israel to preach the Kingdom of God to the people. You, Simon Peter, are the first. You, Simian's brother, Andrew, are the second. You, James, son of Zebedee, are the third and you, his brother, John, are the fourth. Philip, you are the fifth. You, Bartholomew, are the sixth. You, Thomas, the seventh and you, Matthew the publican, are the eight. You, James, son of Alphaeus, are the ninth and you, Lebbaeus, also called Thaddaeus, are the tenth. You, Simon of Cana, are the eleventh and you, Judas Iscariot, are the twelfth.

[4] I am giving you twelve the authority to cast out unclean spirits from men and to heal all kinds of contagious diseases and other ailments. You shall preach the Kingdom of God everywhere, but keep silent about certain special deeds.'

[5] After this selection the 12 chosen disciples asked Me where they should now go, which roads to take and what they should mainly speak about.

[6] To this question I gave them the following extensive answer which the 12 elected did not particularly relish, and only after My ascension they made full use of these instructions.

[7] But the instructions were also given in such a way that they applied mainly to the time after My ascension when the 12, or at that time rather all those who spread My teaching, experienced what I had made known to the 12.

[8] However, before I deal with the extensive instructions to the 12, I must mention, for the sake of a better understanding of the whole, that the Gospels, including Matthew and John, as they are these days available to you in the different languages, are only excerpts from the original Gospel and, thus, do not even by far contain all that Matthew and John did record. Here and there also some small supplementary sentence appears by the later collector and copyist, which obviously could have been added only later, as for instance in Mt. 10:4 the mention of the 12th apostle Judas Iscariot is followed by the sentence "Who later betrayed him." At the time of the selection Matthew, who wrote his Gospel in My presence, had no idea of this could not possibly have added this sentence which was done by some later copyist.

[9] The Hebrew as well as Greek Bibles, therefore, always state: "Gospel according to Matthew," "according to John" and so on.

[10] Therefore, no one should take it amiss if when reading Matthew and John he comes across similar texts which the actual evangelist could not have recorded in his time since the fact mentioned therein occurred only much later. Everything is rendered in the strictest order and I have mentioned this point here in the most suitable place so as to prevent in the course of time rationalistic ponderers from negative criticism.

[11] However, as already earlier in this revelation, supplementary explanations will here and there be given which is all the more necessary since as a result of the transcription many an important fact was not recorded quite correctly and many a thing that did not appear authentic enough to the transcriber was even omitted altogether. Numerous things were recorded at that time, partly by eye witnesses, partly from hearsay, and thus it was for the quite honest transcribers most difficult to stick to the full truth at all times.

[12] And so the 2 Gospels according to Matthew and John are, except for some small matters, the purest.

[13] Here **a critical rationalist** could indeed ask: "Where then has the actual original got to? Is it no longer available on Earth and should it not have been possible to God, in view of the at that time numerous people who were quickened and permeated by the Holy Spirit, to once more bring to light the original Gospel word for word?"

[14] The answer is this: The originals have been wisely removed for the simple reason that before long idolatry would have been practiced with such relics. This does still happen, and even with false and assumed relics, although My true pure teaching strictly forbids this with a warning against the leaven of the Pharisees. Now imagine a historically proven true relic. I tell you that with such a one more idolatry would be practiced than with the so-called Holy Sepulcher in Jerusalem where, except for the locality, not a grain of sand is authentic. That is the real reason why all the originals have been removed.

[15] As concerns the second question, the spirit contained in the originals has been fully retained also in the transcripts, and the letter is of no importance anyway, but only the spirit which is unchanged. Or could there be any difference where the Spirit of God is concerned (i.e. within Him because there is only one Spirit of God) if He as one and the same Spirit is active on this Earth in endless multiplicity in the most diverse forms and in an even more endless multiplicity on a sun? See, it is and remains nevertheless always one and the same Holy Spirit.

[16] Thus it is also with transcripts of My Word. May they seem ever so dissimilar externally, they nevertheless are imbued with the same Spirit from inner depths and no more is needed.

[17] As an extreme case, take the religions of other nations, e.g. the Turks, Parses, Gevers, Hindus, Chinese and Japanese. How they differ from the religion I gave to only the children from the Heavens of all Heavens, yet the same spirit, although hidden much more deeply, reigns also in them.

[18] But it shall be obvious to any moderately scientific person that within the frequently very thick and weathered bark, taken by many to be the tree itself, all kinds of filth as well as worms and insects are found which take their bad food only from the bark. Since it is however the bark which grows out of the living tree and not vice versa, it too has something of the tree-life and it is understandable therefore how within it so many worms and diverse insects find a most marginal and transitory life-sustenance.

[19] Wars, persecutions, devastations are waged only on the meager and

barren bark, while the tree's living wood stays fresh and sound. Therefore no living wood should trouble itself about what takes place within the actually dead bark, because the bark shall be discarded when the wood is brought in.

[20] This interpolation was necessary for a more thorough understanding of what is to follow at a later stage. And since no doubt can arise about it for the present, we can cheerfully return to the main theme.

## CHAPTER 135
### Instructions to the apostles

[1] After choosing the 12 disciples as My messengers and forerunners, giving them a condensed course on what they should do, the chosen 12 nevertheless fervently besought Me for complete directions on what to do, say and teach and on their conduct and on what should be their lot every now and then, because their fear of the many Pharisees and scribes was not little.

[2] **Matthew the tax collector** was the only one with a little more courage, and he addressed the twelve's diverse misgivings as follows: 'What of it. I am a Greek and they can't do much to me. I have a healthy tongue as well and two powerful arms and on top of that I have documented Roman citizenship, on which no cheeky Jew can lay his hands. And so I can at least officially cope with them. Our Lord's almighty Spirit however shall protect us against clandestine and murderous harassment and so I have an abundance of the best weapons even against the most cunning adversary and therefore do not fear Hell even in its entirety. But you are for the most part Galileans, which is tantamount to anti-Temple servants and are more Greek than Jewish, counting the Romans as your friends. What should you fear under such circumstances? Yet we have to in any case be full of courage when it comes to carrying out such endlessly great holy things. Let the Earth be blasted to rubble. A real man has to stand his ground on this, contemptuous of death and not sway like the reeds. But I too am all for exhaustive and full directions for this holy endeavor, because we indeed must know what we are to do and say.'

[3] All took courage with this rousing talk from Matthew the tax collector and they began to itch at the shoulders, as if about to wing away rather than march.

[4] Thereupon I stood in their midst, saying to them: 'Let you concentrate in spirit then. I want to tell you everything you need to know, leaving out nothing.

[5] You shall not actually on your first assignment experience everything I tell you, but after I shall have ascended Incarnate from this Earth to My Heavens, to prepare for you an everlasting dwelling-place in My Father's house, you then shall experience everything that I shall reveal to you for all time to come. Pay attention therefore and take in what is for now and what for afterwards.

[6] But what I shall now tell you, those too shall find out more or less who shall fully step in your shoes after you, in My name. You, Matthew the scribe however take down everything I am about to say, as you did on Gerizim, because this must

not be lost to the world, as it is to be a biting witness against it.'

[7] Matthew gets ready for writing and I say to the 12:

[8] 'First of all do not travel upon the roads of the heathens.

[9] That is, do not like the heathens go about throwing your weight around and avoid also notoriously wild peoples, for you are not to proclaim the Gospel of the Kingdom of God to dogs and swine. Because a swine remains a swine, while a dog always avidly returns to his vomit. This therefore is what I am saying, that I counsel you not to travel upon the roads of the heathens.

[10] Likewise, do not go to the cities of the Samaritans. Why? With these I have in your very presence already placed an apostle and they have firstly no need of you and secondly you would be badly received by the Jews, when they find out that you have joined forces with their most hated adversaries.

[11] When you come to them, preach and say and show them in an understandable manner how the Kingdom of Heaven has come near to them. And if they will hear you and accept your sermon, make their sick whole, cleanse the lepers, resurrect their dead, wherever desirable as shown you by your spirit, physically and spiritually with all and above all. (N.B.: Matthew did not record this, because by the commandment to awaken the dead, mainly the spiritual awakening is to be understood.)

[12] Drive out the devils from the people and safeguard them against the former's return. But, above all, mark well, do not accept payment from anyone because you received from Me freely and freely should you pass it on in My name. This supplement I added at the time mainly on account of Judas Iscariot, who had began to secretly calculate how much payment he would ask for one or the other help rendered. For resurrections, particularly of those dead who had meant much to the very rich, he was going to demand a thousand pounds. Since I at once noticed such arithmetic in the traitor's heart, I also at once added the above supplement, to which the concerned one reacted with a sour face, which did not escape **Thomas**, who was facing him and who could not resist making the comment: 'Now, now, you are putting on the face of someone who wanted to collect interest at usury rates but where justice is now spoiling his plans.'

[13] Says **Judas**: 'My face is none of your business. Shall I in the end have to give account to you for my face? I am called and chosen the same as you, why are you then constantly correcting me?'

[14] Says **Thomas**: 'I am not correcting you, but a question for you on some occasions surely will be admissible? Why was it you did not cut such sour face when the Lord was enduing us with all sorts of powers, showing us how we could and should exercise them? But as soon as the Lord said that we should do it freely, your face turned to vinegar. Why? Did you suffer the cramps, that your cheeks and brow were so sourly distorted? Speak openly if you have the guts.'

[15] Says **Judas** to Me: 'Lord, could you not reprimand him for once, otherwise his constant insinuations might start to offend me?'

[16] I said: 'Friend, If someone imputes sin to the innocent, the latter laughs it off in his heart, for there he knows that he is innocent. If however someone is accused of something, even if by sheer coincidence, of which nevertheless that

person really is guilty, say, will that person also laugh it off? O no. I tell you that person shall be infuriated at the person who reproached him as if by accident and not become his friend for sure. Therefore do not let it trouble you, otherwise in the end you shall be admitting guilt.'

[17] Hearing this, Judas at once cuts the happiest of faces, in order not to betray guilt. But **Thomas** says to himself: 'I know you fox, you won't get away.'

[18] But **Simon of Cana** asked: 'Lord, what are we to nevertheless do if someone were to offer us gold, silver or coined iron, for some healing? Are we to not accept that either? There are many poor to whose aid we could come with such money.' **Judas**, uninvited and quite agreeing says: 'Yes, yes, that's exactly what I think. If anyone has gold, silver or iron forced upon them for some help rendered, one ought to surely accept it for the purpose indicated by Simon of Cana?'

[19] Say I: 'Not so, My brethren. I say unto you: you should carry neither gold, nor silver, nor iron under your belts, because a proper workman is worthy of his gold. But he who will not work, when sound, neither should he be fed. For it is written: By the sweat of your brow shall you earn your bread. But nowhere is it written that a work-shy one should prepare his food from alms, consisting of gold, silver and iron. Yet the weak, old and sick should in any case be taken into care by the community as a whole.

[20] A time shall nevertheless come when mankind shall be ruled by gold, silver and iron, determining their worth before the world. But this shall be an evil time. The light of faith shall then go out, while love of neighbor shall grow hard and cold like the iron.

[21] Therefore you ought not on your journey to take a bag, or two coats, nor a staff, because, as I have said, a proper workman is worthy of his food.

## CHAPTER 136
### The objections of Judas

[1] But **Judas** asked, saying: 'Lord, this is in order and the people on the land shall provide for us, but we shall surely have to also go to the cities and markets, where erstwhile hospitality has come to an end. How shall we get on there and how go about without money?'

[2] Say I: 'When you go to a city or a market, find out (since you know what you are capable of) whether there is someone worthy of you there who needs what you are able to give. If you have found such, stay with them until you are off to somewhere else.

[3] It speaks for itself that you first greet the house you enter, because true love always precedes into a stranger's house with civilized steps. If a house, i.e. its occupants are worthy of you, then your peace shall come over it. If however the house is not worthy of you, then peace shall turn back upon you.

[4] And where an occupant of a house will not receive you or hear you speak,

leave such house at once, as also in the end such city, and shake off the dust clinging to your feet, as a once powerful witness against it. For truly I say unto you: on judgment day in the other world once, the land of the Sodomites and Gommorrhans shall fare better than such city.

[5] See, I send you out as sheep among rapacious wolves. Therefore be clever as serpents, yet without guile, as doves, which are a picture of gentleness.'

[6] Says **Judas** thereto: 'Lord, under such dubious circumstances we shall not get very far. Of what use some future judgment day in the spirit kingdom, on which no man believes. If we cannot or must not with divine power You assigned to us, impose as severe a judgment day as possible upon the rapacious wolf-men, then we might as well stay home. Because if we witness of You with even moderate loudness before such wolves, with which particularly the cities are teeming, we shall be seized, bound and dragged before the city halls and severely judged. And there, if judgment is not over-severe, they shall flog us in front of the Jews in the schools and finally make us free as the birds by thrusting us out of the city. For such present truly I want to say thanks in advance. Of what use all cleverness, truth and fullest sincerity, where confronted by willful power in its blind rage?

[7] Where full truth and proper righteousness have an existence, for which contemporary mankind has not the slightest taste, there the Roman adage has to apply also for us: 'Let the world perish, but righteousness is to be practiced to the full. Let the true virtue always find its sure reward. Let the lie, envy, avarice, guile and all unrighteousness however always find its most relentless punishment.' If we are to accomplish anything with the generally most wickedly depraved mankind, we have to proceed like the angels at Sodom and Gomorrah. He who hears and accepts us in Your name, let him be rewarded through Your grace, but let a plague come over him who shall not hear and accept us. But whoever wants to persecute us and haul us before a worldly court, let a consuming fire fall over him from Heaven and do to him what it once did to the Sodomites!

[8] If You, o Lord, allowed us to act thus, we also shall work decidedly good results from our present mission. If however we are not allowed to proceed thus with the altogether depraved and ruined mankind, then all our efforts and work are for nothing. We shall in the end be stoned. And You Yourself, if it were possible, shall be killed and our countless enemies shall be walking over our bodies laughing and drunk with victory. And that shall be about all we shall achieve with all our untimely goodness, compliance and gentleness. In short, in order to achieve anything with Satan, one has to either be his complete master, or serve him as a slave.

## CHAPTER 137
### The apostles comforted

[1] I said: 'Since you are a man of this Earth you speak also as one of this Earth. But He who is from above speaks differently, because He recognizes and knows

well what man needs at different times for the liberation of his spirit from omnipotence and from God's wrath, in order to achieve true independence for eternity.

[2] Because the life of this Earth gives neither life nor liberation to the spirit, but death, but the death of this Earth is deliverance of the spirit to everlasting life and its true, everlasting liberty.

[3] If I have to speak as just man however, I say unto you that all this and far more has already been undertaken with the human race. Yet ask yourself where in your opinion are the golden fruits thereof.

[4] What did not take place in the days of Noah, yet how much did many improve temporally, above what they were in Noah's time? And what occurred soon after at Sodom and Gomorrah?

[5] And see, except from the black and the Chinese in the far East, all heathens are descendants of Lot, as also many Scythian who degenerated like animals, inhabiting the Earth's western parts. How do you find them, in spite of the lesson their father Lot learned?

[6] Go to Egypt and check out the peoples, how much they improved through the 7 plagues. What did Moses not do and what not some prophets?

[7] It was for 40 years that Jehovah let the degenerate Jews languish most miserably under the Babylonian captivity. They were treated like the most inferior beasts of burden, fed with the fare of swine and dogs, while the lovely daughters of Jews were being mortally defiled by the licentious Babylonians, day and night, with flogging and other tortures, as were the boys and youths, who had been circumcised. Go and ask the high haughty Jews how much they improved through such lessons.

[8] Show Me the period, the year, month or week or a day that the Lord was not punishing degenerate mankind, both individually and collectively?

[9] Therefore your advice is much belated. This has all been here already, having effected for the spiritual path also what it had to effect. Yet for man's exterior earthly state there must and can emerge no evident effect basically, for it is not on account of this that anything ever was permitted from above.

[10] But for proclaiming the Gospel of the Kingdom of God on Earth through repeated thunder and lightning I should not have need of you, because there would be in Heaven mighty angels in overabundance who should be more conversant than yourselves with such spreading of the Kingdom of God on Earth.

[11] But that time has now come which Elijah was shown when he lay hidden in the mountain cave. It was not in the storm nor in the fire, but in the gentle breeze that Jehovah was moving about. And that time of Jehovah's gentle breeze before the world-cave is here now. Therefore we neither want to nor can, move out through storm, nor fire, but in accordance with God's eternal order in all love, gentleness and patience! Yet you are not to disregard shrewdness. Because I am well aware of your moving out as lambs among rapacious wolves, yet if you nevertheless are clever, you shall accomplish much.

[12] Beware of those certain men therefore and do not mix with them, because it are these who shall be handing you over to the courts and also scourge you in

their synagogues – and this shortly, if you are foolish rather than sufficiently clever. So long as a lamb finds itself upon a balcony which the wolf cannot reach, the latter can with all his savagery, nevertheless do nothing to it. But if the lamb cheekily leaves the balcony to look at its enemy more closely, it has only itself to blame if torn up and devoured by the wolf.

[13] But later, after I shall have ascended to the Heavens to prepare everlasting dwellings for you in the Father's house, they indeed shall haul you before princes and kings for My name's sake, for a testimony against them and the heathens, so that it may be fulfilled in accordance with what Isaiah, My prophet, prophesied for all time and about the foolish kings in relation to the establishment now of My Kingdom on Earth: *A fool speaks of foolishness and his heart manipulates misfortune, to simulate hypocrisy and preach error about the Lord, to starve hungry souls yet more and to stop the thirsty ones drinking. The rule of the tight-fisted is harm, finding as he does dodges aplenty to ruin the wretched with false verbiage, when he should be upholding the rights of the poor. But the upright princes will have princely thoughts and dispense justice accordingly. Arise you haughty women and hear My voice. You daughters self-assured, hear My speech but for a year and a day and you self-assured shall tremble, for where there is no vine-crop, there shall be no picking. Take fright, you haughty women. For it is the time of the uncovering and the girding of the loins. There shall be wailing for the fields, for the lovely friends indeed and the prolific vines, because upon My people-field shall be growing thorns and hedges, as also over all the houses of pleasure in the merry cities. The palaces shall be deserted and the crowds of the cities lonesome, the cities and citadels becoming eternal caves, for the joy of the beasts of the fields and pasture of the herds. And this till the days of the outpouring of the Spirit from n high. Thereupon the desert shall turn into field and the field counted among forests. And justice shall prevail in the desert and righteousness reign in the field. And the fruit of righteousness shall be peace and the benefit of righteousness shall be eternal calmness and security. Then shall My people dwell in the houses of peace and therefore in the secure dwellings and lofty silence. But the hail nevertheless shall remain along the forest and the city here below shall be a lowly one.*

*Blessed are ye that sow keenly beside the waters, sending forth there the feet of the ass and ox indeed.*

[14] If you are therefore brought before and handed over to the foolish kings by the wicked fools of this world, as indicated by Isaiah, then do not trouble yourselves about what to say and how to justify yourselves, for it shall be given you in that hour what to say and how to justify yourselves, for it is not you who speak, but My Spirit – the Father's Spirit that speaks through you.

[15] This however applies only to the aforementioned, second sending out, which you shall have to accomplish after My ascension, but for now, your burden is not to be an unduly heavy one.

[16] Because just as the prophet says at the end, so I also say unto you now: blessed are ye that are to sow at the seashores, because you may indeed, for this soil, send your asses and oxen back and forth, i.e. your diligence for goodness

and truth, for which I have called you. There you shall not come upon a foolish king, nor upon haughty women, but upon the poor, the sick, the possessed, the lame, deaf and blind. Naturally and even more so, in spirit. To these go forth, preaching to them the Gospel of the Kingdom of God, healing everyone who believes, not keeping My name secret to them.'

## CHAPTER 138
### The question of Simon of Cana

[1] Says **Simon of Cana**: 'Lord, I would like to raise a question, which seems important at least to me, which you may be inclined to answer for us before we go out – for our instruction and peace of mind. I beg that You would hear me.'

[2] I said: 'I can read your question from your heart more precisely than you can formulate it, but let not this stop you from voicing it for your brethren's sake. For the question is of truly great import and worthy of a true and unspoiled Jew. Therefore bring out into the open by all means what makes you heavy breasted.'

[3] Says **Simon of Cana**: 'Very well. If it be Your will that I too speak, then let you all hear me. The question is this:

[4] We shall presently be going to those who have need of us. We shall be preaching what You taught upon the Mount. This Your Sermon on the Mount is of a purely divine nature and therefore of a heavenly goodness beyond all measure. But this teaching is for the most part in strict opposition to the old Mosaic one.

[5] I am familiar with all the localities along the extensive Galilean sea coast, as also many times no less so with its inhabitants. There are indeed many among them who have thrown Moses overboard for Pythagoras, yet it is not these who would pose too much of a threat for your teaching. But there are among them also many families, who so to say live and die for Moses and actually more still for the Temple – and the parents generally more so than the children – although the reverse is not seldom the case. If therefore the children of some ultra orthodox Jews receive Your in many ways anti-Temple teaching, but not their parents, what shall be the result?

[6] The parents shall reproach the children for disobedience according to Moses and curse them – a phenomenon none too rare among fanatically orthodox Jews.

[7] If this undoubtedly shall be taking place in front of our eyes, what shall have to be our response, because it can doubtlessly be taken for granted that such parents shall persecute and curse us without limit?

[8] In the alternative case however it would be much easier of course, since by mere virtue of political law itself, the children cannot be lords over the parents. Besides blessings therefore, we shall be casting the seeds also of discord, quarrelling, rage, hate and revenge and shall be hated, persecuted and totally cursed by thousands. Who shall make good such damage and remove the thousand fold curse from our loins.'

[9] I said: 'Do not let this overly concern you. See, there comes down from

Heaven not only the mild, all enlivening sun beam of spring, but storm, hail, lightning and thunder as well.

[10] Everyone praises the sunbeam indeed, but nobody wants to praise the hail, storm, lightning and thunder. And winter comes too soon for all, yet winter is more beneficial to all than spring, and storm, hail, lightning and thunder are as necessary as the sunset's mild beams.

[11] I say into you: it shall come and must come that, for My name's sake, one brother shall deliver another to death and thus a father the son and the children shall be outraged at their parents and help them towards death. And you have to yourselves be hated by everyone of the world as it now actually is, for My name's sake.

[12] Whosoever among you shall not be offended thereby, but perseveres until the end, shall gain beatitude, for Satan's paw does not easily let go of his prey. Have you understood Me?'

[13] Says **Judas**: 'It's getting better all the time. If this sending has to draw everybody's hatred upon us, then God help such undertaking. Good luck, those who will hate us are going to look after us and keep us like summer does with the snow. Lord, if this is Your full earnest, then I as a simple but nevertheless quite experienced man say to You: Let You nicely stay home with us, because this seed shall not sprout and bring forth fruit. Hear, if we shall have reached the stage where after our sermon we shall be hated of everyone like death itself, what shall be left us to do? Shall we allow ourselves to also be killed on the quiet side? If that too, who will then spread Your Word? Hey, think of what You are asking. Do You not for the sake of the most luminescent Heaven see You make Yourself sheer impossible, being there with Your own greatest enemy and persecutor? Where, where in the whole wide world is he who, hating me beyond death, will listen to my sermon that is going to fill his house with discord, hate, rage and deadly revenge? Speak, what is to be done in such unavoidable circumstance?'

[14] I said: 'You talk the way you understand it, but we talk the way we do. You understand everything in the terrestrially crude way, while the discussion here is from the Heavens, spiritual.

[15] If however you or anyone else should be so scared of men, then flee from a city where they persecute you, to another. Because, verily I say unto you: you shall not have preached in all the cities of Israel by the time I already, as the Son of Man, come to you again as One who shall kindle judgment for everyone –a ruinous fire in his heart, arousing the evil worm in the evildoer's breast and the fire shall not go out and the worm not die. You yourselves however shall be justified for, let all those beware once who persecuted and laid hands upon you.'

[16] Speaks **Judas** once again: 'Yes, once we shall have been killed, You shall follow us indeed. If however you have now given us the authority over evil spirits and the power to heal all sickness, why do You not also at the same time provide us with the power to call forth fire out of the Earth, under the feet of those who persecute us, and we shall in a short time convert the whole world for You.'

[17] I said: 'And would you be more than is your Master and Lord? I say unto you all however: the disciple is not above his teacher and the servant not above

255

his lord. It is enough for the disciple to be like his master and for the servant to be like his lord.

[18] If however your Master does not avail Himself of extraordinary power in order to force men into His teaching, why should His disciples and servants want this?

[19] Since they have called Me, as the Lord and Master of the house from eternity Beelzebub, how much more shall they call you of My household so?

[20] Since it cannot however remain hidden to Me what they intend to or do to you, you can also count on My help at all times. Does the lioness abandon her young, or in times of danger not hazard her life for every cub that would be taken from her? So, surely, I too shall know how to protect you with My life in times of danger.

[21] Therefore do not fear worldly men. What I taught you at night, that speak before them by day. And what I said to one or the other of you in the ear of your heart secretly, that proclaim from the rooftops [Mt.10,27] and therefore fear none of all those who indeed can kill man's body, but cannot kill the soul, which alone lives and has life and which they are unable to damage in any way.

[22] If however you have to fear, then fear Him who is a Lord also over your souls and can judge same unto hell, whenever He wants to. [MT.10,28] And Him you know now, for it is He who is telling you this now.

[23] Look there before us: a roofed barn. See the sparrows frolicking thereon. They fly up, then literally drop down from the roof. At the market, two are bought for a penny. How little they are worth. And yet not one drops from the roof without the will of the Father in Heaven. [Mt.10,29]

[24] But I say unto you: the hairs of your head are counted, yet none comes off your head without the Father's knowledge and will. If however the Father cares for things seeming so exceedingly trivial to you, will He then not take care of those of you who spread His Word and grace?

[25] Therefore yours is a vain fear and you should never fear, for you surely are better than many sparrows.

[26] Therefore, go ye out without fear and confess Me before men. Verily, he who shall confess Me before men, him also will I confess before the Father in Heaven. But whoever among you shall deny Me before men out of vain fear, him I too shall deny once before the Father in Heaven.'

[27] Here **Judas** takes the word again, saying: 'This all is spoken wisely and nicely and certainly is also quite true, but of what use is all this. The teaching certainly is wondrously glorious, pure and true. We certainly don't want to argue any part, while your deeds, for those of us assembled here, more than testify of Him who basically carries them out. But by prevalent norms, the teaching together with the deeds not only shall hardly ever find general acceptance but, as the main cause for strife in every household to which it is introduced, it shall be either most ardently persecuted, or even totally proscribed by the state, making us impossibilities. What then? When, as the spreaders of Your teaching and deeds on Earth, we shall have certainly soon expired through stoning or the sword, by fire or indeed on the cross or the lion's den, who shall step in our place and carry

on for us?'

## CHAPTER 139
### A promise to the faithful

[1] I said: 'I already said to you that you always speak in accordance with the wisdom of the world. To give the world its peace would be to give it still more death than it is imbued with already in all fullness.

[2] If you are to restore sight to the blind, shall he become seeing if you tear out his eyes, or shall the lame be straightened if you chop off his defective foot, or shall the dumb ever gain speech if you cut out his tongue, pest be healed by more pest, or a burning house be put out with more fire?

[3] See, just so is it with worldly men today. They are spiritually dead and have no life other than the animalistic natural one. Their souls are only flesh and their spirit, as good as dead, resembles the spirits indwelling the stones, chaining together loose matter by their judged steadfastness, to become stones of all kinds and forms – softer and harder ones, some transparent and others not and colored in accordance with their indwelling spirit.

[4] But should you want to liberate the spirits from the stones, will you be able to bring this about with lukewarm water? Definitely not. I say unto you: with such gentle and peaceable treatment, the stone shall remain firmly what it is. Here a mighty fire has to come, so that the spirits within the stone get into a great battle. Only then do they themselves tear the bonds of matter and are liberated. And see, so also it must now be here.

[5] That which liberates the spirits from the stone, the fire, the battle, the mighty pressure and blows that also awakens the hearts of men turned stone, liberating them, especially the hearts of the great and the rich, who have hearts of diamond which no earthly fire can soften.

[6] Therefore take note of what I say: let go of the ludicrous notion that I have come to bring, through you, the peace of the Earth to worldly men, but rather the sword.

[7] Understand Me properly. I have come to arouse the yet softer son against the more unbending hardness of his father and the more unassuming daughter against her domineering mother and the gentler daughter-in-law against her mean and envious mother-in-law. Verily, man's worst enemies shall be those of his own household!

[8] In truth I tell you: whoever loves his father or mother more than Me is unworthy of Me. And who has sons and daughters and loves them more than Me is unworthy of Me. Whoever does not willingly take his burden – even if it should weigh him down like the Roman cross of death – onto his shoulders and follow Me, is quite unworthy of Me and shall not participate in the Kingdom of God.

[9] Truly I tell you: whoever seeks the life of this world, and also easily finds it, shall lose life eternal and on judgment day, following the shedding of his body, I

shall not awaken him to everlasting life, but cast him into Hell for eternal death.

[10] But he who does not seek worldly life, even shuns and despises it out of true, pure love for Me, shall find eternal life, for I shall awaken him immediately after the death of his body, i.e. on his judgment day, or the first day of his new life in the spirit-world, and shall lead him into My Eternal Kingdom and adorn his head with the crown of eternal, immortal wisdom and love and he will then rule forever with Me and all the angels of eternal, infinite Heaven over all the material and spirit world.'


## CHAPTER 140
### The divine secret in man

[1] Asks **Simon of Cana**: 'Lord, would You not tell us where Heaven, wherein the angels dwell, is actually situated, also how large it is and how large the world of matter, which You mentioned, might be?'

[2] I said: 'Friend, you are blind if you do not see and understand this. If I mentioned that Heaven was endlessly vast, how can you ask about its size? The spiritual Kingdom of Heaven is everywhere as endlessly extended as this endless universe of which you can see with your eyes but an unspeakably tiny fraction.

[3] This Earth, the great sun, the moon and the stars all of which are immense worlds, some of them thousands upon thousand million times larger than this Earth – all that taken together is – compared to the endlessly vast creation of the material world, in magnitude and vastness not even as much as the smallest dewdrop compared to the immense ocean which is so vast that a good sailor would need more than twice the age of Methuselah to sail over all of its area. However, the material world up to now, as much as has already been created, still has a limit beyond which there exists an infinite, eternal space compared to the absolutely endless expansion of which, in all directions, the entire aforesaid creation of the whole material world is like a moment compared to eternity.

[4] Thus, the spirit world is quite as endless as infinite space that does not end anywhere.

[5] Although space has nowhere an end in eternity and is thus truly endless in all directions, there is in its most endless depths and distances not a single spot where the spirit of God's wisdom and might is not as much present as now here among you. The true children of God, who will excel in proper love for God, the holy Father from eternity, and also in pure love for their neighbors, shall beyond in the great house of the Father obtain the might and the power to forever fill the infinite space with more and more new creations.

[6] You, however, are still too ignorant and cannot grasp what I have now told you. But this I nevertheless tell you: No mortal eye can see nor ear hear and no earthly sense can ever grasp what beyond in the Kingdom of Heaven awaits those who become worthy of being called children of God.

[7] For, before the eyes of true children of God, the globes, suns and moons

shall be floating like glimmering dust.

[8] Therefore, do not be only hearers, but be doers of My Word.

[9] Only the deed will let you recognize whether the words I have spoken to you, and am still speaking, are coming to you from the mouth of a man or from God's mouth.'

[10] But just as you are yourselves to be complete doers of My Word – if you are to be of an enlivening conviction as to who is He that has given you this teaching and Commandment of love – so you are to also spurn on to the deed all those to whom you proclaim My Word, because as long as the Word merely adheres to the brain, it has no higher worth than the braying of a donkey, which also is audible.

[11] Only when the word penetrates the heart does it become live, taking hold of the will, which is the focus of love, driving the whole man unto action.

[12] Through such action a new man arises within the old and My word actually becomes new flesh and blood.

[13] And only this new-man shall show you that My Words truly are of God, having today the same authority, power and effect as eternities of eternities ago, because everything you see, feel, smell, taste and hear is basically nothing other than God's Word.

[14] He who eternities ago out of Himself commanded the worlds, suns and moons to be, placing them in their extensive tracks, the Same is now placing you into new tracks of eternal life.

[15] But I say to you furthermore that, he who receives you also receives Me, but he who receives Me receives also Him who sent Me unto you – which you ought to understand properly.


## CHAPTER 141
### The first sending out of the apostles

[1] But I say yet more unto you: you are aware of how, as always was, there also are prophets today and there always shall be to the end of the world and to every nation upon Earth, regardless of which faith. Because through the prophets alone, regardless of whether all ties between Heaven and Earth may have already been severed, a secret bond nevertheless is kept up which no dark power is capable of breaking.

[2] There indeed always were, are and will be false prophets among the true, but this affects very little if at all the authenticity of a prophet awoken through Heaven, because the true prophet shall expose the liar to the world and he shall not escape punishment from Heaven.

[3] When a true prophet comes to a house and is accepted as such, then he who has received him as a true prophet, or as a messenger in the prophet's name, hearing and heeding his word in his heart, shall receive a prophet's reward in the beyond in God's Kingdom. And whoever receives one righteous in the name

of one righteous, i.e. where such stands in the reputation of one righteous and merits such title, or where in the absence of such repute, the one receiving him acknowledges him as such without subjecting him to a test as to whether he in fact is one righteous, such shall once receive the reward of a just one in the Kingdom of Heaven.

[4] And yet again I say unto you more: see these little ones here surrounding Me lovingly. Whoever shall, in the name of a disciple, pass even a cup of water unto the least of these little ones, I tell you of a truth, such trifling deed shall nevertheless not go unrewarded.

[5] Now you have everything you have need of in the matter for which I have chosen you. Go now to all the cities I showed you and acquaint those residing, there with the Kingdom of God, and do how and what I have commanded you. Your reward shall not be an inconsiderable one.

[6] When you shall have accomplished in the cities of Israel, of which there are not many, that which you were commanded, then return unto Me again, that I may initiate you into the deeper mysteries in the Kingdom of God, for unto you it is given to understand such mysteries, with which the Kingdom of God is imbued.'

[7] Says **Peter**: 'Lord, are we twelve to move in company or individually into one or the other city, as well as the markets and villages?'

[8] I said: 'That's up to you, but better it is for you to go at least by two's or three's, so that one can act as witness for the other. And My Spirit in you shall act more powerfully when you assemble by two's or three's in My name, teaching and acting thus.

[9] But that you should remain together in full number firstly is not necessary and would secondly make it harder to be taken into a house, due to space and care. Therefore split up into either two's or three's. But choose the cities, markets and villages first and be agreed among yourselves as to who is to tackle them respectively.

[10] In this way you can appear in more cities and win much time, enabling you the sooner to return unto Me again. If you are active, you shall easily have finished in seven weeks or earlier still, but be gone now, as every hour counts.'

[11] Says **Judas Iscariot**: 'Lord, the sun is close to setting. The day hardly lasts another half hour and it is far to all places from here. To reach just the nearest village would take 2 hours treading. Would it not be just as good if we break forth early in the morning?'

[12] I said: 'No, My friend, every minute's delay is a threat. You shall, even today still, after sunset reach a market beyond the mountain towards the East, where they shall need your help and you shall then be well received there, but do not remain there more than three days, nor at another place too easily so. Stay together till then, but then split up at the aforementioned market.'

[13] Following these words, the twelve quickly hit the road and the residents of this destroyed little village, miraculously rebuilt afterwards through My grace, gave them two guides who took them to the shortest road to the market.

## CHAPTER 142
### The first missionary work of the apostles

[1] When after a couple of short hours the twelve had reached the above-mentioned market place, they found the residents before the market-gate huddled in groups, weeping, with some complaining most bitterly, because the Herodian tax-extortionists were terrorizing the market, plundering houses, taking from insolvent parents their most beloved, best and most beautiful children, binding them together with ropes like cattle and throwing them on the oxen-drawn tax-wagons. When the disciples became aware of these abominations, they turned to me in their hearts.

[2] Hearing in their hearts distinctly the words, 'Whatever you want shall at once take place', when they perceived that, they said to the most miserable residents of the market-town: 'Peace be with you. May the Kingdom of God, which we spread in the name of the Lord, be with you. Come with us to your market and we shall fix your problem with those unjust and most heartless tax-extortionists.'

[3] Say **the residents**: 'O, there you shall not be listened to. Because those extorting the most unjust taxes are not humans, but wildest rapacious animals, who shall attack you most vehemently.'

[4] Says **Peter**: 'Dear brethren, accept what we bring you. Everything else the Lord shall accomplish. But gold and silver do not expect of us, but what we have, that you shall obtain from us. But now let us rush to the market, so that the children may not suffer too long.'

[5] Moving upon the place with the residents, the disciples notice several wagons loaded with personal effects, some with children and some with sheep and cattle, with the tax-extortionists already giving the departure signal, not taking any notice of the screaming and wailing of the roped children.

[6] Here **Peter** steps up to the chief tax-extortionist, speaking in the most urgent tone: 'Miserable wretch! With what right do you carry out these abominations?! Do you not know that an almighty God dwells above you who can destroy you and your accomplices at once? Stand back from your abominations and return the lot, or you shall taste the sharpness of God's wrath on the spot!' Says **the chief tax-extortionist** to Peter: 'Who are you, daring to talk to me in that tone? Are you by chance unaware of the power I wield through Herod, who obtains it through tenure from the emperor of Rome? Do you perhaps not know either that I can have anyone getting in my way killed instantly without trial?! Step back immediately! Another word and the edge of the sword will catch up with you!'

[7] Says **Peter**: 'Now then, since you – despite that you are a son of Jacob – are a human no more, but a wild rapacious beast, may God's judgment hit you and your accomplices. Amen!'

[8] When Peter had exclaimed this with great zeal, fire broke forth from the Earth, consuming the chief instantly. Seeing this, his accomplices were so frightened that they fell down before Peter, promising to do anything he orders, if only he would not punish them in this terrible manner.

[9] Says **Peter**: 'So let go of the lot and leave in peace. But do not ever let you crave for such service to a Herod again, because with the first step, it shall happen to you as happened to the chief in front of your eyes.'

[10] Upon these words, the tax-extortionists at once untied and released the children, doing similarly with all livestock, such as sheep and calves, together with whatever they had exacted from this place, to which they, together with Herod, had no right at all. Because this market had already purchased its freedom from Herod a year earlier, from the Romans, as other places too had done, due to the unlimited Herodian oppressions. But Herod was carrying out secret raids nullifying the redemption-deeds and giving his exactors all authority with new deeds, undertaking his accountability to the emperor.

[11] Peter now went about extolling to the extortionists, their injustice towards their brethren, while the former began to curse Herod and execrate themselves for lending the tyrant their ready hands.

[12] Peter however now began to teach the Kingdom of God and see, all the tax-extortionists – nearly 100 in all – were converted and followed Peter, and this was a good catch, because these very tax-extortionists became extremely active in their own right and considerably contributed to the rapid spreading of My teaching.

[13] The residents of this market however hung unto the apostles for 3 days and even permitted themselves to be baptized in My name for the apostles also baptized with water and in My name, anyone who asked for baptism.

[14] They had not yet actually been commanded by Me to do so, but knew it was not against My will.

[15] The residents went to all lengths to host the disciples superbly and at the end also offered them money for having healed their sick. The disciples however did not accept any, nor anything else, which amazed **the former tax-men**, who said: 'Your unselfishness even more than your miraculous works persuades us of the fact that you are messengers of God, because men of this world are full of the blackest self-interest.'

[16] Judas' eyes bulged of course, on seeing much gold, which was offered him, but Thomas was constantly at his side and so the money-hungry disciple did not this time dare accept any, which caused him much inner sorrow.

[17] After 3 days however the disciples split up here into two's and between 10 to 15 of the converted tax-men went with these, rendering the disciples good service, for they had much courage and knew no fear before men.

[18] The twelve now did as I had commanded them and they did well everywhere.

[19] And what did I Myself do after sending the disciples out with the stated instructions?

# CHAPTER 143
## At the sea. The Lord's answer

[1] After the disciples left the place where I gave them instructions, as outlined, I remained there till sunset, blessing the poor little folk and its small children, whereupon I then moved onwards a little with the numerous remaining disciples who were about Me, to the cities upon the Galilean Sea, from where some of these were natives and residents. And there I taught and preached what I had commanded the twelve to teach and preach and everywhere healed the sick.

[2] But John, who had baptized on the Jordan, had by then been already thrown into prison by Herod and that through the priests' of Jerusalem's lobbying, having made strong representations to Herod toward that end, for they could not forgive John for having denounced them as serpents and a generation of vipers. But they did not themselves dare to attack the preacher in the desert, for they were mindful of his being regarded by the people as a great prophet. Therefore they got at Herod, through gold and through all kinds of official ordinances and Herod had him arrested under the pretext of one insane, who was stirring up the people with subversive ideas and driving them crazy in many ways.

[3] But basically Herod was not concerned so much with the substance of John's teaching as making a good haul. Therefore did Herod not confine John too strictly, but allowed everybody access to John in prison, for a reasonable fee. Recognized disciples of the Baptist had to pay only a stater per week, while others had to pay a silver crown for just a day's visit.

[4] And Herod did not forbid John to preach and make as big a noise as possible, in a large hall which had been converted into a large public prison, for it brought in that much more money for Herod.

[5] Herod often went to see John and even encouraged him to make yet more noise than he did in the desert at Bethabara, since he was now safe from the priests and Pharisees and he even confided being a friend and protector of John's.

[6] John was indeed aware in his spirit as to whom he was dealing with in Herod, but he made use of such opportunity and kept on preaching in prison and his disciples had unhindered access to him, naturally for the minimal fee of a stater per week. Priests from the Temple had to pay a pound if they wanted to see John and when they queried Herod on why he let John continue preaching in prison, the cunning fox of a **Herod** replied: 'This I do for state security, in order to track down all the followers of this threatening extremist.' For such answer the priests praised Herod beyond measure and showered him with gold, silver and precious stones. For they reasoned: this is our man – him we must support in every way, for he is destined to rid us of all this prophetic rabble.

[7] But Herod, a Greek by birth, was only after the money and was not in the least concerned about anything else. Next to money, only the most beautiful concubines mattered. On their account he even could show cruelty, if these desired it, but otherwise no one got anything out of him without money, but for

money he was available for every contingency.

[8] From this authentic description of Herod, it shall become clear to all how John could have his disciples around him in prison and how through his disciples as well as others visiting him frequently, he could be kept in touch with My action in Galilee.

[9] Since John found out in prison therefore how I taught and acted, he sent two of his most experienced disciples to Me to ask Me: 'Are You indeed the One who was to come, or are we to wait for another?'

[10] Here it will be asked and said: 'How could John, who at first gave Me the greatest testimony, ask a question like that?' The reason for anyone who could think just one span above the material was most simple and even most natural.

[11] At the time of John's getting acquainted with Me, he also fully understood that I incontrovertibly was the promised Messiah and that through My mere appearance already, the entire Jewish nation was as good as redeemed and that the power of the worldly great was finished forever. When however he ended up in prison, being ever more convinced as the days went by that with My appearance, the power of the worldly great not only had not ceased but only increased, then even John began to slightly and quietly doubt My authenticity.

[12] For he thought: if this Jesus of Nazareth really is the promised the Son of the living God, how can He now let me down and not free me from prison and how could He allow it to happen?

[13] Yet he then heard from those who visited him what unheard of deeds I was performing and so he then dispatched the two of his most experienced disciples to Me, who put the above questions to Me.

[14] I however, knowing quite well the reason for his having Me questioned thus, answered the disciples with brevity, saying to them: 'Go and tell John what ye see and hear. The blind see, the lame walk, the leprous are cleansed, the deaf hear, the dead arise and the poor have the Gospel preached to them. And blessed will be they who shall not be offended in Me.' The two disciples did not know what to say to Me.

## CHAPTER 144
### The Lord's testimony of John

[1] After some time, the older of the two asked Me why it was that John had to languish in prison, since he had never sinned before God or man.

[2] Say I: 'He too could be free if he wanted to. The moon indeed does good service at night, but if it wanted to compete with the sun for prominence, as if its light even by day next to the sun were as important as that of the sun, then the moon is greatly mistaken, for once the sun is up, the moon's sheen is quite dispensable. Do you understand that?

[3] Who prevented John from following Me when I came to him at the Jordan and he recognized Me more distinctly? He remained in his desert and constantly

did rigid penance, yet had never sinned. Why did he do this? He himself delivered him up to Herod. Now he can see how he gets on with the fox.

[4] Say to him however that I did not come to take away the power from the worldly great, but to confirm them upon their seats of power. But he who seeks to dispute with Me shall have a tough battle on his hands.'

[5] Hearing these My words, they said nothing further, but took their leave, setting out upon their road back to John in Jerusalem at once, notifying him immediately.

[6] **John** however beat his breast, saying: 'Yes, it is He. He is right. He must wax and I wane and die off this world.'

[7] Yet, at the place of Seba, a fishing village located at the Galilean Sea, the many people there, as well as those who had followed Me there, were wide-eyed about John the Baptist and said: 'How could he have committed a sin? Was the fact of not following You a major sin of his, which he is now atoning? Lord, are we wrong in judging thus?'

[8] But I answered them: 'When the full moon shines at night, all go out to admire its light and are happy, but when the sun appears, while the moon still shows its weak sheen in the sky, then all turn away from the moon, grazing their eyes upon the mighty sunlight, praising same in every beaming dew-drop, because one drop of water under the sun shines more brilliantly than ten moons in the night.

[9] But does the moon commit a sin if it is darkened by the sun during the day and because even a dew-drop provides the observer more light than the entire moon?

[10] I say unto you all let him who has ears hear. The Son of Man also is a sun and John is His moon. The moon verily shines in the night of your spirit and witnessed of the Light, which has now come unto you, which in your darkness you still have not recognized. If however the moon's glow turns faint when the sun of day shines among you, how can you think of him as with sin?'

[11] Verily I say unto you, there has not since Adam, been a soul among men more pure, indwelling and animating a body.

[12] But I ask every one of you, as there is not one among you who did not go to the desert where John preached and baptized – you all heard his sermon and most of you also let yourselves be baptized: why went you out to see in the desert?

[13] Did ye perhaps go and see a reed blown about by the wind? Or did ye go out to see a man with soft clothing. See, they who wear soft clothing dwell in the houses of kings and not in the harsh desert of Bethabara. Or did you go out to see a prophet?

[14] Verily I tell you: John is more than a prophet. Because it is he of whom it is written: "I send My angel before you, who shall prepare your way." Do you understand now who he is?

[15] Verily, I say it yet more plainly than I already said: of all those born of woman from the beginning, not one emerged greater than this John the Baptist. Nevertheless, I also tell you that from now on, the least in the Kingdom of God

shall be greater than he.

[16] But this too let you keep well in mind: from the days of John even till now the Kingdom of God suffers violence and they that do it violence shall gain it.

[17] Up until John, all the prophets as well as Moses' law have prophesied. He was the last prophet before Me.

[18] If you will receive it, this very John is Elijah who is to come again before the Messiah. He also has come and prophesied before Me and has prepared My ways, as you have found out yourselves. Say it now whether you know who John is.'

## CHAPTER 145
### John the Baptist's spirit and soul

[1] Say **the people**: 'Lord, if so then it is wrong for You to leave him in prison. Judging by Your deeds, which only God is likely to accomplish, it would surely have been easy for You to free him, since he worked for You. Lord, this You ought to do now and not let him be stuck in prison.'

[2] I said: 'He who comes himself accomplishes more than by sending a messenger or a letter. John's spirit is big and bigger than any spirit that ever acted in a body on this Earth, but his body is of this Earth and out of its weakness a weak soul has developed and it is good thus.

[3] For such strong spirit is indeed capable of strongly attract a weak soul, but the flesh and soul of John are weak. Therefore he always sent messengers in his own stead and here messenger or letter never effect what a person does himself in whom reside soul and spirit.

[4] Because I must not and cannot, hang My own strength and power upon someone, be it that someone comes and takes same himself, because on My part none is precluded from taking either life, or judgment, whatever he will, and thus neither My authority nor power for a good cause.

[5] But whoever does not come by himself, to him it shall not be granted, other than the grace of light, through which he would find the way to Me, here or in the beyond and realize along the way that I Myself am the way to life and the Life itself.

[6] John indeed, like no other, attained to near mastery of his flesh. He saw the blessings in front of him yet did not take them by force. Why not? Did he have to be like that?

[7] Here stands before you He who pronounces the 'Must', where necessary. But this One also is telling you that He did not pronounce for John a must in this respect.

[8] His being called to make straight for Me a way, for the people's sake, was a kind of must, behind which nevertheless there was hidden an eternity of freedom, which however you shall not grasp in your flesh, but that he should not have been allowed to follow Me when seeing and recognizing Me, there was neither a

"should not", and even less a "must not". There his spirit listened to the soul, wherewith he also got into doubts about Me and has for this reason sent messengers to Me for the second time. He who asks is not yet in the clear, since every question presupposes either a complete lack of knowledge, or a doubt about whether what one knows is true. If John were fully in the clear, he would not be sending Me messengers.

[9] No one indeed before him had led a life so strict – because he would eat and drink nothing for days if he felt even the slightest carnal desire in his flesh and therefore was the Earth's greatest penitent – without ever having sinned. I nevertheless say unto you all: a sinner who has never mended his ways, approaching Me with a love-filled heart, rates higher with Me than John.

[10] For he who says to Me: Lord, I am a sinner and not worthy of Your entering my house, is preferable to Me than to 99 righteous who need no penance, praising God in their heart for not being sinners and therefore better than an ever so great a sinner. I say unto you: theirs shall not be too great a reward in My Kingdom.'

## CHAPTER 146
### Conversion of Kisjonah, the tax-collector

[1] When I had finished talking, a tax-collector stepped over to Me from the crowd whose heart had already been for a long time aglow for Me, although conscious of many a sin. This one fell on his face before Me, saying:

[2] 'O, Lord, here lies before You in the dust one who is indeed a great sinner, yet daring to love You beyond all measure. See, Lord, it is already high noon. My desire to invite You and all Your disciples to lunch is great, if only I was worthy of Your coming under my roof! I and my house are too unclean and sinful for You, but there are clean foods and drinks in my larder. O, show me sinful one the grace of letting me bring You the foods through clean hands.'

[3] I said: 'Kisjonah, arise and I shall go with you into your house to partake of lunch there. May a great blessing come upon your house, not on account of your sins but your true love and humility. This is also why your sins are forgiven as if you had never sinned.'

[4] After that, Kisjonah the tax-collector got up and I together with a large number of disciples went into the house with him. Over a hundred were served and there was no lack of the best wine as well.

[5] But besides My disciples, a great crowd of people had come together from all the Galilean localities, as well as from Judea, who escorted Me to Kisjonah's house. And as there was no room in the house, Kisjonah had bread and wine handed out to them in the open, on account of their being with Me.

[6] On such occasions, Pharisees were of course not lacking, who followed Me everywhere from Capernaum. Since they once again saw Me eating and drinking with much cheer and gladness and how at the table I was friendly shaking the

repentant tax-collectors' hands, calling them My dear friends even while they were regarded as arch-sinners by the Jews, this again was the last straw for the Pharisees and other ultra orthodox Jews.

[7] But what angered them more than anything else was that after the meal, I went arm in arm with the tax-collectors for a stroll in a lovely big garden upon the Sea and also paid Kisjonah's5 well-behaved daughters much heartfelt attention, because they really were filled with innermost love for Me. I lovingly called them 'My brides', which seemed tremendously sinful to the Pharisees.

[8] When on top of that towards evening I accepted an invitation to stay overnight and I volunteered to stay three days or even longer with Kisjonah, this was the ultimate affront for the Pharisees and arch-orthodox Jews. 'So', they said, 'with such rabble, with such arch-sinners and tax-collectors he is associating, eating and drinking in friendship with them, getting all but drunk and playing gentleman with the sinning daughters of arch-sinners, flattering them and in the end preaching God's Gospel to the arch-whores, instead of calling upon us to seize and burn these monsters. This would be a nice Messiah. And now, with the opulent five whores having seduced him, he even wants to stay God knows how long.

[9] Let's go. Why hang around him longer? Now we know exactly what he is on about. We have been around him for quite some time. Has anyone seen him pray? Who has ever seen him fast? The Sabbath he does not keep, his friend and joy are the greatest arch-heretics and heathens. Greeks and Romans, tax-collectors and arch-sinners and sumptuous and sleek whores, followed by a good meal and many a goblet of the best wine!

[10] In other words, he is firstly nothing but a smart magician from Pythagoras' school and knows how to deal it out. Added to that he is a smooth talker, something all magicians have to be in order to sell their wares. He accepts no money for sure, but is this so praiseworthy? O, all magicians do it in their first year, to get their renown the sooner. Once they have that, then often kings do not have the treasure to satisfy such artists.

[11] But why should this one need money at all? His eating and drinking he gets for nothing – as much of it as he likes and otherwise he needs nothing. To that, he is a glutton and wine-bibber and sinner's associate, enjoying a life of ease. And thirdly he has no need of a God and His commandments, because he deems himself a god or at least his son, whom our God of Abraham, Isaac and Jacob is supposed to have begotten through the notorious Mary of Nazareth. Which one of us is stupid enough to not call the bluff of such newly-baked, typically heathen magic farce instantly?

[12] In short, we are wake-ups and it is high time to let go of him, or he may still get at us and we are of the devil. There! Watch how he flatters the hated tax-man's 5 daughters and how these properly worship him. I would bet a thousand pound to a stater that this prophet and savior, if he were to get to Jerusalem today, would start it up most intimately and sweetly with the queen of all whores – the world-renown Mary of Magdalon and perhaps even with Mary and Martha of Bethany, who are supposed to have the second most frequent visits from the

Greeks of Jerusalem after Mary of Magdalon.'

[13] Says **another** with somewhat sharper eyes, to the first – a Pharisee: 'You are not altogether wrong, but if you think back to a similar occasion at the house of Matthew, the tax-collector, then there too we were judging that way, yet were then so licked by his wisdom that we could not find an answer in a thousand. What if he took it up with us again? Will you take up our defense?'

[14] Says **the first**: 'I know that as well as you do, for I went through it too. He is going to find dodges aplenty and is besides a smooth talker and magician's chief. But our intellect has to show us the way and here it says: "Leave before you are of the devil." And we are surely going to follow such advice? Do we really want to become of the devil? By god no. This be eternally far from us all, for we have Abraham as father, whose father is God and therefore we do not want the wool pulled over our eyes by this magician the way he does it with the heathens.'

[15] Says **the second one** again: 'But his teaching is pure and fully corresponds with man's nature and nothing devilish comes to the fore. Here I do not altogether agree with you, as Moses basically taught us the same thing as this Nazarene.

[16] To love God above all and one's brother neighbor as oneself, to not return evil for evil, to do good even to the enemy and to bless those who curse us and to at the same time be humble and full of gentleness. Here truly nothing devilish will peer through.'

[17] Says **the first**: 'Not for you, because you already are of the devil. Don't you know that the devil is most dangerous precisely when dressed up as an angel of light?'

[18] Says **the second**: 'If old wives tales like that are your yardstick, then one cannot talk to you. Where stands the ox or donkey who has either seen a Satan dressed up as an angel of God, or spoken to one? Truly, here you and all your depressed chaps are not fair to this man.

[19] We know nothing bad about him, but only much good and even unheard-of miracles. Why should we judge him just for seeing him deal as much with sinners as with righteous men, showing them much patience and much loving forbearance?

## CHAPTER 147
### The parable of the children in the market-place

[1] When the second one finished saying this, the arch-Pharisees and ultra-orthodox Jews left the second one with his more moderate supporters. Setting out upon the overland route to Capernaum, because the sea was going strong and they did not trust the shippers who assured them it would be safe.

[2] The entire party however, about one hundred and fifty strong, not being familiar with the correct route, did not get far and that at an insurmountable high cliff jutting into the sea, causing immense breakers. Immediately above this, rose a high and steep mountain range, over which there was no pass from this part of

the sea. And so the party had no option but to back-track the extensive road of about two hours journey, not arriving until midnight and in blackest night under storm and rain with thunder and lightning in Kisjonah the tax-collector's for courts, to seek protection and shelter there, as the whole party was soaked to the skin and in a state of near collapse from exhaustion. And the tax-collector and his people took them in caringly and found them dry quarters, which the soaked ones found most agreeable.

[3] Fairly late the following day the soaked ones re-emerged somewhat tired, drying their apparel under the sun's beams.

[4] It was Sabbath however, but Kisjonah and his people went about their tasks as on any other day. And at midday the tables were set with all kinds of well prepared foods.

[5] Kisjonah invited also the soaked and tired ones, but they not only did not accept but started to grumble and curse such profaners and non-heeders of the Sabbath, for a proper Jew is to neither touch or eat anything before sunset – he is allowed only to drink3 times a day.

[6] Since the invited returned **the tax-collector**'s friendliness in this manner, the latter turned to Me and said: 'Lord, what ought to be done about these fools? I want to do them a good turn and they curse me for it. Please tell me whether God hears the curse of such fools, for the chastisement of those cursed by them.'

[7] I said: 'O yes, but not to the detriment of the ones cursed by them, but only of the cursers. Who has ears to hear, let him hear. I will tell you how things actually are with them. Do you think they observe the Sabbath because this was bid by Moses? Or do you think they fast because of that?

[8] I tell you: in their hearts Moses and the prophets are not worth 3 stater, but they wish to be seen as Aaron's worthy successors by the people who pay the tithe and good money.

[9] How can I describe this miserable generation? Are they not like the little children sitting in the market-place and calling out to their playmates: "We piped for you and you would not dance. We wailed and you would not cry." But I do here not regard the Pharisees and orthodox Jews as such little, but those who are here with us, for they are the ones who yesterday wanted in their heart to keep these fools and total deniers of God here, and the fools have scoffed at them and Me. The sailors wanted to take them across the Sea to Capernaum since there was a good wind, but these fools did not trust the sailors. They went, and a bad storm drove them again back here. Now you have invited them to the midday meal, and they curse you.

[10] You dear little children who are here before Me sitting at the true market of life, I tell you: do not pipe to these fools any longer, for they are lame in their spirit and, therefore, do not want to dance. Thus also refrain from wailing, for their hearts are stones and have no moisture.

[11] John, about whom we yesterday talked so much and to whom I bore a most fair witness, came and led such an austere life that he hardly ate and drank anything except for locusts and wild honey which he laboriously got himself from Earth-holes. And these people, as well as others of this kind of rabble, told him to

his face that he was possessed by the devil who fed and supported him by night.

[12] And has not John piped and wailed more than enough like no one before him? But see, these and many of their kind would neither dance nor cry.

[13] Now the long since promised Son of Man has come into the world in Me. This one eats and drinks. And what do they say now? Yesterday you heard it yourselves what they thought of Me when they shouted: "Look at him. A glutton and a drinker and, besides, a friend of tax-collectors and sinners."

[14] But I tell you: such wisdom has to have itself justified by its children, that is, its own children declare them to be fools, and thus the wisdom with which they have served us has become justified in its children, but so has Mine, for its children recognize and accept it, and thereby both kinds of wisdom, the false and the true, have been sufficiently justified.'

[15] Here **the Pharisees and arch-Jews** rose and said to Me: 'Beware, you are a Jew still. We have the law and the right to ruin you as an arch-heretic, because you want to destroy Moses and undermine the prophets. Woe betide you if you do not let go of such aspirations. We have the emperor's consent to make use of Roman law and any governor has to accede to our demands.'

## CHAPTER 148
### The Lord's pronouncement over Chorazim, Bethsaida and Capernaum

[1] With these threats, **My disciples** stepped over to me and said: 'Lord. How can You listen to this? Do You not have power in abundance to destroy such vermin? The Sycharites were chased away several times when they tried to confront You, yet You had not worked as much at Sychar as at Capernaum.'

[2] I said: 'I naturally would have power for it to excess. But the Lord of life does not need to hold judgment here, because after this life there comes another which, whether good or bad, shall have no end, the duration being the same. And for that eternal time I of a truth now pronounce a just judgment and condemn all the cities in which I had worked so much, yet receive now such reward, as you have just heard.

[3] They have with all My preaching not improved and have remained dumb in their hearts for all My deeds. Therefore beware, Chorazim, beware, Bethsaida! Had such deeds been done at Tyre and Sidon, they should in their days have repented in sack-cloth and ashes!

[4] Yet I say unto you: on judgment day in the other world, they shall fare better than these.

[5] As for you, proud Capernaum, who have been upraised to Heaven, you shall be cast down to Hell! For had such deeds been done at Sodom as have been done here, that city would still stand today!

[6] And yet again I say to you: on the day of judgment in the world to come, it shall be more tolerable for the Sodomites than for you, proud, hard and immeasurably ungrateful city! For this have I healed thousands of your sick and

resurrected your dead, so you would now curse Me?! Woe betide you on judgment day in the beyond! There you shall find out who was He whom you cursed!'

[7] Following this My condemnation, many received a vision and saw how such cities as condemned now by Myself would fare on judgment day, seeing My figure in the clouds and seeing a curse leaving My mouth and strike the condemned cities.

[8] When this vision had passed from most of the unaffected, simple persons of both sexes surrounding Me lovingly, these fell down before Me, lauding and praising Me.

[9] But I raised My hands above them, blessed them and said: 'I too, as Man, now praise You, Father and Lord of Heaven and Earth, for having hidden it from the worldly wise and clever and for revealing it unto babes. Of a truth, holy Father, it is thus well pleasing to You and Me. For, that which You work, I also work, as we have been One from eternity. I never was any other but You, holy Father and that which is Yours, has also been Mine from eternity.'

[10] These last words caused all of them to be gripped by great fear. For there had by now been many disciples following Me who had no further doubts about My deity, yet it was over these that the fear came most of all.


## CHAPTER 149
### The awakening to eternal life

[1] **Nathanael**, who so to say made a spokesman among those left behind, since, without being called by Me, he kept a Gospel in the Greek tongue, which he commanded. And this a more comprehensive Gospel than of all those who undertook it, came over to Me in profound dread and said: 'Lord, You Almighty. I too received the vision, seeing the most dreadful things, so that even my graver failed me from fear. I beg You in the fullness of my love for You, Thou eternally holy One, tell me whether this shall in all earnest take place in the beyond once, as I and many just saw it?'

[2] I said: 'Fear not, for you have nothing to fear. He who lives and acts like you shall in the beyond, as also here already, be awakened to life eternal. And everyone's judgment day shall be whenever awakened to life eternal, either here or in the beyond.

[3] Let everyone therefore strive towards being awakened here already, because he who is awakened already in the flesh shall neither see, nor feel or taste the death of the flesh and his soul shall not be troubled.

[4] But woe betide all these and the later opponents of My order. Verily these shall feel it a thousand fold who He was whom they tried to oppose, burdening Him and His witnesses with the curse.

[5] I verily can say it and do so, for unto you I say: all things are given Me by My Father. But no man knows the Son, who is I, but the Father. And just so, no man

knows the Father, but the Son and he to whom the Son will reveal it.'

[6] Says **Nathanael**: 'In that case not even we, Your most faithful disciples, know You by far, even though You have already revealed much to us about Yourself and who You are?'

[7] I said: 'You do indeed know Me to the extent I revealed and showed Myself to you. Yet you still lack much. But when you shall have recognized the Father, then you shall also get to know Me fully and this shall be when I shall have ascended from the Earth back to My Heavens. From there on the Father shall draw you up to Me, even as I drew you to the Father. And he whom the Father shall not draw, same shall not come unto Me, the Son. Verily, I say unto you: in that time all shall have to learn it from God themselves as to who the Son is. And he who shall not be taught of God shall not come unto the Son and have life eternal out of Him.

[8] But the Son is not harder than the Father, because that which is done through the Father's love, the same is done by the Son's love, and just as the Father's love is the Son, so the Son's love is also the Father.

[9] But the Son speaks to you as to all men: come unto Me all ye that labor and are heavy laden and I shall restore you.

[10] Take My yoke upon you, learn of Me how to carry it and do as I do – for I am gentle and humble of heart – then you shall have rest and all fear shall leave you.

[11] For My yoke is easy and My burden light, for I know what ye are able to do.'

## CHAPTER 150
### The Lord exposes and deals with the Pharisees' maliciousness

[1] The disciples were comforted by such words, while the Pharisees and arch-Jews started asking what it was they had seen and how they could have been so visibly shaken.

[2] Those asked however related what they had seen as with one voice. Here **the Pharisees** became halting, mutually questioning and saying: 'How can a magician affect an appearance with just some yet not with others? Why did we see nothing? If we as staunch Mosaists are cursed and to what extent, (judging by the appearance) by him who also purports to be a Jew, then from his angle it would have been more logical to show us the vision, to frighten us and make disciples of us. But he is clever, not making a show in front of us, fearing that we are awake to him and call it by its rightful name, opening the eyes of many of his followers therewith, to then see who their highly praised master is. We shall have to take more effective measures against this ever more threatening person, otherwise he grows over our heads, therefore making the Romans come and ruin us one and all.'

[3] Say I loudly to them: 'For that you have been ripe a long time and it would take only a word from Me to the Commander-in-chief and by the day after

tomorrow you would be hanging from the stocks by the thousands! Do you think that I do not know of your secret plots against the emperor Tiberius? O certainly not! I know the day and the hour and what the agreed signal for all Judea, Galilee and within Jerusalem's walls consists in! But I say unto you that you shall make wondrously bad business out of it. And the governor Pontius Pilate, who wields a sharp sword, shall hand you your reward for your trouble outside the walls of Jerusalem, and Herod shall have much to do to regain the favor of the governor!

[4] By all means take hold of more effective measures against Me and My disciples and I too shall know what to undertake against you before My time!

[5] John called you a brood of serpents and a generation of vipers! I have never given you such a name yet, but now I too give you that name and call out to you: "get out!", or I let the bears come from the woods to do unto you what was done to the loose boys at the time of Elisha. Because for you the last spark of mercy is gone from My heart.

[6] Had you just in some way blasphemed against Me, I would forgive you. But you exalted and took up arms against My spirit, which is called Love and is My Father from eternity, and this sin shall not be forgiven you, neither here nor in the hereafter! And therefore remove yourselves so that I can spend the remaining few days with My friend Kisjonah, unmolested!'

[7] Says **one Pharisee**: 'We must not let you out of sight, as we have been assigned to it by our primate.'

[8] I said: 'Yes, you are set up over Me like wolves over a flock of sheep. But if you persist with your resolve, I shall at once get bears to come for you from the mountains and set them over you as warders and disciplinarians!'

[9] At this point a tremendous roaring, as of many bears, can be heard from the nearby mountains. On hearing this, the Pharisees and arch-Jews quickly make their escape to the sea, boarding the fishing vessels by themselves and thrusting off shore. But a powerful contrary wind drives them back to shore, where here and there a few bears can be detected. Close on 2 hours they battle the winds that would stubbornly drive them back to shore each time they venture away a few yards, with the intermittent relenting of the storm. After 2 hours of exasperating battling with the wind and sea, a larger ship finally comes, taking up the exasperated and near-collapsed from exhaustion, sailing off with them and that in a mighty storm threatening any moment to swallow up the ship. In this way they are tormented all day and night, only reaching shore at Capernaum at noon the next day.

[10] There they are exhaustively questioned by their superiors as to what they had seen, heard and met with. But they are secretive, not daring to speak, for they had acquired a considerable respect for Me and did not dare to for the present venture forth against Me.

[1] The superiors however appointed others and sent them after Me. But these also had much battle with the storm, for it was nearly early autumn, called the canine days and there were nearly constant storms in Galilee and that much more upon this land's sea. The former therefore did not arrive at the place of My stay until the fifth day, requesting to speak with Me. But I did not admit them, knowing what they were after, letting them know that I shall be staying longer and then visit nearby localities, and that they had to keep quiet or suffer serious consequences.

[2] It was however the day after Sabbath just then, what is today Sunday, and a most clear and beautiful day at that and Kisjonah came to Me to suggest to Me and all present the scaling of a very high nearby mountain.

[3] This was as yet an unnamed mountain, because geography in this time was still in its infancy and therefore most mountains, valleys, plateaus, seas, brooks and rivers had no official names, but only such as they were referred to by neighboring folk. The biggest problem was with mountain names.

[4] Mountains that did not stand isolated, such as a Tabor, Lebanon, Ararat or Sinai, but being part of an extensive mountain chain, generally had no names of their own, except an occasionally local or temporary one, named not seldom after some wealthy alpine owner who grazed his herds there. If the property changed hands, then such mountain was renamed after its owner.

[5] Therefore this place, situated on the border between Galilee and Greece, was a central toll-gate, because from there a fairly well-laid alpine mule-track led from Galilee to Greece, used by thousands of diverse trading folk, transporting their many wares by camels, mules and donkeys.

[6] When the newly-arrived Pharisees heard that we were about to scale the lofty mountain, they asked Kisjonah whether they could join the company. **Kisjonah** said: 'If you are or can be of good will, then this mountain, being my sole property and extending 20 hours in length and five hours wide, shall be sufficiently roomy to receive you too. But as hostile spies of the Capernaum and Jerusalem priesthood, I could not as a Greek and now fervent follower of the holy and by my conviction the only true teaching, of this holy master of all masters, find any use for you at all and would avoid your company with every means at my disposal. Ask your hearts. If they are pure then you have clear passage. If impure, then you better go back from where you came.'

[7] Say **the Pharisees**: 'We are pure and without guile. We are confessors of Moses and are Jews, as Jesus also is a Jew, not being able to destroy Moses' law. But as there is powerful renown about his deeds and teaching, we have to be very much concerned about whether his teachings and deeds do not undo Moses. If they confirm Moses and the prophets, then we too shall accept them, but if they are contrary, then it speaks for itself that we have to be against them.'

[8] Says **the tax-collector**: 'The way you just spoke your forefathers also spoke to the prophets and then stoned them as God-deniers. And to my knowledge very

few only were not stoned. Yet you put on your prophets at every opportunity to boast them. Yet your forefathers were exactly what you are and none of you is better by a hair's breadth than your forefathers who stoned the prophets. Therefore I do not trust you in the presence of this holy prophet of all prophets.

[9] You indeed call yourselves confessors of Moses, but in your doings you are further from Moses than this Earth is from Heaven. Therefore examine yourselves as to whether you are worthy of scaling this my mountain with us.'

[10] Say I to Kisjonah: 'Let them come with us. When it gets too much for them then they will indeed turn back, for none of their kind has climbed a mountain yet. Perhaps this high mountain's pure air shall somewhat clean their hearts.'

[11] Kisjonah was happy with this and we commenced our journey up, with all care.

[12] And the five daughters were not missing either and were about Me like chicks, asking Me all kinds of things about the primordial creation and the coming into being of such mountains. And I explained all to them in accordance with their grasping ability. The disciples too, as well as the large crowd accompanying us listened in on our discussions, to their delight.

[13] And **Nathanael**, who was the most taken in with My deity, talked to the mountain from time to time, saying: 'O mountain, do you feel who it is that is setting His foot upon You?' And each time Nathanael put such exalted question to the mount, its reverberation was perceivable to all.

[14] But the Pharisees became most fearful and started to induce the people not to venture up further – this could be a holy mountain from antiquity, not to be climbed by the unworthy and the mountain starting to quake and rage and ruin all for the sake of the one.

[15] But **the people** said: 'Then you better turn back yourselves, because this mountain, which we have often climbed, has never yet quaked on our account.'

[16] To this the Pharisees started to grumble about the people. And the mountain shook with the Pharisees' grumbling and these turned around and ran as fast as they could from the mountain back to the plain and we were rid of tiresome company.

[17] We then quietly continued our journey, reaching Kisjonah's extensive alpine ranch towards the evening, where we also settled in for the night. Only on the second day, on account of fatigue among the women, did we set out to scale this mountain's highest peak, from where an uncommonly glorious view was to be had over all of Judea, Samaria, Galilee and a large portion of Greece.

## CHAPTER 152
### The spirit world

[1] We spent a day and a night on that summit and enjoyed much that was magnificent and marvelous.

[2] There was, of course, nothing marvelous for Me since within Me rests – and

must rest – the first cause for all the countless phenomena and happenings. But for all those who were with Me there was a great and boundless abundance of all the magnificent and marvelous things.

[3] To begin with, there was the extremely delightful wide view which kept the eyes busy all through the day. Then, when the sun had set, I allowed people's inner vision to open up, so that they could look into the great spirit world.

[4] How surprised they all were to see above the Earth a vast world full of living and acting beings and very vast, partly most delightful regions and areas, but looking very desolate and melancholy towards midnight.

[5] I, however, secretly bade all the spirits be silent about Me.

[6] Many disciples discussed with the spirits life after physical death, and the spirits gave them very obvious proof that after the death of the body there is still another and more perfect life and what it is like.

[7] Also **Kisjonah** said: 'Now all my wishes are fulfilled. By all possess and by this mountain which is standing on my earthly property, I would give one half of all I possess if I could only have some of the principal Sadducees and Essenes here who do not believe in a life after the death of the body. How beautifully these wise people would be knocking their noses against the spirit world. Once I myself was quite captivated by their doctrines, but eventually gave them up again as fortunately a rather weird apparition of my deceased father set me right.

[8] It is extraordinary. One can of a truth deal and converse with these beings as with the like of us. But what astonishes me is that among so many spirits, of whom I personally recognize some very well, there is to be seen no patriarch, prophet nor king.'

[9] I said: 'My dear friend and brother, these are alive in the spirit world just as truly as these, but in order for them to not be accorded a kind of divine adoration by the millions upon millions of spirits, they are kept isolated from the other spirits in a special location called the Limbo, where they wait in their expectation of being, in this very time, freed by Me and then installed in the Heavens of the primordial dwelling place of My angels – which also shall indeed take place shortly.

[10] Besides that however these spirits of the patriarchs, prophets and righteous kings constitute a kind of watch between Hell proper and the world of spirits, to prevent Hell from darkening, polluting and leading them astray.

[11] Satan indeed from time to time is permitted to walk abroad in the natural world to cause mischief, but entry to this spirit world is blocked off to all devils everlastingly. Because where life proper has taken its actual inception, death remains far away forever. 'Satan', 'Devil' and 'Hell' are judgment and therefore death itself and have therefore nothing further to do in the Kingdom of life. Do you really understand this?'

[12] Says **Kisjonah**: 'As well as I can and Your grace permitting it. I understand it, o Lord, but there probably is an immense amount behind it which I probably shall not be able to understand until once a dweller myself, of this rather gloomy than friendly world. Towards the East and South this spirit world truly has a most beautiful and friendly appearance, but toward the West and North it looks more

miserable and sad than the wide desert where the great Babylon once stood. Such sight then spoils the charm of the East and South.'

[13] I said: 'You are right. It verily is as your feeling tells you. But the spirits whom you are seeing now by the hundreds of thousands do not see the West and North the way you do, for a spirit can see only what at any particular time corresponds with his innermost.

[14] Since however neither the West nor North seen here correspond to their innermost, they see neither West and still less the North. Only after they shall once become equal to My angels, shall they be able to see it all the way you do now.'

[15] Says **Kisjonah**: 'Lord, this is somewhat dim and I do not understand it yet, but I figure that this is not necessary for the present. But since, o Lord, You are right now so liberal with these wonderful revelations, how about showing us, besides all these countless spirits, a couple of angels? I have heard so much about Archangels, Cherubim and Seraphim and have read so much in the Scriptures and formed all kinds of concepts about it which probably were highly imprecise and therefore erroneous. You, o Lord, could provide me with a proper concept now if it were Your holy will.' The 5 daughters who were constantly around Me also asked Me for it.

[16] But I said: 'I intend to do so, but not before this Earth's midnight. But for now keep conversing with the spirits, only do not give My presence here away to them.'

[17] All were happy with this promise and anticipated the passing of midnight longingly.

## CHAPTER 153
### Three lunar spirits speak about the lunar world

[1] Kisjonah however, who had a smattering of astronomy, began to estimate whether in accordance with the stars, midnight had been passed yet, because in that age it was a long way still to the clocks of today and one resorted to calculations, unreliable of course, in accordance with the stars.

[2] Says **Kisjonah** after a while: 'In accordance with my calculations, midnight should be over by now?'

[3] I said: 'Friend, your calculation is good for nothing, because we still have an hour to midnight. Therefore it is better not to calculate, because the movement of the stars is quite different to what you think. Even your calculation in itself is wrong and therefore it shall not be likely for you to come up with the middle of the night from the position of and movement of the stars. People who shall be capable of this have still to be born, but now it is not time yet by far.'

[4] But after diverse conversations, midnight nevertheless came and a half-moon rose. Kisjonah's daughters hurriedly asked Me what the moon could be actually and how it can wax and wane like that.

[5] But I said to them: 'My most beloved daughters, directly behind you stand 3 spirits from the moon. Ask them. They shall tell you exactly what the moon is and how it constantly changes its light, sometimes losing it altogether.'

[6] Here **the eldest one** immediately asked the 3 spirits about the moon and these said: 'Lovely one, your asking us about the moon is like us asking about the Earth, which you inhabit. Although you do not know why it is dark on Earth right now, you do not ask about it. How can you ask about the moon, which is much further away from you than the Earth that carries you?

[7] See, our moon, just like your Earth, is a world. Your Earth is round like a sphere and so is ours. Your Earth is half illuminated by the great sun, so is our moon. With you, the duration of the night on average is about 13 of your short hours and approximately likewise your days, but on the moon, one night and one day each last the duration of 14 days and nights of your Earth. And therefore, seen from your Earth, the constant changing phase of the moon – and that is a big difference between the moon and your much bigger Earth.

[8] But another big difference emerges between your Earth and the moon, in that the moon is inhabited by beings like me only on one side – not visible to you, whereas your Earth is inhabitable and mostly inhabited throughout.

[9] Ah, life on the moon is not as blessed as on your Earth. There is intense cold and much unbearable heat, much hunger and not seldom burning thirst. Therefore do not hanker after that small but exceedingly hard world, upon whose fields grow no wheat, or corn and even less, wine.

[10] But on the side which you are able to constantly see, no beings dwell in the flesh, neither animal nor man, but unfortunate, helpless and near helpless spirits. And now you know as much as you need to know.

[11] But do not harbor the wish to find out more about the moon, because such knowledge would in the end make you very unhappy.

[12] Abide in love and let go of all wisdom, for it is better to eat at the table of love, than to lick the scanty dew from lunar wisdom-stones.'

[13] After this account, the 3 lunar spirits left and the daughters asked Me confidentially whether the situation on the moon is as related by the 3 lunar spirits.

[14] And I say: 'Yes, My most beloved daughters, it is exactly so and sometimes far worse. But now let us leave the moon its journey and all look towards the East.

[15] I shall summon several angels from Heaven and you shall see them come from there. Therefore direct your eyes there.'

## CHAPTER 154
### The return of the 12 apostles

[1] All direct their eyes towards the East now where, as with the rising sun, it is getting ever brighter – only for the inner vision of course, although the eye of the flesh also is affected.

[2] Finally, after some time of steady brightening in the East, shapes brighter

than the sun appear, in perfect human form, floating towards us through the air. The light of these 3 angels who on account of their steadfastness, firmness and light are referred to by the general term "Cherubim", the world of spirits nearly was eclipsed and the spirits seemed like alpine mists hovering about the mountain peaks.

[3] When the **3 Cherubim** had come into our midst, they dimmed their light and fell upon their faces before Me, saying: Lord, who in the eternally endless Heavens is worthy of seeing Your most holy countenance? To You alone all honor in eternity and infinity.'

[4] But I said to them: 'Veil yourselves and hasten down to a place where My 12 messengers are waiting. They have fulfilled My will and it is enough. Therefore fetch them and bring them here.'

[5] That instant the 3 angels veiled themselves, departing quickly and bringing, in a few moments, the dispatched 12 to me on the mountain top.

[6] The 12, except for Judas, were filled with joy for having been brought to Me from a great distance in this miraculous fashion.

[7] Only **Judas** said: 'Forever do I say thanks for such journey. It took only a few moments, but was I scared, and the draft.'

[8] The angels had however allowed only Judas to feel this, while the other 11 felt none of all this.

[9] This happening however made the rounds among the people verbally for a long time afterwards, namely, that the 12 disciples were brought to Me on the mountain from a great distance by the angels.

[10] Upon the mountain nevertheless **many** began to fear, saying: 'By Heaven, the goings on here are too miraculous – almost too hard to bear.'

[11] While **the others** said: "This only Jehovah Himself can effect'.

[12] But the 12 had much to tell about their experiences in the short time.

[13] I however commanded the angels to procure bread and wine in proper quantities, as the 12 were hungry and thirsty, as they had not received to eat or drink for a whole day. And the angels at once did as I commanded them, bringing bread and wine in the right quantity. The 12 then took bread and wine and ate and drank what they needed and were fortified.

[14] The 5 daughters however wanted to sample such bread and wine and asked Me for it. But **Kisjonah** chided them for being voracious, saying: 'To be voracious also is a sin. Therefore self-denial in all things is essential, otherwise man cannot achieve virtue, without which there can be no life.'

[15] But I said: 'Friend, let this sin be forgiven your daughters for evermore, for sins which are basically no sins are easy to forgive. Your daughters are in all seriousness hungry and thirsty, and bread and wine there is plenty for everyone here. And therefore let all enjoy it in accordance with need, once the most needy 12 have been fortified.'

[16] That put Kisjonah and his 5 daughters at ease. Whereupon I asked the 12 disciples to hastily hand out bread and wine, and they did so at once.

[17] All in all, there were this time about 800 persons upon the mount, which had a spacious top, with a flat rock of about 10 yards height jutting out of it, which also

was easy to climb from the south.

[18] All ate and drank and were filled, lauding and praising Me for their being fortified so miraculously. And **Kisjonah** spoke down from the aforementioned rock, which he scaled to that end:

[19] 'Lend an ear, friends and brethren. We are conversant with Scripture, starting with Moses right up to our time, as also with the books of the 'Wars of Jehovah', which are mentioned by Moses and many other prophets, which we obtained from Persia, reading the translations, since they were endorsed by many wise men. But of all the miracles described therein, there is not one comparable to that now taking place before our eyes. Such is unheard of not only in Israel but the entire world. Who is it therefore that must be He who accomplishes such deeds, which none besides God can accomplish for sure?'

## CHAPTER 155
### The difference between science and faith

[1] After this I call Kisjonah down from his 10 yard high pulpit, telling him confidentially: 'Keep it secret for now and do not give Me away before time, because there are many around here who have not yet reached your ripeness and must not find out fully yet as to who I actually am, or the enlivening of their spiritual liberation would come under judgment, from which such spirit could then hardly ever ascend.

[2] It is enough that many are now getting a premonition as to who I am, with most of them taking Me for either a great prophet and some for God's Son – which now I am in My exterior. More than this would be of much harm for the present. Therefore we also shall leave them with that opinion and belief for now and you must therefore not give Me away beyond that.'

[3] Says **Kisjonah**: 'Yes Lord, this is certainly so, but I also am a human. Will it not be to the judgment of my soul as well to not only believe without a doubt but be imbued through and through with the knowledge as to who You are?'

[4] I said: 'You I have prepared through word and teaching. When I came to you a few days ago you took Me for a very wise and highly accomplished doctor and when you saw Me accomplish unusual deeds, you began to take Me for a prophet through whom God's Spirit acted. But being a man of much experience, you felt prompted to find out how I had achieved such perfection. Thereupon I revealed to you what man is and what is in him, and also what can become of man when he has fully recognized himself, achieving by that the fullest life-liberty of his spirit.

[5] But then I also showed you how God Himself is a Man and this is why you too – as well as all beings like you – are also men. I then also showed you confidentially that I Myself am that Man and that every man is called to become and be forever what I Myself am. You were astonished, knowing from then on who I am.

[6] And see, this was a purposeful preparation of your soul and spirit, so that

you could now watch Me create an Earth, or men from stones, without being harmed. Because you accepted freely, and that in a fully scientific way, that God can be a Man and man can scientifically true be a god. And so it can no longer trouble your soul and spirit to fully understand that I alone am the One true God and Creator of all things from eternity.

[7] But it is quite different with other people, who on the whole are not accessible to the scientific approach. These only have faith and otherwise little understanding.

[8] The faith of the soul however is nearer to life than the most perfect intellect. If the faith is a coerced one however, then it also becomes a shackle to the soul. If however the soul is shackled, then there can be no talk of the development of the spirit within it.

[9] But where, as in your case, the intellect first was brought to the right insight, there the soul remains free and takes for itself light from the intellect to the extent of her tolerance and digestive capacity.

[10] And thus through a properly educated intellect, a true, full and living faith develops, from which the spirit within the soul receives the right nutrients, becoming steadily stronger and mightier, which can be perceived by any man whose love towards Me and neighbor gets steadily stronger and mightier.

[11] But as stated, where man's intellect quite often is undeveloped, man having only faith, which in its confined state is as it were only an obedience to the heart and its will, such must then be approached with caution, for it to not go numb with delusion, or be hideously side-tracked, as it is only too obviously and unfortunately the case with all heathens and others at this time.

[12] And you will now see why I called you down from the rock before, when you intended revealing Me to the people. Therefore no blind should lead another, but rather one of penetrating intellect, otherwise they both fall into the abyss.

[13] I say unto you all, be assiduous and acquire a proper knowledge in all things. Examine everything you encounter and retain what is good and true and you shall find it easy to grasp the truth and enliven the formerly dead faith, making it into a true lantern of life.

[14] I say into you and therefore also to all: if you want to reap the proper benefit from My teaching, then you must first understand it and only then truly act in accordance with the truth.

[15] Just as the Father in Heaven is perfect in all things, even so you too must be perfect, otherwise you cannot become His children.

[16] You have read Matthew's Scripture and My sermon on the mount in which I taught the disciples to pray and this with the invocation "Our Father".

[17] He who says such prayer in his heart, yet does not understand it in the right sense, is like a blind who praises the sun, yet is not able to see or form a concept of it in spite of its mighty light. He does not of course sin therewith, yet it is in reality of no account to him, for he still remains in the same darkness.

[18] Thus, if you want to truly educate a human heart for life, then do not overlook the proper development of the intellect, or you should make a blind worshipper of the sun out of him, which is fit for nothing.

## CHAPTER 156
### Moses' account of the creation

[1] After this instructive talk, of which Kisjonah said that it left him no further question, the coming day began to dawn in the East. And on the mountain-peak, where we were quite snug, a very cool morning breeze crept in and Kisjonah suggested we should move down to the nearest alpine hut until the sun came up.

[2] I said: 'Let's leave that. This light morning-frost at this height will actually harm no one, but rather strengthen everyone's limbs. Besides, it won't last long and has to be so, otherwise a certain variety of spirits, not to be described further here, would bring bad weather for the day, if not prevented from rising by the powerful peace-spirits.'

[3] Kisjonah was reassured and we tarried on the mountain peak until midday. After midday however we moved down to the alpine ranch again, where we stayed another 2 days, with all sorts of discussions about man's life-responsibility and the nature of the Earth, the stars and all kinds of other things.

[4] Much of it was beyond the rather dull section of the Jews and the Pharisees who remained with Me, but they did not argue about anything, because these Jews and Pharisees, who had turned My way already on the day of My first visit at the tax-collector Kisjonah's house, in reality were more awake and better spirits and more sober thinkers and had already a high opinion of Me and received My Word as Godly. These are therefore not to be compared with those driven back to Capernaum, nor with those who four days earlier had been driven down to the lowland by the mountain's liveliness.

[5] But although the above-mentioned better **Jews and Pharisees** already were quite firm followers of Mine, they shrugged their shoulders at some explanations about the true and graduated coming into being of the creation of the Earth and all things in and upon it, as also about countless other heavenly bodies, saying among themselves: 'Is not this diametrically opposed to Moses. Where are the 6 days of Creation and where the Sabbath on which God rested. What is then Moses' account of the coming into being of all that comprises all parts of the world? If this worker of miracles from Nazareth now gives us a completely different teaching, making Moses obsolete, then what should we say to that? But if he disposes of Moses, then he also disposes of all the prophets and ultimately even of Himself, because if there is no Moses, then the prophets also are nothing, and therefore also the expected Messiah, whom he purports to be.

[6] Yet, basically, this teaching is correct and it could easily be with the creation as he explained it now, rather than Moses' account.

# CHAPTER 157
## The first day of creation

[1] **Jesus**: 'Is it not written: *In the beginning God created the Heaven and the Earth. And the Earth was without form, and void, and darkness was upon the face of the deep. And the Spirit of God moved upon the face of the waters.*

[2] *And God said, let there be light: and there was light. And God saw the light, that it was good: and God divided the light from the darkness. And God called the light Day, and the darkness He called Night. And the evening and the morning were the first day.*

[3] See, these are Moses' words. If you were to take these in their natural sense you should have to at once see their ultimate absurdity.

[4] What of a truth is the Heaven and Earth of which Moses says all was created in the beginning? In man, Heaven is the spiritual and Earth the natural. This still is void and without form – as in your case. The waters are your deficient knowledge of all things, above which the Spirit of God moves indeed, but not yet within them.

[5] Since God at all times however sees the terrible darkness in your material world-depth, God says to you, as manifestly even now: "Let there be light."

[6] It begins thereupon to dawn within your natures, and God indeed sees how good is the light upon your darkness, but it is yourselves who do not want to recognize it. For this reason therefore a division takes place within you, day and night verily are separated, and through the day within, you then recognize the former night of your hearts.

[7] With man, his initial natural being is late evening and therefore night. Since God gives him light however, such light is to him a veritable sunrise, and out of man's evening and sunrise verily come man's first day of life.

[8] Therefore see, if Moses, who most certainly had been an initiate into all Egyptian science had intended in his scripture to indicate the coming into being of the first terrestrial day, then he would, with all his science and wisdom have noted that no day could ever emerge from evening and morning. Night proper surely always follows evening, and day comes only after the morning.

[9] What therefore lies between evening and morning is night. Only what lies between morning and evening is day.

[10] Had Moses said: "…and therefore out of morning and evening emerged the first day", then you would have been entitled to take this in its natural sense, but for good reasons of correspondences he said exactly the reverse, and this signifies man's evening and night, which also is understandable since nobody has seen the highest wisdom in a child yet.

[11] When a child is born, its soul finds itself in utter darkness and therefore night. The child nevertheless grows, receiving all kinds of instruction, gaining all sorts of insights with that. And see, this is dusk comparable with evening.

[12] Indeed you say that it dawns also in the morning, and Moses therefore might have said: "And from dawn and an actually bright morning emerged the first day."

[13] To this I say: indeed, had he availed himself of spiritual correspondences to tell mankind the crassest nonsense. But Moses knew that only evening corresponds to man's terrestrial state. He knew that it was with man's worldly-intellectual education exactly as it is with the gradually waning light of natural evening.

[14] The greater the pursuit of worldly things through men's intellect, the feebler the pure divine light of love and spiritual life in their hearts. Therefore also Moses called such worldly light of men the evening.

[15] Only when God through His mercy kindles a small light of life in the heart, does man begin to understand the nothingness of all that he had previously acquired through the intellect – his spiritual evening, whereupon he starts to gradually see how the treasures of his evening light are as transitory as this light itself.

[16] The right light out of God however, kindled in the hearts of men is that morning which together with the preceding evening brings about the first true day within man.

[17] From this My present explanation however you must see what a vast difference there has to be between these two respective lights or rather cognitions, because all cognition from the worldly evening light is deceptive and transitory. Only Truth lasts forever and deception has in the end to come to naught.


## CHAPTER 158
### The second day of creation

[1] But it can nevertheless happen that the divine light is poured out over the evening light in man's heart and be so consumed or blended that it would in the end be no longer possible to know the natural light within man from the divine.

[2] God then made a divide between the two waters, which bespeaks the two cognitions with which I have now adequately acquainted you, and He thus divided the two waters.

[3] The division itself however is the actual Heaven within man's heart expressing itself in true and living faith and not ever in a void, intellectual musing.

[4] For this reason also I call him who has the mightiest and most undoubting faith a rock, which I place as a new divide between Heaven and Hell, and this fortification, no powers of darkness shall overcome forever.

[5] When this fortification is placed within man and his faith waxes ever mightier, then through such faith the nothingness of natural cognition becomes steadily more apparent. Natural cognition then moves to subordinate itself to the dominance of faith, and with that, out of man's evening and the steadily brightening morning, there arises the other and by far brighter day.

[6] In this second day condition man already recognizes that which alone must maintain itself as ultimate truth forever, but proper order nevertheless still is

lacking within him. Man still continually blends the natural with the purely spiritual, often spiritualizing nature too much and therefore seeing the material also with the spirit, therefore not yet being decidedly on the side of the right deed.

[7] He resembles a world of water which indeed is surrounded on all sides with lucent air – not being clear however about whether his water-world came forth from the translucent air surrounding it or the latter proceeding from the water world, i.e. he is not sure within himself yet whether his spiritual cognition developed from his natural one, or whether the latter secretly came out of a possibly secretly pre-existent and secretly active spiritual cognition in man. Or to put it more plainly still, he does not know whether faith proceeds from knowledge or the latter from the former, and what the difference is between them.

[8] In short, he cannot work out whether the chicken was before the egg and the seed before the tree.

[9] God then comes once again to help man along, provided man has done what he could from the strength loaned to him and therefore his, on this second day of his spiritual education. And this additional help consists in the provision of more abundant light, which then like the sun in spring, not just by greater light intensity but the warmth affected with this, starts to fertilize all the seeds laid in man's heart.

[10] This warmth however is called love, and spiritually constitutes the soil within which the seed starts sprouting and thrusting out its roots.

[11] And see, this is what is written in Moses, that God said: "Let the waters be gathered together in certain separate places, so that the dry and firm land can be seen, from which alone the seeds can grow into living and enlivening fruit."

[12] And it says: "...and God called the dry land Earth, and the water, now gathered at certain places, the seas".

[13] Then the question is: for whose benefit did God call it so? For Himself verily He would not have needed it, since it surely would sound somewhat divisive to attribute to the highest wisdom in God His special pleasure in succeeding with the naming of the dry land as 'Earth' and the gathered waters as 'seas'.

[14] Yet God surely could not do the naming of the dry land and the gathered waters for anyone's benefit, since there was no being besides Himself in this creation period to understand Him.

[15] Such saying of Moses therefore cannot possibly have a material but only a spiritual sense, having only a potentially retrospective spiritual sense in relation to the erstwhile creation of the worlds – i.e. from the spiritual to the material – this being capable of comprehension only by the wisdom of angels. But the way it stands, it has a purely spiritual sense and indicates how initially the individual and society at large develop in time and periods from their necessary original natural state to the gradually purer spiritual.

[16] Man therefore is being sorted out even in his natural state. The cognitions have their place – that is man's sea, and the love emerging from the cognitions as a soil capable of carrying fruit, washed all around by the totality of rightful cognitions, steadily renewed in its strength for the bringing forth of all kinds of select fruits ever more abundantly.'

# CHAPTER 159
## The third day of creation

[1] When man's cognitions therefore surround man from all sides and are progressively lit up and warmed by the love-flame which they had fed, then man correspondingly grows in strength and the capacity to act.

[2] In this state God again comes to man – in Spirit of course, and as love eternal speaks to man's love in his heart: "Let the Earth bring forth vegetation, the herb yielding seed, and the fruit tree yielding fruit after its kind, whose seed is in itself, upon the Earth."

[3] Upon such Commandment from God in the heart, man gains a firm will, strength and confidence and goes into action.

[4] And see, his right cognitions take off like rain-laden clouds above the ordered sea and move over the dry land, moistening and fructifying it. And the Earth begins to turn green, bringing forth all kinds of grass and herbs with seed, and all kinds of fruit trees and bushes and seeds, yielding fruit, i.e., that which the right intellect, translucent with heavenly wisdom now regards as fully good and true, then also desired at once by the love in man's heart.

[5] Because just as the seed laid in the Earth soon sprouts, bringing forth manifold fruit, just so is the effect of the right cognitions if laid in the life-giving soil of the heart.

[6] The seed however acts in the manner of awakening the love-force dormant in the soil, and this then gathers increasingly around the seed-grain, effecting the unfolding of the latter to growth, yielding fruit. In short, the right cognition moves to action only in the heart, and from the action all kinds of works emerge. And it is of this that, out of deep wisdom, Moses speaks in Genesis, and that as already rendered verbatim, from chapter 1, verses 11 and 12.

[7] Man's former evening, raised to proper cognition through the light, thus leads to action, which must be followed by works. And this is the third day in the heart's development and that of the whole man in man, who is the spiritual man around whom everything revolves, on whose account Moses and all the prophets of God came to this world, just as I I now. I think that this subject is now clear enough for you?'

[8] Says **one of the Pharisees**: 'Exalted and wisest friend and master, I for my part underwrite every one of your words, addressed to all of us, since they are totally true and must be so. But move to Jerusalem and explain Genesis to the Temple in this way, and you shall be stoned together with all your following, unless you defend yourself with your evidently divine power. But should you encounter the Temple servants with this might, then they are judged at once and it may differ very little from annihilating them with lightning and fire from Heaven in the first place.

[9] As said, it would in any case be a most daring task, in spite of such truly all-wise and penetrating explanation of the first 3 days of creation, as described in Genesis, being quite straightforward and without a word of self-contradiction. But

now comes the fourth day, on which according to the text, God evidently created sun, moon and stars. How can you explain this differently? To all intents and purposes sun, moon and stars are with us and no man knows a beginning to these large and small lights on the firmament other than what one reads in Genesis.

[10] Now the question is: where is the key to the correspondence by which this fourth day relates exclusively to man?'

[11] I said: 'My friend, have you not often heard and experienced it yourself that there are far-sighted and short-sighted as well as half and totally blind people, and those blind as bats, in the eye of the flesh? The far-sighted see well at a distance but badly at close range. The short-sighted on the other hand see well in the vicinity but badly at a distance. With the half-blind it is half night and half day, i.e. they indeed see objects quite well with one eye, but because the other eye is blind it is self-evident that such seers can only see everything at half light. The fully blind no longer see any object, neither during the day nor at night, although there is a feeble glimmer during the day so that they can tell day from night. Those blind as bats do not have a glimmer and can no longer distinguish day from night.

[12] See, just as men are so diversely constituted in their flesh-vision, just so but much more markedly diverse are they constituted in their spiritual sight. And even you yourself have a strong visual defect and much more strongly in your soul-sight than in the eye of the flesh. Verily I say unto you: the short-sightedness of your soul is extraordinary.'

## CHAPTER 160
### The fourth day of creation

[1] Which way do you read Genesis? Is it not written thus: "And God said, let there be lights in the firmament of the Heaven to divide the day from the night. And let them be for signs and for seasons, and for days, and years. And let them be for lights in the firmament of the Heaven to give light upon the Earth. And it was so. And God made 2 great lights: the greater light to rule the day, and the lesser light to rule the night. He made the stars also. And God set them in the firmament of the Heaven to give light upon the Earth, and to rule over the day and over the night, and to divide the light from the darkness. And God saw that it was good. And the evening and the morning were the fourth day".

[2] See, this is what it says about the creation of the fourth day, which according to Genesis causes the fourth day.

[3] If you illumine this matter a little with even your intellectual power then the crassest nonsense must strike your eyes at first glance, if you take the wording as its meaning.

[4] According to Genesis, God created the light already on the first day. And out of the evening and morning became the first day. Tell Me, what kind of light was this that adequately effected day and night for 3 days? On the fourth day God

again said: 'Let there be lights in Heaven'. The question is: what kind of lights that should divide day and night? Did not the light created on the first day affect this for 3 days? Why on the fourth day more lights for the same effect? On top of that there is talk of only 'lights', but not the slightest mention of a moon and sun. These lights furthermore also affect signs. What signs? Finally seasons. Which ones? And days and years. What days and years? Is night nothing? Does not night count the same as day?

[5] And on top of that the Earth is spherical and always has day on one side and night on the other. According to the revolving of the Earth from evening to morning (west to east) around its own axis, there will always be day where the lands find themselves in the sun, or more precisely, where the steady turning of the Earth pushes the Earth under the sun as it were.

[6] If therefore indisputably the natural day of the Earth is brought about by its peculiar movement, where the sun does nothing other than shine at one point, effecting day through its light wherever its light penetrates, and therefore cannot and does not want to rule the day thereby. The question is: how should Moses have meant sun and moon by his lights? And had he meant the natural sun and the natural moon, then for greater clarification of his revelation to mankind he would have named these two lights, since all men in Moses' time already were able to name these two spheres.

[7] Besides this, Moses speaks of a firmament in Heaven which in the natural outer space exists nowhere in actuality, in that sun, moon and all stars as well as this Earth float freely in the ether, restricted nowhere, maintained in their purposeful position through the law laid within them, having free movement without attachment to any heavenly firmament.

[8] Because there is only one firmament in infinite and free space, and this is the will of God, through which the former is filled with an unchangeable law throughout.

[9] If that which to your eyes appears as an immensely spread-out blue vault, with the sun, moon and stars somehow fastened to same, how could they move and in the case of the familiar planets, continually change their positions?

[10] The other stars, which you call fixed, appear of course as if attached to some kind of firmament, but this is not so. They only are removed so far from the Earth and their tracks so extended that often they hardly cover these in several hundreds of thousand years, and for this reason their movements are not perceived throughout even a hundred human life-times. And that is the reason they appear to you as all but fixed. But in reality it is otherwise and there is to be found no so-called firmament throughout infinite space.

[11] The firmament which Moses means is the firm will within the divine order, gone forth from the right understanding and love, which is the blessed soil of life. Since such will can however only go forth from the fertile fullness of the true divine love in man's heart, just as this goes forth from the heavenly light which God had poured out in man when dividing the latter's inner darkness into evening and morning, just so the Heaven within man is this right love and the right insight and the right intellect, which manifest as a living faith. And the firm will within the divine

order is the firmament of Heaven in man. And into such firmament – if this is in accordance with the love-will of God and the right order – God puts now lights out of the Heaven of Heavens, which is the right Father love in God's heart. And the lights then light up the will, raising it to the insight of the angels of the Heaven of Heavens, and therewith raise the created man to the uncreated one, who had transformed himself, as a child of God, through his own free will within the divine order.

## CHAPTER 161
### Continuation of the fourth day of creation

[1] For as long as man is a creature he is temporal, transitory and cannot endure, because every man in his natural state is merely a suitable vessel within which a man proper can develop through God's constant participation.

[2] Once the outer vessel has reached the right degree of development, to which end God has provided same with all essential parts and properties over abundantly, He then awakens or rather develops His uncreated eternal Spirit within man's heart, and this Spirit in its effect is what Moses understands and wishes to be understood by the 2 great lights which God put in the firmament, the way it also was understood, and never otherwise, by all patriarchs and prophets.

[3] This eternal, uncreated, eternally live light in the heavenly firmament of man only then is the really true ruler of the actual day within man, teaching the former vessel to fully transform itself into its uncreated divine being and to therewith make the entire man into a true child of God.

[4] Every created man however has a living soul, which indeed also is a spirit, with the necessary capacity to know the good and the true, and the evil and the false, acquiring the good and true and banishing the evil and false from itself. Nevertheless it is not an uncreated but created spirit, and as such can never by itself gain the childhood of God.

[5] If however it has in all humility and modesty of heart and from the free will implanted by God, accepted the good and true in accordance with the law given it, then such humble, modest and obedient will has, to put it bluntly, become a heavenly firmament, because it has developed itself in accordance with the celestial placed within it, becoming then fully capable of assuming the uncreated divine nature.

[6] The purely divine or uncreated Spirit of God now placed permanently into such celestial firmament is the great light. Man's soul however which is transformed to an almost equally great light through the great light is the smaller and lesser light, which however like the uncreated great light is placed in the same celestial firmament and transformed to a co-uncreated light, without losing any of its natural nature but instead gaining endlessly in a fully purified spiritual sense. Because by itself man's soul could never see God in His purest divine nature, and the purest uncreated Spirit of God conversely could not see the natural, because

for Him nothing material-natural exists. But through the above mentioned complete conjunction of the purest Spirit with the soul the latter can now see God in His arch-spiritual purest being through the new spirit that he received, and the spirit can then see the natural through the soul.

[7] This Moses is saying, that a great light is to rule the day and the lesser light the night, to determine the signs, i.e. to determine out of all wisdom the basis for every appearance and all created things, therefore also determine the times, days and years, which is to say: to recognize God's wisdom, love and grace in all phenomena.

[8] The stars which Moses also mentions are the countless useful cognitions - every individual thing, which latter of course all flow from the main cognition, and are therefore placed in the same heavenly firmament as the two main lights.

[9] And see, this at last is the fourth day of creation of which Moses speaks in Genesis, which nevertheless, as with the former three, has gone forth from the same evening and morning in man.

## CHAPTER 162
### The fifth and sixth day of creation

[1] So that you would not in this connection ask Me further as to what to make of the fifth and sixth day of creation, I tell you briefly that the ensuing creation of the animal world in aggregate, and lastly man himself signify nothing other than the coming alive in full and realization of all that man harbors in his natural part.

[2] His sea and all his waters come alive and man becomes aware of and glimpses within his now pure divine, uncreated light the countless and manifold fullness of the creative ideas and forms, and in this way becomes cognizant of his purely divine origin. And through the telling of the creation of the first human pair is signified the perfected humanization or inheritance of the complete childhood of God.

[3] Of course you are now secretly asking within your heart: yes indeed, all this is quite good, wise and glorious, and nobody can doubt in the least the fullness of the truth: how then did this Earth, which surely could not have been present like this from all eternity, arise? How was it overgrown with grasses, herbs, bushes and trees of every kind? How and when did all the animals come into being?

[4] And how did man become an inhabitant of this Earth? Was it really just one human pair that was created, as in Genesis, or were men of diverse color, form and character set down on this Earth simultaneously?

[5] To such not altogether unreasonable question I can only say as I said before, namely: if you are imbued with the wisdom of angels, then you shall in a retrospective sense be able to trace also the entire natural creation from the purely spiritual sense in which Moses speaks in Genesis, and shall discover that the natural creation in correspondingly extended periods of course arose almost exactly in the same order told in Genesis – with the emergence of the first human pair falling roughly into the same period and their test and propagation ultimately,

but for a few exceptions, hidden in corresponding images, following in that very order told in the unfolding Genesis text.

[6] But as said, in the absence of angelic wisdom you shall not discover this, were you to possess the wisdom of all the wise of the Earth, who also had already exchanged the most diverse views and opinions on this subject.

[7] But in this world, such knowledge is of no particular use to anyone in any case, since man rarely improves much in his heart through great knowledge, but rather worsens that much more usually. Because not seldom the erudite becomes proud and haughty, looking down from his imagined height upon his brethren with scorn, like a vulture upon sparrows and other small birds, as if these existed only for his catching and devouring of their tender flesh.

[8] Seek ye therefore the Kingdom of God and its righteousness in your heart before everything else, troubling yourselves little about anything else, because all these other things together with the wisdom of angels can be given you overnight. I trust that you have now fully understood Me?'

## CHAPTER 163
### The end of Jerusalem

[1] When the Pharisee and his colleagues had received such an extended explanation of Genesis from me, they all stood in front of Me as if paralyzed, and **the chief Pharisee** said, after he visibly made great effort to deeply think about it: 'Lord. Master of all Masters in all things, I and all of us now see, not without much disappointment, that You are fully right in all things and that everything You say is the complete, pure truth. But I did not say "not without much disappointment" for nothing, because this wisdom is too holy and lofty for an evil, selfish world, and You shall, in the absence of special miracles, preach to totally deaf ears. And if working miracles, You shall have blind spectators and achieve little.

[2] If man, in order to fashion himself into a true human, has to be free in his volition and action, then You can preach and work miracles as much as You like, and hardly one in a hundred shall be converted. Because where someone is already basically too stupid and has no education in any necessary or life-conducive field, he cannot possibly grasp Your teaching. If however he has just one degree more than enough, and therefore a developed intellect, be it either Scripturally or scientifically, or in the arts, tying same to some worldly gain, attaching to perhaps even personal standing, then You can let Jehovah speak, for You under lightning and thunder, yet such people will do what your forefathers did in the desert under Moses, where in the course of Jehovah's talk with Moss on Sinai, under thunder and lightning, receiving the Holy Commandments from Him, they had cast a golden calf, to then dance around it, worshipping it like the heathens.

[3] If I did not know what stuff the Pharisees, Scribes and the priests and Levites are made of, especially in Jerusalem, I would hardly dare to speak to You thus,

but I know this folk only too well and basically have put a good distance between me and it, not visiting it any more.

[4] If however You should return to Jerusalem again, then take a large portion of omnipotence with You, or you shall be stoned as a blasphemer. For anyone wishing to be more clever than even by a hair's breadth than the least Temple sweeper, immediately is denounced as a heretic and blasphemer, and if not reforming, in conjunction with a sizeable offering, stoning without mercy awaits him at the accursed spot outside the city wall.

[5] For Jerusalem, I say unto You, my divine friend, there is only one cure - that of Sodom and Gomorra. Other than that there is no salvation for this city and its inhabitants.'

[6] I said: 'Friend, what you are telling Me I have known for a long time. Yes, I say unto you, this also shall be Jerusalem's end. But prior to that, all the things prophesied over it have to first take place, so that all Scripture will be fulfilled, and its measure filled. And from now on you shall not count 70 years, before not a stone shall be left atop another. If anyone shall then ask: "Where stood the Temple once?" none shall be found to tell such seeker.

[7] Many prophets were murdered within the walls of this city. I know them all. Their blood cried to the highest Heavens for revenge against such evil doers, but the measure with which Hell was meted out to this city is not yet completely full, and it was therefore spared still. But now its measure shall shortly be full, and it shall be spared no more.

[8] But before we leave this mountain, I give you a commandment for strict observance, consisting in that none of you divulge to anyone down below any portion of what you have seen on this mountain, until I have given you authority through the spirit. He who will not keep this My commandment shall be punished with instant dumbness, for the people down in the plain are not ripe for a long time yet, nor are you yourselves sufficiently.

[9] But discuss that which I have taught here among the likes of you as if not emanating from Me, but as if grown upon your own ground. Only after your friends shall have embraced your teaching in a living way you can eye to eye, let them in on where you received such teaching, and what signs preceded it.

[10] But then do not omit to in My name give those instructed the same commandment and with the same sanction as I have given you all here.

[11] But you shall in the short time left us on this mountain witness miraculous things yet, for I thirst for making you as strong as possible in your faith, but keep the said commandment in respect of everything you are still permitted to see and hear, because through non-compliance with this commandment, the threatened punishment would be visited upon you for a year.'

[1] Says **Judas Iscariot**: 'Lord, this is a tough commandment. Who shall be able to strictly keep it?'

[2] I said: 'God also had made dying into an imperative and unalterable law and does not in spite of much human misery retract His holy Word. You may, right now, talk and argue as much as you like, yet in the end you have to die. Only in the beyond will you realize how such dying was most essential.

[3] And see, just so it is with every commandment coming from the mouth of God. Making it into your own commandment, you shall be able to keep it quite easily. But if you prescribe yourself a commandment other than the one I give you, then it shall be hard for you to keep My commandment, because where one commandment is against the other, there abiding by the one or the other shall be difficult or in the end impossible. Do you understand that?

[4] I say unto you: take care indeed and see to it earnestly that a counter-commandment does not arise in you with time, which could become death within you.'

[5] **Judas** says: 'But what is this to mean again? You do indeed perpetually speak in accordance with Egyptian hieroglyphics, which hardly a wise man can still read, let alone understand. What basically is a counter-commandment? I can either abide or not abide by it and this is up to my free will and not a counter-commandment.'

[6] I reply: 'I say unto you, if you remain as foolish as you are now, then it is better for you to return to Bethabara, because that way you are annoying and repulsive to Me.

[7] Where do laws come from? From anywhere other, perhaps, than from the will of him who has the power and authority to give and sanction laws? But does not each man have complete power to do as he will? If he wants to make the eternal laws his own, then he is sure to easily keep them. If he does not want that, then he has his own will as counter-commandment and has in the end to put up with sanction of the external law.'

[8] **Judas**, although cutting a sour face when I said this to him, he nevertheless says: 'Well, now I understand the thing and it is good so. But when You often speak in a veiled fashion, then I get fearful and worried and then I always have to ask until the thing is clear, especially when it concerns a commandment which it may be quite hard for some of us to keep and for myself, which I am not afraid to admit. But see, Lord, when anyone else asks You, then You answer them most friendly at once, yet when it is I that asks, You always get unfriendly and I then hardly dare to ask You again, may it be ever so important to do so.

[9] See, I still cannot get over my peculiar journey through the air the day before yesterday and that with unbelievable speed, so that one could not make out anything on the ground other than a band shooting past at immense speed. Here I want to find out from You how this was possible, because I was possibly the

furthest one from here and that far behind the far sea-coast and would have needed four or five days to walk.

[10] I had just finished preaching at a Greek village, but had unfortunately not found very sympathetic ears and hearts, in spite of healing some of their sick. I became cross and left the stupid nest. But when finding myself all alone some thousand paces from the village – because brother Thomas did not want to accompany me to Greece – there came a whirlwind towards me and before I knew it I was high up in the air. Thereupon an indescribable gust of wind pushed me in this direction and that with the said speed, so that, as said, I could not in this flight make out in the least anything on the Earth's surface – not even the sea itself more than a flash of lightning. I did not even have time to think how I would go if a cliff should be in my path, against which I should have disintegrated into many hundreds of thousands of droplets. But how astonished I was, o Lord, to be set down so gently unto the ground before You after such draft.

[11] Therefore I would like you to just tell me a few words on how such was possible.'

[12] I said: 'Friend, if you know who I am, how can you ask how such is possible to Me, or by what means this was carried out? Are not all things possible with God? See, the clouds. Who carries them? You heard Me before, explaining to everybody the nature of the Earth, the moon, the sun and many other stars which for your concepts are endlessly great suns.

[13] See, these large and therefore immensely heavy heavenly bodies float freely through the ether spaces, endlessly stretched out in all directions, having a speed of movement fantastic for your imagination.

[14] Then a question is: who is carrying these countless ones within an unchangeable order through the free, endless spaces? Think about it and you shall soon see the foolishness of your question. And therefore this question is answered for you with sufficient clarity.'

[15] **Thomas** steps up and says: 'If only you could for once come up with a question worthy of the Lord. Did not all those of us who were sent out go through the same aerial journey to here? We know however that He wanted it that way and therefore, although a most unusual journey over here through the air, it therewith is fully explained to us. If you more strongly believed what and who our Lord and Master is, then such question could not occur to you even in the worst and most foolish dream.'

[16] Says **Judas**: 'Have you got me again? Well, let you have me, if it gives you pleasure. At least I am not upset this time because I myself realize that I have bothered the Lord with a very foolish question, which however I am sure not to do again in future.'

[17] Says **Thomas**: 'Then we shall also be quite good friends and brothers and I shall not counsel you again.'

[18] I said: 'Just be quiet now, for Kisjonah has prepared a meal and we shall afford our body some necessary fortification! After the meal it shall transpire what else there shall be to do. And so let it be and stay so.'

# CAPTER 165
## Why must men be born?

[1] All move to the huts now to partake of the meal, all being in good spirits and therefore cheerful and happy.

[2] After the meal **Kisjonah** says to Me: 'That if I have no objection then he would now make the rounds on his alp before night settles in, to pay his shepherds and take a look at the flocks, checking also how much wool the shepherds had clipped.

[3] I said: 'Listen, tomorrow is the day before Sabbath, which I want to spend on these mountains, but today, since our meal was an extended one, with the day lasting only another two hours, let us just stay happily together here and discuss a few important things. And this evening you are yet to go through quite a few things.'

[4] Says **Kisjonah**: 'Lord, Your every heart's desire is a holy commandment to me. But now I shall come up with a question straight away and this concerns those 3 men who 2 days ago came to us in great splendor, floating through the air rather than straddling the mountain with their feet. These 3 men have now been constantly in our company, speaking with us and eating and drinking with us, being extremely obliging and helpful and, except for a more noble form, they look like ourselves.

[5] It seems almost as if they are going to stay with us, which would please me endlessly. I previously had embraced and kissed them and see, they had bones and a firm and strong body throughout, so that I had to wonder greatly.

[6] My question therefore is to find out from You how this is possible. Earlier on they were mere spirits, whereas now they are physical beings like us. Where does their body come from? And if these spontaneously obtained bodies and as it turns out, much more perfect ones than ours, could not all men be set into this world in that way, instead of through laborious birth?'

[7] I said: 'You would not, to begin with, see and physically feel these three angels, had I not conditioned you for this occasion in such a way that your soul obviously, united with her spirit, could see the spiritual through the body, seeing and perceiving same as if it was on the natural plane and therefore physical. It nevertheless is and remains completely spiritual, including nothing physical.

[8] Men and spirits however are distinguished from each other, in that a spirit like these three angels had from primordial times used his freedom wisely within My order and had thereafter not ever sinned against it, but a proportion of spirits, too vast for your understanding, had misused their free will and therefore plunged into the threatened judgment. And from such spirits, of which this whole Earth and all countless worlds, such as sun, moon and stars consist, go forth by way of an unalterable natural law, the natural men of this Earth as well as those of all other worlds. And this along the familiar way of generation and subsequent birth, having to therefore first be reared and later instructed in human-hood and, after shedding

of the body, developed into pure and completely free spirits.

[9] Since the flesh of man is given him and therefore to the spirit raised up from judgment, mainly to undergo a free will test as if in a separate world, you can now easily understand that for the perfected spirits, a body of flesh would be quite superficial, as the flesh is only the means but not and never can be, the purpose, as everything is to ultimately become purely spiritual and never material again.

[10] I say unto you: this Earth and this whole, actually physical Heaven such as suns, moons and worlds, shall once pass away, after all the spirits held captive within them shall through the way of the flesh have become pure spirits, but the pure spirits remain forever and shall not and cannot ever pass away, just as I and My Word cannot. Tell Me whether you have now understood this.'


## CHAPTER 166
### The fall of woman and its bad effect on man

[1] Says **Kisjonah**: 'O God, o God. What depths of wisdom. Who has ever heard anything like it? Verily, such exposition only God can give. Here the wisdom of all the wise comes to fullest nothingness of all nothingness. No, this truly is too much all at once, for a poor mortal sinner in full measure like me.

[2] Through this Revelation all of Genesis suddenly becomes clear and understandable, as if by magician's master-stroke, so to say.

[3] Now I understand what it means: "And God formed Adam as the first man of this Earth from the clay of the Earth." Out of His eternal order, God willed it that the spirits captive within the Earth under judgment, from the more pliable clay of the Earth build a body corresponding to their spiritual form, with which they can move freely, recognizing their self and from that God, to freely subordinate themselves to the divine order, to attain to their primordially spiritual nature, namely to become perfectly pure spirits, therefore like the primordial archangels.

[4] Yes, indeed, now all becomes clear to me. And it says that woman was formed out of Adam's rib. How clear also this is. Just as the mountains by correspondence are the more solid and therefore more stubborn parts of the Earth and therefore containing also the more stubborn spirits, just so the man's more stubborn part had, as it were, deposited itself in man's bones, which by correspondence relate to the Earth's mountains.

[5] The more stubborn spiritual, the more sensual, proud and arrogant elements of the man were by God's wisdom and might eliminated from him and represented in a female form similar to that of the man which, since it originates from the man, stands in a living correspondence with him and thereby, and through the procreative act, is capable of having a living fruit awakened within it, according to God's almighty will. And since a greater suffering has been imposed on her as the man's more stubborn spiritual part, she can perfect her spirit whereby according to Scripture it can happen, and also does, that finally man and woman become one.

[6] For the expression that man and woman have then one body does not mean

anything else but: although the woman's nature is the more stubborn part of the man, through the comparatively harder trial it eventually becomes equal to his gentler spiritual part and that is what is meant by the expression that man and woman have one body. What do You, O Lord, say to this?'

[7] I said: 'That is absolutely good and true. This is how it is and thus the Scripture should be understood. Then it would be easy to talk to all men and act in their very best interest from the Heavens. But by the second misuse of their free will people have deeply sunk into sensuousness. This is above all the case with women who have begun to abundantly adorn their from Satan inherited more attractive body and because of their selfishness have become inflexible, proud and resentful thereby pressuring the gentler man who, in order to be granted a woman's favor, had to quite voluntarily and submissively to dance to her tyrannical tune and in the end even enjoyed being completely ensnared by her truly satanic cunning.

[8] As a result he fell from all the Heavens dawning within him, became ignorant, lustful, selfish, vain and greedy for power and thus truly of the devil together with the woman.

[9] From time to time the man was softly admonished by his spirit through the awakening of love for life, to read the Scripture and contemplate God's great works. Many also did that by first more or less freeing themselves from the snares of woman. But this did not help much because they no longer understood the Scripture. And since they themselves has become materialistic like the woman they promptly took the literal sense for fully valid and thus turned the Word of God into a monster and God's Temple into a den of thieves.

[10] I tell you and all present: things have advanced to a stage when all men would be completely lost if I, the Lord Himself, had not come into the world to save you from the yoke of Satan and his eternal perdition. And I Myself shall have to go to the greatest lengths in order to begin to raise only a very minor part of mankind to the proper light of the Heavens.'

## CHAPTER 167
### Beware of a tempting women

[1] However, woe betide the world when the women again start to wear finery, bedeck themselves and will sit on the thrones. Then the Earth will be put through the fire.

[2] Therefore, maintain good discipline with the women and let them above all practice proper humility. They should be clean, but never dressed up in finery and bedecked, for women's finery and jewellery is mankind's grave and ruin in everything.

[3] But just as a pure, well-mannered and humble woman is a blessing for a house, a bedecked and thereby proud woman among men, fully comparable to a snake that through its wanton glances lures the Heaven's birds into its venomous

and destructive jaws.

[4] Therefore I advise, but do not wish to make this advice a command:

[5] If someone looks for a wife, let him make sure that the maiden he woos does not bedeck her body, except cleanses it with water which is needed for the body's health, and does not bear an immodest face in the street, which does not befit a woman, and does not parade her attractions, but is in every way modest, has her body well covered with a linen garment and in winter with undyed cloths from sheep's wool, also does not talk much nor boast as if she possessed something, for it is most beneficial for a woman if she possesses nothing but what is absolutely necessary. Such a maiden is then also worthy of a man, and you shall woo her. But I tell you: avoid like a carrion a maiden who is rich, bedecked, wears clothes with striking colors, bears an immodest expression in the street, likes to be greeted by the rich and distinguished, but says to the poor: "Just look at the smelly beggars."

[6] Such a maiden is a true image, on a small scale, of enticing Hell, and who woos such a one commits a gross sin against the divine order and may reckon with it that such a woman, who on Earth hardly ever changes her ways, if she dies before her husband, will – even if he was a righteous man and had loved his wife very much for her earthly attractions – draw him into Hell for at least a very lengthy period.

[7] For in the same way that such a woman used on this Earth tricks to catch herself the man her lewdness had chosen, she will – only a thousand times more destructive – in the beyond come to meet her following husband with all imaginable charm and draw him into her hellish nest. And it will be most difficult for the husband to extricate himself from his wife's influence.

[8] Therefore, keep that in mind and let the one who woos get first will acquainted with his bride and examine all aspects, so that he does not instead of winning an angel become encumbered with a devil of whom it will not be easy to rid himself.

[9] I have clearly shown you the distinguishing marks. Do heed the warning and you will succeed here and in the beyond. I do not actually give you this as a commandment that is to bind you, but only, as already mentioned, as good advice which will be most beneficial to you and all vain women in particular, if heeded.

[10] For the one among you who will reprimand a vain and cunningly seductive woman to make her realize her wicked folly shall once in Heaven be richly rewarded.

[11] Therefore, turn your eyes away from a tempting woman, for such a woman is secretly without knowing it in league with Satan and unconsciously serves him in his seductive designs.

[12] If anyone of you wishes to see Satan in his worst form, let him look at an adorned whore or a decorated woman and he has seen Satan in his for a man most dangerous form.

[13] When Satan comes as a dragon and spits war, famine and pestilence over the Earth, he is least dangerous to men, for in their misery men turn to God and begin to do penance, thereby avoiding Hell and its judgment.

[14] However, when Satan clothes his dragon in the light-garment of an angel, he is most dangerous to the by nature sensually inclined man, just as if a ravening wolf came among the sheep in a sheepskin. If the wolf comes to the sheep as a wolf, they flee in all directions confusing the death-bringer, so that he stops and ponders after which sheep to run and finally has to leave without prey. If, however, he comes in a sheepskin, the sheep do not flee, but on the contrary happily welcome the new sheep that has joined them, which is a wolf that mangles the entire flock without a single sheep fleeing from it.

[15] Look this instruction and this advice you should, therefore, keep in your hearts as a shrine and strictly stick to it as if I had given you a commandment. Then your marriages will have the blessing from Heaven, otherwise the curse from Hell.

[16] Therefore, do not be seduced by the blind and deceptive charms of the world, but be at all times clear-headed and value the world's worth correctly. Do not trade in the gold and pearls which you have now received from the Heavens for the foolishness of the world, then you will always have peace among you and see Heaven open before you. But if you will allow yourselves to be captivated by the attractions of the world, it will be your own fault if Heaven will keep becoming more firmly closed to you. And when in great distress you will be calling to Heaven for help, you will not get it, for it is not possible for a person who loves the world and is firmly attached to it to be at the same time in a blessed contact with Heaven.

[17] Every human being is created and made in such a way that he could not bear evil and good, false and true in one and the same heart side by side. It has to be one or the other, but never both simultaneously.

[18] He can and must indeed recognizes both in his mind, but in his heart there can dwell but one of them as life's foundation.

[19] Have you now understood and grasped this My advice?'

[20] Say all, 'Yes, Lord and Master in all divine wisdom.'

## CHAPTER 168
### The holy Word, the world and mankind

[1] Here **a Pharisee** steps up closer to Me and says: 'Lord and Master, this all is very nice, good and true and not capable of contradiction. But if men do not gather all those materials which the Earth offers them so abundantly, to process them skillfully, then the Earth shall be like a desert and there shall be no sign of any culture. Do there not have to be dwellings and schools of all kinds? Take that away and mankind shall in the shortest time be reduced to a condition like animals. Therefore, the world cannot be set aside, so long as one is an inhabitant of matter?'

[2] I said: 'Your schools are fit for killing all spirit in the tender feelings of children already and therefore their complete disintegration would do no harm, for verily I

300

say unto you: if your teacher be the world, what do you want to learn from it spiritually?

[3] He who is not taught by God in his heart remains in the night of the world, and the light of life shall remain remote from him eternally.

[4] But he who is not shone upon by the true light of life emanating from God is dead, were he to have learned from the world all the wisdom of the angels. How long shall it serve him?

[5] Therefore remain in Me and I shall remain in you, and the wisdom of the Heavens shall eternally fill your hearts. Do you grasp and understand this?'

[6] When **the Pharisee** had received such instruction out of My mouth, he spoke gravely and with a serious countenance: 'O great, holy and vivid truth, how glorious, how great are you. How happy all men could be on Earth if they were imbued with such holy truth and adjusted their life-style accordingly. But, o Lord, an immense "but", so long as one drop of this Earth remains, or the Earth is inhabited by men, there shall be among them greed, envy, meanness, arrogance and the all-destructive domineering, – all those things from the bottom of Hell. And upon such ground this truth, undoubtedly from the Heavens, shall nevertheless never take root and will be persecuted to the last letter by the thousands times thousands of Hell's disciples. Of what use then such celestial wisdom? To expect fruit fit for Heaven, the greatest part of mankind has to be eradicated from the Earth and a new one put on Earth and brought up in this truth from the cradle on, but the way mankind is right now, it is too evil for Hell, not to mention for such truths from the highest Heavens.

[7] Even if You intended founding a small community, which is to endure and grow within this heavenly wisdom and truth, it nevertheless shall everywhere find itself among voracious wolves who, if not able to harm it spiritually, nevertheless shall constantly harass and intimidate it physically, and it shall never be able to maintain itself in its purity. And who but God knows what, after lengthy periods, the descendants of the pure communities shall look like?

[8] Men are and shall remain men. Angels today, devils tomorrow. And therefore even the best are not to be trusted.

[9] Did not Jehovah of a truth visibly lead the children out of Egypt? They saw Him day and night. In the desert where He gave them the commandments He fed them miraculously for 40 years. There it rained wonders upon wonders. Look up history and then glance at the present life, religions and social condition, and see the erstwhile children of God, and no trace shall be found of what they once were.

[10] This is why I say and maintain, without wishing to pre-empt Your love and wisdom: what everlasting waste for such wisdom and deeds of Yours, because they shall never be worthy of them. Fire and brimstone from Heaven yes, of that they are worthy, but not everlastingly of such grace. I speak thus, confident of no betrayer lurking here. But once we get down there again, I shall be silent as a graveyard. Tell me, o Lord and Master, am I right? Is it thus or not.'

[11] I said: 'Terrestrially you are quite right. It is so and shall also become so. But all this must not hold Me back from proclaiming to the world the truth from the Heavens.

[12] Because if the world is to be judged, then it has to be first given that which of itself shall judge and must judge it, namely: the truth from the Heavens, which now is coming through Me into the world and shall remain so, even if persecuted.

[13] Your opinion is a good one and right in respect of the evil world, but most exceptional relationships prevail between God and the men of this Earth, known by none save the Father alone and he to whom the Father reveals it.

[14] But now no more about it. Evening is upon us, and it shall be cold at this height. Therefore we shall turn in at the huts. Let it be.'


## CHAPTER 169
## A Gospel on laughter

[1] After these discussions we move into the big residential hut and many, especially the women and maidens, huddle around the fire. Some of the Jews however, who could also have done with a bit of warmth, were secretly annoyed with the women for completely obstructing the flames. And some of the disciples came over to Me to tell Me this, complaining and grumbling, but I chided them softly for such unseemliness.

[2] All but one calmed down. But one, **a stubborn Jew** of Capernaum, still grumbled saying: 'Eh, what's the use talking? I was freezing almost unbearably already outside. Now when I would warm up a little the women block off the fire and I am nearly stiff with cold. Down below not even in winter is it as cold as it had to get tonight at this height. And I am over seventy and of a cold disposition. I do not want to be churlish. Tell the women therefore to make room for me at the fire.'

[3] Say I to the old man: 'Do you not know that I could warm you also without fire if you had faith?'

[4] Said **the old one**: 'Yes, Lord, I believe. For I have seen many of Your miracles and therefore I believe that everything You say or will, is going to happen.'

[5] I said: 'Then stand with the 3 men who came to us from on high 2 days ago, and you shall get warm at once.'

[6] And the old man did so and he immediately became so hot that he could hardly bear the heat, thanking Me profusely for such favor, but because he is now too hot, he would like to cool down a little.

[7] But I said: 'Do as you like, for I did not tie you up with the 3 men. Go outside, there you shall cool down quickly.'

[8] And **the old man** went outside, but soon rushed back into the hut with a great cry of terror: 'Save yourselves, everyone for himself, the entire mountain is ablaze and the flames are drawing ever closer to this hut! For Jehovah's sake, we are all going to die!'

[9] While the old man is thus lamenting **Kisjonah**, who had been outside for some time, enters and says to Me: 'Lord, You will forgive me that I have prepared a little celebration according to the custom of the alpine shepherds, since You told

us this would be the last evening You are spending on this mountain. My shepherds have gathered brushwood in the forest, and now they have lighted the faggots in Your honor and are singing happy songs and psalms. Would You not like to have a look outside?'

[10] I said: 'O with pleasure, for I love you very much.' And I rose to My feet and went outside all the disciples followed Me.

[11] But the woman laughed at the old Jew for earlier having seen the entire mountain ablaze and making such a fuss as if the whole world was perishing. The old man felt a bit ashamed and now bore the laughter of the woman quite patiently.

[12] But I reprimanded the merry women and warned them. Thereupon the women – the 5 daughters of Kisjonah were not among them for they were engaged in preparing the evening meal in the large host's hut – asked forgiveness of Me and the old man and said that they definitely had not meant it badly.

[13] The old man immediately forgave them from all his heart. But **the 3 angels** turned to the woman and said: 'Listen to us, you women. This old man is a descendant of Tobias who was blind and to whom we restored his sight with the gallbladder of a fish. All descendants of this old Tobias, who was a grave-digger, have in their old age for some mysterious reason known only to God and to us through Him, weak eyes. We tell you that it is a gross offence based on a frivolous heart if someone ridicules a blind person instead of extending his hand and guiding him over footbridges and rough roads. If you had not known that the old man who is also called 'Tobias' is more than half blind and you still laughed, you have sinned and deserve severe punishment. However, as he has forgiven you following your apology, also we shall forgive you.

[14] But woe betide you if you should ever laugh at a disabled person. Then his complaint shall become yours.

[15] Anyway, men should not laugh at all or only very seldom, for laughing is brought about through the awakening of gloating spirits dwelling in the human body.

[16] A friendly pulling of the facial muscles from which an expression of a special goodwill can be recognized is heavenly whereas all other laughing usually stems from Hell. For the devils always laugh when they have succeeded in one of their evil designs. In the Heavens, however, no one ever laughs, but one is at all times filled with the most heartfelt and friendliest goodwill towards all ever so miserable creatures and compassion with every suffering brother who still has to go through his time on Earth. Heed this for all future times.

[17] Once men will be starting to laugh at their brother's' weaknesses, faith will be vanishing like the sun after setting and love in men's hearts will be cooling off as this night has cooled down and there will be misery among mankind the like of which as never before existed on Earth.

[18] Do heed this warning from the Heavens. Punish your children when they laugh. Hear them rather cry than laugh, for the laughing originates from Hell which always abounds with derision.

[19] There are situations where, however, only men are allowed to laugh at

some silly matter and obstinate foolishness, but then the laughing is a well-deserved punishment for the one who deserves to be ridiculed.

[20] But if someone laughs only for fun and seeks things, events and ridiculous talk to be provoked to laughter, he is a fool. For only the heart of a fool can be provoked to laughter. Every reasonably wise person can easily and soon understand life's sacred earnestness and he will not easily laugh about something.

[21] Therefore, do not laugh anymore in future and turn your face away from clowns and comedians who let themselves be paid for preparing you for Hell. Be always of a calm heart, so that you may merit God's goodwill and thereby true honor.

[22] These words made a great impression upon the women and they vowed never in their whole life to laugh again.

## CHAPTER 170
### The healing of the half-blind Tobias

[1] The **old man** however had heard what the three angels had spoken to the women. So he went over and said: 'I hear that you mentioned my forefather's name and showing that my name is not unknown to you. Through God's grace and power, which is in you, you gave life and light to the old Tobias' eye.

[2] See, you dear and eternal friends of God, I am at the point of going totally blind. Sight of the one eye is gone completely and the other one's light is diminishing considerably. How would it be if you gave me the full light of my eyes? This surely would be easy for you. Have mercy on me.'

[3] Say **the angels**: 'Do you not see the One who is watching the blazing flames with Kisjonah, and hearing the shepherd's songs and Psalms? Not we but He it is who gave old Tobias back the light of his eyes. Go to Him. He is the Lord and can do as He likes. He alone can give you back the light of your eyes. We of ourselves can do as little as you of your own self. We only are His servants and wait for His hints.'

[4] Upon these words of the 3 angels, the old man betakes himself over to Me and asks Me for the light of his eyes. I said: 'Were you not for a long time a staunch Pharisee and one singing the praises of the Temple at Jerusalem, taking Me for an Essene, a magician and suchlike. How did you come by your faith now?'

[5] Says **the old one**: 'Lord, I too was present at Capernaum when You awakened the chief priest Jairus' daughter to life. Faith already came to me then. But I needed to see and hear more to strengthen my faith. And I have seen and heard and now believe that You, o Lord, can do anything You will. If only You, o Lord, want to heal me, then You can do it in all fullness.'

[6] After that I said to the old man: 'It is somewhat absurd for night-time. I say unto you however that, spiritually, it is now night and they all are fully blind. And

304

men shall no longer become seeing during the day, but at night, and then for many, their evening and morning will lastingly become their first day. And so let you be made seeing at night.'

[7] With these words, the old one became seeing, admiring the separate fires which previously he had seen blurred and therefore as if one fire.

[8] As he became aware of such seeing light in his eyes, he fell down upon his knees before Me, not able to praise Me highly enough, being overjoyed beyond measure.

[9] But I said to him: 'You too have heard My commandment. Therefore, keep silent on everything you have seen and heard here, otherwise you shall meet with what I warned everyone.' Thereupon the old man rose, promising to be silent as a graveyard.

[10] And so everything was good and accomplished for these heights. And when the fires had burned themselves out, Kisjonah's daughters came and invited Me and all those present to the evening meal. And we all went, consuming a good meal and then going to take our rest.

## CHAPTER 171
### Rhiba invents a story about the Nazarene

[1] The Pharisees however – those of the better disposition, who had also become believers now – some more and others less, about 30 in all, went to a separate hut, to there discuss almost through the night what they should do now.

[2] There was one among them by the name of **Rhiba**, with the reputation of a smart one. This one, after nothing conclusive had been reached took the floor, saying: 'Brethren, you have now traded words for at least 2 hours, yet have not come nearer to a conclusion by a hair's breadth. You have gotten to know me. I have hit the nail on the head in similar scrapes in the past and I presume that my blow shall not miss its mark this time either, after my critical examination and listening and watching of everything that was said and done over here. And so lend me an ear.

[3] It is by no means to be denied that this man, a carpenter's son from Nazareth, accomplishes things and works which should hardly be possible to anyone but God. In short, anyone who is somewhat weak and lacking insight would let himself be easily talked around into believing that this Nazarene is at least a semi-god, after the Greek fashion. I myself came close to being persuaded of this, because the appearance on the heights of these mountains were in all earnest of such an extraordinary nature that they could hardly have been exceeded in Moses' and Elijah's time.

[4] Yet certain things nevertheless did not escape my secret perception, which took the wool off my eyes, making me know exactly where I stand. Did you not notice the 3 men who came to us as angels on the heights?'

[5] They all affirm it. 'Yet do you know who and where they come from?' They all

said no. 'I am going to open your eyes. Hear and see.

[6] It will not be unknown to you that the Nazarene carpenter named Joseph, who has always been in the repute of an initiate into Egyptian and Persian magic, at the same time is a direct descendant of David, at times designating himself with the title "Son of David". Joseph's father, whose name was Eli, also a carpenter, of unblemished repute, secretly aspired to elevate his tribe to the Judean as well as the entire Promised Land's throne. Under the pretext of training his son in the building trade, he let him, in good company, travel to Persia and perhaps even to India, but not on account of the building-trade, but intensive magic, so that Joseph, grounded in such knowledge and craft, could dazzle all mankind as being sent by God, to sit upon the throne of at once the Jews and Romans, because it would then be easier to deal with the idolatrous Romans than the Jews. Joseph would besides his secret craft, of course have to be strict Jew outwardly and without blemish before the law, so that not even the High priests could fault him. Returning from several years of journeying, Joseph, in possession of the art indeed nevertheless did not possess the means and opportunity to put it in practice. He also, as told me by elderly people, lacked the courage, but mainly the speaking capacity, because he was weak and monotonous on that score. Eli realized that he had miscalculated and got his son, who had no capacity to reign, to carry on his own familiar trade. When dying, Eli indeed blessed his son, but telling him quite wisely to drop the agreed plans, because nothing further transpires there. And therefore Joseph did not venture into anything with the children of his first wife either.

[7] But when after the death of his first wife, he by good fortune and probably his magic from Persia came into the guardianship of the beautiful Mary from the Temple, who also was a descendant of David, the regency plans began to reawaken in Joseph. He got Mary – a girl of barely 14 at the time, pregnant, becoming his wife only later – which of course caused him great problems in Jerusalem, but from which he extricated himself through money and magic, at the same time taking Mary for his wife, on the advice of a close friend.

[8] Although the surviving and well-to-do parents of Mary in Jerusalem, a certain Joachim and Anna, are supposed to not have been very pleased with such marriage, Joseph, having a powerful friend in the Temple – the old Simeon and especially Zacharias – the thing nevertheless came off without objection and Mary became Joseph's rightful wife, wherewith her parents also had to be agreeable.

[9] Encouraged greatly by Mary, whom he loved exceedingly, he now did everything in respect of the unborn child, if male – which as a man of experience in such things Joseph could predict with much certainty – towards the said plan, whereto the not inconsiderable means of his in-laws may now have contributed.

[10] Some weeks before delivery he sent messengers to Persia and asked the 3 wise men over, whose acquaintance he had made in his youth. These also came to Nazareth. And since at that very time emperor Augustus had ordered a census in Bethlehem, for all of Judea, Joseph and Mary together with Joseph's children, found themselves on the way to Bethlehem for that purpose.

[11] The 3 wise men, together with their great and dazzling followers of

servants, on arrival in Nazareth did not know which way to turn, traveling up to Jerusalem and unfortunately inquiring of the old Herod about the newborn king of Israel, pouring oil upon the fire: Herod of course could give them no advice other than that firstly this was something entirely strange to him and secondly that, if there was anything to it, this family like thousands of others nevertheless was bound to find themselves at Bethlehem for the census called by the emperor. Therewith the three wise men hastened to Bethlehem, where they found what they were seeking.

[12] That there would have been no shortage of magical appearances for even the Romans to be talked around; can be gauged from the fact that the old Herod would not have otherwise ordered the infanticide. These magicians also loaned, if not actually gave the child such treasures as would help educate it, which it was to then send back to Persia after assuming the regency.

[13] For that reason those 3 magicians never let the child out of their sight, looking after its perfection in magical training to this hour and now appearing again as the purported 3 angels from the Heavens, helping Jesus to carry out his magic works, together with all kinds of wise sermons and miraculous works, to bedazzle the people, who are blind and know nothing of all that goes on in secret.

[14] But they are unable to pull the wool over the eyes of those of us who are conversant with all those kinds of mysteries and it therefore is our sacred responsibility to observe this person in all ways and alleys and put a stop to him if he overdoes it.

[15] The worst would be for him to get the Romans on his side, for that would be the end of all our efforts. Therefore we should try to most methodically proceed to prevent this, or he will grow sky high over our heads in all earnest. Once he has made it, we shall not be able to pull him down. What do you say to that?'

[16] **The others** say: 'You could be right, but if in the end things are otherwise, which could easily be the case, what then with us?'

[17] **Rhiba** replies: 'The question in this particular case is not applicable at all. Is he more and can he be more than a man? Who among us is like the heathens, who do not know what and who God is, taking certain distinguished men and even certain animals for gods, to worship and honor them.

[18] Is this Nazarene anything more than an exceedingly distinguished man, a genius, unsurpassable in his ways and means?

[19] If he tried to remain what he is, exercising his craft for man's benefit and also teach them a few things in those fields where men are blind and without insight, then he would be of indispensable worth and the land which could count him a citizen should be envied. But the way things are, David's throne, crown and scepter are itching him and this makes him contemptible to all orthodox and pure Jews, who have the spirit to regard and grasp all human appearances within the right light and understanding and not have the wool pulled over their eyes as easily as half-heathen tax-collectors and sinners.

[20] Of what use to mankind in any case the many dazzling teachings dividing it into diverse sects, which then only hate each other on account of their disparate beliefs – more than the voracious beasts of the forest. Those of the old faith hate

the unbelievers and the latter those of the old faith and thus such religion achieves the opposite always of what it preaches. Instead of friendship, love and peace, it often creates irreconcilable enmity, hate and the most furious wars. And these have always been the fruits of all religious revivals upon Earth. But if the fruits after such happenings, as experience always teaches, are the same ones, then it becomes the imperative responsibility of us enlightened ones and leaders of the peoples to in time cut the path of such revivalists, along which thousands are threatened with downfall and ruin. Is it not better that such domineering magicians should be dispatched from the world, rather than thousands having to be led astray by such eccentrics and be bumped off and destroyed?'

## CHAPTER 172
### The curse of a Pharisee

[1] Says **another**: 'You are not altogether wrong, if we look at the matter from a purely worldly viewpoint, but if there is yet another life for man's soul after death, which I have never doubted yet, then all these worldly considerations and relationships are altogether worthless and then this Jesus is a sun for the night of man's spirit, showing us the right way along which we can already in our bodies catch a glimpse of the great beyond, taking from the Father's house the glorious fare for eternal life.

[2] And such He teaches, wanting to show blind men how without further assistance, the air can offer and has to yield bread and wine, therefore food proper, as we saw upon the heights a couple of days ago and of which we ate and drank.

[3] That the old night always has to do battle with the coming day not only human history but the entire nature of things teaches us as occurring before our eyes and unfolding. Yet this is God's order, permission and will, against which no worldly power ever has prevailed.

[4] What do you intend doing if this Jesus, surely suffused utterly with God's power, were to seize you with His thoughts and utterly destroy you. What opposition could you offer Him?

[5] Now listen. A man who is instantly obeyed by wind and sea and all evil or good spirits – a man who calls the dead back to life, healing through mere will every ever so old and stubborn illness, without medicine, surely could be somewhat more than a mere genius in magic. Have not you and I often watched and observed the magicians, how these are surrounded with all kinds of magic symbols, magic formulas, amulets and magic wands and always make the greatest fuss out of every trivia they produce.

[6] This Jesus however has neither amulet, nor anything pertaining to conjuring, nor any magic ointments, nor herbs or roots and is not at all secretive or mysterious, or a show-off, but a completely plain, good-natured and courteous, civil philanthropist and in Himself a man in the ultimately perfect sense.

[7] He is not downhearted and always good-tempered and His Words flow like milk and honey. And yet, with all His simplicity everything happens in the most miraculous way. I am more than convinced that He could create a new Earth just through His will. I have known Him almost from birth and can tell you that as a little boy He was already performing all the things that He performs before us now as a man.

[8] If however a man accomplishes deeds which are possible only to God, what should hold me back from taking such a person to be God?

[9] I have been a Galilean from birth and am over 70 years and my eyesight has been very feeble for 30 years, having been fully blind already in one eye and of a completely blurred vision in the other. How many doctors from all parts of the world, who nearly all regarded themselves as supernatural in their vocation, who tamed snakes and wild beasts, who decapitated birds and then miraculously fused the heads back, have I not consulted and strictly followed by prescription for my dear money, but to no avail.

[10] Two hours ago, just after supper, He helped me through one Word in such a way that I now see probably more perfectly with both eyes than any of you.

[11] Look into the history books and see whether the Earth ever was trodden by a human being with such miraculous power. Moses indeed accomplished a lot through God's power, bestowed him on account of his mighty faith, like the great promise made to Abraham. But how small are Moses' deeds compared to those which this Jesus performs before our eyes.

[12] And yet you are actually consulting on how to get Him out of the way. Bah! This is shameful of you and you deserve everlasting punishment by God's sharpest scourge.

[13] Truly, in this Jesus seems the most complete fulfillment of what the great prophet Isaiah prophesied of the most exalted Servant of God, when he spoke: *See My Servant, whom I have chosen. Mine elect in whom My soul delights. I will put My Spirit upon Him and He shall proclaim judgment unto the heathens. He shall not cry nor quarrel nor cause His cry to be heard in the street. A bruised reed shall He not break and the smoking flax He shall not extinguish, until He accomplish judgment for victory and the heathens hope upon His name. (Isa 42:1)*

[14] If He were after crown and scepter, by Heaven, He would be mighty to excess for that. Because if He can carry His disciples together through the air from all parts of the world in a moment through his invisible servants, what we saw with our own eyes, then He could carry together all rulers of the world and quite simply tell them: "I am the Lord and you all have ceased ruling everlastingly. If you want to be My servants, you may remain with Me, but if you do not, then depart from Me and be undone."

[15] But He, who is almighty in the truest sense of the word, threatened us even against divulging in the plain even a syllable of what took place here. He does not therefore seek honor from men in any way, but exclusively man's spiritual refinement and perfection. The kingdom He wants to establish among men is a spiritual one, to lead back to the lost Paradise those who no longer know where they come from. And for this we should want to, if it were possible, remove Him

from this evil world? Never. The curse be upon him who makes way for such thought in his heart.

[16] The Earth never has carried a greater philanthropist, or anyone more selfless than He, and you are going to lay hands on Him? Ask yourselves of whose spiritual children you are and Satan, resident in your breast, shall tell you and reply: "I am your father."

[17] What is your Messiah to look like? Perhaps like yourselves? Or is He to make an appearance as a thousand fold Sampson and with Sampson's weapons kill millions of men, with one blow, so as to not seat Himself but you upon the seat of power, afterwards letting Himself be slavishly ruled by you and playing for you the donkey of burden, the camel, the guard dog, a lion fighting your enemies in the desert, a falcon espying from on high the approach of your enemy, so that you can consume the Earth's booty in peace, fornicating with the most tender and beautiful maidens of the Earth? This would be the right Messiah for you.

[18] You are going to be lords and the Messiah your servant. You would have your Messiah only in this way. But that you should have to say "Lord" to the Messiah does not agree with you, which is why you would have Him out of the way.

[19] Look into your hearts and ask them whether this is not exactly so and your hearts shall say yes.

[20] But if I have been wrong, then tell me what your Messiah is to look like and what qualities He needs to have.

[21] Shame on us who call ourselves children of the Highest, yet the heathens, tax-collectors and sinners have a start on us in everything. The Greeks, Romans, Egyptians, Persians, Assyrians and nearly all heathens known to us, out of gratitude towards their idols, idolized the great wise men, because they assumed that such were given them by their gods' grace and they accorded them divine worship, building them temples, hallowing the localities of their residence. There are very few precedents of atrocities on their part against such men.

[22] We Jews however who call ourselves "God's people" have stoned a large number of the prophets sent us by God and have uttered curses over them, yet still dare call ourselves "God's children".

[23] Elijah, one of the greatest and mightiest prophets, had to flee nearly to the end of the world, to save himself from the rage of "God's children" and their neighbors.

[24] We are the ones who stoned God's messengers and now also want to dispatch this good Jesus from the world, if it were possible. If however this were to become possible – for God allows evil mankind the most wicked deeds, so that their measure for Hell be filled – then I prophesy an everlasting curse over all Jews, that they should never again have a homeland on Earth and their name, before which even the heathens have bowed down, shall be an abomination to men.

[25] As truly as God lives this shall take place. And such our heinous deed shall find a never-ending retribution in Hell.'

## CHAPTER 173
## The Pharisees want to stone Tobias

[1] Some accepted what this old man, whose name as pointed out was Tobias, said, but the greater number were so enraged that they wanted to tear up his clothing and stone the old Tobias and all who supported him.

[2] But the old **Tobias** said: 'O, by all means proceed against us who have become a thorn in your eyes. The 3 angels still here will give you out a praiseworthy reward in Hell and the devils will finish the tear in your coats.'

[3] As Tobias had finished his vigorous words to his furious colleagues, with the latter starting to look for stones, the 3 angels entered the hut, their faces shining like the sun.

[4] On seeing this, the stubborn ones were gripped by great fear and they fell upon their faces, asking the three for forgiveness, wailing.

[5] But these said: 'If you will be adversaries of them who are driven and drawn by God's Spirit, who then are your friends? We tell you to your faces: it is the devils. Therefore let you be converted, or you are going to taste the might of the Highest.'

[6] Those shaking with mortal fear scream: 'What must we do?' Say **the three**: 'Humble yourselves and believe on the One, true Son of God, whose soul is One with the Father, because the Father is in and not without Him.' With these words the 3 angels vanish and the Pharisees start to get up, desisting from their exceedingly vociferous plans.

[7] **Tobias** now asks them, saying: 'Now then, what's up, what will you do? Where are the cursed stones? Why did you not lay hands on the three, seeing you took them earlier for the three disguised magicians from Persia?'

[8] Say those hit hard: 'You know of a truth that we have to abide by Moses' laws, to which we have sworn by Heaven and Temple. But if this Jesus now teaches the opposite everywhere, how should we be able to exchange our oath with this anti-Mosaic teaching, just like that? But we will ponder and see what can be done. At this stage we are saying neither yes nor no, because it is written that no prophet shall ever arise from Galilee. Thus the thing, wondrous though it may be in its uniqueness, nevertheless always shall be associated with many a disturbing feature.'

[9] Says **Tobias**: 'That indeed is true, that no prophet is supposed to arise from Galilee, but I ask: is it also written that the Messiah shall not arise in Galilee. I am not aware of anything being written about that, or of any special locality being indicated for the Messiah's appearance. If, according to Scripture, there is to be no prophet from Galilee, it can nevertheless be the case with the Messiah. For there surely is bound to be an unlimited difference between a prophet and the Messiah.' Say **the affected ones**: 'There you are right. That is why we want to think about it.'

[10] Says **another Pharisee** at the back, who had quietly listened to the lengthy proceedings without once contributing his view: 'Friends and brethren, to get to

311

the bottom of this most miraculous thing requires a sober and wakeful state. We however all are more or less drunk since supper and full of sleep as well. How can we arrive at a credible judgment upon a matter that is so miraculous and also important and serious?

[11] Therefore my view is that we now rest a little and continue our proceedings somewhat more wisely tomorrow. Because if am not mistaken, it is dawning already and the morning shall not be long in coming. Therefore we should anticipate the Sabbath in a somewhat appropriate manner and not with arguments and debates.

[12] The big crowd of Jesus' followers appears to be on the rise already. We want to or ought to observe them, but how so when full of sleep. When they may leave even before we awaken if we should now take a little nap?'

[13] Interrupts **another**: 'That is easy. We will set up a watch.' Says **the former speaker**: 'Who? You perhaps or someone who is just as full of sleep as you and I and will fall asleep like us?'

[14] Says **a third**: 'Sleeping will not do as the others are getting ready for departure. Therefore we shall have no alternative but follow their example. Because the way down to the plain is drawn-out and we shall not be in the village for some time after rise!'

[15] Says **a fourth**: 'Ah, the Master Jesus also is before the hut, making preparation for departure. We shall therefore have no option but to quickly break forth.'

[16] Says **the first**: 'Ah, here we have it. Just as I thought, now we have it. This will be a nice trip, without sleep and quite drunk from last night's supper.'

[17] Say **a number of them**: 'Well, there just is no alternative. They, having rested, are not likely to wait for us. Therefore away! We shall catch up with our sleep in the village.' All rise and quickly move outside.

[18] With the Pharisees all being ready for departure, but with Myself not actually starting off at once, all but a few get a little indignant, asking Me whether I was not pulling out yet.

[19] But I tell them: 'I am Lord, doing as I please and none are to ask Me 'Why thus?' But if someone is not pleased with how I will have it for Myself and Mine, he can do as he will, for I bind no one. If anyone wants to go, let him. But if he will wait, then let him wait patiently. I shall not be breaking forth before sunrise and shall first partake of a morning meal, for the road is long and tiring.'

[20] Say **the Pharisees**: 'In that case can we take a short rest?'I said: 'Most certainly. For the Earth does not need the light of your eye for sunrise, but of a truth the light of My eyes, so that there be light in the depths.'

[21] Say **the Pharisees**: 'Let him who can or will, understand this. We cannot understand that.'

[22] Says the old **Tobias**: 'I understand it indeed and therefore remain in the open. Perhaps a brightness shall enter upon my depth as well.

[23] Say **the others**: 'You old codger do as you like, but we shall return to the hut to get some sleep.' With these words all quickly return to the hut, throwing themselves on their bunks.

312

[24] Tobias however comes over to Me with reverence, to tell Me everything that took place during the night. But I comfort him, saying: 'I know it all, for if I did not, how could I have sent you help at the right time? Leave it at that. Because whoever rises up against Me before My time shall have to kick hard against the pricks. Therefore do not fear. For from now on no more disgusting things shall get to you.

[25] But let us now go a bit further up. There on that hill towards the East. From there we shall be able to see a most glorious sunrise. And that kind of thing fortifies the soul as well as the bodily limbs, cheering up heart and kidney.'

[26] With these words all betake themselves with Me up the alpine slope, eagerly awaiting the rise of the sun, which was not long in coming.

## CHAPTER 174
### Conduct for judges and law-givers

[1] When after about an hour, it, the sun came up with indescribable majesty and splendor, all were uplifted and moved to tears, singing Psalms to the glory of Him who created all this so wondrously and gloriously.

[2] Said the old **Tobias**, after such solemn morning-hour: 'O Lord, this is a different temple to that in Jerusalem, which latter always is full of filth and obscenity. How often in my life have I sung psalm after psalm, yet my heart was as dry as ten year old straw and cold as ice. And how warmly it now beats towards my Creator. How often was I in the Temple, yet always glad to leave its stinking halls. Yet here I feel like spending eternity, and from the deepest love-warmth praise the great God who created all the countless glorious things. You beloved Master, how can I thank you for such previously never-felt supremely holy elixir of life?'

[3] I said: 'He who ventures forth into the creation feeling and perceiving what he owes his Creator as warmly as you do, already has shown Me the best and most pleasing gratitude.

[4] Stay with such feelings and perceptions and do not close off your heart towards your poorer brethren even if they had once been your enemy, and you shall once merit a great grace from the Heavens. When seeing all kinds of sinners, neither judge nor condemn them, for, understand Me well, it mostly is not them who sin but the spirit that drives them. You yourself are not able to say what spirit drives them. There are many who in their piousness can become haughty, wanting to then look down from their imagined virtue-heights upon sinners with contempt and revulsion, wherewith they then unconsciously turn into greater sinners than those whom they despise. There then comes a spirit who drives such people towards some sin and the proud virtue-hero discovers on himself that he is not a god for a long time yet, but just a very ordinary, weak human.

[5] Such person then becomes humble again and repents, something for which.

[6] And therefore no one should hate a sinner for being a sinner, but all have

done enough to just hate sin and detest it in deed. Only a hardened criminal, who had become one with his sin, you should not help. But when, as a result, he sinks into just extremity, for his betterment, then you should think of him and if he pleads with you then do not stop off your ear. And if you see a criminal led to his execution, you should not feel joy at such his miserable fate, even if he were to have committed the crime for which he is led out to death against your own house, for see, it is not impossible for such a criminal to attain to beatitude in the other world.

[7] Each person's predominant trait should be love in all things. Justice which is not grounded in love is no justice before God. And if carried out by a judge therefore, then he is ten times a greater sinner before God than the one he sentenced, and God shall once judge him as mercilessly as he judged his neighbor.

[8] Therefore judge and condemn no man, even if he were to have offended you ever so grievously and you shall then not be judged and condemned, because with whatever measure you mete out, with the same you shall be rewarded in the other world. The strictly just by whatever law, but cold and loveless judge, shall find just as inexorable a judgment over himself, while henchmen and executioners shall never see God's countenance.

[9] He who has caught a thief or murderer has done his part if he hands them over to a just court. But the judge should not forget that so long as the criminal still lives in the world, he is not a complete devil yet, but a maladjusted person led astray, on whom every possible reformation attempt should be made before he can be condemned to death as an incorrigible devil.

[10] But the right procedure for the execution is that the sentence not be carried out immediately, but that such a person should be tied to the stake by the hands and feet, publicly, five feet above ground for the whole day.

[11] If he pleads with genuine remorse that he shall better himself, then he is to be taken down from the stake and placed in an appropriate, love-righteous reformation centre, yet not freed until his betterment has shown itself unquestionably. But if the criminal strung up shows no sign of betterment the whole day, then he is a complete devil and therefore, if still alive on the stake, after sunset is to be put to death and then burnt on the place of execution, together with the stake.

[12] Such I tell you for your future adherence, because you too were a judge and still are, among the Pharisees, having had to look after burial places for the dead and places of execution for the criminals.

[13] Blessed are they who shall act accordingly. Their names shall shine in the eternal book of life.

[14] But now we shall move down to the huts. Our Kisjonah has prepared a moderate morning meal and is awaiting us with his wife and daughters.

[1] We now quickly made our way down and Kisjonah hastens towards Me to ask Me and the disciples to the morning meal, at the same time he apologized for a rather moderate meal than usual, as the supplies are exhausted and that he had not more brought up, being aware of My moving – on this Sabbath – down from the mountain to the plain. If therefore the meal is a rather moderate one that I would not attribute it to his lack of will but that he was unable to change it.

[2] I assured him, saying: 'Do not be troubled. All is in order and according to My will. I want to say unto you, as a beloved brother and friend, that you have indeed outdone yourself in these last few days.

[3] As regards the uninvited guests – the legion of Pharisees – there you would by no means have committed a sin by not setting them a table, for these, having gold and silver in great quantity, could have, if they had wanted to, paid their way around here. But you have of course not sinned by providing for them free of charge. I shall not rebuke you if you want to write them a bill. But the old Tobias is My guest.'

[4] Says **Kisjonah**: 'That I also shall do. There are plenty of poor whom such payment shall benefit. But now, o Lord, be pleased to partake of the moderate meal with your disciples. The Pharisees are still asleep in the big resting hut and I do not wish them to eat with us.'

[5] I said: 'Let it be. Wake and invite them to the meal. I shall be fasting till midday with all of Mine. We shall then take a proper meal down in the plain.

[6] Kisjonah at once does as I told him, although somewhat heavy-heartedly. The Pharisees and their colleagues quickly get up from their sleeping places, rushing to the morning meal which they consume with all haste, in spite of the Sabbath, for they fear that the sun, which had indeed been up for quite some time, may soon reach the hut, which was shielded by a great cliff, along which it was built, which would then prevent them from eating until sunset, or till the agreed Sabbath-evasion ritual in the Temple of Jerusalem.

[7] **Kisjonah** notices this and says to Me: 'This business really is quite funny. The Sabbath with these does not begin until the sun shines upon the spot where they find themselves. As You, o Lord, have now seen a number of times, the sun does not come to this hut until midday and therefore these hypocrites would not commence their Sabbath till noon, to honor it. It would be hard to find anywhere else on Earth fellows like these.'

[8] I said: 'Let us leave them. There shall yet be multiple opportunities for rubbing their Sabbath into their noses even before we reach the plain. This is as nothing compared to how they outflank the Sabbath when they want to and when the Sabbath does not promise to yield much of a harvest in their Synagogues. They then shut the windows and doors, so that the sun cannot cast its rays into the rooms of such hypocrites, whereupon there then is no Sabbath in the house. Neither does a dull day serve for a full Sabbath, unless they light their seven-

branched candlestick in their Synagogues, for the occasion of a substantial offering of course. For which reason a dull Sabbath always is preferable to them to a fine one like today.

[9] But an opportunity shall yet offer itself today, as I have said, where we can bring this out in the open. But let us now get under way, because today shall be very hot and traveling is not too pleasant in such heat.'

[10] Thereupon we break forth with hasty steps from the mountain towards the plain and the Pharisees behind us are gasping for breath and angry about our rapid steps. **One of them** even calls out to us: 'Why are you rushing so nonsensically? Did you by any chance steel something upon the heights?'

[11] **The younger Matthew**, the disciple, won't let that pass, saying: 'We walk with our own feet and you with yours and therefore walk as speedily as we please and do not have to account to you, we hope. Neither did we agree with you beforehand how fast we shall go. Therefore shut up and go your way as you will. We are not bothering with you, why should you bother with us?'

[12] Says **one Pharisee**, quite furious about that: 'What are you silly tax-collector reeling off? Do you not know that it is Sabbath today, when none should argue?'

[13] **Matthew** replies: 'Should the Sabbath apply only to me and not you? Who was the first to argue? It surely is not written that one cannot walk quickly on a Sabbath? You quite on the contrary demand that one should not be tardy going to the Synagogue on a Sabbath and therefore we are not breaking even your own regulations by moving more quickly on a Sabbath than on another day. There is a Synagogue down in the village which we can still reach if we walk quickly. What more do you want of us?'

[14] Say **the Pharisees**: 'Those who hasten to the Synagogues and schools indeed look like you. It is funny when a tax-collector speaks about a Synagogue. Do we perhaps not know you?'

[15] Says **Matthew**: 'Time is up for you putting bridles on your mouths, or we shall take the liberty of breaking the Sabbath on your backs with clubs. Just look at these eternal loafers, what rights they would like to grant themselves over us. Another offending word and I shall give the Sabbath and my humanity a miss and put on bear nature for you.' To this threat the Pharisees say nothing, but are secretly filled with rage.

## CHAPTER 176
### The gleaning of the wheat on a Sabbath

[1] After a while however, much nearer the plain, we came to a field of near-ripe grain, spread out before us. The path led through this field and we set upon this one through the field, as it was the shorter one to the village. We therefore traveled through the grain, on a Sabbath of course. The disciples however, having together with Myself had no morning meal, began to pluck some of the riper ears,

rubbing the grains into their hands and eating.

[2] Noticing this, the furious **Pharisees** step hastily up to Me, speaking with self-important mien: 'Do you not see the unseemly thing your disciples are committing on a Sabbath?'

[3] Say I to them: 'Have you not read what David did when he and those who were with him were hungry how he entered into the house of God and ate the showbread, which neither for him nor those who were with him it was seemly to do, but only for the priest? Or have you never read in the law how on the Sabbath, the priests profane the Sabbath and are blameless?

[4] You have witnessed My works upon the heights and heard My teachings and were repeatedly told who I am. If all this is not enough to you, then I tell you straight to your faces: He who is in Me is greater than the Temple.

[5] But if you knew what is meant by: "I will have mercy but not sacrifice", then you would not in your hearts have condemned these innocents. You blind and deaf Pharisees, be told that the Son of Man, who is Myself, is Lord also over the Sabbath.' These words so frightened the Pharisees that they stepped back at once and stopped denying the gleaning of the wheat to the disciples.

[6] **Kisjonah** however, who constantly walked by My side and whose field this was, said to Me: 'Lord, I shall hasten ahead at once to arrange an ample meal, for I feel sorry for the disciples and their obvious hunger.'

[7] I said: 'There you shall indeed do well. But I shall nevertheless first visit a school with My disciples, so that the Pharisees' anger should not wax. For they already cannot stomach Matthew for having proven to them that we hasten on account of the Synagogue. Were we to now by-pass the village-school, that would be the end with them and they would start making trouble. If however we go to a school first, then we have shut their mouths and you can without further ado then present them with your bill, i.e. at the end of the Sabbath.' With these words Kisjonah and his went straight home, where they found everything in the best order.

[8] We however turned slightly left towards the school which was situated highest up in the village. Arrived there, we at once entered the rather sparsely attended school.

[9] With the Pharisees at our heels, secretly fuming at having been laughed off by the disciples out on the field, on account of their blindness, after I had chided their objection to the gleaning of grain.

[10] On our entering, the Pharisees at once started throwing their weight around, ushering a person to Me whose hand had been withered for a lengthy period and who therefore was capable of hardly any work at all. Here they wanted to know, seeing that I had said that I am Lord also of the Sabbath, whether it is lawful to also heal on a Sabbath. But they only asked to have a witnessed case against Me, for their evil hearts were burning with rage and fury.

[11] But I spoke to them: 'Why are you asking Me as if you yourselves were capable of enlivening this one's long-dead hand? But if I intended healing him, surely I would not ask you for permission to do it?

[12] Which one among you would be foolish enough not to pull a sheep from a

ditch because it fell in on a Sabbath? But how much better is a man than a sheep. For this reason it surely ought to be lawful to do a man good on a Sabbath?'

[13] The Pharisees were silent, but I called the person over and said to him: 'Stretch forth your hand.' And he stretched it out and it became whole as the other that had never been sick.

[14] This was the last straw for the Pharisees. They left the school to discuss how to kill Me.

[15] But Matthew, who was a bit of a spy, slipped out, unnoticed by them, soon returning near-breathless and proclaiming aloud what he had heard. Upon this I at once dispatched a disciple to Kisjonah, letting him know that I shall not be able to dine with him for prudence' sake, as the Pharisees were after My life and with My not wanting to make bigger criminals of them than they already are, I shall make Myself scarce to this area for a while. The disciple was off with arrow-speed, knowing where to catch up with Me later.

[16] Hardly had he passed it on to Kisjonah, when the latter let everything go, speedily gathering a large number of folk, rushing to the school and arriving just as the Pharisees were entering, well-provided with stones.

[17] That on this occasion the Pharisees were served up by Kisjonah good and proper hardly needs mentioning, whereupon I then departed with a larger number of folk, healing their sick on the way, because this area at harvest-time, being located on the Galilean Sea, was fever-stricken and there always were many sick, especially the female gender and these, getting news of Me, ran after the crowd and, catching up with Me on the road, asking that I would heal them. And all who followed us were healed.

[18] After their healing I warned all not to divulge it at home nor to mention the place where I healed them and which direction I left. They promised to strictly keep it and I let them depart with peace.

## CHAPTER 177
### The fulfilling of the prophecy

[1] When these had been dealt with, **the apostles** stepped over to Me, saying: 'Lord, sometimes You are a little puzzling. See, we have already seen so many wondrous things about You and ourselves experienced so many, that we could no longer even for one moment have doubts, even if we wanted to that You in the truest sense must be the Son of the living God, because the deeds which you accomplish have not heretofore been possible to man. Yet You nevertheless have certain moments when You seem in all earnest to fear men, notwithstanding that we convinced ourselves of countless hosts of angels from the Heavens standing at Your service.

[2] The Pharisees, of whom each one is more cowardly than the other, together with their 50 or so unarmed adherents, we ourselves could have fixed up properly, while one little almighty word from Yourself and the Pharisees' desire to persecute

You should have left them forever. How You could therefore, with all Your Godly might take to your heels before these fellows is a puzzle to us which we cannot grasp with the best of will. Could You not let us in on such intriguing behavior therefore?'

[3] Said I: 'You still are fairly weak and blind, not to work this out at first glance. See, this took place so that you may become aware of the fulfillment of what the prophet Isaiah prophesied of Me when he spoke: *"See, My servant, whom I have chosen, Mine elect, in whom My soul delights. I will put My Spirit upon Him and He shall proclaim judgment to the heathens." (Here judgment signifies Truth, Light and Life, for it is Truth that brings about righteous judgment). "He shall not argue or cry and His crying shall not be heard in the streets. A bruised reed He shall not break and the smoking flax shall He not quench until He executes justice (the full Truth). And the heathens shall hope upon His Name".*

[4] See, therein lies the reason why I did not want to, nor could, enter upon an argument and even less some scuffle with the Pharisees.

[5] I by the way knew in advance that Kisjonah would not let them go unpunished. Their punishment now is tenfold of what it would have been in a possible scuffle with us, firstly because they were grievously clubbed by Kisjonah and his people and secondly because of all that they went through, they are not allowed to mention a syllable in Capernaum, which is what annoys and embarrasses them most of all.

[6] Because, as threatened upon the mount, if any one comes out loud with even a syllable of it, he shall turn dumb, deaf and where necessary, blind on the spot. That also is the reason for their attempt on My life, for therewith they hoped to also eliminate what they believed to be the certain consequences of My threat upon the mount.

[7] For they still take Me for a wicked magician, who indeed can perform while still alive, but not dead. The worst to them now is not to know where I have gone. They have indeed already sent emissaries eastwards to track Me down, having seen us flee east from the school, but they do not know that we should have suddenly turned west after an hour in the forest and then sail over the sea to the other side and therefore their search shall be a futile one. Now, is your puzzle solved therewith?'

[8] Say **the 12 as well as many others** traveling with Me: 'Yes, now everything is clear to us. Therefore it is actually much better than if we had laid hands on the wicked ones ourselves. Now everything is in the nicest order again.'

[9] Says **Judas** somewhat laconically: 'Except for our stomachs. Nothing has gotten inside yet, considering it is evening, except a few grains of wheat. Therefore it should be nice if something could also be done about our stomachs before we sail over the sea.'

[10] I said: 'Today it simply is going to be fasting, at least to the other shore. Something is bound to turn up on the other side.'

[11] **Thomas** however reproached him for such crudeness, saying: 'But how can you, after such exalted teaching on the Lord's part, come up with such low comments? Do you have no sense of decency or shame in your body? If you

319

actually are of such wolf-like voracity, then take some provisions with you in future, but to make such remarks in the Lord's presence is too endlessly crude to lose more words on it.'

[12] Says **Judas**: 'Yes, yes, I forgot we still have you in our midst. You are and stay my task-master and you seem to enjoy every chance to hit me. Very well, keep doing it if it makes you happy. It shall not bother me in future.'

[13] Says **Peter**: 'That will be best. Thomas nevertheless is right, although he is a bit rough at times. But in my view we should always look up to the Lord. If He says something then it is good for it to have been said and we should all abide by it. But if the Lord is not saying anything, then it is even less fitting for us to say something. In my opinion we should always observe this in the Lord's presence, for peace and harmony to be among us.

[14] My dear brother Thomas, if the hungry Judas will not keep silent before the Lord, he shall be even less afraid of you. If we do have to correct one another however, then let us avoid shrillness and harshness, so that those words of Isaiah which the Lord mentioned can apply also to us, His disciples.'

[15] I said: 'That is correct, My dear Simon Jona. So it ought to be among you and all mankind. Because he who is wounded and puts something rough over it shall not heal but only make it worse and bigger. But if he covers it with balm and pure oil, he shall also heal it soon and will thus repair the injury to the flesh.

[16] But now My friend Kisjonah's boatmen already are steering towards the shore and he is himself among them. Therefore let us go down to the shore and be around when the skippers cast the mooring, that we may pull them ashore, for their wind is contrary and makes it hard for them. But the wind shall come in handy for our crossing and shall quickly set us on the other side. So let us hurry, that their efforts would not be futile.

### CHAPTER 178
### Healing of the possessed, dumb and blind

[1] We rush towards the shore, arriving just as the skippers are casting the moorings. Peter, a skillful boatman himself, grabs hold of it and we quickly pull in the boat and board it and it takes us to the opposite side in an hour and a half, and this at the spot where half the population consists of Greeks and the other half Jews.

[2] We reach the shore at dusk, enabling us to still make out the district quite well. Kisjonah sends out two messengers to provide the place for accommodation for about a hundred, but they return without success. And so we stayed on board overnight, for the wind had dropped and the sea was near calm.

[3] Kisjonah then brought out plenty of bread, wine and well roasted fish from the hold and his wife and daughters, who were not missing either, were serving us. That Judas, who had already felt empty on the other side, was highly pleased with this development hardly needs recounting.

[4] Kisjonah asks Me whether to light a fire, seeing the nights can turn quite cool, notwithstanding any heat of day. I consented and a fire was quickly lit in the big flare, which was well provided with clean resin, oil and other combustibles. This ship's flare was soon blazing away, spreading a great light over the entire area. This soon lured a great many onlookers to the shore, with many among them recognizing Me from the short distance, and they began an immense cheering for the renown, miraculous Savior's presence in their district, for there were many sick there.

[5] Many others rushed home from the shore, telling the whole place that I am to be found on the ship.

[6] It did not take long before one dumb and blind at the same time and thereforeask juergen to redo the whole the whole sentence possessed in this fashion, was brought to the shore and the people asked Me whether I could and wanted to heal him.

[7] **Several local Pharisees** however had also hastened to the shore to see what would happen there, saying to the people: 'To heal this one he shall well and truly leave alone.'

[8] But their possessed one I healed from the ship instantly, so that he could both see and speak. All the people of this place were horrified and Jews who were not of the same persuasion as the Pharisees, yelled: 'This is truly David's Son, on whom all Jews hope.'

[9] There was however **a man** in this place, upright and just. This one stepped up close to the boat, saying: 'Divinely great, wondrous Master, why should you have to let the wind and a rather fresh night on a rocking boat deprive You of a night's probably overdue rest? The notorious feature about this district is that the heat of day usually is followed by proportional freshness of the night, resulting in all kinds of disease among the local residents. I am however in possession of a roomy and well-equipped house that could provide You and Your disciples with more than sufficient room and you can stay for as long as You like. Neither shall there be any shortage of provisions.

[10] Say I to him: 'Yes, I shall accept your invitation, for I know that your soul is without guile. But Kisjonah with his wife and daughters are also here. His is the boat and he is a disciple and a man after My liking. Do you have room for him too?' Says **the old man**: 'Even if there were more such families. Whoever is with You is welcome in my house.'

[11] I said: 'In that case a great blessing shall come over your house' (and to Kisjonah): 'Therefore, let the boat by fully beached, for your easier disembarking.' This was done and we soon reached the old man's house, who at once got his people to organize the most comfortable lodgings.

# CHAPTER 179
## The old host's humility

[1] After the quarters had been organized, **the old man** came to Me with his sons, who mostly were fishers, boatmen and carpenters, saying: 'Lord, as quickly as it was possible, everything has been made ready for Your accommodation, and You are now invited to make full use of it at once. You now are, as always, the Lord also of this house, which I have built with my seven sons. Let you command it and I with my house shall be Your servants.

[2] I said: 'You are the way you are, and I also am what I am, but since you are so humble, lowering yourself, you shall once be elevated in My Kingdom. Our needs for today are just a little rest. But let the sick come here tomorrow, so I may heal them.

[3] Says **the old man**: 'There You shall have much to do, for it is not an inconsiderable district and it would be hard to find a house without a sick. Although the area along the coast is one of the most fertile, it nevertheless is one of the least salutary for man's health – nothing but fevers and boils of every kind.'

[4] Say I: 'Let that be. Tomorrow all that shall change, but provide yourself with fish for tomorrow, so that My disciples, who mostly fasted today, can be filled again tomorrow. Everything shall be compensated to you.'

[5] Says **the old man**: 'Lord, forgive a little rejoinder here. Thousands have already been lodged and satiated here, and never yet have I accepted anything from anyone and how much less from You. My bills I hand over to the winds and these carry them aloft to the stars where the almighty Father dwells. He has so far always been My best payer and compensator and shall be so again this time as well! How many sick and ailing have not been cared for here for months on end and yet in spite of the harmfulness of the area, none of my household has become ill. Lord, this is a grace from above and therefore let You not speak of compensation or payment, for I would accept neither the one nor the other.'

[6] I said: 'Yes, but there is actually a snag to this. For if I do not compensate you, then the compensation from the stars shall turn out somewhat meager as well, because My say and direction extend even to the stars and beyond.'

[7] Here **the old man** is taken aback tremendously, not knowing what to say. Only after a while does he say somewhat timidly: 'For Jehovah's sake. Are you perhaps an angel from the Heavens or is one helping you, or is given You as a servant by the Father from the Heavens?'

[8] I said: 'Let you just take yourself some overdue rest now, but much shall be revealed to you tomorrow. But go out to the people, who still are noising about and ask them to retire and to bring the sick here tomorrow. I shall heal them all.' The old man went and did as I commanded him.

[9] And **the people** started cheering wildly, yelling: 'Praise be to the exalted Son of David! He came to us to free us of every plague! Although we do not know where He comes from, one thing is certain: God's Spirit is with Him, as it was with His forefather David! For were it not with Him, He would not have healed the

possessed!'

[10] **Some Pharisees** however also had set out with the people to observe, as Jerusalemite Temple police, everything else that I, of whom they had been hearing much, would do. The healing of the possessed, who was deaf, dumb and blind as well, had jolted them mightily, and they were constantly plotting on how to cast suspicion on Me before the people as a tramp, rogue, deceiver and even as a magician in league with the devil. This is why they said to the people: 'Tomorrow it shall transpire of what spirit he is. We shall no doubt be seeing in what fashion he shall heal the cripples, the lame and leprous.' Say **the people**: 'If he has healed the most difficult case suddenly, then he is certain to heal the others with greater ease. But you should yourselves not be talking about such things at all, because no man has yet been healed through your expensive prayers and still less through your amulets, which you highly recommend and sell to the sick for dear money.

[11] That One has the Spirit of God in His body, for this He has proven to us amply already through the mere deed. But you yourselves have no spirit in you at all, other than that of haughtiness, avarice and domination.

[12] You want to be the first after God and to receive divine honor from us men, but we say unto you that to us you are the last, and worse by a hundredfold than the heathens. For you do nothing at all for our benefit. You do no work and those who attend your schools become so stupid and dark after 2 years that no angel is likely to fix them up without special power from God. And this is still the best of your care and efforts for our supposed well being.

[13] The wives of your Jewish co-religionists you seduce a hundredfold, fornicating with their daughters, yet this is nothing. If however some other poor devil were to go that far he is stoned, if poor, but if rich and of repute, he can buy himself out and beside that remain your friend.

[14] Your colleagues, the Jews, do not of course know you as well as we Greeks do and even if they know you, they must not speak up. But we know you and can speak. Wherefore we take this opportunity to tell you what we really think of you.

[15] But take yourselves home soon, before a storm of Greek fists comes over you. We however shall keep watch here. Do not dare to as much as touch this Person, or you shall have to deal with us.

[16] We indeed also were Jews once, but are happy to be Greeks in name and law. We nevertheless in our hearts are true Jews, but not like you of course, who sell their God-glorifying prayers for money, ascribing to such the most fabricated effects.

[17] We ourselves worship God because He is God and because we as His beings owe it to Him. Therefore get yourselves moving, because your presence is more repulsive to us than a stinking carcass.'

[18] Upon these unambiguous utterances from the people, about half of whom were resident Greeks, the Pharisees made off as quickly as possible, with the folk cheering with victory, and at having rubbed the naked truth into the nostrils of these idlers, which they normally called the Pharisees.

323

## CHAPTER 180
### The plan of the young Pharisee

[1] This district, otherwise, was notorious for its witty residents. Anyone wishing to take it up with them, especially with the Greeks, would have to be of sound mind. And the Pharisees therefore were conscious of what it was like arguing with the people and therefore retorted very little this time, and made their way home. But they brooded the more at home over how to cast suspicion on Me before the people, or to even basically destroy Me.

[2] **One of a better spirit** among them however, to whom the deliberations were getting too drawn-out, finally said: 'Brethren! For whatever my opinion may count, I suggest we now get our sleep, so that tomorrow we are all there with head and heart. Of what use all our brooding and scheming today? Tomorrow is another day. Let us see what tomorrow will bring and then we shall with Jehovah's help be in the clear about what this man is about. That this is something most singular, cannot be questioned in the least, because the healing of the possessed at the shore, just from the boat, without him being touched is a phenomenon that to my knowledge has not been with us yet.

[3] And therefore let us wait for what else follows tomorrow and we shall be more likely to judge properly. For it would be too risky to blindly condemn him, especially the way the people are worked up, since they have for a long time been siding with the Greeks rather than us, who have been a thorn in their flesh for some time. Therefore take note of my well-considered opinion. Tomorrow is another day, which could turn out more favorably for us than today.'

[4] Says **another**: 'Should we not do something about our being abused that way by the people? Should we go to sleep on that too and grow no gray hair over it and forget it as if it had never happened, taking no revenge?'

[5] Says **the better one**: 'Shake them down for a sacrifice, if you can. Or call the culprits to account today or tomorrow, if you can. What can one do against many? Keeping quiet about it seems the most advisable thing to me, at least for the present. But if you want to take action straight away, then no law will keep you from it. I for one however shall first wait for the outcome to this story before taking the appropriate action. Let ripen the apple on the tree, if you do not like biting into a sour one. Do you get me?'

[6] After these words of the better Pharisee, who still was young and zestful and did not feel much solidarity with the old money-bag heroes, several Pharisees and scribes went to take their rest, but nevertheless still appointed one of their servants to keep watch, so that they would not over sleep the start of the magician's story.

[7] **The better Pharisee** however, after all the others, including the watch, had fallen into heavy sleep, went outside to work out how to sabotage the old ones' evil schemes. He reasoned thus: 'If only I could get to this wondrous man, I could show him how he could carry out his healings without my colleagues' molestations. But how get to him? The agitated people surround the house and I

notice that the sick already are being escorted and carried there. But I know what I will do. I will go over to the people and tell them straight where I stand, showing them my hostility towards the old money zealots and that I intend to confide something to the wondrous man, without which he shall hardly be allowed to carry on his healings. If the people let me, good, if not, I shall at least have followed my conscience.'

[8] With these thoughts he goes back to the people, who in the moonlit night can make him out quite well as the familiar young rabbi.

[9] Those Greeks who had formerly been Jews go to meet him at once, asking in a brutish manner what he is up to at such hour and whether he actually is a spy. But he says amicably and confidingly: 'Dear men and friends, my skin is indeed covered with Pharisaical clothing and as you know I am a Pharisee in actuality, for as first-born of a well-to-do home in Jerusalem, I had to become what my unprincipled parents wanted. And therefore I am externally indeed a Pharisee, yet in my heart less so than all of you, although you now are Greeks.

[10] My intentions are simply this: you know my colleagues as well as I do and what rights they arrogate to themselves. They are theologians and no one other than they is allowed to understand Scripture, although between ourselves, they probably understand any other thing better than Scripture, but they are selected for it by the Temple and they exercise their purported rights and you can do nothing about it.

[11] They also are doctors and do not like anyone to come along and through his skill diminish their income. Through this also they enjoy a Temple privilege and know how to fight for their rights and you can do nothing about that.

[12] They are also, in certain cases prescribed by Moses, judges and Lords of life and death over their subordinates, and can exercise such rights when and on whoever they like without being accountable for it. They have only to submit to the Temple, besides the yearly amount of lease for the Synagogue and school, a list every year and are praised the more for the length of the list of those whom they have judged.

[13] Because all of these offices have for a long time been either sold or leased, here we are only lessee and I myself only a sub-lessee.

[14] I tell you, such Synagogue or school costs much money in the Temple. And in order to bring in the more from those to whom assigned, it is loaded by the Temple with all kinds of frills which such renter then will not, with the law on his side, suffer to be diminished too easily.

[15] One cannot of course become a buyer or renter of a Synagogue or school until consecrated by a Pharisee by the Temple, under the strictest oaths. Once a Pharisee however, it is no longer easy to become a non-Pharisee.

[16] And see, although a true Jew should spit at such Temple fraud, they nevertheless are even acknowledged and sanctioned by the state and you can do nothing about it. I could tell you more, but it is sufficient to at least show you within what rights the Pharisees are moving, against which, for the time being, nothing can be undertaken.

[17] Had I not used my good offices in the good cause with the old, vindictive

colleagues, then you would have already been in big trouble, because they were about to send for a legion of soldiers to Capernaum, to hand the entire house over to the court. I therefore am your friend and not your enemy and even less a capricious, hostile spy. Only do not betray me please. But if some good advice on my part does not seem too remiss to you, then hear me with all patience.'

[18] Say **the three**: 'You seem genuine to us and so tell us what we should do. But do not dare to deceive us, or it would cost you your life.'

[19] Says **the young Pharisee**: 'I do not fear that, and if I had a hundred lives, I would give them as testimony to my sincerity. And so hear me: you know that, with the Pharisees, what matters to the exclusion of everything else, is income. Go over to them in the morning therefore and agree with them upon a sum for which the wonder-doctor residing here can heal the sick tomorrow morning without objection. And the old money-brokers shall give you the authority without further ado. If however you are not able to immediately put down the money, then promise to do so and it will still work out.

[20] I would only add the following for the wondrous man: that he firstly leaves this area after the healing of the sick, or else the money-hungry Pharisees would straight away demand a second money-payment from you. And that secondly, since such wonder-doctors normally extend into the prophetic field, starting to work on the people spiritually, he should not start such here, not because of me, but the old ones, who in this respect are intolerable here precisely on account of you Greeks.

[21] And finally, that the people do not refer to him as Son of David in front of the old foxes, for this is the scariest of all scares for my old colleagues. If all this is adhered to, then everything – as I wish with all my heart – may come off quietly. In the alternative case it may come to a terrifying row.

## CHAPTER 181
### The young Pharisee's artfulness with his colleagues

[1] Say **the three Greeks**: 'Your advice is quite well-meant, yet we are not completely happy with it. For how much longer is this cruel control by these public deceivers to last? We are fed up with them, although we have nothing more to do with them, yet they keep jeering at us, holding diatribes against us in their school, cursing and condemning us at every turn. For how long are we to put up with that? On top of that they are our judges in official matters and if we want to enjoy any rights, we must buy them dearly. See, this is a terrible state of affairs, and therefore we think of putting an end to this control once and for all tomorrow. Because tomorrow all resident Jews are transferring over to us, and the Pharisees shall be thrown out as useless, except for yourself, if you desire to remain with us. See, this is our plan, already put in motion, in that there are to be found no more actual Jews among the residents of this area. What do you say to such plan?'

[2] Says **the young Rabbi**: 'If you succeed, then nobody shall have less to

object than I. But proceed with the caution of ravens, or you and I shall not fare too well. Because no one knows the outreach of these old foxes' paws better than I and their eagle's eyes see through walls and their ears hear many hours (walking) distance, whatever is said anywhere. But let me return home now, so as not to arouse their suspicion, for it is dawning and the foxes shall wake up soon, and if they found me missing, that would be the end.'

[3] Say **the three**: 'Go then. But mind you do not betray us to the old foxes, for then you would be done for.'

[4] The young Pharisee makes his way home and finds everything soundly asleep, including the watch. These he wakes however, making a big fuss over their sleeping. That awakens the old foxes, and some go to check on what is going on.

[5] The young Pharisee however, feigning fury, said that having found no sleep, he went to check out the watch: 'And see and share my anger, they slept more soundly than any of us. Ah, this is a bit thick. Had we not had Jehovah's especial protection this night, we could have all been murdered by the incensed people.'

[6] The old ones shudder at the thought, suddenly realizing the danger they had found themselves in, and praising the young colleague beyond measure for watching over them like an angel of God.

[7] The young one almost burst out laughing of course, barely containing the urge to give his throat to full throttle. He kicked the watchmen not too heavily, commanding them to get out of the way. They left immediately, seeming to make out what the young man was at.

[8] After the watch was gone and day-break had advanced, **the young man** said: 'Brethren, I do not think we have much time to lose, wherefore we should get on our way, so that nothing of what goes on should escape us.'

[9] Say **the old ones**: 'Yes, you are right, we must miss nothing. But did you send to Capernaum for soldiers in case of obduracy?'

[10] Says **the young man**: 'Had I waited for your instructions, we should be done for. All's attended to. Whether the soldiers will arrive soon is another matter, because it is quite far to Capernaum, and even further to elsewhere. Therefore patience is the thing, waiting for what comes – being or non-being.' (An expression of the young one).

[11] It speaks for itself that the young one had not even thought of sending to Capernaum for soldiers, because he was in secret a foe of the old Pharisees, because he also was a secret adherent of the teaching of the Essenes and therefore would have desired nothing more fervently than to cause the old Temple heroes trouble.

[12] The old ones however had not yet had a morning meal, and said to **the young one**: 'Well well, if only those soldiers would turn up. It is of course high time we went over there, but we could eat breakfast before they come, for surely the magician is not going to carry on before sunrise?'

[13] Says **the young man**: 'O, certainly not. If you do not mind I shall go for a minute to check if anything is stirring at Baram's house yet, and you could have your breakfast meanwhile.' (Baram was the carpenter's name, at whose house the

Lord had taken his lodgings. The name of the place however was Jesaira, currently a prairie).

[14] Say **the old ones**: 'Will you be fasting today?' **The young one**: 'That, no, but as you are aware, I can never eat before sunrise. Therefore, leave me something for after. Say **the old ones**: 'All right, therefore go quickly and bring us good news, especially about the soldiers, because without them we are done for, as you would say.'

[15] The young one leaves straight away, while **the old ones** shout after him: 'Don't forget – the soldiers!' Shouts **the young man**: 'Just trust me!' Then to himself: 'Then you are done for'.


## CHAPTER 182
### Ahab called by Jesus

[1] As the young man comes to the house, he already finds it surrounded with the sick and the sound. He asks someone whether I am up yet. One **old, upright Greek** says to him: 'Yes, he is up, and has been before the house once, when the old Baram called him to breakfast, whereupon he went back into the house.'

[2] Asks **the young man**: 'What was he doing before the house?'

[3] Says **the Greek**: 'Nothing more than raise his eyes towards the firmament, seeming to as it were draw power from it. But his gaze was that of a great general, whose sign millions of men and animals must obey. Although there was something immensely friendly in his countenance, there was yet an earnestness that my eyes have not beheld previously. I was only glad that he did not give me a solid stare. Truly, I admit I would not have been able to bear it. And yet I nevertheless felt irresistibly drawn to him with an inexplicable power, which I would not have been able to resist, had not Baram called him to breakfast.'

[4] Says **the young man**: 'What do you make of him after that? What could there be to him in all probability, and who and what could he be, according to your usually well-considered opinion?'

[5] Says **the old man**: 'I am indeed Greek, and in accordance with your saying, an idolatrous heathen, but I am in truth no more heathen than yourself, believing in one highest Being. But this wondrous man quite easily could persuade me of idolatry, because if he is not at least a demi-god, then I renounce my humanity.'

[6] Says **the young man**: 'I really am most anxious to see him. If only one could get into the house, then I would soon get acquainted with him. Just to trade words with such a man would be of the highest interest.'

[7] Even while the young Pharisee is saying so, I come out of the house and call to him, saying: 'Come, Ahab – Thomas of Toreh's son. If you hunger and thirst after truth, then you shall be filled.'

[8] Says **the young man**: 'Lord, we never saw each other, and to my knowledge you have never been to Jesaira. How can you know me and my father?'

[9] I say: 'Quite a lot of things yet do I know of you and your entire house, but

328

that would not be to the point here, but that you kept watch for me and risked much, that is of much worth before Me, and such your sacrifice shall not go unrewarded. Come.'

[10] Ahab quickly makes his way to Me through the crowd, and cannot get over how I can know all this.

[11] I say: 'Do not be overly astonished, for you shall be witness to things of quite another kind. It is good that you put the old ones at home to fright. They would disturb these people in their faith, without which it would be hard to help these many sick. Once these are healed, then they can by all means come to satisfy their money-bag conscience. Let you therefore stay here, and let them wait for you until I have finished. I know everything. You have indeed told them an immense lie, but God always forgives a sin for such a cause. Do you understand that?'

[12] Says **the young man**: 'I am indeed familiar with the law, and know that Moses said "Thou shall not bear false witness" – an exceedingly portentous commandment – which however none heed less than precisely my colleagues, because they say that false witness in favor of the Temple and its servants is well-pleasing to God, whereas God condemns a just witness against the Temple and its servants and such should be stoned.

[13] Nothing like that indeed is written in Moses, but the Temple servants say that the written word in the Book is dead, but that they are the living book, into which God daily writes His will through the angels. And we have therewith actually a completely new Bible which is the exact opposite of everything that Moses and the prophets taught.

[14] According to this new Temple Scripture therefore, the lie at the right time and for a good purpose, not only is allowed, but in certain cases commanded, especially for Temple benefits, because he who can lie the best and most stubbornly and demonstrably in the Temple's favor, counts for much.

[15] It may not be unknown to you that the Temple always is cleaned before feasts, with a lot of Temple dung and all kinds of unclean stuff accumulating. All of the dung – being too dry, containing too much soil and sand – is hardly worth the removal fee, but there are certain true dung-prophets. These go all over the country, selling the mire even by the minutest quantities, asking for a piece of silver the weight of an egg. The Temple-dung thus is the soul of the other varieties of dung, with which the gullible manure their fields, with actual conviction that without the Temple-dung, their fields shall not bring forth fruit, and even if bringing forth some, same shall forego God's blessing and therefore benefit no one.

[16] It happens that quite often, the dung-prophets get rid of the loads they scoop up at the Temple for sale in all areas quite quickly, whereupon they load their carts along the way with whatever street-dung, selling same as real Temple-dung, so that each of the hundred prophets of dung sells ten times more dung than they picked up at the Temple. See, here the initial sale amounts already to grossest deception, since the Temple-dung is sure to be vastly inferior to any other stable-dung, yet that's not enough. The blind and spell-bound people in the end must also purchase the street-dung for genuine Temple-dung.

[17] But never mind. Such deception being for the Temple's advantage, this not only is no sin but even virtue – and since well-pleasing to the Temple, thus naturally also to God. Ah, Moses.

[18] But let someone just dare tell the folk the truth about the Temple-dung effect, which is as good as none, even if only in respect of the second deception, with the street dung sold as Temple-dung, and he shall be cursed a sinner against the Temple, and then let him see how he gets away with it.

[19] And as with the dung, there are a hundred things that are nothing but lies and deception. Let someone expose it to the people, Lord, and Jehovah's grace and mercy be with him.

[20] That I lied to my old colleagues by fathoms I do not regard as sin, especially where, as is here the case, I can protect a man such as yourself from the hounding to which anyone in whom my colleagues sense a spark of insight and brighter intellect is subjected. But let you now do your thing with these sick or else the old buggers might get here before I call them.'

[21] Say I to Ahab: 'See, they already are healed. The blind see, the lame walk, the deaf hear, the dumb are speaking. And all who had been brought here suffering from any illness whatsoever are now vital and well. I shall now just tell them to go home, after which you can bring your colleagues here, after first telling them what you witnessed here.'

[22] After this I bid the healed to go home, warning them to make it known neither here and still less in Jerusalem, if ever they go there. They all promise Me to keep quiet about it, thanking Me with tears in their eyes.

[23] But I say again: 'Let you depart now. Your faith has helped you, but from now on let you not sin again, otherwise a second affliction shall be worse than the first.' Thereupon all who were healed depart, praising and glorifying God, who gave man such power.

[24] Says **Ahab** completely amazed: 'No, this has not been seen by human eye before – without rites, word or touch. No, this is powerful stuff. This is too much all at once for a man of limits like me. They actually all got fully well – no drugs, no prayer, no word or touch. Lord! Let me in on just a little of this capacity of yours.

[25] I said: 'This you cannot understand yet, but if you want to become My disciple, then you are bound to recognize and understand it. But now you can go and inform your colleagues if you wish.'

[26] Says **Ahab**: 'Yes, I shall go and tell it exactly the way they want to hear it. I shall strew their eyes with a desert storm, to blind them in the ultimate way, possessing a knack for that. They shall find out nothing about today.'

[27] I said: 'Good, good. Do as seems best to you. We are friends. Free yourself and then follow Me, and you shall find Truth and Life, and Truth shall make you free.'

# CHAPTER 183
## Ahab the Templer with his colleagues

[1] Ahab goes off, rushing over to his colleagues. Arriving there, **they all** besiege him, saying: 'For Temple's sake, what kept you? What we have been through because of you. Where are we? What's the magician doing? How did you fare? Are the soldiers on the way? We are in dire straits. Are you unaware of this?'

[2] Says **Ahab**: 'Why? What should I know about?'

[3] Say **the old ones**: 'Imagine, barely half an hour ago, three residents were here, Jews of this place, telling us that the entire Jesaira market city have one and all gone over to the Greeks, leaving us with nothing further to do here. What do you say to that? And listen, for all this we can thank this cursed magician, who is nothing but an apostle of Hell, harboring Beelzebub's spirit in his breast. Yes, what say you to this?'

[4] Says **Ahab**: 'If so then we are done for, and can start looking for an exit. I indeed heard a whisper yesterday, but could not work out the drift of it. But it serves us quite right. I have told you many times that the stupidity and darkness into which the Temple initiated us won't get us far with the wakeful Greeks, and that it is an easy matter for them to have us over the barrel. But this was pouring oil on the fire. Now that has come to pass which I kept working out for you by the fingers of one hand, and I can't see why you should now be surprised. I said to you often, let's not pull wool over the people's eyes, because there is a limit for everything in the world. What good will it do us to systematically confound the people into darkest fools. The stupidity will relapse into malice and we can then take to our heels, and that's it.

[5] The people placed great store by Moses and the prophets, yet we were saying, these are dead, and Scripture with them. God reveals His will in the Temple and indicates what to make of Moses and the prophets. It now is the High Priest's, the Levites' and the Pharisees and the Scribes who are the living Moses and Prophets. That is our doctrine.

[6] Only too clearly had I told you a hundred times that this presumption shall have dire consequences. But you laughed me off with this having no hope of a possibility. It is here now. Would you still call it impossible?

[7] But I say again: it serves us all absolutely right, because whoever does not accept advice on serious issues cannot be helped.

[8] Over at Baram's house I went to great lengths to calm down the stirred-up folk. I told the hotheads that soldiers shall shortly be arriving from Capernaum to discipline them. And they laughed, saying: "For these you shall do a little waiting, because your messenger is in our hands, as are all of you. See to it that you leave of your own accord, or you shall be moved by other means." That was the commendable response to my warning and threats of the people. It wasn't worth the bother.

[9] Concerning the magician however, he is in the clear on that score, for he together with his disciples and Baram might now be the only Jews in this place.

That he could be a magician I will not dispute, but I would not hazard to assert that he acts through Beelzebub, although I don't wish to dismiss your view completely. Go over now yourselves and talk to him, and be convinced of everything.'

[10] Ask **the old ones**: 'Has he healed the many sick yet?'

[11] Says **Ahab**: 'Could well be, although I did not notice. There still is a crowd of people of both sexes outside Baram's house, mainly familiar Greeks, talking with the really very plain magician, or whatever else he might be, but I saw no more sick people. Perhaps he healed them at the time I was keeping watch here for you. But as said, let's go over now, and you shall find out how matters stand.'

[12] Say **the old ones**: 'Is there no hazard to life.' Says **Ahab**: 'How foolish a question again. Can you say you are safe here? The way things have turned out against us, the open ground surely is an advantage, when we can use our legs rather than be knocked off behind four walls.'

[13] Say **the old ones**: 'You are quite right. Therefore let's go outside, and lock up our considerable treasures first.' Says **Ahab**: 'Very well, just let's get going. Who is about to rob us of our treasure? The people of this place now have quite different things to watch rather than our treasures.'

[14] After this the old rise, locking up everything and not telling even their servants what they are on about.


# CHAPTER 184
## The people against the Pharisees

[1] Getting over to Baram's house, they take in the big crowd, which is still quite shocked and perturbed at the great instant healing. Not having witnessed the great healing, the Pharisees are assuming **the people** to be still astonished at yesterday's healing of the possessed, as these continue to exclaim as they did yesterday: 'Glory be to David's Son! This truly is the Son of David!'

[2] Hearing this, **the old Pharisees** get annoyed, saying to the people: 'Why are you wondering all that much? We know better than you how this took place. He, this magician, drives out the devils by means no other than Beelzebub, the devil's chief, and you would praise him as David's Son.' Here some of the weaker became hesitant, asking the Pharisees to clarify this, and how this is possible. And whether the devils' chief can on occasion also accomplish godly deeds.

[3] Not bargaining for this question, the old foxes did not know how to reply. But since **the inquirers** sensed the Pharisees to be out of their depth, due to the long silence, they said: 'Why do you give us no advice upon our very reasonable question, that we might get to the bottom of how this purported magician drives out the devils, and how Beelzebub can work also godly deeds? It is relatively easy to accuse a person, regardless of exceptional procedures, to be a servant of the devil, thereby making him suspect, but it is quite another thing to provide proof. Why do you keep silent if you are sure of yourselves?'

[4] Say **the Pharisees**: 'We keep quiet because, enlightened by God's Spirit, we

are always aware of what man needs to know, and when therefore to speak. It is not because we should not know this, but because we must not and therefore don't want to give you verifiable proof. Your business is to just believe everything we teach and not to probe on your own, for God has placed us for this reason, to probe the innermost substance of all things, keeping secrets to ourselves and telling people only as much as is good for them. Do you understand us?'

[5] Say **the people**: 'O yeah, we have understood you quite well, and having understood you thus for a long time, we have, following such vivid understanding, gone over to the Greeks, with whom there is no such mystery-junk. There we have an Aristotle, a Pythagoras, a Plato, a Socrates, and these writings are clear and true. But with yourselves all is constantly wrapped in the deepest fog-night, to the extent of no visibility by even a span forward or backward.

[6] Why do you try to cast suspicion on this emissary Savior to us from God? He has done good to us and healed all our sick, and for this you denounce him a servant of Satan?

[7] What then are you, who have never yet done us a favor ever so small? When have you, with your inane devices or pretended prayer, healed anyone'

[8] Say **the Pharisees**: 'Have we perhaps no credentials?'

[9] Say **the people**: 'That you have, of course, from the Temple, and highly boastful ones at that, but where are the deeds, which according to your qualifications, you are supposed to be capable of performing? Of these, nothing has seen daylight yet.

[10] Yet this one came to us without credentials, but accomplishes deeds the like of which, one can quite properly say, man has not accomplished since the world's existence. We can see quite clearly as to why you want to make this godly human suspect to us, in spite of your refusal to tell us the reason. Listen, we take it upon ourselves to rub it into your noses, and the reason is the following:

[11] This divine human carries out deeds in all actual, wondrous reality, which according to your Temple credentials, you are supposed to be capable of. Yet up to date you have come up with no deed, for the 30 years you have been with us.

[12] How much of the best money and other costly things did you not obtain from us, so that you would act in our behalf? Where are the effects? You indeed took our gold and silver, but we received nothing but empty promises, which never were fulfilled. When we asked you when they shall be fulfilled, you pointed to the rich harvests and, praise god, our healthy herds. We however referred you to the even richer harvests and healthier herds of the Greeks, who are cursed by you seven times every Sabbath before sunrise. There you said: "This abundance is affected by Satan, and that the bread from such harvests and the meat from such herds serves not for life but damnation." But you nevertheless did not scorn the yearly tithes which the Greeks rendered you by way of all kinds of grain. Tell us therefore what you actually did with this wheat, blessed by Satan according to you?'

[13] **Say the Pharisees**, brimming with bitter fury by now: 'We sold it to heathens, such as the Romans and Greeks, for them to receive that much more damnation on judgment day!'

[14] Say **the people**: 'How very nice. It is said that the devil is stupid enough and his lies thick enough for grasping with the hand. Yet you are ten times more stupid. Your lies can be grasped with heavily shod feet. Was it not us who carted your sundry grains to the Jerusalem market, with our oxen and asses, and we surely will know to whom we sold it? And you have the hide to tell us that you sold the Greek grain to the heathens for their greater damnation. If you have to whitewash yourselves with lies, then lie more smartly and not make us even more stupid than yourselves, buying black for white and white for black without further ado. No, such lying-atrocity. Such has not been heard yet.'

[15] Say **the Pharisees**: 'You know nothing and understand nothing. Do you not know that a Pharisee is incapable of lying? For Temple-law states for all who are ordained into God's service that they are not able to lie even if they desired it, for in their mouth, even the thickest lie turns into the most luminescent Truth.'

[16] Here **the people** start laughing, saying jokingly: 'Indeed, indeed, we too are aware of the Temple-law you quoted, where it also is supposed to say: "Where a Pharisee puts excrement in his mouth, it instantly turns into gold."

## CHAPTER 185
### The Lord calms down the people

[1] With the Pharisees realizing that the people saw through them, and that they now were the subject of derision, they began to spawn thoughts of retribution. I therefore said to the people: 'Let them be, for they themselves are blind leaders of the blind, and where they come to a ditch with their charges, they fall into the ditch together with those they lead. In a land where they hold dominion as superiors, they can do you more harm than you can do them. But now you set them a trap, where they can easily fall in the ditch, more so than yourselves, for they bragged of having sold accursed grain to the Romans and Greeks for damnation. If you report this to the Roman chief, he will have them all over the barrel for it. But it ought in no way to come to that. But we intend retiring into the house for now, and I shall try to make also this spiritually totally bat-blind lot to see.'

[2] Following which I move into the house, and the Pharisees follow Me at once, and are inside greeted by My disciples. But behind them, a huge crowd followed as well, so that it came to a great crush inside the room. This however did not matter over-much, as I and the disciples still had plenty of room.

[3] When things quieted down inside the house, I opened My mouth and began to speak, mainly to the Pharisees, since I saw their evil thoughts only too well and clearly: 'That it has come to this with you, no one is to blame, other than yourselves. Have you not of a truth been with these people here in Jesaira these 30 years, yet not noticed their kind of spirit. Now it is, at this time, too late to again force the wakeful spirit of these people into sleep. Your anger is therefore a vain one, for you and no one else is responsible.

[4] I came here as an authentic Jew, and as such, truly in full possession of

334

God's Spirit and all its power.

[5] When I came to shore and you were enticed by the fire on the boat to rush to shore with the people. I healed the blind, dumb and possessed before your eyes. The people, instantly recognized the divine power in Me and greeted Me as David's Son. You yourselves internally recognized it the same way. Since however you deemed such recognition to set limitations upon yourselves, in everything, you asserted against your inner convictions: "Such deeds I carry out with the assistance of the devils' chief." Who was it you harmed therewith? See, no one other than yourselves.

[6] Had you only thought about this thing with greater openness, examining it more closely, you should have instantly seen the sheer absurdity of your assertion, recognizing therewith that with this most untimely and foolish assertion, you of necessity lost the last shred of integrity and faith from this awoken population.'

[7] Say **the Pharisees**: 'What then should we have done? Tell us, since you are so clever.'

[8] I said in a somewhat more somber tone: 'You should have thought, judged and spoken thus: "Every nation that is divided against itself, perishes, and every city, or household at odds with itself, cannot endure." This surely can be grasped with the hand.

[9] If I however, being a perfect Jew too, according to your assertion cast out devils through Beelzebub, then tell Me through whom actually do your children, who even now travel every country as saviors, healing the sick and casting out devils? I say unto you: your children too, and not only these people, shall be your judges.

[10] If I nevertheless, as clearly understood by this population, cast out the devils through God's Spirit, then the Kingdom indeed has come unto you, for which reason you, as Jews, should be particularly happy in front of the Greeks, who are heathens since this sign reestablishes the Jews' privilege which they had lost for already a long time. For only in this way can the authentic Jew show the whole world that he alone is the man upon this wide Earth who stands in manifest association with God, working deeds through the might of God's Spirit that are possible to no other man.

[11] When the outsiders see such in a Jew, they shall congregate around the mighty Jew by the thousands times thousands and say: "The Jew alone is of God. Through him works God's omnipotence most miraculously – he is powerful and wise, and shall be our lord forever."

[12] If then the true Jew ever shows himself thus strong, then his entire household and nation ought to be that strong. How could anyone then enter such a strong man's house to rob him of its contents? Be it that he first binds the strong one, which is impossible, and then robs the contents, as the Romans actually have done to us in our house, finding us drunk and asleep in our house, binding, robbing and making us slaves, which serves the Jews right, as they have departed from God completely.

[13] But God has mercy on His people, and again wants to help them,

wherefore I have been sent to you from God. Since however, as you can see for yourselves, this now obviously is the case, why do you scatter where I am gathering?

[14] For he who is not for Me is against Me, and he who does not gather with Me scatters and manifestly is against the Spirit of God, who wants to make you free.

[15] Wherefore I say unto you, after all that has already come over you: all sin and blasphemy shall be forgiven man, but never so the blasphemy against God's Spirit, for you knew quite well that I healed the possessed through God's Spirit, but for despicable worldly gain and honor you nevertheless blasphemed against God's Spirit in Me, wanting to save you. And thus you have received the deserved reward also from the heathens.'

[16] Say **the Pharisees**: 'We did not blaspheme God's Spirit, but only yourself, and you yourself surely are not with flesh and blood going to be the Spirit of God? For you are no more than ourselves, a son of man.'

[17] I said: 'Yes indeed, that I am by appearance, but in reality perhaps somewhat more. But if I am no more than a son of man like you, that does not excuse your blasphemy in the least. For I as a son of man surely am not working such deeds any more than you. But within this son of man standing before you, the Spirit of God alone is manifesting, and it is this One against whom you have blasphemed, for not I but God's Spirit has accomplished such before your eyes, and you blasphemed against it.

[18] Indeed, whosoever speaks against Me as a mere human, such shall be forgiven, but he who speaks against the Holy Spirit, such shall not be forgiven, neither here, nor in the beyond.

[19] Because where a tree is by its whole nature already bad, there the fruit also is bad, but if a tree is already by its nature good, its fruit also shall be good. By the fruits therefore the tree is recognized. You are the tree, and there, the Jews turned into heathens are your fruit. Judge for yourselves whether it is good or bad.'

## CHAPTER 186
### The different types of possession

[1] Say **the Pharisees**: 'This is not our fruit. This is the fruit of vagabonds such as yourself, who come from the whole world from time to time, in the shape of all kinds of artists and magicians. To our faces they indeed carry on this miserable trade, but comes night, and they turn into proselytes for heathen philosophy, having great persuasive powers for casting suspicion on us and the Temple, together with its God-given ordinances, to the most scandalous degree. See, such heathen-Jews as dwell here in Jesaira are then the fruit of such individuals. We have at all times spoken good and true, and taught them according to Moses, rightly and fairly. But if Beelzebub turns the people away from us through individuals like you, is this our fault? Wherefore it is not us who are the evil tree,

when Satan destroys and robs the fruit on our branches. Our teaching and speech is good, but your talk and deeds originate with the devils' chief, and seduce the gullible population. Therefore you ought to be stoned, together with your followers.'

[2] While the infuriated Pharisees spoke such words, the people began to murmur and betray intentions of laying hands on the Pharisees.

[3] But I said to the people: 'Let it be. It is enough that these evil ones are everlastingly defeated. This is why they should be spared for now. But they are now to receive My well-deserved testimony.'

[4] Say **the people**: 'Yes, Lord, we implore You to show these wretches who and what they actually are.'

[5] I now turn to the Pharisees again, saying in full earnest: 'O you generation of adders! How can you speak good, since in your hearts you are evil through and through? But with whatsoever the heart is filled, the mouth overflows. A good person at all times brings forth the good from the good treasure of his heart, but an evil person brings forth from his treasure. Yet I say unto you that men shall once be called to account for every evil and useless word they uttered, on the day of judgment. It will be as written in the book of Job: "For by thy words you will be justified, and by your word you will be condemned".

[6] I have showed you before why I came here and also to other places, but the evil sense in your heart cannot accept this, and still less grasp it, that you should become free and blessed.

[7] For all the good that I do you freely, you want to stone and kill Me. O you generation of adders, you brood of vipers! True indeed is every evil testimony the prophets foretold you, verily only too true: "With dead ceremony and mere lips you honor God, but your heart is far from Him."

[8] There were however **a few Pharisees** and Scribes among them whose heart was struck somewhat by My speech. These cut a somewhat human face, saying: 'Master, we cannot fully dismiss your teaching, but we were prevented yesterday and today from being witnesses of your wondrous deeds. Work another such sign, as we want very much to see one. (Mt.12,38) Perhaps this will suffice our intellect, and we could in the end embrace your doctrine ourselves.'

[9] But I turned to the people and spoke thus: 'This evil and adulterous generation looks for a sign. But no sign shall be given it, other than that given to the prophet Jonah once. (Mt.12.39) For just as Jonah was in the whale's belly 3 days and 3 nights, so likewise shall the Son of Man be in the middle of the Earth 3 days and 3 nights. (Mt.12,40) *(Note: Here, at the outset, middle of the Earth signifies the grave. Spiritually however it indicates that the soul of the Son of Man shall descend to the captive souls of the departed and there make them free).*

[10] Here **the Pharisees** looked at one another, saying: 'What's this, what will he do? How shall he get to the middle of the Earth? Where is that? Is this not everywhere and yet nowhere? Who can know how big the Earth is, and where its middle is? This person is insane, or an evil spirit is trying to get hold of him, for it is said that any man about to go insane, can work diverse wonders. How would he compare himself with Jonah, who preached at Nineveh?'

[11] Here I say again, as if to the people: 'Verily, verily, the men of Nineveh shall rise in judgment with this generation and shall condemn it, because they repented at the preaching of Jonah. And see, a greater one than Jonah is here. Likewise, the queen of the South shall appear in the beyond with this generation and shall condemn them. For she (Semiramis) came from the end of the Earth to hear the wisdom of Solomon, and see, here is more than Solomon.'

[12] Say **the Pharisees**: 'Very well then, since you believe we all are of the devil, and that we shall be condemned by one and all on judgment day then drive the devils out of us, as you did with the blind and dumb yesterday, and we shall then be as well able to praise you as the one healed by you.'

[13] But they did not speak thus out of a sincere desire to be rid of their many evil spirits, with which they already were fully at one, but only to make out some case against Me. Because once an evil spirit has made everything subject and subservient to himself within a man, he does not manifest in an obvious fashion, but acts in a clever and worldly way, so that none should believe such person to be possessed, notwithstanding that he is possessed more thoroughly than some other who is still being tormented by some spirit because not yet master in his house.'

[14] Therefore also I said to the Pharisees and Scribes: 'This can for several reasons no longer be effected in you, for the evil spirits have for a long time been completely at one with your soul and therefore fully comprise your very own evil and adulterous life. Were I to take them away, I should also remove your life with it. But were I to somehow still maintain your actual original life, this would still be of no use to you, for your entire nature now is of the devil through and through. Because even where through My power such unclean spirit departs from such people, he then wanders through arid regions, looking for rest and finding none, i.e. the devil seeks to tempt virtuous men and knocks, but he finds no admission, and these for him and his purposes are arid regions and deserts, where no herb grows for him. He then says to himself:"I shall return again to my old house, for in the steppes and deserts there is for me no place of rest, while in the dwellings already harboring the likes of me I shall find no admission." When resolved thus, the devil comes back to his former dwelling, and he of course finds it empty, swept and garnished. (Mt.12,44) Whereupon he withdraws, calling seven other spirits, who each are more wicked than he. With their help he then easily obtains access to his former dwelling, and all live in such house. And with such person, the last state then is much worse than the first.

[15] And this is how this generation would fare. Therefore it shall not be made more damnable through Me than it already is.

[16] On hearing such, the Pharisees are aglow with rage, and would have liked to tear Me to pieces but for fear of the people.

# CHAPTER 187
## Jew or Greek

[1] Ahab, the young Pharisee, however, stepped aside from the old ones, being happy that I said such truths to the old ones. But he asked Me in confidence whether he too is such a wickedly possessed one.

[2] But I said to him with friendly face: 'If you were so, you would not ask Me thus. You also have been an arid region for Satan so far. See to it nevertheless that you don't become a fertile field for him. Therefore beware of your evil colleagues.'

[3] Says **Ahab**: 'Lord and Master, if only You will not leave me, then the power of Hell is sure to have no effect on me. There shall be no lack of zeal on my part.'

[4] I said: 'Go over to them. Let you be strong through your faith and zeal for Me. But see to it that your colleagues don't drive you into a corner, for their devil has a fine nose, and sharp ears for their purposes.'

[5] Says **Ahab**: 'Lord, You are bound to know me better now than I do myself. My cunning is artful and clever. The devil however, it is said, is blind, and therefore they shall all see how I have them on the ice. I shall even today put them to the test. I shall now exchange a few sharp words with You, that they may not become aware of what I discussed with You, but You must not bear ill-will towards me for this.'

[6] I said: 'Do as you think fit, but be good, clever and truthful in all things, because a lie, regardless of how good a variety, helps only temporarily, and shortly thereafter gets men into disadvantage and harm.'

[7] Says **Ahab**: 'I am easy, and therefore shall say nothing for the present.'

[8] I said: 'That will be better. For to keep silence at the right time is better than a most resourceful lie.'

[9] With these instructions, Ahab makes his way back through the crowd to his colleagues, of whom one nevertheless had noticed his conversation with Me. This one at once started to sound him out. But Ahab stood his ground well, to the extent of finding himself praised by the would-be detective.

[10] But I turned away from the Pharisees and began to talk to the people. I showed them how it is not pleasing to God to abandon Judaism, because salvation comes to all men from the Jews, and that, as some had done already in their hearts, they should in all truth return to Judaism, or it is not otherwise possible to attain to the childhood of God.

[11] Says **one Greek**, asking: 'Are we therefore to once again bend our knees before the puffed-up Pharisees, eating their old, indigestible leaven? Friend, you of a truth are a grand master of the deity's might and authority, being good, wise and righteous, yet here you are asking something very odd of us. To Moses we have no need to return, as we have never left him in actuality, and in our hearts, the God of the Jews also is our God. The outward name of Jew and Greek surely shall not detract from God's wisdom? Yet to us it nevertheless is a bastion against unremitting hounding and goading by the Pharisees. Why should we again be

339

called Jews and Greeks?

[12] See, this is not a very clever demand of yours upon us. What does it matter that besides Moses, we familiarize ourselves also with the wise men of the Greeks, besides their richly poetic theosophy, whose wise parallel poetry surely is something quite different from the expensive Temple-manure? Particularly since we don't place much store by this, knowing only too well how the Greek and later Roman Gods came into being, and that Jehovah alone is God over everything, who has created all and maintains and guides everything.'

[13] I said: 'Friend, even though you speak, you have not understood Me, while those who understood Me are not saying anything, being Greek as much as yourself. There is of course not much in the name, but in the faith of the heart. But this also has to be taken into account: that it is better to make a pilgrimage to Jerusalem and to there with proper and intelligent devotion partake of the feasts, than to make a journey to Delphi to ask the foolish Pythia for advice.

[14] The immense Temple excesses verily are better known to Me than yourselves, and you heard how I am against them. But with all its evil, the Temple nevertheless is incomparably better than the one at Delphi, whose priests and priestesses are nothing more than fine dialecticians, knowing how to give just that answer to every question which always makes them right in the end.

[15] After you had at one stage decided to take a wife, you first made a trip to Delphi, and there for a lot of money asked Pythia whether you shall be happy with the woman you intended marrying. Tell Me, what was the answer?'

[16] Says **the Greek**: 'All right, thus, with the woman you shall be, not unhappy indeed.' And see, the oracle told me the truth, because I really am happy with my woman.'

[17] I said: 'See, the oracle would have been right even if you had been unhappy with your woman.'

[18] Says **the Greek**: 'I don't see how that is possible.' I said: 'Because you are spiritually blind. See, the sentence goes as follows: "With your woman you shall happy be, not unhappy indeed", but if you divide the sentence after the negation, then the oracle is right when you are unhappy, because then, without any alteration to the chain of words, the sentence would go: "With your woman you shall happy be not, unhappy indeed."

[19] If nevertheless you don't believe Me, then ask your neighbor, who a year later went to Delphi on similar business, and whether the answer he got is not the same to the dot. Yet he is very unhappy with his wife who is an immoral woman. Yet with him, the oracle is just as correct as with you, and yet you highly regard it. Judge for yourself what is better, the Temple at Jerusalem or the oracle of Delphi?'

[20] Here **the Greek** is wide-eyed, and says: 'Master, now everything is clear to me. This, only God and no man can know. You are either God Himself or a Son begotten of God, but not a son of man like us. Therefore we intend turning back to the Temple, although not under the Pharisees' rod, but freely. These Pharisees however must go, for they have too greatly deceived us, relieving us of nearly all our goods, both spiritually and materially. We therefore shall remain pro-forma Greeks, but in truth confessors of Moses and the prophets. We also shall go to

Jerusalem annually and visit the Temple. And if it is closed to us, then the hall of strangers remains open to us, which also is part of the Temple.'

[21] I said: 'Do as you think fit. Only protect your hearts against falsehood, anger, vengefulness and persecution. Let you be of chaste and pure predisposition. Love God truly above all and your neighbors as yourselves. Bless those who curse you, doing no harm to those who hate and persecute you. This way you will be pleasing to God, peaceful, gathering burning coals over your enemies' heads.'


## CHAPTER 188
### 'Who is My mother, who are My brothers?'

[1] While I yet spoke to the people, mother Mary arrived with My brothers, for she had found out at Kisjonah's house that I had gone and might be staying at Jesaira. It was half a day's journey on foot, and she was well capable of being in Jesaira at noon on Monday, having left home very early morning.

[2] Her concerns were on the one hand domestic, which she wanted to discuss with Me, while on the other hand they reached into the spiritual, for she had found out quite a few things about Me at Capernaum, about which she wanted especially to talk to Me. But due to the crush, she could not get into the house so that she had to wait outside till I came out.

[3] But because she had been waiting a long time in vain, she asked someone from Baram's house to tell Me she has been waiting outside for a lengthy period and needed to urgently talk to Me. So the messenger forced his way into My vicinity, saying: 'Master, see, your mother and brothers stand outside, wanting to speak to You.'

[4] Here I said to the messenger in an earnest tone: 'What are you saying? Who is My mother, and who My brothers?' Here the messenger drew back somewhat scared.

[5] But I raised My right hand over My disciples and said: 'See, these are My mother and My brothers. For he who does the will of My Father who is in Heaven, truly, those are My brother, My sister, My mother. But step outside and tell those tarrying that I shall come.'

[6] Some found this saying hard, reproaching Me and asking whether I am not aware of Moses' commandment regarding parents.

[7] I however rebuked them for such question, saying: 'I know who I am, and My disciples and My earthly mother also know, and therefore I can speak according to the truth. Let you therefore sweep before your own door diligently, for I know best what I must do.' All kept their silence after this and none dared say anything for or against it.

[8] After a period of silence, **Baram** the host stepped over to Me, saying: 'Lord and Master, noon is with us, and the meal is ready for You, Your disciples and Your earthly relatives, who are tarrying for You outside. Would You perhaps do

me, a poor sinner, the honor to partake of the ready meal?'

[9] I said: 'For today I actually had planned another meal, which I am going to consume at the sea, but since you have invited Me in such an honorable way, I intend granting you the honor and grace at the table. But this I shall also say, that none of the Pharisees is to come into the room where I shall dine, except for the young Ahab, whom I am taking up among My disciples. Because with his colleagues, who have become deeply suspicious of him as a result of seeing him speak with Me before, he shall no longer be able to get on. But let you now tell the people that I shall be saying and doing no more in this house, so that they would go outside and leave us room, because in this crowd it would be hard to make an exit in a natural way.'

[10] After these My words, **Baram** turns to the people, saying: 'Beloved neighbors, the godly Master has now finished speaking and shall not be saying and even less doing anything further in this house. Would you all except Ahab therefore oblige me by quietly stepping outside, because the Master would like to speak with him.' In response to these words all the people except the Pharisees move outdoors.

[11] When the people were gone, the old Pharisees furiously stepped over to Me and quite impudently demanded to know what I had in mind with Ahab, whether he too is going to be prepared by Me for Hell. On hearing such question, **Baram** is filled with justifiable anger and says to them: 'My taxes have I paid annually to the last farthing, and am therefore the lawful owner of this house built by myself, and will not tolerate any strangers like yourselves to molest in my very own house a guest I am honoring and hosting! I therefore command you to instantly leave this my house and remove yourselves beyond the boundary of my property, or I shall make immediate use of my owner's privileges.'

[12] Say **the Pharisees**: 'So you too have become a Greek now, threatening us with owner's rights? Should you not be aware of the fact that with the Jews, there are no owner's rights in the presence of a Pharisee? Is not every Pharisee the perfect lord in every Jewish house he enters, with the actual owner resuming his lordship upon the Pharisees' departure? Do you not know as well that as a Jew you are only a steward and no lord of your house, nor your grounds and that we can take grounds and house away from you whenever we please and rent it out to someone else for fifty years?

[13] Says **Baram**: 'This I have as a Jew indeed known to my immense anger. Therefore I am a Greek today, or more precisely a Roman, and in return for a given rate of taxation have procured for myself an irreversible property deed, of which I shall at once give you a taste if you don't immediately comply with my request.'

[14] Say **the Pharisees**: 'Show us the deed from the Roman court.' **Baram** pulls out a still well legible deed, stamped with the emperor's seal, holding it up before the old ones and asking: 'Do you know this?' They yell: 'So you too are a traitor to God, Temple and us?! For this we can thank this son of David? Therefore let you too be cursed together with your house.'

[15] As the Pharisees pronounce such curse, **Baram** quickly took a decent rod

and proceeded with all his strength to hit the Pharisees, exclaiming: 'Wait, you servants of Satan, I'll pay you the right wages for your curse!' Yells **one Pharisee** still out of range of the rod: 'It is written: "Let him beware who lays a hand on God's anointed." Says **Baram**: 'I know that quite well. That's why I used a rod!' And Baram lets also this "anointed" taste the rod. With this, the wicked Pharisees and scribes with the exception of Ahab, flee outside, where they are also served up by the people.

## CHAPTER 189
### Ahab warns against the Temple's revenge

[1] After these were gotten over the border, **Baram** returns, somewhat fatigued, saying: 'Lord, forgive me, I truly find no pleasure in what I just did, but this evil and adulterous lot became intolerable. One cannot of a truth imagine Satan to be more wicked than these fellows, who earnestly think the entire Earth to be their property already. But this would not have upset me personally overmuch yet, but when these fellows started to properly confront you I could no longer suppress my just anger and had to make use of my owner's rights. But do not let it trouble you, for should these fellows lodge a complaint, I shall know how to handle my defense, and how to vindicate you wisely and cleverly.'

[2] Says **Ahab**: 'Friend, there is no harm in you taking the necessary precautions, because these old buggers shall now have nothing more urgent to do than report this incident in the worst possible light. Firstly, their most unfavorable prospects by virtue of the works of this godly Master, together with the total apostasy of all Jesaira from Judaism, together with my own behavior, and secondly to Herod, and how he has lost all his subjects through their purchase of Roman citizenship. This shall awaken all evil spirits of Jerusalem, with probably quite sinister repercussions for this place. Therefore let you take precautions and assure yourself of imperial assistance, or these evil spirits shall play up wickedly with you.'

[3] I said: 'Ahab, let it be. That nothing will befall Baram's house I vouch for you, but that the old inhuman ones shall do as said by you is the truth, yet neither Baram nor yourself need to trouble yourselves. But now let us go to the meal, where I also intend hearing Mary and Joseph's sons.'

[4] Says **Baram**, surprised at the mention of Joseph's name: 'What, my master at Nazareth, whom I owe so many thanks? He was in those days still a young man, yet already a master of his craft when I was his apprentice. With what patience and lovingness he showed me all the high points of his craft, and then bringing me all the best work, supporting me with advice and deed without fee. This truly I shall never forget.'

[5] I said: 'Well, Mary is his second wife, becoming his through the Temple. The two men with her however being Joseph's sons by his first wife, now carrying on their father's craft. I Myself however physically am Mary's son, My name being

Jesus.'

[6] Says **Baram**: 'O, how fortunate for me, that my house should meet with such honor and grace. But let us now quickly attend to the tables, to avoid undue waiting on the part of the glorious mother and Joseph's two sons'. We at once move to the dining room, where Mary with Joseph's two sons await us.

[7] On seeing Me, Mary burst into tears of joy, for she had not seen Me now close on 2 months, as also the two brothers, who loved Me exceedingly. After we all exchanged heartfelt greetings, we all started toward the tables, saying our thanks and then consuming the good and abundant meal, shared by Kisjonah, who with his wife and daughters still had not left Me, and who had much to talk about with Mary and the two brothers.

[8] After the meal, sitting at the table and drinking watered down wine on account of the heat, Ahab asked to speak, for he had an important disclosure to make, especially concerning My security, for he had only during the conversation established that I am that Jesus of Nazareth, highly esteemed by the people, but held in contempt by the Pharisees, yet of unprecedented renown throughout the land. I say to him: 'Say what you know.'

[9] Speaks **Ahab**: 'Lord and Master, You of a truth resurrected our chief Jairus' daughter from the dead – the entire region knows this – as also about the daughter of a Roman centurion. whoever would even in the least doubt that even the most terrible and cruel tyrant would show everlasting gratitude for such wondrous deed, and make way to the right of his throne for the miracle worker, as did Pharaoh with Joseph once, after the latter's prophecy.

[10] What however does this Temple-brood do, these true Satan-servants? They brought out a report, which I myself too was obliged to sign, although I had not at that time either heard about any of Jesus' teaching nor seen any of His deeds. In accord with this report all kinds of spies and assassins have been sent out by the Temple as well as Herod and the Roman governor, for the purpose of getting rid of You.

[11] In this report You are denounced to Jerusalem as a deceiver of the people, a seducer and agitator, in a way no man had been denounced before. Jairus' daughter was not supposed to have been dead at all when You were called to heal or resurrect her, but that she was perfectly well, but made to act to test You. On going and saying to her: "Talitha Kumi", the chief realized that You are a deceiver, having no real knowledge of healing, for were You as a Savior capable of assessing a person and their sickness, You would have known at first glance not only that the maiden was not dead, but on the contrary bursting with health.

[12] The Roman chief, named Cornelius I think, whose servant or daughter You are supposed to have resurrected from death, takes exception to this, but what is he against such mass of false testimonies.

[13] Beloved, dearest friend, Master and Lord, I could tell You a lot still, but I can see that my account has saddened You. As this slandering of You is too despicably devilish, I shall be silent about the rest. It is enough that I told you the main part. The only good thing about it is that Satan is stupid and easily excelled by the truly wise and clever. What should be that much easier for You on account

of Your exceeding wisdom. Let it be left at that.

[14] Although I am quite a simple man myself, I nevertheless quite easily can twist these buggers around each of my fingers, and don't consider it a sin to have Satan heftily run up against the wall. This lets him depart from the place of conflict for a while, tail between legs, and a wise and clever man's spirit gains time for something more uplifting than the constant tussle with Satan.'

## CHAPTER 190
### Sermon on the Kingdom of Heaven

[1] Mary now says: 'My Lord and Son, what this young man told You just now is strictly true, and it is my being driven from my house on Your account that has caused me to come and tell You. What am I to do now, with Your brothers and sisters, speaking terrestrially of course? For I know that You have no relatives on Earth, other than the disciples, at heart.

[2] Our little lot is gone. The wicked Pharisees have seized hold of it and have sold our hut together with the well-tended garden to strangers. Know that I and Your brothers and sisters are no longer young enough to do strenuous labor for a living. And even if we tried, these evil Temple autocrats have threatened to punish any Jews that were to give us work or even alms. What are we to do and where to live from now?'

[3] Says both **Baram and Kisjonah**: 'Highly esteemed mother through whom God has shown the endless grace of bringing the most exalted Son of all Heavens into this evil world, do not let this trouble you in the least. See, we firstly are no longer Jews from the civil aspect, but Greeks – outwardly, although fully Jews according to Moses by conscience. We both are – all praise to the Lord – wealthy. Therefore let you move in with all your relatives, and you shall be lacking in nothing.'

[4] I said: 'Friends, your offer is balm poured in My heart. My blessing and grace shall be with you forever. But I shall nonetheless presently go home, to see by what right these wicked ones have robbed the mother – the rightful wife of Joseph, of their small and well earned property.

[5] And I shall then also trade a few words with Jairus, for his daughter is to once again fall sick, and he shall come to Me, after which I shall speak to him. But for now, since matters indeed stand thus, with the infernal brood having laid traps everywhere, we shall arise and take to the sea, which has set us no trap.

[6] But I shall in the first instance from the sea reveal a few things about the Kingdom of Heaven to the people through images, so that none should once be able to find excuses and say: "How should have believed and kept it, since I never heard anything about it?" When the old wicked ones arrive, let the people not obstruct them, so that they shall once have that much less to excuse themselves with.

[7] Let you friend Kisjonah however go and make ready your big ship, for we

345

shall be much in need of it.' Kisjonah rises with his and goes to attend to My wish.

[8] Baram however asks for permission to accompany Me, since I am not able, or minded to stay at his home.

[9] And I say: 'As far and as long as you have a mind to. For no honest or just request has ever been rejected or left unheard on My part.' Baram therefore makes domestic arrangements with his wife and children, including on how to respond to the evil persecutors. Taking some gold with him, he then comes over to the sea with us, even as we also are tailed by an outsize crowd.

[10] Nor are the old evil Pharisees missing, but in disguise, to avoid being recognized by the people. Arriving at the shore to the people's exclamations of: "Hail to David's Son" – the crowd swelled to where I and My relatives could not retain a foothold, and the much multiplied disciples even less.

[11] I therefore said to Kisjonah: 'Let the half-landing be dropped, for we must go out to sea, the land is getting scarce.' Kisjonah quickly dropped the landing, and we boarded the ship. On seeing Me board ship the people thought I was departing and loudly pleaded with Me to let them have the promised teaching on the Kingdom of Heaven.

## CHAPTER 191
### The parable of the sower

[1] When we all were aboard ship and the landing retracted, I asked the people to calm down and to search for a place at the shore. And the people did so, with the only exception being the old Pharisees, who did not settle down but stood close, near their ship, for they were determined to not let Me out of their sight again, and were therefore ready to also follow us at sea.

[2] But I took a seat on the spacious deck and began to speak a few things to the people in parables, so that the stupid Pharisees would not understand it. The people however, of a more wakeful spirit over here, on the whole understood Me quite well.

[3] To begin with, I compared Myself to a sower, saying: 'See, a sower went out to sow good and wholesome grain. And as he sowed, some seed fell upon the wayside, and the birds came and devoured it. Some fell on stony ground, with little soil and sprouted quickly, not having depth or weight of soil over it, but when the sun came up glowing with many beams, the sprouts that sprang up in the cool and moist of night, withered and dried, being without roots. Some fell among thorns, and these, with their more abundant growth choked them. And some fell on good soil, bearing fruit, some a hundredfold, some sixtyfold and some thirtyfold. He who has ears, let him hear.'

[4] Here I was about to carry on without a break, but **some of the disciples**, not understanding these parables themselves, stepped up to Me and said: 'Why do you suddenly now speak to them in parables? Those of us who have been around You for quite some time now, hardly can understand them? Do you not see how

they are shrugging their shoulders, some even thinking that You are either having them on, or speak of indifferent things on account of the Pharisees, and that everybody knows that grain should not be sown along the wayside or upon stony ground or upon thorns. We do indeed grasp what You are getting at, but those on the shore really think You are having them on. Or can You be seriously instructing them in a way not comprehensible to them?'

[5] Say I to the disciple: 'What are you saying and interrupting Me? I know why I speak to those people in parables which they are not to understand. To you it is given to understand the mysteries of the Kingdom of God, but to these it is not given. For it is thus: he who has, to him it is given, that he may have in fullness. But he who has not, from him shall be taken what he has. For which reason I as Lord speak to them in parables. For, having eyes, they see not and having ears, they hear not, for they do not understand it.

[6] All the things I have worked here. And for what do they take Me? They all are blind and deaf. A parable for them you saw yesterday, with the blind and mute. As was he in body, so are they in their soul. This is why I speak to them in parables, that it may be fulfilled what Isaiah prophesied: "With the ears you shall hear yet not understand, and with seeing eyes you shall see and yet perceive nothing.

[7] For this people's heart is obstinate and their ears dull and their eyes slumbering, lest with their eyes they might see, with the ears hear and with their heart understand and be converted, and I could help them.

[8] But blessed are your eyes for seeing this, and your ears for hearing it. For verily, I say unto you: many prophets and righteous men desired to see and hear what you see and hear, yet did not see or hear it.

[9] But I have said, that, unto you it is given to understand the mystery of the Kingdom of God. Yet I perceive that, basically, your understanding is not much better than those on the shore. Then hear and listen as to how the parable of the sower has to be understood:

[10] If anyone hears the Word of the Kingdom of God that I speak but does not understand it in his heart, which with its worldliness is trodden smooth as a roadway, then the wicked one soon sees the Word not fallen in the Earth but unto the trodden world-smooth outer and exposed surface of the heart, easily plucking off what actually is sown in the heart, yet clinging to the world-smooth outer surface. And see, such man is like unto a wayside unto which the grain i.e. My Word, has fallen. And of this variety there are many standing at the shore.

[11] But the following is a case of the seed falling on stony ground: where a person hears the Word, receiving it with much joy. But, because like a stone, such man has little life-moisture or proper stoutness of heart, and too little soil, or firmness of will, in or above himself, being like the stone dependent upon the weather, whether it be moist or dry, and therefore changeable, then such person, when on account of My Word he comes to be tried by all kinds of tribulations and persecution, turns full of anger and fury, resembling the sun-heated stone, upon which of course My word cannot take root, in the end having to wither away.

[12] And see, there upon the shore stand many such stones, who indeed now are offended in Me on account of the Pharisees, but then seeing My Words

directed to them being immediately followed by all sorts of tribulation and persecution, they deaden the Word in their heart by, on the one hand being too much offended, and too fearful on the other. For in spite of all the signs they saw and all My living assurances that I can adequately protect them against all kinds of trouble, they still don't believe and therefore resemble the stone upon which the seed fell.

[13] But the falling of the seed among thorns signifies the following: where a person hears the Word and even accepts it, but is immersed in all kinds of worldly business, and worries associated therewith on account of deceitful gain and even more deceitful riches. Such trivial worries accumulate by the day, richly proliferating in the heart like all weeds, to but easily smother My sowed Word.

[14] And again see, of such there stand many at the shore, resembling the thorns among which the seed fell.

[15] And the following is the seed sown into good soil, where a person hears My Word, receiving it into the depth of his heart, where alone it is at all times understood validly, rightly and animatedly. Such man then is such good ground into which the seed falls and, depending on man's will and strength, brings forth the fruit of good works a hundredfold, sixtyfold or thirtyfold. And a hundredfold is when he does all for Me, sixtyfold where he does much for Me and thirtyfold where he does a good portion for Me.

[16] By analogy, there are in My Kingdom 3 Heavens. The first for the hundredfold fruit, the one below it for the sixtyfold and the lowermost for the thirtyfold. Lower than the thirty receives no consideration, and he who has less than thirty shall have it taken from him and added to him who has thirty, sixty or a hundred. And it shall thus be taken from him who has nothing and added to him who already has, that he may have in all fullness.'

[17] Say **all**: 'Yes, Lord and Master, for Your wisdom exceeds all our ever so great and presumably wise thoughts. Therefore we ask You to continue speaking thus.'

## CHAPTER 192
### The parables of the tares among the wheat, and the mustard seed

[1] I now however speak loudly enough for those standing upon the shore to hear: 'Now then, he who has ears, let him hear, and he who has eyes – in the heart, let Me emphasize – let him see! I want to give you another parable on the Kingdom of God: listen!

[2] The Kingdom of Heaven also is like unto a man who sowed good seed upon his ground. But while his servants slept, the owner's adversary came, casting sheer weeds among the wheat, which then sprang up with the wheat. Wherever the wheat came up with its fruit, there the weeds also came up.

[3] When the servants saw this they came to the landlord and said, "Lord, did you not cast prime wheat upon the field? Wherefrom came the weeds?"

[4] The landlord however spoke, saying: "This my enemy has done." And the servants replied: "Lord, shall we go and weed it out?" And the lord said: "Let it be, so that you would not trample and pull out the wheat with the weed. Let them both grow together till harvest. At harvest time I shall say to the cutters: "Gather up the tares into bundles first and remove them from the field to a place for burning, but afterwards gather the clean wheat into my barns." See, this is an appropriate parable of the Kingdom of Heaven. But hear Me further. I want to give you more parables, which all depict the Kingdom of God. Therefore listen:

[5] The Kingdom of Heaven is like unto a mustard seed which a man took and cast into his field. This seed of a truth is known to be among the smallest among the seeds. But when it grows it is the biggest among the herbs, and finally a very tree, so that even the birds of the air come to build their nest among its branches.'

[6] Here **the disciples** looked at each wide eyed, saying: 'What's this, who can grasp this? Now the Kingdom of Heaven looks like a mustard seed?'

[7] I said: 'Wonder not but listen further. Yet another parable I want to give you on the Kingdom of God.

[8] The Kingdom of Heaven also resembles leaven, which a woman took and mixed into three measures of wheaten flour, until all was leavened.'

[9] All the disciples as well as the 12 wakeful **apostles** once again looked at one another, saying among themselves: 'Who can grasp and understand this? Or does He want to have the people on, because of the Pharisees? It is impossible to understand why He now talks in these most muddled images?'

[10] **Ahab** however, who was exceedingly well-versed in Scripture, overhearing the disciples talk, said to them: 'If this One is what I now firmly believe Him to be, then the following prophecy of Isaiah would probably apply to Him, which speaks about Him constantly, speaking in parables: *'I will open My mouth in parables. I will utter things which have been kept secret from the foundation of the world.'*

[11] See, thus spoke once the great prophet, and so sang David once in his Psalm 78, verse 2, and this, besides a lot of other things, exactly applies to Him. And despite of this, you can still ask: "how so" and "what does it mean?" being with and around Him for a considerable time now. He shall, if necessary, reveal these parables to us indeed. And if not necessary, well, then we can still boast that we are ourselves able to see and hear, what all the patriarchs and prophets would have much liked to see and hear.'

[12] All the disciples are quite happy with this interpretation. The people however, now that I kept silent during Ahab's talk, asked Me whether I am going to say more of such inconceivable things or whether they should go about their business – they who were waiting at the shore for a good teaching but which did not come.

[13] But I said: 'Let you return home, for it was not for you that I opened My mouth, knowing full well your uncomprehending heart. Wherefore also your children once shall be your masters and judges.' Therewith all the people soon departed from the shore, and each went to their dwelling.

[14] Only the Pharisees, noticing that Kisjonah was getting his boat ready, soon boarded their ship, held in readiness, and took to their oars ahead of us. But

secretly, My will was that they should be seized by a strong wind. And see, a mighty wind soon began driving their boat, completely covering it with waves time after time.

## CHAPTER 193
### The Lord stills the sea

[1] We however took off from Jesaira in a totally different direction and it was necessary that we too had to be overtaken by a great storm on the high sea, whereupon the disciples together with all on board were gripped by much fear, as once before, starting to scream with fear for My help, or all should perish.

[2] And as once before, I commanded the wind and the sea, whereupon immediate calm of wind and sea set in, with **all the people** in the boat exclaiming: 'Who is He whom wind and sea obey?'

[3] **Ahab** however, who had not chimed in with this question, said to the disciples and a few others: 'Friends, this once again was a most untimely and foolish amazement. You surely have been such a long time with and around Him, and still can be as amazed as if this were His first sign that you saw Him work. I have been hardly one day among you, and yet all this is as comprehensible to me as anything can be to a man. If He is that, namely the great promised Messiah, who according to David is neither more nor less than Jehovah Himself, acting through flesh and blood, then it should be easy for Him to terminate a sea storm, since it would hardly have been difficult for Him to create the whole world. If such is indisputably the case, and you know Him, how does such question and astonishment arise in your heart?'

[4] Says **Judas**, somewhat indignant at Ahab's comments: 'Friend, should we no longer be astonished at what the Lord does before our eyes, just because we have seen this and much else of His?'

[5] Says **Ahab**: 'Brother, such be far from us. But I look at it this way: we should indeed be amazed in all meekness of heart that He should work such before our eyes, and that He should consider us not so worthy beings worthy enough of His love, wisdom and power, and for working such deeds before our eyes and senses. I for myself at least do not consider myself worthy of the least of this. But since we know who He is and then wonder that He who has made Heaven and Earth should work extraordinary deeds, as if this had been done by a mere man, then in the end we would consider Him, the Lord, as no more than some other, albeit extraordinary human. And in this context I consider your astonishment, ensuing upon the sudden stilling of the storm, as somewhat out of place.

[6] Would it not be ridiculous to also start wondering at sun, moon, stars and Earth and all the most wonderfully equipped and shaped creatures, which surely are as much His work as the extraordinary stilling of this powerful storm upon the sea? If however we have to wonder, then let us wonder only at how the unspeakable almighty God Jehovah lowers Himself so endlessly as to come to us

350

mortal and exceedingly weak mankind from His eternal, immeasurable heights, which should be almost unbelievable if not already prophesied since Adam, Henoch and all the prophets right down to Zacharias and his son John, as is now happening in the fullness of truth.

[7] The greatest wonder, it seems to me, is that, as prophesied by hundreds of prophets with one accord, all this is here now. What is now taking place is but a natural consequence of the prior and most wonderful manifestation upon this Earth, namely: the aforementioned appearance of Jehovah in the flesh and blood.'

[8] Say even **the 12 disciples** to me: 'Lord, wherefrom this one's speech and lucid wisdom?'

[9] Said I: 'It is not his flesh and blood inspiring him, but his most wakeful spirit, so that it won't take much to the full rebirth of his spirit. It does not do you much honor however that he is a teacher to you rather than you to him, but his advantage over you is his being deeply versed in Scripture, and I love him as I love you, there being much meekness in his heart.'


## CHAPTER 194
### Man's spiritual house

And now **the disciples** at the water's edge ask Me: 'Where, o Lord, shall we be going now?' I said: 'We shall head straight for home.' The disciples replied: 'Lord, there we shall not fare too well. For have not the Pharisees taken everything away from Your earthly mother of Your body. And so home in our opinion is in a somewhat sad state, even though we know that everywhere is home to You, and You therefore are at home.'

[2] Said I: 'You ought to by now be more versed in the language of the spirit. If I say that we are heading straight for home, do I want to go to Nazareth? Understand, for once. When I speak of going home, I mean man's interior, which is man's true gathering point of life, strength, power and all wisdom. There we therefore are going. We are in need of inner, spiritual rest, and this is a proper home. Within it – not on My but your account, we shall find what the outer flesh and blood is in need of. Do you understand that?'

[3] Say **the disciples**: 'Yes Lord, now we understand it.'

[4] I said: 'Terrestrially however we are going to Kisjonah again. In his home we are safe, because this is a free house, and it pays a large tribute for this to the emperor, and the Pharisees shall be kept away. But a few days thereafter we shall indeed be going to the terrestrial fatherland, and shall attempt to make straight what has become exceedingly crooked.'

[5] Says **Kisjonah**: 'Lord, I would that it were Your pleasure for not just a few days, but preferably, that You stay at my, or rather in all truth, exclusively Your house, together with all Yours, for a few moons (months), or at least a few weeks, because in Nazareth You shall, unless You let fire and brimstone rain from the sky, find little or no reception, especially with the Scribes and Pharisees, who are

increasingly after Your life.'

[6] I answer him: 'Friend, banish such cares, for I can only be got at or harmed to the extent that the Father who is within Me as I am within Him allows it. And all the things that will be allowed for the salvation of mankind and the fulfillment of Scripture I have already known in advance for an eternity. All the prophets would never have been able to prophesy this without My knowing it in advance. For the same Spirit now dwelling in all fullness within Me and speaking to you has also spoken to the prophets what you read in the Scripture. Since now the same Spirit is personally here, He must also fulfill what He has prophesied of Himself through the prophets. You should not worry about it. For this almighty Spirit will surely know how to help Himself.'

[7] **Kisjonah**, understanding Me, keeps silent. Then, after a while, beating his breast three times, he says: 'I am not actually worthy of Your sheltering under my roof, but show me poor sinner grace and mercy nevertheless, and stay a few days for my comfort.'

[8] I said: 'Feel at ease nevertheless. Because for as long as I have work to do on this Earth, I shall stay with you, together with all who are with Me, for your house shall be My house of rest. But I shall nevertheless have to frequently leave it on account of My work, but I shall never leave it spiritually' (laying My hands on Kisjonah's heart).

## CHAPTER 195
### Reunion with Jairuth and Jonael

[1] By the time we spoke thus, we hit shore, and that at the very landing place of Kisjonah's from where, through a big and beautiful garden, one could get to Kisjonah's spacious buildings and dwellings, within which everything had been readied for our reception. Because I had already secretly notified Kisjonah at Baram's house that I shall be returning to his place, whereupon he at once sent home a small conveyance of messengers with instructions.

[2] And who did we run into there? Jairuth, the wealthy merchant of Sychar, who owned and occupied Esau's old castle. And Jonael, the high priest of the same place with whom we have been acquainted. Both were escorted there by the angel who was with Jairuth, for they had worthy things to discuss with Me. And so this indeed was a pleasant surprise of a celestial nature.

[3] These two, touched to the core with fervent joy on seeing Me, were not able to utter a word. Deeply moved, they greeted Me with placing their quivering hands on their chests with all the love of their hearts.

[4] But I said to them: 'My cherished friends and brethren. Save yourselves the effort of your tongue, for the language of your hearts means more to Me than a thousand ever so beautiful words spoken by the tongue, of which the heart is often only marginally conscious.

[5] First recover from your long and arduous journey. Only then do I intend to tell

you, My Jonael, what you shall need to do at home against the High priest appointed by the arch-Samaritans in addition to yourself for officiating in the trivial and blind ministry at Gerizim. But, as said, you have need of first resting and recovering, so first take to rest and recovery.

[6] You, My brother Kisjonah, bring them refreshment, availing yourself of the servant who escorted the two friends from Sychar, for this one is not tired, and he shall give you speedy and good services, and is an initiate to your household as if a senior servant to you of many years. Therefore let you avail yourself of him untroubled, letting also your weary people rest a while. The day is indeed coming to an end, yet it shall not be retarding your household if the weary ones retire a little earlier than usual, for this servant shall adequately substitute for them all.

[7] Says **Kisjonah**: 'That all things are possible to You o Lord, of this I am vividly convinced, and of a faith quite like unto Ahab's our young Pharisee, but how this delicate boy rather than youth, can not only carry out the many tasks still remaining, then serve us, several hundreds, as well, this o Lord, although not doubting in the least, nevertheless baffles me exceedingly.'

[8] I say: 'Friend, at home you are short of milk, cheese and butter, whereas you have an abundant supply on your alps. Let all your supplies first be brought down from the alp pastures by this servant. It serves you better if your supply is here rather than in the mountains, which shall be skimmed by a horde of wild Scythians overnight to spy them out for robbery.'

[9] Says **Kisjonah**: 'Ah, I am catching on. This boy is probably one like those three who served us in the alps?' I said: 'Well yes, only ask and speculate no more, or it shall be too late.'

[10] Kisjonah quickly moves over to the youth to ask him amicably. Says **the youth**: 'Let you not be troubled, dear friend of my Lord and God. It shall all be fixed in a few moments, because with me, here, there or anywhere is all the same, and although I am one of the feeblest, the entire Earth has to shake under the power of my feet.'

[11] Kisjonah was exceedingly astonished at such talk, being unable to imagine such possibility and in his amazement hardly noticed that with these words, the youth had left the room to attend to his errand.

[12] Kisjonah however, had not yet done with astonishment, and was about to ask Me how such were possible, when **the youth** already stood before him supple, saying with a smile: 'Well now, you are still pondering over how such is possible, and see, I already have it under control. Even that which your scribes did not manage to record at the busy tolls today, notwithstanding their laboriousness, I managed to fill in, so that now they have leisure and are un-engaged.'

[13] **Kisjonah**, confounded, not knowing what to make of it, says full of astonishment: 'But, my cherished friend, you have hardly left the room, but are supposed to have already accomplished what would take all my people together, with all their diligence, a whole week. This seems just a shade unbelievable to me. You would need to have a thousand hands and the speed of lightning.'

[14] Says **the youth**: 'Well, then go out and be convinced.'

## CHAPTER 196
### The power of the angel

[1] **Kisjonah** goes to the larder and finds the neatly arranged supplies of milk, cheese and butter in their respective places, then goes to the barns, finding them full, for even the ripened harvest of the field had been brought in. He then goes to the great stables for cattle, sheep as well as donkeys, finding everything properly attended. From there he goes to his big office building, checks the books and finds everything in proper order, checking the tills and finding them all full. He rushes to the large kitchen and there finds everything fixed up by the right quantity and selections, fully cooked, asking **the men and women cooks** how this may have taken place. These can tell him only: 'A beautiful youth came into the kitchen, saying: "Place the foods in the bowls as they are already well prepared." We checked the foods and it was as the youth said, who immediately left us. Taste them, and you shall see it is so.'

[2] Sampling the foods, Kisjonah finds the cooks are telling the truth. He quickly betakes himself back to the big room where I was, and **the youth** asks him: 'Now, are you happy with me Kisjonah?'

[3] Says **Kisjonah**: 'Much of the supernatural has indeed already taken place in my house, for which I could not account other than say, with God all things are possible. Yet this nevertheless is the most incredible so far. To carry out in a moment a task that could have taken a solid day's work, that as said, through a man filled with God's spirit is understandable. But that a hundred tasks in widely separated locations can be simultaneously carried out by one human being in just one moment is a completely different thing, and to a mortal is entirely beyond grasp or intellectual acumen, and I can only once again say, Lord, have mercy upon me, a poor sinner, for never shall I be worthy of Your living under my roof.'

[4] Say I to Kisjonah: 'Let you now cease your astonishment and have your people bring in the foods, for we are all now in need of the same.

[5] But if you are already so much taken aback with this, what will you say if I tell you that, of a truth, on the entire Earth, only one angel is assigned the task of caring and acting upon all the grass, shrubbery and trees for the bringing forth of all the most diverse fruits, as well as take care of all the animals of the sea, air and upon the land? This also you cannot understand, and yet see, so it is and so it happens. Therefore do not be astonished unduly, but go and let the foods be brought in through your servants.'

[6] Says **Kisjonah**: 'Lord, my only love and life, what if You were to permit this wonderful youth to assist me with getting the large quantities of food in here, since it is bound to take my servants a full hour?'

[7] I said: 'Just so, avail yourself of him. Only cut out the excessive amazement, for you know that with God all things are quite easily possible.'

[8] Kisjonah is fully satisfied with such advice and implores the amicably beaming youth to assist in getting the foods from the kitchen unto the set tables.

[9] Says **the youth**: 'But without all that astonishment dearest friend. Just take a look at the tables. It already took place while you were still contemplating asking the Lord of all glory for my assistance. But where do you have your wine?'

[10] Says **Kisjonah**, casually mustering the tables and secretly amazed: 'Verily, we nearly forgot the wine. Would you be so good and get it from the cellar?'

[11] Says **the youth**: 'Take a look, once again it is taken care of. The wine is on the table with the foods in the right quantity.'

[12] Kisjonah eyes the 40 large tables set in the big dining room, and nothing is lacking. Chairs and benches are in the most beautiful order, and the lamps, for lighting up at dusk, provided in right number on all the tables, already are burning with clean flames.

[13] On seeing all this, **Kisjonah**, inwardly stunned, says after a while: 'O God, O God, You my Jesus, my love eternal. If this is kept up, then all my dwellings shall come apart yet today, and all wood and stone therein shall come alive'. And turning to **the youth**: 'My fairest young man, human or angel – whatever you might be – tell me just a little of how this is possible to you.'

[14] Says **the youth**: 'You are indeed inquisitive. I tell you that nothing is possible to me without Him who now dwells with you in this house. He alone carries out all these things. But on how this is possible to Him, you shall have to seek His advice, for the power within me to act thus is not my possession but the Lord's possession, who right now is taking abode at your dwelling. Therefore go and ask Him.'

[15] Says **Kisjonah**: 'That, dearest friend, I do know indeed. Only the ways and means on how this is possible, that is where I would like a hint. Surely you need motion? But how speedy and sure this must be. For compared to this, lightning itself is a snail's pace. Ah, ah, I must think no more about it. If only you had needed at least a hundred moments for all this, then the thing would still be understandable, but like this – without discernible span of time – and in best order at that, this is what yanks me right out of my usual thinking mode, so that I hardly dare to breathe for reverence and admiration.'

[16] Say I to Kisjonah: 'Now then, friend, are you not finished with your astonishment yet? I suggest that we now take our seats at the table and first eat supper and discuss further points on God's omnipotence and His most distinct love and wisdom thereafter.'

[17] Says **Kisjonah**: 'Forgive me, Lord. I nearly forgot why the foods and drinks are on the table, for all the astonishment over astonishment. Therefore I would ask You and all Yours to get down to the table. But where is the mother of Your body Mary, and those she brought with her, Your supposed sisters, that I may go and fetch them to supper?'

[18] I said: 'Just ask about your wife and daughters. That's where also good Mary is, together with the daughters of Joseph, who was My earthly adoptive father. These are now busy with each other taking in everything, for which they would of course still have tomorrow, the day after tomorrow and even later. Our young and nimble servant shall indeed fetch them and bring them here. So be at ease.'

# CHAPTER 197
## Explanation of the parable of the tares

[1] I hardly had spoken this when the youth was already here with the women, and we all sat down at the tables, soon consuming the supper in good cheer. But after the meal, I said to everybody: 'Listen, since it is a beautiful, starlit night, we shall not immediately take our rest, but settle down on the lawn under the sky, for today I have yet much to say unto you and show you.'

[2] This offer was agreeable to all, and we soon rose from the tables and proceeded into the open and unto a hill of some 40 meters height which gently rose at the end of the garden some 30 paces inland from shore. Kisjonah remarked of course that although this hill affords a lovely view of the entire sea, there nevertheless was the perpetual unpleasantness that it was massively infested with snakes, adders and vipers, probably on account of its proximity to the sea. He had indeed tried everything to chase off the vermin, unsuccessfully.

[3] I said: 'Let it be. From now on it shall not be serving this vermin for an abode, of this you can be fully assured.'

[4] Says **Kisjonah**: 'If so, which I don't doubt in the least, then firstly I would thank You from the bottom of my heart for such riddance, and secondly, in remembrance of You, a proper school shall be built here for both the great and small, young and old, expounding Your purest teaching.'

[5] I said: 'Such school, if abiding by the fundamentals, shall at all times enjoy My blessings. Unfortunately however, the way the world is, it shall with time not spare this school, just as with My purest teaching. Therefore nothing is lasting in this world, because the whole world is now in a bad condition and circumcised by Satan. But let us now go up the hill.' I and Kisjonah move ahead, with all the disciples and with Kisjonah's servants at our heels.

[6] As we come to the hill however, **Kisjonah** notices a hefty adder in front of him moving up the hill, and he soon sees several of them and says to Me: 'Lord, did I actually not have enough faith for this vermin to have cleared out?'

[7] I said: 'This is for the purpose of your seeing and recognizing the fullness of the Son of God's glory. And so pay attention. I now shall command these animals to leave this area and not inhabit it for all time, for as long as any of your offspring occupies this garden or hill, and you shall see how even these exceedingly dull beasts have to obey My voice.'

[8] Here I faced the mountain and threatened the beasts. And these shot like arrows out of their holes by the many thousands and fled into the sea. And thus the mountain was cleansed of this vermin for evermore, and there was not seen again upon this hill any ever so small worm.

[9] We however then moved up the hill unconcerned, and since there was already some dew on the grass, Kisjonah had brought a great many carpets, covering nearly the entire hill, once again enjoying also the youth's useful and fast services. Thereupon we happily settled down on the fairly choice carpets.

[10] My disciples however, who, notwithstanding all their thinking, brooding and

meditating about the parable of the tares in the field could not get to the bottom of it, came over to Me on the hill and asked Me to clarify the parable of the sower who cast good grain into the soil but later found tares in among the wheat.

[11] I said to them however: 'Did you not hear what Kisjonah is preparing to build on this hill in memory of Me, and how I told him how such institution would fare in view of the world? See, this has an application with the good field that was sown with the purest of wheat and yet sprouted a great many tares in its midst afterwards. See, the signification of the parable is this:

[12] I, or like the Jews are saying, the Son of Man is sowing the good seed (Mt.13,37). The field is the world; the good seed are the children of the kingdom; the tares are the children of wickedness (Matth.13,38). The enemy who sows them is the devil; the harvest is the end of the world and the gatherers are the angels. (Mt.13,39) But like the tares are weeded out on the field binding it to be burned, the same will happen to the world. (Mt.13,40)

[13] The Son of Man shall send out His angels and they shall gather together from His Kingdom everything that offends, and all those men who act unrighteous (Mt.13,41) and who have neither eyes nor ears for the want of their brethren, and still less a heart, and shall cast them into the fiery furnace, where there shall be wailing and gnashing of teeth. (Matth.13,42) The fiery furnace however shall be for the children of malice – by which is to be understood pride, selfishness, domination, hardheartedness, indifference towards God's Word, avarice, envy, jealousy, falsehood, cheating, false promises, fornication and whoring, adultery, false witness, slander and everything that is contrary to love of neighbor – their own heart.

[14] For just as Heaven in all glory shall sprout from the hearts of the righteous, so shall sprout what is in the unjust heart. A bad grain shall never bring forth good fruit.

[15] A heart like stone shall yield no soft fruit, and a heart that does not keep its promises will never be able to master itself, and the wrath shall be the fire that shall never be extinguished. Therefore beware of all this and become righteous in everything, in accordance with the commandment of love.'

## CHAPTER 198
### Not keeping a promise is most reprehensible

[1] Do not ever promise a person something you then cannot or – even worse – do not wish to keep for whatever reasons, if you truly want to become children of God. In truth, I tell you, the worst thing is a promise that is not kept.

[2] For the one who is angry sins within himself and harms first himself. Who practices lewdness buries his soul in the judgment of the flesh and again harms himself, but the evil of evils is the lie.

[3] If you have promised to do something for a person and circumstances arise that make it impossible for you to keep your promise, do go to him without delay

357

and tell him honestly what has happened to you, so that he can help himself at the proper time in some other way to overcome some difficulty.

[4] But woe betides everyone who makes promises and does not keep them, even if he could do so, for thereby he causes far-reaching trouble. The one who expected his help cannot fulfill his duty, and the hands of those who relied on him are tied, and thus such a broken promise can cause greatest embarrassment and distress to thousands. Therefore, a promise that is not kept is the thing most opposed to the love of one's neighbor and, therefore, the greatest of evils.

[5] It is better to have a hard heart because that will not raise any deceptive hopes with anyone. One knows that nothing can be expected of a hard-hearted person and, therefore, other means are sought for the preservation of the necessary order. But if someone expects something that was promised to him, he abstains from seeking other ways and means, and when the time comes that the business of the one expecting help has to be attended to and the one who promised him lets him down and does not tell him in advance that for some reason, which must of course be absolutely true, he will not be able to keep his promise, such promiser is like Satan who from the very beginning made mankind brilliant promises through his prophets none of which he has ever kept, thereby plunging numerous people into misery.

[6] Therefore, beware above all of such promises which you cannot keep and, even worse, for whatever reasons do not want to keep, for that is the attitude of the chief of devils.

[7] Be loving and righteous in all things, for in the Father's Kingdom the righteous once shall shine as the sun at noon.

[8] He who has ears let him hear. For I want to give you another two parables about the Kingdom of Heaven.

[9] The Kingdom of Heaven also is like unto a treasure hidden in a field, which a man found. And as it was too big and heavy for him to carry home, since he was still too far away, he went and buried it in the adjacent field at night, then went home happily, sold everything at home and bought the field at any price, for the treasure in the field was worth thousands of times more than what he paid for the field. And since the field was now his, he could safely take the treasure out of the field since no one could dispute its ownership. Now he could easily move the treasure to his new house, which he had bought with the field, and no longer had to earn his living by the sweat of his brow, for he now enjoyed vast excess for life. Do you understand this parable?'

[10] Said **the disciples**: 'This is an easy parable, for the finders of the treasure are those who hear Your Word, and the field is men's worldly heart, which they first must spiritually buy for themselves through acting upon Your Word, so that Your Word becomes their possession in their hearts and with that they then can work all good for self and their brethren.'

[11] I said: 'You have understood the parable well, for thus it is with the true Kingdom of Heaven. But hear another.

CHAPTER 199
## Parable of the great pearl and the net

[1] The Kingdom of Heaven also is like unto a merchant who searched all the lands for good pearls. And he found a pearl of enormous value, inquiring of its price, and when told, he returned to his city, sold everything he had and then went and bought the big pearl, which in turn was of thousands-fold greater value than what he paid. Have you understood this image?'

[2] Say **the disciples**: 'Yes, Lord, this too we understand, for such merchant we all are, having left everything on Your account. You, however, to us are the big, priceless pearl.'

[3] I said: 'This parable also you have understood in all truth, for thus it is with the Kingdom of Heaven. But listen unto another parable.

[4] The Kingdom of Heaven yet again is like unto a net that is cast into the sea for the catching of all kinds of fish, and when the net is full, the fishermen draw it to shore, whereupon they take out the good fish, placing them in a container, but the sick and foul they throw away.

[5] Thus it shall also be at the end of the world. The angels shall go out and separate the wicked from the righteous and shall cast them into the furnace of their own wicked hearts, and there shall be great wailing and gnashing of the teeth, which is a true darkness of the evil soul, which shall constantly be in search but not find what will gratify its evil love.' And after a while I asked the disciples, who were in deep thought about this image: Have you also understood this parable?'

[6] And **these** said: 'Yes, Lord, this parable too we have properly understood now. It resembles the one You told at the coast of Jesaira: "He who has, to him shall be given that he may have more abundantly, but he who has not, from him shall be taken also what he has."

[7] And **Ahab** added: 'By the sick and foul fishes I understand mainly the Pharisees and all those idle Scribes who constantly proffer their old wares, praising nature and its productiveness, but despise and persecute everything ever so brilliant that this time has to offer. These too surely would be foul and sick fishes? What is there in being a scribe and Pharisee in the brain but take oneself to be measurelessly better than other men, and to even receive sacrifices and tithes from those men, probably better brothers and sisters, yet having a hollow, stone-hard and unfeeling heart?

[8] Therefore I believe that in future, he who is initiated into the Kingdom of Heaven in his heart according to Your Word shall surely have to discard the old, spoilt and foul doctrinal junk of the Pharisees, laying an entirely new foundation for Your teaching, for Your teaching is wise and just, and therefore diametrically opposed to that of the Pharisees.

[9] Well do I know indeed that Moses and the other prophets prophesied out of Your spirit, but how distorted are they now. And since You are now here Yourself to reveal Your will to us, what for still the foul and sick Moses, as also all the

359

prophets?

[10] Who in his heart according to You, o Lord, has actively become a learner in the Kingdom of Heaven, no longer needs a Moses and prophets.'

[11] I said: 'You are quite right in what you are saying, except for a small detail which consists in the fact that a true teacher of the law, that is one who has become a learner in the Kingdom of Heaven, must be like a wise householder who produces from his store both old and new to offer to his guests for their enjoyment. Or should one, when the new wine is filled into the skins, pour out the good old wine, or throw out the old grain when the new crop has been gathered into the barns? Therefore, a true teacher of the law, a learner in the Kingdom of Heaven, must know and observe the old Scripture as well as My new Word.'

[12] Says **Ahab**: 'But surely only Moses and the prophets, excluding the no doubt partly distorted laws of the land, the empty rules of divine service, which can no longer be of any use since all of us are politically subject to the Roman laws anyway?'

[33] I said: 'That goes without saying. What has to be omitted from the ancient law for the sake of true love of one's neighbor, you find already written down. Here are now My two friends from Sychar who are witnesses to My extensive Sermon on the Mount which deals with all these things.' With this Ahab is quite satisfied.


## CHAPTER 200
### Why does God not always help immediately?

[1] But now I call over the two Sycharites, to put to Me the case for which they came here. And **Jonael**, the spokesman, says: 'Lord, You actually had already touched upon the correct reason earlier, and so it is. It nevertheless is hard to believe that people, who together with us have the enduringly great signs of Your divine power before their eyes, should be so evil. They acknowledge the truth and persecute it for the very reason that they have to acknowledge it as truth. Me they have expelled. Had brother Jairuth not taken me in, together with my family, I should be without roof over my head.

[2] Lord, how fervently and how often I had prayed to You in spirit for You to come and stand by me against my enemies, yet it was in vain, and you did not come to help us out of our worst plight.

[3] While it is true that You left us in Your stead visible angels to serve us, these don't want to always act, or in a manner I consider as desirable, for they say that they can do nothing without Your will, for only Your will is their entire power and authority. This is all true of course, yet with the offended old arch-Samaritans expelling hundreds of Your followers from the country, so that they have to seek shelter with the heathens, with the necessary consequence of the expelled themselves becoming heathens, then surely it ought to be in order for Your angels to intervene, to put an end to such evil doings, rather than watch all this and hang their faces with us, sighing and exclaiming with us. Are not the Lord's counsels

always mysterious and unfathomable His ways.

[4] But what does this help? Hundreds turn into heathens, hundreds are caned and mocked in public places for Your name's sake.

[5] Joram had to leave Sychar for a time, and the house that Jacob built meanwhile stands empty and locked up. And Joram and his wife now also find themselves in brother Jairuth's house, like many other respectable families who no longer were tolerated in Sychar on Your account.

[6] Yet against all this Your angels, who dwell with us, have taken not one step. Lord, Lord, in Your holiest name. What is the good of all this?

[7] Must all power and might over You be ceded to Satan on this Earth? Or is his Hell in all earnest more powerful than Your Heavens? Lord, if this continues, then mankind of a truth shall be forced to erect temples and sacrificial altars to Satan, and pull Yours down. A most sorry state of the times.

[8] What is now the divine service in Gerizim and even in the Jerusalem Temple, other than sheerest Satan service. I know it through Your own mouth, Yourself being the Lord Himself who dwells within You in all fullness bodily, how God wants to be honored and worshiped. Then look at the service at Gerizim, and you have the truest and most authentic Satan service, for there, in all earnest and not denied even by Your angels, incense is scattered to Satan in full measure.

[9] Faithfully and truly, Lord, thus it goes on, and cannot be a secret to You that it does so, and yet You are allowing it to be so and to go on. Lord, how are we to take this and to understand Your holy Word?

[10] And even the honest brother Jairuth, fully devoted to You, together with his entire house, day after day is receiving threats to either declare himself a Samaritan without delay, or suffer dispossession of all properties.

[11] Many who had already staunchly embraced Your teaching, o Lord, have let themselves be intimidated by daily threats and prescribed cursing and oaths, and have reverted to the purest Satan service.

[12] See, Lord, such things are taking place, to which Your angels indeed are at all times veiling their faces, but to what end such formal sympathy?

[13] Lord, You can see into my heart, totally devoted to You. And thus I speak to You without reservation and say, here a sympathetic watching is as untimely as a fig just 3 days after dropping of the blossoms. Here only weighing in forcefully with all power will do, or Satan gains ground and root.

[14] And if already now Your disciples cannot prevail against him, what shall they do after he has attained to full power, which should not be too hard for him, if continuing unopposed, as is the unfortunate case up till now, when not even Your angels dare to undertake anything against him?

[15] For the sake of Your holy name and for the sake of all those who, like us, still cling to Your name unshakably, stand by us and free us from Satan's traps.

[16] Did You not Yourself up on the mountain teach us how to pray? Yet see, it is getting worse by the day instead of better.

[17] We are willing to offer up everything to You and to suffer poverty to the limit out of our love for You. But some spot upon Earth surely you will not begrudge us, for in order to follow You, one cannot live among wolves, hyenas and bears,

unless one wished to become like unto those beasts.

[18] We are not asking for a peaceful paradise in this world, but only that we should not have to live among devils in the most perfect Hell. From this, o Lord, protect us.'


# CHAPTER 201
## Twofold nature of tolerance

[1] 'Friends, I did indeed know that this would soon happen, so that Satan may complete his work. However, the ones who fled to the heathens could also have found refuge here in Galilee, and those who cursed My name in order to save their earthly possessions would have done better to free themselves from all their worldly ties than by cursing My name to safeguard their possessions to which eternal death is attached.

[2] How hard it will be for a person with many things to part with them one day. And how easy will he depart from the world who did not possess any goods from its poisonous bosom and suffered persecution for the sake of My name. The latter scorns the world and will surely not be sorry when, clearly seeing it as it is, he will be leaving this place of darkness to enter the Kingdom of Heaven.

[3] See, as the gold is proved in the fire only thereby gaining its great value, thus it must be with you who truly wish to be My disciples and followers. My Kingdom for which all of us are now working is not of this world, but of that vast, eternal, everlasting one which follows this earthly, material, short trial life.

[4] Therefore, I do not give you peace for this world, but the sword, for you have to attain to the freedom of eternal life through the battle with the world and all it offers you.

[5] For My Kingdom suffers force, and those who do not seize it forcibly will not enter it.

[6] It is of course an easy matter, in a safely walled city and well provided for life, to stand fast as My disciples and teach virtue to the lambs, watering them with clean water. Verily, this does not take much. But quite another thing it is to tame lions, tigers and panthers, transforming them into useful animals. For this, of course, more cleverness, courage, strength and endurance are required than for taming sheep.

[7] Wherefore you need to take this phenomenon in Sychar as you find it and join the fight, whereat I shall support you, but if you immediately allow men's blindness and evil to provoke you hands over heels into rage, straight away calling for consuming fire from Heaven over such evildoers, then you can fare no other than you have done.

[8] Nor can My angels be of service to you in such cases, for such service would be diametrically opposed to My eternal order.

[9] If you intend to be victorious fighters for My Kingdom, then prepare yourselves a sharp sword from pure truth, but this is to be fashioned from the

purest and most unselfish love. Then fight courageously with such sword, not fearing those who in extreme cases can kill your body but then can harm you no more.

[10] If however you must fear, then fear Him who is a true Lord over life and death and who can reject or accept man's soul.

[11] He who loses his earthly life in a just fight for Me shall regain it to full measure in My Kingdom, but he who strives to cling to his earthly life in his fight for My sake is a coward, and the victorious crown of everlasting life shall not be his. What rewards has he who fights gnats and kills flies? Verily, I say unto you, such hero is not worth to urinate on.

[12] Ah, it is something quite different to, well-armored and with sword in hand, enter a herd of lions and tigers. After cutting down the herd and returning home victoriously, triumphal arches shall await him, and a great reward shall not be withheld from him for his heroic feat.

[13] Return home therefore and fight as I have shown you, and you shall not forego your proper victory.

[14] To what state Satan has brought this Earth I verily know best, and I lack not the power to finish him off. Yet My great love and patience will not allow it.

[15] Because he who seeks to defeat his enemy only to destroy him is a cowardly fighter, for not his courage but his great fear has prompted him to rid himself of his enemy by killing him.

[16] He who wants to be a real hero must not annihilate his enemy, but take the trouble to win his foe with all cleverness, patience, love and wisdom in his heart. Only then he can boast of fighting a true victory over his enemy, and his greatest reward shall be the hard-won foe.

### CHAPTER 202
### The true church and Sabbath

[1] If you two have now understood this then return home soon with your angels, and there do according to My word, and all the unpleasantness there shall soon take on a different aspect.

[2] But there you must not make your appearance as angry judges but as truly wise teachers and friends of the blind, deaf and dumb, and they shall then let themselves by guided by you.

[3] Who would advisedly turn angry to a blind one stepping on his foot? Withdraw your foot from the blind one's step, and you shall not be trodden upon.

[4] If however you see a blind one near a precipice, then rush over, grab him and bring him to safety, leading to the light which heals every soul blindness, and he shall become your most thankful friend and brother.

[5] If however, when teaching the people in My name, then always do as I do, first through good deeds and then with plain and simple words, and with that you shall soon count many true disciples.

[6] But if you dress yourselves up in mysteries, way beyond the stars, and try to impress upon men that you are called of God to judge, bless or curse them, and besides that get angry if My angels don't want to support you therein, then it must be clear to you that such conduct is not at all My will as revealed to you, but that you have created a new order and from this tried to build a safe church in place of the old Mosaic one, before which your lambs were to bend their knees already from afar.

[7] See, thus it was with the mosaic church. And when it had been fenced in, it did not bring any or only little, and usually stunted fruit.

[8] I am now giving you a completely free church that does not need any other fencing than with everyone his very own heart wherein the spirit and truth are dwelling and where alone God wants to be recognized and worshiped.

[9] Because I gave you My Spirit first, you shall not imagine yourselves by a hair's breadth better than any other person, and you shall not make any particular office of this gift as is done by the heathens and the twice as dark Jews and Pharisees for there is but One who is your Master and all of you are equal as brothers and sisters, and there shall never be any discrimination among you.

[10] Thus there shall not be any rules among you, and you shall not observe any particular days or times as if they were better or worse as if God had laid down only certain days on which He wants to hear your prayers and accept sacrifices. I tell you: with God all days are equal and the best among many is the one on which you have done a truly good deed for your neighbor. And thus only your deed shall in future determine the true and sole Sabbath day pleasing to God.

[11] On whatever day you will be doing a good deed, that will be the right Sabbath which is considered by God, but the usual Jewish Sabbath shall be an abomination in God's eyes.

[12] However, if you wish to erect a so-called house of God, then build hospitals and homes to care for your poor brothers and sisters in which you serve them with all they need. Thus you will perform the truest divine service which will be most pleasing to the Father in Heaven.

[13] By such a genuine and solely true divine service one will recognize that you are truly My disciples.

[14] Do go home now and act accordingly, then your work will be blessed.'


## CHAPTER 203
### Jonael's song of praise to the Lord

[1] After these extensive instructions, **the two** say: 'Lord, forgive us our sin. For now we clearly see that actually we, rather than the people, are at fault, and with Your grace and help we shall put matters right where possible.

[2] Only now have we discovered the true spirit of Your most holy doctrine, and shall endeavor to eagerly spread same to the people. But many have gone over to

the heathens, and we hardly know how to win them back. What shall we do?'

[3] I said: 'Do with them as I do with the heathens, and they shall be your disciples, together with the heathens.

[4] See, this house too is now a heathen one, having for a lengthy period already embraced the doctrines of the Greek wise men, and yet it is now more on My side than ever a house was in Jewry. Do likewise, and soon more heathens than Jews shall rally around you.

[5] For, he with an empty stomach more avidly consumes a meal than a person with full stomach, especially when the stomach already is quite spoilt, as is that of the Pharisees and Scribes.'

[6] Say **the two**: 'What shall become of those who cursed Your name for the sake of their worldly goods not being taken from them?'

[7] I said: 'He who has fallen, him raise and lead unto the right path, that he may become aware of his sin and repent committing it. Let this be your special charge.

[8] I have not come to judge and destroy this world, but to seek what was lost and rise up the fallen. If you know that now, then go and do so.'

[9] After these words the two bowed down deeply before Me and asked Me if they could remain with Me for a few days.

[10] I gave them My approval, saying: 'Although I said to you beforehand that you can now return home, I wanted to therewith indicate the willingness of your heart and its comprehension, rather than to directly return to Sychar by a specific time. And so you are welcome to tarry here for a few days, which I shall be still spending here with My friend.'

[11] The two, quite happy with My advice, gave Me thanks and honor, and **Jonael**, deeply stirred emotionally, said: 'Oh Earth, you aged field of weed, thorns and thistles, you life's dark tomb, deliverer of sin and death. Are you indeed worthy of the Lord your God and Creator's walk upon you, with His own most holy feet, breathing in your pestilential air and partaking of your evil fruits?

[12] We humankind, together with the animals and plants, are not worthy enough for His glance. It all is endless grace and mercy.

[13] Therefore let everything get up and praise Him forever.

[14] And you stars up there upon high Heaven, veil your unholy countenance, for it is God your Creator upon whom you are looking down from your height, haughtily.

[15] Oh Earth, what has become of you? What name shall be given you – not on your own account but on account of Him whom you most unworthy one now are carrying?

[16] Ah, the more I think about who it is that is tarrying here among His chosen, the tighter my breast. How in any case ought this limited one to contain what all the Heavens and angels are unable to do.

[17] O, you holy of all holy times on Earth, where that One now dwells who gave the light to sun and moon and determined their grand way of His love and wisdom and to give the Earth its time, night and day.

[18] Wherefore let all praise the Lord of glory from all the Heavens, for His alone is all praise, honor, tribute and love of eternal infinity.'

[19] On hearing such exclamations, **the disciples** say: 'Do You not hear Jonael's praise, as if David's spirit had taken possession of him?'

[20] I said: 'I indeed hear his praise, and am well pleased with it. From yourselves however I have not as yet received such, but it should not at all harm you if at times you really gave thought to who He is that speaks to you now. But let us now take a little rest, as the middle of the night is long past.'

[21] After these words, soon everything becomes quiet around the hill, and most of them fall asleep. Only Jonael and Jairuth are deeply immersed in all kinds of reflections, and are quietly praising Me.


## CHAPTER 204
### Parable of the mother with her two sons

[1] As the near approach of sunrise in the morning, Jonael and Jairuth's angel awaken all those still asleep, while Kisjonah, whose quarters were next to Mine, instructed his wife and daughters and the sundry servants to organize a proper morning meal.

[2] But I say to the hospitable Kisjonah: 'Leave that for today, for see, we should also let brother Baram of Jesaira have the pleasure occasionally. Look over there on the sea. There, not too far from shore, Baram's fully laden ship stands, and his sons and he are right now striving to get the morning meal over here. Therefore let you be relaxed for the day – for besides that the ship also holds a big lunch and supper, as well as 40 skins of the best wine from Greece.'

[3] Says **Kisjonah**: 'Ah, look at the tight-lipped Baram. He mentioned not a syllable of his intentions; in the evening he simply got lost. I think he became invisible just after our arrival, and now he is here with a fully-packed ship. He must have had a good wind, otherwise he could not have made it by a long while yet, what with all the work. For it takes a whole day's rowing from here to Jesaira normally.'

[4] I said: 'Brother, believe it, he who has good intentions shall always be guided by a good wind, whereas the one with bad intentions shall also be guided by a bad wind.

[5] There once were two brothers, whose mother had many a treasure. Both loved their mother exceedingly, so that the mother could not make out which loved her more, for the purpose of giving him the greater inheritance. But only one loved her in actuality, while the other kept only the large inheritance in mind and for that reason constantly showed more concern for his mother, and not infrequently excelled his brother, who truly loved his mother.

[6] The good son, truly loving his mother, had not the slightest suspicion of his brother and was only too glad about his brother's making the beloved mother happy. This went on for several years.

[7] The mother, however, getting older and weaker, called her two sons and spoke: "I am unable to say which of you two loves me more, for giving him the

larger inheritance. Therefore I want you to share it equally after my departure."

[8] Whereupon the good son said: "Mother, it was through your care that I learned how to earn my living for all my needs, but I shall ask God with all the fervor of my heart to keep you alive as long as me, and that you would manage your wealth for the best of the whole house. For if I were to possess the inheritance without you, it would become my greatest torment, making me disconsolate each time I looked at it. Wherefore, dear mother, keep the inheritance and give it to whoever you will. Your heart is my dearest inheritance – would that God would keep it alive as long as possible.'

[9] On hearing such talk from her good son with deeply stirred heart, she spoke, hiding her real feelings: "Most beloved son, your confession indescribably gratifies my heart, but this is still not a reason to give your inheritance to a stranger. If you insist on having no part of it, then let your brother take the whole inheritance after my expiry, and let you serve him and earn your keep by the sweat of your brow.'

[10] Says the good son: "Dearest mother, when serving and working, my heart shall always be gratefully mindful of you and speak "see, this is the way your mother taught you to work". Were I to possess the inheritance, I would in the end become work-shy, throwing myself into a useless life of wealth and finally even forget you. Therefore I don't want your hard-earned treasure, which does not bear the imprint of your heart but only that of the emperor's authority. Yet that which I have taken from your heart also bears the latter's imprint, and has a lasting seat in my heart. Therefore, beloved mother, this inheritance, which you have given me already from the cradle and with which I have already earned much of the good and the costly, is to me indescribably more precious than that which you earned for yourself with the work and struggle of your hands. Its sight would only perturb me, as the thought would keep returning: "see, this has cost your mother's hands much strain and work. Did she perhaps cry often from pain – for being concerned about giving you an inheritance". And see, dear mother, I could not then possibly be of good cheer, because I love you so exceedingly.'

[11] Moved to tears, the mother calls upon her other son to say what he thinks and wants.

[12] This one answered: 'I have indeed always thought my brother noble, yet in some ways an eccentric. There I am quite a different man. Just as much as I honor and regard you, dear mother, just so I also respect everything you want to and will give me. Therefore I accept the entire inheritance with the most thankful heart, and my brother's intended services shall not go unrewarded. If however, dear mother, you so wish, you could issue me with half the inheritance in advance, which will enable me to purchase land and take a wife.'

[13] Says the mother somewhat heavy-heartedly to the second son's answer: "What I have spoken, by that I abide. The inheritance you shall receive only after my death.'

[14] Thereupon the second son was downcast and left the room.

[15] A year later the mother became very ill, and a maid came out to fetch the two sons working in the field, so that the most worthy could receive the mother's blessings in accordance with her will.

[16] Here the good son was filled with sorrow, and on the way prayed to God loudly that He would preserve the mother's life.

[17] But the bad son was upset, saying to the son steeped in prayer, "Do you in all earnest want to prescribe laws to nature? Whoever has once matured, whether father, mother, brother or sister, has to die. Here no asking or praying is of avail. Therefore my watchword is "what God wills, that also is right by me."

[18] But the good brother was still sadder, and prayed yet more fervently for his dear mother's life.

[19] As they came to the mother's sick room, the bad son said: "I knew that you wouldn't die so quickly." Whereupon he began dissuading her from fearing death.

[20] But the good son cried and prayed loudly. God, however, listened unto the good son's groans, sending an angel to the mother's bedside, who made her fully well.

[21] Therewith the mother soon rose, becoming aware of a higher power restoring her health. And upon noting the strength in her limbs, she said: "For this I have the fervent prayer of my son to thank, who rejected the proffered inheritance out of his true love for me. Truly, I say to you, my most beloved son: because, for true love's sake, you wanted nothing, you shall now have everything. Whatever is mine is yours. But you other one, having loved me only for the inheritance, fervently desiring my end – for being good to you and making everything over to you – shall receive nothing, and become man's slave for evermore."

[22] Note this parable well. Which of the two sons do you think had the good wind?'

[23] **The disciples** said: 'Obviously the one who truly loved his mother.'

[24] I said: 'Well said. But I say unto you, as this mother acted, so shall the Father in Heaven do.'

[25] He who does not love Me for My own sake shall not come to where I shall be.

[26] Man should love God without thought of gain, just as God loves him, or he is completely unworthy of God.'


## CHAPTER 205
### The nature of love

[1] **Kisjonah** says: 'That is an exalted and deep truth, but I would like to comment on this that – at least among humans – there cannot exist a completely unmotivated love. Having often pondered on love, I find that love, be it ever so pure, always more or less goes on the prowl.

[2] Look, I surely love You as deeply as anyone can ever love You. If it were possible I would like for love to fully absorb You with my body and place You in my heart.

[3] But the question is whether I can feel that also for another person of no interest to Me? Why not? Why do I feel it with You? The answer is supplied by the

matter as such.

[4] I know who You are and know what You can do and also know what I can achieve through You and the observance of Your teaching, and that is the unquestionable basis for my ardent love for You. For if You were not what You are, my love for You would surely be considerably weaker. Thus, I have an enormous interest in You and, therefore, I want and love You.

[5] I do not want to say that I love You for the sake of some particular gain, for I am giving up everything in the world for love of You. But nevertheless my love here goes on a special prowl, for it aims at You because You are more to it than the whole world.

[6] The greater worth – either material or spiritual – always determines the prompting of love. The merchant who was looking for pearls sold everything and bought the finest pearl he found. Why? Because it was worth much more than everything he had so far possessed. The interest is indeed a noble one, but it is still an interest and without that there is no love, at least not with man. And to the one who would like to convince me of a love without an interest, which at the most may be found in God, I say: "Friend, you may be very wise, but you have never as yet pondered deeply on the subject of love."

[7] Of course, the divine, true love differs from the hellish one quite considerably in so far as divine love is also on the prowl as is the hellish one, but it returns it all again. It only gathers for the sake of returning, whereas hellish love robs only for its own benefit and will not surrender anything.

[8] However, if we adopt heavenly love, we know that we shall thereby never end up with a loss or suffer damage, but are going to gain ever more the more we give.

[9] There we may be compared to a hole dug in the ground. The more Earth it loses the larger becomes its inner cavity for the reception of light and heavenly air. Lord, I think that I am not wrong there. What does Your endlessly superior wisdom say to it?'

[10] I said: 'Nothing but that you are quite right, for if love were not a robber in one way or another, it would not be love, since all love desires and wants to have.

[11] However, there is an endless gap in the motivation for having, and that separates Heaven and Hell for all eternity.

[12] But now Baram's people are bringing the morning meal. We want to therefore, having for hours cared for the spirit, also for a few moments think of the hungry body.'

[13] Baram brings me a most precious fish in a bowl, prepared in the finest manner, together with a full beaker of wine, begging Me for grace to be worthy of serving Me a morning meal from his hand.

[14] And I say to him: 'This your deed shall not go without reward, for you have taken the trouble out of your great love for Me, and equal love for brother Kisjonah, with whom you empathized, thinking that perhaps, after a few days, caring for several hundred guests may become a strain on him.

[15] I say unto you: Kisjonah indeed suffers no want, as all of us could not consume his provisions in 10 years. But because you thought so in your heart,

and that Kisjonah could in the end run out of supplies coming to meet him with help from afar, your reward shall be as if you had done it for a destitute. For God sees only the heart of the giver.

[16] But let you now sit down and share the bowl with Me and Kisjonah, for the fish is too big to eat for even 3 people.' Baram did so, as well as Kisjonah.

[17] And so starts the morning meal, with the sun risen, and lasts for close on 2 hours. For the meal was nowhere near finished with the fish, with many other refreshments to follow.


## CHAPTER 206
## Human nutrition

[1] It hardly needs saying that at such morning meal, all is exceedingly cheerful and talkative, for the wine has loosened all tongues. Even **Jonael and Jairuth** completely cheered up and even asked Me to make them return to Sychar in such frame of mind. And I let them do so after their departure.

[2] Thereto they said: 'It is good that You allow this, for then we shall commit no sin in being cheery, but the great question is whether we shall be able to be so.'

[3] I said: 'Well then, you shall and will be cheerful.'

[4] But their angel cut a sad countenance to the prediction. Noticing this, Jonael asks Me for the reason.

[5] I said: 'Because the angel knows only too well that no great distance separates the greatest exuberance from sin. He foresees the effort he shall have, protecting you against sin on your way home. This is why he is sad. Pass him some wine too, and maybe he shall brighten up.'

[6] Whereupon Jonael hands the angel a beaker of wine. He takes it and empties it completely, which amazes the two, for such they had not noticed with him before.

[7] But **the angel** says: 'For quite some time I have been with you now, why did you never pass me a beaker at home?'

[8] Says **Jonael**: 'But how could it have occurred to us even in a dream that an angel takes in any material sustenance on Earth?'

[9] Says **the angel**: 'Strange. Have you not seen how the Lord of all Heavens also ate and drank, and yet He is the highest and most perfect Spirit. How then should we angels not also eat and drink, when we have to put on a body in order to serve you in the physical?

[10] Give me also some fish and bread, and you shall see how I can not only drink but also eat quite well, for where the Lord takes terrestrial sustenance, the angels also do so.'

[11] Whereupon Jonael passes the angel a whole fish and fair-sized lump of bread, the angel taking and consuming both.

[12] After the angel showed the two how a spirit also can consume material sustenance, Jonael asks him how such is possible, since he is fundamentally only

a spirit.

[13] Says **the angel**: 'Have you ever seen a dead person eat and drink?' Says **Jonael**: 'No one has ever seen that.'

[14] Says **the angel**: 'But if a soulless and even more spiritless body which is almost pure matter does not and cannot take nourishment, it is obviously the soul and its living spirit that take food. Since the body being no more than an instrument for the soul does not need any nourishment for itself, it is the soul with its spirit that takes nourishment from the Earth as long as it dwells in the body and sustains the latter by letting it eat its excrement. For the body is nourished with the soul's excrement.

[15] Since in the still material man only the soul, while it is in the body, takes nourishment from the Earth, should not I, as soul and spirit, be entitled to partake of earthly fare during my stay on Earth where in order to serve you I also have a certain body which I created for myself from the matter of the air? What do you think about this?'

## CHAPTER 207
### The right kind of fasting

[1] Both of them and still many others who had heard the explanation by the angel open their eyes in surprise and **Peter** asks Me: 'Lord, is it right what Jonael's servant has just said? It does sound a bit peculiar. How can the body be nourished with the soul's excrement? Does then the soul too have a stomach and maybe even an anus?'

[2] I said: 'The angel has spoken truthfully, this is how it is. Therefore, feasting and carousing makes the soul itself sensuous and material. It is overloaded, the body cannot absorb all the soul's excrement and as a result this stays in the soul, oppresses and frightens it, so that it makes every effort to rid itself of the too much accumulated excrement. This is done through all kinds of lewdness, fornication, adultery and so on.

[3] However, since these things offer the soul a certain stimulus for lust it keeps becoming increasingly lustful, turns more and more to feasting and carousing, becomes finally most sensual, absolutely ignorant in spiritual things and as a result hard, unfeeling and in the end evil, proud and arrogant.

[4] For, once a soul has lost its spiritual value – and it had to lose it through the here described way of life – it begins to literally erect itself a throne from excrement and finally even finds honor and authority through the fact that it is so rich in excrement.

[5] I tell you: all people who in the world enjoy the things that please their sensuality are over their ears and eyes in their thickest dirt and, therefore, spiritually completely deaf and blind and no longer want to see, hear and understand that which would be of benefit to them.

[6] Therefore, you should always be moderate in eating and drinking to avoid

falling ill in your soul so that this may not perish in its excrement.'

[7] **Peter**, looking very doubtful, says: 'Lord, if so, which cannot be doubted, one should probably fast more than eat?'

[8] **I** said: 'He who fasts at the right time does better than the one who is always feasting. But there is still a difference between fasting and fasting. A proper fasting consists in abstaining from sin and in all worldly things denying oneself with all one's might, carrying one's cross (in those times figuratively: misery, want and oppression) and following Me without being too scrupulous in eating and drinking, but also not exceeding what is needed by guzzling. All other kinds of fasting have little or no value at all.

[9] For there are people who by a certain castigation of their body wish to penetrate into the world of spirits and with their help conquer the forces of nature. That is then not only useless for the soul, but extremely harmful. There the soul falls from the tree of life as an immature fruit whose core of life is always rotten, hollow, empty and thus dead.

[10] Such a castigation and fasting is therefore not only no virtue, but it is a very gross sin.

[11] Therefore, who wishes to live in accordance with the true order, let him live as I Myself do, and as I teach him to live, then he will see the living fruit of life blossom within him and fully ripen. In this fruit there will not be a dead stone, but a fully alive one for the once to come everlasting life in the spirit will be growing and forming into the most alive self-awareness in the best of order and beneficial progress. Now you know also in this matter what you have to do in full accordance with the divine order. Act accordingly, and you will have life within you.

[12] But now the sun's rays are gathering strength. Therefore we shall make our retreat from this hill to the shady garden, and you My scribe Matthew can sort out your writing tablets for a fuller rendition of the happenings and teachings but we shall now allow ourselves a little rest.'

## CHAPTER 208
### Earthquake, sea and thunderstorm

[1] We leave the hill and move to the shady trees. There was a nice grassy bank under a wide fig tree, where I sat down and fell asleep, and all the others, even Mary near Me, took their places and slept. Only Jonael, Jairuth and Matthew sat at a garden table, where Matthew started ordering his tablets, with Jonael and Jairuth's angel making him aware of certain deficiencies.

[2] Towards the middle of day Baram, who meanwhile found himself aboard the ship with Kisjonah, noticed immensely heavy storm clouds rising over the horizon in the west, with the water surface growing progressively calmer, it being a sure sign of imminent and destructive tempest, combined with Earth tremor.

[3] Baram therefore at once had all edibles brought up from the ship, tying the latter down in the firmest possible manner. He had hardly finished the work when

the sea already began to rise prodigiously from afar.

[4] Said **Kisjonah**: 'We shall have to awaken the Lord and His disciples, for such, the like of which I have not seen before, may submerge the whole garden, and those asleep could suffer harm, and the chances are that the ship will be cast ashore.'

[5] Says **Baram**: 'Yes, friend, failing the Lord restraining the storm this time, there could be nameless destruction. But I count upon the Lord. He is certain to prevent our perishing. And I reckon that so long as He quietly sleeps, we shall have nothing to fear from the imminent storm; let us nevertheless go up to Him and make Him aware of the approaching storm.'

[6] Thereupon the two, together with the deck hands, rush over to Me, trying to awaken me, for good reason this time however I do not awaken, and **the angel** steps over to them saying: 'Let Him rest, and do not waken Him, for it is on account of this necessary storm that He sleeps. The immediate future however soon shall tell the good reason for this necessary storm.'

[7] Says **Kisjonah**: 'But what if the mountainous seas shall soon be washing over my garden with the wildest floods?'

[8] Says **the angel**: 'Don't be troubled by that. Do you think that while appearing to you asleep the Lord is not aware of this storm? See, this is His will, therefore it is so. Therefore settle down.

[9] Asks **Kisjonah**: 'Do you know the reason?' Replies **the angel**: 'Even if I knew, I would not be allowed to tell you until that is the Lord's will. Inquire no further and do not fear, but settle down. The eyes of you all shall be opened by what follows.'

[10] After these words of the angel, who then quietly helped Matthew to upgrade his tablets, **Baram** spoke: 'I must confess that in my whole life I have not seen a more threatening storm, yet at the same time I never before watched a storm so undaunted and indifferently. Just look, no more than a quarter hour average travel time further on, the length of this bay. In just a few moments the storm should hit us.

[11] Yet watch now the billowing rollers move along the length of the sea towards Sibarah, a mere quarter hour's distance outside the bay, resembling swimming mountains being smashed by thousands of lightnings. And yet the bay is so calm that one can see the storm in its external aspect, like a section of the coast; this truly is a rare phenomenon. One has to admit that, observed calmly, it takes on a rare and frightfully beautiful aspect. But for those perhaps finding themselves out in that high sea shall feel quite differently to us near the mirror-smooth bay.

[12] It is at least a half hour from the weather front, yet what mighty roar of the thunder. It must be downright deafening at that front. Now I also feel a marked Earth tremor. Do you not notice anything?'

[13] Says **Kisjonah**: 'Indeed, I just wanted to tell you. However, it is a wonder of all wonders that my bay still remains calm. For I know the spectacle of what this bay is capable of, once it starts raging. Yet the bay, together with a considerable stretch beyond, is totally calm. But listen, the tremor intensifies. If only the

dwellings escape harm. I am seeing a peculiar circular swell in the bay, and the start of a tidal wave further out. We haven't long to go. In the name of the Lord, we can't lose more than this earthly life, and so let come what may. The Lord and His angel in any case are with us. But it has a terrifying look. May the Lord have grace and mercy on all sinners.'

[14] Now the bay too is getting rough. Powerful wind gusts are tearing through the trees, and countless flashes of lightning through the heavy clouds. Several hit the bay with an unbelievably frightening racket, causing a roaring froth, yet there still falls not a drop of rain from the glowing cloud. Lightning hits the hill on which we spent the night; the exceeding racket of this flash now wakens all from their good sleep except Myself.

[15] As the many awakened ones take in the unprecedented din, and the storm of all storms, fully awakening with the tenfold simultaneous flashes, they leap off the ground, with the disciples rushing over to Me to awaken Me, shouting with fear.

[16] Says the nervous **Judas**: 'But Lord, how can You sleep with these raging elements? It is raining lightning from the sky. Who could be safe from death for a moment? Help Lord or the entire Earth is rubble!'

[17] I said: 'Has lightning actually hit you?' Says **Judas**: 'Not yet of course, but what hasn't happened may easily still do so with this storm. I therefore speak while I still live, the next flash shall probably finish off all my talking for good.'

[18] And see, while Judas is speaking, the tidal wave is heading for the bay with a mighty roar. And with the wall of water seeming to exceed our garden position by several fathoms, all disciples are yelling, with some even turning heels towards the next rise, driven back however by thousands of lightnings. 'Lord help us, if You can or will, or we perish', hundreds are screaming. Only Matthew, Jairuth, Jonael and the angel remain unperturbed, putting the finishing touches to their business.

[19] This time however I don't curb the storm, letting it roam, simply not allowing it to do any ever so small damage.


## CHAPTER 209
### The purpose of this storm

[1] Peter however steps over to Me, saying confidingly. 'Lord, has the Father's Spirit within You retreated to the extent where You are no longer Master of this storm? Could You not try to silence this storm if possible?' I said: 'There are wise grounds why this storm, which shall not last long, has to rage its course. If you don't doubt it however, then be advised that there are 10 hostile ships upon the sea pursuing us for our destruction. This storm is doing to them what they intended doing to us. If so, why beg Me to halt this most essential storm of our grace. Let it rage until it has achieved its aim, and it then shall cheerfully stop. Look over there and tell Me what the mountainous waves are carrying on their furious backs like nasty and spiteful children tossing their mischievous toys up and

down.'

[2] Peter looks over the exceptionally stormy, high and wide seascape and straight away notices several shipwrecks, together with one somewhat less damaged, intact ship, and how wrecks and ship are being tossed about by the mighty breakers like chaff. He also sees some people clinging to wreckage and trying to reach shore with a last desperate effort, while being buried by wave after wave and intermittently tossed up again.

[3] Having watched this spectacle for a while, **Peter** says to Me: 'Forgive me Lord, for You know that I am still a sinful man and therefore burdening You with a basically stupid question. Now I am in the clear. The wicked Pharisees from Jesaira went to get help from Jerusalem. Ten ships with Roman centurions were fitted out to seize us over here. They had to move by sea, as it is not easy to get here to Kis (a city belonging to Kisjonah) on foot, and they have received their well earned reward for their trouble. These shall harm us no more, and judging by the course of the tide, the wrecked ships are being driven towards Sibarah, where there are plenty of reefs which with this unprecedented storm rage, are not likely to let anyone escape alive. Oh, this is highly appropriate, that this evil, adulterous brood for once received this judgment. This episode may appropriately have robbed the Pharisees of the guts to take up arms against You again'.

[4] I said: 'Satan can take it on the chin a thousand times a thousand, yet after a thousand times a thousand blows he steadily remains the same, most wicked enemy of God and of everything good and true emanating from God's Spirit. Those floating dead upon the sea shall indeed harm us no more, but others shall take their place and force us to retreat to cities of the Greeks. And not many weeks shall pass until then'.

[5] Says **Peter**: 'Lord, surely we shall be left alone during our stay here?'

[6] I said: 'That indeed, but other men and nations of the Earth have need of the Gospel as you do, and they are created by the same Father who created you. To these we must go in spite of all persecutions still awaiting us, bringing them the good news from the Heavens. They shall indeed persecute us as well, but by and by shall be converted, and join our pen as lambs.

[7] We are good, yet the world is evil, therefore we can expect nothing good of it, save an occasional sweet strawberry among the weeds. But see, the storm has abated, and for this time all danger has passed.'

[8] (To Baram): 'Friend, the storm has settled down, and midday has passed with the storm, and therefore we shall partake of lunch, to make us sufficiently strong for the afternoon work.'

[9] It will not be necessary to say more about the lunch, or shed more light on the effects of the preceding storm on mainly the 10 ships. It suffices to know that of the 1,000 men aboard the ships, only 5 escaped with their lives, the others becoming prey to the sea. And upon the Sibarian reefs for over a year, human remains, partly gnawed away by fish, were being found, together with a host of Roman arms and chains earmarked for me and My disciples.

[10] It will hardly be necessary to relate the chastening effect such a storm had upon the Pharisees as well as the Romans, especially at Capernaum and

Nazareth, and I and those with Me were left in peace for some weeks.

[11] After lunch on that day, nothing much of note was undertaken, and the disciples therefore went to sea with Kisjonah's fishermen, and by evening brought in 5 big catches of the choicest fish held by this sea, taking them to Kisjonah's fish tanks, who was greatly overjoyed therewith, and about a hundred of them had at once to be most superbly prepared, with all kinds of spices and herbs. And so the day came to an end, with a rest taken after supper, which had become most essential for all.

## CHAPTER 210
### Excursion to Cana in the valley

[1] The following day we made a so-called excursion to a valley which wound along half way between the two mountain-chains toward Samaria, through which a main road led to Damascus, and from there to all the small and great cities of Central Asia, for which reason Kisjonah's toll at Kis was one of the most profitable in all of Galilee.

[2] In this valley there were of course a great number of small villages which were occupied by large numbers of Jews and Greeks, mainly for trade's sake. Most adjacent to Kis was the locality named Cana, for which reason the Cana near Nazareth was referred to with the appendage 'of Galilee'. If Cana was mentioned on its own, then it was understood to mean the above-mentioned Cana in the valley, whose location already was in the region of Samaria, the reason also for a toll at Kis, a border city between Galilee and Samaria.

[3] This Cana was inhabited mainly by Greeks, Greek families outnumbering the Jewish by at least five to one. The Jews subsisted mainly from working the land, and stock breeding, whereas the Greeks only from trading.

[4] We therefore visited this Cana, and namely the resident Jews who quite often were immensely cheated by the sharp and crafty Greeks, and as owners of the land were almost exclusively subject to all the taxes and other burdens, and therefore quite often sank into all sickness and infirmities from grief and wretchedness.

[5] As we arrived in Cana, with the Jews as well as the Greeks noticing the familiar Kisjonah, they rushed over and greeted him, pleading forbearance for their debts, as both the Jews and Greeks owed him substantial sums of money.

[6] But **Kisjonah** said: 'If I had wanted to make demands on you, I need not have made this journey myself, but just have sent my servants to you. But I came to bring you comfort, which I announce to you all publicly: your arrears are more than paid, for my and your Lord has paid them and restituted me, and you can cheer up and be untroubled.'

[7] On hearing such, the Cana residents joyfully probe Kisjonah as to who and where such Lord would be, who did them such great favor, that they may go and thank him and do him honor.

[8] **Kisjonah** places his hand on My shoulder, saying: 'This is He before whom to bend your knees.'

[9] Hearing this, **the residents** fall on their knees before Me, calling: 'Hail You, our as yet unknown benefactor. What favor are we supposed ever to have done you that you have shown us compassion in our immense plight? Since you have now as a perfect stranger and benefactor shown us such unheard-of grace, have the forbearance to tell us how we can repay such grace, to show ourselves more worthy of your goodness than we are, and can be, as perfect strangers to you.'

[10] I said: 'Let you from now on be righteous in everything, love God above all and your fellow men, who all are your neighbors, as yourselves. Return good unto those who do you evil; bless those who curse you, and pray for those who persecute you. In this way shall you be accepted as children of the Most High, and in this shall consist your only real gratitude for all I have done for you. This is all I ask of you.'

[11] Say **the Greeks**: 'Lord and friend, we have many gods. Which one of the many gods should we indeed love above all: Zeus, Apollo or Mercury, or any other out of the 12 chief gods? Or should we love the God of the Jews thus? For the God of the Jews, in the final analysis, appears to be no more than our Kronos. How can we love this mythological god above all?'

[12] I said: 'The gods whom you Greeks worship are no more than idle machination, made from matter by human hands. These you can beg, worship, honor and love more than your own lives for thousands of years, and yet they shall neither hear you nor do you a good deed, for the simple reason that they, in living truth, are nothing and exist nowhere.

[13] The God of the Jews however, whom the vast majority now are no longer able to or want to recognize in fullness and in truth; and instead, in spirit and in Truth of heart, which in reality is love, worship and honor with only the filthiest and dead sacraments, nevertheless is the only true, eternal God, who out of Himself once created Heaven and this Earth, with everything on it, in it and under it, that lives and has its being.

[14] I am however His Messenger from eternity and have now come to you to proclaim this Gospel to you.

[15] It is this God therefore whom you are to love above all, keeping His Commandments, which briefly consist in loving Him above all and your neighbors as yourselves, as I said to you before.

[16] Besides that however you are to believe that this very God, who is My Father and therefore My love from eternity, has sent Me into this world, so that all who believe on Me should have eternal life and therefore become a child of the Most High.

[17] In order for you to believe more easily however, bring all your sick, and I shall make all of them well, regardless of which sickness they may suffer from. Therefore go and bring them all here.'

[18] They were astounded at this My saying, calling out as **with one voice**: 'A great blessing has overtaken this place. How mighty and marvelous is the sound of the divinely true words of this our greatest benefactor. Verily, no guile could

reside in such kindness and goodness, nor falseness or deception. Therefore we shall do without misgivings whatever He is pleased to ask of us. For he who was our friend before seeing us, will be the more so after he has spoken to and seen us in our great plight. Praised be the God of Abraham, Isaac and Jakob, that He should have remembered and be merciful to us".

[19] With these commendable words they all rush to their dwellings, quickly bringing about 200 sick over to Me.


## CHAPTER 211
### Great healing miracle in Cana of the Valley

[1] When the sick; some escorted, others sitting on mules and some carried on stretchers, were assembled around Me in a semi-circle, **the elders** of this place stepped over to Me with a supplication, saying,

[2] 'Lord. You who have freed us of our debt to the mighty and exceedingly wealthy Kisjonah – a deed for which we shall never be able to thank you sufficiently – heal these poor if You can, that they too may enjoy with us the fullness of the great favor you bestowed upon us.'

[3] I say: 'Yes, I have urged you to do this and can, and will keep My promise, but to begin with, I ask whether you can and want to believe this? Your faith would help you much'.

[4] Say **the elders**: 'Lord, it seems to us that You are capable, wherefore we believe, so to speak blindly, that You will heal our sick with wondrous remedies as yet unknown to us.'

[5] I say: 'But what if I have no special medications with Me, neither healing oil nor healing potions, nor any usual healing substances; how do you think I shall then heal these sick?'

[6] Say **the elders**: 'Lord. How could we possibly understand that? For we probably have more knowledge in any field other than in the art of healing. We indeed have a doctor in this place, who however is as good as none, for he has helped no one yet, other than into the grave. If therefore we knew even as much as our doctor, we could still not tell You anything about Your method of healing without medication; therefore we cannot possibly know how it is possible for You to in a natural way make the sick whole.

[7] Perhaps You have supernatural means at Your disposal, something we cannot know. Or You could be perhaps a disciple of the famous wonder-doctor of Nazareth by the name of Jesus? Then of course such cures could be possible to You.

[8] It is an everlasting pity however that we hear how the Pharisees in Jerusalem persistently pressure Herod to arrest and jail this most famous Savior. Oh, this is a tragedy for poor, suffering mankind.

[9] But by good fortune he is supposed to have instructed several students in His art. It is of course rare for a disciple to become as perfect as his master. But

with the right amount of diligence, he could have in any case learned something from him. And that which we suppose as indwelling You to a high degree, is already a considerable something to give us the faith You... but... what is this? Even while we are trying to represent our faith as based on Your being a disciple of Jesus... all the sick are getting up. The blind are seeing, the lame walking, the dumb speak, the leprous are clean. And among them had been several choleric and some with consumption, and they are well. Surely this is unheard of from the foundation of the world. In the great almighty God's will, how did this take place? Did You perhaps heal them all? Or has an angel descended to this valley from above and invisibly touched all the sick and healed them? What... what went on here?

[10] You did not even look around to the sick, dealing only with us, yet all the sick are well. Oh, tell us how this came about.'

[11] I say: 'What does the 'how' matter, as long as the sick, through My will and through My inner Word, to which all things are subject, became completely well, something you surely will no longer doubt? But this deed did not take place so much on account of the sick as on your account, who indeed are whole in body, but nonetheless more sick of soul than were those physically sick.

[12] But I should be very happy if I could also heal your souls the way I healed the physically sick. But this is not so easy, as each soul has to be its own doctor.

[13] But the spiritual medicine I have already given you before, use it in actuality and you shall become well in your souls, and shall therewith transform yourselves into the true children of God.

[14] The word that I spoke to you nevertheless must be kept without the slightest addition or subtraction. And you few Jews of this place are to be perfect Jews in heart; and you Greeks are to become true Jews, that there may be peace and unity among you.

[15] Likewise you Greeks, through your clever spirit of usury, are from now on to desist from forcing the already poor Jews to borrow money on prescribed land-rent rates, in order to achieve your unjust demands.

[16] Is it you that created this Earth with its diverse treasures, that you should now act as if it were your property?

[17] Why do you demand rent from the Jews, seeing that the land was given to the Jews by God, and that they alone therefore have the right to levy land rent from you? You are strangers in the land of the Jews, who are children of Jehovah more than you, and ask land rent on fields, meadows and woodlands which are the possession of Jews since Abraham. Ask yourselves whether this can be just before God and before all righteous men.

[18] I therefore earnestly warn you against such blatant injustices in the future, or you shall in all seriousness fare badly.

[19] Restore without remuneration the property and possession seized by you most unjustly and regard yourselves in the land of the Jews as that which you are - namely strangers - and you shall have a blessed part in all now bestowed upon the Jews, as promised in the Word; otherwise the curse of thousands with its effects shall be your portion.

[20] Regard the matter for once in its true light, and you shall see that in your eyes, the Jews are no more than beasts of burden.

[21] You indeed cede political right of possession to the Jews, and the Jew can still say, this land belongs to me, but you are there with your tempting wares, you have made the beautiful daughters and wives of the Jews into vain fashion merchants, and fools out of the blind Jews, who prefer their women and daughters dressed up Greek fashion rather than in their simple Jewish apparel, whereupon they signed over to you the harvest from their fields, gardens and woodlands. And since they still needed their life-support, and to reap some of the harvest from their fields, they had to go into a secondary lease for land use and in addition then tithe you from the harvest. And on top of that you let them, as the true owners, carry all taxation and other burdens.

[22] I say unto you: such injustice cries out to Heaven and calls for punishment from above. Let you therefore suffer My rebuke, or you shall not escape the sharpest scourge from above.'

# CHAPTER 212
## The hardened stoic

[1] The talk makes the Greeks hesitant, with **some** saying: 'The usually stupid Jews have worked this out very well. This miracle-working Jesus they assigned here so he may have us against the wall. But we stand on solid ground.'

[2] This time however I became indignant Myself with the Greeks' intransigence, saying to the hard-nosed speaker, who tried to dissuade the somewhat better Greeks from doing the right thing: 'Listen, you hard-hearted person. Watch that the ground does not shake underneath you and the firmness of your stand. There have been a great many already who called out to their surroundings with super-heroic voice: "Let the Earth be demolished, and the left-over pieces shall carry me about unflinchingly through infinity".

[3] I say unto you braggart of a Greek who calls himself Philopold, that the fly that sometimes makes a business trip unto your nose stands more firmly on your nose than you do on the ground. For should your nose suffer shipwreck, the fly still has a second foundation on which to preserve itself quite well, such as air; where however is your second support if the ground under your feet loosens?'

[4] At these My rather intentionally sarcastic words, **Philopold** the Greek, who was by nature a bit of a satirist, became piqued, saying; 'Look at the rare sight. Even a Jew sarcastic? Probably the first and last in Israel. Friend, when a Greek speaks of courage it is factual. For a Greek knows how to escape from life, seeking death. Greek history acknowledges Greek chivalry only, but is not ignorant of the incomprehensible cowardice of the Jews. Let the Earth shake, or let all the dragons out, and watch whether a Philopold's expression changes by the smallest degree.'

[5] I said: 'Let go of your vain bragging, and do as I commanded all of you, or

you shall earnestly force me to put your courage to a tough test. Because the God of the Jews will not be trifled with in such serious things, for even God's great patience has its fixed limits in certain things.

[6] If however you and your followers want to push your luck, then you shall be properly convinced that an angry God is not so easily appeased as to let a crude sinner get away without a well-earned punishment.'

[7] Says **Philopold**: 'This sounds typically Jewish. The Jews had certain seers. These never opened their mouths, except for sheer warnings of which some came true upon certain usually unspecified times. Most of them however were empty air, for the Earth's nature surely always has been stronger than the mouth of a Jewish prophet. The Greeks are stoics in general, and a true stoic has no fear, therefore neither I, for I too am a staunch stoic.'

[8] Says **Matthew**, the apostle, to Me privately, (until recently the tax-collector at Sibarah), 'Lord, this one I know quite well, a thoroughly annoying person. This one always kicked up a fuss outside my tax office, whenever he was taking his wares to Capernaum or Nazareth. With him I am still quite annoyed and feel like working him over.'

[9] I said: 'Let it be. I have a little test for him, and it will shortly come about.'

[10] Matthew stands back, but **Philopold** recognized his tax collector from Sibarah, saying to him: 'Well well, you miserly turnpike jockey, how come you are here too? What is your barricade going to do without your watching it from every angle with your lynx-like eyes? No need for you to actually stir up this wonder savior against me, for he shall know what to do if I get too stiff for him. But from the natural aspect you two could have a tough fight with me, for a stoic is no rope or string that one can bend any old way.

[11] See, the miraculous healing of the 200 sick has confounded nearly all the inhabitants of Cana. Why not me? Because I am a true stoic, to whom nearly all of creation is hardly worth a bump on the nose, and myself and miserable life even less. How would you therefore punish me? With death? I tell you I long for it, together with eternal annihilation, because I owe thanks to no god for this ignominious life. Or should one feel obliged to anyone for the most despised gift of all? Surely it isn't much for an almighty God to call a human into being. Who could prevent God from doing so? The man still-to-be created surely won't be asked whether he wants to be created, so that as the only one really concerned, he may utter his yes or no. Of equal unconcern to the as yet un-created one is it for the already created one as to whether or not he is followed by an as yet uncreated one. For a God therefore, the act of creating is nothing special, but indeed so for the created one, because he has to be something that he has never been able to request. What could indeed be more deplorable than having to be without ever having wanted it?

[12] Give me to eat and drink without my work or effort, and I shall be satisfied for at least the duration of Earth-life. But having to work unreasonably hard for maintaining this being, and therefore suffer like a hunted wolf, and on top of that be obliged to thank some god for it and at the same time keep certain commandments, only for the creator's selfish benefit, for this let me 'thank you,

not' to all Jewish and Greek gods or half-gods.'

[13] Says **Matthew**: 'A few more such people on Earth and Satan himself has a school he can attend for a hundred years. Lord, what is to be done with this one? If he really is the way he speaks, then all the angels together can achieve nothing with him in the normal way.'

## CHAPTER 213
### About reincarnation

[1] I said: 'Just let it be, you shall soon convince yourself that something can be done with this one.' And turning to Philopold, the stoic: 'Do you think that you did not enter upon a prior contract with God, your Creator, fulfilling all the oft-stipulated conditions essential for life upon this planet? See, you fool, this is already the twentieth heavenly sphere on which you live physically. Your cumulative age in the flesh in terrestrial years far exceeds the number of sand grains in all the terrestrial oceans. Yet besides that, what eons of time, hardly imaginable to men walking the Earth physically, had you already existed as a pure spirit of the fullest being and in the clearest self-consciousness within endless space, together with countless other spirits, consummating the fullest life and power.

[2] When however, living upon your most recent solar world, called Procyon by the wise of this Earth, but named Akka by the inhabitants of its wide Earth (pronouncing it with uniformly, because the inhabitants there speak only one language), you expressed the most ardent desire (after hearing from an angel that the great, almighty, eternal Spirit and sole Creator and sustainer of infinity and everything within it, is to take on the flesh Himself and the full human form upon one of the most insignificant planets orbiting within infinite space in countless numbers), that you would be set down here for the purpose of seeing and hearing Him who created you. Whereupon the same angel whom you see here as the seventh person, but who nevertheless is a fully free spirit, came to you and acquainted you in smallest detail with the difficult conditions you would have to suffer if wanting to become an inhabitant of this planet upon which you now stand, for the purpose of achieving the childhood of God.

[3] You accepted all the conditions including the one that, in common with all the inhabitants of this planet, you be barred all retrospection to your previous existence on other heavenly spheres until such time as this same angel would call you 3 times by the name by which you were named on Akka.

[4] If however things are of a truth just so, although of course incomprehensible to you, then how unfair is your assertion that there was no contract entered into between you and your Creator for your existence upon this Earth.'

[5] Says **Philopold**: 'What kind of raving lunacy is this? I am supposed to have already lived, in the flesh, on some nicer and obviously better world as a human? No, this is getting too thick. Listen, you seventh one on the right, referred to as an

angel by the Nazarene, what do they call you and me?'

[6] Says **the angel**: 'Just wait a little, and I shall in all haste fetch evidence from your previous world, and give it to you for your greater insight and identification.'

[7] With these words the angel vanishes, re-appearing in a few moments to hand Philopold a scroll on which, clearly inscribed in ancient Hebrew, appear the angel's and his name, together with a second scroll in which were recorded the conditions he promised before his transfer.

[8] Handing such over to Philopold, **the angel** says: 'Here, read and understand, old Murahel, Murahel, Murahel. For I myself, named Archiel, have picked it up from the same altar where you made me the great promise. But do not now ask how such was possible in just a few moments, for with God, the most wondrous things are possible. Read it all first and speak afterwards.'

## CHAPTER 214
### Relationship between body, soul and spirit

[1] **Philopold** is absorbed with reading the scrolls, and as his inner vision opens therewith, he says after a good while, with the greatest astonishment: 'Yes, it is so. I now am seeing into all the endless depths of my being, seeing all the worlds upon which I have already lived, together with the places and locations I lived from birth to departure from those worlds. I am seeing what I was and what I did on one or the other celestial spheres, seeing also all my next of kin. And see, upon Akka (Procyon) I also see even my parents, my many brothers and most dear sisters. Yes, I even hear them talk about me with concern, saying: "What could have become of Murahel? Will he have found the great Spirit in human form within endless space? He will not be thinking of us, because Archiel the messenger of the great Spirit has veiled his retrospection, until he will call him 3 times by his real name.'

[2] See, thus I hear them speak now, even as I'm seeing them physically as well. Now they are going to the temple to look up the documents with the difficult life-conditions; yet they don't find same. But the high priest of the temple is telling them that Archiel picked up the documents a few moments ago on behalf of Murahel, but that they shall be restored in a short while. And now they are waiting in the temple, giving a sacrifice for me.

[3] O love, love, you divine power! How endlessly far have You stretched Your holy arm. Everywhere the same love. O God, how great and holy art You and how full of mysteries is free life. What man on Earth can probe the depths that I see now? With what insignificance miserable man walks this lean Earth, waging mortal combat not infrequently for a span of Earth, even while carrying within himself what billions of earths cannot grasp.'

[4] With these words, **Philopold** falls silent, going over to the angel to return the two scrolls to him, remarking: 'Restore them to where they are waiting for them.'

[5] But **the angel** says: 'See, I also brought a writing utensil, the very same one

with which you wrote the documents in the temple up on Akka. Sign yourself doubly on each document and your name here, and keep the writing utensil for remembrance.'

[6] Philopold does that, and the angel takes the documents and vanishes.

[7] After a few moments, those he needs to talk to the high priest on Akka, he is back among us, asking Philopold what he thinks now.

[8] Says **Philopold**: 'As I handed the two scrolls back to you, the vision disappeared, and I hardly remember more than a dream, where consciousness tells only that there was one, whose details however no amount of memory-tugging will recall. I also notice that I hold some strange writing utensil in my left hand, yet I hardly recall how I came by it. Therefore I would like to know why one retains either very little or nothing at all of the phenomena from the domain of the inner life. Why so?'

[9] Says **the angel**: 'Because here it is all about becoming a completely new creature out of and in God. Once you will have become a completely new creature out of God, and achieve the childhood of God, everything shall be added back unto you.

[10] In all the other countless worlds, you are created externally and internally what you are to be, but here God hands the external formation to the soul, which builds its own body in accordance with its created order. But the task of the spirit placed into every soul, primarily is to develop the soul by keeping the commandments given him from without. Once the soul as a result has achieved the right degree of ripeness and development, the spirit spreads into the entire soul, and the entire man is then perfected, a new being, and that fundamentally out of God, since the spirit within man is no less than a God in miniature, because fully out of the heart of God. But man is then so, not through God's deed but through his fully own, and is for that reason a true child of God. And I repeat to you in all brevity: in no other heavenly sphere do men have to form themselves, for they are so of God, or what amounts to it, are so through His children. But here men have to develop completely by themselves, in accordance with the revealed order, or they could not possibly become children of God. And thus a perfected man on Earth, as a child of God, is fully identical with God, although an undeveloped one, in contrast, is below the kingdom of animals.'


### CHAPTER 215
### Archiel speaks about the Lord's incarnation

[1] **Philopold** again asks the angel: 'But who will show us this most mysterious order?'

[2] Says **the angel**: 'The same who referred you to me. Go to Him, He will tell you what He has already told you. Because to live as He teaches already is that divine life-style, through which alone one can attain to the childhood of God.

[3] And He also is the same One on whose account you and many others have

spiritually left Akka, and for the Lord's sake were incarnated on this Earth, into the flesh of this Earth.

[4] But throughout all of Creation, and that upon all celestial spheres inhabited by intelligent beings in human form, the incarnation of the Lord has been proclaimed by us, but only a few spirits from a small number of worlds were allowed to enter the flesh of this world. For the Lord is familiar with the nature of all the worlds in endless space, together with the nature and capacity of their inhabitants and spirits occupying one or the other such world. And He therefore knows best as to what spirit is capable of entering upon the flesh of this Earth.

[5] Whoever was fit was also transferred here, and the number transferred here is not much over 10,000.

[6] But among these you are one of the most fortunate, because if you so desire, then you can be accepted by the Lord as a disciple, like those who arrived with Him here.'

[7] Says **Philopold**: 'My Archiel, since you have already done me such great favors, please do me also the favor of taking me over to the Lord, for now that I have recognized Him, I lack the courage to go over to Him again. If it were left to me alone, I would rather run away as fast as possible and hide so that no man would find me. But since I am here now, and everybody knows me only too well, I can't do so, for the entire valley would be filled with laughter. Therefore be so good and take me to the Lord, as my advocate.'

[8] Says **the angel**: 'It is not necessary to do so, as the Lord knows what we have need of. Therefore go to Him yourself, and He shall not pull your head off your trunk.'

[9] Upon these words of the angel, **Philopold** plucks up courage and comes to Me cautiously, saying from some 30 paces away: 'Lord, will You let me approach You? If not, then I shall make my retreat.'

[10] But I say: 'He who wants to come, let him come, for no man has advanced while hesitating.'

[11] Hearing this, Philopold hastened his steps and is therefore quickly by My side, achieving what many hesitate doing and therefore frequently don't achieve, as they are not to be moved from the spot they occupy, in spite of being called.

[12] For as long as someone, no matter what he does, will not direct his steps to Me in a straight line, all his doing, going and standing will be futile for his life. And were he to win the whole world but not Me, then the whole world will be useless to him. And if, in this time of revealing the Gospel, I call to someone, saying "come", but does not come, then he shall die the spiritual death. And for this reason, Philopold is a good example that everyone should follow. He who calls after Me, let him not hesitate once called. For from now on I shall not remain in Cana (meaning: filled with grace in this world) but shall move on, turning My eye and ear away from all who hesitate upon My "come".

# CHAPTER 216
## The last will be the first

[1] On coming over to Me, **Philopold** said: 'Lord, I have sinned without limit against You, but only my great blindness was responsible for this. But now that You o Lord, made me see in the most miraculous way, and I recognize who You are, I beg You for the sake of Your eternal love and wisdom that You would forgive me a poor, blind sinner, the transgressions I have committed against You and my neighbors, as you pointed it out to me before. Had I written down Your holy Word, then by all the Heavens, not even one accent should have remained unfulfilled. But I believe myself to have memorized Your will and shall follow it to the letter. You paid off all our debts with Kisjonah, and healed all our sick miraculously, without charge and all this You did ahead of any due request. And I therefore believe that You will not cast off a begging sinner.'

[2] I said: 'I say unto you: you are accepted. For he who comes shall be accepted. But go and first put your affairs in order as specified by Me. Then come and follow Me, for you are not to cling to this world, as you are not of this world or from below, but from another world, and therefore from above.

[3] Because, of all those you count as around Me, there are some from your world – others from another light-world, and only a few from this world. And these few don't mean much, for the world still matters more to them than I. Therefore they are capable of only little or nothing.

[4] I selected this Earth however because its children are the last and lowliest throughout all of infinity, and therefore I put on the garb of the deepest lowliness, to make it possible for all the creatures of My most endless creation to come unto Me. From the lowliest planetary inhabitants to those of the highest arch-primordial central suns, all are to be enabled to come unto Me along the same path.

[5] Therefore let it not astonish you that you meet Me on this most imperfect and last planet of My entire creation, for it is I who want it thus. Who therefore is to prescribe to do it differently?'

[6] Says **Philopold**: 'Lord, whoever would want to or could give You advice, if he believes and recognizes that You are the Lord from eternity? But now I shall depart, in order to attend to Your holiest will immediately.'

[7] With these words, Philopold rushes off, together with all the local chiefs, but while quite a few Jews accompany them, to see what the Greeks would work out on their behalf, I Myself am instructing the healed on how to conduct themselves in future, in order not be re-visited by their old illnesses.

[8] Everyone received this teaching gratefully, and they thank Me also most ardently for the great favor bestowed upon them.

[9] I however command them, one and all to tell no stranger what they had seen and heard here and to as it were betray Me before time, the non-keeping of which would cause them to fare badly. But they all promised that no other place shall find out.

[10] I then let them go and also tell the disciples not to make known this deed

anywhere outside Kis. And to Matthew's query regarding whether to record this matter, I reply: 'No, because you as My closest witnesses indeed can bear and also grasp it. But if everything I do and say before you were recorded in books, the world not only would not comprehend such books, but on the contrary be offended beyond measure, and denounce you below every carcass on Earth. Therefore nothing should be recorded by you, Matthew, other than what I expressly direct you to record.

[11] Says for once also **John**: 'But Lord, my purest love, this would all be fine, but if once with time the world is handed down only fractious original documents about Your presence and action in this world, then it shall go over into all doubts about Your being and operation and regard such fractions as the work of mere priestly self-interest.'

[12] I said: 'This is however exactly how I want it to be for the actual world, which is Satan's house, for regardless of whether you cast corn or the most precious pearls before swine, it shall do the same with the pearls as with the corn.

[13] Therefore it is better to present the thing to the world fully veiled, whereupon the latter is free to wrestle with the husk, within which the living corn remains unharmed.

[14] When once nevertheless it becomes necessary, I shall indeed awaken men and reveal to them all that took place here, and what the world can expect on account of its incorrigible wickedness.

[15] But how all this shall take place I shall, My brother John, once reveal to you for the rest of the world in veiled images while still in this world, when I shall again be dwelling in My Heavens.

[16] But now the Greek and Jewish local chiefs are returning from the city. We shall see how they attended to My request.'

## CHAPTER 217
### Warning against Satan's traps

[1] Philopold together with **several Greeks** steps over to Me, saying: 'Lord, as far as was possible in the short time, we gratefully attended to Your request, but we shall not fail to attend to the minor details too. So far as my family is concerned I am now free to accompany You 1 or 2 or 3 years, if only I let my family know from time to time where I am and what You are doing. For see, my entire household now believes and hopes in Your name. If You are pleased with that o Lord, then please communicate it, or any further request.

[2] I said: 'For the present you have done everything that is right before God and before all men who feel and think righteously, but be on your guard against all sorts of traps with which Satan enchants you and you then fall out into all kinds of quarreling and wrangling, where such future state would then be worse than was the present one from which I liberated you.

[3] For the wicked spirit never rests, neither by day nor night. He runs to and fro

and like a hungry lion, rapaciously falling upon anything at all coming his way.

[4] Were he visible, then some men of courage would hazard a fight with him, yet be defeated even sooner than if visible, for he can transform his appearance to a beauty surpassing an angel of light, or on the other hand clothe himself with the shape of the most frightful fiery dragon. Who would dare then to take him on in that appearance? For Satan would then vanquish millions through either the beauty or petrifying hideousness of form alone. Where he cannot and must not reveal himself however, with every man nevertheless being capable of easily recognizing his evil whisperings, which always make the soul hard-hearted, selfish, domineering, deceitful, mean, merciless, indifferent towards truthfulness and godliness, unfeeling towards the poor and suffering but attuned to all worldly indulgence. There man can openly confront these efforts on Satan's part, for Satan can affect only the soul's senses, but not its will.

[5] I have now given you the signs that show you – when they try to overtake your soul – how you can easily recognize what spirit is close to you and what he has in mind with you.

[6] Whenever you perceive such upon yourselves, then listen back to this My teaching. Lift up your souls and do the contrary to the initial enticements, to thus become master of the wicked one. And once you have defeated him in the aspects indicated, he shall leave you alone and you shall have no more fights with him. But if you allow yourselves to get caught in one or the other aspect, or relent in even a small way, then you shall not easily be rid of him again to the very end of your Earth life.

[7] Thus, heed all those points that I brought to your attention. Because once when the evil one has brought a certain soul to the point – which is not so hard to do for him – that he gives in to something, leading of course to sin, then it already takes a fierce fight to fully repair the damage to the soul.

[8] But when someone is firmly determined to do all he can by himself, and spiritually hands his weakness over to Me, for such the full victory over Satan shall be easier. But note well, only after the calling upon My name in living faith.

[9] Now you know everything you need to know. You know the One true God, and now His will.

[10] Verily I say unto you: the Father in Heaven has well-provided you with everything you have need of. Now it is up to you as to how conscientiously you want to employ it for your true and everlasting benefit.

[11] Out of your own doing or omission all effects shall proceed, and your words and deeds shall be your judges.

[12] You, Philopold, wait here 3 more days and try to order everything. Then come out to Kis where you shall meet Me.'

[13] Philopold promised to do so. Thereupon I blessed the place, and we made our way back to Kis.

[1] On arriving home, several servants come to meet us and tell us that shortly after our leaving for the valley, a great many strangers had arrived, insistently inquiring about Me, what I was up to and to where I had headed for. But they, the servants, who presumed to recognize them as Pharisees in disguise, told them that I had left the area a long time since, and that, in their opinion, for Damascus or possibly even to the heathens in Persia, for I am supposed during My stay here to have repeatedly stated: the grace shall be taken from the Jews and given to the gentiles.

[2] At this the inquirers were visibly angered, and **one of them** was supposed to have said: 'Boys can shake the fruit off young trees indeed, but not from an old one that has to be climbed cautiously, if one wants to get to the fruit-laden branches. This magician shall have little effect upon the Jewry!'

[3] At this, they, **the servants**, laughed and said: 'Just watch that the tree does not get blown over on account of its rottenness. It seems to us that your tree has already had it for a long time, so far as fruits are concerned, and its dried-out branches hung by you with dried figs, for a dirty-trick wonder.'

[4] At this, the obvious Pharisees were supposed to become indignant and to start threatening the servants.

[5] But **the servants** said: 'To begin with we are Greeks, and embrace the religion of our emperor, and therefore can laugh at your stupidity that you call God's doctrine, and you can do us no harm if we don't do so in your temples and schools. And secondly, there are many of us serving at mighty Kisjonah's big house. And if therefore you don't leave this place soon, then we shall start showing you the way out with clubs.' Thereupon they bit their lips balefully and went their way up the coast leading to Jerusalem.

[6] But we would ask You, Lord Jesus, whether we acted in an appropriate manner?'

[7] I said: 'Except for one thing: it was not right that you knowingly told them an untruth. It would have been better if you had told them the truth. In that case they would have waited for us and we would have effected changes on them. For these were mostly sick, with some Pharisees among them indeed, but of a better variety. They are still camping upon the hill that rises from the upper end of the bay. Therefore hasten over to them with donkeys and mules and bring them all here. Say to them: 'The Lord has arrived and waits for you. Load the sick upon the mules and donkeys and let the healthy walk.'

[8] Although it is already late dusk, the servants get under way as I requested, bringing all those over whom they had driven away with blind zeal.

[9] 5 Pharisees step over to Me at once with proper deference, complaining of how roughly they were treated by domestic staff, which abused and lied to them.

[10] But I reassure them, telling them that it was not from ill-will, but out of blind love for Me, since they thought they sensed you My enemies. This is why I also

commanded them on My arrival to convey you here in as good a state as possible. And so they had to therewith make good their transgression against you. And I regard this matter as fixed up.

[11] Say **the Pharisees**: 'Quite, it is all in the best order. But now to another matter.

[12] We have come all the way from Bethlehem, having heard of Your extraordinary healing-miracle power. Therefore we brought along our sick. Those still strong enough had to walk of course, and the weaker ones we transported by beasts of burden. We beg You to have mercy on the suffering and heal them of their maladies.'

[13] I said: 'Where are they whom you brought upon the beasts of burden? The staff did not mention them.'

[14] Say the 5 **Pharisees**: 'We left them at the inn beyond the bay, as we could not know whether we could meet up with You. Because it was hard to even find out that You were to be found here, intermittently, and that You could not be met with certainty. And so we ventured here to either find You, or to most likely find out here where You might be, or when You might return. Due to this uncertainty we left our rather feeble sick at the aforementioned inn, so that they may receive care while we try and reach You and beg You to have mercy on these acutely suffering. Therefore we also set up camp on the mountain above the inn, in order to be as near as possible to our sick, quartering at the inn with barest essentials.

[15] We now have, Lord and Maser, told you everything, and we can tell you no more. If therefore You are that way inclined, then have mercy on the poor and suffering.'

[16] I said: 'It is indeed so. If you don't see miracles and signs, your faith is weak but without the power of faith, little can be done for mankind's well being. If you believe however, then you shall see the glory of God's power in man.'

[17] Say **all**: 'Yes, yes, indeed Lord. All of us believe. He who can, as You have done, call back to life a deceased daughter of the chief Jairus, can also heal all other sickness, which is no death by a long shot. Because, of this deed we heard as far away as David's city of Bethlehem.'

[18] Say **I** with raised hands: 'So then, let it be in accordance with your faith.'

[19] **All the sick** awaiting healing in the courtyard instantly became completely well, and started to jubilate and cry for joy, exclaiming: 'We saw a light enter our bodies, and we are well. And we now feel as if there had never been anything wrong with us. Hail to Him who has made us whole so suddenly.'

[20] The Pharisees can hardly utter a word for astonishment. After a short while however they hear more shouting and jubilation in the Kis area. The Pharisees, as well as the thoroughly healed sick, go to at look at what the noise was. They quickly realize it is **their sick from the inn**, all leaping about like lively stags, shouting; 'Hail to the Man who healed them so miraculously.'

[21] As the healed ones join the 5 Pharisees, the latter ask the jubilant ones when and how they were healed. All those healed – about 30 in number – tell with one voice: 'At such and such a time, and that they saw a light entering their bodies.'

[22] Here the five realized this was at the time **I said:** Let it be in accordance with your faith, and that those in the inn were healed by a light.

[23] All are astonished, and **the healed** are exclaiming: 'Take us to the Savior, so that we may say our thanks and praise to Him personally.'

[24] The Pharisees lead them to Me and they fall down before Me, praising God for imbuing man with such power.

[25] But I command them to rise, and while showing them to their dining room, warn them not to make any of this known, neither at Jerusalem nor at David's city.

[26] And they promise with one voice that they will heed this as far as possible, but that they shall fare badly in their city when returning completely fit. But they shall do everything not to betray Me.

[27] Calling their intentions good, I lead them into the dining room, where refreshments and fortifications of all kinds await them. I bless the food and drinks for them and invite them to eat and drink according to need, assuring them of no harmful effects. And they start eating and drinking, while I Myself withdrew to another chamber, where honest Baram had prepared an exceedingly plenteous supper for Myself and Mine, with Kisjonah and his family partaking at My side.

## CHAPTER 219
### Parable of the fattening bull

[1] Said **Ahab**, after supper: 'It goes without saying that I am clear about Your nature since Jesaira, and there would have been no need for such immense signs for either myself or the likes of me, to convince us all abundantly that You are Jehovah Himself, acting through a physical body, borrowed as it were from this Earth. But I am curious about whether the 5 Pharisees, seemingly upright people, in all earnest do not sense who might the One who healed their sick in a truly miraculous way. If they had but the faintest clue, they would have to be capable of grasping by hand that an ordinary human could not possibly accomplish this in all eternity. In my opinion, one should go and sniff them out a little and it should quickly transpire as to what they actually make of You.'

[2] I said: 'Friend, you will surely not doubt that I know what they think of Me. So I don't consider it necessary to interrupt them in their deliberations. Therefore, tomorrow is another day on which a few initiatives can be taken in that respect. Let us leave them to some real fermentation overnight. Because just as cider needs fermenting to become a spiritual wine, just so every man's emotions need fermenting, if he is to transcend to the truly spiritual.

[3] See, if a man has everything that he needs, then he feels quite snug. He cares about nothing, does no work, takes it easy and inquires little about the existence of God or life after physical death, or whether man is more than the animal, or vice versa. Mountains and valleys are the same to him, winter and summer don't concern him, for in summer he has shade and cooling baths, and in winter well-heated fire-places and warm clothing.

[4] Neither does he care whether the year was plentiful or not, for he is provided firstly with all stores for ten years and secondly with plenty of money for acquiring anything he lacks.

[5] See, such a person then enjoys the leisure of a fattening ox in the stable, prone to little more thought than the ox, and is therefore no more than a hedonistic animal in human form.

[6] If you came to such a man to preach the Gospel of the heavenly kingdom, he would do to you what the ox in the stable does to the blowfly, swinging his tail over it to make it take off or be killed or at least suffer considerable harm.

[7] And see, such carefree glutton shall direct his servants, who also are no more than the carefree hedonists' fly chasing and repelling tail, to chase you away. You obviously shall quickly turn on your heels, and at a safe distance contemplate the effect of your gospel on the glutton.

[8] But I know how to give such oxen quite a different introductory sermon. I let one terrestrial accident after another overtake them. This fills them with all sorts of troubles and fears, causing them to think, seek to find out and ask how it is possible for them to now be beset by all sorts of extremities, since they had never been unjust to anyone, having always been orderly and respectable citizens.

[9] This however is only on account of the necessary fermentation.

[10] When such people then undergo a proper fermentation, they long for friends who could bring them comfort. Go to them then to preach the Gospel, and they shall hear you and not raise their furiously swinging tail against you.

[11] And see, for this reason it is good for these guests to undergo real fermentation this night; this shall make them internally more spiritual, and your work shall be easy with them tomorrow. Do you follow this?'

## CHAPTER 220
### A late-riser will soon age

[1] Says **Ahab**: 'O wisdom, o wisdom. See your grasp of the exalted and true, and how immensely stupid the likes of us. It is an eternal truth that nothing can arise without a struggle, yet I was going to hurry over to the people of Bethlehem to start enlightening them. O, centre of stupidity that I am. Do not the Greek wise men say: Every activity is generated from struggle, and every effect its outcome. Yet I did not see this. Why do I see it now?

[2] Indeed, if there is no preceding contention between the inner life-elements in man, then all external efforts with man are futile.

[3] I am now in the clear about human instruction, and could almost pronounce a life-fundamental, without straying too far afield.' **I** said: 'Let it be heard. I intend not to review it within Myself until you have voiced it.'

[4] **Ahab** says: 'What man has not initially acquired himself from the properties given him at the outset, no God can give him without ruining him. To God, of course, all things are possible, but thereby man does not gain anything.

[5] Who does not know himself first, how can he know another and, finally, even God? That would be my principle. Am I far off the mark, Lord?'

[6] I said: 'No, friend Ahab, you have in truth hit the nail firmly on the head. Thus it is. What man does not acquire for himself independently with the abilities bestowed on him, God cannot and may not provide without judging him.

[7] Therefore, all of you should not be just idle hearers of My Word, but diligent doers, only then will you begin to notice its blessings within you.

[8] For life is action and not stagnation of the powers on which life depends. And so life must be preserved even for eternity through the constant activity of all its powers, for in the lying-down-to-rest there is no permanent life.

[9] The certain feeling of well-being you gain from rest is nothing else but a partial death of the powers needed for living. The person who then increasingly enjoys the inactive rest, especially of the spiritual life-powers, thereby also slides ever more into the arms of actual death from which no God will easily free him.

[10] O yes, there does also exist a proper rest full of life, but that is in God and for everyone an indescribably blissful feeling of contentment to be active in accordance with God's will.

[11] This most blissful feeling of contentment and the clearest realization to have always truly acted according to the order of God is that proper rest in god which alone is full of life because it is full of energy and respective action. Every other rest that consists in the ceasing of the life-powers is, as already mentioned, an actual death to the point to which the various life-forces have withdrawn from activity and no longer resumed it. Do you understand this?'

[12] Says **Judas Iscariot**: 'Lord, if so, then man should flee sleep like the pestilence, for also sleep is a rest of a number of life-forces, although external ones.'

[13] I said: 'Certainly. Because of that late-risers will never reach a particularly great age. Whoever grants his body 5 hours of sleep in his young days and 6 hours in his old age will usually reach a great age and look youthful for a long time, whereas a late-riser soon ages, gets a lined face and gray hair and at a somewhat advanced age walks around like a shadow.

[14] And just as the body gradually dies off through too much sleep, in the same way, but on a larger scale this applies to the soul if it increasingly slackens in its activity according to My Word and will.

[15] Once idleness has made itself at home in a soul there soon follows also depravity. For idleness is nothing else but a self-indulging love which all the more flees any activity for someone else's sake because it basically want only one thing, namely that all others should work for its benefit.

[16] Therefore, beware particularly of idleness, for this is an actual see for all kinds of vices.

[17] The various beasts of prey may serve you as an example. Look, these beasts become destructively active only when driven by burning hunger. Once they have captured their prey and satisfied their hunger, they again return to their lairs where they rest often for days, especially snakes.

[18] Now look at a robber or murderer. This man who shuns all work, who is

actually a devil in the flesh, lies often for days in one of his dens. Only when his pies tell him that a rich caravan is due to pass his den, he lies in wait together with his accomplices, ruthlessly attacks and robs the caravan and kills the merchants to prevent them from betraying him. And that is a fruit of idleness.

[19] Therefore, I say once more: Beware above all of idleness, for it is the road and the wide door to all imaginable vices.

[20] After the work has been done moderate rest is good for the limbs of the body, but excessive rest is worse than none.'


## CHAPTER 221
### Rest and activity

[1] If someone has walked a long distance and finally reaches a shelter he will, if he does not go to bed immediately, but continues with small movements and on the following day is on his feet already before sunrise, not feel any tiredness all day, and the longer he will thus continue his journey the less tired it will make him.

[2] If, however, someone after a day's march arrives quite as tired at a shelter, immediately throws himself on a bed and maybe leaves it only at noon on the following day, he will be continuing his journey on completely stiff feet and with a totally drunk head. After having covered a certain distance, he will from utter exhaustion long for a rest, and it can even happen that he collapses on the road and perishes there if no one comes to his aid, which can easily happen.

[3] And what has caused it? His own too great desire for rest and the delusion that rest strengthens a person.

[4] If someone wished to achieve a great, amazing accomplishment in one or the other art where a high degree of skillfulness of hands and fingers is required, then I ask you: will he achieve it if instead of constant diligent practice every day he idly strolls around day by day with his hands in his pockets motivated by a kind of anxious concern not to tire his hands and fingers to prevent them from getting stiff and unfit for the striven-for accomplishment?

[5] Truly, even I Myself with all My boundless wisdom could not make a prophet and determine the time when such a disciple of art will become a virtuoso. Therefore, My dear friends and brothers, I repeat:

[6] Only activity upon activity for the common good of people brings you salvation. For all life is the fruit of God's constant, never tiring activity and therefore can only be maintained and preserved for eternity through proper activity whereas nothing but death does and must result from inactivity.

[7] Place your hands on your heart and feel how it is constantly active day and night. The life of the body depends solely on such activity. Once the heart stops, that would mean the end of the natural life of the body, I should say.

[8] And just as the rest of the physical heart obviously constitutes the total death of the body, this same rest of the soul's heart is the death of the soul.

[9] The heart of the soul, however, is called love, and its pulsating expresses

itself in true and full love-activity.

[10] Thus constant love-activity is the never wearying pulse-beat of the soul's heart. The more actively the heart of the soul pulsates, the more life is generated in the soul and once thereby a sufficiently high degree of life, this awakens therein the life of the divine spirit.

[11] This spirit – being pure life because it is the untiring supreme activity itself – then flows into the soul that has become equal to it through love activity, and everlasting imperishable life has fully begun within the soul.

[12] And look, all this arises from activity, but never from idle rest.

[13] Therefore, shun rest and seek full activity, and eternal life will be your reward.

[14] Do not imagine that I have come to bring peace to mankind on this Earth. O no, only the sword and war instead.

[15] For, men must be impelled to all kinds of activity through distress and hardships or they would become lazy, fatted oxen that fatten themselves for eternal death.

[16] Distress and hardship bring about fermentation upon fermentation in man from which in the end something spiritual could develop.

[17] One could, of course, say: "Through distress and hardship also anger, vengeance, murder and manslaughter arise, also envy, hardheartedness and persecution." That is indeed true, but bad as all that is, the result is nevertheless better than from idle rest which is dead and brings neither good nor bad results.

[18] Therefore I tell you: let a person be really warm or completely cold where I am concerned, but a lukewarm one I will spit out from My mouth.

[19] I prefer an energetic enemy to a lukewarm friend, for the energetic enemy will challenge Me to full activity, so that I may either win him over or make provision to prevent him from harming Me. Beside a lukewarm friend, however, I become lukewarm Myself and if I should get into difficulties, will the lukewarm friend be of any use to Me?

[20] Therefore, also a lukewarm ruler is a pest for his people, for then the nation's spirit decays and the people all turn into voracious oxen and beasts of burden. But a severe and even tyrannical ruler causes the people to be alive and there is activity everywhere so as not to incur punishment. And if a tyrant goes too far the people will rise in great numbers and rid themselves of their tormentor.

[21] I think I have now said enough about the value of activity and am convinced that all of you have understood this lesson. Therefore, if someone wants it and feels a need for a sleeping rest for his body, let him seek a bed, but who wants to sit up with Me through the night, let him remain here.' There **they all** said: 'Lord, how could we sleep when You are sitting up? Only the mother Mary seems to need a rest for her body, and so You could send her to bed.'

[22] But Mary, although she had dozed a little in an armchair behind Me, heard these words, sat up and said with great friendliness to the speaker: 'Friend, you who usually speak for your fellow-disciples, I tell you that your concern for me is rather futile. For, see, for the sake of my Lord I have sat up for probably hundreds of sleepless nights and am still alive – and if it is His will I will again go through as

many sleepless nights and not lose my life. Therefore, do not concern yourselves about me all of you, it is sufficient that One looks after me.'

[23] These words had been addressed to Thomas and he came to Mary and asked her not to regard his good intention unkindly. But Mary comforted him and was very kind about his concern for her, and Thomas felt easier in his mind and soon, quite relieved, resumed his seat.

[24] For a while there was now silence. No one spoke, for they all pondered on what had been said and found the truth of it shining ever brighter.

[25] Only **Matthew** said after a while to himself: 'Tomorrow at daybreak this teaching about activity and rest will be recorded as best as possible on a special tablet, for this so extremely important lesson must on no account be lost to the world.' And when soon it began to dawn, Matthew kept his word, and this lesson was preserved for a long time and through Jonael and Jairuth reached also Samaria, but in the course of time was considerably distorted and, therefore, also got lost. But while it was still around the people knew it under the name of "the night-sermon."

## CHAPTER 222
### The 5 Pharisees washing the Lord's feet

[1] In the morning, the 5 Pharisees came over to me, greeting Me and My disciples in the friendliest terms, after their fashion, and even showed Me an especial honor by asking me whether I would find them worthy of washing My feet.

[2] For in Bethlehem, it was still an old form of especial reverence the following morning for the host to wash his guest's feet or alternatively for the principal guest to wash the feet of the host. Therefore I permitted the 5 Pharisees to wash and dry My feet.

[3] Only after this action did **the 5 Pharisees** ask me, saying: 'Verily, inexplicably supreme master, would you not tell us something of the method by which you achieve such unheard-of healings. There can be no doubt that in general terms, You obviously perform this through God's power, but it is another question in what way, and in unheard-of perfection. Only of this give us a few hints, if You find us worthy, whereupon we shall be joyfully and everlastingly grateful to You, and undertake our journey back to Bethlehem.'

[4] I said: 'Even if I were to tell you that, you would nevertheless not believe Me, for Moses' threefold veil hangs also over your eyes, that you may not discern who it is that now speaks to you. Were you to know Him, you would not put such a question, but because you don't know Him, you ask the way you do.

[5] And were I to give you the right answer, you would still not accept it. Because you see indeed what is and happens in the world materially, but concerning the Spirit, its Kingdom and action, this is strange to you, wherefore you are unable to grasp or feel what is the being and action of God's kingdom in man.

396

[6] But go and do penance on account of your many sins, and you shall perceive that the Kingdom of God has come near unto you.

[7] Love God with all your strength, worshipping Him in spirit and in truth, but loving also your poor brother and sister neighbors. Do not persecute your enemies, nor curse those that curse you, doing good to those offending you, and you shall heap coals of fire upon their heads and God shall regard such your works and reward you a hundredfold.

[8] Do not lend your money to those who can repay you with high interest, but to the truly poor and needy, and your money shall be invested for high interest rates in Heaven, and your Father in Heaven shall be paying you interest and capital everlastingly.

[9] Do not crave the world's praise, thanks and reward for your good deeds, for doing so, what reward shall be due to you from Heaven? I Say unto you: he who receives any reward whatsoever for a good deed performed on a neighbor, forfeits his reward in Heaven.

[10] He who works for Heaven shall be rewarded by Heaven, temporally, and once everlastingly, but he who works for the world shall receive the world's base and perishable rewards. But in Heaven he shall find his earning-record void, and his reward shall be gone, and there shall be hardly an end to his spiritual poverty.

[11] If you take this to heart and act accordingly, you shall soon be in the clear on how I heal your sick. Now you know all you need to know. Further asking would gain you nothing, even if you were told.

[12] But see to it that neither I, nor My action and My disciples are broadcast, either in Jerusalem or in the city of David, for this would bring you no blessing.

[13] But when you shall have partaken of the morning meal, you can start upon your homeward journey with cheer.'

[14] This My saying brought forth a baffled expression from the five, yet they dared ask no further question, bowing down before Me and then moving over to their dining room, hitting the road for their homeland after the morning meal.


## CHAPTER 223
## Hints on teaching

[1] Following this, the disciples step over to Me, asking why I was so secretive with the Bethlehemites.

[2] I said: 'Are you still so unwise, as if you had never heard Me utter a wise word yet? These regard Me as no more than an exceptionally gifted doctor, who performs such healings with the help of secret natural forces.

[3] They are not ignorant of the Essene sect that has some very remarkable knowledge in the secret art of chemistry, by means of which they are capable of healing quite a few sicknesses and also are capable of producing quite a few phenomena which the layman regards as obvious miracles. If you consider this, then you can't expect anything to come out of this other than their taking Me for an

Essene chief, therefore of the highest rank, whose knowledge is supposed to be capable of harnessing the most diverse natural forces and direct them to his liking.

[4] Had I therefore revealed Myself to them straight-out as the Son of the Most High, and therefore the promised Messiah, how would these steel-hard Jews have started raging beyond measure, taking Me for a self-arrogating magician, in league with Satan, and then also as such blasphemed Me beyond measure, and the healing of their sick would then have been the ultimate bone of contention. But since they take Me now for an Essene of the highest order, they go home happily, praising God for enduing man with such secret knowledge and power as to enable him to render suffering man the surest and most miraculous help.

[5] My instruction to them therefore was just enough to, upon quieter and more mature reflection at home, conclude that I might not be an Essene after all, since the moral and social fundamentals I expounded to them flatly contradict those of the Essenes. At home they shall be soberly comparing My exposition with the doctrine of the Essenes in their possession, and after detecting the most glaring contradictions, begin to pause, just as the five already stopped in their tracks on hearing My Words, because as said, My teaching of them is more than just the exact opposite to that of the Essenes.

[6] They would have liked to question Me further, but I cut them off, and they left, not daring to put another question, for they realized that regarding My deed, I could be on the one hand an Essene chief of the highest rank indeed, yet not according to My address to them. But on their way home, and pre-occupied only with this phenomenon, they are thinking: "Could the Essenes perhaps have two doctrines – one exoteric and official, just for blind mankind, and one esoteric for themselves? But that, on the other hand, that I had been direct with them and as one versed in Scripture, gave them throw-away lines of the inner doctrine, leaving them to work out the rest by themselves.

[7] One of the five however is maintaining that there must be something totally different to me than an Essene of the highest order. He now is saying to the other four: 'I on my part cannot take him for an Essene, because I only recently discussed all their doctrines and customs with one Essene who was most forthright about it. Yet he knew nothing about a second, secret doctrine. I therefore regard the Nazarene Savior as a totally different and unprecedented phenomenon. He is either a god or a devil, which however I doubt very much, as his doctrine is one of the most altruistic I ever encountered. A devil on the other hand is a supreme tyrant and therefore a self-proclaimed enemy of socialism'.

[8] See, such a conversation the five are already having on the way, and they are so steeped in it that they are hardly aware of whether their feet are carrying them forward.

[9] My cherished friends, when teaching, one has to proceed most carefully. One need not blurt everything out straight-away, or serve all foods at once at a dinner. One enters a house quietly, and quietly knocks at one or the other door. And when giving a dinner, one serves a second course only after the guests have consumed the first. Otherwise, in the case of being a visitor, one's rudeness shall become notorious; and as a cheeky gatecrasher, one will achieve little or nothing

on the host's premises. While, on the other hand, the host would take away the guests' appetite if he were to set a medley of different foods on the table simultaneously, whereas, in proper sequence, the guests' appetite would be preserved, and the latter would praise the host for his superb hospitality.

[10] And see, just so must one proceeds with teaching, if one is to accomplish something. Do you understand this now?'

[11] Say **the disciples**: 'Yes, Lord, we understand it all now, as You have spoken with exceeding wisdom, as always.'

[12] I said: 'Very well, then let us all go to the morning meal.'


## CHAPTER 224
### Importance of introspection

[1] Thereupon we rise from our resting benches, going to the garden where an abundant morning meal awaits us that Baram had continued to prepare for us.

[2] **Kisjonah** however remarks to Baram: 'Brother, what are you doing? Do you think my storehouse, larder and wine cellar are empty?'

[3] Says **Baram**: 'I know only too well, brother, that a thousand guests a day would not consume your reserves in a thousand years, but praise God that I don't count among the poor of this land, and so allow me the pleasure of serving the Lord with my limited means. Let it be a lively day at your cooking stoves again tomorrow.'

[4] After that, Kisjonah and Baram embrace and kiss one another and then sit down at the table too, consuming a splendid fish, with bread and wine.

[5] After the meal however, Kisjonah inquires about what shall engage us in the afternoon, or whether perhaps I planned another excursion, so that he may provide for our needs.

[6] I said: 'Friend and brother. Let nothing trouble you. Whatever time shall present, that shall be seized upon. But today's and tomorrow's time shall deliver nothing or little other than ourselves, and therefore we shall have no need for special preparations. Towards evening tomorrow, Philopold shall arrive, and he shall have a few things to relate.

[7] But until noon we shall do some exercises in introspection, by the cool of the shady trees.

[8] For truly I tell you: nothing is of greater benefit for the whole man than a temporary introspection. Whoever wishes to become acquainted with himself and his powers must sometimes search and contemplate his within.

[9] Since this is so very necessary we shall before noon practice this, and following the midday meal we shall go out to sea and see what will be happening there.'

[10] Some do not know how to go about this introspection and ask Me what to do. But I say: 'Relax and think quietly on your actions and the to you well-known will of God and whether you have complied with it at different times of your life,

then you have contemplated your within and have made it increasingly difficult for Satan to enter your heart. For Satan seeks eagerly through all kinds of external meaningless trickery to prevent a person from such introspection.

[11] For, once man has through practice acquired a certain accomplishment in introspection, he easily discovers within himself the traps Satan has set him and is then able to properly destroy and eliminate them and energetically take precautions against all further deceitfulness of this enemy. Of this Satan is quite aware and is, therefore, busily occupied with engaging the soul in all kinds of diverting trickery and then finds it quite easy, unnoticed behind the scene, to lay a snare for the soul in which it gets so entangled that it can no longer manage an introspection, and this is very bad.

[12] Thereby the soul is more and more separated from its spirit which it can no longer awaken, and that is already the beginning of the second death within man.

[13] Now you know wherein introspection consists. Practice this quietly from now until noon and do not let any external thing disturb you. For Satan will certainly not refrain from diverting you through one or the other external spectacle. But then remember that I have foretold you this and return again quickly to your within.'

[14] Now they all relax and everyone begins quite energetically with his introspection. This continues without disturbance for a full hour.


## CHAPTER 225
### The Leviathan

[1] After an hour, however, there is suddenly a resounding bang as if a violent flash of lighting had hit a house nearby. All get a mighty shock and start up, but then remember My words and return to their quiet.

[2] But Satan does not waste any time, soon after the bang the relaxed but spiritually active hear an uncanny hissing and whistling and before long an unusual monster emerges at the seashore. The head resembles that of a wolf, but is at least a hundred times as large. The long tongue sticking out from the jaws resembles a wildly writing python. Both the immense ears are like those of an ox. The eyes look like two large sheets of glowing iron. The fore-feet resemble those of a giant bear, the hind-feet those of a lion of immense size. The body is like that of a crocodile with the tail of a basilisk (African vampire). Its cry is a resounding bang and its breath an uncanny hissing and whistling. Thus it emerges from the sea.

[3] Sheep, oxen, cows, calves and many donkeys are grazing on the shore and the monster immediately begins to hunt these domestic animals and devour one after the other. The animals now flee, but the monster heads in our direction.

[4] When **several** notice this, they rise to their feet and say: 'Lord, this test is a bit too hard. The horrible monster has already devoured some calves, about 10 lambs and 2 young donkey-foals. Now it is after some delicacy here and has,

guided by its sense of smell, surely selected something among us since it is slowly approaching in our direction. In this case it should surely be advisable to get out of the way of this death bringer. For by natural means a fight with this beast could not possibly lead to victory.'

[5] I said: 'Do not let this disturb you in the least. Externally all of us together could not master this monster which is a fully developed Leviathan, but form your inner power he will have to flee to the end of the world. So be completely unconcerned. Another short hour and you will have broken through the barriers and boundary defenses of Hell and the domination of all the Hell and its army shall be your reward.'

[6] Immediately following these My words the monster again sounds its detonation-like voice several times in succession and then quietly, but rather fast, proceeds in our direction clearly demonstrating its voracity by the violent movement of its serpent tongue and the constant lashing of its long, tree-sized tail. The disciples, however, are now in a good frame of mind and without fear and faint-heartedness allow the monster to approach them.

[7] When it has come to about 10 paces from us, I – only in My mind – give the angel **Archiel** a sign and he suddenly steps up to the beast and asks it: 'What do you want here, Satan? Withdraw, or I shall destroy you.' The monster now opens its jaws as if it wanted to speak, but the angel once more bids it to withdraw. Then the beast gives off several banging sounds and with loud hissing and whistling rushes into the sea.

[8] After it had sunk back into the sea, it for some time stirred the water in the large bay as if by the worst storm, but all that no longer confounds any of the disciples and with the greatest inner zeal everyone now rested in God during this last hour.

[9] Towards the end of that hour of rest there suddenly arises a mighty thunderstorm. Wild lightning is flashing and strong gusts of wind are bending the trees almost to the ground while heavy drops of rain mixed with hail are already falling from the dark clouds.

[10] Some of the weaker disciples were already the point of escaping in the house, but **the angel** says: 'Stay and recognize Satan's empty trickery.' So they stay and easily put up with the empty rain. The rain does get worse and the hail stones are dancing on the ground, but no one is hit by one and the rain hardly wets anyone's skin.

[11] Then the angel threatens the clouds which promptly disperse and it becomes immediately a clear day. In a few moments the time of introspection has ended and **Baram** says: 'Lord, whatever You prefer, here or in the house. The meal is prepared.'

[12] I said: 'Let another half hour pass, then everything will be in order. I still have to say a few words to My disciples.'

[13] Baram returns to his ship where in a large case several skins with the best wine are kept. These he has now taken to the kitchen by his servants there to be emptied into jars. He also tells his cooks to wait for half an hour and only serve up the dishes when he gives them a sign. Then he again returns to Me and listened

to what I tell the disciples about this introspection and its usefulness.


## CHAPTER 226
### The way to rebirth

What was said is this: 'You have now seen a new way in which man can pass from matter into the increasingly purer spiritual and how in this way he can become a master over himself and thereby finally also over all nature in the world. Therefore, from time to time do practice this method in My name and you will gain great power over your passions, thereby over the entire natural world and in the beyond over all creatures.

[2] You have seen the evil phenomena Satan presented to you. They caused you fear and terror, but relying on My word you returned to your rest and in this rest you have become complete masters over all the bad events.

[3] But do not think that you have already completely discouraged Satan. Wherever you will again practice this introspection you will be bothered by him as long as you are not completely reborn in the spirit.

[4] Once you are reborn in the spirit Satan has lost all power over you forever, and you shall be judges over him as also over all those whom he has seized hold of and whom you will rescue from him forever.'

[5] Asks **Peter**: 'How is one born again? Will the soul and the spirit have to enter and then be born out of another woman's body, or how is this to be understood?'

[6] I said: 'This you shall not be able to fully grasp for a long while yet. But when I shall once have ascended from where I came, with My spirit liberating your spirit, then you shall be able to grasp the rebirth of the spirit and understand it in all depth and fullness. But right now this would not be possible to you, nor anyone else. But through following My teaching, and such life exercises, you shall in the end attain to such light within yourself.

[7] This can be grasped through no exterior doctrine or instruction, but has to be won from within oneself, along the path now shown you for all time by Myself.

[8] Says **Judas**: 'Lord, I have seen powerful magicians and conjurers and exorcists. These spoke with the souls of the departed, and these actually spoke and revealed things hidden. How did these enter the kingdom of spirits? Would not this also be a type of spiritual rebirth?'

[9] I said: 'Indeed so, but not for Heaven, which is God's throne, but for Hell, where Satan and his angels dwell.'

[10] Says **Judas**: 'If so, then Satan is also a lord, furnished with great power, albeit evil. In my view therefore it would be better to destroy Satan than let thousands times thousands be destroyed through him. Why must there be a Satan within the divine order.'

[11] I said: 'For the purpose of also catching you in the not too distant future, for being too much his advocate. You are still far from even feebly recognizing yourself, let alone God's great order, which upon Earth has called forth, for wise reasons, both night as well as day. Do you fundamentally understand the Earth's

terrestrial night, or the eternal day of every sun, each of which is an Earth just like the one that carries you? If you don't understand such, then I ask how you can put a question which is not appropriate for a human to ask before his Lord, God and Creator. Would you not also ask why a stone is hard and water so soft, or why fire hurts you but not cool water?

[12] I say unto you: if you don't understand anything, then first learn something, going about it quietly and with wakeful spirit. And only after understanding something from its foundation can you talk, and put tricky questions to your brethren.

[13] And see, it is with you as with all human stupidity. They are secretly embarrassed by it, but nevertheless would cover up with all kinds of seemingly wise questioning, not reckoning that with that they uncover their stupidity even more. Let these My gentle words therefore serve you as a rebuke or you may yet run into something, and I shall not then hurry to pull you out of the mud.'

[14] These words cooled down Judas' questioning zeal considerably, and he also casts meaningful glances at Thomas, but the latter wisely feigned not to have noted the rebuke, and so did the other disciples. And Judas felt comforted, and wisely withdrew.

[15] But I said to Baram: 'And now, brother, you could have the meal served up, but this time in the rooms.' Baram hastens to the kitchen, and has everything served up quickly, and we follow him, and in an hour's time the meal has been unhurriedly consumed.

## CHAPTER 227
### A voyage at sea

[1] After the meal, the day being nice and clear, a sea voyage is undertaken. Baram quickly gets his ship ready, and Kisjonah makes his own big ship sea worthy too, and it easily accommodates half the disciples.

[2] I, and the principal disciples and Baram and Kisjonah, board Baram's solidly built ship, which had 2 sails and 6 rudders on each side, being capable of moving by wind or rudders. From the Kis locality, we traveled in the Capernaum direction, not however making same our destination.

[3] But after moving in the direction of Capernaum for some 2 hours, we noticed a ship quickly steering towards our 2 ships. It carried the Capernaum colors, and when we deviated from our course to test if it deliberately steered our way, it also deviated from its course and hastily set out in our direction. When Baram's boatmen took this in, they asked him what was to be done, as the Capernaumian ship did not seem to have good intentions. Baram asked Me what I might say about it.

[4] And I answered: 'Just let it come near us, and we shall soon see its intention.' In response to My words Baram had the sails lowered, and the rudders retracted, while the boatmen on Kisjonah's ship did likewise.

[5] A quarter hour later the Capernaumian boatmen have caught up with us, asking Baram whether I am aboard, for they had established at Capernaum that I was staying at Kis. For they had been dispatched by the High Priest Jairus to ask Me to come to Capernaum, for Jairus' little daughter, whom only a few weeks earlier I had resurrected from the dead, once again had fallen so ill that no doctor was able to further help her. 'The Chief fears her death. A great reward would await you if you can put us unto Jesus of Nazareth', the boatmen said to Baram and his boat people.

[6] However, **Baram** said: 'Judging by your talk, good intentions have led you our way, and I say unto you: Him whom you seek is aboard, but whether He intends to hear you and accede to your request I cannot say. But I shall go below and speak to Him in the cabin.

[7] The Capernaumians are happy with that, and Baram comes down to my open cell, to acquaint Me with the Capernaumians' petition.

[8] But I say unto him: 'Save your breath, brother, for I already know it all, and have already told you at Jesaira that this slanderous brood shall fare thus. In order to persecute Me and cast suspicion on My teaching, they denied that Jairus' daughter had been sick and dead. She is supposed to have just slept soundly and I am supposed to just have awakened her in a very natural way, and to have then pretended that I awoke her from death.

[9] Now then, since such My deed was fullest deception, they shall let the little daughter again fall soundly asleep, and she shall then also be again capable of awakening in a natural way through any normal human.

[10] Verily, this one shall not be touched by Me until she has lain 3 days in the grave. Go on deck and tell them so, but then set the sails, and a fast wind shall carry us seawards over the great bay at Kis, and these shall not know to where we traveled.

[11] **Baram** rushes up to deck, saying. 'My esteemed messengers of the Chief, I heavy-heartedly let you know that I can bring you no favorable reply from Jesus, the Lord. But the Capernaumians themselves are to blame, for when at the other occasion He had awaked the Chief's little daughter from visible and perceptible death, back to fullest life, it did not take long for the Pharisees of this city, condemned by Him, to declare Him a deceiver, telling all folk that Jairus only wanted to put Jesus to the test by laying his healthy daughter upon a makeshift death bed, whereupon the deceiver Jesus, having no notion of the trap set Him, was easily able to awaken her from death to life, which He effected as I heard it said by some, after having in the end discerned that she lives, by applying much pressure when seizing her by the hand. And that she finally rather rose than continued to bear the painful pressure.

[12] According to what I heard, the Chief's intention was for the little daughter not to let herself be awakened, so that Jesus would have at once been apprehended as an accomplished scoundrel. But through the daughter's awakening, this lovely plan was foiled, for the people were supposed to have been firmly convinced that the daughter, who had for that purpose been kept artificially sick the previous two days, really was awakened from death.

[13] Wherefore she shall not be looked at by Him, save perhaps when half decomposed in the grave.

[14] I now let you depart with this advice and tell your Chief Priest that, so that he would realize of what blackest ingratitude his heart is filled. Under no circumstances shall He go to Capernaum, for He has blessed that locality from its foundations forever.'

[15] Upon these words, Baram quickly sets the sails, whereupon the wind was at hand, driving the 2 ships forward so quickly that the Capernaumian ship, having no sails and being also otherwise quite unsightly, and a low vessel, in a few moments was left so far behind that we completely lost sight of it. And after landing above the great bay at Kis and stepping ashore, we let the ships run into the bay by themselves empty, the wind changing and blowing heftily towards Capernaum.

## CHAPTER 228
### The doctor of Nazareth

[1] Having climbed the considerable hill that rose above the bay, at whose foot the aforementioned inn was built and across which the main road to Jerusalem led, we saw from a great distance how the Capernaumian ship was battling the waves and as the wind began to trouble it more, it raised its rudders and let itself be driven in a straight line for Capernaum.

[2] It speaks for itself what face Jairus would have cut, on receiving My communication from the messengers he had sent to Me.

[3] Jairus immediately had all the doctors from the surrounds called in, including the Nazarene one, for the latter stood in good repute as also a disciple of Mine, with miraculous healing capacity, by having actually cured even the seriously ill instantly by the mere laying on of hands.

[4] But when he arrived at Capernaum and looked at the sick daughter, he shrugged his shoulders, saying to all the doctors surrounding the sick bed: 'Only He who created her can help her. See, the girl at some feast had consumed some cold drink and contracting an active lung infection. Her time will be and has to be up, in another 7 days at the most. We cannot create a new lung for her, and therefore there is no possibility to help her.'

[5] Says **Jairus**: 'What do you think? Could the divinely renown Jesus, who once already awakened this my daughter from real death and who awakened also the centurion Cornelius' daughter from death, where my daughter contracted the disease a few days ago, not heal her either?'

[6] Says **the Nazarene doctor**: 'Oh yes, He indeed, if He wanted to. But you have already dispatched messengers there, I think to Kis, where He is now staying, mainly at Jonah's, but He has quite rightly given you a negative answer, only following which we have been summoned here, and we can achieve nothing more.'

[7] Says **Jairus**: 'But I had begged Him in all civility and He as the One who preached only love, and how one should do good even to one's enemies, answers my dispatched messengers like that?'

[8] Says **the Nazarene doctor**: 'None other than you all deserve, who call yourselves servants of the Most High. Tell me, what kind of person could still be your friend after such behavior on your part? Verily, God Himself could not bestow greater favors on you than this purely divine Jesus has done upon you in fullest measure. But how did you return His favor? You persecuted Him like a most hideous criminal, and had you been able to apprehend Him, you would have already killed Him long since, but because God's hand obviously protected Him, you still did everything evil you could do to Him.

[9] What did His poor, exceedingly pious and God-fearing mother Mary do to you, that you had to take her tiny house and the 2 little gardens from her, and then drive her away, together with Joseph's children, publicly disgracing her as if she were a common criminal?

[10] Why, I ask, have you done this?'

[11] Says **Jairus**: 'Because He casts suspicion on us, and denigrated the priests and God's Temple. This surely is cause enough?'

[12] Says **the Nazarene doctor**: by the name of Borus, who was a Greek by birth: '*Ah - hince ergo illae lacrimae?* (which means: so that is why you cry?). Listen, as You all know, I am a Greek by birth, and therefore have nothing to do with your theology, although I am not ignorant of it. Far be it from me to belittle your Moses and your prophets, who were mistreated by your forebears one and all, for their teaching and admonitions were no different from those my most sincere friend Jesus has dressed you down with, and are therefore full of truth and of God's Spirit.

[13] Alongside that, look at your current theology and your most miserable Temple regulations, beyond all lambasting, together with the commendable Temple set up itself, and you shall yourselves have to exclaim: *Quam mutatus ab illo* (what a difference).

[14] Just read the prophet Isaiah with unshakable faith, according to which Jehovah, Moses and the prophets of a truth should appear as considerably more than a welcome fable for your selfish and hedonistic aims, and you shall step back with a shudder at the sheer heinousness with which you carry on upon the holy precincts.

[15] If, now, the godly Jesus upbraids you in the manner of Isaiah on account of your monumental transgressions, desiring as a true friend to lead you back to the God from whom you have distanced yourselves beyond all measure, then I ask you: does He earn such treatment from you?

[16] Verily, were I imbued with His truly godly – I should say omnipotence – then we should have been squared off a long time from now, just as the 10 ships are now squared off upon the cliffs of Sibarah, which you had launched out after Him and His most harmless disciples from sheer altruism. Probably, on this occasion for once, He ran out of even His godly patience.

[17] I repeat: if imbued with His factual omnipotence, I should have a long time

since emptied the entire sea of Galilee over you, to drown you like mice and rats.'

[18] Over this Borus' forthright address, **several of the attending Pharisees** were infuriated, saying to him: 'Bridle your loose Greek tongue. For this you were not summoned here from Nazareth. Fear us, for we have plenty of power to ruin you.'

[19] Says **Borus**: 'Oh, this I believe you with all my heart, for your notorious philanthropy attests that to me. But there happens to be a big 'but', in consequence of which Borus the Nazarene does not fear you in the least.

[20] Borus is certainly not omnipotent like a godly Jesus, yet he possesses sufficient secret power to ruin you all in a moment, without being, as a doctor, accountable to anyone. Have you understood me? Jesus however is a God, and I only human. This is also why He has more patience than I. But let you not take it much further, or my patience runs out.'

[21] Here **Borus** pulls out a tiny bottle from his pocket, showing it to the vitriolic Pharisees, with telling words: 'See, this weapon has more power than ten legions. I know how to protect my own person, but upon opening it, you are all dead instantly. And see, over this tiny bottle too, the big portent 'but' is written. If you want to have a go at me, we shall be square soon.'

[22] The Pharisees take terrible fright at the sight of this deadly little bottle which contained exceedingly noxious and rapidly spreading poison fumes, instantly numbing and killing whosoever's nostrils it reached.

[23] This poison however was an extract which subsequently suffered extinction. It had been extracted from a shrub that occurs sporadically in the remote parts of India, destroying all life within a wide radius of its growth. The Pharisees know of this, making them mute with fear, and Jairus asks Borus to pocket the bottle.

[24] **Borus** does so indeed, but says to Jairus: 'Friend, how can one let a Jesus, who did you an unheard of favor, be so shamefully persecuted? Tell me, do you actually not realize that He is right in every one of His holy Words, or do you in all earnest intend not to see this?'

## CHAPTER 229
### Jairus' cowardly and timid answer

[1] Says **Jairus**: 'Friend, I understand you better than you think, yet there are things which in the light of status in the world, must not be understood at all.

[2] As a person of standing, you have quite often to laugh when you would cry, but often mourn when you would rather leap and dance for joy. But what can you do as an individual in isolation? Can you swim against a raging stream once you get caught up in its power?

[3] We humans however have a sensitive skin, and a still more sensitive stomach. These two want gratification, and it therefore it is better for us to either let go of all understanding and common sense, or run with the crowd, or feebly

expire in some corner as a scorned beggar, like a beast wounded in the hunt.

[4] Believe me that, speaking between ourselves, I know Christ better than you do, but what does that help in the face of Rome and Jerusalem? If you make a move it is your last day.

[5] Jesus may in all earnest be a Son of the Most High, which I personally don't doubt in the least, but can I confess this openly, considering my official position? And if I did so, what then with the likes of us?'

[6] Says **Borus**: 'What then, what then. The world always has, on account of worldly advantage thrown up such questions at some friend to whom pure truth counted far more than all the kingdoms of a cursed world. Therefore holy truth always found its grave in the skin and belly of hedonistic men.

[7] Whoever cares more for worldly advantage and exalted status than about godly truth, may he yet be born of a congenial disposition, he shall get caught up in such questions and considerations, then withdrawing from the divine light to the darkness of the world, denying God and all the light out of Him. Ask why? What lays that burden into his heart? See, nothing but his bent for worldly comfort of every kind. Avidly he seeks after everything that can assure him worldly comfort. And having achieved it often through much effort and trouble, seeking same on account of worldly sensuality, he soon chucks all truth overboard. If he fears the least constraint to his glittering worldly living standards, then he chooses to become a tyrant against everything that is imbued with just a spark of genuine truth.

[8] But on getting miserable and sick, and coming to the doctor, he wants nothing but truest help. Why truth here but nowhere else?

[9] Look, there. Your daughter has been laid low with an incurable illness. What would you not now give for a true medicine to bring help to your daughter's body. As an experienced doctor, I tell you that there is indeed one medicine which would bring your daughter immediate relief and such medicine in relation to the physical sickness of your daughter would then surely be a perfect truth. Yes, for such truth you would indeed give everything. Yet for truth that would heal your soul you not only give nothing, but you actually persecute it wherever it shows up, for worldly comfort. Say: where does such behavior belong?

[10] You know as well as I do, that there is no curative effect in the Temple manure. You know that such things are blatant superstition, well suited to stifle the last spark of faith in the weak folk, yet you would persecute such 'profaner of the Holy of Holies' with fire and sword if any of your fellow believers were to go public with it.

[11] Think of an eternally just God however who Himself is the Light and the most unchangeable eternal Truth and who will not be bargained with. What will such say to servants like you once?

[12] Verily, not one of you shall justify yourselves. Whether you believe or don't believe, there nevertheless is a hereafter beyond grave's portals, where each shall be rewarded in accordance with one's doing and dealing.

[13] I am no stranger to it, for I sought and found it. My eternal life is in my hands, and I would give a thousand physical lives if that were the price.

[14] But I have it, and eternal life has taught me to scorn the life of the flesh and only cede it enough value to benefit the everlasting life of the soul in all fullness. That I have attained to such in all clarity and truth I thank none other than Jesus alone, who showed me the hidden path to it.

[15] And this Jesus, this God among men, you persecute with fire and sword, and shall hardly rest until you have done to Him what your forebears did to all the prophets.

[16] But then beware. God has sent you, who most shamelessly call yourselves His people and His children, a God from the Heavens. Each of His words in an eternal truth out of God, which can be grasped even with the hand by every honest person. Yet you want to kill Him because He dismisses your old Temple rubbish.

[17] Woe betides you. God's wrath shall overtake you soon.

[18] Yes, I could still help your daughter; I now feel the power within me. But I don't want to help her, because you are all devils, and no longer men. And I shall never offer my helping hand to devils.'

[19] This went to the Chief's heart like glowing arrows. He indeed saw the truth of it in its depth and was ready to lay down his ministry, but feared the uproar, saying to Borus:

[20] 'You may not be subtle by any means, but your words have the ring of truth. If I could, without causing as it were a destructive disturbance, I would chuck my high office overboard. I would be quite prepared to do so for the sake of my beloved daughter's recovery. But consider the upheaval this step would cause. Therefore I have to put it off to a more appropriate occasion.'

[21] Says **Borus**: 'I have finished and can now continue a better way again than the one that led to you. Because this is obviously Hell on Earth, and here no angel can do any good, let alone myself as a still weak, carnal and mortal man.'

[22] With these words Borus leaves the chief's house unstoppably, rushing away in agitation. The above went on in Capernaum the day after we encountered the dispatched messenger.

[23] I however took a rest upon the hill, foretelling the episode in detail a day before it actually took place in all truth.


## CHAPTER 230
### Death of Joseph and his testimony on Jesus

[1] After this narrative, during which all the disciples felt like embracing and kissing the well known doctor Borus, we nevertheless headed back for Kis, arriving there just as the sun was setting.

[2] Baram however was holding the supper in full readiness, and we enjoyed it much, after accomplishing an important work. The meal also put Judas in a better frame of mind, and he praised the courage of Borus, whom he too knew well.

[3] It was our topic for some time after the meal, and even mother Mary could

not bless Borus sufficiently, for standing up for her with the chief, who had initiated the seizure of her small property.

[4] Said **one of Joseph's elder sons**: 'Our well earned property might then be restored to us in the end?'

[5] Says **Kisjonah**: 'Friend, don't make it your wish. See, over here you have a much better existence, safe from all persecution. And I'm making the inn over there, at the upper end of the bay, your own, including a hundred acres of ground. And with this swap, you may get over the loss of your small property, and you are also closer to Jerusalem by over half a day's journey, compared to Nazareth.' Joses is happy with this, but asks Me also for My advice.

[6] And I say: 'What is better is always better; therefore take it, but never regard it as your own, but only a thing on loan to you from God, for this brief time.'

[7] Says **Joses**: 'Lord and brother. Such, our father Joseph has already taught us, and therefore we never regarded even the small property at Nazareth as some kind of possession, but something loaned to us by God for this short Earth time, for which we also, including Yourself, thanked Him daily, asking Him to also preserve such treasure for our earthly needs. He also preserved it for so long as it was His holy will. But I now say with Job: "The Lord gave it to us, and now it pleased Him to take it away again". His holy will be done, and His alone are the honor, praise and glory. Whatever God takes He can richly restore. Indeed, as Your earthly brothers and sisters, we are now in the clear about it. But they also took our tools and household implements. Here we consider that such at least, or the equivalent, should be restored to us.'

[8] I said: 'Don't trouble yourself. In 3 days we are moving to Nazareth, and everything shall have to be returned to us. Have we not an angel of the mightiest order among us? Just one hint, and all is fixed up. And if one were not to suffice us, legions are at our disposal every moment.

[9] Verily I say: whatever in My heart I ask My Father, that He will do. And what the Son wants, that also the Father wants eternally, and there is never a difference between the Father's and the Son's will. For let you all believe it: Father and Son are not two but fully one in everything. Therefore be still and believe that it is so.'

[10] Says **Joses**: 'Lord and brother, all of us do believe, and how could we not believe as we have since Your birth always been near You and seen countless signs that proclaimed to us who You are. Brother James has even written a whole book about it beginning with Your birth until Your twentieth year from which time until the present You did not work any more signs and worked and lived with us like an ordinary man. So that we would almost have forgotten who You are if the physical death some years ago of our beloved father Joseph has not mightily shaken us up.

[11] For, as Joseph was dying in Your arms, his last words, accompanied by a blissfully radiant smile were:

[12] "O my God and Lord, how much grace and mercy You have bestowed upon me! O, now I see that there is no death. I shall live forever. O how glorious Your Heavens are, God. Children, look at the One who is now supporting my dying

head with His arm. It is He, my God, my Creator. O what bliss it is to die to this miserable world in the almighty arms of one's Creator.'

[13] After these words he passed away and all of us wept aloud, but You alone did not weep. We all understood why You did not weep.

[14] And see, from that moment on we could never forget who You are, for Joseph had declared it only too clearly in the last hour of his temporal life. How should we now not believe everything You say since we do know who You actually are?'

[15] I said: 'Quite so, My dear brethren. It is well that you spoke thus, for we are in fully initiated company and such knowledge can no longer have judgmental effect on any, except one if it will offend him. (Judas was meant).

[16] But when we find ourselves among strange children of the world, then we must keep strict silence. But now we shall go for our rest, so that tomorrow we can attend to some work early.' Thereupon all went happily to their rest.


# CHAPTER 231
## Kisjonah's people capture a band of Temple robbers and smugglers

[1] Only Kisjonah, Baram, Jonael and Jairuth, together with the servant Archiel, go outdoors, and Kisjonah checks out his big household. All is in the best of order, and the barrier-keepers and guards are of good cheer, telling their lord that an important catch shall be made, as they were notified.

[2] Kisjonah asks briskly wherein this would consist, and whether it may not consist in some poor carrying their meager stores to some market to cover their tax dues.

[3] Here **the barrier's chief** says: 'Lord and master, You are quite aware of how we all honor and respect your most just and exceedingly fair rules regarding poor mankind, but no poverty is involved here, but rather a most shameful disgrace on the part of the Jewish Pharisees, Priests and Levites.

[4] These have undertaken a diversity of the most shameless seizures and exactions through a wide area, and at midnight shall be taking all sorts of cattle, grains, wine and implements to Jerusalem for sale, but not along the public highway, but a surreptitious path secretly run through the mountains.

[5] You are aware of the lack of a possible passage by land to Sibarah, where your advance toll that you always rent out is located, owing to the massive cliff jutting its high and steep face into the sea, the reason for having to bring people, cattle and other effects to a certain landing place for marine travel, unless one travels by calm sea, a rarity in a straight line to Pirah, where also the toll is located that is leased out for ten years.

[6] In order to bypass all your tolls however, the wealthy Pharisees have, with hired slave labor built a secret road through the mountains, and that through what are already Samaritan regions, and this passage they are trying out for the first time today.

[7] They shall break forth some 2,000 paces into the valley, at the spot where we built the bridge over the brook – the road which runs through your ground still for a long stretch, over the brook, winding along the left side of the valley towards Cana, but we had some 200 well-armed guards positioned quite early along strategic points. I tell you, father and lord, a mouse would not get through. We want to teach Jehovah to these evil scoundrels in a way that will them think of Him for the rest of their lives.'

[8] Says **Kisjonah**: 'You have set it up well and truly and you shall not go unrewarded. The money the merchants have on them shall be taken as spoils, while all cattle, grain, flour and implements shall remain here until the culprits have named all those from whom they have extorted them, so we can restore same to them in good conscience.

[9] But for running a road through my mountains and woods without my permission, they shall be fined 1,000 pounds of silver as penalty by the Roman judge, who has set up office in my dwellings. Two thirds of it by law falls due to the emperor and a third goes into my till.'

[10] At this point however the Roman judge comes over to inquire what is going on at the barrier and whether suspects are being anticipated, and whether military assistance is needed. The barriers' chief however briefs him on what had already been reported to him during the day.

[11] Says **the judge**: 'So that's it. Well, see to it that you catch the miserable scoundrels. Then we shall give them a few lessons on Rome's customs and laws. These shall lose their bent for making beggars out of Roman subjects for good, making the latter incapable of rendering their due taxes to the emperor, while not a penny can be gotten out of the dark scoundrels themselves. These fellows pretend to perpetual poverty, while burying gold, silver, pearls and precious stones in massive quantities. And those of Capernaum are the same to boot as those of Chorazim. Well, well, have a good time, you villains, your game is up in a way that will make you think about it for the rest of your lives.'

[12] The judge had hardly announced these words when much yelling could be heard from the distant valley, while **the barrier keeper** was rubbing his hands with glee, saying: 'Ah, they have hooked up. They shall be here in a quarter hour. Quick, let us light the flares and turn the valley into day, so that not one of these scallywags may get through.'

[13] 40 flares are lit, and the entire location turned into light. And the lighters were hardly done when the first bunch consisting of 12 Pharisees arrives, who as agents were to move the loot for sale in Jerusalem.

[14] **The strong escorts** line up the 12 bound Pharisees at the barrier, saying to Kisjonah: 'Lord, here are the main culprits. 5 of Capernaum, 3 of Nazareth and 4 of Chorazim, all assassins worth their weight in gold. At the rear follows all sorts: masses of oxen, cows calves, goats, sheep. About 400 donkeys laden with grain, together with fillies, with that many mules laden with wine casks, and another 500 donkeys and pack animals carrying superbly shaped boys and girls, between the ages of 12 and 18 who had all been destined for the Sidon market. And besides that, a great many servants to these main culprits. All this shall be here shortly.

Therefore organize space: let's make room for the lot.'

[15] Says **Kisjonah**: 'Let the big impounding stores on the shore be opened at once. There, everything can be fitted in, and for the children, the big inn here on the mountain. And see to it that they receive to eat and drink, because these brutes are sure to have given them meager rations on the way. O God, o God, why do You allow such devils to power monger upon Earth, over poor and peaceful mankind?'


## CHAPTER 232
### Preparation for the trial

[1] The wailing of the children, who had been torn from their parent's arms, can now be heard. Kisjonah and Baram, Jonael and Jairuth, together with the angel, rush to meet the children. The judge however has the 12 seized and escorted to a sturdy prison.

[2] Shortly afterwards the file of children arrive. The angel instantly releases them from the donkeys and mules. The number of children exceeded the first reports by the escorts who brought the first 12 scoundrels, as some were bound in threes on their mules. The children were all shaking with fear, expecting something nasty. But the angel chats to them most friendly, telling them that here they shall find themselves in the arms of their mourning parents already the following day. This calmed the children down.

[3] Some however were lamenting the pain the fetters had caused, some having bloodied spots upon their tender bodies, for they had been beaten for crying, to prevent them betraying the entire caravan. Most were naked, for they could have been recognized if dressed on the way from Capernaum to Sibarah, which was by-passed. Therefore the barest clothing-needs had to be provided.

[4] Kisjonah at once issued a large quantity of linen, and all got stuck into making skirts so that in the morning every child had received one. Many hands make short shrift of a large task. The children were then taken to the big inn which Kisjonah had erected just above the barrier.

[5] No sooner had the children been lodged at the inn when the main transport of cattle and other things arrived, and all was received into store, while the servants of the twelve also were bound and thrown into a large jail.

[6] After this hustle and bustle was over and the guards dispersed, Kisjonah and his 4 companions also took to their rest, which nevertheless did not last long, beginning late, while the approaching day promised many and large concerns.

[7] All was at rest till day break, whereupon everyone was on their feet and Kisjonah's first move was over to me, to appraise Me of all that took place during the night, and to of course also seek My advice on how to deal in a God-pleasing manner.

[8] But I anticipated him, telling him what took place this night, but also giving him advice on how to best deal with it all in haste. The advice consisted in the

following:

[9] 'Brother, as a first step, dispatch hastily a messenger to the centurion Cornelius at Capernaum, with power of attorney from the local imperial Court of law, that he would send a commissioner for examining the 12 sinners, to enable him to return a verdict on them and to restore to all concerned victims, as confessed by the 12, the stolen cattle, but mainly to return their children in the shortest time, because, for the scale of this culprit-case, the special court here is too small and incompetent. But no mention shall be made of Myself.

[10] The 12 Pharisees shall yet create trouble for the High Court. It shall not be able to get them regarding the robbery. And the avoidance of the toll shall not worry them either, as they hold freedom of passage passes throughout the country. And since they are children of the nation, no toll can lawfully be taken from them, so they also did not avoid the toll for that reason, but out of fear of the people, for they had already paid their tuition fees on previous occasions, and for that reason forged a secret road to Jerusalem.

[11] Therefore they are lawfully accountable for only one Cause, on account of which they may be sentenced only for substantial damages, this being for breach of forestry law committed in your woodlands. This would not be covered by all the impounded chattels, not even together with all the money they have on them.

[12] Therefore, as a second prerequisite, let expert estimators, in company with a court official, hasten to the forest to assess the damage, so that when the High Court comes here for a sitting, everything is in readiness for arriving at a verdict, in the absence of which the Court would drag out lengthy examinations, and the victims perhaps not be compensated for a year. If however all that the Court considers material is at hand, then a sentence can quickly be passed and carried out.'

[13] Upon this advice, Kisjonah hastens to his administrators and arranges everything I advised.

[14] A sail boat quickly takes off with good wind for Capernaum, while the Roman judge himself, together with 8 assessors under oath, quickly leave for the mountains bordering the left side of the valley from Kis, dispatching at the same time a commissioner together with 8 other assessors under oath, to the right of the valley.

[15] By the fourth hour, a High Court commissioner with 2 scribes arrives, as do the two parties of assessors from both mountains, together with their assessments.

## CHAPTER 233
### Intensive interrogation of the 12 Pharisees

[1] Preliminary hearings quickly get under way, and at their rapid conclusion, the

414

12 are brought before the judge. In response to the Chief Judge's interrogation, they say: 'We are lords to ourselves and have our own court at the Jerusalem Temple. Other than to God and that other court we are not answerable to anyone for any doings or omissions and therefore you can question us as much as you like and still receive no answer from us. For our stand is based very firmly upon law, and you shall not be capable of bringing up anything against us.'

[2] Says **the Judge**: 'For this type of intransigence I carry a special remedy: it consists in rod and scourge. These are bound to make you speak. For the court is no respecter of persons. All are equal before the court.'

[3] Says **the leader of the 12 Pharisees**: 'O, this remedy we are fully aware of, together with its power and effect, but we are also aware of yet another remedy. If we should choose to, and probably will make use of this one, then we probably are the last ones you shall ever be putting on trial. Are you acquainted with Caesar Augustus' prestigious certification, written in his own hand for the Jerusalemite priests, which reads as follows:

[4] "*This particular priestly caste is more pleasing to the imperial throne than any of the others, wherefore their laws and privileges are to be protected as sacred. Whoever would attack these, beware. Such offender shall be severely prosecuted as traitorous.*" This law is as current as it was 30 years ago. Should it not have been known to you, then we have now called it to your mind. Proceed now as you will and we shall do likewise.

[5] We have completely rightful possession of our seizures, and none can or has the right to take them. Temporary power can indeed do so, for our counter-force is too small. But when we get ourselves through this, we must be set free, whereupon we shall know how to institute other proceedings.'

[6] Says **the chief judge**: 'Nor do I sit in judgment here over the seizures which, before God and all righteous men, you have wrested unto yourselves as ignominious robbery rather than through just possession, for I am well aware of the privileges you have wrung out of the emperor with your artful hypocrisy.

[7] Had an Augustus known you the way I do, verily, you would have received a quite different certification. Unfortunately, he let himself be deceived by false glimmer, looking upon your lamp shine as upon sunshine, giving you a concession on that account.

[8] But now it is up to me and the centurion Cornelius to present you to the emperor in your true colors, and you shall soon part company with your concession. You may, by the way, counter-threaten me as it pleases you, for I too move upon the foundation of law, and we, chief judges of this land, have only just recently received new instructions concerning your intrigues, of which the emperor is no longer ignorant – this with the request that we keep the closest possible watch over you. And I assure you that we, chief justices, comply with this latest instruction from Rome in full faith and conscience, having already sketched you out in a manner that is certain not to please you. Understood?

[9] In the fashion of African basilisks you suck the last drop of blood from the emperor's subjects, making them beggars, and whatever you leave over, the despot Herod takes to keep his 1,000 concubines fat and voluptuous. The poor

people have to languish in sheerest misery. Is this right?

[10] If there is a God with only as much sense of justice as my own and as much love for mankind as my robe, then it is not possible for Him to let devils like yourselves and Herod to lord it over poor mankind for much longer.

[11] In your Book, it says: "Love your neighbor as yourself", as supposedly given you by your God. How do you keep this nonetheless?

[12] Of a truth, the law that you practice unceasingly with diligence consists in hating all who don't support you strongly in your life of utmost lustfulness and lasciviousness. For this purpose you have unfortunately obtained deviously an ordinance on which you lean for effecting unheard of extortions of all kinds.

[13] By good fortune however you have, for this impending case, in the course of this purported rightful seizure, perpetrated a deed which no known sanctions, a deed for which you alone stand before me at court, a lawbreaking coming under the crime of forestry infringement, which you have committed over an extensive area in the beautiful woods of Kisjonah, who is a Greek and a staunch imperial subject, whose rights every Roman emperor would defend with an entire legion if infringed to only the slightest degree, since he pays the emperor a 1,000 pounds annually for this, which is no small matter.

[14] For a stretch of road extending to nearly 5 hours, you have in the course of secretly lying down your smuggle road, devastated nearly a 1,000 beautiful young cedars, and several thousand lesser tree trunks, causing Kisjonah damage exceeding 10,000 pounds, according to the deposition of sworn estimators. Now then, how will you make restitution for such damage?'

[15] Says **the chief Pharisee**: 'Are you not aware of the Earth being God's, and that we are His children, to whom alone He gave this Earth? Just as God has however the right to do with the Earth as He pleases, so we, as His children, can do with the Earth as we please. Even if some pagan power has wrenched such right from us for a time, it shall not possess such for long. God shall take it from them and return it to His children.

[16] From the point of view of our God-given rights, we are not liable for restitution of forestry infringements, since the Earth is ours and we can do with it as it pleases us. But on account of your greater, but of course only apparent worldly power, which you Romans unjustly wield over us, we shall indeed condescend to restitution. Yet of the 10,000 pounds, up to nine tenths can be dismissed. For that much we also know: that we are capable of assessing the worth of the trees that we felled, using only a minimal portion thereof for random bridge-building. And what, fundamentally is the damage? A new road now exists which the tax collector Kisjonah can employ very well indeed. Had he himself laid it, then this would have come to at least a 1,000 pounds. Now he can erect a new barrier there, and in one year his takings shall have amounted 3 times the cost of the road.'

[17] Says **the chief justice**: 'In the name of the emperor and his wise law, and in view of the damage having been assessed by sworn estimators, and because by making yourselves out to be children of God, you arrogate to yourselves power over the entire Earth, consequent to which the Emperor himself is subject to your

416

power, something he probably would not as yet have dreamt of. Such shameful presumption makes you into the barest criminals. Your seizures are declared forfeited herewith.

[18] Since however either the death penalty or permanent banishment is irrevocably set for crime against the crown, you now have your preferred choice: either beheading by axe, or permanent banishment to Europe's ice region. I have spoken in the name of the emperor and his wise law. It is to take effect immediately. Even if in the mean time the whole world would perish, justice will be done.

[19] See, thus acts a chief justice of Rome, fearing none but the gods and the emperor.'

[20] Thereupon, in accordance with Roman custom, he signals that water be handed to him, wherewith he washes his hands. A bailiff breaks a rod in two and casts it under the twelve's feet.

## CHAPTER 234
### A good catch

[1] Here the Pharisees get apprehensive, and **the rather bold one** says to the Judge: 'Lord, cancel the second fine, and we shall deliver the first fourfold, and that within 48 hours'.

[2] Says **the Judge**: 'I accept the offer, but stick with the banishment for 10 successive years. Are you satisfied with this?'

[3] Says **the Pharisee**: 'Lord, we pay fivefold if you fully remit us the banishment.'

[4] Says **the chief justice**: 'So be it, but with the High Court reservation that you remain under Roman police supervision for 10 years, and that any unlawful attempt to lead the state or its titular head up the garden path, or any evil aspersion cast upon Rome, as well as any high-handed omission to report or confess any seizures regardless of nature, shall carry the aforementioned banishment to Europe for 10 years, for which there then shall be no further release. The money however needs to be deposited to this court chamber within 48 hours. 1 hour overdue and it would not be acceptable under the present moderated conditions, but instead under the conditions of the first verdict.

[5] And a further matter. Before freedom can be restored to you, you must give the names and addresses of all the parties that were so shamelessly dispossessed by you, so that I may summon them here and restore to them all the things you robbed, such as children, cattle, grains and wine.'

[6] The Pharisees went along with this demand, giving all the precise names and addresses. And the Judge immediately dispatches messengers to all the named locations, and 10 hours hardly passed before all the parties arrived who had anything to pick up.

[7] The 12 Pharisees at once uncover their wagons, harnessed to mules, and

everyone was astounded beyond measure at the immense masses of gold and silver. They carried enough silver and gold to easily pay their fines 5 times over. The chief justice felt sorry that he had not imposed higher damages.

[8] A wise thought struck him however which made him to interrogate the 12 again, and he said to them: 'Hear me, you have indeed correctly paid on demand, and you have the receipt for it in your hands. But since I discover on you now a colossal sum of money, this has to make it appear to me impossible that you came by such masses of gold and silver through rightful means. Verily, if the emperor came here today with his cash, it would be extremely doubtful whether this would equal yours, wherefore explain to me briefly how you came by such masses of gold and silver, for this seems to me suspicious to the highest degree.'

[9] Says **the chief Pharisee**: 'What suspicious, what suspicious? This is 50 years' pay saved for the Temple by all the Pharisees, priests and Levites of this country; and the time being up, we have to deliver to the Temple. It nevertheless is the smallest sum ever delivered from Capernaum to the Temple. These are nothing but offerings, legacies and special Temple donations, and therefore perfectly rightful earnings and consolidated moneys.'

[10] Says **the chief justice**: 'Let's leave the word 'rightful' out of this. Even if so, they are extortion and base legacy hunting, and so, rightfulness is remote from this wealth.

[11] A month ago, the following was reported directly from Rome to myself and all high courts: "For a half year now, taxation moneys have been awaited from Asia Minor and some of the localities in the Pontus. They are supposed to have been collected and dispatched a long time since, and consist in gold, silver, precious stones and pearls – the gold and silver largely not in the form of coins. The said sum in gold alone would amount to 20,000 pounds, in silver 600,000 pounds and approximately a similar amount in precious stones and pearls".

[12] I notice another 5 unopened wagons. Uncover them so that I may view them too.'

[13] Visibly embarrassed, they also uncover the other 5 wagons, and see, these were filled with all sorts of precious stones, in a mostly still rough and unpolished state, while one wagon, weighing over a ton, was filled with small and large undrilled pearls.

[14] On examining these carefully, **the chief judge** says: 'It seems clear to me where the dispatched taxes and treasures from Pontus and Asia Minor ended up. With all due respect to your cunningness, it shall be hard for you to come up with proper evidence, but I dare to swear before all gods and their heavens that the overdue tax moneys and other treasures, awaited in Rome long since, here lie open before me, and are as good as in my hands. Let you then hang around here. On arrival of the concerned parties I shall institute a big inquiry.'

[15] On hearing such words from the chief judge, they turn pale and are gripped by fever, which does not escape the observant **judge**, saying also to the judge of Kis: 'Brother, I think we have netted the big birds of prey.'

## CHAPTER 235
### The chief judge Faustus and the Lord

[1] Says **the judge of Kis**: 'Friend, the renowned Jesus of Nazareth has been staying here for 3 weeks already, intermittently, and shall be probably spending a few more days here. I say unto you, He is a god to whom all ever so hidden things are as clear as the sun, of which He has given us hundreds of living demonstrations; what if we should now turn to Him in this matter? He could give us a mighty light, and that even more because he is by no means a friend of the black thieves and robbers, on account of the Temple's contemptuous manipulations, for I heard with my ears how he condemned Chorazim and Capernaum, i.e. their respective priests and Pharisees, down to basest scum. Wherefore I am convinced that through him we would get to the bottom of this.'

[2] Says **the chief justice** with astonishment: 'What? This God- Man is here?! Well, well, why has none of you told me straight away? Verily, I should have immediately let Him conduct the trial in my stead, and saved myself 3 quarters of the work. Would you take me to Him quickly, for the centurion Cornelius only recently urgently advised me to make inquiries about this godliest of all men at the earliest opportunity and to let him know at once.

[3] If the centurion finds out with certainty about Jesus' staying here, then he shall be here rapidly with his entire family. For he and his entire household actually worship this man, and I myself stand firmly with them on this. All praise to a true God for the unspeakable fortune, to for once see and speak with my most pure, celestial friend Jesus. Take me to Him quickly, quickly. All is won now.'

[4] Even while **the chief justice** is going towards the big house, fervently longing to see and speak with Me, I am coming to meet him. And on seeing Me, he shouts with joy: 'Here, but here You are, You my most godly friend and brother, if I can still call You so.

[5] O let me embrace You and cover Your holy countenance with a thousand friend and brother kisses. O, You my holy friend You. How unspeakably happy I now am that I have You again at last. Verily, wherever men find themselves in greatest distress, there You are at hand to help them. O, I can't help myself for joy at finding You here.'

[6] I said, firmly pressing him to My heart: 'Greetings to you too, endlessly. For in spite of the burdens of your judge's office, your heart has not been shipwrecked, so I love you also constantly beyond measure, and fully bless your works.

[7] Verily, for the fact that you got to the bottom of this wicked tax robbery, you can thank only Me, and Him who dwells in Me.

[8] But let us now go inside, where a plentiful evening meal awaits us. We shall talk more about this after the meal.'

# CHAPTER 236
## Marital hints

[1] The chief and the assistance judges, together with Kisjonah, Baram, Jonael, Jairuth and Archiel, now come with Me to the dining room, and at a half hour past sunset, partake with Me, and all Mine, of a well prepared and abundant meal while **the chief justice**, a single man, finds great pleasure in Kisjonah's eldest daughter, saying to me: 'My most esteemed friend, you know how much I always loved You, notwithstanding our religious or theosophical differences, because I found in You no sly or one-sided Jew, but rather a most frank and liberal one, yet also a man of many sides, and well informed in every science.

[2] I therefore confide to You that Kisjonah's daughter pleases me immensely. Notwithstanding, I am as You know a Roman and she would undoubtedly be a Jewess, who is not allowed to give her hand to a pagan, as the Jews call us. Tell me, friend, what is there to be done here? Could she not become my wife under any circumstances? Let me have Your solution.'

[3] I said: 'You are a Roman and she is a Greek and no Jewess, and therefore, from the point of view of nature, nothing stops you from seeking her as a wife from Kisjonah, who shall also certainly give her to you. But the fact that, spiritually, she and the entire household is now Jewish, in accordance with My teaching, of which you are not ignorant, shall it be no bone of contention for you?'

[4] Says the Chief Justice, named **Faustus, Caji Filius**: 'Why should it. Am I not in my heart one of the most fervent adherents to Your most purely godly doctrine? For in my view, a God who knew how to build a world and then call a whole range of beings into life thereon, including man himself in the end, must be exceedingly wise. If such God were to give man a doctrine, then he could surely give no other doctrine – I say – to His humans, than a most wise one, as should be in the most precise harmony with nature and with the sustaining principle among men.

[5] Now then, Your doctrine is imbued with such spirit and character and is therefore perfectly divine, wherefore I have accepted it for my very life as completely true, and therefore also accordingly act the preacher to my entire household, and to all my many subordinate officials. If indeed so, then that leaves only the father's consent.'

[6] I said: 'Well, this you have already, together with beautiful Lydia's love. See, behind you, the thoroughly happy Kisjonah, who can hardly help himself for joy at the honor his house is encountering.'

[7] Faustus takes a look behind him and **Kisjonah** says: 'Lord and commander over all our Galilee and Samaria, can it be that You desire my Lydia as wife?'

[8] Says **Faustus**: 'Indeed so, as the only one among thousands, if you will give her to me.'

[9] Kisjonah calls Lydia, same coming over visibly embarrassed with love and great joy, **Kisjonah** saying to her: 'Well, dear daughter of mine, would you be blessed with this glorious man?'

[10] And **Lydia**, eyes to the ground, says after a while: 'How could you still ask?

When this glorious Faustus arrived today and I saw him for the first time, I heard the words in my heart: "How blessed must be this glorious man's woman", and now that he desires me, should I encounter him with a no?'

[11] Says **Kisjonah**: 'But what shall your beloved Jesus say to that?' Says **Lydia**: 'His we all are. He is the creator and we His creatures, whom He is now making into real children. Despite that, He remains in my heart's depth of all depths.'

[12] At this **Faustus**' eyes bulge, fully astonished at this unexpected testimony of Me by Lydia: 'What, what? What do I hear? Should a recent dream I had, turn out to have true meaning? I saw all of Heaven open. All was light, all countless beings light, and at the depth I saw You, You my friend Jesus, and all beings tarried impatiently for a sign from You, in order to instantly proclaim Your commands throughout infinity.

[13] At that time I thought to detect Zeus in Your countenance, which far outshone the sun in brightness, and it took me by surprise that You should resemble Zeus to such extraordinary degree. And since that time I secretly took You to be an earthly son of the prime deity, which however identified with the Jews' Jehovah and the Indians' Brahma, taking all other gods to be just His earthly children resembling You, which He procreated with the Earth's daughters intermittently for the purpose of providing men with earthly leaders, teachers and enliveners from such sons.

[14] But now this dream takes on an entirely different meaning. You Yourself are the living Zeus, Brahma or Jehovah, carnally among us, teaching us personally Your divine wisdom, probably because your former children on this Earth taught it wrongly, not properly applying same in action.

[15] Since unquestionably so, I am receiving this most beautiful woman by the hand of my very God, my creator, and therefore do not need to ask whether I shall be happy with her.

[16] But my desire has now taken on a much different aspect. Most beautiful Lydia, see the Lord. Now it is not up to our mutual desire, but up to the most holy will of this One and only, this Lord of all glory, this God of all gods, out of whom went forth all Heavens, sun, moon and this Earth with us all.

[17] You, my godly Jesus, in the fullness of truth. If it is agreeable to You that Lydia becomes my wife, then she is my wife. Should it however be displeasing to You in the least, then say so, and my life shall be no more than the active expression of Your will.'

[18] I said: 'My most noble brother, I have already blessed you, and with that you are fully one body. Remember this however:

[19] What God has joined, no man should separate, and thus a true marriage remains indissoluble for all eternity. A false worldly bond is no bond before God in any case and therefore can be dissolved like worldly men and all their bonds, which are nothing but plain whoring in advance, through which Satan's children are brought into miserable being. You two therefore are now fully husband and wife, and one flesh before God, Amen.'

[20] With these My words the two embrace, and greet each other with a kiss.

[21] It speaks for itself that this quick union created quite a stir throughout Kis, while Kisjonah was now thinking of giving a great present.


## CHAPTER 237
### The trial of the Temple robbers continues

[1] When the excitement of this event calmed down, the now familiar Philopold arrived from Cana, coming up to Me at once to appraise Me of how he brought everything in order in Cana.

[2] But I greeted him most friendly, saying to him: 'I am aware of it all. You are My disciple, go over to My other disciples, and these shall have much to tell you. This night however I have much to attend to. Tomorrow however we two shall have much to discuss, for you are to become an effective weapon for Me.'

[3] Philopold now moves over to the disciples, even as the keepers are announcing the arrival of those summoned from Capernaum and Chorazim, asking what is to be done.

[4] But I say 'Take them to their children first and give them to eat and drink. Meanwhile we shall have an extraordinary session with the Pharisees.'

[5] The keepers leave and Faustus asks Me whether it would not be better for Me to examine the 12, while he would act merely as executive secretary.

[6] But I say: 'No, brother, this won't do, for as far as they are concerned, you are the only one with the official rank, wearing for that reason the emperor's token ring of authority, together with sword and baton. Therefore you must examine them yourself. But what and how you ask, I shall place on your tongue, and they shall not be able to wriggle out. Let us therefore hurry to the task, for it is not early in the night.'

[7] We move out to the Court House, where the 12 and their 30 main accomplices are detained in custody under strong guard, waiting in the great fear for the arrival of the chief justice, for they now did not have any more time and opportunity to get hold of a dozen or so false witnesses, to lie for them under oath. Especial grace was promised by the Temple to all servants who bore false witness for the Temple, when circumstances made it necessary. These had to be of course fully informed in advance, which in the present case was impossible.

[8] We entered the court room in company with Kisjonah, Baram, Jonael, Jairuth and the angel Archiel, together with the assistant Judge and several scribes.

[9] Already at our entering, **the infuriated chief Pharisee** asks Faustus: 'What manner is this towards us, priests of God, after we already complied with all demands, to treat us like common criminals, in not setting us at liberty. As surely as we are servants of God, if we are not set free at once, then God will treat you badly.'

[10] Says **Faustus**: 'Keep your silence, or I may be forced to silence you, for we have quite extraordinary things to settle with you. Listen to me now with attention.

[11] I have already remarked to you earlier on that your immense treasures

appear to me to be the very self-same, about which I had made questionable mention to you earlier. I am now quite sure in all but one aspect about this would-be assassination attempt, during the transfer to the emperor in Rome of tax moneys and other treasures from the Pontus and Asia Minor. And this one aspect consists in:

[12] According to the report, the taxation moneys and various treasures were escorted by a quarter legion of Roman soldiers. It could not therefore have been a light matter for you to overpower such powerful escort, and to either completely wipe it out or at least force its retreat.

[13] It is now clear to me that these moneys and treasures were whisked from their Roman escort either through trickery or power of arms, either on your own part or on the part of still more cunning colleagues. For this we need no further proof, for we already have over a 100 witnesses to testify for it. But, as said, I only lack the method and means, and the correct sum, what size it had been to enable me to dispatch an exact report with the moneys and other treasures to the emperor in Rome.'

[14] Says **the chief of the Pharisees**: 'Lord, this slander of us is too great for us to let rest upon us. And if you had a thousand witnesses against us it would not help you, for our case is too firm, and you shall not with all your power bend one hair. Therefore save yourself all further effort, for from here on you shall not be dignified with further answers, unless for your undoing.

[15] If you have not come to know the Pharisees by now, then you soon shall get to know them. For such immense blot we cannot allow to rest upon us. We yielded on account of the forestry infringement, although we need not have done so in accordance with our laws. But for the sake of peace we accepted your most unjust verdict. But from here on we break it off, and if you should unscrupulously dare but touch one cent, be it gold, pledge or treasure, you shall not only have to restore it a hundredfold, but also there shall be an end to all your glory. Because they shall in the Temple have by now found out how most brazenly they carry on with us here.'

[16] Says **Faustus**: 'Well then, it is in this fashion that you intend to get yourselves off the hook? Good. Then I know exactly what I have to do with you. Your trial is at an end. The matter is verified through a 100 witnesses, and your guilt surfaced. I say to you no more, giving you an ultimatum – the executioners stand outside.

[17] Should your 30 accomplices wish to talk, their lives shall be spared. If however, they too refuse to talk, then this very night the axe shall be theirs as well as yours. This ought to convince you how much I fear you.'

[18] To these cold-blooded, forceful words of Faustus, **the 30 accomplices** step forward yelling, 'Lord, preserve our lives, we intend to give detailed descriptions of how this matter took place.'

[1] Says Faustus: 'Well then, speak. By all my honor, not one hair on you shall be bent.'

[2] Says **one Pharisee**, shaking uncontrollably from fear of death: 'Lord, will you spare my life too if I talk?'

[3] Says **Faustus**: 'Yours too, for you are one of the least among them.'

[4] **The other 11 Pharisees** scream: 'Don't you know that one should rather die than turn traitor on God?'

[5] Says **the one Pharisee**: 'That I know indeed, but here there is no talk about God, but only about your most shameful deception of the Romans. You knew how to elegantly relieve the Romans of the big booty with such artful cunning, that truly, the entire world would be astounded.

[6] You prime villain wore the regimentals of the governor in chief, who is now stationed at Sidon, and intermittently at Tyre. You wore the emperor's token ring of authority and a golden sword and ruler's baton for all of Palestine, Assyria and Asia Minor and the whole Pontus.

[7] Besides this, you are of an apparently equal age to that of the venerable old Cyrenius, assuming his name and putting together a retinue and royal household, similar to that of Cyrenius, mounted upon a magnificent steed. When greeted as Governor by the escort, who half a day's journey from Tyre handed the order of command roll, drawn up by himself to you, the supposed Governor, together with the moneys and treasures, received into possession by your Roman soldiers in disguise, you commanded him to withdraw to the Pontus as quickly as possible, in that you had heard from reliable sources that disturbances had broken out there on account of oppressive taxation, and the inhabitants of the far Pontus had combined with Scythian hordes against Roman rule. To delay would be dangerous, wherefore he as the governor had, on instructions from Rome, come to meet him, the toughest chieftain of Pontus and Asia Minor, part of the way, in order to shorten his trek back for the emergency.'

[8] It goes without saying that the supreme commander of Pontus and Asia Minor and his 3,000 horsemen at once tuned back, and were at such a distance in a few hours as to leave us nothing further to fear from him. We all were threatened with secrecy upon death and they would give us 200 pounds of silver each, which however we have never received yet, but are not to receive until at Jerusalem. Fate however decreed otherwise, and the prospects for the 200 pounds look somewhat slim.

[9] The moneys and treasures were then moved to Capernaum by night, where it had now rested for some two moons, while the secret road was built only on account of the great treasure, and does not as far as I know lead to Jerusalem, but towards a great hidden cave in these mountains, within which rather than the Temple, quite many a 1,000 pounds of gold already are awaiting retrieval.

[10] Only the 12 of us were initiates to this secret and beside us no Pharisee

knows anything about it, but for our 30 accomplices, although these are not aware of the purpose. They are told this is being preserved for the coming Messiah, who shall imminently liberate the Jews from their Roman yoke. But I of course know a quite different purpose, namely, first: a life of luxury over luxury and secondly: mighty corruption powers in important emergencies, where it is intended to have the mighty Romans dance according to one's tune, or to purchase a supreme position at the Temple, which of course is always worth a fortune of gold. Now you know the lot, and you can now examine all the 30 and they shall tell you the same thing.

[11] Only the pledges were destined for Jerusalem, in order to win the Temple's favor; the moneys and treasures however would have joined their likes in the cave, had they not suffered this mighty shipwreck here. Now you know everything and can act as you see fit, only let you not be too hard and inexorable towards myself and the 30 misguided ones.'

[12] Says **Faustus**: 'Towards you and the 30 I shall not be acting as judge but as protector. What is to be done with the 11, Cyrenius shall decide. Only tell me one more thing, whether any of the moneys or treasures has been stolen or whether all that was brought from Asia Minor is here together and whether you know about the famous cave.'

[13] Says **the Pharisee**: 'Just as it all was taken into possession, together with the wagons, so it still is here, undamaged and complete. Regarding the famous cave however, I as a co-sworn know of everything it contains of course, and without one of us 12, no one could find either entry or exit.'

[14] Following this, **Faustus** praises the more destitute Pharisee named Pilah, saying to Kisjonah: 'Well, friend and now most esteemed father-in-law, the cave, located in your mountains, obviously, shall be given to you as pronounced in the initial verdict. The Emperor's moneys and treasures however, let you take into custody for the present, for they shall be safest in your custody pending the conclusion of this major trial.

[15] Let Pilah be placed on my bill, but let the 30 be given good accommodation for the night. I cannot give them freedom until the cave is cleared. Then afterwards they can go wherever they choose. Nor do I intend to have them whipped, since their co-operation led to big revelations.'


## CHAPTER 239
### The Temple treasures

[1] Thereupon Faustus turns to the 11 saying: 'Well now, where is the ruin with which you threatened me in such domineering fashion? What do you anointed servants of God say to this story? Verily, it must be heinously bitter for purported, would-be anointed servants of God to stand there as state villains. Nevertheless, just wait, as worse is yet to come over you. This was only an easy prelude.

425

[2] Verily, you can be grateful to but One, for my not having you now taking your clothes off, pronouncing the emperor's curse over you and then handing you over to the henchmen thirsting for justice. And this One is at my side, the godly Jesus of Nazareth, whom you have been cursing now for a long time, persecuting Him from place to place, and that for taking the supremely honest liberty of enlightening you in front of the poor people, deluded through you.

[3] Turn within yourselves and say whether, next to your Satan, can there be anything more evil than yourselves?

[4] You make the people believe in a God you yourselves never believed in. For, were you to believe in a God, in Jehovah, whom also Moses clearly proclaimed, and in whom your forefathers vividly believed and hoped, then you would not be playing a game of jeering mockery and brazen shame with Him.

[5] As purported anointed servants of the Most High, you receive godly honor from your spiritually killed people, on top of that demanding exorbitant sacrifices, so as to then block with bolted steel doors their way to the portals of God's light and life-filled kingdom.

[6] Ask yourselves whether there can be found anywhere greater criminals against God, emperor and poor mankind than you.

[7] O for the incomprehensible patience and long-suffering of the great God. Had I but a spark of divine power over the elements, then Heaven would not have enough of the fire that I would rain over you day and night.

[8] Lord, why were You so hard on the 10 cities of Sodom and Gomorra in Abraham's time, and yet their inhabitants, but for their lust of the flesh, evidently were angels compared to these evildoers whose numbers throughout Judaism now are greater than those of the 10 cities?

[9] You call yourselves God's children, saying that God is your Father. Verily, I shall not eternally be able to make out a God who sets down such children into the world, for with us Romans, such God, in accordance with the myth of Pluto, is named Satan or Beelzebub. That is your father.

[10] You are the live, wicked seed that your father always casts among God's wheat, that it may suffocate the divine seed, yet you call yourselves the anointed servants of God? You servants, you are of Satan. He anointed you for the destruction of everything godly upon Earth.

[11] If you were only a trifle less devilish than you are, then on account of the one who is here, I would have pronounced the lightest possible sentence over you. But because you are too exceedingly and devilishly evil, I don't want to sully my name with you, handing you over to the *Judicio criminis atri* (trial of a black transgression) at Sidon. There every *Judex Honoris* (judge of honor) washes his hands 7 times.'

[12] Hearing such words from Faustus, they are starting to lose courage, begging for mercy, promising to completely change their ways to betterment, and wanting to make a hundredfold restitution of all the damage they ever inflicted on anyone.

[13] Says **Faustus**: 'But with what? The rich cave is now in our hands. Wherefrom will you get more money and treasure? Do you have other caves

bristling with gold, silver and pearls?'

[14] Say the 11: 'Lord, we have another, the other side of Chorazim, where old treasures rest, which were moved there from the Temple and other houses of God during the Babylonian captivity. Nobody knew about it down to our time. About 7 years ago we went hunting for woodland birds and forest bees and honey. There, some 30 fields away, quite close to the Greek regions in the vicinity of a rising mountain chain, we found a spot where honey and wax literally flowed from a steep and vertical wall about 8 meters in height. At the top was an opening the height of a boy of 12.

[15] Another wall of about 140 meters in height rose above this entrance, so that without a ladder, the presumably honey and wax-rich opening, swarming with bees, would have been inaccessible. A ladder was soon put together and also straw and diverse grasses for bring out the bees, which operation soon had been successfully completed except for a few bee stings. We recovered several 100 pounds of the purest honey and a similar amount of wax, for quite a number of hives numbering some 1,000 cells each were already empty.

[16] Busying ourselves with the removal of the ground wax, we hit upon Temple tools of metal, and on closer examination the metal turned out to be gold and silver. We moved deeper into the widening cave and in its depths continued to find ever greater hoards of priceless treasures. We left all the treasures in the cave intact, and blocked the cave entrance off with stones and moss, putting it under the watch of sworn guards from the hour of discovery to the present moment. And see, all these treasures we put in your charge if you deal with us mercifully, remitting us the terrible punishment you pronounced over us.'

[17] Says **Faustus**: 'I intend to consult about it. But now tell me also conscientiously what there is to the cave in Kisjonah's mountains. Did you also discover this during another chase for honey, and already filled, or did you fill it. And if the latter, wherefrom did you obtain the treasures and how long has this cave been filled?'

[18] Say the 11: 'We earned same over a course of 15 years through lawful trading. But because, owing to the recent Temple regulations, we are allowed to have only a certain minimum sum to cover our basic needs, and to hand every excess over to the Temple then if those of us placed in the country during annual checks are found to possess substantial excess, we are ruthlessly and mercilessly punished as deceivers of God. To escape the punishment and yet posses enough for certain eventualities, we have chosen the most concealed cave in Kisjonah's mountains and therein preserved our considerable excess. This is all there is to the secret attaching this cave.'

[19] Says **Faustus**: 'Does the road you laid down lead right up to the cave?'

[20] Say the 11: 'No, your honor, only as far as the densest scrub, through which one can reach the cave, detectable only to us, by a path known only to ourselves.'

[21] Says **Faustus**: 'Good, then you shall be our guides tomorrow. For today – tonight – this court now retires in this matter, because for the present we know enough.'

[22] The 11 plead for mercy on their knees before Faustus. **Faustus** says: 'This

is no longer up to myself, but someone entirely different. If He forgives you, then so shall I, Amen.' With that we leave the court chamber and head for a desirable rest for the body.

[23] Lydia awaits Myself and Faustus, now her husband, at the entrance to the dwelling, greeting us and voicing regrets that it probably caused us a couple of hours heated debate.

[24] **Faustus** returns his young wife's greeting, saying to her: 'Yes, dear Lydia, this was indeed a heated contest, but one obtaining a desirable and most brilliant solution, owing to the purely godly help of this equally godly friend Jesus, to whom be all praise. But let us leave that for tomorrow; much shall yet be dealt with.'

[25] All save the necessary guards now went to take their rest.

## CHAPTER 240
### About the true honoring of the Sabbath

[1] The following day, a Sabbath, Faustus, although a Roman, asked Me whether the Jewish Sabbath is honored over here and what is to become of the 11 Pharisees.

[2] I said: 'Dearest friend and brother. Every day that is filled with good deeds is a true Sabbath, and on any day on which one has carried out something decidedly good, one has precisely therewith truly celebrated the Sabbath. Wherefore you should do as much good as possible this Sabbath, and it shall truly not be reckoned to you as sin, except by the evil fools of the world who curse even the wind if it blows on a Sabbath, as well as the rain and the flocks of flying birds. Such fools shall never be honored by us as models, but only serve us as an instance of loathing. For they curse the good and would like to have their evil praised by the whole world.

[3] Regarding the 11, let them also go free, after you will have sized all their treasures. Transmit to the emperor what is his, and notify him of any reason for the delay you wish. But give also to the Temple its due, from the Chorazim cave, notifying also the High Priest on how the treasures were discovered by the said 11 Pharisees several years ago but withheld from the Temple, whose property they basically are. Then the Temple itself shall undertake quite a decent investigation of the 11.

[4] Regarding the treasures in Kisjonah's mountains, share out one third to him, one third to yourself in the name of the Emperor, while one third shall be handed out to all the poor who came here on account of the things of which they were robbed, after which all the proceedings shall take their end for all time of times. Do this today.

[5] Baram has good ships and in just a few hours you shall be fully done with the cleaning of the Chorazim cave. Let one party attend to the clearing of Kisjonah's cave, and if you move but moderately, you shall have both treasures here by evening, and have them dispatched to their destinations tomorrow.

[6] I could of course move the treasures here in a moment through Archiel, but there are too many people here right now, and such miracle would cause too great a sensation. This is why I do not want to do this, yet secretly help speed up the work to the extent that instead of taking you three days in the normal course of things, it will be finished in one, namely today. But let you not tarry, but to and fro.

[7] Take only one Pharisee to where you go and let the others stay here in custody.

[8] Pilah shall stay here, for he is already too good for these things, with which children of God should have as little as possible to do. Therefore you need not personally attend to the said locations either, for a commissioner shall be enough if you give him the necessary authority. Meanwhile we ourselves shall undertake the distribution here of the catch and the children to their respective parents.'

[9] Who would have been happier with these arrangements than Faustus, this being to his threefold advantage: firstly he stays with Me, secondly with his young wife whom he now loves exceedingly and thirdly he has some leisure for sending the Emperor an informative report, as well as accompanying regulatory and legal documents, written upon good parchment. And can have all the moneys and treasures dispatched to their destinations the next day.

[10] Once the 2 commissioners had departed to pick up the aforementioned treasures, we at once set about the distribution of the catch and the children who had already mostly located their parents during the night. But there were some whose parents were laid up sick at home, from grief and sadness, wherefore they could not come to Kis to pick up their children and other things. These sick parents then requested their neighbors to receive the children and things on their behalf, if these still existed in accordance with the announcement. At the distribution, this too was kept in sight, and everything accurately found its way to its owner, as well as a sum of a 100 pounds, handed to each party by Kisjonah, as directed by Me, for a portion of the one third of the treasure from the cave on Kisjonah's property, after which all the parties, several hundred of them of course, were discharged from Kis, after some good instruction and exhortations from Faustus to all.

[11] Kisjonah had all the trading ships readied, and the entire great throng, residents from Chorazim, Capernaum and Nazareth, were transported therewith back to their homes, the distribution together with their transportation home, taking hardly over 7 ½ hours.

## CHAPTER 241
### A word for our time

[1] It could indeed in these times be asked, even as these long past events are being recounted anew, through an especially chosen scribe on behalf of mankind, by Myself, the same Christ who nearly 2,000 years ago, as God and Man, taught and acted:

[2] "What's this? Maybe more than half of these children, as security of the Pharisees, had they not been intercepted here, would have been in 10 or at the most 12 days sold by packed slave traders in Sidon, Tyre, Caesarea, Antioch or even Alexandria, yet would have been well bred children. Nevertheless, there is no indication that I, as a foremost friend of the little ones, ever visited them or spoke a word to them, whereas I normally would let the little ones come unto Me, hugging and blessing them before all men."

[3] On this question I give the following answer: For a start, these children were of course mostly aged already over 9 years, and there were girls of 14 to 16 among them as well as youths, and one could not therefore enter a roomful of such half-naked people without causing offence. And secondly, these were no longer such as could still be innocent children, such as had still found here and there, but basically mostly spoilt, carnally and morally. For pedophilia and defilement were nowhere as prevalent as in the border regions between Jews and Greeks. And so, even for these very depraved children, their recent lesson, permitted by Me, was not altogether useless, because this experience had to firstly appear as a powerful punishment for depravity, and secondly they were warned thereby to from now on avoid serving the sensuality of the lewd Greeks and live a God fearing life, in all earnest, if they did not want to be punished by God most severely for the very next sin, something Faustus had driven home penetratingly in his exhortation speech to the parents and children.

[4] Appraised thus, it shall hopefully be understood that I, although filled with all godly love towards each human being, on account of the same godly holiness nevertheless cannot and must not personally approach such sinful and unclean flesh, for the good of its own continued existence, wherefore the familiar 'do not touch me' applies in all such cases.

[5] For there is an immense difference between a pure and a most impure child. The first can be guided by Me directly, while the second only indirectly and that along essentially, or as need be, thorny paths.

[6] It should not therefore be rashly asked why, not seldom children, who surely have committed either no offence at all or who at least are not yet of an accountable age, are afflicted by Me sometimes more harshly than aged sinners, who would find it as hard to number their sins as the sand of the sea.

[7] Here I say: whoever has notions of making a tree lean towards some direction, must start to do so while the tree is still young and tender. Once the tree has grown old, then extraordinary means would need to be applied for giving it any possible new direction; a very old tree however shall accept no other direction than the final one, when hewn down.

[8] And it therefore happens that I, speaks the Lord, sometimes worked children and even little ones over more severely than someone ripe in years, because nowhere are the evil spirits busier and more ready to serve than with the children, in helping the soul to build her body in such a way as for her body to harbor free and comfortable dwelling places for a large number of their kind.

[9] But what does the Lord, to whom nothing can remain unknown, do then?

[10] See, He sends His angel and has the work of the wretched helpers pulled

down and removed as foreign parts through outwardly apparent sickness.

[11] Consider the diverse sicknesses of children and little ones, and I say unto you, these are nothing but castings out of the evil foreign substances, through which evil and dishonest spirits, assisting the soul in building her body, wanted to build for themselves free dwelling places in that self-same body.

[12] If such mischief were not constantly tackled in children most decisively, then the numbers upon Earth of the possessed, deaf and dumb, idiots and cripples would swell to such proportions that hardly a single healthy individual could be found upon the Earth.

[13] It is of course asked again and said: "But how can the most wise God allow such at the start, so that such evil and impure spirits can smuggle themselves into the young body of a soul?"

[14] And I say: thus asks the blind man, who does not know that the entire Earth and indeed the entire creation, in its outer apparent, material aspect is to be, so to say, defined in all its so-called elements, as a combining of spirits held under judgment, or imprisonment for a determined time.

## CHAPTER 242
### Our daily food

[1] Whenever the soul demands material food for her body and such is handed to her, she also therewith always receives a legion of liberated and still evil and impure spirits into her body, which then must aid her in the ongoing body-building process.

[2] The spirits gradually seize one another, soon forming their own souls, intelligent after their kind. After raising themselves to such level, they abandon the soul, as authorized possessor of the body, starting to make such arrangements within the body as will suit their imagined well being.

[3] With such spirits once reaching a high degree of imagined well being, as is easily the case with rapacious souls within young bodies, then one or the other phenomenon can and must make its appearance with such children.

[4] The foreign matter must be cast out through either an appropriate illness, unless it is intended to let the child go over into virtual spirit possession; or, in order to not torment some weaker child's soul too much, one allows a soul to live on wretchedly within such half-foreign body until a certain time, to then cause it, through instruction either by the external or internal spirit world, to bring it to a level of insight where in the end it voluntarily starts to drive out her parasites, through fasting and all sorts of other self-depravations; or, where the parasites are too stubborn, one takes the whole body away, and then develops such a soul in another world, for life eternal.

[5] Such cause also underlies the occasionally early physical death of the child, so bitter for the parents. Therefore, especially parents of terrestrial wealth should be particularly concerned about their children obtaining the appropriate external

food.

[6] If the mother eats unclean foods, as proscribed through Moses, then the mother should not breast-feed the child but let it be breast fed by someone eating clean food, or she shall have much trouble with the child.

[7] For this reason, since Abraham, and mainly through Moses, the clean animals and fruits were prescribed to the Jews, and all who kept such commandments conscientiously, never had sick children and achieved ripe old age, dying from old age feebleness.

[8] In the present time however, when one makes a grab for even the most exotic delicacies, no longer even thinking whether a morsel is clean or unclean, where in some lands almost anything is constantly stuffed into the body that is not either stone or clay, there it is in any case a wonder that blind mankind has not yet sunk back into the animal forms corresponding to what, surely, they already attained in their psyches.

[9] If, currently, children in their first few years already are stricken with all kinds of maladies, then the obvious cause lies in the most inappropriate nutrition, through which a multitude of evil and unclean spirits are conveyed into the body, which not seldom has to be completely removed for the good of the soul; and therefore nothing but inexcusable parental blindness alone is responsible for the early physical death of the child, because such parents would rather follow anything than the divine advice in the holy Book.

[10] See, through My angels I undertake an annual thinning out of all fruit trees, from whose fruits men feed, upon which no apple, pear or fruit of any kind whatsoever must ripen, within which during flowering, some unclean spirit has settled in up to the fruit stage. And such fruit is cast down from the tree or bush while still completely unripe.

[11] Similar care is taken with all types of grains and plants destined for human consumption.

[12] But blind man not only does not recognize this but, akin to a polyp, eats everything that seems a tidbit to him. Any wonder that he soon gets sick, sluggish, toilsome, crippled and therefore miserable through and through?

[13] Therefore also all varieties of so-called potatoes are more than bad, especially for children and breast-feeding nannies, as also for pregnant women, even while coffee is worse still. But blindness sees nothing, avidly consuming both for the pleasant flavor. But children get physically miserable, and in the end the woman and the man. This does not concern the blind: does he not consume poisons far worse? Why shouldn't he eat these two lesser forms of poison?

[14] But I intend to once again advise the foods congenial for man's consumption. If he will heed same, he shall get well, be well and stay well. However, if he does not heed same, then he shall also be ruined, like the savage beast in the desert.

[15] But now an end of this most essential explanation, and therefore a return to the main theme.

End of Volume 1

**GREAT GOSPEL OF JOHN, VOLUME 1**
**TABLE OF CONTENTS**

found Messiah

435

**EXPANDED TABLE OF CONTENTS**

Chapter 1: Spiritual interpretation of the introductory words  of the biblical gospel of John. [John 1, 1-5]

with celestial fare brought to the newly-created hall by celestial servants. 'I am wealthier than you'.

lying mates. Joram's resoluteness and the disciples vigor against the liars. The Lord's rebuke and His guidelines in dealing with men's wickedness. 'Do not return evil for evil'. Parable of the master and servant. The evil of dogmatism and retribution.

Chapter 75: At Sychar. The drawbacks to being good. Zoological example. About redemption from evil. The new Way to freedom for children of God. About dealing with criminals. Parable of the lion. About apostolic ministry.

Chapter 76: Peter's commendable talk and request (the Lord's Prayer). The Lord's instructions on national policy for keeping order and peace. 'You shall achieve everything with love'. Force awakens the devils - for evil. Peter's humane suggestions for the spreading of Truth. The Lord discusses the work of guardian angels, and the nature of miscreants.

Chapter 77: At Sychar. The Lord and the troublemakers. The commander's dark thoughts about mankind's depravity. Jonael indicates trust in the Lord. 'He shall do it in His time'.

Chapter 78: At Sychar. Continuation of the discussion between Jonael and the commander about tolerance. The chief's commendable testimony to Jesus, and his anger about the blind and evil Jews. A hint about allopathy. Consequences of sin, and a medicine. Gentleness and patience more effective than anger. Better to follow than forestall the Lord.

Chapter 79: At Sychar. Jonael's comments on the treatment of the soul-sick. Evil consequences of over-strictness. About the death penalty. Revenge by the departed. David's killed enemies as example. The blessedness of peace and friendship. Revenge by departed enemies.

Chapter 80: At Sychar. 'Live in peace and unity.' About guardian spirits. Hints about the order in the divine household. A pertinent question: how and when shall it get better on earth? When shall the kingdom of God take effect?

Chapter 81: At Sychar. The Lord's instructions regarding the treatment of criminals. The death penalty and its effect. A hint for judges. The main reason for God's Incarnation. The erection of a bridge between here and the beyond. Guides for the ignorant in the beyond. Commendable request.

Chapter 82: At Sychar. Promise of a secret visit from the Lord. A prophet is more effective abroad. Matthew accompanies the Lord as a scribe. The high priest's thanks. Jonael receives his calling as a teacher, with miraculous powers and an angel as companion. Irhael's and Joram's deep sorrow at parting. The Lord's reassurance [John 4:43-4].

Chapter 83: At Sychar. Important missionary hints. The power of truth. About the essence of the Lord's Word. The grace of man's calling to the childhood of God. The Lord wants no pessimists or condemners of the world. Life-hints. What the world is, and how it is to be utilized. Departure from Sychar.

Chapter 84: Matthew's reproach of the Lord. About God's nature and the creative process. The sun's beauty, distance and size. An eclipse. 'A little fear does not harm sensual man.'

Chapter 85: Continuation of journey. Arrival in Galilee. Diverse opinions about the Messiah. Hints about the kingdom of God. Further journey to Cana in Galilee.

443

Matthew's and John's Gospel: Matthew's is a factual report whilst John's highlights correspondences. The meal at Peter's hut. The miraculous catch. Peter's humble witness to the Lord's Deity. Allusion to the traitor.

Chapter 101: Interruption of Peter's testimony to the Lord. Dinner at Peter's. The occasion between Peter and the boastful Judas. An unusual wine-miracle. Judas drunk. Great miraculous healings.

Chapter 102: The case of the Jewish believers at Capernaum. A great healing miracle. The Lord's warning against the temple vipers. The leading scribe gives good testimony to the Lord from Isaiah. A crowd. The Lord puts the clever scribe in place.

Chapter 103: 'Let the dead bury the dead!' The Lord and His in the ship, avoiding the crowd. The storm. The Lord sleeping in the small boat, awoken by His. 'Oh ye of little faith'. The storm stilled and the people astonished.

Chapter 104: Landing among the Gadarenes. The spectacle with the two possessed. Their healing through the Lord's word. A pagan sermon. The Gadarenes' fear. The Lord's departure. Good missionary work by the two healed.

Chapter 105: Return to Nazareth. The Lord's morning meal at His earthly home. Diverse views about why Jesus worked no signs here. Visiting a synagogue. 'To speak is good but silence is better.' The nature of the temple clan; their hypocritical retort and furious questioning after Jesus. [Mt. 9:1]

Chapter 106: A righteous man gives a good and true testimony of the Lord in the Synagogue. Comments on the personal and public life of Jesus of Nazareth - His life, deeds and teaching. The Pharisees' heated reaction. The man's renewed attack on the Pharisees' wickedness and his testimony to the Lord's Deity, causes the accused's furious departure. The believers try to elevate Jesus to teacher and high priest.

Chapter 107: Simon the host's gladness about this fitting defeat of the Templers. The Lord's guidance on when to feel rightful joy and His warning against bad jokes. Examples: the healed Gadarenes and the duped blind man. The comedy of the world is a tragedy to God's children.

Chapter 108: The Lord relieves Mary's domestic worries. Her thanks and His admonition. The disciples' and the Master's praise of Mary. The Lord's foretelling of the idolizing of Mary. Warning against presumption. Vanity and haughtiness, women's weaknesses.

Chapter 109: Peter and Simon discussing the future prospects for the Lord's teaching. The Lord urges trust in God. 'Do not trouble yourselves about future events but willingly attend to what you have been called'. Parable of the artist and his tool. 'You are a winnowing fan in the Father's hand'. 'What art Thou, Lord?' Hints about Father and Son.

Chapter 110: Judas offended. The Lord's hint on him. Judas the glutton and trader in pots. The Lord and the three Pharisees, including Jairus of Capernaum.

Chapter 111: The holy One with His company in the boat. Return to Jairus' house. The healing of the Greek woman with the issue. Her life-story in brief.

Chapter 112: The death of Jairus' daughter. The Lord's comfort and promise.

450

who My brethren'. Baram inviting the Lord to supper; dismissal of the people. The Pharisees' curse over Baram and their just mugging. [Matthew 12:46-50]

firstly through good deeds and then with simple words'. The truly free church. 'Ye all are brethren'. The right Sabbath. A proper 'House of God', and 'Divine Service'.

and crime against the crown.

End of Volume One